JOHN A. MACDONALD

The Old Chieftain

JOHN A. MACDONALD

The Old Chieftain

By

DONALD CREIGHTON

TORONTO
THE MACMILLAN COMPANY OF CANADA LIMITED

Reprinted 1965, 1968, 1973, 1979

Canadian Cataloguing in Publication Data

Creighton, Donald, 1902 –
John A. Macdonald, the old chieftain

Covers the years 1867-1891.
Sequel to John A. Macdonald, the young politician.
Includes bibliographical references.

ISBN 0-7705-0074-9 pa.

1. Macdonald, John Alexander, Sir, 1815 – 1891.
2. Prime ministers—Canada—Biography.
3. Canada—Politics and government—1867–1896.°
I. Title.

FC521.M3C74 1979   971.05′0924   C55-2390
F1033.M13C74 1979

PRINTED IN CANADA
Macmillan of Canada
70 Bond Street, Toronto
M5B 1X3

PREFACE

I have to acknowledge Her Majesty the Queen's gracious permission to make use of material in the Royal Archives, Windsor Castle. I am grateful to the Duke of Argyll, the Marquess of Lansdowne, the Earl of Kimberley, the Earl of Iddesleigh, and the Earl St. Aldwyn for generously giving me access to their family papers relating to Canada. I have been fortunate in the number of diaries and letters that have been placed at my disposal; and I am particularly indebted, for the privilege of using such material, to Mrs. D. F. Pepler, Mr. C. P. Meredith, Mr. Oscar Orr, and Mr. W. F. Nickle. I should like to thank Sir Archibald Nye, High Commissioner for the United Kingdom in Canada, for enabling me to become better acquainted with Earnscliffe, Sir John Macdonald's old residence; and I am under obligation to Professor W. L. Morton of the University of Manitoba and Miss Heather Donald for permitting me to read in manuscript their studies on this period in Canadian history. Mr. Norman A. Robertson, High Commissioner for Canada in the United Kingdom, Mr. E. H. Coleman, Brigadier J. M. S. Wardell, Dr. T. P. Morley, Mr. J. S. Moir and Mr. G. D. Scroggie have all kindly assisted me in my search for material, or have furnished me with valuable information; and I should like to record my appreciation of their help. I am again indebted, for generous assistance, to Dr. W. Kaye Lamb, Dominion Archivist, and his assistants in the Public Archives of Canada, especially Miss Norah Story and Mr. W. G. Ormsby of the Manuscript Division; to Miss W. D. Coates and the staff of the National Register of Archives, London; and to Colonel C. P. Stacey, of the Historical Section, General Staff, Ottawa.

For help in finding illustrations and for permission to republish cartoons, my thanks are due to the Public Archives of Canada and to Rapid Grip and Batten, Limited, of Toronto.

Finally I should like again to acknowledge my indebtedness to the University of Toronto, the Rockefeller Corporation, and the Nuffield Foundation for the grants which have enabled me to carry this work forward to its completion.

TORONTO, DOMINION DAY, 1955   D. G. CREIGHTON

CONTENTS

ILLUSTRATIONS

ix

JOHN A. MACDONALD

The Old Chieftain

Chapter One

The Pacification of Nova Scotia

I

On Thursday afternoon, November 6, 1867, Macdonald, along with the other members of the Commons, stood waiting expectantly and somewhat nervously in the Senate chamber of the Parliament Buildings at Ottawa. The Governor-General, Lord Monck, was reading the speech from the throne to the first federal Parliament of Canada. The legislative history of the new Dominion was about to commence. Outside, though the season was far advanced in autumn, the day was fine. Most of the shops in town were shut. A great crowd had pressed behind the rows of regulars and militia which lined the carriage drive up to the great central door of the building; and inside, in the Senate chamber, the galleries were crowded with people.[1] Behind the rows of Senators, nearly a hundred ladies, the wives and daughters of the members, gay in crinoline toilettes, watched the ceremony: and out in front, close to the Governor-General's chair, a little group of seats had been specially reserved for Lady Monck and the wives of the Cabinet ministers. Susan Agnes was prominent among them. For the first time in Macdonald's career, his wife was taking her appointed place in the ceremonial of Canadian politics. He noted appreciatively how much she seemed to enjoy such affairs and how instinctively expert she was at them. She was a tall woman, dark, with rather large but regular features, and fine, serious eyes. Her grave, almost statuesque appearance, her poised, easy manner made her an appropriate part of the formal scene.

Macdonald wore his court costume. He was fifty-two now —getting on for fifty-three; but it was difficult to see his age in his tall, slight, erect figure, in the easy nonchalance of his pose. The crested wave of his black hair had subsided only a little. The skin of his long oval face was still boyishly unlined; and his sardonic smile was as quick and genial as ever. He tired more quickly than he had done. Now, when he read, he liked to lie extended on a sofa, and, after luncheon, he would often seek a quick midday rest. Sometimes there was a weary pallor in his face that brought Agnes a sudden pang of fear. But he had remarkable powers of recovery. His spirits seemed as resilient and mercurial as ever. "He can throw off a weight of business in a wonderfully short time," his wife confided to her diary. "Oftentimes he comes in with a very moody brow, tired and oppressed, his voice weak, his step slow; and ten minutes after he is making clever jokes, and laughing like any school boy, with his hands in his pockets, and his head thrown back."[2] His high spirits were just as refreshing as they had been before. His good nature seemed to have lost none of its old easy-going tolerance. "I tell him," his wife wrote admiringly, "his good heart and amiable temper are the great secrets of his success."[3]

He had need of his secret recipe still. In a very few minutes he would have to confront the faithful Commons of the first Parliament of the Dominion of Canada. For years now this very day, the beginning of a new parliamentary history, had seemed the objective of all efforts. Now it had become merely the starting-point of a new and laborious series of endeavours. He was well armed for them, of course; he had seen to that. The first general election of Confederation, fought out in the previous August, had been a triumphant success for his government. The forces of the coalition had won handsomely in both provinces of Ontario and Quebec; they had better than broken even in New Brunswick. The party, in general, was full of good heart and lusty confidence. There had been, it was true, a rather unseemly row among three or four members for the Speakership. Galt, the temperamental, touchy, changeable Minister of Finance—"he is as unstable as water" Macdonald complained despairingly—had decided to mark the opening of the first federal Parliament by the emphatic device of sending in his resignation. Yet all this—even Galt's rather tiresome vagaries—was familiar enough. Macdonald could afford to dismiss it with his ironic smile. He knew that the coalition, for the present, was irresistibly powerful in Parliament. But he also knew that, beyond Parliament, an enormous, continental task still awaited it. The four provinces which had been united were only a fragment of British North America; and even in the existing union, it would be a long time, indeed, as he put it, before the gristle had hardened into bone. The process had not even begun in Nova Scotia. Nova Scotia was the violently unruly member of the union. Its opposition, he knew, made the electoral triumph look equivocal, and the future terribly uncertain. "You will have seen," he had written a few weeks earlier, "that we have carried everything before us in the two Canadas and New Brunswick. Our majority is, in fact, too large. Nova Scotia, on the other hand, has declared, so far as she can, against Confederation; but she will be powerless for harm, although that pestilent fellow, Howe, may endeavour to give us some trouble in England."[4]

"That pestilent fellow Howe"! As Macdonald settled himself in the chair to the right of the Speaker which he was to occupy for nearly twenty years and glanced with scrutinizing interest over the first House of Commons of Canada, it was to Joseph Howe that his gaze most frequently and curiously returned. On the other side was the opposition, ranged out in seven rows of beards, whiskers, moustaches, bald heads, oiled locks, and tall tile hats. On the whole, it had a rather depressingly familiar appearance. There were, of course, a number of unknown newcomers—a few unaccountable absentees. George Brown had been defeated in South Ontario; and although Macdonald probably expected that his old antagonist would quickly find another seat, Brown was never to become a member of the House of Commons of Canada. His absence was the greatest portent of change; but there were other signs of the arrival of new generations and the challenge of new problems. Prominent in the opposition—by no means a back-bencher—

was a thick-set young man with a broad, fat, rather babyish face, and a near-sighted, studious expression which gave him the air of a precocious infant. It was Edward Blake, the son of William Hume Blake, whom Macdonald had challenged to a duel nearly twenty years before. He was the most conspicuous newcomer in a phalanx of old and not very terrifying opponents. John Sandfield Macdonald, the new Premier of Ontario, who had campaigned for the unionists during the recent election, briefly and somewhat inexplicably occupied the seat of the leader of the opposition. Close to him were the familiar faces of Dorion and Holton, and the bleak, unsmiling, whiskered countenance of Alexander Mackenzie. Macdonald could afford to regard them all with the tolerant contempt of long familiarity. He had out-manoeuvred them, and others better than them, a dozen times before. The real danger came from Joseph Howe. He glanced at the ageing man with the untidy fringe of hair, the tired yet still luminous eyes, and the coarse, rather bulbous, features. Here was mischief whose potentiality he could not yet calculate.

What would Howe do? He and the anti-Confederates had overwhelmed the unionists in the Nova Scotia elections, both federal and provincial. There were only two supporters of union in the new provincial assembly at Halifax; and seventeen out of the eighteen Nova Scotians who came up to Ottawa were anti-Confederates pledged to support Howe. Their mere presence in the capital was, Macdonald realized, at least somewhat reassuring, for it proved that they had no intention of boycotting the Canadian Parliament or flouting its authority. But what part would they play in it? As the House settled down into the debate on the speech from the throne, his curiosity grew. Would Howe and his sixteen followers act as an intransigent bloc? Or would they co-operate, and how far? On Friday, the second day of the debate, when Howe rose to state his position, the House and the galleries were crowded.[5] It was a respectful rather than enthusiastic audience. People were disappointed by the uneven quality of Howe's oratory, and puzzled by his odd, rather unparliamentary mannerisms. But these personal oddities and verbal infelicities scarcely mattered to Macdonald. What Howe's speech chiefly brought him was an enormous sense of relief. It was true that the old tribune kept on insisting that the Nova Scotian members had not the slightest interest in Canadian politics, that they would support neither the government nor the opposition, and that all they wanted was the repeal of the union so far as Nova Scotia was concerned. But, at the same time, Howe made it quite clear that he and his supporters had not come to Ottawa to interrupt the business of Parliament and exasperate its members. Macdonald was surprised, relieved, even a little encouraged. "We have commenced in a most amicable mode," he wrote a few days later to a correspondent in Nova Scotia. "Howe made a very good-humoured speech on the address to which he moved an amendment for the purpose of defining his position. From his tone it is very evident that he will by and by be open to reason."[6]

This was far too optimistic. Three days later, provoked by Tupper to make another explanatory statement, Howe left his listeners in no doubt that the Nova Scotian agitation for the repeal of the union would be carried on with all the force which the anti-Confederates at Ottawa and Halifax could bring to it.[7] Yet, as Macdonald had expected, Howe and his followers soon showed that they were not anti-social and unparliamentary fanatics. They kept their detached position, but they never relapsed into sullen eccentricity or deliberate obstructionism. The business of the first session of the first Parliament of Canada went promisingly forward. Macdonald himself introduced the bill which provided for the immediate construction of the Intercolonial Railway, which was to link the Maritime Provinces with central Canada. William Mc-Dougall sponsored resolutions which declared Canada's readiness —at no cost to itself—to acquire Rupert's Land and the North-West Territories. East and west, the work of nation-building had been undertaken in an impressive fashion; and the anti-unionists had not been able to interrupt or perplex it.

Yet they remained unrepentant and unconverted. Macdonald's first sense of relief was succeeded by a growing feeling of annoyance. The mere presence of a group of irreconcilable

men, who were prepared to do almost anything to break the
union, was a small, daily exasperation to the spirit. ". . . I must
say," he wrote almost irritably to the Archbishop of Halifax,
"that they tried our patience extremely. Howe talked a great
deal of nonsense and some treason, but we bore with it all."[8]
Yes, he had borne with it all. But now he was tired of indulgence, and anxious to be finished with suspense. "There must
be an end to this kind of thing, however," he told the Archbishop
grimly, "and language of the same kind will not be permitted
when we assemble again." It was time for Howe to emerge
from his ambiguous inactivity and make whatever last effort
he had planned for the repeal of the union. Macdonald felt
himself ready and anxious to meet him.

II

The riddle of Nova Scotia seemed only a symbol of the mass
of uncertainties and novelties which now surrounded him.
His life had become for a while a comprehensive task of
settling into new conditions. Almost everything was different.
He was a husband not a widower, a householder not a lodger,
a citizen of Ottawa instead of a Kingstonian, and a sole, rather
than an associate, Prime Minister. All these changes demanded
adjustments; and the change from the widowed to the married
state was perhaps the most important of all. Isabella had been
dead for ten years, and for ten years before that she had been a
chronic invalid. But Susan Agnes, who was nearly twenty
years his junior, was a young and vigorous woman, full of
vitality and naïve enthusiasms, and yet with a mind and a
character which were evidently her own. He could tell easily
—the signs were plentiful—that she was very much in love.
She waited for him humbly in the square outside the East
Block, worried over his occasional tiredness and pallor, responded
quickly to his high spirits, and wondered musingly whether her
heart's devotion, which was "so entirely given up to him",
could be so "all-engrossing" as to be sinful.[9] She watched him
proudly as he led the House. She was consciously thrilled to

be "a great Premier's wife". "I do so like to identify myself with all my husband's pursuits and occupations," she wrote heartily,[10] and as a chatelaine and political hostess she had all the qualities which poor Isabella had conspicuously lacked. She thought herself a "laborious" and "awkward" housekeeper; but she presided with dignity over Macdonald's political dinner parties, and gave him the support of her grave, statuesque elegance on all public occasions.

As time went on, he began to discern at least two separate and distinct "Agneses" in her character. There was one Agnes, a girlishly excitable and pleasure-loving Agnes, who irrepressibly enjoyed a long succession of "visitors, engagements, parties, letters, and all sorts of excitement". This was the Agnes who was quick to notice the colour of the sky or the glitter of sunlight upon snow, who was sensitively aware of the atmosphere of a room or the moods of a face, who never failed to appreciate all the details, big and little, of the crowded life that she led. For this Agnes, the physical world of time and place seemed all absorbing. But there was a second Agnes, a devout, repentant, and serious Agnes, who sometimes entirely replaced the first, and for whom these temporal things could be judged only by eternal standards. This second Agnes was a woman who looked back upon her own—and other people's—"frivolities" with grave disapproval, who strove to remember the moral purpose of existence, who held up for herself the idea of a dedicated religious life. In her Anglicanism, there was a tincture of both the evangelical and the puritanical. "I am afraid," she confessed, "that my turn of mind is getting Methodistical."[11] She gave up wine—"this for example's sake"—deplored "the fashionable delineation of passion in novels *à la mode*", sighed over Mrs. John Rose's worldly sophistication, and hoped that "I may be enabled to give something of a higher tendency to the thought of the set among whom I live".[12]

Under her sober and thoughtful management, Macdonald's house began to take on a new order, decorum, and cosy comfortableness. It was the old "Quadrilateral" at the corner of Daly and Cumberland Streets, one of a terrace of houses, where he and Galt and Brydges had lived a few years before. He may very well have wished to move to larger and slightly more distinguished quarters, which would be better suited to the size of his new household and the importance of his new position; but at the moment a bigger house was something which he simply could not afford. At the beginning of his career, his professional income as a lawyer had very acceptably augmented his official salary; but during the 1860's the practice at Kingston had gradually ceased to be an asset and was rapidly becoming a serious liability. For years now he had been quite unable to give it any close personal attention; and during his long absences and the long and ultimately fatal illness of his principal partner, A. J. Macdonnell, the affairs of the firm had gone from bad to worse. It was at this most unfortunate moment that there occurred the failure of the Commercial Bank of the Midland District, the bank which his first employer, the great George Mackenzie, had helped to found thirty-five years before. Macdonald was one of the bank's shareholders and directors; he had been its solicitor since the early years of his practice. But at the moment the crucial aspect of the relationship was that his firm owed the bank considerable sums of money. A heavy obligation hovered over him. He would not know its full extent until the affairs of the Commercial Bank were finally settled. But meanwhile it was no time to be moving to more expensive quarters.

Despite this enforced simplicity and the financial worries that accompanied it, Macdonald was becoming rapidly and most agreeably domesticated. The house on Daly Street was crowded but not uncomfortably so. Old Mrs. Bernard and her son Hewitt, who had been Macdonald's secretary and who had become Deputy Minister of Justice, were permanent residents; and a room was always kept vacant for Hugh, who was away now at the University of Toronto but who came back to Ottawa regularly during the holidays. Macdonald's family, and his wife's, and the servants certainly took up most of the space; but there was enough left to permit him a separate study, and he worked there often far away from the importunate callers of the East Block, in the luxury of complete seclusion. He valued the study highly; but the room he most enjoyed was the dressing-room on the first floor, where Agnes did her sewing and her correspondence and where a cheerful fire was always burning on autumn and winter evenings. It was pleasant to drive home to these domestic comforts on November and December days after a long day in Council or the House. Winter had set in early that autumn; the wind roared in across the Ottawa River from the north-west, and there were great slanted drifts of snow on the square on Parliament Hill.

Often Agnes would be waiting for him in the antechamber of his office; the carriage or sleigh stood ready at the door of the East Block; and they would drive off together across the canal bridge and down Rideau Street through a winter dusk that was often lightened by a white blur of snowflakes. Once or twice a week, at least during the session, they would have a dinner-party; and he would notice approvingly how tactfully Agnes spoke French to the Quebec members, and with what gracious efficiency she played her rôle at the head of the table. But on most evenings there were no visitors; and he would play innumerable games of patience—Agnes reflected complacently that patience had been approved by "Albert the Good"—and lounge on the sofa reading *Phineas Finn* or Carlyle's *Frederick the Great*. On Sundays they would go to church, usually to St. Alban's, Church of England, and sometimes, by way of variation, to the "Scotch Church". In the early days at Ottawa, Macdonald had been accustomed to a number of Sunday visitors and a good deal of Sunday political talk. But Agnes discouraged these profane conversations. "I made it for months a subject of very earnest prayer," she confided to her journal, "that my husband might prevent Sunday visitors and Sunday interruptions. . . . He, my own kind dear husband, has been mercifully taught to see the right in this thing. . . ."[13]

The novelties of domestic life were matched and exceeded by the strange and unaccustomed conditions of political existence in a federal union. Even the capital itself was relatively new to Macdonald. Since the autumn of 1865, when the parliament of the old Province of Canada had moved to its new home, he had probably spent as much time in London as he had in Ottawa. And Ottawa, despite the great natural beauty of the rivers which encircled it, was a raw, overgrown, lumber town, with rows of ugly mid-Victorian terraces and semi-detached "villas" and a fringe of untidy lumber-yards, littered with stacks of boards and piles of dirty yellow sawdust. In such a setting, the Parliament Buildings stood out with incongruous magnificence; and even the Parliament Buildings, which George Brown had thought so absurdly grandiose only a few years before, were now found to be not nearly so spacious or comfortable as had been expected. The heating system, which was fed with wood instead of coal, was disconcertingly capricious; and the Commons chamber, which had been built for the one hundred and thirty assembly men of the Province of Canada, was certainly a tight fit for the one hundred and eighty-one members of the first Parliament of the Dominion.[14]

Confederation itself was not unlike a new and unfamiliar building. One was always blundering into new passages, bumping up against unexpected walls, discovering unfinished rooms; and periodically the uneasy suspicion returned that not enough provision had been made for this or that need, or that something had been completely forgotten. "The whole of our present system is an experiment," Macdonald wrote to one dissatisfied correspondent.[15] As the chief author of the experiment, he was always being called upon to explain and defend its processes, to say what could be done under the new rules and what decidedly could not. He would have to see the whole complicated process through to the end—to watch over the new system until, as he said, it had "stiffened in the mould". It was exciting and dismaying to realize that he could not yet be in the least certain how it was going to turn out.

The winter adjournment of Parliament gave a welcome temporary relief from all these perplexities. For a time, during the Christmas holiday season, many of the ministers scattered. The little town was buried in drifts of snowy peace. On his birthday, January 11, he did not go to the Departmental Buildings until late in the afternoon; and then he and Agnes drove back by sleigh over a countryside which was one even, unbroken expanse of glittering snow. They dined that night— the occasion was in his honour—at Rideau Hall. He wore the

star and the broad red riband of his order. He could catch
Agnes's surreptitious admiring glances; and it was pleasant to
see her being grandly taken in to dinner on the arm of the
Governor-General. When they left at a late hour, he and
Agnes and Hewitt Bernard were in high good spirits, and
they drove home gaily in an open sleigh, half-smothered in fur
wraps and buffalo robes, through the icy, deserted Ottawa
streets.[16]

He thrived during these days of relaxation. But they could
not last indefinitely. Council reassembled, Parliament was
due to open again early in March; and then, from one quarter
after another, really bad news began to pour in. In the previous
autumn, when it had passed its addresses to the imperial
Parliament respecting the Hudson's Bay Company, the Canadian Parliament had affected to assume that, in taking over
Rupert's Land and the North-West Territories, it need accept
only the obligation of providing government for the region. This
comfortable delusion was shattered by a dispatch which arrived
from the Colonial Office early in the New Year. The British
government stoutly insisted that the Hudson's Bay Company
held chartered rights which, until they had been successfully
challenged in the courts, could not be surrendered without
compensation. The business of western expansion was evidently
going to be extremely costly, as well as extremely difficult and
dangerous. There would be trouble and delay in the west. But
the west was not the only place where trouble and delay could
be expected. The problem of Nova Scotia suddenly emerged
from the state of ominous inactivity in which it had lain ever
since the autumn meeting of Parliament. The anti-Confederate
legislature at Halifax passed a series of resolutions which, in
scandalized and vehement tones, denounced Confederation and
demanded the release of Nova Scotia from its toils.[17] The
anti-Confederate government appointed Joseph Howe, William
Annand, H. Smith, and J. C. Troop as delegates to present this
peremptory demand for freedom at the feet of the imperial
throne. Another pilgrimage for the repeal of the union so far
as Nova Scotia was concerned would infallibly take place.

What were Macdonald and the Canadian government to do about it?

He studied the problem anxiously. Confederation was not a neat and finished job. There were loose ends lying untidily about in all directions. The long Cabinet meetings were succeeding each other rapidly now. He was "on the stretch", as Agnes called it, once more; and as he played his little games of patience in their sitting-room at night she could easily divine the worries that lay behind the drawn face and weary eyes. Early in February, Dr. Grant, who was Macdonald's physician, warned Agnes that her husband was dangerously overworking, and towards the end of the month he repeated the warning.[18] Her inward distress showed itself in a nervous and over-solicitous care; and then, just at the moment when she most wanted the house to be a refuge of comfort for him, a domestic calamity occurred. Something went wrong with the drains, and, in the middle of winter, it was difficult to have them repaired satisfactorily. The air of his study, where he did most of his business at home, was finally condemned as impure; and after protesting for days that he did not wish to disarrange the entire household, he was finally persuaded to move upstairs.[19] Yet even this shift of quarters did not stop his headaches; and for several weeks he felt out of sorts and depressed. Late in February, when the meeting of Parliament was less than a fortnight away, he had a long talk with his old friend, Alexander Campbell, in which he hinted vaguely but none the less unmistakably at retirement from public life.[20]

III

Yet, despite his troubles, he had no real doubts about Nova Scotia. He was conciliatory by instinct and long practice; but he had not the slightest intention of making compromises about the newly created Dominion of Canada. The object of Howe's mission to England was the repeal of the union so far as Nova Scotia was concerned. Macdonald refused to discuss such a subject officially. The only concessions that he ever considered making were small adjustments, chiefly financial, inside the unaltered frame of the union. He was willing to bargain about these, but about nothing more. There were those who argued that the best plan would be to persuade the Nova Scotians to give the new system "a fair trial", with the inevitable implication that if they continued to dislike the union at the end of the trial, they would be free to withdraw from it. "That, it seems to me," Macdonald wrote bluntly to Jonathan McCully, "would be giving up the whole question. The ground upon which the Unionists must stand is *that repeal is not even a matter of discussion*. I hope that the Colonial Office will be firm in this matter. If the Duke of Buckingham says at once to Howe and his confrères that they have nothing to hope or expect from the British government, I think the matter will end there; but if he should be weak enough to say—'You should give this system a fair trial for a year or two'—the consequence will be that the professional agitators will keep up the agitation for a year or two and then will return to the Colonial Office and plead their own factious course and its success as an evidence of the persistent refusal of the people to be incorporated in the union."[21]

That would be an absolutely fatal result. Surely the Colonial Office would never make such a ruinous concession. And yet, in such a matter, was it wise, he wondered, to rely upon dispatches and telegrams for the presentation of the Canadian case? Would it not be better to have a stout unionist at Westminster who could answer Howe's arguments and counteract his poisonous propaganda? He knew, of course, that such an agent could not be a member of the Canadian government, for that might be taken to imply that Canada regarded the repeal of the union, so far as Nova Scotia was concerned, as a matter for official discussion. But, beyond the limited circle of the Cabinet, there were others who were close in the confidence of the government and who might be equally suitable appointees. There was, for example, the temperamental Galt, who had resigned his portfolio at the beginning of the session, and whom it might be useful to propitiate with the offer of another job. There was also Tupper, who had disinterestedly declined a place in the first federal cabinet, but who had headed Nova Scotia's delegations to both the Quebec and London conferences. Galt, who was inclined at the time to be sulkily jealous and resentful of Macdonald, declined the post, alleging that Tupper's appointment as the second commissioner would inevitably defeat the object of the mission. Poor Tupper's unfitness, as the man whom the anti-Confederates of Nova Scotia most abominated, was the target of most of the opposition's criticism, when Macdonald got up on March 19 to explain the government's policy.[22] He defended Tupper stoutly, declaring that it was only fair for his Nova Scotian colleague to have the opportunity of vindicating his policy against its critics. When he sat down that night he must have felt fairly certain that there would be no more fuss in Parliament about the mission to England.

Physically he was feeling a good deal better than he had a month or so before. The coming of spring nearly coincided with the re-opening of Parliament; and, if the winter had been exceptionally severe, there was now ample compensation in the long, cloudless, balmy April days. He still had his unexpected lapses, his bad off-days. But he felt less depressed than before—more ready for parliamentary combat; and when, on April 6, "that sneak Parker", as he informed Tupper, brought up again the question of the mission to England, he composed himself to listen to a late debate with more equanimity and interest than he might have thought possible a month before. He pointedly took no part himself in the discussion. The debate was really beneath the attention of ministers! And the only prominent debater on the government side of the House was Thomas D'Arcy McGee. McGee was not at the top of his form—the occasion hardly required that; but, as Macdonald realized with satisfaction, he was eloquent and adroitly persuasive. He defended Tupper as a man who had risked a little temporary unpopularity in order to gain enduring fame. He promised that the Dominion would give real consideration to Nova Scotia's practical grievances. And he ended by appealing to both sides in the dispute to give time a chance to soften existing irritations.[23]

The debate drew to a close some time after one o'clock, and Macdonald drove home through the silent spring night to the "Quadrilateral" on Daly Street. It was cooler than it had been. The sunny, chill, uncertain day had ended in a sharp return of frost. A bright full moon hung high in the sky; and, as he drove along Rideau Street, the thin brittle patches of ice in the rutted road were picked out clearly in the moonlight. It was nearly half past two when he reached the house. Agnes, who had waited up, flew down to open the door for him; and he had his late brief supper in her dressing-room, while the last remains of the fire glowed in the hearth, and the gas sang serenely overhead. He was in a relaxed and cheerful mood. The Nova Scotian protest had been met and silenced for the second time, on the highest grounds, and in the most effective fashion. And, in his amused and amusing fashion, he told her something of the debate. The day had been long and full of exasperation; but it had ended at last in contentment. He lingered, savouring the peace of the silent house.[24]

He was not yet in bed before the low rapid knocking began at the front door. In a minute he flung open the dressing-room window and looked outside.

"Is there anything the matter?" he called softly.

Then he saw the messenger, his lifted frightened face pale in the moonlight.

"McGee is murdered—lying in the street—shot through the head."

Macdonald roused Hewitt Bernard. Together they drove back again, up Rideau and along Sparks Street toward McGee's lodging. Just beyond where Metcalfe Street crossed Sparks he saw the little group of still dark figures—McGee's landlady, the doctors, the police, and the printers from the Ottawa *Times*. He knelt beside the body, close to the pool of blood, to the half-smoked cigar, and the useless fallen new hat, and helped to lift his colleague and carry him into the house.[25] He listened while the witnesses told their first excited stories. He went down to the *Times* office and telegraphed to the police of the neighbouring towns. It was five o'clock and the streets were grey with dawn, when he reached the "Quadrilateral" again;

but he was back again at his office in a few hours, setting in
motion all available machinery for the capture of the murderer
whom everybody expected from the start to have been a Fenian.
That afternoon, when the House met, there were several
tributes, moving or laboured, to the dead man; but it was
Macdonald who, in his practical fashion, proposed an annuity
for McGee's widow, and a small settlement for each of the
daughters.[26] In the galleries his voice could scarcely be heard.[27]
His face was white with fatigue, and sleeplessness and shocked
regret.

The tragedy moved him deeply. McGee was dead at forty-
three, "just at the beginning of his usefulness". He had been
Confederation's most eloquent prophet. In the minds of many
British North Americans he had almost come to stand for it;
and at his death it was still ringed round with the old enemies,
anti-Confederates, secessionists, annexationists, and Fenians.
Macdonald and all the unionists, young and old, drew a fresh
determination from the dreadful event. With almost his last
breath, McGee had defended Tupper and the Nova Scotia
mission; and to ensure the success of the mission had now
become a duty to the dead as well as to the living. Confederation
must not be destroyed "just in the beginning of its usefulness".
Tupper must succeed. He must, in the first place, persuade the
British government, through the Colonial Secretary, to put its
foot down, flatly, firmly, and finally, upon the secessionist
appeal. He must, in the second place, prevent John Bright or
any other gullible member of the imperial Parliament, whom
Howe and his friends could influence, from kicking up another
ineffectual row in the House and thus prolonging the agitation
for repeal.

Yet this, as Macdonald knew very well, was not the final
objective of Tupper's journey to England. The defeat of Howe's
anti-Confederate appeal to the British government and Parliament was, in reality, only a negative achievement. The ultimate
goal of the Canadian government could be nothing less than
the pacification of Nova Scotia—the reconciliation of the Nova
Scotians to the "fixed fact" of Confederation. And the Canadian
government, Macdonald also realized, could only approach

anti-Confederate Nova Scotians through their own anti-Confederate leaders. Howe was the head and front of the repeal movement. Macdonald's final objective was to persuade him to abandon it and to identify himself publicly with the union through membership in the federal government. Much of the vigour of the anti-Confederate movement could be attributed to Howe's leadership, he knew; and time merely served to increase his estimate of the old tribune's importance. "The Antis have dwindled into insignificance in Howe's absence," he wrote to Tupper at the end of April, "and I see more than ever the importance of arranging matters with him."[28] The importance— and also the possibility! For Tupper, who had made occasion to see Howe several times since his arrival in England, was convinced, in his hopeful fashion, that the Nova Scotian leader would be open to reason if the anti-Confederate mission failed. Howe could then honourably lay down his arms. He could appeal for the submission of his followers. And this was exactly what Macdonald hoped to gain.

His hopes grew stronger as the summer advanced. In June, the Colonial Secretary, the Duke of Buckingham and Chandos, decisively rejected the petition for the repeal of the union, and John Bright's motion for a royal commission of inquiry on the position of Nova Scotia was ignominiously defeated in the imperial House of Commons. Tupper, who immediately announced the return of himself and the Nova Scotian delegates, wrote in a tone of confidence and jubilation. Macdonald, he insisted, must write at once to Howe. Tupper himself, immediately after his arrival, would set off through Nova Scotia to hold a series of public meetings which would finally convert the wavering inhabitants to union! Macdonald shook his head doubtfully. "Now in all this, *entre nous*," he wrote cautiously to Archibald, "I discern zeal without discretion."[29] He could not help but feel that the present was "the most inopportune time to hold such meetings, as the people have not yet recovered from the feeling of injury caused by the rejection of the motion for inquiry". As for Howe, he still believed that the Nova Scotian should make the first move. He feared to risk a snub.

Within a month he had changed his mind. For circumstances were changing rapidly also. Tupper came up to Ontario to report the results of his mission and to plead the need of action. Tilley and Archibald, who had seen Howe immediately after his arrival in Halifax, reported that the Nova Scotian leader was prepared to consider "pecuniary concessions"—or, in plain words, better financial terms for his province in Confederation.[80] This was the kind of arrangement—an arrangement which did not change the constitution vitally—which Macdonald had always himself believed possible. It was the kind of arrangement which the Colonial Secretary had discreetly hinted at, when, in the dispatch rejecting the anti-Confederate appeal, he had promised that Canada would be willing to consider all legitimate Nova Scotian grievances. Macdonald wavered. All that he now needed to meet Howe half-way was an occasion. And, as it happened, the occasion was miraculously provided for him. Down in Nova Scotia, it had been decided that the delegation to England would present its report to a convention or general caucus of all the members of the provincial Assembly as well as all the Nova Scotian Members of Parliament. The convention would then presumably plan the future of the repeal movement. It was to meet almost immediately, on August 3. Why should not Macdonald present himself in Halifax? Why should he not offer to discuss Nova Scotian grievances informally and amicably with the convention? There was just enough time. He decided to go. And Monck enthusiastically approved his decision. "I think," the Governor-General wrote, "all the evidence tends to show that you should *strike while the iron is hot*, and the iron *is* hot at the present time."[31]

IV

The trip down to Nova Scotia marked an interesting term in the history of Canadian Confederation. The Dominion was just over a year old. The federal Parliament and all the provincial legislatures had finished the first of their legislative sessions. The whole system was settling down into its own orderly routine.

He watched the process with anxious scrutiny. How far was his ideal design being realized in fact? He had planned a predominant central government. In his view the provinces were just as subordinate to Ottawa as they had once been to London. He had taken good care, in the British North America Act, to grant the federal government and the lieutenant-governors important controls on provincial legislation; and he had provided that all the great subjects of legislation should be entrusted to the federal Parliament. In fact, the legislative powers of the Dominion were very great. But they were not yet complete. There was one great gap that remained to be filled. "Property and civil rights" remained with the provinces until the laws respecting these subjects in the common-law provinces of Ontario, Nova Scotia, and New Brunswick had been assimilated in the manner authorized by section 94 of the British North America Act. Once this assimilation had taken place, "property and civil rights" could, with the consent of the provinces concerned, be transferred to the federal Parliament. He was eager to make this transfer. During the spring and early summer he had been planning for a commission which would settle "the great question of the uniformity of the laws".[32] He began to suspect, also, that despite all his careful planning, the division of power between the provinces and the Dominion was not so clear and definite as had been assumed. It occurred to him that the different governments might agree on a declaratory act which would settle the disputed points. Even this did not complete the legal structure which he was anxious to raise. The crown of the whole edifice was to be a Supreme Court. He hoped, he said, to "submit a measure for the establishment of a great Dominion court of justice, with original as well as appellate jurisdiction".[33]

This was his general programme for the completion of the new federal system. But the immediate particular object was the pacification of Nova Scotia. That must come first. On July 28, he set out from Montreal, accompanied by Agnes, Hewitt Bernard, Tupper, Cartier, and by an additional and special emissary of good will, John Sandfield Macdonald, who was both an old personal friend of Howe's and a Liberal who had opposed Confederation until it became an accomplished fact. It was nearly as large a delegation as that which sailed off down the St. Lawrence to Charlottetown nearly four years ago. But if the initial reception at the capital of Prince Edward Island in 1864 had been indifferent and unenthusiastic, the greeting now at the capital of Nova Scotia was positively hostile. There was a forbidding silence when Macdonald stepped off the train at Halifax, on Saturday, August 1; and all the members of the provincial government unanimously and conspicuously stayed away from the dinner-party which General Doyle, the Lieutenant-Governor, gave that night in honour of the visiting Canadians.[34] Yet, despite this frigid public reception, Macdonald had already gained a secret but important success. He had written to Howe, suggesting that they should meet together for a quiet talk in the General's office at Government House immediately after church on Sunday. And Howe had replied that he would be there at half past one o'clock.[35]

As he sat in the General's office, warm with August heat and tranquil with Sunday silence, Macdonald realized that, so far as Howe himself was concerned, the game was won. The man who sat before him was beaten—and knew it. The big head, with its rather coarse features and grey, untidy hair, was heavy with the dull, stupefying realization of final defeat. Despite his great talents and his greater ambitions, Howe had spent much of his life in demeaning jobs and dubious enterprises; and now, in this last and most ill-considered crusade of his career, he had been forced to recognize his complete and irremediable failure. What was he to do? His pride rejected a third appeal to the imperial Parliament—to the god that had failed. His loyalty made impossible the very thought of active or passive resistance. Why should he not discuss any remedial measures which the Canadians had to propose? Macdonald told him earnestly that the government of Canada was ready to "remove any proved grievance" concerning Nova Scotia's financial or commercial condition, and pressed him to become a member of the federal Cabinet.[36] Howe drew back. Could he carry his people with him? His unhappy doubts returned. He must, of course, wait for the convention to declare itself. He had, he told Macdonald, great hopes of the convention. Perhaps it could be persuaded to sanction friendly negotiations with the Canadians.

Macdonald withdrew to the side-lines to await developments. The General was an affable and generous host; the frivolous entertainments which Agnes liked so much and chided herself so severely for liking, continued pleasantly. And, in the meantime, the convention met and debated in a state of baffled indignation. In the end it did what all bewildered assemblies invariably do. It appointed a committee—a committee of seventeen, with Howe as chairman, to recommend a course of action for the future. If Macdonald wanted a conference, it was obviously to this body that he had to address himself; and in a short note he requested "a frank and full discussion of the position of Nova Scotia, and the best means of removing any feeling of dissatisfaction that may now exist".[37] In its reply the committee took up a stiffly formal position. It "affected to consider," Macdonald later explained to Monck, "that our visit there was an official one, and that we were charged by orders from England to make certain propositions to them".[38] Macdonald had no intention of placing himself or the government of Canada in a false position. He replied flatly that the Canadians were ready to discuss alleged grievances, but had no propositions whatever to make. This blunt announcement almost broke up the hope of a conference. But Howe still kept pressing his colleagues for a free and informal discussion; and in the end, by the casting vote of the chairman, the committee decided that it would listen to "statements" as well as accept written proposals.

By now it was Friday, August 7, nearly a week since Macdonald had arrived in Halifax. The committee's resolution, inviting the Canadians to a meeting but without specifying the time, did not reach him until nearly the middle of the afternoon; and a few more minutes elapsed before a second hurried note from Howe arrived, informing him that the appointed hour was three o'clock. By that time it was already three o'clock, and the members of the Canadian delegation were scattered on a variety of employments.[39] But Macdonald was determined to meet the committee. He spent a frantic hour in collecting the nearest available Canadian Cabinet ministers—Cartier, Kenny, and Mitchell—and in driving down to the Province Building. There, as he explained later to Monck, they were received "with sufficient courtesy". Howe could hardly be his naturally pleasant self; and at least half the members of the committee watched in sullen, disapproving silence. The atmosphere was glacial. But Macdonald spoke for some time, explaining that the Dominion could not alter the constitution, but was quite prepared to discuss financial grievances with representatives of the provincial government. Then Cartier spoke briefly, and Howe asked a few questions. The meeting was over. It had lasted about an hour.[40]

There could be no disguising the fact. He had failed to gain his objective. The convention, after having wrangled half of Friday night on the subject, did not authorize a renewal of the discussion with the Canadians. The meeting with the committee of seventeen had no sequel. Yet it was not entirely without consequences. Howe assured Macdonald that the Canadian explanations "had given considerable satisfaction, even to the violent". The convention significantly decided that the agitation for repeal could be carried on only by lawful and constitutional means; and the provincial legislature, which people had feared might refuse to work the new constitution any further, in fact continued its legislative functions in a fairly ordinary fashion. There were gains, then, even among the provincial politicians, who remained the core of the resistance movement. But with the Nova Scotian Members of Parliament Macdonald was having much more success. He had gone furthest of all with Howe. Howe and he had at least one long discussion over the week-end; and before Macdonald boarded the train for Pictou on Tuesday morning, they had reached a secret and significant agreement. "So soon as the prorogation takes place," Macdonald confidentially explained to the Governor-General, "I am to address a letter to Mr. Howe, the terms of which will be settled between us, and which, though marked 'private', he is to use among his friends, with the view of inducing them to come to his support in case he or some leading man of his party should take office."[41]

V

The government steamer, *Napoleon III*, was waiting at Pictou to carry them up the gulf. There was a day's stop at Prince Edward Island, for it was wise to take every opportunity of being courteous to the stand-offish Islanders, and a two-days' visit to Quebec, which had many pleasant memories for Agnes.[42] By August 18, they were back in Ottawa. The late summer was brilliant with cool, tranquil, cloudless days; and after the sultry weeks at Toronto, and the uncertain and exacting visit to Halifax, it was pleasant for Macdonald to slip into an easy administrative routine. A morning's work in the quiet of his study, a light luncheon at home, an afternoon's visit to the East Block for a meeting of Council or a session in his departmental office—this was his day. He was free while it was still early. As he walked down the long, cool corridors, clerks or petitioners were often waiting to beg a last-minute instruction or a brief interview; but beyond the final, importunate hanger-on was the door, and the open square of Parliament Hill, where Agnes was waiting for him. In the warm, yellow sunlight of late afternoon, they would walk together down Rideau Street and back to the "Quadrilateral".

Now his small family was complete, for Hugh, who had spent most of the summer with his Aunt Louisa in Kingston, returned to Ottawa about the middle of September.[43] Macdonald was well aware of the fact that he did not know Hugh as intimately as most fathers know their sons. The boy had lost his mother when he was seven, and for years had seen his father only infrequently and briefly; and he had grown up in Kingston under the inevitable assumption that his aunt's house was home. He was eighteen years old now—a youth who had suddenly and strangely become a man; and Macdonald began to wonder a little about his career. He had always intended to offer Hugh a place in his own law firm in Kingston. But, at the moment, there was no satisfaction whatever in making such plans for the future. The firm had been in a bad way for years. For years it had really existed on the sufferance of the Commercial Bank of the Midland District; and now that the Commercial Bank itself had failed, Macdonald's private affairs were really in jeopardy.

His family and its future welfare were often in his thoughts that autumn. He had to accustom himself to the presence of a young man who would soon be "keeping his terms" as a law student at Osgoode Hall in much the same way as he himself had kept them nearly forty years ago! An astounding novelty! Yet the prospect of Hugh's coming-of-age disturbed him far less than the thought of another event, far more imminent and perilous, to which he must look forward. It was certain now that some time in the coming winter Agnes was going to have a child. He watched her anxiously. Occasionally when she lay for long hours listless and "ailing" upon the sofa he could scarcely quiet his apprehensions for the future. But usually, as he knew well, she was supremely happy with what she called "my New Hope". "I can hardly express what a new life it has given me," she wrote. "I often think what an unsatisfactory existence women must lead who passing girlhood and having no particular vocation never realize the joys of wife and mother and spend their lives in trying to fill the void which nature has decreed they should experience."[44]

While the still September days passed by, and while he waited for Howe to give the signal they had agreed on for the letter, Macdonald took up once again the matter of the Hudson's Bay Company. He knew now, as everybody did, that Canada was not going to obtain an empire in the north-west for nothing. He had swallowed the unpalatable fact that compensation, provided by Canada, would have to be paid for the surrender of the Hudson's Bay Company's chartered rights; and whereas before he had been worried at the prospect of an overgrown colony assuming the burden of western dominion alone, he was eager now that the expansion of Canada across the continent should be completed. By the middle of September Council had reached the point of discussing the personnel of the delegation which was to go immediately to England to arrange for the transfer of Rupert's Land and the North-West Territories to Canada. There were exasperating difficulties about the matter, for, although William McDougall and Cartier—he was Sir George now and a baronet—were two certain delegates, the proposed third, Alexander Campbell, first asked for the job, and then unexpectedly declined it. Macdonald was so furious that he upbraided Campbell publicly in Council. Campbell dispatched just as much public business as it suited his convenience to do! But he, Macdonald, was blandly expected to go everywhere and to carry all burdens! He knew he could not possibly go to England in the autumn of 1868. He must stay and meet the new Governor-General, watch over the expiring efforts of Fenianism, draft his Supreme Court Bill, and get up a show of legislation for the next session. Above all he must stay to gain Howe and encourage the union cause in Nova Scotia. He stuck to his decision, though there were many influential voices which urged him to take the opposite course. "Lord Monck writes me urging very strongly that I should go to England," he confided to Rose, "but the more I think of it, the more I am satisfied that that is out of the question."[45]

It was past the middle of September before he heard from Howe. The old tribune was cautious and non-committal; but there could be no doubt that he meant business—that he hoped some positive result would issue from the correspondence. "The first step," he wrote to Macdonald, "should be for you to put in writing the substance of your oral statements to the committee. Let this be done without delay. I will then show the paper to a few friends and perhaps give you our views in writing."[46] Macdonald waited until the end of the month, for Council was to reassemble then, and he wished to base his proposals on the concurrence of all his colleagues. He warned Howe that his letter would be "merely a repetition of the statements made before the committee"; and, in fact, the lengthy communication which was finally sent off on October 6 contained nothing new.[47] He pleaded that the "purely constitutional provisions" of the British North America Act should not be lightly disturbed; he promised a generous consideration of Nova

Scotia's financial and commercial disabilities under the union. He offered to consider verbal amendments to the letter if Howe would send on his suggestions by telegraph. But Howe was amply satisfied. "Letter received, well expressed," he wired, "will write you soon."[48] This was on October 13; and for more than another fortnight Macdonald waited while Howe passed the letter about and consulted with his friends. Then suddenly the Nova Scotian broke the enigmatic silence which he had maintained all that summer and autumn in the face of the slanderous attacks of his enemies. In the Halifax *Morning Chronicle* of October 26 he began a series of public letters which advocated negotiation with the Canadians for the readjustment of the terms on which Nova Scotia had entered the union. "As you truly say," Macdonald wrote to Tupper, "Howe has not only abandoned the ship 'Repeal' but has burnt the ship. Now everything depends upon the game being played properly."[49]

Yet the game was an extremely difficult and dangerous one to play. Macdonald realized, only too clearly, that in order to win Howe and an uncertain number of his anti-Confederate friends, he ran the very real risk of alienating the faithful unionists of Nova Scotia. He had been obliged to promise that, pending the conclusion of the negotiations which he had started, he would make no federal appointments in Nova Scotia; and Tupper complained bitterly that not a single member of the union party in the province had "influence enough to get a tide-waiter appointed". Macdonald wearily agreed with much of what the resentful Nova Scotians said. He knew that he could not expect Howe to bring more than an intelligent minority of his anti-Confederates with him. He knew also that he must continue to rely on the faithful unionists for eventual success. But the brutal fact was that the unionists were already gained, and Howe was not. He must win Howe. He must be allowed the latitude necessary to win him. He pleaded for patience. "I can particularly sympathize with you and Tupper," he wrote to Archibald, "as you must hear, every day, complaints from our union friends of the manner in which they are treated by the local government and the cold shoulder given them by the government of the Dominion. This kind of thing cannot last much longer, but I do not desire, by any impatience or by yielding to the pressure of friends, to break off the understanding with Howe, which was commenced by me at Halifax and which is not yet closed. . . . The union party will have their triumph and their turn if Howe accepts the position, as he must throw himself upon the union party and cultivate their good graces in order to secure a majority in Nova Scotia. . . ."[50]

Howe would eventually need the union party. But in the meantime the union party desperately needed Howe. All that autumn Macdonald sought to gain him for the federal government by every persuasive art in his power. "From all I can learn of matters in Nova Scotia, and I hear much from both sides," he wrote, "I am satisfied that you have only to declare your will that the present constitution should have a fair trial, and your will will be law."[51] Howe had been the inspiration of Nova Scotian resistance; he was, Macdonald believed, the indispensable instrument of Nova Scotian pacification. He could bring peace alone and without assistance; and once his help had been gained the opposition of the irreconcilable provincial government became a matter of comparative unimportance. At first Macdonald had hoped that, through Howe, he could persuade Annand, Wilkins and company to sit down amicably and discuss "better terms" for Nova Scotia. But, in the end, the futility of all such hopes was borne in upon him. The existing Nova Scotian government would never negotiate. The plan must be abandoned. But, in its place, another much more brilliant and daring scheme could be substituted. The Dominion government would simply disregard Annand and his stubborn associates. The Dominion government would deal only with Howe, and the friends whom Howe might nominate, such as McLelan. All the credit for achieving "better terms" would go to Howe and his supporters, and to them alone. "This, you will say, is a bold game," Macdonald wrote to Howe, "but 'out of the nettle danger, you will pluck the flower, safety'. . . . There is a glorious and patriotic game before you; let me urge you to play it."[52]

All autumn he continued his patient exercise in persuasion.
Monck finally departed for England about the middle of
November. Less than a fortnight later the new Governor-
General, Sir John Young, arrived by way of New York; and
Macdonald, along with several other Cabinet ministers, took
the morning train down to Prescott to greet him.[53] Canadian
policy would not be greatly affected by these changes, Macdonald
knew; but the political upset which occurred in England early
in December was, he realized, decidedly more serious. Disraeli
and the Conservatives, after only a little over two years of office,
were defeated in the general elections; and a new government,
with the formidable Gladstone as Prime Minister and two such
notorious "anti-colonials" as John Bright and Robert Lowe in
the Cabinet, was installed in Whitehall. Cartier, who was
over in London, deep in negotiations for the cession of the
Hudson's Bay Company's territories, was frankly worried that
the change in government would have the most unfortunate
results for Canada. Lowe, he reported darkly to Macdonald,
"will not favour us very much"; and he suspected that Bright
was "full of American ideas and sympathies".[54] Macdonald
feared most for the Hudson's Bay Company negotiations which
had just been getting nicely under way when the Conservatives
went out of office. He did not really believe that the Liberals
would take up the cause of Nova Scotia, and thereby disavow
the policy of Confederation which originally had been their
own. Yet Bright had sponsored the motion for an inquiry.
His presence in the Cabinet might arouse false hopes in Nova
Scotia. It was essential, in the interests of the Canadian plan,
that the new British government should make its position clear at
once. At Macdonald's request, Sir John Young quickly sent off
a dispatch urging the new Colonial Secretary, Lord Granville,
to confirm the policy of his predecessors in unequivocal terms.[55]

In the meantime, Macdonald realized, Howe was being
rapidly manœuvred into the rôle which he had designed for
him. At the beginning, the Nova Scotian had seemed anxious
to discuss a rather frighteningly wide range of possible changes
in the British North America Act. But, by degrees, these
demands were forgotten, as Howe's whole energies became

absorbed in the desperate struggle to convince his sullen fellow-countrymen. He dropped his concern for "constitutional questions". He began to assume—what Macdonald had always wanted him to assume—that a favourable readjustment of the financial terms of union was the one essential point in the pacification of Nova Scotia. "Better terms", Macdonald argued, could only be effectively arranged in conference; and John Rose, the Canadian Minister of Finance, stood ready to discuss the whole matter with Howe and his friend McLelan as soon as they gave the word. The meeting could not be held at Halifax, for then Rose could hardly avoid communication with the members of the provincial government. But Portland was an acceptable "neutral point"; and if agreement were secured at Portland then Howe and McLelan could "come on" to Ottawa.[56] The New Year arrived before Howe made his final decision. Rose departed by the Grand Trunk Railway for Portland. "Nova Scotia is about to take the shilling and enlist," Macdonald wrote to one correspondent, "though I am afraid it will consider itself for some time, a conscript rather than a volunteer."[57]

VI

It was a milder January than the last and lovely with clear skies, bright sun, and shimmering blue shadows on the snow. Macdonald's health was much better than it had been a year before. He was in high spirits, and almost every prospect appeared favourable. Even the approaching domestic crisis could be looked forward to with joy only slightly mixed with apprehension. Agnes was close to her time; but there was nothing in her trials which reminded him of the half-forgotten terrors of Isabella's confinements. Sometimes his wife felt "headachy" and unwell, and when he came home from Council in the late afternoon he would find that she had spent most of the day stretched out on the sofa reading a novel. But mainly she was well and confident, ready to receive callers and to preside at the dinner table; and sometimes she would venture out for a short walk with him, or he would persuade her to take

a drive into the snowy countryside. His own light-hearted
cheeriness was a strange contrast with his mood of a year ago.
Agnes noted delightedly how often he came in "in great fun
and spirits" to greet her.[58]

In fact, everything seemed to be going well. Everywhere
Confederation appeared to be capturing the trophies of victory.
Over in London, Cartier and McDougall grew more hopeful
about the prospects of the Hudson's Bay Company negotiations;
and from Newfoundland, which had almost been written off
as a possible member of the union, the Lieutenant-Governor,
Anthony Musgrave, wrote to Macdonald, assuring him that he
thought his ministers really meant business about Confederation
in the approaching session of the legislature. The timing of
this new union movement, Macdonald realized, could hardly
have been more fortunate. It would help to discourage and
confound the repealers in Nova Scotia, just as Howe's entrance
into the federal government would strengthen unionism in
Newfoundland. Could he gain both the island and the peninsula
in 1869? He began to plan in a mood of eager expectancy. The
next session of Parliament would have to be postponed until
late in the season in order to give time for Howe to join the
government and win his by-election, and for delegates from
Newfoundland to arrange terms of union at Ottawa. Then,
about March 1, Parliament could be assembled to receive and
endorse a splendid and comprehensive programme of Canadian
expansion. "What a glorious programme it would be," he wrote
enthusiastically to Tupper, "to go down to Parliament next
session with Nova Scotia pacified, Newfoundland voluntarily
joining, and the acquisition of Hudson's Bay."[59]

On Monday, January 18, Howe, McLelan and Rose
reached Ottawa from Portland. The next day Howe came to
lunch at the "Quadrilateral" and talked Nova Scotia affairs
with Macdonald until far on in the afternoon; and on Wednesday Agnes gave a dinner party for eight in honour of the visiting
Nova Scotians. It took only a few days to arrange the "better
terms"; and although, as Macdonald confided to Tupper, there
was "a good deal of protocolling", nothing was permitted to
disturb the main basis of the plan which the Canadians had

already put forward. Nova Scotia was simply to be put on a financial equality with New Brunswick. Henceforth Nova Scotia's federal subsidies were to be calculated on the basis of the rather more generous rate which had been granted to New Brunswick by the Quebec and London Conferences. These were important concessions, looked at from one point of view; looked at from another, they were simply necessary adjustments of the unfortunate irregularities of the original settlement. It was made clear that the new terms were all that the Dominion would concede, and all that the imperial government would sanction. On January 13 Granville sent off the desired dispatch to Canada rejecting the Nova Scotian demand for repeal, and confirming the new Liberal government's support of Confederation. It was the last card necessary to complete Macdonald's winning hand. "This, coming from a government of which Bright is a leading member, cuts off the last hope of the repealers, and justifies Howe's prognostications and his course."[60]

On January 30, a mild snowy day, Howe came again to the "Quadrilateral" to complete the last details of the arrangement; and after luncheon he and Macdonald went down to the East Block together. Howe was sworn in as President of the Council, and Macdonald publicly announced a government measure of "financial relief" for Nova Scotia. He had scarcely ever had a more complete, or a more carefully guarded, success to disclose. By evening everybody was talking about the wonderful news; and when he got home that night, he and Agnes spent a happy time recalling the amusing episodes in Nova Scotia's triumphant pacification. Agnes reminded him of the time, shortly after their marriage, when they had met Howe on the street in London.[61] For a few minutes the two political opponents had chaffed each other pleasantly, for they had always remained on good social terms. "Some day soon," Macdonald had insisted jocularly, "you will be one of us!" And Howe had replied, "Never! never! you shall hang me first." Well, he was "one of them" now! The victory was complete —or it would be as soon as Howe had won his by-election in Nova Scotia. He was well armed for that encounter. He carried back with him both Granville's dispatch and Macdonald's "better terms". "He will go back to Halifax," Macdonald wrote proudly to Langevin, "with the dispatch from the government of which Bright is a member, cutting off all hope of repeal, in one hand; and the substantial concessions made by us in the other."[62]

If it had not been for his worries about Agnes, he could have settled down into a state of satisfied relaxation, once Howe had left for Nova Scotia. But Agnes was very close to her ordeal. She was moving with greater difficulty now; and once, when, according to her own account, she "crept" into her husband's office, she found that he had been giving a brief sitting to a sculptor who had come to do a bust of him, and that the two were joking heartily over the bump on the sitter's large nose. Macdonald accepted few lengthy engagements that winter. He declined an invitation to the party which the Governor-General was giving in Montreal. He stayed close to the house on Daly Street, fussing over his wife protectively; and early on the morning of Sunday, February 7, when she woke him and told him that her time was coming, he first took her in his arms and held her there for a long time comfortingly. Then the doctors and nurses assumed control; and the long struggle began. It lasted while the clock ticked out a full day; and far into the grey hours of Monday morning, Agnes and the child she carried lay in peril.[63] She faced death that night and almost accepted the still peace in his eyes. But there was a final strength in her weary body which was wakened with exultance when she heard the first cry—when she knew that she and the child who was to be called Mary would live.

Chapter Two

The West in Jeopardy

I

Towards the end of February, the winter, which had been so mild and beneficent, lashed out in a sudden violent fury. The roads and railways were blocked with huge drifts of snow, and for a week, early in March, no mails whatever reached Macdonald's office in the East Block.[1] He lived in a curious state of isolation and helpless inactivity which was like a physical expression of the miserable suspense of the past few weeks. For a time it seemed that there were no foreseeable happy endings ahead. The reports of Howe's progress in his by-election contest in Nova Scotia were contradictory and a little disquieting, and Cartier's letters from London gave discouraging accounts of the negotiations with the Hudson's Bay Company. Macdonald was worried about his debts to the Commercial Bank, about his small daughter Mary, and about Agnes who seemed to recover so slowly from the dreadful crisis of Mary's birth. It was not until Sunday, April 11—nine weeks after her confinement—that she was permitted to go to church again, and they knelt side by side in thankfulness in St. Alban's.[2] Physically his wife was well once more. But how could he possibly gain real security for his small family while the tangle of his indebtedness remained unresolved? He had known now for some time that the Merchants' Bank of Canada had taken over the assets and liabilities of the old Commercial Bank. But the months went by, and no word—good or bad—came from the head office in Montreal. Finally, when he could bear the suspense no longer, Macdonald wrote directly to Hugh

Allan, the great ship-owner, who was president of the Merchants' Bank. Allan replied politely, protesting that he had left the matter in abeyance "till it suited your convenience to bring it up", but, at the same time, quite obviously expecting and welcoming a full settlement.[3] He did more. A few days later he presented the grand total of the claims against Macdonald. They amounted to $79,590.11.[4] The full consequences of Macdonald's absences from Kingston, and his debts, and Macdonnell's far heavier borrowings had now come back to him— and to him alone.

He could see no glimmer of light at the end of this long tunnel of trouble. The feeling of grinding pressure, the desperate need to scrape together some solution out of inadequate materials, was always with him now. It affected his whole outlook, although he had always tried, not unsuccessfully, to keep his public and his private life separate. He remained depressed, although in fact spring brought a return of his old luck in public affairs. On April 9, two days before he had gone thankfully to St. Alban's, Granville had cabled Sir John Young that the officials of the Hudson's Bay Company had finally accepted terms for the surrender of Rupert's Land; and less than two weeks later, on April 23, the telegraph brought the exciting news that Howe had been elected with a majority of nearly four hundred votes. Parliament reopened. The Conservatives, their numbers swollen now by the adhesion of the Nova Scotians, mustered in a mood of gay confidence. Only eight months before Macdonald had told Rose that he must stay in Canada and get up a show of legislation for the approaching session of Parliament. A show of legislation! What he had in fact was a magnificently substantial list of measures to submit to Parliament. "Better terms" for Nova Scotia, the acquisition of the north-west, provision for the prospective entrance of Prince Edward Island into union—they could all be announced in the speech from the throne.

But even this was not all. The session was scarcely a month old when it began to seem probable that still another province, Newfoundland, would soon join the federation. On May 24, the Queen's birthday, the island delegates arrived in Ottawa, and early in June it was announced that terms of union had been agreed upon. "We hope to close our session this week," Macdonald wrote triumphantly to Sir Hastings Doyle on June 16, "and a very momentous session it has been. We have quietly and almost without observation, annexed all the country between here and the Rocky Mountains, as well as Newfoundland."[5] "All the country between here and the Rocky Mountains"! It was an empire in itself. Yet it had its limits. Beyond the Rocky Mountains was British Columbia; and now, for the first time, British Columbia, which had been a mere speck on his mental horizon, moved up into the middle distance of his thought. With the acquisition of the north-west, the entrance of the Pacific province into Confederation became practical politics. He began to marshal his forces. They would need a new lieutenant-governor in British Columbia, "a good man at the helm", in place of the obviously unsympathetic Seymour. Who should it be but Anthony Musgrave, who was just finishing his term in Newfoundland, and who had already proved his devotion to Confederation by successfully promoting the union movement there?[6]

Yet it was not the governorship of British Columbia but the governorship of the new North-West Territories which was, at the moment, the really important office that Macdonald had to fill. By the terms of the "Act for the Temporary Government of Rupert's Land", a lieutenant-governor and a small council were to administer the new territory. Their rule must begin very shortly, for the date of the transfer of the territory was fixed for December 1, 1869. Who was to be the first governor of the newly acquired, Canadian Rupert's Land? Macdonald pondered the problem in his usual deliberate fashion, but there was never much doubt in his mind about the solution. He had, in fact, already picked his man. It was William McDougall, the former Clear Grit, the Liberal who had entered the coalition government along with George Brown, and who had held the post of Minister of Public Works in the first Cabinet after Confederation. McDougall had not been an easy colleague.[7] A tall man, heavily built, but erect of carriage, with a thick jowl, and dark, luxuriant hair and moustaches, he stood out, a somewhat portly model of elegance, in any fashionable Canadian gathering. His public manner was composed and courteous. In the House he spoke with restraint and consideration for others. Yet he was, in fact, a somewhat assertive and moody individualist, who had not found political association very congenial and who, as the record proved, had changed his loyalties fairly frequently and with apparent ease. His importance in the coalition Cabinet had declined, but he himself seemed unaware of the fact. The Reformers, his political followers, were bringing less and less support to government; but he still talked and wrote with an air of cold command, as if he had a legion at his back. He refused to accept Macdonald's reasonable suggestion that the number of Ontario Liberals in the Cabinet should be reduced from three to two. He complicated and embarrassed the task of filling the places of the retiring Liberal ministers. He was becoming, at one and the same time, more tiresome and less useful.

Macdonald may have been slightly bored with McDougall's political company. He may have been ready enough to take a dignified method of dropping a difficult colleague. But it was quite out of his character to make such an important appointment as that of the Lieutenant-Governor of Rupert's Land on such purely personal grounds. He knew that the situation in the north-west required an able first administrator; and, in many ways, McDougall was the obvious choice. McDougall had publicly advocated western expansion ever since the 1850's; he, along with Cartier, had made the final arrangements with the Hudson's Bay Company for the transfer of Rupert's Land; and under his direction, the Department of Public Works had already, with the consent of the authorities of Assiniboia, sent out road-making and surveying parties to the Red River. In the public mind, his name had long been associated with the north-west; and he probably knew more about it than any other man in Canadian public life. To Macdonald the appointment must have seemed an unexceptionable one; and when, late in the session, he finally offered the governorship of the North-West Territories to McDougall, he can have had no inkling of future trouble. Early in July McDougall accepted; and everybody seemed satisfied.

Yet McDougall's resignation, if it was a relief, was not an unqualified relief. It helped to make a general reconstruction of the federal Cabinet more than ever necessary. McDougall was the second Liberal minister to leave the government since the beginning of the year; and John Rose, Macdonald's old friend and crony of early days, the urbane and amusing companion of so many travels and escapades, announced, at the end of the session, that he would soon be leaving Canada to begin a career as a private banker in England. His departure was certainly the severest personal loss that Macdonald would have to bear. But it did not create the greatest political difficulty. Good ministers of finance were hard to get. But genuine Reformers were even harder. There was no doubt at all that the Liberals, in both the House and the country as a whole, had been steadily withdrawing their support from government during the past session. But, in Macdonald's view, the government had begun as a *bona fide* coalition in 1867, and as a coalition it must continue, at least until the next general election. Liberals were still necessary. But where were they to be got?

At this point, Macdonald thought of Sir Francis Hincks. Hincks was a veteran antagonist, the leader of the Reformers of Canada West in succession to Baldwin. He had retired from Canadian politics shortly after the formation of the Liberal-Conservative coalition in 1854, and had subsequently entered the British Colonial service as an imperial administrator. He had been Governor, first of Barbados and the Windward Islands and later of British Guiana. He had then been given a knighthood, but not a third appointment; and finding it difficult to live in England on the half pension to which his services entitled him, he came out to Canada for a visit.[8] Exactly fifteen years before, during the summer of 1854, he had been Macdonald's most notorious political enemy; but these old battles, if they were partly an embarrassment, were also partly a help. They at least served to remind Canadians that Sir Francis had been a very prominent Reform leader, with a record of service in party warfare which was as good as George Brown's

and better than that of any of the new Liberal front-benchers.
The dry, precise, ageing little man, with the mutton-chop
whiskers, had once been a power in Canadian politics! Perhaps
he could win back his old followers from George Brown and
persuade them to give their support to the coalition government! Macdonald wondered. He hastened to show Hincks a
flattering attention. He travelled down to Montreal to meet him,
invited him up to Ottawa to stay at the "Quadrilateral", and
organized a large public dinner in his honour at the capital.[9]
Hincks, he was becoming convinced, was a real possibility for
the vacant Reform post. The last of his serious worries seemed
to be dissolving. It was August now, and he went off to
Portland "for a fortnight's sniff of the salt water". He could
hardly remember the time when he had taken a recognized
formal holiday.

II

Some time during the summer—and probably soon after the
session had ended—Macdonald had sent off to Hugh Allan a
detailed proposal for the settlement of his debts to the Merchants'
Bank.[10] The savings of a professional career which had begun
nearly forty years ago in George Mackenzie's office in Kingston
were, quite literally, to be wiped out. Macdonald put in all
the cash which he could realize; but these liquid assets were
far from being enough, and he had to fall back upon the one
large piece of landed property which he had ever been able to
acquire. It was a tract of land at Guelph, which he had
bought long years ago, and which, as the village began to
grow more populous, he had subsequently divided into town
lots.[11] Upon this property, which was his biggest asset, and
other lands in his possession, he offered to take out a mortgage
with the Merchants' Bank for the remainder of his debt. Allan
had not immediately accepted the offer. He had told Macdonald
that he would submit his proposal to the board of the Bank
and let him know its decision in due course. But there was no
answer from Montreal when he left for his holiday at Portland

and none when he got back again at the end of the first week in September. He was profoundly worried. He had another account to settle—a much smaller account, fortunately—with the Bank of Upper Canada, and some time ago the trustees of the Bank had tentatively commenced an action against him. If they resumed the action and secured a judgment, it would be quite impossible for him legally to carry out the proposal he had made to Allan. And if that arrangement fell through he knew only too well that he was at the end of his tether.

Yet even this was not the sum of his trouble. He carried with him always now knowledge which had begun as a torturing suspicion and had developed into a hideous certainty. Over six months ago—with what agonizing difficulties—his daughter Mary had been born. Death had almost claimed her in the moment of deliverance. And could the very desperateness of her first struggle for existence be a portent for the future? He had watched her as she lay, terribly tiny and fragile, upon the pillow, with a curiosity which from the first was touched with disquiet. For a dreadful moment, a suspicion, like a threatening cloud, formed in his mind, only to be hurried away by the fresh winds of his sanguine temperament. It was absurd, at this early stage, to attach any importance whatever to what seemed to be the little anomalies, the tiny irregularities, in her appearance and behaviour. The child cried heartily at times, she was fractious, she kept Agnes and himself up for long, wakeful nights; and these small childish disorders, these little outbursts of childish temperament, were surely only the reassuring signs of normal, healthy growth. He almost persuaded himself; and then suddenly, as if he were a boxer with his guard relaxed, the doubt struck him like a smashing blow upon the face. Why did Mary lie so inertly upon her pillow? Why did she not kick, and wriggle, and struggle to lift herself with the strenuous eagerness of a healthy child? What was the explanation of that frightening enlargement of the small head, which, despite all his denials and reassurances, was always there, in whatever light and from whatever angle he looked at it? There was something wrong with the child—dreadfully wrong—how wrong he did not yet know. The sickening realization of her abnormality was a wordless secret which he and Agnes shared between them.

These were the burdens which he carried with him always now. There were days when they seemed too heavy to be borne. It was a long time since he had tried to forget his worries by drinking to excess. In the past he had drunk more often when he was happy than when he was heartsick; and for over two years now he had hardly drunk at all. When he had married and come back to Canada as the first Prime Minister of the new Dominion, he had obviously tried to effect a complete change in the conduct of his private life. This small reformation was something which he felt he owed, not only to himself, and his new country, but also to his wife, Agnes. A much more sedate and regular existence stretched before him and Agnes was certain to be the main agent of the change.

He had known from the start that she was a distinguished woman who would grace the position to which he called her. He began to realize as time went on that she was also a woman of deep religious faith and strong moral purpose. She strove earnestly for the moral improvement of others—as well as of herself. The urge towards betterment was not always a pious, private aspiration. At times it seemed to ring in the air like a command; and there were flashing hints of a steely will which flickered like a sword-blade drawn suddenly and imperiously from its scabbard. On these occasions she might have seemed almost a self-righteous and domineering woman; but she was saved from moral arrogance both by her critical intelligence and by her simple, joyous enthusiasm for life. She broke her own rules and neglected her own exacting standards with hearty human frequency. She subjected her own pious impulses to a sharp and disarming self-criticism. She realized only too well that she sometimes confused devotion to duty with love of domination, and she frankly confessed the muddle of her motives to Macdonald. "Often," she wrote contritely in her diary, "I find what I thought at first to be a principle proves itself only an evidence of a selfish love of power."[12] Macdonald, in his tolerant realistic fashion, tried to persuade her to moderate her moralizing urge, and to drop her habit of self-analysis. He knew the weakness of her strength; but he also knew its greatness. He had come to rely heavily upon her, and upon the supports with which she had buttressed his existence.

Then suddenly—it was just after his return from Portland, in early September—he began drinking heavily again.[13] There had been no letter from Allan awaiting him, and he had come back to realize that the appointment of Hincks was not going to be nearly such a generally acceptable solution of the ministerial difficulty as he had hoped it would be. In September Cartier insisted on making one last attempt to persuade Galt to re-enter the ministry; and when that failed Macdonald went up to Toronto to talk over the matter of appointments with his western supporters. It was annoying to encounter so much opposition to Hincks and it was a grievous shock, when he got back to Ottawa, to find that there was still no communication from the Merchants' Bank. In the meantime, while the new appointments exasperatingly hung fire, the old ministers were certainly departing. On September 28, Macdonald came down to the railway station to say good-bye to William McDougall, outward bound for the Red River;[14] and the next day John Rose came up specially from Montreal to bid them all farewell. "It is more of a wrench to one's heartstrings writing the enclosed than I care to express," Rose had declared when he sent in his official resignation;[15] and to Macdonald this was a departure which carried with it something of his own youth. He was still in a reckless, desperate mood when he went west again to pay court to Prince Arthur, who was visiting Canada, and who had been travelling about Ontario attended by the Governor-General. Despite his company, he kept on drinking, careless of consequences; and Hewitt Bernard, who had gone west with him, reported that he had been kept in a state of miserable anxiety the whole time they were away.[16]

Then the bout gradually ended. It was over; but, like other more important things that had gone before it, it left its mark on Agnes and his relationship with her. They had faced tragedy together that year. But it was inevitably she who had suffered most from the appalling disappointment of her first-born. Her "new hope" had been turned into a cruel frustration; and although nothing could ever equal the shock of that terrible discovery, her husband's lapse into his old habits only served to confirm her sense of inadequacy and failure. Up to that time, their life together had been marked by a succession of small wifely triumphs. The improvement in his health, the praiseworthy alteration in his Sunday routine, the increasing regularity of his church-going—she had recorded them all with pride. But now she was obliged to admit defeat. That autumn she had reason for sorrow; and one dreary November Sunday, when the first thin flurries of snow were driving across the darkening landscape, she looked back with resignation on the events of the past twelve months. "What has changed with me since this day last year, when I sat writing, as I write now, in my big diary?" she asked herself. "Wonderfully little—and yet wonderfully much. . . . I ought to be wiser, for I have suffered keenly in mind since I last wrote here. Only *One*, who knows all our hearts, can tell how keenly and painfully or how for long weeks and months all was gloom and disappointment. I was over confident, vain and presumptuous in my sense of power. I fancied I could do too much and I failed signally. I am more humble now. . . ."[17] Yes, she was more humble. She was wiser than she had been. She began to have a better understanding of this complex man, her husband, who at long intervals seemed to run so quickly out of the power of self-control, and who on most occasions could draw on resources rich and varied beyond her understanding.

In the meantime Macdonald had recovered his balance. The Merchants' Bank had accepted his proposal, and he knew now that although he would face the future penniless, he could face it at least without public disgrace. The annoying question of the ministerial replacements had ended in the appointment of Hincks; and he was free to survey the political scene once more, plan for the future acquisition of British Columbia and Prince Edward Island, and estimate the prospects of the union forces in the approaching general election in Newfoundland. All these matters were certainly important to the maker of a transcontinental federation. But it was McDougall and the new empire in the north-west which were capturing the public imagination; and Macdonald found that the affairs of Rupert's Land were bulking large in his correspondence, and occupying more and more of his thoughts. Yet he did not want to make any important decisions about the north-west until his knowledge of its problems had largely increased. It was precisely for the purpose of obtaining this information that McDougall had been sent west before the actual transfer of the territory to Canada. His mission was not a rashly premature assumption of authority; it was simply a modest preliminary survey of a little-known situation. The Act under which his appointment had been made was an "Act for the Temporary Government of Rupert's Land". His government was essentially a provisional government. And nothing would be done—and in particular no western positions would be filled—until the results of his inquiries were made known. ". . . Until McDougall has time to look about him and report," he wrote to one correspondent who was enquiring about a job, "we desire to make no appointments lest they might jar with the prejudices and feelings of the people at Red River."[18] Surely this caution was sensible, and surely McDougall's mission was a wise preliminary move. Yet he remained vaguely uneasy. "McDougall goes with a large party," he wrote in one of these doubtful moments, "and I think is safe from all molestation. I anticipate that he will have a good deal of trouble, and it will require considerable management to keep those wild people quiet. . . ."[19]

He was not entirely unprepared for trouble. He did not magnify it when it came. It was about the middle of November that the American newspapers first reported that McDougall had been prevented by half-breed rioters from entering upon his prospective dominions; and a few days later a dispatch and a long personal letter from McDougall himself gave Macdonald all the first details of the ignominious repulse. The first Canadian Lieutenant-Governor of Rupert's Land had arrived at the border of his jurisdiction on October 30, only to discover that the trail to the north was barred against him. Despite protests and remonstrances, the organized *métis* continued to maintain their armed blockade; and on November 2, they completed their effective control of the settlement by the capture of the Hudson's Bay Company's post, Fort Garry. It was still too early to be at all sure of the seriousness of the affair. The American newspapers had obviously returned with zest to their favourite habit of exaggerating every Canadian difficulty and rejoicing in every Canadian misfortune. But, despite the confusion and exaggeration of the reports, it was clear that Canada had suffered a dreadful humiliation. What was to be done? Macdonald sat down to consider the appalling disaster, interviewing people, piecing evidence together from a variety of sources. One conclusion was unavoidable. Canada was at least partly to blame. Dr. Schultz and the "Canadian party" at Red River, together with Dennis, Snow, Mair and the other Canadian surveyors and road-builders who had been sent up in advance of the cession, had done more than he could have believed possible to exasperate the native population. "You must bridle those gentlemen," he told McDougall curtly, "or they will be a continual source of disquiet to you."[20] Stoughton Dennis had been "indiscreet", Snow and Mair "offensive", and Schultz and his party were "disliked" and "distrusted" by the inhabitants. Together they had made the *métis* dread the coming of Canadian sovereignty.

It was all unhappily true, he realized. But he also began to realize that the indiscretions of a few Canadians had not been the only incitement goading the *métis* to action, and that the *métis* themselves were not the only group that was opposed or unsympathetic to the advance of the Canadian frontier. The affair was much more complicated and dangerous than that. It was true, of course, that the French half-breeds formed the active advance guard of the movement. Their strong sense of community, their loyal belief in the validity of *la nation métisse* gave them inspiration; and the semi-military organization which they had developed in the buffalo hunt enabled them to take the initiative effectively. Yet it was obvious also that they had not acted in isolation or with complete spontaneity. On the contrary, their resistance, Macdonald began to suspect, had been tolerated, if not actively encouraged, by other important groups, which were either unfriendly or positively hostile to

Canada. In his private letter of October 31 McDougall had written of "the apparent complicity" of a few of the missionary priests from old France. The officials of the Hudson's Bay Company appeared to be behaving with an equivocal inertness; and there was no doubt that the citizens of the north-western American states were watching the affair with an ominous, greedy curiosity. Canada, in fact, faced a sinister complex of antagonisms in the north-west; and, by a deplorable coincidence, nobody with any position and authority in the little colony was at hand and ready to defend Canadian interests.

William Mactavish, the Governor at Fort Garry, was seriously ill; Alexandre Antonin Taché, the Archbishop of St. Boniface, had left the settlement some time before to attend the Vatican Council at Rome. The British and French-Canadian leaders were absent or incapacitated or unwilling; but a small group of American agents, less vocal but more influential than the "Canadian party", sought, by every means in their power, to exploit the troubles at Red River for their own political purposes. Their aim was nothing less than the annexation of all or part of the British north-west to the United States; and they were well and strategically placed for the work they had in hand.[21] W. B. O'Donoghue, an Irish-American of strong Fenian sympathies who became the treasurer of the provisional government at Red River, was very close to Riel in the early stages of the revolt. General Oscar Malmros, the American Consul at Winnipeg, and Colonel Enos Stutsman, the Treasury agent at the American customs house at Pembina, were both accepted, for a time, as confidential advisers to the rebel leaders; and the editorship of the *New Nation*, the one newspaper whose publication in the colony was permitted by Riel, was given to Major Henry Robinson, an American-born annexationist. Back of these men, in the United States, was a group of journalists, politicians, and railway men, including Jay Cooke, the wealthy promoter of the Northern Pacific Railroad, who were ready to assist the movement with propaganda, political influence, and money. Back of them all was the government of the United States, which had never settled its account with Great Britain for the *Alabama* claims, and which viewed the whole north-west

with an interested and acquisitive eye. From the start the
American government was very curious about the troubles at
Red River; and it appointed J. W. Taylor, the greatest authority
in the United States on the British north-west, as a secret agent
to keep the State Department informed about the development
of the affair.

Macdonald suspected the existence of these American ma-
chinations. But, for the moment, he focused his attention upon
the Hudson's Bay Company which, until the transfer had
taken place, was the only legal authority in the region. Was
Mactavish's unfortunate illness a satisfactory excuse for his
curious, irresponsible detachment? Macdonald shook his head
sceptically. He would never know that Malmros had reported
to the State Department that many of the Hudson's Bay
Company's servants desired the union of the settlement with
the United States. He would never know—what Donald
Smith, the chief Canadian representative of the company later
confessed to its Governor, Sir Stafford Northcote—that there was
some foundation for the charges levelled against the loyalty of
the company's employees, and that, in particular, John McTav-
ish, "was undoubtedly leagued with Riel".[22] He had little
positive evidence as yet; but the incredible silence and passivity
of the entire organization of the Hudson's Bay Company, from
the head office in London down to the smallest outpost in
Rupert's Land, seemed to suggest ill-will if not bad faith.

No official notification of the date of the transfer of the
territory, or even of the transfer itself, he discovered, had ever
been sent from the authorities in London to their subordinates at
Fort Garry. "It was the business of the Hudson's Bay Company,"
he told George Stephen indignantly, "to instruct their officers
in Rupert's Land of the arrangements as they made progress
in London."[23] Yet the Company had sent no official information or instructions; and at Fort Garry, Mactavish and his
officials, though they were well enough aware of what was
about to happen, had maintained exactly the same misleading
and provocative silence. "No explanation, it appears," Macdonald wrote to Cartier, "has been made of the arrangement by
which the country is handed over to the Queen, and that it

is Her Majesty who transfers the country to Canada with the same rights to settlers as existed before. All these poor people know is that Canada has bought the country from the Hudson's Bay Company, and that they are handed over like a flock of sheep to us. . . ."[24] In such circumstances the growth of discontent was almost inevitable. Mactavish must have been conscious of the increasing tension in the settlement. Why had he made no use of his authority to prevent an outbreak? Macdonald's indignation mounted. What part of all this, he asked himself angrily, was mere neglect, and what was positive malice?

In the meantime, the Canadian government must act. In the west, Macdonald decided, it must behave in as patient and conciliatory a fashion as possible. In winter, a military expedition was physically impossible, even if it were politically desirable as a first step. Until spring came, troops could not be sent through British-Canadian territory; and the unfriendly American government would certainly not permit them to reach their objective through the United States.[25] All that Canada could do at the moment was to send out emissaries of peace. The government selected two, the Very Reverend Grand Vicar Thibault and Colonel Charles de Salaberry. Both of them had previously spent some time at Red River, and they were now sent back to give their old fellow-citizens the explanations and assurances which the Hudson's Bay Company had failed to supply. McDougall himself must help to quiet the excitement by cultivating the virtues of patience and kindliness. He must remain in the vicinity, of course, and not return ingloriously to Canada; but, at the same time, he must not even dream of thrusting his way uninvited past the inhospitable boundary of Rupert's Land.[26] It was a difficult and frustrating rôle, a rôle which McDougall was not likely to find very congenial. Yet there he was—on the spot! They would have to trust him. They would have to pray that he would not snap in their hands like a highly tempered instrument of steel.

It was a waiting game in the west. But, in the east, Macdonald decided, the Canadian government must take immediate and decisive action. Canada had very nearly blundered into a catastrophe, and his quick lawyer's eye spotted the one sure path away from the overhanging avalanche of responsibility that threatened to overwhelm them all. They could still escape. There was just time enough. The surrender of the territory from the Company to Great Britain, and the transfer of the territory from Great Britain to Canada would not take place finally until December 1. The fatal date was still over a week away! The authority of the Hudson's Bay Company was still the only legal authority in the north-west. The £300,000 compensation money had not yet been paid over by Canada. John Rose, in his new office in Bartholomew House—"We are between the Bank and Rothschilds," he had written a little complacently, "so we are well placed"—was waiting expectantly for orders to pay it over. But he could be stopped. Canada could refuse to accept the transfer until peace was restored, and the whole responsibility could be flung back on the imperial government and the Hudson's Bay Company. It was the one neat, quick way out. And Macdonald determined to take it. "Canada cannot accept North West," he cabled Rose on November 26, "until peaceable possession can be given. We have advised Colonial Office to delay issue of Proclamation. . . . Meanwhile money should remain on deposit but not paid over."[27]

III

On the night of December 1—the very day on which the transfer was to have been effected—Macdonald sat in the upstairs dressing-room of the "Quadrilateral", by the side of a blazing coal fire, tranquilly reading a Trollope novel.[28] The house was very still. Early in the day it had turned sharply cold after a period of thaw and rain; and now the frost gripped the deserted street outside in an icy stillness. Agnes was writing in her diary. Old Mrs. Bernard and Hewitt were playing backgammon together in their sitting-room. Little Mary, who had not cried all day, was sleeping peacefully in her cot; and downstairs, in the kitchen hall, the servants were reading the papers by the kerosene light and gossiping quietly. His mind was more at ease than it had been for weeks. Barely a fortnight ago, the first

dreadful news of the trouble at Red River had burst in upon
an unprepared Ottawa. But in the meantime he had taken the
best means to vindicate the Canadian government and pacify
the unrest. Above all, he had extricated Canada, at the very
last minute, from the frightful responsibility that was about to be
unloaded upon her. December 1 might have been a day black
with forebodings. Now it was bright with a glad sense of
release.

Everything was not settled yet, of course. The Colonial
Office had regarded Canada's refusal to complete its contract
with astonished disapproval. Granville had cabled to Sir John
Young that, in accordance with the terms of the imperial act,
the transfer to Canada and the payment of the purchase price
must legally follow the surrender of the territory to the Crown.
"Government by Company has become impossible," he wired,
"government by Canada only alternative and ought to be established promptly. . . ."[29] But how could it possibly be established
promptly, Macdonald demanded, with the half-breeds already
resisting the peaceable entrance of McDougall? A military
expedition was out of the question in the depth of winter; and,
at the moment, any assumption of authority by Canada which
was not backed up by force of arms, would simply expose
the weakness of the Dominion and invite interference from
the United States. "I cannot understand," he wrote to John
Rose, "the desire of the Colonial Office, or of the Company, to
saddle the responsibility of the government on Canada just now.
It would so completely throw the game into the hands of the
insurgents and the Yankee wire-pullers, who are to some extent
influencing and directing the movement from St. Paul that we
cannot foresee the consequences."[30] It was easily conceivable
that the American government would decide to interfere. It
was quite possible that Canada would lose its inheritance in
the north-west.

"Our case is unassailable," he declared emphatically. Granville
retreated before it. "We could not force the territory upon
Canada, if they put up their backs," he had written realistically
to Gladstone as soon as he had heard of the Canadian decision;[31] and time convinced him that it was not even desirable to

try persuasion. Responsibility for Red River, for a while at least, was deposited once more in the laps of the Hudson's Bay Company and the imperial government; and Macdonald confidently looked forward to rapid and decisive action. He may even have hoped that the imperial government would send out its own lieutenant-governor to Red River and actually convert the region into a temporary Crown colony. He certainly expected that the Hudson's Bay Company would take the most energetic steps to put an end to the anarchy in its dominions. The fact that Governor Mactavish had at last issued a "strong and well-considered" proclamation from Fort Garry gave him a good deal of satisfaction; and he was even better pleased when Donald Smith, the Company's principal representative in Canada, called on him and offered loyal co-operation in restoring order in the west. Smith was a tall Scotsman from Speyside, only five years younger than himself, with a nose almost as big as his own, a great spade of a beard, extravagantly bushy eyebrows, and calm, determined, far-seeing eyes. Why not take him at his word? A capable Hudson's Bay man at Fort Garry would at least give the feeble Mactavish "some backbone". Smith could be sent up to Red River ostensibly on instructions from his Company, and at the same time he could be commissioned, with powers larger than those of Thibault and de Salaberry, to treat for the peaceful transfer of the territory to Canada.[32] In a few days it was all decided, with the Hudson's Bay Company's hearty agreement; and early in December, only a little while after the departure of his predecessors, Smith left for the north-west.

During the first fortnight of December, Macdonald grew increasingly optimistic. "There never was much in the insurrection," he wrote rather complacently to Archibald, "but it has been tremendously exaggerated by the American newspapers which, at first, were our only source of information."[33] There were good reasons for this reviving confidence; but it was still qualified by a lingering and awful doubt. What might McDougall, in his forlorn position at Pembina, be tempted to do? From the very beginning he had tried to impress upon his incalculable western Lieutenant-Governor that, until the transfer

JOHN A. MACDONALD

had been completed, Rupert's Land was foreign territory, into which he could not enter without the consent of the local authorities. Even when Canada had expected shortly to assume control, this had been true. It was doubly true now, when the transfer of the territory had been indefinitely postponed, and at Canada's own peremptory request.

Power had not changed hands. There had not been even a moment's interregnum. Riel had no legal justification whatever for his provisional government; but McDougall equally had no right to proclaim Canadian rule. If, out of mere impatience, he tried to exercise an illegal authority or to use force, he would upset the *status quo* which Macdonald had effectively re-established and he might bring on the international crisis which Macdonald was desperately trying to avoid. "An assumption of the government by you," Macdonald had warned him emphatically, "of course, puts an end to that of the Hudson's Bay Company's authorities. . . . There would then be, if you were not admitted into the country, no legal government existing, and anarchy must follow. In such a case, no matter how the anarchy is produced, it is quite open by the law of nations for the inhabitants to form a government *ex necessitate* for the protection of life and property, and such a government has certain sovereign rights by the *jus gentium*, which might be very convenient for the United States, but exceedingly inconvenient to you."[34] He was exaggerating the legal position, perhaps deliberately, in order to intimidate his lieutenant. McDougall was so impulsive and high-handed! Yet, for the sake of Canadian prestige, he could not be abruptly recalled. He would have to stay on the borders of Rupert's Land. Macdonald could not quiet his apprehensions. "I very much fear," he confided to Cartier, "that he will not go the right way about settling matters."[35]

No man ever fulfilled expectations more completely than McDougall. He was reported to be high-handed. He now acted with a high hand. Before he could possibly have received any instructions in answer to his reports of half-breed resistance, he chose to assume, without any confirmation, that the northwest had been transferred to Canada on December 1. On the

very day which Macdonald had ended in a peaceful fireside
reading of Trollope, his western lieutenant illegally inaugurated
Canadian jurisdiction on the prairies by issuing a solemn
proclamation in the Queen's name. In it McDougall announced
the transfer of Rupert's Land, and proclaimed his own appointment as first Canadian Lieutenant-Governor; and by another
instrument, issued on the same fatal day, he empowered the
ex-surveyor Colonel Stoughton Dennis to raise and equip an
armed force for the chastisement of the rebels. Armed with
this formidable document, Dennis began what Macdonald later
called "a series of inglorious intrigues" among the Indians and
Schultz's "Canadian party" which ended on December 7 in
the abject surrender of McDougall's "army" to an overwhelming
force of aroused *métis*.[36] Louis Riel—the man whom Macdonald
had saluted at the start as a "clever fellow"—had completely
triumphed. He dominated the situation as he had not done
before. And he now took precisely the action which Macdonald
had predicted would be the terrible result of any premature and
unsuccessful attempt to assert Canadian authority. On December 8, he proclaimed the establishment of a provisional government at Red River.

Macdonald was almost in despair. It was Christmas now—
of all seasons in the year! The holiday had been sadly marred
by "this infernal western news", though not by that alone. In
the last few weeks everything had gone wrong. Carter and his
fellow pro-Confederates in Newfoundland, of whom everybody
had hoped so much, had been overwhelmingly defeated, towards
the end of November, in the provincial general election. There
was now no prospect of the island joining Confederation; and
the union with British Columbia, which a few months before
he had considered such a likely possibility, must be postponed indefinitely. It was idle to dream of the Pacific Coast
until Canada was in possession of Rupert's Land. And when
the peaceful possession of Rupert's Land would come about,
he had now not the slightest idea. The Canadian emissaries—
Thibault, de Salaberry, and Donald Smith—would probably
have reached Fort Garry by this time. He still hoped that they

could pacify the excitement; but it was obvious that they would encounter a most formidable opposition.

Had not the balance of probabilities tilted against Canada already? The American annexationists, realizing that the crisis of the whole affair was now at hand, would do everything in their power to prevent the Canadians from reaching a peaceful settlement. O'Donoghue and the other pro-American advisers still kept their places in the inner councils of the provisional government; the *New Nation*, which made its first appearance early in January, 1870, began a vigorous propaganda in favour of the union of the colony with the United States. Riel had the clear prospect of American aid; and already, without any external assistance whatever, he had successfully put down an armed protest against his authority in the colony. Had not the whole situation deteriorated so irretrievably that it was beyond the power of the Canadian emissaries to negotiate a peace? "As it is now," Macdonald wrote gloomily to Rose, "it is more than doubtful that they will be allowed access to the territory or intercourse with the insurgents."[37] And even if they were admitted, they would still have to confront men whose pretensions had been encouraged and whose power had been confirmed through the criminal stupidities of McDougall and Dennis. "The two together," Macdonald wrote bitterly, "have done their utmost to destroy our chance of an amicable settlement with these wild people, and now the probability is that our Commissioners will fail and that we must be left to the exhibition of force next spring."[38]

The exhibition of force! He had kept the idea in reserve from the beginning. Now it moved slowly into the forefront of his mind. Perhaps a military expedition was the only certain way of settling the whole complicated and threatening business. But it was a desperate expedient, and he dreaded its possible international consequences. He knew very well that the troubles at Red River were being watched with a steady, eager scrutiny from south of the border. The Fenians, it was reported, were in communication with the half-breed insurgents; the "Yankee wire-pullers" in the American north-west were doing everything they could, with money and propaganda, to exploit

Canadian difficulties. These guerrilla annexationists were dangerous enough in themselves; but far more ominous was the curious interest shown by the American government in the state of affairs in Assiniboia. The accounts which reached Washington of the pro-American attitude of the Hudson's Bay Company's servants aroused the interest of Hamilton Fish, the American Secretary of State. He instructed Motley, the United States' ambassador to the United Kingdom, to make inquiries; and late in January Motley subjected Sir Curtis Lampson, the Deputy-Governor of the Hudson's Bay Company, to a prolonged and surprisingly searching interrogation on the views of the Company's servants concerning the political future of the Red River colony. "I am convinced," Lampson wrote to Northcote, "that the government at Washington feel a much greater interest in this Red River affair than anyone supposes, and the settlement may possibly take a very different turn from what we supposed two months ago."[39]

Macdonald, of course, had no knowledge of this disturbing conversation. But he strongly suspected that such diplomatic manœuvres were going on. He knew that Fish was certain to be interested in the pro-American sympathies of the Hudson's Bay Company's servants and in the annexationist influences which were so strong in the inner councils of Riel's government at Fort Garry. Fish was attempting to acquire all, or a large part, of British North America, by peaceful "constitutional" means. He had inquired of Sir Edward Thornton, the British Minister at Washington, whether his government would object to what was described as a "free vote" being taken in Canada to decide the question of annexation to the United States! Any sign of disaffection, of annexationist sentiment, in any part of British North America would, of course, be valuable to him. He would, Macdonald felt sure, attempt to exploit the troubles at Red River to advance his scheme of peaceful territorial aggrandizement. This "blackguard business" of Fish's both worried and infuriated him.[40] "It is quite evident to me," he wrote to Brydges of the Grand Trunk Railway, who had informed him of another ominous conversation with an American, "not only from this conversation, but from advices from Washington, that the United States' government are resolved to do all they can, short of war, to get possession of the western territory, and we must take immediate and vigorous steps to counteract them."[41]

Yet what steps should he take? Could Canada undertake a military expedition by herself? He knew that at the moment she had neither the prestige nor power to act alone. The risks of separate action, in the circumstances, would be appalling. No, the western expeditionary force must be a mixed force, composed both of British regulars and Canadian militia. The British government must prove to the whole world, by the convincing demonstration of military co-operation, that the United Kingdom was solidly behind Canada in the extension of its authority over the whole British American north-west. He had always been convinced that the Anglo-Canadian alliance would alone enable Canada to secure and maintain its separate political existence in North America. "British North America must belong either to the American or British system of government," he told one correspondent frankly. "It will be a century before we are strong enough to walk alone."[42] They were not nearly strong enough to walk alone yet. They needed British military assistance badly in the north-west. And yet this was the year, of all years, when anti-colonial feelings and separatist tendencies seemed to be gaining rapidly in strength.

It was the attitude of Great Britain which really worried him. He could afford to treat Galt and the other "few fools at Montreal" who were suffering from mild attacks of "independence" with tolerant contempt; but the purposes and policies of the Gladstone government were a different and a much more serious matter. From the start he had been a little suspicious of Gladstone and his colleagues. His doubts were certainly not allayed when Rose reported from London that he had been "a good deal pained to find indications of indifference" in quarters where he would not have expected to find them.[43] How serious some of these "indications" were, Macdonald probably did not realize. He almost certainly did not know that, in the previous June, Granville had actually gone so far as to enquire of the Governor-General whether there was any feeling in Canada in favour of a friendly separation.⁴⁴ He would have been appalled to learn that Sir Curtis Lampson had gone away from a recent conversation at the Colonial Office about the Red River rising with the uneasy impression that "negotiation with the United States is a possible contingency under certain circumstances".⁴⁵ Macdonald was almost certainly ignorant of all this. But at the same time he was very well aware of the equally intimidating fact that Granville and Cardwell, the Liberal Minister of War, had announced with all possible definiteness that the imperial garrisons would be immediately withdrawn from central Canada. The regulars were going in a year when their presence was as necessary as it had ever been before. All of them must not go! Some at least should remain to become part of the western expeditionary force. They must prove, to the United States, the reality of Anglo-Canadian solidarity on the North American continent. "It has got to be a fixed idea at Washington," he wrote to Rose, "that England wants to get rid of the colonies, indeed Mr. Fish has not hesitated to say so."⁴⁶ British regulars in the west would be at once a denial of American hopes and an assurance of Canadian expansion.

IV

February was a month of anniversaries. It was three years now since he had married Agnes, and a year since his daughter Mary had been born. The child had reached the first important stage in the awakening of human energy and intelligence; but her first birthday came and went, and the little struggles and accomplishments which would have delighted Macdonald's heart were so laggard and so few. "She lies," Agnes wrote in her diary, "in spite of her thirteen and a half months, still on the pillow in her little carriage, smiling when she sees me and cooing softly to herself."⁴⁷ She might walk—there was still good hope for that—but not surely with great vigour. She might do many things, but feebly, imperfectly. The terrible enlargement of her head was grievously obvious.

He came away, sick at heart, from these visits to the nursery. In his private life he had met failure after failure. That winter he carried out the arrangement that he had made with Allan and mortgaged all his assets to the Merchants' Bank of Canada. At home he lived with sorrows and worries; and at the office there seemed no end to the state of uncertainty and suspense in which he had existed ever since the troubles began in the north-west. McDougall, "very chop-fallen and at the same time very sulky", returned to Ottawa;[48] and Archbishop Taché, recalled from momentous theological debates at Rome, reached the capital, discussed the whole western imbroglio at length with Macdonald, and departed for Red River as the fourth peaceful emissary of the Canadian government. There was nothing to do now but wait for reports from these western representatives, and for the British reply to Macdonald's request for military assistance. In the meantime, Parliament opened, with Prince Arthur gracing the ceremonies, and "no end of festivities going on". A debate on the Red River fiasco was inevitable; and McDougall, who had now worked out a complete explanation of how his ruin had been accomplished by the malice and stupidity of others, took advantage of the occasion to fling the wildest accusations in all directions. Huntington and Galt, those two advocates of a very carefully qualified form of "independence", introduced resolutions supporting the treaty-making power for Canada, a customs union with the United States, and—as Macdonald explained tolerantly to Rose—"all that kind of nonsense".[49] No, there was nothing very much to be feared from the opposition of McDougall or Galt. Neither the plan for the pacification of Red River, nor the scheme for a joint Anglo-Canadian military expedition was likely to be much affected by their manœuvres. "I have got complete control of the House," he told Rose a little boastfully, "and can do with it pretty much as I please."[50]

Then the long-awaited news began to arrive from Red River. Macdonald looked at it, and looked at it again, with growing misgivings. In one sense, it was reassuring, even encouraging, yet it filled him with disquiet. Donald Smith, who had reached Fort Garry on December 27, had apparently achieved a good deal in a relatively short space of time. Within a few weeks he had somehow managed to acquire a considerable influence in the settlement; he had succeeded in appealing over Riel's head to the whole community of Red River. On January 19, a large number of citizens assembled in Fort Garry to hear him explain his mission. On January 20, a second and still more largely attended mass meeting decided that a convention, composed of twenty representatives from the French-speaking parishes and twenty representatives from the English-speaking parishes, should be called to consider the needs of the settlement and the proposals which Smith had brought. The convention, which met less than a week later on January 26, proceeded to draw up a statement—called a "list of rights"—of the claims and wishes of Assiniboia. On February 7, the list of rights was presented to Smith; and Smith then invited the convention to send delegates to Ottawa to discuss the affairs of the settlement with the Canadian government.

These were favourable results. But they had been obtained only as a result of protracted explanations and debates at Fort Garry; and these long negotiations had other and less fortunate consequences. They strengthened the political consciousness of the settlers and confirmed their improvised political institutions. Up to this point, Riel's rule had been accepted only by the French-speaking part of the community. But now the *métis* leader urged the convention to approve and reconstitute the provisional government; and the English and Scots delegates, after having obtained—incredible as it seemed—some kind of sanction from Governor Mactavish, agreed to recognize the régime and to elect Riel president. All this was disturbing enough; but it was quickly followed by a still more sinister piece of news. The irrepressible "Canadian party" in Assiniboia had chosen the peculiarly unfortunate moment of Riel's political triumph to make another suicidal attempt at resistance; and this second outbreak was as abject a failure as the first. Macdonald was deeply perturbed. "The foolish and criminal attempt of Schultz and Captain Boulton," he wrote gravely, "to renew the fight has added greatly to Riel's strength. He has put down two distinct attempts to upset his government, and American sympathizers will begin to argue that his government has acquired a legal status, and he will be readily persuaded of that fact himself."[51] It was only too true. Riel was persuaded that his government was legitimate. It was founded on popular will. It had withstood the shock of attack. It had become, in fact, what Macdonald had always feared it would become, the *de facto* government at Red River.

There was no doubt now, in Macdonald's mind, of the need of the military expedition. It would probably come to fighting yet. What did he know of Riel's purposes? Was the half-breed acting in good faith when he had agreed to send delegates to confer with the Canadian government? Or was he secretly determined, with American assistance, to continue the fight—to found an independent republic—to take the Red River colony into the United States? ". . . The unpleasant suspicion remains," Macdonald confided to Rose, "that he is only wasting time by sending this delegation, until the approach of summer enables him to get material support from the United States."[52] Canada might have a real struggle on its hands yet, he realized, and he waited impatiently for the answer of the imperial government. It came only after considerable discussion in the Liberal Cabinet, for, as usual on a Canadian matter, Gladstone was full of doubts and reservations.[53] But in the end Granville brushed these misgivings aside without much ceremony. "I see no alternative to our standing by the Canadians," he told his chief, "and if so the prompt assertion of authority is probably the safest."[54] On March 6, the official cable promising British military co-operation arrived at Ottawa.[55] The offer was, of course, accompanied by conditions—the first of a growing list of conditions. Canada must grant reasonable terms to the Roman Catholic settlers, and the transfer of the territory to the Dominion must accompany the movement of troops. Yet the matter was settled. There would be help from overseas.

It would be needed, he was more and more convinced. Before the month was out, a last and most appalling piece of news arrived from Red River. Riel had given one final proof of the fact that military power was the one solid and constant basis of his provisional government. On March 3, one of his Canadian prisoners, an obstreperous youth named Thomas Scott, was charged with having taken up arms against the provisional government (of which offence all the other prisoners were equally guilty), with insubordination, and with striking his guards. For these crimes he was tried in a summary fashion before a military tribunal, sentenced to death, and executed within twenty-four hours. Riel may have decided to strike fear into the hearts of his opponents by a savage example; or his hand may have been forced by the murderous temper of his unruly followers. But the execution of Scott, whatever its motive, utterly changed the problem of the Red River rising. It made Macdonald almost despair of a peaceful settlement.[56] He was more than ever doubtful of Riel's good faith. He feared a desperate half-breed resistance. And he was only too well aware that the execution of Thomas Scott, unlike any previous incident in the Riel rising, had aroused a passionate controversy over policy in central Canada.

English-speaking Ontario, which identified itself with Scott and the "Canadian party", clamoured for the dispatch of a military expedition to Red River, and insisted that there must be no negotiation with emissaries from the murderers of Scott. French-speaking Quebec, which instinctively sympathized with Riel and his *métis*, denied the need for force, and demanded that the government seek a peaceful settlement through negotiation with the delegates from Red River. Macdonald could have groaned in spirit. From the start the Red River affair had been full of international complications. Now it was perplexed by all the rancours of Canadian domestic politics. He foresaw a racial division in the House—an inevitable split in the Cabinet, with the Ontarions and the Maritimers demanding a military expedition, and Cartier and Langevin obstinately opposing, and himself almost torn to pieces by the struggles between the two.

It was at this inopportune moment that the rumour of a new Fenian raid burst upon Ottawa. John O'Neill, the Fenian leader at the Battle of Ridgeway two years before, was expected, according to McMicken's espionage service, to invade in force about April 15.[57] The last complication had now been added.

Yet, in the circumstances, it was an inevitable complication. Macdonald had expected it. From the very beginning of the troubles at Red River, he had feared that the Fenians would try to take advantage of Canada's western difficulties by launching an attack in the east. Now the attack was coming. And it was coming at a time when Great Britain had publicly announced the recall of the imperial garrisons from British North America, and when the western military expedition, in which she had agreed to co-operate, was being held up by annoying British conditions and stipulations. He felt like the solitary defender of a beleaguered city. "We are glad to know," he wrote to his old friend, Lord Carnarvon, on April 14, the day before O'Neill's raid was expected, "that we have in you a friend —I may almost say a friend in need—for we greatly distrust the men at the helm in England. . . . At this moment we are in daily expectation of a formidable Fenian invasion, unrepressed by the United States government, and connived at by their subordinate officials. And we are at the same time called upon to send a military force to restore order in Rupert's Land. Her Majesty's Government have been kept fully informed of the constant threats from the Fenian body for the last five years, and they have been specially forewarned of the preparations for the present expected attack. And yet this is the time they choose to withdraw every soldier from us, and we are left to be the unaided victims of Irish discontent and American hostility. . . ."[58] It was a bitter reproach, its tone perhaps heightened for Carnarvon's benefit, yet in a fashion not unjustified by the circumstances. The crisis seemed to mount about him. "We must however bear it as best we may," he ended his letter to Carnarvon, "and we intend, with God's blessing, to keep our country, if we can, for the Queen against all comers."

V

Not even the arrival of the delegates from the west could take place peacefully. On April 11, the first two of them, Father Ritchot and Alfred H. Scott, reached Ottawa; but they

had not been in the capital more than two days when they were
arrested, charged with aiding and abetting the murder of
Thomas Scott, on warrants sworn out by ardent young Ontario
patriots who deeply sympathized with the "Canadian party"
at Red River.[59] In the meantime, while the first two delegates
cooled their heels in custody, and Ritchot protested indignantly
at this violation of their "diplomatic" immunity, the third
representative, "Judge" Black, the Recorder at Red River,
arrived in Ottawa. Macdonald saw him privately and unofficially
at the earliest possible moment. Black was a servant of the
Hudson's Bay Company, a moderate man, very different from
the fanatical Ritchot and the pro-American Scott; and Macdonald hoped that, with his help, it might be possible to
reduce the extreme demands which the delegation as a whole
was only too likely to make. He did not want to recognize
the delegates officially. He much preferred to receive them
as representatives, not of Riel's provisional government, but of
the convention, of the people of the north-west. The negotiations, he was convinced, must be kept at the level of informal,
private discussions; and their basis could be only the list of
rights which the convention had adopted after long public
debate.

He began to realize that he would likely have to give way
on many of these points. He was not negotiating with the
representatives of a real frontier democracy. Black, Ritchot,
and Scott were not simply and solely the deputies of the whole
community of Red River. They were something rather less
—and more. They were, to a large but indefinite extent, the
agents of a remarkably astute, extremely dictatorial half-breed
leader, Louis Riel, who was determined to manipulate the Red
River rising in the special interests of his own people, the
French-speaking *métis*. It was all over Ontario now—A. H.
Scott had revealed the fact in a newspaper interview before
his arrest—that the delegates had come armed with a new
and revised "list of rights".[60] This second list had never been
submitted for approval to the convention, or to the "legislature"
of the provisional government, which was actually in session at
the time the delegates left. It had simply been privately drawn

up by the French-speaking members of the executive alone; and, as Macdonald speedily discovered, its terms were not only much more exacting than those of the first list, but also in some vital respects completely different. The second list included a demand that Assiniboia enter Confederation as a province, despite the fact that the convention had considered a proposal for provincial status and had expressly rejected it by a considerable majority.[61] The Red River community, democratically organized, did not want provincial status. But Riel did. And so did the French-speaking members of the executive and their clerical advisers, Archbishop Taché and Father Ritchot. Their purpose was evident. They wished to establish the character and institutions of the new western province at a moment when the French-speaking Roman Catholic half-breeds were still in a majority, and therefore at the most favourable opportunity for preparing defences against the approaching influx of Protestant, English-speaking settlers.

He realized that he would have to accept provincial status. This first western province would be an absurdly premature creation, a top-heavy, needlessly expensive establishment, which he had never expected and did not want. Yet, in the circumstances of Canadian politics, it was apparently unavoidable. It was the price that he would have to pay for the military expedition. He still doubted Riel's good faith, and feared his intentions. He still believed, despite the presence of the delegates and their apparent readiness to negotiate, in the necessity of the military expedition; and he was sustained by the welcome knowledge that Cartier emphatically agreed with him. Cartier's support was vitally necessary. But Cartier did not stand alone. Back of him, giving him political strength, were the Quebec members, his docile troop of "moutons" who usually followed him submissively enough, but who now began to show unmistakable signs of obstreperous restiveness. Like most of their fellow French Canadians, they identified themselves emotionally with the cause of Riel; they opposed the use of force against his government; and it was now rumoured on all hands that they had threatened to desert Cartier in a body if it were decided to send a military expedition to Red River.[62]

Macdonald knew very well that there was one obvious method of meeting this threat and of ensuring Assiniboia's entrance into Confederation on his own terms. With the help of the opposition, which was ready and eager to exploit the fury of Protestant, English-speaking Ontario, he could disregard Cartier's followers, authorize the military expedition, and insist that the list of rights adopted by the convention could alone be accepted as a basis for negotiation. No doubt he could do all those things. But it would mean abandoning Cartier, ruining the Liberal-Conservative party, breaking up the Anglo-French *entente* upon which Confederation itself was based. He did not even consider the possibility. At all costs—or nearly all costs —Cartier must be sustained. He must have something with which to satisfy his "moutons", and they would be satisfied only if Ritchot were satisfied. "The French," wrote one shrewd observer at Ottawa, "are earnestly bent upon the establishment of a French and Catholic power in the north-west to counteract the great preponderance of Ontario."[63] There was no way out. Provincial status—whatever its value ultimately for French-Canadian ambitions—would have to be conceded. They must negotiate on the basis of the exacting terms demanded by the executive at Red River.

On Saturday, April 23, Father Ritchot and Alfred Scott were finally discharged.[64] The negotiations with the three delegates were scheduled to begin on Monday; and on Sunday night, along with a large party, he and Agnes dined at Rideau Hall.[65] The crisis of his difficulties was at hand. It was true that the prompt muster of the militia had apparently intimidated the Fenians, for there had been as yet no real sign of John O'Neill's threatened raid. But the British government was still haggling about the terms on which it would permit imperial soldiers to be sent to the north-west; and Macdonald was now beginning to fear that the Americans, although they had used the Canadian canals freely for the transport of military stores during the American Civil War, would refuse passage on the Sault Ste. Marie Canal for the Red River expeditionary force.

He was uneasily conscious of dangers hidden or only partly disclosed, of the watchful scrutiny of a ring of pairs of eyes—eyes that were curious, or questioning, or admonitory, or hostile. The Colonial Office had sent Sir Clinton Murdoch to watch over the negotiations with the delegates; and Sir Stafford Northcote, ruddy, cheerful, and curious, the new Governor of the Hudson's Bay Company, had hastened across the ocean to protect the interests of his shareholders. He was present that night at Sir John Young's dinner party, politely pumping Macdonald for information. And there was still another interested visitor to Ottawa, who had not been invited to Rideau Hall that evening, but who had, oddly enough, been having long and intimate conversations with the delegates from Red River. It was J. W. Taylor, the special agent of the American State Department, who had found that business called him imperatively to the capital of Canada.[66]

On Monday, when he and Cartier met the reunited Red River delegation, Macdonald quickly found his worst fears realized. Ritchot was the most powerful of the three delegates, and he was both peremptory and uncompromising. He threatened to return to the north-west if the delegates were not given official recognition. He refused to negotiate on any other basis than that of the list of rights which the executive government had drawn up. He himself had brought a special copy of this list, different in one very significant particular from those which had been supplied to Black and Scott. The Ritchot version contained what had been included in no previous list, a demand for Separate Schools for Roman Catholics, supported by public money, on a basis of population.[67] The convention of the people at Fort Garry had made no request whatever for Separate Schools. It is not even certain that the French-speaking members of the executive ever authorized the demand; and the new clause may have been inserted by Riel alone, at the earnest solicitation of his clerical advisers. In any case, however it got into the Ritchot version, the request for Separate Schools was emphatically made at Ottawa. Macdonald knew that it would have to be conceded. He had no means of getting past these delegates to the people of Red River whose known wishes were being so freely altered. If he questioned the validity of the revised list of rights, he would merely arouse the French-Canadian members at Ottawa, imperil Cartier's position, and bring on a racial war. He gave way. "We are nearly through our troubles with the delegates," he wrote at last to Sir John Young on Wednesday, April 27, "and then we can take up the military matter."[68]

He was weak with fatigue. Yet fatigue was not the only thing that oppressed him. He was burdened with a general distress which lay heavily upon both body and spirit. For some time now he had not felt really well. Usually his trouble seemed to be nothing more than a malaise, a vague, unhappy feeling of discomfort. But sometimes, at rare intervals, there were more precise and much more disquieting symptoms. Occasionally he felt, high in his back, an odd, uncomfortable sensation of tightness, as if some organ, or organs, had been unnaturally distended; and once or twice, some terrible force—it was almost like a cruel, grasping hand—had closed briefly but agonizingly upon these stretched sensitive surfaces. He shuddered with pain and bewilderment. Yes, there must be something wrong with him. When the session was over, he would see a doctor. Yet there was another and a far more serious trouble, which, he knew now, was probably beyond the cure of any doctor. There could no longer be any real doubt that Mary's condition was irremediable. She would never be a normal girl and woman. In a sudden clairvoyant vision, which illuminated the future like a beam of harsh, pitiless light, he saw a dreary procession of treatments and manipulations, an endless repetition of hopes and doubts and deceptions, which could end only in despair. He could not even guarantee material security for this helpless, dependent being—or for Agnes, or for Hugh and himself. Everything that he had scraped together in half a lifetime of professional effort had gone to meet his obligations at the Merchants' Bank. . . . He was sick of Riel, and Red River, and these interminable negotiations. The piled papers lay on the desk in front of him. The gaze of the delegates was fixed upon him with implacable ferret-like intentness. Laboriously they worked their way through the clauses. It was Thursday night and the business was nearly finished. Tomorrow they could put the last touches to the act which would transform Assiniboia into the new Province of Manitoba.

He walked down the corridors of the Parliament Buildings and into the bar. The next morning, when Sir Stafford Northcote went down to breakfast, he was greeted by the alarming intelligence, "Bad news, Sir John A. has broken out again";[69] and, at intervals during Friday, Macdonald was seen about the House and in Russell's Hotel, obviously intoxicated, and keeping himself erect with difficulty.[70] People had half expected, Northcote went on to tell Disraeli, that the Prime Minister would "break out" once the crisis of the Red River affair was over. But Macdonald, for reasons that lay beyond the knowledge or the imagination of most, had anticipated the event. For at least a day he tried at one and the same time to continue his work and to satisfy the insatiable craving within him. But it was no use. The papers before him became a muddled chaos. The realization that this was another bout broke through the disorder of his mind, and he took the last precaution which he had taken often enough before. "His habit is," Northcote informed Disraeli, "to retire to bed, to exclude everybody, and to drink bottle after bottle of port. All the papers are sent to him, and he reads them, but he is conscious of his inability to do any important business and he does none." He did none for at least two days, while the *Globe* began charitably to denounce his drunkenness, and the government papers ascribed his temporary breakdown to pressure of overwork. Friday and Saturday and Sunday went by. The week-end was over.

Then, with a great effort, he roused himself. After all, the work of the last six months was almost finished. The military expedition, with its complement of British regulars and with Colonel Garnet Wolseley as its commander, was about to leave for Red River; and a political settlement of the north-west had finally been achieved in the Manitoba Bill. The session was nearly over. Only a little more effort was required. But it was absolutely essential that he himself should make it; and, in his absence, everything was going wrong in the House. The ministers were leaderless, intimidated, and uncertain of their following. They fumbled, hesitated, and lost direction. "The House is becoming rapidly demoralized," wrote one experienced observer, "and the government is losing its control over the members."[71] There was not a moment for delay, Macdonald realized. He must appear immediately in the House. The Bill was ready, though printed copies were not yet available to members; and on Monday afternoon, May 2, he went down to the House to make his first explanation of the Manitoba Act. He was pale, his face was drawn, and he looked and felt ill.[72] His voice, which was never very strong and sometimes indistinct at the beginning of a speech, seemed unusually feeble. But he had summoned up all his old skill in presenting an argument, all his old ingenious dexterity in avoiding pitfalls and anticipating criticisms.

"The Bill affecting Red River," he wrote to Sir John Young on May 4, "was received last night with great favour by the House, and will pass without any serious opposition."[73] The first reading was over. He was confident that the party was reunited and that the House would do his bidding. It was true that there would have to be one major amendment to the Bill for the boundaries of the new province had been somewhat curiously drawn to exclude the settlement at Portage la Prairie where the "Canadian party" was strongest, and McDougall and the opposition had leaped triumphantly upon this pointed omission. But the enlargement of the boundaries was the only important change that would have to be made; and on Friday, May 6, he waited for the debate on the second reading without much apprehension. It was early afternoon. He had come from the Council chamber only a little while before; the last caller had just left him; and he sat in his office preparing to eat the sketchy luncheon which, during the crowded days of the session of 1870, was often brought in to him. He rested for a moment, savouring the welcome peace; and then, without warning, the pain was upon him, like a wild animal, savage, implacable, immitigable. He stood up twisting, writhing, trying to bear the pain, knowing he could not bear it; and somewhere in his back, the pressure, like a great iron hand, closed inexorably on his vitals. He felt his senses whirling, spinning, dropping into a dark void of agony. He clutched the table, swayed, tried to recover his balance, and fell blindly across the carpet.

Chapter Three

Fish and Diplomacy

I

Dr. Grant, who arrived in a few minutes and found Macdonald in a state of collapse, diagnosed the disease as "biliary calculus" or gall-stones. Obviously the dreadful seizure had been caused by the passage of a stone, and there could be no doubt that the patient was in a most alarming condition.[1] His pulse barely fluttered; he was almost insensible with the pain he had endured; and, as Dr. Grant explained to the fearful Agnes, it was utterly impossible to think of moving him for a while at least. He would have to lie, almost literally, where he had fallen. The office where he had worked and eaten his hurried meals, where he had done everything but sleep, was now, by a preposterous exaggeration, to become his bedroom. In these incongruous surroundings, all the paraphernalia of the sick-room would have to be improvised and at once. It was a task that exactly suited Agnes. Her devotion to her husband, her strong sense of duty, her uneasy, recurrent suspicion that the life which she and her friends led was largely frivolous, all helped to fortify her for the work that now lay ahead. Under Dr. Grant's direction, she assumed control of the sick-room. She watched, waited, anticipated needs, and multiplied attentions with an unwearied and slavish devotion. If her nursing could accomplish it, he would live.

Yet nobody really believed that he would live. May was a month of brief recoveries and dreadful relapses during most of which his condition remained critical. Friends, assuming in secret that their old leader had not long to live, began to make discreet enquiries about the state of his affairs and discovered his almost penniless condition with horrified surprise. The general public, kept informed by a series of gloomy newspaper bulletins, was convinced that death was inevitable in a matter of days. At the end of the month he was still frighteningly weak.[2] The doctors virtually gave up all hope of his recovery. And it was perhaps the very desperateness of his condition which induced them to take advantage of a brief period of improvement to move him in a litter from the cramped quarters of his office in the East Block to the relative ease and convenience of the Speaker's chambers in the Parliament Buildings. Edward Blake, in a kindly letter of condolence and sympathy, called this migration a "march of recovery".[3] So it proved to be. Macdonald stood the little journey of June 2 well. The next day he was better again. And all during June, while Ottawa sweated and suffocated in one of the hottest summers in its history, he steadily improved. By the middle of the month, he was definitely past the crisis.[4] He would live now. The period of convalescence had begun. And for that it was best for him to get away from Ottawa, which was baked with drought and heat, and which, a few weeks later, was to be covered by a thick, grey pall of dust and smoke from a dangerously encroaching ring of forest fires.

He had to be carried on board the steamship when, on July 2, he finally left Ottawa, in company with Agnes, and Mary and Dr. Grant. The government steamer *Druid* brought them slowly down the St. Lawrence and into the cool breezes of the gulf; and it was not until the morning of July 8 that they finally tied up at Pope's Wharf in the harbour of Charlottetown, Prince Edward Island.[5] Colonel Gray, who had acted as host to the Charlottetown Conference nearly six years before, was waiting hospitably at the quayside with his carriage; and when Macdonald had been lifted ashore in an easy chair, they drove off cautiously towards Falconwood, a comfortable house on the banks of the Hillsborough, in the near vicinity of Charlottetown, which had been fitted up as a temporary residence for the patient and his family. There Macdonald rapidly improved. Within a week he was taking short walks in the grounds of

Falconwood. Now his convalescence had entered the final, not unpleasant, stages which lead towards complete recovery. And all that summer, while Europe rocked with the Franco-Prussian War, and England doubtfully considered the diplomatic future, he remained placidly fixed in the deep peace of Prince Edward Island. People respected his temporary retirement. He received few letters and sent fewer replies. He spent more time over the articles on the war in the English periodicals than he did on the ferocious controversies of the Canadian newspapers; and instead of worrying about party manœuvres in the constituencies, he followed the cavalry charges at Mars-la-Tour and Gravelotte, and watched the inexorable encirclement of Sedan.

On September 16, when they finally left Charlottetown, he walked aboard the steamship in what was almost his old jaunty style.[6] He had made a marvellous recovery; and he could have counted the summer of 1870 as one of the happiest and freest from worry that he had ever spent, if it had not been for the deepening tragedy of little Mary. The child was now a year and a half old. Her terrible physical abnormality, the enlarged head, was more conspicuous than ever; and her slow responses, at a time when a spring-like spontaneity was natural, left no doubt of the impairment of her mind and spirit. On the journey up the gulf from Prince Edward Island, she became ill; and, in the end, she had to be left at Quebec, in the care of old Mrs. Bernard, while he and Agnes came on alone together to Ottawa. The station platform at the capital was sumptuously carpeted when they stepped out of the train on the morning of September 22, and there were dozens who rushed forward eagerly to shake Macdonald's hand.[7] It was a joyful yet an awed reception. He might have been risen from the dead.

At home there was a great pile of congratulatory telegrams and letters, and oddly assorted gifts, including a basket of grapes from Moll and Professor Williamson, and a suit made of Canadian tweed and sent by an admiring Conservative woollen manufacturer. "I see," he wrote jovially in reply, "that you are resolved by sending me such an outfit to keep me politically consistent; with such a nice suit of new clothes I have no pretext for turning my coat!"[8] He smiled as he worked easily and rapidly through the huge pile of correspondence. He was flexing political muscles which had remained unused for months and which yet responded with reasonable elasticity. It was good to be back. He was not laid on the shelf yet, thank God! At the station everybody had been obviously surprised by the apparent completeness of his recovery. He had been told a dozen times enthusiastically that he had never looked better in his life. The truth, he knew very well, was a little less wonderful. He had made an extraordinarily successful recovery. There was nothing organically wrong with him now that any doctor could discover. But his strength had not entirely come back. He would have to take things easy for a while. "I shall not do much work for some months," he told his sister, "but act in the government as consulting physician."[9]

II

He picked up the old design—the union of British North America—where he had dropped it so hurriedly. On the whole, it was an encouraging moment for a reassessment. The forces which he had set in motion had travelled surely on towards their objectives during his absence. In the east, it was true, he had made no progress whatever. Both Prince Edward Island and Newfoundland had refused the better terms which had been offered them, and in the circumstances it was better to let the question of their entry into Confederation drop quietly for the moment. He would have to wait a while yet for the remaining provinces in the east; but in the west the territorial expansion of the new Dominion was about to be triumphantly completed. The Red River military expedition had reached its objective without incident, and had confirmed British-Canadian occupation of the north-west. The Province of Manitoba had been set up; and the delegates from British Columbia had come east and had agreed to the terms on which their province was to be united with Canada. These terms, of course, had yet to be ratified by the Dominion Parliament and the British Columbia legislature; and although the Red River affair had ostensibly been wound up in a satisfactory fashion, there remained a perplexing, annoying loose end—the question of an amnesty for the leaders of the rebellion, a question hideously complicated by the execution of Scott. Still, this was not an immediately pressing problem. It could be left, Macdonald thought, to "time, that great curer of evils". But the union with British Columbia was another and a much more urgent matter. Canada had, as part of the compact, agreed to begin a railway to the Pacific within two years, and to complete it within ten years, of the date of the union. "The terms can, I think," Macdonald wrote to Musgrave, the Lieutenant-Governor of British Columbia, "be fully justified on their own merits; but we may expect considerable opposition in our Parliament on the ground that they are burdensome to the Dominion and too liberal to British Columbia."[10] It would help greatly, he thought, if the legislature of British Columbia accepted the terms as they stood at once. The Dominion Parliament, when it met next winter, would hesitate to change an approved arrangement.

These were matters of tactics. He had no real doubt of a successful issue. The forces inside British North America which favoured a transcontinental union had not yet lost their potency. What worried him most, as he took stock in the early autumn of 1870, was not so much the association of the parts as the security of the whole. Confederation, as he knew very well, had been to an indefinitely large extent a response to a potential danger from the United States. That danger had not yet manifested itself in coercive diplomatic pressure, or taken the horrid shape of open war. But, on the other hand, it had never been entirely cleared away. The disputes and animosities which had grown up during the American Civil War between Great Britain and British America on one hand and the United States on the other, remained unsettled, to everybody's chronic dissatisfaction. The damages claimed by the United States for the losses wrought by the *Alabama* and the other cruisers built in British shipyards had not been honoured by Great Britain; and Canada had never got a copper of compensation for all the needless worry, expense, and loss of life which

had been caused by the Fenian Raids. Canadian-American relations had been extremely bad before 1867; and the years since
Confederation had certainly brought no improvement. In
1870, and particularly during Macdonald's illness, there had
been, in fact, a further marked deterioration; and this, as he
knew well, was the consequence of the termination of the Reciprocity Treaty which the Americans, with an angry desire for
retaliation, had brought about in 1866.

So long as the Reciprocity Treaty lasted, American fishermen
had been permitted to ply their trade freely within the three-
mile limit of British North America. But, once the Treaty had
been abrogated, these spacious freedoms came to an end.
Citizens of the United States were flung back upon the privileges which had been guaranteed to them by the Convention
of 1818; and by the terms of this Convention, American fishing
vessels could enter the bays and harbours of Nova Scotia,
New Brunswick and Prince Edward Island "for the purpose of
shelter and of repairing damages therein, of purchasing wood
and of obtaining water, and for no other purpose whatever".[11]
The complete exclusion of Americans from the inshore fisheries
of British North America was thus an unquestionable treaty
right. But the provinces, realizing that American fishermen had
come to take their long-accustomed fishing privileges almost for
granted, decided to assert their rights of exclusion in a gradual
and conciliatory manner.

During the seasons of 1866 and 1867, they permitted American fishing vessels to fish within the three-mile limit on the
payment of a small fee; and for the following two years licences
were again issued at somewhat higher rates.[12] But the Americans
abused the licence system without scruple; when the fee was
raised, only a very small fraction of them bothered to take out
licences. And Macdonald decided to make an end of this
régime of unappreciated indulgence. He was perfectly ready
to exchange the inshore fisheries for tariff concessions in the
American market, as had been done in the Reciprocity Treaty;
but he saw no point in surrendering property to people who
were determined to appropriate it for nothing. "We are going
to put an end to all fishing licences," he had written to Rose

during the previous January, "as the system has proved abortive."[13] During the summer, while he had been ill, the Canadian government had fitted out several marine cruisers to protect its inshore waters from marauders; and when he got back to Ottawa in the autumn he discovered that the American State Department had been indignantly protesting against the resulting seizure of fishing vessels, and that the fisheries had become an international issue once again.

For a while after his return, he tried to take things easily. He was determined, if it were possible, not to prejudice his complete recovery with overwork. His illness, his long convalescence, his long absence from Ottawa, all combined to invest this resumption of his old activities with something of the significance of a new departure in his career. He decided —it was in keeping with the opening of a new chapter in his life—to leave the "Quadrilateral", with its recurrently defective drainage system, for a new and more spacious house on the outskirts of the town. "I am now in the agonies of moving into Reynolds' house for the winter," he told David Macpherson early in November. "I am regularly driven out of my present one by the stench from the drains."[14] "Reynolds' house", known later as Earnscliffe, the house in which he was to spend the last years of his life, was a comfortable, rambling, many-gabled house, which stood about a mile or more north-east of town, on a great cliff fringed with low trees, overlooking the broad expanse of the Ottawa River, and the sombre masses of the Laurentian Hills beyond. The house was secluded and relatively inaccessible; and as the uninterrupted mornings and peaceful evenings succeeded each other, he began to feel progressively better. "I am, thank God, in good health and spirits," he wrote to one correspondent, "and I think have got a new lease under more easy terms than the old."[15] Yet he tried carefully not to overtax his new-found strength. "I do not do much office work," he told Archibald reassuringly, "but my attendance at Council is absolutely necessary."[16]

In Council that autumn the most important matters that came up for discussion were the problem of Canadian-American relations in general and the problem of the fisheries in particular. During the summer, while he had been convalescing, Macdonald had wondered anxiously whether Peter Mitchell, the Minister of Marine and Fisheries, was not enforcing the new policy of exclusion with more rigour than was strictly necessary; and, when autumn came, it became quite clear that Great Britain, upon whom Canada depended for diplomatic and moral support in her fisheries policy, was even more apprehensive of possible trouble with the United States. "A very unpleasant dispatch respecting fisheries has come from England," he wrote to Alexander Campbell, who had been pleading with him to go away for another holiday, "in consequence of the too energetic action of the irrepressible Minister of Marine. I must take that subject into my own hands."[17] It was easy to modify the strictness of Mitchell's policy slightly, in the hope of satisfying the British and soothing the Americans; but Macdonald had no intention of making an abject surrender of Canada's main exclusive rights in the fisheries. And what worried him now was the possibility that this ominously growing concern of the British government over the policy of exclusion really implied an anxiety to come to terms with the United States at any price.

For Great Britain, the need for a reconciliation with the United States was now more urgent than ever.[18] The Franco-Prussian War had involved England in serious embarrassments in Europe. As soon as Metz fell and the defeat of France seemed imminent, Russia took advantage of the situation by denouncing the clauses in the Treaty of Paris of 1856 which forbade her to establish naval or military bases on the Black Sea. England would have to meet this challenge without support from Europe. And why, in such dangerous circumstances, should she continue to run the risk of trouble with America? Once again, as had happened with such tragic frequency in the past, the Anglo-Canadian resistance to the United States had been weakened, at the crucial moment, by the distracting events in Europe. And once again Macdonald feared, and with reason, that the United States would attempt to exploit the British desire for appeasement by extracting ruinous concessions at Canada's expense.

He knew that important voices in the republic had urged the cession of all or part of Canada in payment of the *Alabama* claims, and that Fish, the American Secretary of State, had actually been trying, under the guise of a disinterested concern for British North American "freedom", to persuade Great Britain to abandon Canada.[19] He did not believe that even the Gladstone government could be induced to give more than a glance at this blatant manœuvre of American imperialism. No, there was no real need to fear the abandonment of British withdrawal. But, if the surrender of Canadian territory was unthinkable, could one be equally sure of the defence of other Canadian property rights? As the autumn wore on, it became obvious that Great Britain was earnestly considering the establishment of an Anglo-American Commission which would deal, not only with the problem of the fisheries, but also with all outstanding disputes between herself and the republic. Would Canadian fishing rights suffer by being included in this general agenda? Macdonald was distinctly apprehensive. He suspected that the Convention of 1818 was the weak point at which the United States would strike for the purpose of dividing Canada from Great Britain; and early in December, when President Grant gave his annual message to Congress, his fears were bluntly confirmed. "The imperial government," declared the President in a tone of mingled hostility and condescension, "is understood to have delegated the whole or a share of its control or jurisdiction of the inshore fishing grounds to the colonial authority known as the Dominion of Canada, and this semi-independent but irresponsible agent has exercised its delegated power in an unfriendly way. . . . It is hoped that the government of Great Britain will see the justice of abandoning the narrow and inconsistent claim to which her Canadian provinces have urged her adherence."[20]

III

On New Year's Day, 1871, he called another Cabinet on the everlasting fisheries question. It was deep winter now.

The Ottawa River, which had been so charming in its ruffled blue two months before, was stilled and white with ice; and the strident winds blew harshly from the north-west. "More fires," Agnes wrote in her diary, "is our war-cry, our watch-word, our hourly, nay, momently entreaty."[21] Reynolds' house, with the trees on the cliff side bent to the gale, was certainly exposed; but it was also spacious and well-appointed; and, as the night of January 1, 1871, came on, it was pleasant to think of going back to it, with its fires all crackling and its furniture all polished in readiness for the annual parade of New Year's visitors. When he got back, it was nearly dinner-time. Snow was falling now, in great, wind-blown showers, and his shoulders as he entered were thickly powdered. Inside, on the sideboard, were the remains of the sherry and the hot oyster soup with which Agnes had entertained her visitors. Over one hundred and thirty gentlemen had called to pay the Macdonalds the compliments of the season! Agnes was full of the day's doings. But she watched Macdonald's tired face with anxious interest. ". . . I think this American fishery question bothers Sir John," she wrote. "I suppose it is ticklish business as Brother Sam may show fight."[22] It was indeed a ticklish business. Council continued to prepare the Canadian case respecting the fisheries and the Fenians, as if there were a near prospect of a settlement. But nothing happened until the second day of February. Then Macdonald received a short significant note from the Governor-General, newly raised to the peerage as Lord Lisgar.

He hurried over to Rideau Hall. There on the Governor-General's desk lay a decoded cable which had arrived the day before from the Colonial Office. "If Joint Commission is appointed to consider questions pending between the United Kingdom and the United States," it read, "will Macdonald serve as Commissioner for Canada, or Rose, or both?"[23] Obviously the matter was nearly settled. The Joint Commission was a virtual certainty; and, as Macdonald had feared, its agenda would be a general one, with all questions mingled together, perhaps to the prejudice of Canadian rights and interests. He did not definitely know yet whether the British interpretation of the Convention of 1818 agreed substantially with the Canadian one,

and whether he could count upon a united British-Canadian
front in defence of the fisheries. This was a crucial point
which must certainly be cleared up before the arrangements
for the Commission were very far advanced; and there was
now no time for dispatches. "Important that Canada should
know," Lisgar cabled to Kimberley, "points of agreement and
difference between England and herself as to fishery rights."[24]

In the meantime, while they waited for the reply from the
Colonial Office, Macdonald considered Kimberley's invitation.
He did not like it very much. His first impulse, as he told
Lisgar frankly, was to advise the Governor-General that Canada
had better not be represented on such a Commission at all.
Yet, as soon as he had tentatively framed such a reply, he
realized immediately that it would be impossible to submit it.
". . .We must consider," he told Lisgar, "that if Canada allowed
the matter to go by default, and left its interests to be adjudi-
cated upon and settled by a Commission composed exclusively
of Americans having an adverse interest, and Englishmen
having little or no interest in Canada, the government here
would be very much censured if the result were a sacrifice of
the rights of the Dominion."[25] No, Canada would have to be
represented on the Commission, whatever dangers were involved.
But what kind of a representation would be best? Should Rose
and he both go? Or should one of them go alone?

Rose was one of his best friends. Rose had been active in
Canadian politics for years, had resigned his portfolio as
Minister of Finance barely eighteen months before, and, since
his removal to England, had served Canada in a variety of ways
as an interested and informed unofficial agent. Macdonald was
very fond of him. Personally, he told Lord Lisgar, he "would
like no better colleague to fight Canada's battle on the Commission". But no, it would not do. Rose was not a Canadian
by birth. He had left the country to become a permanent
resident of the United Kingdom; and he was a member of an
Anglo-American banking house, which had important interests
in the United States and which at the moment was vitally
dependent upon the good will of the American government.
Politically, it would be very dangerous for the Canadian govern-

ment to sponsor him. He was unacceptable either as a sole, or as an associate, representative for Canada.[26]

There remained Macdonald himself. It was obviously his duty to go; and, although the prospect worried him, some at least of his misgivings had been allayed by the Colonial Office's cabled statement of its views about the fisheries. "It would be impossible," Kimberley replied to the Canadian cable of inquiry, "to pledge ourselves to any foregone conclusion on any particular point before entering upon negotiations, but as at present advised we think the right of Canada to exclusive fisheries within three mile limit beyond dispute and only to be ceded for adequate compensation."[27] It was true that this highly satisfactory statement was followed by a couple of qualifications. The Colonial Office was willing to compromise on the subject of fishing in bays less than ten miles wide at the mouth, and it considered that the exclusion of American fishermen from trade in Canadian ports, though perhaps justified by the letter of the Convention, was an extreme stand which might be modified. Yet despite these qualifications, the statement was a reassuring one. It would be possible, on this basis, to defend the fisheries at Washington. His colleagues would certainly expect him to represent Canada.

He did not really want to go. He had been desperately ill. He had spent a long summer in convalescence, and a long autumn relatively free of administrative routine. The strength which he had missed when he resumed his duties last September, had not yet come back. "*Entre nous,*" he wrote to David Macpherson on February 6, when his final decision had not yet been taken, "I do not feel as strong as I ought to be, and I may want to talk to my friends about the future."[28] To a person who was hinting, however obscurely, about his possible retirement from public life, the prospect of an exacting and probably ungrateful diplomatic task was definitely not attractive. "I contemplate my visit to Washington with a good deal of anxiety," he wrote to Rose. "If things go well, my share of the kudos will be but small, and if anything goes wrong I will be made the scapegoat at all events so far as Canada is concerned."[29] There was danger in his presence in Washington:

there was also danger in his absence from Ottawa. All sorts of misfortunes were possible in the Canadian Parliament while he was away. Yet he did not really hesitate. Probably he had never hesitated from the start. ". . . I thought," he told Rose, "that after all Canada had done for me, I should not shirk the responsibility."

On Monday, February 27, he set out from Ottawa, accompanied by Agnes, Colonel Bernard, and the Deputy Minister of the Department of Marine and Fisheries. At Washington, no American officials and no members of the British Commission had thought it necessary to come to the station to meet him; but Sir Edward Thornton had sent his carriage, and one of his attachés, and the Canadians were soon comfortably installed in the Arlington Hotel.[30] The first few days were crowded with a succession of dinners, receptions, courtesy calls on the American Commissioners and the officials of the State Department, formal visits to the Senate and the House of Representatives, and long and amiable conversations with such notorious Anglophobes and Canadian annexationists as Charles Sumner, Benjamin Butterworth, and Zachariah Chandler. It was the first time that Macdonald had met Hamilton Fish, the Secretary of the American Department of State and the head of the American section of the High Commission. Fish was a rather sluggish-looking man, with a long, solemn face, and a big jowl whose size was accentuated by a bristle of beard fringing the under side of his chin. He was perhaps more tenacious than swift in his mental processes. But there could be little doubt that he was much superior in ability to his four rather nondescript American associates on the Commission.

Macdonald was probably more interested in his British colleagues than he was in the Americans. He knew most of them, at least vaguely, by reputation, and one or two by personal acquaintance. He may already have met the dyspeptic and lugubrious Thornton, the British Minister to Washington, who on rare occasions came up to Ottawa for visits; and he had seen something of Sir Stafford Northcote, the one British Conservative on the Commission, when he had come over in the interests of the Hudson's Bay Company, at the time of the negotiations

SECRETARY TO THE BRITISH COMMISSIONERS   JOHN A. MACDONALD   MONTAGUE BERNARD

SIR STAFFORD NORTHCOTE   EARL DE GREY AND RIPON   SIR EDWARD THORNTON

THE BRITISH HIGH COMMISSIONERS, WASHINGTON, 1871

with the Red River delegates. The other members of the
Commission, and its secretary, Lord Tenterden, were new to
him. Montague Bernard, the Professor of International Law at
Oxford, a slight, dapper little man who was distantly related to
Agnes, seemed a friendly, kindly, rather retiring scholar. Earl
de Grey and Ripon, the head of the British Commission, was
physically perhaps its most distinguished member. His was a
handsome and striking personality, which, outwardly at least,
seemed made for leadership. His forehead was high and broad;
the lines of his mouth and nose were cleanly and decisively
drawn; and his dark, deep-set, piercing eyes seemed to suggest
conviction, determination, and authority.

The presence of Macdonald—an indubitable colonial statesman—among these people was a slightly embarrassing novelty.
It was the first time that a British North American had ever
participated on terms of equality in such a general imperial
negotiation; and everybody—though Macdonald probably least
of all—was sensitively aware of the fact. The British ministers,
Gladstone, Granville, and Kimberley, had made a consciously
revolutionary decision; and the High Commissioners and many
British officials regarded their daring innovation with scepticism
and inquietude. Sir Edward Thornton made little secret of the
fact that he would have preferred John Rose—who, after all,
had been restored to respectability by his return to England—
as the fifth Commissioner;[31] and Lord de Grey was disposed
from the start to regard Macdonald as a member of some strange
and unidentifiable species, whose habits puzzled him, and whose
nature he feared would be malevolent. The mere fact that
Macdonald had brought with him two officials of the Canadian
civil service was looked upon doubtfully as a possible pretension
towards separate status. Fish had actually been inquiring for a
definition of Macdonald's position! "I shall take an opportunity
for which Fish's inquiry yesterday will afford an opening,"
wrote de Grey in a tone of lofty condescension, "of letting Macdonald understand that he is here as the representative not of
the Canadian, but of the British government, and is in precisely
the same position as any other member of the Commission.
If I find any difficulty with him, I will telegraph to you, and

a hint from Kimberley may be required to keep him square."[32]
Certainly no nonsense could be tolerated from colonials. Macdonald must be kept very firmly in his place. De Grey hoped
that Canada would not attempt to take advantage of the great
concession which had already been made to it. But he instinctively feared that the Dominion would try to assert its
special claims against the general imperial interests. It was
exactly the counterpart of Macdonald's own apprehension.
The Canadian feared that his country's rights would be sacrificed
to the achievement of Anglo-American concord; the Englishman was perturbed lest the welfare of the Empire should be
imperilled by the intransigence of Canadian claims. It was
a curious, equivocal situation which portended trouble, and
trouble came.

IV

On Sunday, March 5, just after church, de Grey came down
to the Arlington Hotel specially to see Macdonald. He had a
disturbing story to tell. On the previous evening, after dinner
at de Grey's house, Fish had drawn his host aside and had
informed him that the American Commissioners did not wish
to begin a protracted discussion on the nature and extent of
Canada's exclusive rights in the fisheries, but that they were
prepared to buy these rights, whatever they were, and that
they intended, as soon as the formal preliminaries were over,
to make an offer for their purchase in perpetuity.[33] It was this
astounding piece of information which had sent de Grey hurrying down to the Arlington Hotel that Sunday morning. Macdonald heard the news with surprise and disquiet. Where, he
wondered, had this embarrassing notion of the sale of the fisheries come from? Who had suggested it? Although he was
ignorant of the fact, it was his own chief, Lord Lisgar, the
Governor-General of Canada, who had ventured to propound
to Thornton the idea of granting the liberty of the fisheries for
a term of years in return for an annual money payment; and
Thornton, assuming, of course, that Lisgar would not have

made such a suggestion, even in a private letter, without the concurrence of his ministers, had informally discussed the possibility of a sale with Fish.[34] Fish had appropriated the idea enthusiastically, and had made it his own. But to Macdonald the prospect of a sale was unexpected, unwelcome, and disquieting. He had the uneasy impression, which was to return at frequent intervals during the negotiations, of being manœuvred rapidly and expertly into a position which he did not like and had never dreamed of occupying. All he could do, on that Sunday morning in March, was to ply de Grey with arguments against a sale and in favour of commercial concessions. The Canadian Cabinet, he told his chief solemnly, "had not even taken into consideration" a "pecuniary equivalent" for the fisheries.[35] On the contrary, the Canadian Cabinet had put all its hopes in a reciprocal trade agreement which would be as close as possible to the vanished Reciprocity Treaty.

De Grey listened to his Canadian colleague with rising impatience. He had quickly conceived a slight distaste for Macdonald. From the start the Canadian's reserved, non-committal manner had inexplicably irked him. At the end of the first meeting of the British Commissioners, he had come to the rapid conclusion that Macdonald was going to be extremely difficult in his insistence on Canadian rights. He confided to Granville, in a tone of curiously childish self-satisfaction, that the British Commissioners had determined to pay Macdonald's expenses with imperial money, "as it would not do to give the Dominion government the claim to interference which would result from any charge being made on their funds".[36] He had expected opposition. Now it was coming. Macdonald was demanding a broad reciprocal trade agreement in exchange for the fisheries. But Fish, in their conversation on Saturday night, had informed him bluntly that it was quite impossible to persuade Congress to accept a broad trade agreement. What was possible, de Grey had already convinced himself, was a comprehensive arrangement in which Canada would trade her fisheries, her canals, and the navigation of the St. Lawrence for a few tariff concessions and a good-sized lump of money. It would be a good bargain, he thought. He would, of course, make an attempt to get what Macdonald wanted from the Americans. But if this effort failed—and he had little doubt of its failure—he wanted to start negotiations for a sale of the fisheries at once. Without delay, he wrote to Granville requesting permission to do so, Macdonald or no Macdonald. ". . . I expect Macdonald to be very exacting," he intimated a little irritably, "and I look forward to having a good deal of difficulty in bringing him to accept moderate terms."[37]

The next day, when the Americans informally presented their revolutionary proposal, de Grey replied on behalf of the British Commissioners that a sale of the fisheries, particularly a sale in perpetuity, would be unwelcome, and that Canada would much prefer a trade agreement in exchange for her property. Outwardly, the British front was unbroken; but when Her Majesty's Commissioners met alone, Macdonald could hardly be unaware of the chilly air of disapproval that was creeping about him. It was already strangely apparent that his colleagues were spending almost as much time arguing with him as with their American counterparts. His uneasiness grew. What did the other British Commissioners really intend? Did they mean to sell the fisheries to the United States, despite the solemn protests which he had repeatedly made in conference? He did not know, he had no means of knowing—so completely was he shut out from the familiar, confidential discussions of the "bachelor" establishment on "K" Street—that his colleagues had already determined to force his hand. But, at the last moment, some hypersensitive political sixth sense warned him of impending danger. He decided to appeal to the British government over the heads of his unsympathetic colleagues. He could not, of course, communicate directly with Granville, the Foreign Secretary—that was de Grey's prerogative. He would have to approach the British government through the regular channel of communication between the Governor-General at Ottawa and the Colonial Office. His excuse would be Kimberley's last dispatch on the fisheries, of February 16, which had been sent on to him at Washington. "Cable should be sent on dispatch to this effect," he telegraphed to Charles Tupper at Ottawa, "Canada considers inshore fisheries her property and that they cannot be sold without her consent."[38]

He was only just in time. The very next day, March 9, the Americans, as de Grey had anticipated, rejected the British proposal of a reciprocal trade agreement in exchange for the fisheries, and instead proposed purchase for a term of years. This time, however, the unpalatable dose was sweetened with a small teaspoonful of tariff concessions. Fish suggested, in deference to Macdonald's well-known wishes, that in addition to sanctioning a money payment, Congress might be persuaded to reduce or even repeal the duties on a small number of commodities—coal, salt, salt fish, and firewood.[39] It was a shrewd offer, cunningly devised, as Fish was well aware from his previous conversations with Thornton and de Grey, to win the approval of the British members of the Commission. And its success was fully up to his expectations. De Grey and his English colleagues, with that easy alacrity which characterized all their decisions about Canada, were instantly convinced that a better offer could not be expected. But neither Macdonald, nor the Canadian ministers up in Ottawa, were in the least impressed.[40] Coal, salt, salt fish, and firewood! Firewood, of all things! This niggardly little list was not even remotely comparable with the generous arrangement for which they had hoped. The Canadian Cabinet turned down the revised American offer, and Macdonald communicated the rejection to his colleagues in Washington.

He bore their not too well concealed disapproval with fortitude. For the reply to the cable to Kimberley had arrived in time. "We never had any intention," it announced conclusively, "of selling the inshore fisheries of Canada without consent."[41] Macdonald carried these fortifying words around in his pocket, prepared for any emergency. He had not long to wait. For de Grey had also received a reply—an equally satisfactory reply —to his cable of March 7 to Granville. Granville had authorized him to discuss the sale of the fisheries, and had even gone so far as to express a preference for a sale in perpetuity.[42] De Grey was elated. The supreme authority of the Empire, speaking *ex cathedrâ*, had delivered judgment. He would be able now to overwhelm the contumacious Macdonald. And, at the

very next opportunity, he solemnly read the portentous words.
The other British Commissioners listened approvingly and with
eager interest. But, strangely enough, the heretic seemed im-
penitent and unabashed. Instead of capitulating, he proceeded
composedly to read a second pronouncement, from the
same supreme authority, which was strangely inconsistent with
the first, if, indeed, it did not exactly contradict it! De Grey
was mystified and annoyed.⁴³ He even toyed with the idea
that Macdonald had falsified the words of Kimberley's cable!
But this ludicrous suspicion brought no permanent comfort.
The shock and bewilderment were great. It was a "floorer", as
Macdonald wrote briefly and with colloquial complacency, to
Tupper. He had outmanœuvred them all. It was his first
great moment of triumph during the conference.

Yet had he really gained anything more than a temporary
advantage? It was true that he could force his colleagues to
require the Americans to produce still another offer for the
fisheries. But would de Grey and the others willingly accept
this virtual Canadian veto over their proceedings? In their
present temper, would they not try immediately to clear up the
apparent contradiction in British policy, and to their own
advantage? "Lord de Grey," Macdonald wrote to Tupper, "is
now, doubtless, communicating with Lord Granville as to the
apparent discrepancy between his statement and that of Lord
Kimberley."⁴⁴ It was only too true. De Grey was writing in
reproachful astonishment to the Foreign Office. What had the
British government been thinking of? And the British government, confronted with the muddle of its own making, had now
to reconcile the two sincere but conflicting impulses by which
it had been guided. Gladstone and his colleagues had no desire
to sell Canada's property without its owner's consent; but at
the same time they had a very anxious wish to reach a general
settlement with the United States. In the old days the problem
might have seemed insoluble. But the Gladstone government
was an innovating government in colonial affairs, and it now
discovered a quick way out of its perplexities. Canada's consent
would be safeguarded by a special clause in the treaty providing
that all articles relating to the Dominion could take effect only

after ratification by the Canadian Parliament. Canada would have its say in the end; but in the meantime it could not be permitted to frustrate the negotiations at Washington. De Grey was authorized to negotiate for a settlement of the fisheries, without any restriction as to the kind of equivalent that Canada might be given for her property.

Macdonald was surprised and perturbed. He had never expected such a solution. The power of ratification was undoubtedly important for the future; but it was not the power that he wanted at the moment. So long as Canada's consent meant his own consent, given in conference to his fellow British Commissioners, he occupied a position of commanding importance. But now negotiations could be carried on, arrangements made, and even, presumably, a treaty signed and sealed, entirely without his approval! Canada was left with public and formal methods of expressing non-concurrence; and formal methods, as he knew very well, were clumsy and dangerous to use. "If a majority of my colleagues," he explained to Tupper, "should at any time conclude to accept terms which I do not approve of, I must, of course, either protest and withdraw, or remain on the Commission and trust to non-ratification of the treaty by Canada. If I take the first course it will disclose to the Americans the fact of a difference of opinion, a conflict, in fact, between Canada and England. This the Americans are anxious to establish, in order to get up a sort of quarrel between the two, and strengthen that party in England which desires to get rid of the colonies as a burden. If I continue to act on the Commission, I will be attacked for making an unworthy sacrifice of Canada's rights and may be compelled to vote in Parliament against a Treaty which I had a share in making."[45] Yet could he really vote in Parliament against a treaty which he had helped to frame? Was it conceivable that Canada could reject an agreement which had been accepted by the senior partner in the Empire? Did he even possess the option of withdrawing from the Commission or of refusing to sign the treaty? He did not know. He felt his power to influence the negotiations slipping rapidly and irretrievably away.

V

The Commission had by now got well into its stride. At first Macdonald had found in the work the relaxation of novelty. The mild March of Washington, so different from the drab late winter of Ottawa, delighted him, and for a while the politics and society of the Capitol were an amusing change. But the entertainment had been extravagantly lavish from the beginning; and it soon became a tedious superabundance. "Our life here," complained de Grey, "is rendered very intolerable by the endless feasts. We work all day and dine all night. And some wag in the newspapers says we are not a Joint High Commission, but a High Commission on Joints—the joke greatly delights the Washingtonians."[46] It also mildly amused the British Commissioners, for they accepted the sobriquet of "High Joints" and called their secretaries and assistants "cutlets". But these pleasantries did not reconcile them to the mountainous dinners. "Even in this Lenten season," Macdonald grumbled, "we are overwhelmed with hospitalities which we cannot refuse."[47] At first he found this nearly the only drawback of a pleasant situation. But not for long. The climate, which had been so charming at the outset, began to seem "relaxing", and within a month of his arrival he was anxious to be home. "I am very tired of Washington," he wrote to Colonel Gray towards the end of March, "although everybody has been very civil since I have been here; but I want to get back to my work again."[48]

There was a simple explanation for his home-sickness. He viewed the work that he had to do with growing distaste. The British Commissioners seemed to be no nearer to an agreement with the Americans; but they were perilously close to an open disagreement among themselves. The United States had, for the moment, withdrawn its offer of a "pecuniary equivalent", plus a few small tariff changes. It had apparently accepted the Canadian plan of a primarily commercial arrangement, and it now proposed, as a basis for discussion, the free entry into the American market of Canadian coal, salt, all kinds of fish and all types of lumber.[49] Macdonald was still seriously dissatisfied. The second offer was so much like the first; it was so utterly unlike the old Reciprocity Treaty, by which all Canadian natural products, without exception, had been freely admitted to the American market. Could he surrender Canada's biggest commercial asset for these trifling concessions? He did not see how he could. But his English colleagues, who were as quickly convinced on this as on the two previous occasions, decided for the third time that a better offer could not be had. Macdonald had wanted a trade agreement. Well, here was a trade agreement! Yet he still declined to accept! They could not understand it. But now there was no need for them to do so. With Granville's express authority, they could exchange the fisheries for any kind of reasonable equivalent, despite Macdonald's protests. It was time to call a halt to all this nonsense. They decided to make a definite offer to the United States, based largely on the American suggestion of free coal, salt, fish and lumber.

Macdonald had protested verbally before. He now renewed his protests in a long and somewhat formal letter to de Grey.[50] This document, without rehearsing the previous efforts of the British Commissioners to get a fair equivalent for the fisheries, concentrated on the current proposal. It condemned the proposal as insufficient and frankly predicted its rejection by the Canadian Parliament. De Grey objected heatedly, and an unpleasant row ensued, in which the leader of the British delegation openly accused his Canadian colleague of "misrepresentation".[51] Macdonald gave way. He had no intention of presenting such an obvious opportunity to a man who seemed determined to put him in the wrong if he possibly could. The obnoxious letter was withdrawn; and a short informal memorandum, briefly stating the Canadian case, was substituted for it and sent over to the British government for its information. A new struggle for the verdict of the Colonial Office was at hand. Macdonald had done all he could, but he was probably less hopeful now than he had been on the previous occasion. His position had been seriously weakened as a result of Granville's decision to give de Grey a free hand in the negotiations. And he can hardly have failed to suspect—what was, of course, the truth—that de Grey, in every private letter to England, was attacking his arguments, belittling his objections, impugning his motives, criticizing his conduct, and urging the British government to coerce him.

Yet—as he also had some reason to suspect—there was far more sympathy for his views in Whitehall than at Washington. To the shocked amazement of de Grey and his British colleagues, the Gladstone Cabinet did not at once perceive the truth in all the simple purity in which it was apparent at the "bachelor" establishment on "K" Street. Gladstone, indeed, seemed strangely unimpressed by the horrifying story of Macdonald's formal protest to de Grey. He told Granville frankly that after reading it he did not feel any more like coercing Canada. "We ought not to let our credit," he went on, "or even that of our Commission weigh a single hair in the balance. If we place a burden or an apparent burden on Canada, we shall pay for it dearly, shall never hear the last of it, nay, may perhaps tempt Canada to say, 'if gifts are to be made to the United States at our expense, surely we had better make them ourselves and have the credit of them'."[52] All these considerations suggested circumspection and delay. Gladstone was not disposed to be "hustled" into an agreement by his over-zealous Commissioners at Washington. He told Granville that the Cabinet was "of a mind to hold a little with Macdonald about the fisheries";[53] and Granville agreed that "Macdonald seems to have more to say for himself than his brother Commissioners admit. . . ."[54] The result was a cable which once again lifted de Grey's eyebrows in pained surprise. The British government would not undertake to compel Canada to accept the newest American offer of free coal, salt, fish and lumber.

Incredibly, Macdonald had won again! He had expected a final defeat. He had gained one more temporary victory. But the contest was not yet over; and de Grey and his colleagues, who believed sincerely that Macdonald's selfish obstinacy was endangering a just and necessary peace, bent themselves with grim-lipped determination to overcome his resistance. Throughout the British side of the High Commission, annoyance, suspicion, and resentment were in the air. The ambiguous relations between these five men inevitably produced misunderstandings. England and Canada had just begun the long and painful process of redefining their respective rôles in the conduct of foreign policy; and the British Commissioners at Washington were the inexperienced and easily exasperated victims of a daring experiment in imperial diplomacy. Macdonald regarded himself as the representative of a national state, with separate and important national interests which it was his business to defend and promote; and actually this was the conception of Canada's place in the Empire with which the Gladstone government had publicly identified itself. In theory, British Liberals were always protesting their readiness to welcome the growth of colonial separatism; but in practice, so long as the Empire endured, they tended instinctively to think of it as a strict diplomatic unity, with Great Britain in complete and unquestioned control.

To de Grey and his British colleagues it seemed unnatural and almost indecent that Macdonald, a mere serviceable subordinate, should actually try to employ diplomatic devices, even against themselves, in the defence of his country's special interests! The fact, communicated by Lord Lisgar, that Macdonald had inspired some of the answers to his own telegrams to Ottawa, and that the Canadian Cabinet had been willing on occasion to take lower terms than he had indicated, seemed, to the horrified de Grey, to reveal not so much a talent for diplomatic bargaining as a dreadful propensity towards "slippery" moral behaviour.[55] "Candour" was at one and the same time a duty which Macdonald owed to his colleagues and a favour which they were under no obligation to confer upon him. It never apparently occurred to de Grey that the confidences of a colonial were something which had to be requited. On at least one occasion he urged Granville to maintain greater secrecy about the private letters and cables which they habitually exchanged. ". . .I have to carry on quite as difficult a negotiation with Macdonald as with the United States Commissioners," he wrote, "and it would never do to cut me off from telegraphing to you privately without his knowledge."[56]

In the midst of this unpleasantly sultry and electric atmos-

phere, Macdonald and the other British Commissioners stuck
to their task. In the full meetings of the Joint High Commission,
de Grey was outwardly doing his best to persuade the Americans
to improve their last offer for the fisheries; but privately he
was bending every effort to induce the British and Canadian
governments to come to terms as quickly as possible. The
Gladstone Cabinet had shown a strange tenderness for Canada's
interests, and an inexplicable respect for Macdonald's views.
It must be rescued from these absurd delusions, if the peace
were not to be lost; and Macdonald, who had been acting with
irresponsible, self-seeking obstinacy, must be taught to see
where his "true interests" lay. De Grey and his English colleagues set about the work in deadly earnest. Sometimes,
Macdonald reported to Tupper comically, "they made speeches
at me". Sometimes they wrote long letters, full of admonition
and reprimand. More and more often, as time went on, they fell
back on a judiciously compounded mixture of threats and bribes.
De Grey was at pains to point out to Macdonald that if any
"unpleasant consequences" were to follow the failure of the
negotiations, "the people of England will not be much inclined
to help the Canadians out of their scrape".[57] But these dark
and sinister suggestions were suitably varied by other, very
different, deliciously tantalizing hints. "I have had a talk with
Macdonald," de Grey wrote Granville, "which I hope has done
good; the word Privy Councillor somehow escaped my lips as
a distant vision that individually I should like some day to see
realized in the person of an eminent colonial minister; but I
have committed no one and yet I think done what I wanted."[58]
Surely the "hard, needy, greedy" colonial, in Robert Lowe's
elegant phrase, would not remain insensible to this blandish-
ment!

Yet Macdonald seemed unmoved. He kept to his course.
The British government had backed him. It had agreed with
him that free fish, coal, salt and lumber were not a sufficient
return for the fisheries. He was determined not to make a sacrifice of Canadian property; and he was still bargaining for
further tariff and other concessions from the United States,
when suddenly, without warning, the whole basis of the discus-

sion was drastically changed. On April 15, Fish informed de Grey that the current American proposal, which the British Commissioners had not yet finally accepted, would have to be withdrawn, as a result of the pressure of important vested interests in the American Congress. All that he could offer now was his original proposal of a purchase of the fisheries, not in perpetuity, but for a term of years, the amount of the payment to be settled subsequently by arbitration; and he suggested that, in addition, the United States might concede the free entry of Canadian fish. Macdonald was discomfited and deeply chagrined. His British colleagues could hardly conceal their jubilation. Macdonald, they agreed sagely, had "overstayed his market". He had "dropped the bone out of his mouth like the dog in the fable".[59] And it was almost a pleasure to confront him with the painful necessity of reaching a decision upon this last and probably final American offer. The conference was coming to an end. Most of the matters on the agenda had been settled. There remained only the wearisome problem of the Canadian fisheries. What were they to do about it?

Macdonald knew that the crisis of the whole negotiation was at hand. He had won tactical victories before. But now he was boxed in an extremely vulnerable position, and in his heart he expected nothing but defeat. Yet he maintained his stand with apparently unaltered firmness. He rejected, with the hearty agreement of the Canadian Cabinet, the new American offer of a money payment to be settled by arbitration, plus free fish. He reminded his colleagues that the Joint High Commission had originated in a proposal put forward by Canada for a diplomatic settlement of all disputed points under the Convention of 1818. ". . .What Canada desired," he told his colleagues, "was if she could not get a satisfactory equivalent for her fisheries, that she should be allowed to remain in exclusive possession of them, leaving the questions as to ports and headlands, the only matters in dispute, for adjustment by the Commission."[60] De Grey was horrified. Such a conclusion to their labours was unthinkable! The final American offer must be accepted, and Macdonald must either be persuaded or forced to yield his consent. He struggled to convince the obstinate man with argument. He even lost his temper, lecturing the Canadian, like an angry pedagogue, upon his duty as a Commissioner! But he quickly saw the futility of tirades. There was a better method available. On Sunday, April 16, after church, he came down to the Arlington as he had come exactly six weeks before, to reason with Macdonald.

Most of the interview was taken up with a long, serious recital of the reasons for Canadian acceptance of the latest American terms. Macdonald had heard these often enough before, and it was not until the conversation was nearly over that de Grey produced his astounding novelty—the last, gorgeous inducement, which the Gladstone government had authorized some time before, but which he had been keeping carefully in reserve for just such an extremity as this. As far back as February, when the Commission had first been appointed, Gladstone himself had suggested that de Grey should be provided "with the means of smoothing over any difficulties which may arise between us and Canada in the course of the negotiations by some undertaking on account of the expenses of the Fenian Raid".[61] That was when it was still hoped that the Americans could be induced to repay Canada for her losses. But it now began to look as if the United States would be able to avoid paying any compensation whatever for the raids. As a result of some singular defect in the official correspondence which had settled the terms of reference, the Americans were claiming, with a show of plausibility, that the Fenian Raids were not on the agenda of the Joint High Commission at all! It was very odd! Had the best Foreign Office in the world actually blundered? Nothing, in either explanation or apology, would ever be said to the Canadians. But the British Cabinet authorized de Grey to "hint" about the possibility of imperial compensation to Macdonald.[62] Clearly it was time to begin "hinting" now. And at the close of the long conversation at the Arlington Hotel that Sunday morning, de Grey informed his colleague of the British government's offer.

Macdonald accepted this proposal gratefully. But it did not change his attitude to the final American scheme for the settlement of the fisheries. He protested, and his protests, and those of his government, were cabled to England. The British government must finally decide. He hoped. But, at the same time, he had very little doubt as to what Great Britain's decision would be. He was only too well aware of his colleagues' eagerness to close with the American offer. He expected that they would urge the British government to accept. But even he could scarcely have imagined the desperate urgency with which de Grey and the others tried to convince the Gladstone Cabinet of the necessity of acceptance. They had tried appeals and exhortations before. What they now presented—in still another of the long list of private telegrams—was a virtual ultimatum. "If you do not back us up against Macdonald," de Grey wired to Granville, "he will be quite unmanageable, and I see no chance of coming to an arrangement."[63] This dreadful prophecy, which, de Grey assured his chief, was the collective opinion of all the Commissioners—with, of course, the exception of Macdonald—was enough to set the British government pondering deeply. Gladstone and his colleagues were eager to complete an otherwise successful negotiation. Nothing, apparently, would satisfy the Canadians; and Gladstone, reading carefully through the last protests of Macdonald and his fellow-ministers, pronounced them to be "rampantly unreasonable".[64] It was impossible to support Macdonald any longer. Yet there remained Kimberley's promise not to sell the fisheries without Canadian consent; and despite the proviso requiring ratification by the Dominion Parliament, this was still a slightly embarrassing pledge. A cabinet was held on the subject, while for days the British Commissioners in Washington waited in an agony of expectation. Then, at long last, came the eagerly awaited, the enthusiastically applauded, answer. De Grey was instructed to concede the inshore fisheries in return for a money payment, the amount to be determined by arbitration, and free fish.

VI

"Your fisheries telegram has arrived," de Grey cabled triumphantly back to Granville, "and Macdonald has yielded with a good grace which was almost laughable."[65] It was a strangely optimistic interpretation, which revealed more of de Grey's state of mind than it did of Macdonald's. Outwardly Macdonald had—at least for the moment—accepted; but inwardly his sense of exasperation, futility, and failure had now reached its culminating point. "My first impulse, I confess," he wrote to Tupper, "on the arrival of the cable message from England, authorizing the reference to arbitration of the value of the fisheries, was to hand in my resignation of my position as Commissioner, procurator, and plenipotentiary to Lord de Grey for transmission to Lord Granville. . . ."[66] It was a first impulse of disgust and anger. But it did not last the night; and by morning he had decided to remain on the Commission, even if only with a watching brief, to guard Canadian interests during the last stages of the negotiations. "It was fortunate that I did so," he explained to Tupper later, "else the articles would have been much worse than they were." Even so, they were bad enough. There was no compensation whatever for the Fenian Raids. The free navigation of the St. Lawrence—though not of the canals by which alone it was navigable throughout—was conceded for ever in return for similar rights on three remote Alaskan streams; and of all the long list of Canadian natural products, fish alone was to be admitted free to the American market. "Such are the articles," he complained bitterly to Tupper, "and a precious lot they are!" He was sick at heart. "Never in the whole course of my public life," he told Alexander Morris, "have I been in so disagreeable a position and had such an unpleasant duty to perform as the one upon which I am now engaged here."[67]

What was he to do now that the treaty was at last complete? His decision to remain on the Commission had simply postponed the difficult decision that he had to make. Should he sign the treaty or not? "Canada," he told Tupper, "is certain to reject the Treaty *in toto*." He clearly implied to Alexander Morris that he expected publicly to oppose it himself. If he signed the treaty now, how could he retain his moral right to liberty of action thereafter, how could he escape the charges of disingenuousness and inconsistency which might inflict irremediable political damage upon him? To withhold his signature was the easiest, simplest, most completely effective way of protecting himself from the inevitable accusation that he had concurred in the betrayal of his country's interests. It was the course which he first thought of taking, which many of his Canadian colleagues would have preferred him to take. But, on the other hand, there were a number of serious objections to it, all of which were pointed out to him with solemn emphasis by de Grey. He was, like all the other British Commissioners, a plenipotentiary of the imperial government, acting on behalf of the imperial government, and now instructed by the imperial government to sign the treaty. ". . .I fancy," he wrote to Francis Hincks, "it would be an unheard of thing for an envoy to refuse to carry out the instructions of his principal."[68] It might also be a highly dangerous thing politically, for the rejection of the treaty by the American Senate was a very possible result, and with it the loss of the dearly-won settlement of the *Alabama* claims. No, he could not accept such a heavy load of responsibility. He would have to put his name to the treaty.

But need he sign without explanation or qualification? He would, in fact, be acting under the orders of the British government. Was there not, he wondered unhappily, some way in which he could prove to the world in general and the Canadians in particular, that in signing he had merely done his duty as an imperial Commissioner and had in no way compromised his future liberty of action as a member of the Canadian government? Possibly, he suggested to de Grey, they might insert a paragraph in one of the protocols, stating that although the Canadian Commissioner had signed in obedience to the orders of the Queen, he considered the arrangements distinctly disadvantageous to his country. De Grey rejected this suggestion instantly and authoritatively. It would never do. Macdonald must sign *tout court*. Obviously there was only one way out. If his objections could not be indicated on the face of the treaty and the protocols, then it could only be put on record in letters between himself and the other people concerned. De Grey accepted this idea with alacrity. He promised to write a letter which Macdonald could use in Ottawa; and Macdonald set about composing formal statements of his position for Lord Granville, and the Governor-General.

This discussion—it took place early in May—was the last occasion on which Macdonald talked at length about the treaty with de Grey. Before they separated, Macdonald made a final request that the British government would not delay in honouring its principal Commissioner's pledge of compensation for the Fenian Raids. "I pressed him, therefore," Macdonald told Cartier, "to take the matter up and have it finally settled the moment he returned to England. This he promised to do. He thanked me very much for the course I was taking."[69] Gratitude may have been on de Grey's lips; but there was little in his heart. He had striven, he reasoned with himself, for a settlement in the interest of the whole Empire. Macdonald had opposed him stubbornly, from a purely Canadian viewpoint, and by methods which, he had become convinced as a result of Lord Lisgar's disclosures, were unquestionably underhand. Lord Lisgar, who had been permitted to see some of Macdonald's private communications to his Canadian colleagues, quoted from them freely in his letters to Northcote at Washington;[70] and although Macdonald's accounts of the proceedings had been in general scrupulously temperate and fair, he had made a few disrespectful remarks which affronted his English colleagues. As the proofs of Macdonald's semi-independent course increased in number, de Grey's sense of injury grew. It seemed to him monstrous that the Canadian should have dared to forward separate Canadian interests by methods which, though a commonplace for Great Britain and any other national state to pursue, were completely inadmissible in a colony. When it came to the point, colonial "nationalism" in diplomacy was nothing more or less than "treachery" to Great Britain. ". . .Macdonald," de Grey wrote to Granville in still another of those private letters from which his Canadian colleague would never have a chance to quote, "has acted with a pretty strong amount of treachery towards us."[71]

Macdonald believed that promises had been given him, and that Canada had made sacrifices which deserved reward. But de Grey felt no sense of obligation whatever. Macdonald's conduct had been simply deplorable. If he really wished to prove that he could be "of service", then let him get the treaty through the Canadian Parliament. And until that was safely accomplished, everything could be held up. How fortunate that de Grey had been so discreet in making his little hints! "I merely dandled before his eyes," he assured Granville again, "the idea of giving occasional admission to the English Privy Council to distinguished Canadian statesmen; but I was throughout the conversation, which was a short one, very careful to avoid saying anything that would bind myself or anyone else."[72] No, he was not in the least committed. Macdonald had nothing owing to him. Macdonald would get nothing. All the other Commissioners and all the secretaries —the "joints" and the "cutlets"—had been superlatively co-operative and helpful. Without exception, they all deserved well of the British government. But Macdonald was different. "Macdonald has puzzled us all," he summed up to Granville. "I do not know whether he is really an able man or not; that he is one of the duskiest horses that ever ran on any course I am sure; and that he has been playing his own game all along with unswerving steadiness is plain enough. If he gets the consent of the Colonial parliament to the stipulation of the treaty for which it is required, he will deserve reward; but if he does not, he ought to get nothing."[73]

On May 8, at ten o'clock of a brilliant spring morning, Macdonald appeared at the State Department for the final ceremony of the conference. The High Commissioners and the secretaries were all there; most of the clerks of the Department had come in to watch what was evidently an unusually solemn event.[74] The room was sweet with bright masses of spring flowers; and on the sideboard an unusual but not unappetizing morning collation—strawberries and ice cream—lay waiting to be eaten. A relaxed elated feeling of accomplishment was in the air. Macdonald alone did not share it. He was only too well aware that something that he did not want, but could not prevent, was about to be done, and done irrevocably. Even as they chatted a little nervously together, and exchanged photographs and autographs, the seals were being affixed to the two precious copies of the treaty by an awkward and extremely nervous clerk, whose operations were not assisted when Tenterden, that most invaluable of secretaries, dropped quantities of burning sealing-wax on his fingers. The poor man somewhat inauspiciously burst into tears when the work was done. But done it was, and the copies lay ready on the table. Then the final, solemn act began. Macdonald, being the junior member of the British Commission, was one of the last to sign.

"Well," he said in a half-whisper to Fish, as he took up his pen, "here go the fisheries."

"You get a good equivalent for them," Fish countered swiftly.

"No," Macdonald retorted with cheerful cynicism, "we give them away—here goes the signature!"

He signed his name with the usual small flourish under the final "d", and rose from the table.

"They are gone," he said slowly.[75]

Chapter Four

Design for the Future

I

He did not return to Ottawa as a conqueror. He did not feel like a conqueror and he did not want the pretence of a conqueror's reception. A conqueror would be expected to receive tributes and furnish reports. He had no desire to take the one or to make the other. At the back of his mind was the troubled realization that the first Parliament of the Dominion of Canada was nearing its inevitable end, and that in twelve months' time or a little more he would have to face a general election—a general election in which the unpopularity of the Washington Treaty might prove absolutely fatal to his government. A brief respite was essential to him. He did not want, for the moment, to show his hand. He had taken good care to suggest, indirectly, to the editors of the faithful Conservative newspapers, the Montreal *Gazette*, the Toronto *Leader*, the Ottawa *Times* and *Citizen*, and the rest, that they should hold back, for a few precious days at least, any expression of opinion on the Treaty. In the meantime, the Reform leaders and the Grit newspapers, assuming readily that he would support the work of the Joint High Commission, would rush forward, in their usual unthinking and intemperate fashion, to attack the Treaty. That was what he wanted. The whole Grit party must be fixed in an unchangeable position, pinned down immovably to ground which had been hastily chosen but which could not be abandoned without fear of disaster. "It is therefore," he wrote to Alexander Morris, "of very considerable consequence that Brown and the

Globe should be committed irretrievably against the Treaty."[1]
In the meantime he himself would have space to manœuvre and
time to consider his dispositions.

Time was valuable, whatever his final decision might be.
At Washington, during the last gloomy days of conscious failure
and defeat, he had talked and written as if his own public
opposition to the fishery clauses in Canada were a certainty.
But, despite these confident predictions, had he ever really
dismissed the possibility that he might have to defend the
Treaty for the sake of the Anglo-Canadian alliance by which
alone Canada had survived in the North American continent?
In any case, a protective silence was undoubtedly the best
policy at the moment. If, in the end, he came to the conclusion
that he must oppose the Treaty, then Brown and the Grits
would find themselves occupying a thoroughly false position
without hope of withdrawal. If, on the contrary, he finally
decided that acceptance of the terms was the only possible
course for Canada to take, then the delay would give him a
chance to better his own position, to improve the prospects of
his doubtful cause. Time would permit the violent denunciation of the Treaty in the Canadian press to burn itself out.
Time was necessary also to enable the American Congress to
legislate upon the subject, and the Canadian government to
come to a satisfactory agreement with the British government
about the promised compensation for the losses of the Fenian
Raids. In six months many things would certainly be clarified,
and his own chances would probably be much improved.
Meanwhile he and his colleagues would maintain an unrevealing
reserve.

And so, while the whole country rocked with debate over
the iniquities of the Washington Treaty, he gave not the
slightest indication of what the Canadian government proposed
to do. It was not, of course, that he was uncommunicative
about his own view of the Treaty, or about the outraged sense
of betrayal which it had awakened everywhere throughout the
country. In letter after gloomy letter to Lisgar and de Grey
he affirmed that the violence of public disapproval exceeded
even his own expectations, and that he did not yet know

whether he could control the storm. "The feeling in Canada against the Treaty," he told de Grey, "has increased and is increasing and I cannot foresee the result. An utter feeling of distrust in the imperial government has arisen in the public mind and every clause in the Treaty is therefore discussed in a jealous and prejudiced spirit."[2] He was always ready to expatiate upon the endless and awful difficulties which confronted him; but, neither in private or public had he a word to say about the course which his government intended to pursue.

"The line the government takes is simply this," he told one correspondent, "that the Treaty is satisfactory to them in every respect except as regards the fisheries, and that as to the fisheries they are free to act as they please."[3] He had signed the Treaty, he reminded de Grey—and signed it expressly reserving his future freedom of action—simply because the British government had instructed its commissioners to sign. The British government had, in short, accepted responsibility for the Treaty; and if it wished the Canadian Parliament to ratify the clauses relating to British North America it must explain and justify satisfactorily the solution which it had imposed.[4] "It will be for the home government to make out a case with us," Macdonald wrote to Gowan. "After giving every consideration to the arguments of Her Majesty's government, we will have a policy on the subject which we will submit to Parliament next session."[5] In other words, if Great Britain wanted Canadian compliance in the appeasement of the United States, it would have to strengthen the Canadian government's hand. And, as Macdonald reminded de Grey, one of the first things to be done was to implement the promise of compensation for the Fenian Raids.

He had no doubt at all about the form which the compensation should take. He wanted, not a money payment, but a British guarantee for a part of the great sums of money which would have to be borrowed for the Canadian transcontinental railway to the Pacific. During the late winter, while he had been away in Washington, Parliament had ratified the terms of union with British Columbia, though only after a struggle which Alexander Morris described as the

worst fight the party had had since Confederation.⁶ On July
20, only a few short weeks away, British Columbia would
become the sixth province of the union; and the Canadian
government was committed to begin a railway to the Pacific
within two years, and to finish it within ten, of this new addition
to Confederation.

It was true that this formidable commitment had been
explained, if not exactly qualified, by an interpretative resolution
introduced by Sir George Cartier on behalf of the government, soon after the terms of union had been accepted by the
House. According to this resolution, the railway was to be
built by private enterprise, not by government; and the contribution of government to the project was to consist in liberal
grants of land and in such subsidies of money as would not
be "unduly pressing on the industry and resources of the
Dominion". Was this a valid gloss upon the contract? It was
highly doubtful. But even if it had not been doubtful, the
Dominion was still left with an enormous and clearly defined
responsibility. It must choose a company. Its own preferred plan
required a commercial company, worthy to act for the nation,
and to receive the nation's financial support, in what was perhaps
the greatest of all national undertakings. Very soon now
Macdonald and his colleagues would have to choose, and choose
well, from among the various little groups of capitalists which
were in the course of formation and which would soon be
openly competing for the prize of the Canadian Pacific railway
charter. One of them, indeed, had already appeared. Macdonald
had not been back in Ottawa for six weeks, and British Columbia had not yet become a member of the union, when the first
of these associations of railway promoters presented itself in his
office towards the close of a sultry day in July.

It was a little group of seven people.⁷ There were four Canadians—two Toronto lawyers, and two rather shadowy "capitalists",
Waddington and Kersteman, who speedily turned out to have
more pretensions than financial resources. These, as Macdonald
probably knew very well from the beginning, were not the
real men of substance in the group. The real men of substance
were the three Americans, Hurlburt of New York, and Charles

Smith and G. W. McMullen of Chicago, who brought with them, not only their own financial strength, but also the support of a number of well-known American bankers and contractors. It was the first time that Macdonald had ever met McMullen, the ex-Canadian, who had grown up in Prince Edward county, and had gone off to Chicago to acquire control of the *Evening Post* and to interest himself in a variety of canal and railway undertakings. Macdonald was, of course, affable with the visitors, but he told them frankly that nothing whatever could be done at the moment. "We saw the American gentlemen who came from Chicago," he told George Jackson a few days later, "but their movement was altogether premature, and was improperly hurried by that respectable old fool Waddington."[8] The government could not act without a survey of the country and the authority of Parliament, and at the moment it had neither. Besides, Macdonald instinctively disliked a syndicate so obviously dominated by Americans. Yet the interview, he realized, was important despite its inconclusiveness. The government would have to make an agreement with a group very much like that which faced him, and in short order. It was for this reason, among others, that he wanted to clear up the matter of the British compensation for the losses of the Fenian Raids. The Treaty, the guaranteed loan, and the Pacific railway would together make a formidable instrument to develop the country and defeat the opposition. He waited comfortably for the offer from England—the offer which would reward Canada for its sacrifices and himself for his submission.

What he got instead was a hard and sudden shock. The first dispatch from the Colonial Office, which was a loftily paternal lecture on the benefits which Canada would derive from the Washington Treaty, made no mention at all of compensation for the Fenian Raids; and although Lord Kimberley alluded to the subject a few days later in a private letter to Lisgar he did so in a fashion which was surprising and annoying in the extreme. "What does Sir John A. Macdonald mean to do?" he inquired of the Governor-General. "If he is prepared to do his utmost to carry the treaty through we shall be ready to strengthen his hands with respect to the Fenian claims, but he

must understand that there is no chance of obtaining concessions such as a guarantee of the Pacific Railroad. . . . The
Fenian claims being omitted from the treaty are a fair subject
for consideration but it is only fair to Sir John Macdonald
that he should not be under the impression that further concessions can be obtained from us."⁹ These hard, wary, bargaining
phrases, communicated to Macdonald by Lisgar, brought both
bafflement and exasperation. What did Lord Kimberley mean by
"further concessions"? Why had the Colonial Office begun
to quibble about the solemn engagement respecting the Fenian
claims? Macdonald had believed that the promise to pay
compensation was an unconditional commitment. Now it began
to appear that in England it was regarded merely as a conditional
liability contingent upon the ratification of the Treaty by the
Canadian Parliament. The order of obligation, as he saw it,
had been exactly reversed.

The fact was, though as yet he did not fully realize the
truth, that the Gladstone government was viewing him with a
mixture of dislike, suspicion, and cold hostility. He had
opposed the settlement with the United States, opposed it
persistently, and by methods unbecoming a colonial. In letter
after letter de Grey and Lisgar had depreciated his services and
criticized his conduct; and now their successive disclosures of
his shortcomings were completed by a final and astounding
revelation. Lisgar had already quoted freely from Macdonald's
private communications to his colleagues in Ottawa, tearing
phrases and sentences from their context in order to show
his Prime Minister in a most unfavourable light; and now
he transcribed a last damning extract from a confidential letter
which Macdonald had written to Hincks in the last days of
the conference at Washington. "Our true policy," Macdonald
was alleged to have written, "is to hold out to England that
we will not ratify the treaty; and I have strong hopes that in
her desire to close every possible cause of dispute with the
United States we can induce her to make us a liberal offer."¹⁰

This startling fragment handed around among a few members of the Gladstone Cabinet, provoked some very acid comment. "If I understand it rightly," Kimberley wrote, "he means

to play a game for which knavery is hardly too strong a word."[11] Gladstone was equally definite in a different way. "I hope," he wrote, "the 'liberal offer' which Sir John Macdonald intends to conjure from us will be *nil*."[12] And Kimberley summed up the feeling of his colleagues accurately with the biblical quotation, "in vain is the net spread in sight of any bird".[13] The mood of suspicious niggardliness in everything that concerned Canada became a habit. The Cabinet decided that there would be no further delay in the recall of the garrisons from the Dominion, that nothing would be done to carry out the promise about the Fenian Raids until Macdonald had declared himself, and that no honour whatever should be granted him until he had got the Treaty safely through the Canadian Parliament.[14] "Payment for results," wrote Kimberley firmly, "is the safest course in his case."[15]

Macdonald was unaware of all this. But the incredible inquiry in Kimberley's letter was, in itself, sufficiently enlightening. He sat down towards the end of July to write a long private letter to Lord Lisgar which would be in effect a rejoinder to Lord Kimberley. What was he going to do about the Treaty? "The more pertinent question," he wrote, "would have been, what is the Canadian government going to do?" He promised that, when the holidays were over, the Cabinet would assemble and consider the question "in all its bearings". But he took care to remind the Governor-General that the Council had already objected to the fisheries articles and had stated its belief that the Canadian Parliament would not ratify them. "There has not been, so far as I know," he went on, "any change of opinion in the Council. . . . Meanwhile, I would venture to suggest that you should press upon Her Majesty's Government the expediency of giving satisfactory assurances as to the Fenian claims and the notice on the termination of the treaty. I hope that no attempt will be made to make the settlement of the former contingent on our acceptance of the Treaty. Such an attempt I should consider a breach of the understanding, and would at once abandon any attempt to reconcile my colleagues or the people of Canada to the adoption of the Treaty."[16]

This was plain speaking. A few days after he had finished

his letter, he went off to Rivière du Loup, for he badly needed a holiday, leaving behind him a difference of opinion which was rapidly becoming a portentous dispute. He was nettled by the condescending, temporizing communications that came from England; and Lisgar and Kimberley were annoyed by what they considered to be the deliberate non-committal evasiveness of his attitude. "It is no doubt a serious crisis in the relations of the colony with the home country," Kimberley wrote gravely to Lisgar, "but I do not despair of a satisfactory result."[17] Macdonald's letter, which had, of course, been sent on to him, was described as "very unsatisfactory", and towards the end of September he dispatched his answer to it using the somewhat formal vehicle of a secret despatch to the Governor-General for the purpose. He confessed to Lisgar that the dispatch was "controversial". It was scarcely an overstatement. The Colonial Secretary began by agreeing with Macdonald's account of the promise made by de Grey in respect of the Fenian claims. But he went on to remind his readers that compensation had been offered "if it was clearly understood to be no precedent for the future, but part of a great and final settlement between Great Britain and the United States". How then could Macdonald possibly claim that the promise made by de Grey was unconditional? "On his own showing," Kimberley continued argumentatively, "the assurance given by Lord Ripon as to the Fenian claims was contingent upon all the other questions being settled with the United States. . . . How all the questions between Great Britain and the United States can be regarded as settled, if Canada rejects an important part of the Treaty, and the fishery question is thus left unsettled, I am altogether at a loss to imagine. Her Majesty's Government will abide strictly and honourably by the promise they have given but they entirely decline to admit that a conditional promise can be construed as if it were unconditional. . . ."[18] The promise must continue to be regarded as conditional; and Kimberley implied, though he did not insist too dogmatically, that the condition could be nothing less than the acceptance of the Treaty by the Dominion Parliament.

II

Macdonald did not hurry with his answer. It was autumn now, but the American Congress had not yet met, and he had an interval which he could give to private as well as public affairs. His law firm, now Macdonald and Patton, was being prepared for its transfer from Kingston to Toronto; and late that autumn he and his family moved again, to a new house in the eastern suburbs of Ottawa, in a district which soon would be known as Sandy Hill. He had to take possession, in fact, before the house was properly finished, and in November he was laid up with a severe attack of quinsy, which he thought had probably been caused by the premature removal.[19] "I have had a run of ill luck," he wrote a little later to his old friend Alexander Campbell. "No sooner was my quinsy got rid of, than I was obliged to go to the dentist, who so bedevilled my mouth that I have had to be lanced and probed and blistered."[20] He had never enjoyed exceptionally robust health. He could look back on a long series of minor ailments, and little debilitating troubles; and he knew now, one year after his convalescence in Prince Edward Island, that the terrible illness of 1870 had left its mark on him for life. Yet he had no intention of giving up the task he had set himself. ". . .I think there is some work left in me yet," he told his friend Gowan. "I greatly desire to complete the work of Confederation before I make my final bow to the Canadian audience before whom I have been acting my part for so long."[21] At the back of his mind there was the consciousness of a definite historical rôle. There was a creator's zest for the completion of work which he knew was so largely his own, which he was determined to realize in all the finished perfection of his inner design.

That autumn he took stock of the electoral chances of the future. In Quebec province, Cartier had become alarmingly unpopular with the English-speaking population of Montreal, which before had always supported him so heartily. In Manitoba there occurred a stupid, abortive Fenian escapade, which unhappily brought Riel back again into the limelight, revived the old campaign for an amnesty for all political offenders in the Red River Rebellion, and provoked another outburst of Protestant anti-French fury in the Province of Ontario. It was, in fact, in Ontario, the most populous and politically powerful province, Macdonald's own special bailiwick, that difficulties and signs of Conservative weakness seemed to accumulate most ominously. The Ontario farmers would gain no benefit whatever from the Washington Treaty. The Ontario Orangemen had been infuriated once again by the revival of trouble in Manitoba. Worst of all, the provincial administration at Toronto, which, under Macdonald's old opponent and new ally, John Sandfield Macdonald, had been a strong support since Confederation, was now obviously weakening under the attacks of the re-invigorated provincial Liberals; and on December 20, 1871, after a defeat in the provincial House, Sandfield Macdonald resigned and Edward Blake formed a new Reform government. "I need scarcely say," Macdonald wrote, "that I look upon the defeat of Sandfield's administration as a most unfortunate event, of which one cannot see the results."[22] Yet the results were all too likely to be unfortunate also. Sandfield had lost power at the moment when his support was most vitally necessary. A defeat in provincial affairs was a very inauspicious prelude to a victory in a federal general election.

He badly needed new policies—policies that were positive and popular. But his new policies—the guaranteed loan and the Pacific railway—were both stuck in embarrassing uncertainty. Early in the autumn, the American railway promoters, Smith and McMullen, returned to Ottawa, bringing with them this time, as a more effective Canadian associate, the white-bearded Montreal ship-owner, Hugh Allan, the proprietor of the Allan Line of Ocean Steamships, who had just been knighted for his services to transatlantic commerce. "Allan has joined himself with a number of American capitalists," Macdonald wrote to a newspaper friend, "and they are applying to the Canadian government to be allowed to build our Pacific Railway. The government is, of course, glad to receive all such applications as they show an interest in the undertaking and indicate its value; but as yet we have come to no conclusion with respect to it. You may depend upon it we will see that Canadian interests are fully protected, and that no American ring will be allowed to get control over it."[23] It was, of course, impossible, without parliamentary authority, to make an arrangement with any syndicate; but, as he talked with the members of the Allan group, it was not merely this legal barrier that held Macdonald back. He was worried by the still obvious predominance of American capital in the syndicate and by the complete absence of any financial support from the Province of Ontario. Allan represented Montreal finance; but Toronto was Montreal's jealous and aggressive rival. And Toronto was the capital of Ontario, where, at the moment, his political weakness was most alarming.

In all these perplexing circumstances, the Treaty still remained his biggest political embarrassment. His policy was still a policy of reticence and delay. All that autumn he made no public appearances whatever, for he knew that if he accepted invitations to political dinners, he would have to speak, and speak of the Treaty, "and that it would stultify all my policy which I have carried through this whole summer if I did so".[24] Delay and silence—the silence appropriate to doubt, uncertainty, and difficulty—were best from all points of view; but, at the same time, it was absolutely essential that the Canadian and British governments should come to some agreement about the Fenian claims before the opening of the last session of the Canadian Parliament in the late winter or early spring of 1872. Late in November he finished his rejoinder to the protests of the Colonial Office. It was at least a little more conciliatory than the long letter he had written to Lisgar in July. He still harped upon the general detestation of the Treaty and the great difficulty of his own position; but he now admitted that there had been a slight abatement in the violence of popular disapproval, and he held out some hope that the Treaty might be ratified, if the British government suitably strengthened the Canadian government's hand. He denied emphatically that the promise of compensation for the losses of the Fenian Raids had been contingent upon any further action of his own or of the Canadian Parliament. The promise had been made to him during the negotiations, with the purpose of furthering the

progress of the negotiations, by inducing him not to press the
Fenian claims and to accept the objectionable fishery clauses.
If the interminable talks had not issued successfully in a treaty,
then, he admitted, it might have been claimed that the promise
was void. "But," he reminded Lord Kimberley, "a Treaty has
been made, and all other matters but the Fenian claims have
been settled so far as the two governments could settle them,
and I therefore hold that the engagement of Her Majesty's
government has thereupon become absolute and unconditional."[25]

The long, solid argument of the letter perhaps made a
greater impression upon the members of the Gladstone government than they were ready to admit. It was true that their
unpleasant suspicions of Macdonald remained largely unaltered.
They found it difficult, Kimberley confided to Lisgar, to treat
him with confidence after all that had passed.[26] But at the
same time it was impossible to deny the force of his argument
and the pressure of his surrounding difficulties. The attitude
of frigid negativism in which the Colonial Office had apparently
stiffened began to be relaxed. Lord Kimberley suggested to
Gladstone that the British government should be prepared to
consider the substitution of a guaranteed loan for a money
grant, and that it "ought not to make the assent of the Canadian
Parliament to the Treaty the condition of our payment for the
Fenian claims".[27] Three days later, at a Cabinet meeting which
considered the problem of compensation, it was decided, so
Gladstone informed the Queen, "that it would be expedient
to place in the hands of the Canadian government the power
of assuring the legislature that this question would be entertained
and submitted to Parliament, independently of the course
which that legislature might adopt with respect to the Treaty".[28]
Three days later again, the dispatches and private letters embody-
ing these proposals were sent off from the Colonial Office to
Lord Lisgar.[29]

They reached Ottawa in the third week of January; and,
with a swiftness that equalled or surpassed that of the Gladstone Cabinet, the Canadian government made up its mind.
Macdonald had had great difficulty in holding his colleagues
together, in reconciling them—and himself—to the sacrifices of

the Treaty. Indeed, as time had dragged on without a decision, Lisgar had come to believe that "instead of Sir John Macdonald trying to convert his colleagues, the ablest of his colleagues are trying to convert him".[30] It had not been easy for Macdonald to accept the difficulties in which the Treaty had landed him, or to forget the slights he had received at Washington. But now the British government's air of Olympian displeasure had softened; it had shown a willingness to compromise, to meet his requests half way; and, as he wrote still another letter to Lord Lisgar on the subject, he could not prevent a slight note of triumph from creeping into his account of the past. "I therefore took the course, as you know," he reminded the Governor-General, "of urging on my colleagues not to come to any hasty conclusion, to let the Treaty be discussed on its own merits in the press, and to trust to time, liberal legislation on the tariff by Congress, and prompt action by Her Majesty's government in the Fenian matter, to afford us a justification for accepting the Treaty with all its demerits. . . . They were thus kept together and in hand, and the result has been their gradual conversion to my views. Hence the minute of Saturday."[31] The minute of Saturday was a Council decision to support the Treaty in Parliament in return for a guaranteed loan for railways and canals.

III

As soon as this decision had been taken, he started west for Toronto. It was the first of his pre-election reconnaissances in Ontario. He must try to repair, if possible, some of the damage caused by Sandfield Macdonald's defeat; he must make some specific arrangements and, in general, put new heart into his friends. For three weeks he moved rapidly about Toronto, Hamilton, and Kingston, dining urbanely with Roman Catholic bishops, trying to regain the support of the hierarchy which Sandfield Macdonald had lost, begging merchants, bankers, and industrialists for money to establish a really respectable Conservative newspaper in Toronto. Journalistic opposition to George Brown's *Globe* had been ineffective for longer years

than the Conservatives cared to count; and recently, just when
the need of a vigorous government press was being felt acutely
again, the Conservative newspapers had seemed to become even
more lamentably feeble. "The *Leader* is so completely run
down as to be of no value. . . ," Macdonald complained, "the
Telegraph is a mere blackmail paper, and the sooner it is
crushed the better."[32] No, they must have something new—
something distinguished, authoritative, yet lively—the *Mail*!
He was busy with plans for the new paper, with Pacific railway
negotiations, and with efforts to convince the Roman Catholic
bishops that he could be relied upon to give the Catholic body
its full share of positions in government and jobs in the civil
service. "The Catholic priests are crazy to have representatives
in Parliament," he observed, "and that is the best way to catch
them."[33] He was certain that he had won the support of the
Bishops of London and Kingston; "and I believe," he added,
"the Archbishop is favourable, although from his peculiar character we cannot tell how long the impression I made on him
may last."[34] Altogether the western trip had been difficult but
reasonably rewarding. "I have had hard work for the last ten
days here," he wrote from Toronto, "but have put heart into
our friends and on the whole have made satisfactory arrangements."[35]

For a few days, while he dealt with this very familiar stuff
of Canadian politics, he had almost forgotten that tangled,
bungled, unlucky, vexatious affair, the Washington Treaty. He
had thought comfortably that he was done with it—or almost
done with it. But suddenly, without warning, the troubled
international issues which it had apparently settled, were raised
again in all their dangerous complexity. Early in 1872, the
board of arbitration, which had been established according to
the terms of the Treaty of Washington to settle the *Alabama*
damages, met and began its hearings in Geneva; and to the
utter consternation of everybody in England and Canada, the
United States, in presenting its case, filed claims not only
for all the "direct" losses which the *Alabama* had occasioned,
but also for all the "indirect", "consequential", damages which,
it was asserted, had led to the prolongation of the war! The

British government had never for a minute admitted these outrageous claims. The British High Commissioners at Washington had clearly understood that the United States had agreed to waive them in the coming arbitration. Yet here they were —perversely and discreditably revived! The Gladstone Cabinet prepared for resistance. It was morally certain that the arbitration would be at an end if the Americans persisted in presenting the "indirect" claims. The dearly bought settlement of the *Alabama* difficulty was in danger. The whole of the great diplomatic reconciliation between the British Empire and the United States was in jeopardy.

It was obvious to Macdonald—and to everybody else who was intimately concerned with the affair—that this put the question of Canadian ratification of the Treaty in a new and very different light. Up to this point it had been chiefly Canada which had expostulated at American diplomatic chicanery, protested against the sacrifices demanded of her, and predicted that it would prove impossible to ratify the Treaty. But now the position was reversed. Great Britain herself, by refusing to continue with the *Alabama* arbitration, might wreck the Treaty, wholly, or in large part; and if she did so, the most potent argument in favour of Canadian ratification, the plea of imperial necessity, of the desirability of a general Anglo-American understanding, would—at least for Canada—lose much of its force. Yet, for the harassed Gladstone government, it would remain a weighty argument. The Gladstone government would be anxious to save as much of the Anglo-American settlement as possible—to escape, if possible, the imputation of having repudiated the Treaty in its entirety. For Great Britain, rejection by the Canadian Parliament was now doubly to be feared. "It is more our interest than ever," Kimberley argued to Gladstone, "to come to terms if possible with the Canadian government";[36] and John Rose significantly reported that the proposal of the guaranteed loan had been received in official circles in London, "in a much more friendly spirit than I supposed it would have been".[37]

Macdonald may have enjoyed a certain ironic amusement at the change in the situation. It was now Great Britain's turn to

feel embarrassment and anxiety. The Gladstone Cabinet solemnly debated the new problem in its relations with Canada. "What
effect has been produced in Canada by the Alabama difficulty?"
Kimberley wired privately to Lisgar.[38] Would Canada consent
to ratify the fishery articles of the Treaty, even if the *Alabama*
arbitration fell through? It was in her own interest to do so,
Kimberley argued.[39] It was impossible, John Rose hinted, for
the British ministers to come to any decision about the guaranteed loan until they had some assurance of Canada's intentions.
But Macdonald was not greatly moved by these eager hints,
these anxious invitations. He was not to be easily cajoled into
reassuring declarations. Apart from a very general statement
of solidarity with the United Kingdom, the Canadian Council
remained unresponsive and uncommunicative. Lisgar, who had
expected that complete assurances would be given with loyal
alacrity, raged over this impudent delay. "This arises," he
growled, "from Sir John A. Macdonald's jealous reticence and
inveterate habit of waiting upon providence."[40] The Canadian
Cabinet politely reminded the Colonial Office that it had not
as yet received any reply to its proposal for a guaranteed loan.[41]
Until that had been satisfactorily answered, it could obviously
do nothing. The worried Kimberley promised a reply as soon
as possible. In the meantime it was decided to delay the opening
of the Canadian Parliament until early in April. That, it was
hoped, would give time for the matter to settle itself.

Meanwhile, whether the last session opened early or late,
the term of Parliament itself was inexorably approaching. Within
a very few months now the general election would be upon
Macdonald; and although the difficulty over the Fenian compensation made the completion of his programme impossible
for the moment, he tried to set out his other policies in preparation. The *Mail*, which was soon to appear, was henceforth to
be the distinguished and sonorous vehicle for the oracles of
Conservative truth; and with its editor, T. C. Patteson,
Macdonald carefully talked over the name, nature, and programme of the Conservative party. The very adjective "Conservative" itself seemed to him, as it had often done before, a
little unfortunate, though he was sure it could not be entirely

dropped. "I think, however," he wrote to Patteson, "that it should be kept in the background as much as possible, and that our party should be called the 'Union Party'; going in for union with England against all annexationists and independents, and for the union of all the Provinces of British North America, including Prince Edward Island and Newfoundland, against all anti-Confederates. . . . What think you of such a name as 'the Constitutional Union Party'?"[42] This was essentially the great national programme which he had undertaken nearly ten years before and which he was determined to complete—the union and expansion of British North America under the protection of the Anglo-Canadian alliance.

It was a political programme. But it was rapidly becoming an economic programme as well. The Canadian people were committed to the great enterprise of the settlement of Rupert's Land, to the equally great undertaking of the transcontinental Canadian Pacific railway; and the nationalistic impulse which lay back of these two great decisions, the ambition to build up a Canadian economy for the benefit of Canadians, had just been emphatically steeled by the blunt denials and disappointments of the Washington Treaty. The Washington Treaty had dropped a thick curtain on all the tenaciously held hopes for a renewal of reciprocity. The United States, which seemed openly determined to starve Canada into annexation, had refused all proposals for a reciprocal trade agreement; and this conclusive rejection came at a time when Canadian manufacturing industry, which had grown rapidly during the American Civil War, was stronger, more varied, and more ambitious than it had ever been before. The manufacturers were the angry advance guard of an unorganized but potentially huge army of increasingly nationalist-minded Canadians who resented the undisguised attempt to break their hopes, who believed in the potential value of their own resources, and who were determined to develop their national economy independently of the United States, and, if necessary, by every coercive device which the United States had employed against them. The army was great; it would certainly become greater. It stood, at that moment, waiting for a political leader.

Macdonald determined to put himself at its head. "The protection of manufactures is a delicate thing to handle," he had told Adam Brown, a Hamilton mill-owner, during the previous December, "but it can be dealt with, I think, so as to weigh heavily against the Grit opposition."[43] In February, when he went up to Toronto for his first western reconnaissance, he found that the Ontario farmers, who had hoped for much and gained nothing from the negotiations at Washington, were ready and eager for retaliation against the United States. "It is really astonishing," he told George Stephen, "the feeling that has grown up in the West in favour of encouragement of home manufactures. I am sure to be able to make considerable capital out of this next summer."[44] He had, indeed, high hopes. But it would not do—it would never do—to be precipitate. Canada was still too much a country that exported raw materials and imported manufactures to accept the doctrine of tariff protection with general and unqualified enthusiasm. The very word "protection" must itself, for a while, be taboo; but the impulse towards economic nationalism was potent nevertheless; and with a sure instinct for the telling slogan, he appropriated a phrase, "National Policy", which others had used incidentally, but never so purposefully before. "The paper," he told Patteson of the *Mail*, "must go in for a National Policy in tariff matters, and while avoiding the word 'protection' must advocate a readjustment of the tariff in such a manner as incidentally to aid our manufacturing and industrial interests."[45]

Eastern manufacturing and western settlement—they were two closely related national policies. The third of the trio was the transcontinental, all-Canadian railway, which would provide the physical link between the other two. That project had advanced rapidly during the winter, but in an unsatisfactory fashion which slightly perturbed Macdonald. Early in March, Sir Hugh Allan's syndicate, the Canada Pacific Railway Company, handed in to the government its preliminary proposal to build the railway. Unfortunately, Allan had not yet got rid of his American associates, McMullen, Smith, Jay Cooke and others, most of whom were deeply interested in the obviously rival American undertaking, the Northern Pacific Railroad. Perhaps even more unfortunately, he had utterly failed to attract Toronto capitalists, or even other important Montreal capitalists, to his scheme. Brydges of Montreal, who had been general manager of the Grand Trunk Railway, and David L. Macpherson, the leader of the Toronto group of promoters, had both refused to join Allan's concern, on the ground that the Americans would exercise absolute control over it. Macpherson, not satisfied with mere abstention from the hated enterprise, proceeded promptly to form a rival syndicate, the Interoceanic Railway Company, which in its turn presented a proposal for building the Pacific railway.

What to do? How could Macdonald choose between the Montrealer and the Torontonian? Sir Hugh Allan, whom he knew much less well than he knew Macpherson, was obviously the senior of the two in age, experience, and international prestige. Macpherson was a personal friend, a very warm and devoted friend, indeed, for he had acted as chairman of the small committee which that winter had collected and donated to Macdonald a "testimonial fund" of more than sixty-seven thousand dollars, in part replacement of the heavy losses which had been discovered during his serious illness of the previous year.[46] Yes, Macpherson was a friend for whom he would like to do much. Macpherson was a good Conservative. He and his associates in the Interoceanic were far from being negligible financially and above all they were Torontonians; they represented a metropolitan, a provincial, interest which it was his business to promote and which he would neglect at his peril. He did all he could for Macpherson. He wrote to him as soon as he had received the Interoceanic Company's proposal, pointing out a few places in which it suffered fatally by comparison with Allan's scheme.[47] He did not want Macpherson to fail. But he knew, in his heart, that the Interoceanic Company could not be given the charter. He knew, with equal certainty, that Allan and his dangerous American associates could not be given the charter either. Both companies were ruled out—while they stood alone. But if they united, they could be instantly acceptable. The solution was really absurdly simple. Allan's dubious American friends would be compelled to withdraw; and their places would be taken by Macpherson's band of worthy Torontonians. A coalition between the Montreal and Toronto rings was, he told Rose, the probable answer to the problem; "and Allan will, I think, be obliged to abandon his Yankee confreres".[48]

But Allan was determined not to surrender his "Yankee confreres". Macdonald had counted on submission, but submission was refused him. For Allan had taken the one inexplicable decision in his otherwise straightforward career. A mature and successful man, who had prospered without reliance on politics, and who now, with his knighthood, his great house "Ravenscrag", and his little fleet of ocean liners, stood at the respectable summit of his career, he suddenly descended, in a moment of blind infatuation, down a dangerous course of dissimulation and intrigue. It was perfectly clear to him, when he came up to Ottawa early in the session, that the Prime Minister, the government as a whole, and the great majority of the members of both parties, were utterly opposed to the inclusion of any substantial American interest in the national transcontinental railway. It was so obvious, indeed, that he at first instructed his solicitor, J. J. C. Abbott, to prepare a bill for the incorporation of his company which would have absolutely excluded all foreigners from the directorate. Outwardly, he was prepared, in the most ostentatious fashion, to conform to public opinion; but secretly he still kept up his contacts with his American associates. He had no hesitation in attempting to evade the known wishes of the nation. He was equally ready to do everything in his power to get the better of the government plan for the amalgamation of the two syndicates.

Throughout the session, the government tried studiously to maintain a position of absolute neutrality. The rival companies were incorporated in two statutes, drawn up in almost identical terms; and by a third act the government was given authority to grant subsidies of land and money to the company which it should decide eventually to charter. On the face of it, a difficult choice seemed unavoidable; but in fact it was perfectly clear from the beginning that the Cabinet hoped to avoid this dilemma by effecting an early amalgamation of the two competing concerns. Allan professed himself perfectly ready to accept an amalgamation; but it must be an amalgamation upon his own terms. And his terms were nothing less than the presidency and a controlling interest for himself—a controlling interest which he would secretly share with his American associates. He would force the government to accept these terms; and the vulnerable point at which he intended to put the full weight of his pressure had already been cunningly chosen. It was Cartier, who was past his prime now, and none too well, who had already lost the support of the British in Montreal, and who in the circumstances of the moment could fairly readily be made unpopular with his old French-Canadian following. Cartier was still the solicitor of the Grand Trunk Railway; and the Grand Trunk, with its main lines south of the St. Lawrence, was naturally assumed to be hostile to the project of a new railway, running along the north shore of the river between Quebec and Montreal, and from thence to Ottawa. But the North Shore route was popular in Montreal. It could be made much more popular easily; and Allan, who was president of the Northern Colonization Railway, the North Shore's western extension between Montreal and Ottawa, appropriated the whole scheme and made himself its principal backer. He engaged French-Canadian newspapermen to write up the North Shore route and French-Canadian politicians to speak about it in public. He began to dispense cash with a lavish hand. "I think you will have to *go it blind*," he wrote his friend Smith in Chicago, "in the matter of the money (cash payments)."[49] He proceeded to go it blind. The muttering volume of opposition to Cartier began to mount.

At the moment Macdonald did not properly appreciate what was happening. He was not aware of the gradual intensification of Cartier's difficulties, still less did he suspect that malice was at the back of it. He was, in fact, feeling fairly cheerfully confident, for the session was not going at all badly and he had just had an enormous stroke of luck. All during the winter the Canadian trade unions—the mere fact of their presence in numbers was a sign of the growth of the new industrialism—had been actively crusading for a reduction of working hours.

From Ottawa Macdonald had watched this so-called "Nine
Hours Movement" with curious interest, his big nose sensitively
keen like an animal's for any scent of profit or danger. Montreal,
Toronto, and Hamilton were evidently the key centres of the
working-class agitation; and at Toronto, where George Brown's
Globe was printed and published, the strongly organized typographical union went out on strike towards the end of March.
By great good luck, the *Mail* had not yet appeared, and was not
involved in the resulting controversy. By even greater good luck,
James Beaty, the proprietor of the *Leader*, the Conservative
paper which Macdonald had described so contemptuously only
a little while before, granted the strikers their demands, continued to publish his newspaper, and strongly supported the
nine hours movement in its columns.

All this was highly satisfactory; but the crowning mercy was
yet to come. The crowning mercy was the infatuated conduct
of George Brown. Brown put himself at the head of the master
printers who fought the strike, excoriated the strikers in his
newspaper, and was popularly supposed to have inspired, or
actually engineered, the arrest of twenty-three of their number
on charges of conspiracy. As soon as their trial began, a regrettable, an almost shameful, fact was revealed. The legislatures
of Canada had evidently never dealt with the subject of trade
unions and their activities. The only law governing the subject
in Canada was the common law; and by it the twenty-three
arrested printers, merely because they belonged to a union and
had gone on strike, were convicted as parties to an illegal combination in restraint of trade. George Brown had apparently
won; but it was an unwanted, an unpopular, victory. He had
been found guilty, in the eye of the public, of dredging up out-
worn and half-forgotten legal precedents in order to deal an
unfair blow at opponents that were weaker than he.[50]

Macdonald seized his advantage at once. He had already
concerned himself with industry; now he saw where he could
espouse the cause of labour. He had a quick instinct for the
kind of Tory democracy which Disraeli was to proclaim only a
little later. He had been presented, as if by magic, with an
opportunity of gratifying the working-men and of discomfiting

the Reformers. The circumstances could hardly have been more favourable; the means lay right at his hand. Only the year before, Gladstone had rescued the trade unions of Great Britain from a somewhat similar anomalous position by passing the Trade Union Act and the Criminal Law Amendment Act. All that Macdonald had to do was to re-enact, with suitable modifications to suit Canadian conditions, the two British statutes of 1871; and the unimpeachable orthodoxy of Gladstonian legislation would remove all doubts and silence all criticisms. The situation must have amused Macdonald immensely. He could confound George Brown with William Ewart Gladstone! He could silence the disciple with the latest revelation from the master!

In the meantime, the long and involved negotiations over compensation for the Fenian losses had come to an end. On March 16, the Gladstone government finally offered to guarantee a Canadian loan of £2,500,000 for railways and canals; and at the same time it suggested, in order to remove the Canadian objection to ratifying the fishery clauses before the *Alabama* imbroglio was cleared up, that the statute of ratification should come into force only by order-in-council.[51] There were still delays, hesitations, vain attempts by the Canadian Council to get the amount increased, and other last-minute efforts at bargaining; but after the opening of the Canadian Parliament on April 11, Macdonald drew rapidly towards the end of his long exercise of patience and persuasion. He had had far greater difficulty in convincing his colleagues than Lisgar and Kimberley had been disposed to give him credit for, at least in the early stages of the deliberations. It came as a shock to Englishmen in general and the Colonial Office in particular, when Joseph Howe, one of the Cabinet ministers whom Lisgar had fondly believed to be friendly to the Washington Treaty, took advantage of an address to the Young Men's Christian Association of Ottawa, to launch out in denunciation of "England's recent diplomatic efforts to buy her own peace at the sacrifice of our interests";[52] and after that outburst, which nearly resulted in Howe's resignation, there was rather less talk about Macdonald's zealously loyal colleagues "converting" him to the necessity of the ratification of the fishery clauses. "Meanwhile," he wrote to John Rose a few days after the opening of the session, "I have screwed up my colleagues, after very many months of labour and anxiety, to the sticking point. We have finally agreed to go to Parliament this session for an Act to bring the fishery articles into force, with a clause suspending its operation until an order-in-council is issued here, Her Majesty's Government giving us the guarantee of two and half millions."[53]

In all probability he had never believed in, or hoped for, any other solution. "The great reason why I have always been able to beat Brown," he told Matthew Crooks Cameron, "is that I have been able to look a little ahead, while he could on no occasion forgo the temptation of a temporary triumph."[54] Macdonald would never be betrayed into a temporary triumph or a temporary revenge. With him the short view was lifted habitually to the long view, the gaze was steadied towards the distant objective, the eyes, wise with the remembrance of the past, sought the certainty of the future. The studied discourtesies at Washington, the long haggling with the Colonial Office, the exasperating suspicion, which he confided to Rose, that somebody was privately belittling his difficulties, were all, in the long view, merely the small inevitable frictions, the blunt familiar give-and-take of a family relationship by which Canada could alone survive as a separate and independent nation in North America. An occasional concession, a bad bargain, even something which, in the eyes of the inexperienced Canadians, could only seem an enormous diplomatic sacrifice, must all be regarded, in the long view, as a small price to pay for the indefinite continuance of the Anglo-Canadian alliance, which was the reality behind the imperial connection, and the condition and guarantee of Canada's autonomy in the new continent.

Macdonald believed he could rely on the indefinite continuance of that alliance. It was true that he had never had any very great confidence in the loyalty of Gladstone, Lowe, Cardwell, and Bright. He suspected that, in the existing British Cabinet, there were men who, in Lord Kimberley's words, made "no secret of their opinion" that England would be well rid of the colonies.[55] Yet these well-founded suspicions had never weakened his belief in the permanence of the imperial partnership. "Little Englanders" had been fairly prominent for some time now in the English governing class; and, as Macdonald had good reason to suspect, even extreme "little Englanders" were conscious of the claims of historic loyalties and obligations. Gladstone himself had admitted that the compact could never be dissolved by the action of one of the parties to it. "Let separation come if it must," wrote Kimberley, "but I will be no party to any step which tends to bring about a separation in anger."[56] The present British ministers, Macdonald realized, were simply temporary actors in a long, complex imperial drama, which had brought England greatness in the past, and which would never be permitted, even by its severest critics, to end in ignominy. Back of the Gladstone government was England and its people, and all that they had ever thought and said and done for British North America, all the effort and daring, the political wisdom and the political magnanimity—Brock leading the volunteers up the heights at Queenston, Mackenzie toiling north towards the mouth of his great river, Colonel By driving the canal through the forest towards the Ottawa River, and Carnarvon rising in his place in the Lords to move the first reading of the British North America Bill.

The third of May was a dull, cool spring day; and, when Macdonald got up to move the ratification of the Canadian clauses in the Washington Treaty, something of its uninspiring chilliness seemed to have stiffened the opening passages of his speech.[57] He often began badly, in a hesitant, feeble, not too easily audible, fashion; and on this occasion the first awkwardness was perhaps emphasized by the technical difficulty of the subject itself, and by the embarrassment of its surrounding political circumstances. It was not until after the recess for dinner that he began to warm up. By this time the long quotations were mostly finished, the legal explanations were done. The subject took hold of him, and for two and a half hours he spoke his best, defending each clause in the treaty, emphasizing the sacrifices which it called upon Great Britain to make, driving home the realization of Canada's interest in the achievement of Anglo-American peace, and ending with a personal explanation which was both a defence of his own conduct and an appeal to the mature judgment of his countrymen. "I have not said a word," he told the House, "for twelve months. I have kept silence to this day, thinking it better that the subject should be discussed on its own merits. How eagerly was I watched! If the government should come out in favour of the Treaty, then it was to be taken as being a betrayal of the people of Canada. If the government should come out against the Treaty, then the First Minister was to be charged with opposing the interests of the Empire. Whichever course we might take they were lying in wait, ready with some mode of attack. But 'silence is golden', Mr. Speaker, and I kept silence. I believe the sober second thought of this country accords with the sober second thought of the government; and we come down here and ask the people of Canada through their representatives to accept this treaty, to accept it with all its imperfections, to accept it for the sake of peace, and for the sake of the great Empire of which we form a part."[58]

Chapter Five

Blackmail

I

The brief remainder of the session was an unbroken success. The Washington Treaty passed the House by the large majority of one hundred and twenty-one to fifty-five. The Trades Union Bill, the repeal of the tea and coffee duties, the Redistribution Bill allocating the six new seats due to Ontario as a result of the recent census all slipped through with a minimum of trouble and difficulty. "We had a most triumphant session," Macdonald wrote to Rose, "not having experienced a single check of any kind. The opposition were completely demoralized and I am going to the country with good hopes of success in Ontario."[1] All the preparations were finished. The most favourable ground had been chosen, the best possible dispositions made. Even the patient propitiation of the Roman Catholic authorities was at last having gratifying results. "I cannot conceal from you the thought," wrote Archbishop Lynch genially at the conclusion of a reassuring letter, "that (now that I am warmed up about you) I will have you a good Catholic yet."[2] A most satisfactory letter! The skies seemed to smile over the home ground of Ontario. And abroad, the threatening storm on the Anglo-American horizon, instead of darkening, had cleared up with magical suddenness. The United States withdrew the "indirect" claims. The arbitration of the *Alabama* damages at Geneva continued placidly through its legal involutions. The peaceful settlement between the British Empire and the United States was saved.

Not inappropriately, the coming of peace, the achievement

of security for the new, transcontinental Canada, was marked by a change of governors-general. Lord Lisgar, the Governor who had come over as Sir John Young—a "mere Bart." in his own phrase—was now about to yield his place to "a man of high rank and the first water of fashion", the Earl of Dufferin. Lisgar's governor-generalship had coincided with the rapid political expansion of the young Dominion and the settlement of its outstanding political differences with the United States. Lord Dufferin, who was as elaborate and complimentary in his manner as Lisgar had been simple and downright, would have to preside over what was expected to be the more sober work of national organization. It was true that the projected Dominion was not yet complete. Newfoundland and Prince Edward Island had yet to come in; but the importance of their entrance into Confederation was hardly comparable to that of the acquisition of Rupert's Land or the union with British Columbia. The days of Canada's most rapid territorial expansion were past; and the task that remained, now that the United States had accepted the existence of the transcontinental northern nation, was to weld its vast domains into a working and prosperous unity. It was for this purpose—to clinch the sudden victory, to make fast the claim that had been merely staked—that Macdonald wanted another five years of power. "I am, as you may fancy," he wrote to John Rose, "exceedingly desirous of carrying the elections again; not from any personal object, because I am weary of the whole thing, but Confederation is only yet in the gristle, and it will require five years more before it hardens into bone."[3] It would require far more than five years, of course, to people the west and build up a strong eastern industry. These were long-term, comprehensive national projects, which depended, for their success, upon the inflow of men and capital, and which the Canadian government and Parliament could never realize by legislation alone. The Pacific railway was an entirely different affair. It must be built in ten years, if the Dominion kept its compact with British Columbia. It ought to be finished in less than ten years, if Canada were to give the world a convincing proof of its enterprise and resources.

Macdonald wanted to begin quickly. The Pacific railway

was his biggest task and his most important policy. But—within six weeks of the election—it had also become his principal source of anxiety. The Interoceanic Railway Company and the Canada Pacific Railway Company confronted each other in intolerable opposition. He realized that he would have to make a very earnest effort, before the elections began, to end this stupid rivalry by persuading Macpherson and Allan to unite in a joint undertaking. But what enormous difficulties confronted him! Macpherson, who still doubted Allan's good faith and who suspected that he had not, in fact, got rid of his American associates, was obviously in no mood for generous compromises. But neither apparently was Allan. Allan seemed flushed with ambition and a growing sense of power. Did he possess enough influence to force Allan to make the real concessions which were necessary to gain Macpherson's support? He was very doubtful. Within the last two months his chances of imposing a reconciliation between the two promoters and an amalgamation of their rival companies had perceptibly worsened, as he was now very well aware. His strength in Montreal, and in everything that concerned Montreal, was nothing more or less than the strength —or weakness—of George Etienne Cartier. And Cartier, the pugnacious, masterful companion of the past, was very far from being his old self, either physically or politically, in the first summer months of 1872.

Allan had, in fact, chosen his victim with extraordinary cunning. Cartier was not well. He was troubled by various disquieting symptoms, by swellings in his limbs which seemed ominously to suggest some grave disorder. But he was determined to run in the election and to run in Montreal East. Montreal and its district was his old political empire; Montreal East was his old constituency. It was all true. But it was also true that, in Montreal East, the natural public interest in the North Shore route and the Northern Colonization Railway had been so magnified and strengthened by Allan that it had now become an apparently irresistible political force directed against Cartier. Cartier, like Macdonald, had been deeply suspicious of Allan and his American connections. "Aussi longtemps que je vivrai et que je serai dans le ministère," he told one delegation

which had come to ask his opinion of Allan's pet scheme of an
amalgamation of the Canada Pacific and the Northern
Colonization Railways, "jamais une sacrée compagnie Améri-
caine aura le contrôle du Pacifique. . . ."⁴ He had seized upon
the vital defect of Allan's project as a national, Canadian
scheme. But, in Montreal East, nobody would believe that the
solicitor of the monopolistic Grand Trunk Railway could be
a really unprejudiced witness. The thunder of Cartier's typically
explosive, typically anti-American criticisms was stolen before it
ever really began to roll. By the end of June it was clearly
evident to most people, if not to Cartier himself, that he could
not possibly win in Montreal East unless Allan and the railway
interests which he represented were in some fashion appeased.
"I hear on all sides," Alexander Campbell wrote to Macdonald
early in July, "that the Allan North Shore interest is wanted to
put Cartier in for East Montreal."⁵

By this time, Macdonald was ready to move to Toronto for
the opening of the campaign. The Pacific railway, although
at the moment it caused him most concern, was far from being
his only worry. He expected that the general election in Ontario
would give him the hardest fight of his political career. He had
made all prudent preparations, he had had several strokes of
real luck; but it was impossible to blink away the plain fact that
every mistake that the government had made, every misfortune
it had suffered—Riel, the Manitoba settlement, the bargain with
British Columbia, the fatal omissions of the Washington Treaty
—would be felt more severely in Ontario than in any other
part of the federation. In Ontario, the new provincial
administration, flushed with its triumph over John Sandfield
Macdonald, and eager to complete the defeat of the Conservative
party, would bring all its power and influence and patronage to
bear against him. He might be defeated; he might be able to
do no more than break even. And even to fight a drawn battle
would, he was perfectly certain, require his constant presence in
the hottest of the fighting. He would have to take to the
stump, *more Americano*, as he called it, through all the central
and western part of Ontario. It would mean two solid months
of strenuous, exhausting campaigning. He had never done

such a thing before in all the twenty-seven years of his political career; he hoped never to have to do it again. But he persuaded himself that this time it was inescapably necessary. "I only wish," he told Rose, "that I was physically a little stronger. However, I think that I will not break down in the contest. We will carry all the other provinces, I believe, with sweeping majorities."[6]

II

In the first week in July he and Agnes travelled to Toronto and settled down for what was certain to be a long summer's visit. He left his own election in Kingston to Alexander Campbell's care. There were more general and more important matters to consider, and the amalgamation of the two Pacific railways was the most important of all. A meeting of the principals involved, with himself, a benevolently diplomatic broker, hovering in the background, was surely the best means of achieving an amicable union; and he had barely established himself in the Queen's Hotel when he wrote to Montreal inviting Allan and Abbott to come up to Toronto for a personal conference with Macpherson. He had made up his mind about the broad lines of the arrangement that he wished to impose. The board of directors of the united organization would have to be a board which, from the point of view of the government, would be politically defensible; and no board would be defensible which did not reflect the political pre-eminence of Ontario. Thirteen directors, of whom Macpherson would nominate five, Allan, four, and the government the remainder, choosing one from each of the other provinces, would make a very acceptable governing body.[7] This much he would have to insist upon, for the sake of Ontario and Macpherson; but all the details of the amalgamation he left to the principals, hoping that they could reach a friendly agreement between themselves. His hopes were disappointed. Allan—it was possibly an ominous indication of the Montrealer's sense of conscious power—found it inconvenient to accept Macdonald's

invitation. Abbott, his solicitor, alone put in an appearance for
the conference at the Queen's Hotel; and as soon as he and
Macpherson got down to a detailed discussion of the terms of
the proposed amalgamation, a fundamental conflict of interest
at once appeared. Macpherson utterly refused to accept Allan
in advance as president of the united company;[8] Allan was
plainly unwilling to grant Macpherson the nomination of the
larger number of directors. There were no compromises and no
agreement. Almost as soon as it began, the conference was over.
And Macdonald's first attempt to secure the amalgamation had
failed.

That night—it was the night of July 11—he went with Agnes
to the Toronto Music Hall to keep another engagement—an
engagement which was to reveal him to shining advantage in
his new rôle as the "working-man's friend". A fortnight before
he had received a rather shakily spelt, shakily punctuated letter
from John Hewitt, corresponding secretary of the Toronto
Trades Assembly, which informed him that the trades unions of
Canada wished to make a presentation to Lady Macdonald "as
a slight token of our appreciation of your timely efforts in the
interests of the operatives of this Dominion".[9] It was a handsome, gold, jewelled casket that was presented to Agnes that
night; and along with it went a laudatory address, which
sketched the efforts of the Typographical Union to forward the
nine hours movement, and referred poignantly to the "harsh
and uncalled-for" arrest of the twenty-three printers—an arrest
"instigated by the proprietor of a newspaper whose animus
leads him to follow, even to the death, those who cross his
path".[10]

Macdonald thanked the assembly of working-men on his wife's
account and his own, promised that he would give "respectful
and prompt attention" to any representations the Trades Assemblies cared to give on the subject of Canadian labour legislation,
and ended up by identifying himself, in a jocular fashion, with
the highly sympathetic audience before him. ". . . I ought
to have a special interest in this subject," he said, while his
listeners laughed their approval, "because I am a working-man
myself. I know that I work more than nine hours every day

myself; and then I think that I am a practical mechanic. If you look at the Confederation Act, in the framing of which I had some hand, you will admit that I am a pretty good joiner; and, as for cabinet-making, I have had as much experience as Jacques and Hay themselves."[11] It was all a tremendous success. The meeting ended in a storm of cheers and hand-clapping; outside the audience formed a torch-light procession, and a carriage carrying Sir John and Lady Macdonald, Beaty, the proprietor of the *Leader* and McCormick, the president of the Trades Assembly, was drawn in triumph through the streets. "The workingmen," Macdonald wrote proudly to Alexander Campbell next morning, "are at white heat in my favour just now."[12]

The next move in the campaign was to Hamilton, the "ambitious city", at the head of Lake Ontario. He and Hincks had decided that an important announcement of government policy was to be made there. And he was just about to leave Toronto on the following morning when a most ominous telegram arrived from Sir Hugh Allan. "It is very important," the message ran, "in the interest of Sir George and of the government that the Pacific question should be settled without delay. I send this from no personal interest but a storm is brewing."[13] It was only too obvious what had happened. Allan had been informed at once by Abbott of the denial of his demands, of the inconclusive ending of the interview with Macpherson, on the previous day. Sir Hugh had decided peremptorily to apply pressure himself. He was using threats—blatant, obviously disingenuous threats. But his power was real. Macdonald felt himself pressed, suddenly and savagely, by a force stronger and more unscrupulously wielded than he had ever felt in the past. He had only time enough, before his departure, to beg a favour of Macpherson. Would he, for the sake of peace, go and see Allan in Montreal, since Allan would not come to Toronto to see him? The only hope lay in a real meeting of the principals. Macpherson reluctantly consented; and with that Macdonald tore himself away.

Hamilton was a manufacturing town, already specializing in heavy industries in iron and steel, and in the last few years

growing rapidly in population. Macdonald had decided to give
it one of the six new seats allotted to Ontario by the Redistribution Bill. The town had been represented in the last Parliament
by a Grit; but he was determined to regain the old seat and to
win the new, and, with his new programme, he believed he had
an excellent chance of succeeding. The Trades Union Bill
would, he was certain, win the Hamilton mechanics. To the
Hamilton manufacturers he had already been clearly hinting
that the removal of the tea and coffee duties would make it
necessary for the government next session to propose an increase
on the tariff on articles that Canada could produce;[14] and on
July 13, at a big public meeting in the city, Hincks and he
made the first public announcement of the Conservative policy
of incidental protection.[16] Two days later at Brantford, which
was another growing manufacturing town, he repeated the
announcement, dwelling proudly on the industrial growth of
the country during recent years and insisting that Canada,
irrespective of free-trade or any other theories, must have a
commercial policy "of its own".[16] "Incidental protection" and
"national policy" were the main themes of their speeches as he
and Hincks travelled westward through the province. They
were together at London on July 16. Then they separated and
Macdonald went on to Stratford.

It was while he was still in western Ontario that the bad
news began to catch up with him. There was a letter from
Campbell, who had been given charge of his campaign in
Kingston; there were letters and telegrams—increasingly demanding or importunate—from Macpherson, and Allan, and
Cartier. Campbell wrote to inform him that Carruthers was
to be the Reform candidate in Kingston, that a severe contest
was expected, and that everybody hoped he would come back,
establish himself at the British American Hotel, and "go into
the contest as of yore".[17] He felt like a commander-in-chief of
combined operations who is suddenly invited to step aside and
meet one of the enemy in single combat. It was a nuisance, but,
of course, he would have to go back to Kingston, at least for
the nomination meeting. That was clear enough; but what was
not clear, what was, in fact, shrouded in complete obscurity, was

a way out of the dangerous mess of the Pacific railway affair. Macpherson had done all he had promised. He had gone to Montreal, and, on the afternoon of July 18, he had discussed the whole matter at length with Allan. He had apparently agreed to an amalgamation and had even consented to an increase in the number of directors, with himself and Allan each appointing an equal number and the government the rest. But he absolutely refused to accept Sir Hugh beforehand as president, and he insisted that the free choice of both president and vice-president should be left to the board after it had been constituted.[18]

The turning-point had been reached. Nothing had yet been settled, but an agreement was possible, if only Allan would make some concessions. And, in fact, he seemed outwardly to be prepared for compromises. Outwardly only. Secretly he was determined to get his way. He insisted that if a board as now proposed were set up, the directors appointed by the government should be given clearly to understand that they were to vote for him as president and that, in addition, over fifty per cent of the stock must be assigned to his "friends".[19] These demands were, as Macdonald knew perfectly well, dangerous and possibly fatal to grant in the circumstances. But they were demands which were no longer made by Allan alone; they were endorsed and supported by Cartier, who now, on the eve of the election, had at last realized the desperateness of his situation, and who was ready to capitulate to the man who had mastered him. On July 19, he telegraphed to Macdonald at Stratford, giving him an account of the meeting of Macpherson and Allan on the previous day, and urging that the affair must be settled "on account of elections in Ontario and Quebec".[20] Three days later, when Macdonald was at Toronto hurrying to get back to Kingston for nomination day, he received another telegram from Cartier which this time gave Allan's final ultimatum. "If the government will pledge itself," Allan had wired unequivocally, "to appoint directors favourable to me as president and to the allotment of stock as stated in my letter of yesterday I will be satisfied." And Cartier had added a desperate, importunate postscript: "Matter could be settled at once thus between him and Macpherson. Important it should be settled without delay."[21]

But Macdonald—even with Cartier's fate in the balance—was not willing to settle on Allan's conqueror's terms. He would grant nothing until he had had another conversation with Macpherson, and that was impossible at the moment, for Macpherson was still away in Montreal. Macdonald hurried on to Kingston, and the mental and physical strain to which he had been subjected for the last few weeks was only too evident on nomination day when, on a public platform at Kingston, before a large, disorderly crowd, he completely lost his temper with his opponent, Carruthers, and, as the newspapers put it discreetly, a "slight contretemps occurred".[22] He could not leave Kingston, when the struggle was fiercely and all too evenly joined; but he telegraphed Macpherson begging him to stop off on his way back from Montreal. And on July 26, their meeting finally took place. Macdonald pressed Macpherson to accept the unpalatable fact that Allan must be president on political grounds. Macpherson was stubbornly suspicious of Allan, and his American friends, and the sinister influence which they might exercise together. But he did not appear to reject the idea of Allan's presidency without qualification, and he seemed prepared to wait until after the elections for a final decision. Macdonald seized the opportunity. He telegraphed to Cartier, authorizing him to assure Allan "that the power of the government will be exercised to secure him the position of president" and postponing the settlement of the other details until after the election.[23] He had made only one promise—the presidency. And it could be argued, of course, that Allan was entitled to the presidency on grounds of age, experience, and prestige.

He closed his telegram to Cartier with the peremptory word "Answer". But for four days no answer came. And then, on July 30, a telegram from Cartier and a letter from Allan shocked him with the realization that Sir Hugh was still not satisfied, that he had made a final effort to extort the desired concessions from Cartier's weakness. The presidency—the one promise that Macdonald had thought it possible to make—was not enough for Allan. He wanted more. He insisted that he and his friends must have a clear majority of the stock and "government influence" in their favour; and he now demanded, for the first time, that if the negotiations for the amalgamation should not succeed within a brief period of two months, the charter would then be given to his own company, the Canada Pacific Railway Company.[24] In this last gambling effort, he had raised his demands to their most extravagant limit. But he had also baited them with his most seductive inducements. At the frantic Cartier's own suggestion, he had agreed that "the friends of the government will expect to be assisted with funds in the pending elections", and he had accepted a list of "immediate requirements" for Cartier, Langevin, and Macdonald, totalling sixty thousand dollars.

Macdonald stared at the telegram with amazement and apprehension. He desperately needed the money. In the mêlée of the election the rival forces surged uncertainly backward and forward, and from all over Ontario the demands for funds had become a roar in his ears. But it was utterly impossible to yield to Allan's demands. The whole agreement, into which the wretched Cartier had been betrayed by his weakness, must be instantly repudiated. In the first few moments of worried excitement, Macdonald decided that there was only one thing to do, and that was to go immediately to Montreal himself. He even began to make preparations for departure, giving Campbell hurried, last-minute directions for the conduct of the election during his absence. Then he drew back. The election! How could he leave Kingston at this moment of all others! Today was July 31. Tomorrow, August 1, the poll would begin. He had only a few hours more in which to clinch his uncertain chances of success. He could not go—not, at least, for the moment. He telegraphed instead, rejecting Allan's absurd demands, repudiating the dangerous agreement into which Cartier had been forced, throwing the whole arrangement back to the terms of his own telegram of July 26.

The next morning, in the early hours of the poll, the longed-for answer arrived from Cartier. "Have seen Sir Hugh," Cartier telegraphed. "He withdraws letter written you since you make objection to it, and relies for basis of arrangement on your telegram to me of which I gave him a copy."[25] This was definite enough, and the blessed assurance was confirmed by another telegram from Allan, in very much the same terms. A great load of anxiety rolled off his back that hot August morning; and, as the day waxed and waned, and the polling continued, his released spirits mounted mercurially. By the end of the day, the vote stood seven hundred and thirty-five for Macdonald, and six hundred and four for Carruthers.[26] He had won Kingston, and by a safe majority of one hundred and thirty-one. He was free—free of his own election contest, free of Allan's threats and his own worries for the Pacific amalgamation, free to return to Toronto and resume his command of the general election at a time when most of the contests in western Ontario were yet to come. He was free—yes. But he was also armed, as he had never hoped to be, with the sinews of war. He had rejected Allan's extreme demands. But Allan had not revoked his offer of funds for the election. The sum of twenty-five thousand dollars stood to Macdonald's credit in the Merchants' Bank of Canada. He used none of it for his own election in Kingston; but before he left Kingston for Toronto, he had already distributed a large part of it to important Conservative candidates in Ontario.

In Toronto he plunged again into the sticky fatigues of an August election. He had never worked so hard, or so continuously, or with such doubtful prospects of success. It was true that the government gained some big, popular, well advertised victories. Witton, the "labouring man", and Chisholm, his fellow Conservative candidate, captured the two new Hamilton constituencies; and Conservatives took two out of the three seats in Toronto. But, all over the province, riding after riding was falling to the opposition. Macdonald was conscious of the unpopularity of his own past mistakes and failures, of the pugnacious strength of the provincial Liberal electoral machine, of the large sums of money—he estimated over a quarter of a million dollars—which the Grits had put into the contest. Like a general desperately throwing in the last of his fresh troops, he flung his own campaign money broadcast across Ontario with reckless generosity. Already, he had approached Abbott, Allan's solicitor, for another ten thousand dollars. Hincks had been given two thousand, Carling fifteen hundred, Stephenson, Grayson Smith, and Ross a thousand each.[27] He did not know exactly where the money went. It seemed as if he could not keep himself going without constant recourse to wine and spirits; and the days slipped past him indistinguishably in a muddled confusion of effort. He knew only that the money dribbled away with incredible rapidity. It was going. It had gone. And once again—how often had it happened already? —he found himself wiring another appeal for assistance to Abbott. "I must have another ten thousand," he telegraphed on August 26. "Will be the last time of calling. Do not fail me. Answer today."[28] And Abbott answered that day—affirmatively.

The final polls were held. Six days later, on September 1, Macdonald was back in Ottawa. He had taken at least forty-five thousand dollars of Allan's money. It was a huge sum. But even so it did not represent the total of Allan's contributions to the Conservative party, as Macdonald now discovered to his dismay. Cartier had taken eighty-five thousand dollars, nearly twice as much as he himself had accepted; and Cartier and Langevin between them had been given a total amount of a hundred and seventeen thousand.[29] Macdonald felt a cold chill of uneasiness. The Conservative party had put itself in a most dangerously equivocal position. It was true that it had made only one promise—the promise of the presidency; but it had accepted sums whose size implied other and far less legitimate undertakings. At the moment when it was about to make a contract of the highest national importance, involving millions of money, the government had become deeply indebted, for purely party purposes, to one of the principal capitalists with whom it was negotiating.

III

What had the Conservative party got from this dubious, hazardous connection? It was strange, and vaguely disquieting;

but Allan seemed from the first to be followed by a grey familiar, ill-luck. Of course, he had not been the only contributor to the campaign fund and of course money alone never won elections anyway. But certainly the Conservatives had not experienced any very bountiful good fortune in the contest of 1872. They had, it was true, won the election as a whole; but only by virtue of the Maritime and western seats. Macdonald's estimate of forty-two out of the eighty-eight Ontario constituencies turned out, in the end, to be over-optimistic; and in Quebec, where Allan had spent most money and claimed to have most influence, Langevin and Cartier had been able to secure only a bare majority of the sixty-five seats. Cartier himself was defeated in Montreal East, in a constituency which, as Macdonald knew very well, was not *Rouge*, and which another Conservative might have captured with ease. It was a curious commentary upon Allan's vaunted political influence that he had been totally unable to allay the popular storm which he himself had helped so much to arouse against Cartier. Poor Cartier had given his unhappy pledges for nothing. He had yielded only to incur defeat, a defeat which must have seemed all the more bitter because it had come when his once splendid vitality had been sapped by illness, and when he faced a future which was dark with uncertainty. Macdonald had been present at the fatal interview in Montreal when the doctor had informed Cartier that he had a confirmed case of Bright's disease. He tried to spare his old colleague fatigue, and to hasten his departure for England, where Cartier was to put himself under the care of Bright's successor in the treatment of kidney diseases. But he did not believe that the greatest of all his French-Canadian team-mates would ever again take his seat at the Council board. "I cannot tell you how I sorrow at this," he wrote to Lord Lisgar. "We have acted together since 1854, and have never had a serious difference."[30]

Yet poor Cartier's defeat and illness, about which he could do nothing in any case, was not his main preoccupation at the moment. His main preoccupation was the amalgamation of the Interoceanic and the Canada Pacific Railway Companies—an amalgamation already complicated by the secret assurance given to Allan. Allan had been promised the presidency; and on no account could that engagement be disturbed. If Sir Hugh had not brought Cartier and Langevin a smashing victory in Quebec, he had at least saved them from an annihilating defeat; and they would certainly insist upon the complete and literal fulfilment of the government's pledge. It was a "political necessity", as Macdonald knew, to satisfy Quebec; but, as he also knew, it was a "political necessity" to conciliate Ontario. And since the presidency of Allan was now one of those "fixed facts" about which nothing could be done, then his first task was obviously to persuade Macpherson to accept the inevitable, in the interest of Ontario, as well as in the interest of the railway and the government. He knew that it would be a hard task; but he saw quickly that he had underestimated its difficulties. He picked the negotiations up where he had dropped them so hurriedly late in July, only to discover that in the meantime Macpherson had simply become more embittered in his opposition. Why, Macpherson inquired indignantly, did the government feel obliged to make any concessions whatever to Allan? Allan had failed it during the elections. Allan had not even been able to save poor Cartier from defeat.

Macdonald did his best. In two long letters, he tried to reason with Macpherson, pointing out that Allan had a fair claim, on grounds of seniority, to the presidency, that all the members of the Cabinet had agreed that his pretensions could not be denied, and that a scheme which, as Macpherson himself admitted, was in many other respects good, could not be rejected out of hand simply "because Sir Hugh sits at the head of the board instead of the side".[31] But Macpherson was not to be mollified. He was furious with wounded pride and mortification. He told Macdonald angrily that Allan's operations from start to finish had been nothing less than "an audacious, insolent, unpatriotic, and gigantic swindle—the greatest ever attempted in this Dominion".[32] He kept insisting that on such terms the Interoceanic Company would never accept the amalgamation; and very rapidly these confident predictions were confirmed by an official rejection. "I received this morning," Allan wired to Macdonald on October 4, "a letter from the secretary of the

Interoceanic Railway Company, Toronto, declining peremptorily to enter into the scheme of amalgamation."[33]

It was a crushing refusal. But Macdonald was not yet ready to give up. He thought he saw a way in which the Toronto capitalists' uncompromising position could be turned. The one legitimate objection of the Interoceanic Company was to Allan's alleged American associates; Macpherson's one valid fear was that the Pacific railway, under Allan's presidency, would inevitably fall under the control of Canada's most dangerous rivals. Macdonald himself had felt exactly the same fears and objections. And it seemed to him that if they could only be removed, once and for all, to everybody's satisfaction, Macpherson would, in all honesty, have to give way, and the scheme could go triumphantly forward. A thorough clarification of the Canada Pacific's somewhat ambiguous position was due—if not, indeed, overdue. Government itself could help to supply the necessary reassurance. It could insist upon the inclusion in the charter of clauses which would make it impossible for foreigners to get control of the railway. But it could not possibly win Macpherson without Allan's help. Allan must make a full and complete disclosure of his affairs. The memorandum in which the Interoceanic Company had justified its rejection of the amalgamation must receive a candid, explicit, and detailed answer.

It was at this point, a few days after Macpherson's formally renewed charges had made further concealment impossible, that Macdonald received a letter from the President of the Canada Pacific Railway Company.[34] Allan was full of protestations and assurances. Yet his letter was curiously disquieting as well. He reminded Macdonald that it was Hincks who had told him originally of the visit of the Americans to Ottawa and had suggested that he get in touch with them. The implication that the alliance between Allan and his American associates had had the previous sanction of government was annoying to Macdonald; but, bad as it was, it was not the most disturbing feature of Allan's letter. The dismaying fact which now unmistakably emerged was that Sir Hugh, despite all his previous solemn assurances, had yet to break conclusively and finally with the

Americans! He had hinted to them, he told Macdonald, of the popular Canadian suspicion of anyone connected with the Northern Pacific Railroad. He had pointed out the great and increasing difficulties in the way of American participation in the Canadian line. He had done all he could "gradually and not in too rude a manner" to prepare the way for a rapidly approaching separation. But the fact remained that he had not yet taken the final step. He was, however, just about to take it, he assured Macdonald eagerly. He would now inform his American friends that, as a result of popular Canadian opposition, their syndicate would have to be broken up.

Macdonald considered Allan's letter doubtfully. It certainly posed almost as many questions as it answered. It left Allan's good faith in doubt. It awakened fearful speculations about possible American reprisals in the future. Yet, for the moment, Macdonald could afford to put these worries aside. The main burden of Allan's letter was satisfactory. And a week later, in a formal reply to the accusing memorandum of the Interoceanic Railway Company, Allan and his principal Canadian directors solemnly protested that they had never contemplated combining with American capitalists or asking aid of them. It was possible, Macdonald believed, to build policy on the solid foundation of these assurances. If Macpherson remained obstinately sceptical of these new proofs of Sir Hugh's financial independence, then surely other and respectable Ontario capitalists would be convinced by them. And if an amalgamation of the two companies proved impossible to carry out, then the government would promote the formation of a completely new company, with a board of thirteen representative directors chosen from all six of the provinces, and free from the rivalries of the past. There remained, of course, the question of the presidency. For a moment he toyed vainly, longingly, with the idea of a new president. But, no! It would not do. The commitment to Allan could not be broken. Yet might it not be modified—just a little modified? Could Allan be made "provisional" president? "Provisional" was an agreeable word. Could Macpherson be induced to accept the provisional presidency of his rival?

Early in November, Macdonald boarded the train for Toronto.

Three weeks before, Alexander Campbell and Hewitt Bernard had been sent up as his ambassadors, and they had failed.[85] Now he was about to make a last personal effort to gain Macpherson. Safe in the Queen's Hotel, surrounded by his Toronto cronies, and far away from the dull routines of Ottawa, he began to drink a good deal. The jocular high spirits with which he approached the crucial encounter with Macpherson were fortified by a long succession of brandies and soda; and every art of persuasion which he possessed was lavished upon his obstinate fellow-Scotsman and his Ontario business associates. He told Macpherson of his plan for the "provisional" presidency. He promised that, in order to prevent the railway from falling into the financial control of Americans, the government would retain a veto on the distribution of stock for the first five years of the new company's existence. But Macpherson remained obdurate. For a little while, it was true, he wavered. But as soon as he discovered that the "provisional" presidency could mean nothing less than the presidency for a year, he drew back coldly and implacably. A whole year! It was far too much. In a year Allan could—and probably would—ruin the entire enterprise.[86] Macpherson would have nothing to do with it on such terms. The final words were spoken and written. And Macdonald realized that the long, fruitless pursuit of the president of the Interoceanic Railway was at an end.

He returned wearily unsuccessful to Ottawa. Yet he was not entirely defeated. He had, he informed Lord Dufferin, collected enough financial support in Ontario to make him virtually independent of Macpherson's refusal.[87] The formation of the new company could now be pushed forward with some prospect of success. But it would be a difficult, unsatisfactory business; and besides there were now other and more sinister perils which he could vaguely discern ahead. Allan had been hinting, not very obscurely, that it was going to be very difficult for him, at this late stage, to free himself from the clutches of the Americans; and already, Hincks reported, rumours were current in Montreal that Allan had contributed enormous sums during the elections in return for some unspecified but important promise by Cartier connected with the

Pacific railway.[38] Cartier's promise! Macdonald recalled with something of a start that he had never known exactly what the promise was. He and Cartier had agreed, by telegraph, that his wire of July 26 was to be the "basis" of the agreement. But had the rapacious Allan succeeded in extorting some dangerous additional concession? Macdonald did not know. He could not be certain that Allan would never present another of Cartier's I.O.U.'s for payment. He did not expect to see Cartier again. But he knew that the responsibility for all that Cartier had said and done during those last crucial weeks in Montreal would be his, and his alone.

"We have fixed next Tuesday for Pacific railway matters,"[39] he wrote Langevin on November 28. "There are rocks ahead of the most dangerous character, and I therefore think that you must be here without fail on that day." Early in December, Allan and a few of the directors came up to Ottawa to discuss the terms of the charter. Macdonald put on a brave front about the matter. ". . . We are making the best company we can," he wrote cheerfully to Cartier a few days before Christmas. "The thirteen directors are not all chosen yet, but they will all be settled by New Year's Day." New Year's Day![40] On New Year's Eve he was in his room at the East Block, working away at the details of the arrangement, when a card was brought in to him. As he stared at it, he realized that this was the visit he had been dreading for months past. George W. McMullen, the proprietor of the Chicago *Post*, the shareholder in the Northern Pacific Railroad, the principal American associate of Sir Hugh Allan, was waiting in the ante-room to wish him the compliments of the season! Happy New Year! Would it be—could it be—happy now?

IV

McMullen stayed in his office a solid two hours. He had a great deal to say, and he said it carefully and emphatically. He was a man who obviously knew exactly what he wanted, and, equally obviously, was determined to get it. He had about him the blunt, uncompromisingly authoritative air of conscious power. Like all successful blackmailers, he came heavily armed with documents. He produced the original contract between Allan and his American associates. He produced Allan's letters. With unsmiling satisfaction he read the more damning portions of the papers aloud while Macdonald listened in silence.

Macdonald was appalled. All his worst apprehensions, doubts, and fears about Allan and Allan's conduct were now confirmed with prodigal conclusiveness. Allan had committed errors—and something worse than errors—on a positively gigantic scale. It was as if the very grandiose magnitude of the Pacific enterprise had exaggerated every one of his defects and failings, had blown him and his vices into a size larger than life, had transformed a sober, inhibited Scottish merchant into a Roman emperor, free of restraint and drunk with power. Ambition, cunning, vanity, incredible indiscretion and incredible duplicity were all exhibited without reserve in the letters that McMullen held firmly in his grasp. Allan had boasted about his triumph over Cartier, had misreported his agreement with the government, had told, in garrulous detail, a most dangerously compromising story, compounded of truths, half-truths, and vague insinuations. During all the long months that he had been promising so profusely to break with his American colleagues, he had in fact done virtually nothing to prepare them for the end of the partnership. He had even had the sublime impertinence to demand repayment from McMullen for the $343,000 which he had paid out, chiefly to insure his own election to the presidency in a railway from which his American associates were certain to be excluded. For weeks, for months, he had carried on this unabashed double-dealing; and it was not until October 24, over a fortnight after his solemn declaration of purpose to Macdonald, that he had given McMullen the first real intimation that the syndicate would have to be broken up.

Rapidly Macdonald considered the position. He was under no obligation whatever to shield Allan, for Allan had grossly and inexcusably deceived him. A little commiseration for his fellow dupe, he felt, could be afforded. He admitted to McMullen that if all he said were true, he had been very badly used; but his tone clearly implied that redress for McMullen's grievances could be sought only from Allan. McMullen seemed unimpressed by this attitude of benevolent detachment; he obviously believed that the Canadian government was deeply implicated in the affair. He calmly pointed out the evidence which the letters supplied of the corrupt bargain between Sir Hugh and the Cabinet; and when Macdonald denied that he and his colleagues had been bribed, McMullen unpleasantly replied that, in that case, Allan must be even more of a swindler than the Americans had suspected, for he was now demanding repayment for nearly $4,000,000 which he had never expended. Macdonald made no reply. There was no use in arguing; and McMullen proceeded to state his demands. Either, he told Macdonald, the government must permit the agreement between Allan and his American associates to be carried out in its original terms, or else Allan's name must be completely omitted from the proposed new company.[41] Macdonald was staggered. He could do neither the one nor the other, he announced flatly. And then, as he expected, McMullen became very unpleasant indeed. He and his colleagues, he announced truculently, had no intention of acting as so many stepping-stones for the personal advancement of Sir Hugh Allan. If the Canadian government persisted in putting Allan in as president, if it permitted him to break faith with his American colleagues in this outrageous fashion, then the Canadian public would be promptly put in possession of all the facts.

Macdonald could only beg for time. He must, he told McMullen, consult Allan and Allan's solicitor, Abbott. McMullen acquiesced. He would withdraw now. But it was also certain that he would return—that this was the beginning, not the end, of a highly dangerous affair. Macdonald began to make discreet inquiries. From Allan, he learnt that McMullen had already been pressing him for money—a large sum, two hundred and fifty thousand dollars, was mentioned—which would include compensation for the time and thought which the Americans had given to the scheme as well as repayment for the small advances they had made to Allan's political fund.⁴² Allan had jibbed indignantly at the preposterous total. The man who had been prepared to squander hundreds of thousands of dollars to ensure his appointment as president of a railway company was now unwilling to risk a smaller amount to save the railway itself from probable disaster. Allan's sudden obstinate parsimony was certainly disquieting. But even if he were prepared to meet the formidable American demands instantly and in full, could he really purchase complete safety by these means alone? Did the Americans merely want money? Or did they want something different and much more sinister? Did they want revenge—on Allan, or on the government itself? Macdonald did not know.

One thing at least was certain. There was no chance that the Americans would let the matter drop. Late in January, the pertinacious McMullen appeared again in the East Block, accompanied this time by two of his associates, Smith and Hurlburt.⁴³ The same ground was gone over; the same documents were produced; the same protests were made. Macdonald freely admitted the justice of the Americans' grievance. He told them that, if he were in their place, he would certainly take legal action against Sir Hugh. But, beyond this, he would concede nothing. He was not prepared to acknowledge that this was a concern of government; and he had gone so far with the new Pacific railway company that concessions were impossible, even if he had been willing to make them. All he could, and did, suggest was that the Americans see Allan and Abbott and try to reach a friendly arrangement. He bowed his visitors out, his heart full of foreboding. All during February, while he prepared for the new session of Parliament, and reopened negotiations for union with Prince Edward Island, he hoped, hoped desperately, that Allan had made a private settlement with his discarded American friends. The days went by. A reassuring silence descended over the affair. He almost began to regain confidence. And then, towards the end of February, the hard blow fell. A long threatening letter from Charles M. Smith, McMullen's principal associate in Chicago, drove home the brutal facts that no settlement had yet been made, and that the Americans were determined to get satisfaction, not only from Sir Hugh Allan, but also from the government of Canada itself. "Sir Hugh Allan *came to us* . . . ," Smith wrote bluntly. "*We* did not go to him. . . . The government alone had the address of our syndicate, and Sir Hugh's approach could not be viewed by us in courtesy or practically as resting on less than direct authority from the cabinet, and we accepted him as their representative."[44]

Macdonald knew that the end had come. Something must be done and at once. Allan must on no account be permitted to depart for England, in a vain effort to get funds, while this enormous avalanche of disaster hung suspended over their heads. McMullen was expected in a day or two at Montreal; it was probably their last chance to disarm and appease him; and Macdonald wrote hurriedly to Hincks, who was about to leave the ministry and whose home was in Montreal, begging him to bring the principals together immediately and to use all his influence to effect a settlement. Hincks replied at once reassuringly. The matter was in train at last. And three days later, a second letter brought the hoped-for relief. At a dinner in Allan's honour before his departure for England—of all ironical occasions!—Hincks had been secretly informed that an agreement had been reached. "I know no particulars," Hincks went on, "as of course conversation was impossible at the dinner, and I was quite content with the assurance that it was quite satisfactorily arranged."[45]

Macdonald nodded. In one important way, he, too, was "quite content" to know as little as possible about what had been done. As Hincks had said, it was absolutely essential for the government to keep itself clear "of all responsibility for any settlement with M.". Yet, at the same time, Macdonald secretly wished to know the truth. The whole business had been settled with such suspicious rapidity. Was McMullen really satisfied? Were they quit of the affair? He shook his head doubtfully. He feared McMullen. He profoundly distrusted Allan. "*Entre nous*," he wrote to John Rose, "Allan seems to have lost his head altogether, and has made a series of stupendous blunders with respect to the whole matter, and the company is not yet out of the troubles caused by his imprudence. He is the worst negotiator I ever saw in my life."[46] It was a terrible indictment to have to make of a man to whom he and his country were now committed beyond repair. But the whole history of the railway had been one long, unbroken misfortune. The new board, with its elaborately graduated scale of provincial representation, and its almost complete lack of capital, was a pompous fraud. Everything depended on Allan's success in London; and Allan, as Macdonald knew only too well, was a selfish, unskilful, unreliable man. The railway and the government were far from being out of the woods. Macdonald might yet have to admit the failure of his railway policy; and in Montreal a rumour persistently circulated that the overthrow of the government at the next session was a certainty. Yet, for the moment, there was peace. There were no more frightening visits from McMullen, or threatening letters from C. M. Smith. Allan and Abbott departed for England; and down in Montreal their offices seemed sunk in unaccustomed repose.

Yet—though Macdonald, of course, was unaware of the fact—Abbott's office was not quite so undisturbed as might perhaps have been expected. Sometimes, after six o'clock, when all the clerks had departed for their dinners, the legal establishment of Sir Hugh Allan's solicitor was the scene of activities which an onlooker, if one had been present, would have found it difficult to explain.[47] Two men, one young, one not so young, entered the deserted rooms, moving very unostentatiously indeed. From the fact that the elder of the two had unlocked the outside door with a key, it might have been presumed that he was an employee, perhaps a confidential clerk, of Mr. Abbott's; and this impression would have been strengthened by the sight of the quick, systematic efficiency with which he went about his curious work. He busied himself with Mr. Abbott's files, going rapidly but carefully through the letter books, the shorthand books, the docketed packets of incoming letters and telegrams, while the younger man, who was clearly a subordinate, assisted his superior in the searches in various ways. Then, having tidied everything very carefully, they quietly departed. The younger man went ahead and got a cab. They both got in it and the cab drove away into the darkness.

V

Macdonald was in his place in the House when suddenly, without warning, the vague persistent rumours of impending trouble took the concrete form of an opposition attack. On April 2, Lucius Seth Huntington, member for Shefford in the Province of Quebec, rose in his place and moved the appointment of a select committee of seven persons to inquire into the circumstances surrounding the grant of the Canadian Pacific railway charter to Sir Hugh Allan's company.[48] Huntington was a prominent but not very commanding figure in the opposition, "a man of no great political capacity," Lord Dufferin remarked confidentially to the Colonial Secretary, "but the most agreeable speaker in Canada".[49] It was the supreme moment of Huntington's political career. Two charges, each grave in itself and graver far in combination, supplied the justification for his demand for an investigating committee. He asserted that the Canada Pacific Railway Company, ostensibly a Canadian organization, was in reality financed with American capital; and he further claimed that its president, Sir Hugh Allan, had advanced very large sums of money, including American funds, to the Canadian ministers in aid of their elections and that in return for this they had promised to award the contract for the construction of the railway to his company.

Huntington read the solemn indictment of his resolution aloud very slowly. Then, without any effort whatsoever to substantiate his charges, he sat down. What was his game? Some, including Lord Dufferin, assumed that he was hoping to provoke the ministers to angry protests—to inveigle them into an impromptu debate in which all the advantages would be on the opposition side. But Macdonald was not to be caught so easily. He did not deign to say a word himself; he imposed an absolute silence on his followers. The members were called in, and Huntington's motion, regarded as a vote of want of confidence, was rejected by a majority of thirty-one, which was one of the largest majorities which the government had obtained so far during the session. "This vote was very satisfactory," Macdonald re-

ported to the absent Cartier, "but Council felt that we could
not properly allow it to remain in that position. I accordingly,
the very next day, gave notice that I would move for a committee. It was fortunate that we took that course, as we found
great uneasiness among our friends. . . . It looked so like
stifling an inquiry that they were afraid of the consequences to
themselves in their constituencies."[50]

On April 8, less than a week after Huntington had first made
his charges, Macdonald got up to move the appointment of
a select committee of five.[51] Blanchet, McDonald of Pictou,
and John Hillyard Cameron, Macdonald's old rival for the
leadership of the party, were the three Conservatives elected
to it; Blake and Dorion represented the opposition. It was a
foregone conclusion that the investigating body should be
divided three to two; and, in the House, interest centred more
on the committee's powers than on its personnel. The session
was already pretty far advanced, and the committee was almost
certain to take a good deal of time in its investigation. Should
Parliament not try to ensure, in some way, that the inquiry
could be continued after the prorogation? And should it not
empower this specially important special committee to take
evidence on oath? There was no real division of opinion in the
House about the desirability of either of these arrangements;
but, as Macdonald saw quickly, there were technical difficulties
in the way of carrying out either of them.

It was clear on the one hand that committees of the House
of Commons could not survive the prorogation of the body
that had created them; and, on the other hand, it was not at
all certain that the Parliament of Canada was competent to
empower parliamentary committees to take evidence on oath.
By section eighteen of the British North America Act, the
Canadian Senate and House of Commons were granted the
privileges, powers and immunities enjoyed by the imperial
House of Commons at the time of the union. Unfortunately, in
1867, the British House had not yet seen fit to empower any
one of its special committees to take evidence on oath. This
circumstance was sufficient to arouse very strong doubts in
Macdonald's mind about the competence of the Canadian

Parliament. But others, including John Hillyard Cameron and several prominent members of the opposition, were very confident that all would be well. Macdonald yielded, and the Oaths Bill was rushed through the House with great rapidity.[52] He had given way here against his better judgment. He was equally accommodating about the prolongation of the work of the committee. He offered at the beginning to transform the committee into a royal commission of inquiry as soon as the prorogation took place; and when the opposition objected to this on the ground that it would "at once place the committee in the hands of the government", he discovered an ingenious and unobjectionable alternative. Parliament would not be prorogued. It would simply adjourn until some time late in the summer when the committee was certain to have finished its investigation. It would then reassemble, in a purely formal meeting, with the Speaker and a quorum only in attendance, for the purpose merely of officially receiving the report.[53]

Macdonald was seriously worried. All during the debates on the committee and its powers, he kept wondering unhappily how the government could best defend itself. He assumed, of course, that Huntington's charges were mainly based on the Allan-McMullen correspondence. McMullen, he knew now, had accepted the first instalment, twenty-five thousand dollars, of Allan's blackmail money; but this had not prevented the Chicagoan from closing another deal with the Liberals for the same documents only a few weeks later. Macdonald had doubted the blackmailer McMullen from the moment he had laid eyes on him; and McMullen had fulfilled all his worst expectations by double-crossing Allan and himself. The letters would certainly discredit Sir Hugh. But they would not, he believed, ruin the government—not, that is, unless they were supported by other evidence. Had Huntington any further evidence? Macdonald did not know. The member for Shefford was in no hurry to disclose his hand to the newly established committee. And it was only after several weeks' delay that he suddenly handed in to John Hillyard Cameron, the committee's chairman, a long list of the witnesses whom he intended to call. As soon as he saw the list, Macdonald realized that the investigation was certain to be both comprehensive and searching. The problem of the government's defence became more acute than ever. He himself would obviously have to make a detailed and carefully prepared statement of his own part in the whole affair; and if Huntington's witnesses began to be called, and the inquiry got seriously under way, he would have to make it very soon, in self-defence. But how could he possibly commit himself to a formal statement until he knew exactly what the unpredictable and unreliable Allan was going to say? The government's explanation would have to be based on Allan's evidence. Allan must speak first, or he might bungle or betray Macdonald's defence. But he could not speak first, for he was in England. In mere prudence, should not the whole investigation be held up until his return?[54]

Once again, as so often in the past, Macdonald's first impulse, in the face of difficulty or danger, was to seek delay. Delay was almost always useful; in this case, it seemed absolutely essential. And, moreover, it could be justified on the simplest grounds of equity. In the absence of three of the principals involved, the inquiry would necessarily be "partial" and unfair. He decided to demand a postponement on those grounds. In his capacity as one of the principal persons involved in the indictment, he appeared before the committee and made a long statement in defence of the absent Cartier and Abbott, both of whom were Members of Parliament. It was on the basis of this representation that the committee, by a majority of three to two, decided to recommend to the Commons that its proceedings should be adjourned until July 2, by which time, presumably, Cartier and Abbott would have returned. The next day, May 6, when this recommendation came before the House, Macdonald supported it vigorously.[55] It was a travesty of justice, he expostulated indignantly, to try men during their absence. The worst criminals in the country, charged with the most heinous crimes, could, as of right, obtain a postponement until they were prepared to meet an indictment. Why should a similar privilege be denied the ministers of the Crown in Canada? If the inquiry were continued now, Cartier and Abbott would not have a chance, until Parliament met next February, to reply to the unrefuted calumnies levied against them.

The House decided to accept the committee's recommendation. The inquiry was adjourned until July 2. But, in the meantime, an effective opening on that date had been rendered very uncertain by still another development. On May 7, Kimberley reported by cable that the law officers of the Crown had given it as their opinion that the Oaths Act was *ultra vires* of the Parliament of Canada.[56] Macdonald had dealt very fairly with his opponents here; he had, on at least two occasions, openly expressed his honest doubts as to the competence of the Canadian Parliament to pass the Oaths Act. And now the unreflecting over-confidence of the opposition had given the game into his hands once again. The imperial government would be obliged, of course, to disallow the Oaths Act. The committee would be unable to carry on the investigation in the way Parliament had clearly intended; and since it would be manifestly unfair to the accused to postpone the whole inquiry until the next session, there was every justification for appointing a royal commission to carry on the work which the committee would be compelled to drop. He had always preferred a royal commission. Now he would get it. Huntington, Dorion, and Blake had been out-generalled once again.

But there was no satisfaction at all in this small tactical success. Details did not matter. What mattered really was that the Pacific enterprise as a whole was a colossal, ruinous failure. If, in spite of all that had happened, Allan had been able to float the railway successfully in the London money market, then something of essential importance would still have been saved. But Macdonald knew now that there was very little hope of solid financial support in England. The news that came from London was gloomy, without relief. John Rose, who busied himself introducing the Canadians to his friends and acquaintances in the City, regarded Allan as "about as bad a negotiator as I have ever met";[57] and Allan himself could do nothing but report the successive refusals of all the important financial houses—Glyns, Barings, and Rothschilds—to have anything whatever to do with the project. Rose, he informed Macdonald sadly, "has uniformly told us that our mission has no chance of success".[58] Macdonald agreed with Rose. The railway in its present form was finished. Any chances that it might have had in London had been effectively killed by the publication in England of the full story of what was already beginning to be called the "Pacific Scandal". The City would have nothing to do with the enterprise. He was beaten.

He was beaten. And he stood alone. On May 20, the cable from Rose announcing Cartier's death reached Ottawa. Sir George had died in London, fighting his disease to the last with the same patient, dogged courage that he had shown in a hundred political encounters. The man whose love for Canada amounted to a blind obsession, who had grasped eagerly, while the strength slipped from him, at every bit of news from the homeland, had gone off on a longer and stranger journey than that which he had hoped and "always purposed" to take to Canada on May 29.[59] The schemes and stratagems which they shared together, the tough battles that they had fought side by side in the House, the long convivial evenings, with Cartier robustly singing his French-Canadian songs, and the endless discussions of the entwined destinies of the two Canadian peoples which had taken shape in the British North America Act and the great experiment of Confederation—they were all ended. They were ended just at the moment when the House was about to accept the terms of union with Prince Edward Island, and when all British North America—with the sole exception of Newfoundland—would be united in a single great Confederation. With almost his last breath, Cartier had given thanks for the completion of union. But now he would never see it. He had gone far too soon. Macdonald could hardly control himself sufficiently to read Rose's cable in the House.[60] He was alone now—for there would never again be anybody like Cartier—alone at a time when the burdens of solitary responsibility seemed heavier than ever. He had not been well since the session commenced. He was overworked, harassed, driven by worries.

It was too much for him. "As a consequence," Lord Dufferin wrote to Kimberley, "for the last few days he has broken through his usual abstemious habits, and been compelled to resort to more stimulants than suit his peculiar temperament. It is really tragical to see so superior a man subject to such a purely physical infirmity, against which he struggles with desperate courage, until fairly prostrated and broken down. . . ."[61] He was down indeed. Cartier's elaborately solemn funeral in Montreal, on June 13, brought the realization of his loneliness home to him with terrible force; and when, a few days later, he arrived in Quebec for the christening of the new Dufferin baby, Victoria Alexandrina Muriel May, he had obviously been drinking heavily again. "Cartier's funeral had been too much for him," Dufferin wrote, "and he was in a very bad way—not at all himself—indeed quite prostrate, but he contrived to pull himself together on the morning of the day he was to appear in church in a most marvellous manner. . . ."[62] He was weary to death of the never-ending labour and distress of office. He vainly tried, he reported to Dufferin, to resign his post on the grounds of ill health and overwork.[63] But it was plain, from the answers of his colleagues, that his retirement would bring about the instant collapse of the already shaken ministry. He squared his shoulders, pulled himself together again, as he had done on the morning of the Dufferin christening, as he had done so many, many times before. He would have to go on.

VI

He moved down to Montreal for the impatiently awaited meeting of the committee investigating the "Pacific Scandal". He wanted to be on the ground. On July 2, the day of the first session in the Montreal Court of Appeals, he wrote to the chairman, John Hillyard Cameron, reminding him that the Oaths Act had been disallowed by the imperial government, and renewing the offer, made on the floor of the House, to issue a royal commission for the continuance of the investigation.[64] He did not, of course, attend the committee's session in the Court House, nor did any member of the government; but it was a public meeting, freely reported, and very soon he knew

all about the debate which had been the chief feature of the
first day's proceedings. The committee had divided sharply on
the question of the course which it ought to take in view of
the imperial disallowance. Cameron, McDonald, and Blanchet
argued that proceedings should be suspended, since the committee was unable to take evidence on oath, as the House had
obviously intended it to do. Blake and Dorion combatted this
view vigorously, demanding that the inquiry be carried on in
the same way in which all such parliamentary inquiries had
been prosecuted in the past.[65] The wrangle lasted all afternoon,
and it was not until the second session, on July 3, that the committee finally decided, by the usual majority of three to two,
that its task must be postponed until Parliament reassembled on
August 13.[66] The chairman then read Macdonald's letter, offering to change the committee into a commission—a commission
which would be required to report to Parliament. But Blake
and Dorion would have nothing to do with this offer, and late
that evening Macdonald received their formal refusals. "I
believe," Blake wrote, "that it would be of evil consequence to
create the precedent of a government issuing a commission of
inquiry into matters of charge against itself, the commissioners
being as they are subject to the direction and control of
the accused."[67]

Macdonald had been checked. But so also had the opposition.
The inquiry was stopped dead. It looked like an interminable
stalemate. But this, as Macdonald knew very well, was not the
fact. In reality, a simple move, as easy as it would be spectacular,
was open for Huntington and his friends to make. They could
publish in the newspapers some of the evidence they had been
prevented from giving to the committee. And this, it now
appeared, was exactly what they intended to do. During the
afternoon of July 3, the rumour began to run rapidly through
Montreal that the Allan letters had been bought from McMullen
for twenty-five thousand dollars and that they would appear
the next morning in the *Herald*. There was not a moment to
lose. That night Macdonald saw Allan and tackled him firmly.
He insisted that, if any seriously damaging evidence appeared
in the press the following day, Allan must make a formal state-

ment "of all the facts as to his relations with the government, the railway, and the elections. . . ."[68] Sir Hugh, who was in no position to refuse, agreed to do so; and Macdonald felt reasonably secure. If, as the report ran, it was the Allan-McMullen correspondence which was to be published the next day, he felt that he could estimate the effect of its appearance fairly accurately, for he knew exactly what the letters contained. Publication would seriously discredit Allan; but it would not ruin the government. There would certainly be damage; but damage might in large measure be repaired by a lengthy statement from Allan with supporting documents.

The next morning, July 4, a great batch of Huntington's evidence was published in the Montreal *Herald* and the Toronto *Globe*. The public rumour and Macdonald's expectation had been quite correct. It was the Allan-McMullen correspondence which was published—nothing more, and, in fact, a little less. The documents were printed in full, but with two very significant exceptions. The two letters which Sir Hugh had written in the autumn of 1872, breaking off all connection with the Americans, were, as Macdonald explained to Dufferin, "most uncandidly omitted". He had never expected such a thumping piece of *suppressio veri* from men like Huntington, Dorion, and Blake. But he saw that manœuvres of this kind, which could easily be exposed, would quickly discredit the opposition; and he was fairly well satisfied with the long account of the whole affair which was prepared for Allan's signature during the course of July 4. "The affidavit," he told Lord Dufferin, "is very skilfully drawn by Abbott. He has made the old gentleman acknowledge on oath that his letters were untrue."[69] It was sad, but it was inevitable. Allan had brought about his own destruction and had seriously endangered others. He was expendable. It was the others whom every effort must be made to save.

On July 5, Allan's sworn statement with supporting evidence was published in the newspapers. It took well, Macdonald was immensely relieved to see. The excitement began at least slightly to subside. "The Huntington matter," he wrote three days later, "has ended in a fizzle as I knew it would do."[70] In part, of course, he was whistling to keep his courage up; but at the same time there were some good reasons for a revival of confidence. The Allan affidavit had proved that the concessions made by Cartier on July 30, 1872, had been revoked at Macdonald's instance, and that the government had compelled Sir Hugh to break with his American associates. This told in Macdonald's favour, while, on the other hand, Blake's and Dorion's refusal to accept the proffered royal commission, and the shameless "editing" of the Allan-McMullen correspondence aroused a good deal of suspicion of the validity of the opposition case. Judgment had not yet been suspended, but the scale was falling less rapidly against Macdonald than it had been.

In these circumstances, his best move was to demonstrate his eagerness to court a full inquiry. The royal commission should be established in the near future and preferably before the meeting of the adjourned session of Parliament on August 13. The meeting of August 13, which had originally been regarded as a most perfunctory occasion, had now, in the light of recent events, acquired a much greater significance. In the House, Macdonald had insisted that, in order to save the members' time and expense, Parliament would meet only *pro forma*, to receive the committee's report. But now there was no report to receive. There was, instead, a mass of highly exciting evidence which the House might like to consider, in part because its own committee had been prevented from doing so. The opposition had already begun to insist that Parliament must not be prorogued on the fatal thirteenth. Macdonald shook his head. The prorogation would take place exactly as had been agreed. But, at the same time, it would never do to give the appearance of stifling inquiry. The royal commission must be launched immediately before, or immediately after, the meeting on the thirteenth. It was over a month away. He was limp with strain and fatigue, the July sun was oppressive, and, after all that had happened, he badly needed a holiday. He stole away to Rivière du Loup, and his modest cottage by the riverside.

He was pleasantly established there when, on July 18, the opposition loosed its second and annihilating thunderbolt. On that day there appeared simultaneously in the Toronto

Globe, the Montreal *Herald*, and the Quebec *l'Evénement*, a
fresh and terrible instalment of revelations.[71] There was a long
statement by McMullen of his relations with Allan and the
government; there was a letter from a Canadian Senator, A. B.
Foster, supporting McMullen; and then, in cold black type,
there appeared the telegrams which Macdonald and Cartier
had sent to Abbott in the last feverish days of August, 1872.
"Immediate, private," the damning words stared up at him.
"I must have another ten thousand. Will be the last time of
calling. Do not fail me. Answer today." How, in the name of
God, had the opposition managed to obtain this appalling evidence. Had his own files been rifled? Had Abbott's office
been searched during his absence in England? He shook his
head in bewilderment. In his worst moments of despondency he
had never even dreamed of such a dreadful disclosure. Nothing
like this had ever happened to him before. "It is one of those
overwhelming misfortunes," he confessed to Lord Dufferin,
"that they say every man must meet once in his life. At first
it fairly staggered me. . . ."[72] He was more than staggered. He
had been felled to the floor. He was down and out.

Yet something must be done. The next day he roused himself
and took the train from Rivière du Loup up to Quebec.
Alexander Campbell had telegraphed from Montreal, suggesting
a meeting of Langevin, Macdonald, and himself in Quebec city;
and the three sat down together miserably to consider the disaster
that had overtaken them.[73] Campbell, fresh from Montreal,
was able to clear up at least one minor but baffling mystery.
The theft had taken place in Abbott's office during his absence
in England with Allan. George Norris, Abbott's confidential
clerk, had rifled his employer's files, copied his employer's private
documents, and sold the lot, as a straight commercial transaction,
to the Montreal Liberals. It might be possible to persuade Norris
to confess, to get him into a court for theft, to expose the des-
picable methods by which the opposition had acquired its
information.[74] He could carry the war into the enemy's country.
But what positive defence could be made of his own conduct?
Everybody knew that elections were fought with money, large
amounts of which could be quite legitimately spent; that

throughout the English-speaking world political parties habitually received substantial contributions from their wealthy supporters; and that in Canada, where no party clubs or permanent party organizations existed, these campaign funds had been traditionally distributed by the political leaders. It was all true. There was really no indictable offence here. But, as he knew very well, this was not the crime with which he was charged. His crime was the crime of accepting campaign funds from the very man with whom he was negotiating a contract of major importance in the national interest. And for that, as he and Campbell and Langevin gloomily realized, it was difficult to devise any effective defence. They concocted a "disclaimer" which appeared a few days later in the press. They told themselves that the party must not permit itself to be panicked into a disastrous rout. The government must struggle to keep control of the explosive situation. It would press forward the establishment of the royal commission. It would resist to the last the mounting opposition clamour against prorogation on August 13.

All these measures were the merest palliatives. What confronted him in reality was an unavoidable and immediate political disaster. He could not face it, and for the next few weeks he went completely to pieces. He had been drinking a good deal in Montreal during the early days of July; and now, in a fashion which had become habitual with him in moments of acute tension, he went back to the bottle for escape from this most desperate crisis of his entire career. The days passed drunkenly with the black depression of awakening consciousness alternating with the muddled forgetfulness of stupor. ". . . Sir John A.," Dufferin confided a little later to Kimberley, "has been in a terrible state for some time past."[75] It was only toward the end of July, when the meeting of Parliament was rapidly approaching and the appeals of his friends had become increasingly importunate, that he finally roused himself, got into communication with Dufferin, who was away in the Maritime Provinces on a vice-regal perambulation, and made the necessary arrangements for the appointment of the three royal commissioners. Dufferin, as always, was courteous and sympathetically friendly; but it was plain that he took a very serious view of the situation. He volunteered the suggestion that it would be impossible to prorogue Parliament until the usual time of meeting in the winter, and that an early autumn session was absolutely unavoidable.[76] Moreover—and this was perhaps the most ominous feature of the correspondence—he announced his intention of coming back to Ottawa for the adjourned meeting of August 13. When Macdonald had parted with him in the early summer, it had been agreed that the perfunctory duty on this occasion could be performed by proxy. But no proxy could be adequate in a crisis. And Dufferin was coming back.

The brief spurt of activity was over. The drinking, which had never really stopped, was heavily resumed again. In a few days now he would have to face Parliament and the public in general. The eyes of his enemies, derisive and triumphant, would be fastened on him. He clung desperately to these last moments of respite, of seclusion. In the past, at these times, he had always tried to secrete himself, to "exclude everybody", in Sir Stafford Northcote's phrase; and now, more than ever before, he wanted to be alone, to crawl away and lick his wounds, like a dog that had been beaten and humiliated. Rivière du Loup was a small, smug, gossipy summer colony. He was conscious, everywhere, of prying eyes and sibilant whispers; and one day, when he could bear it no longer, he stole away from his modest farm cottage and took the Grand Trunk Railway train west to Lévis. Nobody knew where he was; the frantic Agnes was ignorant of his condition and his whereabouts. For a few days at least he lay, as Dufferin later informed Kimberley in horrified tones, "*perdu* with a friend in the neighbourhood of Quebec".[77] Finally, the ever-inquisitive members of the opposition got wind of the fact that he was absent from home. An interesting piece of information which might be exploited with advantage! This time mere rumour would do the trick. Early in August they industriously spread about what Dufferin called "a dastardly report" that Macdonald had committed suicide.[78]

VII

On Sunday, August 10, the suicide returned to Ottawa. He had recovered himself once more; but he seemed pale and shaky to some observers, and he waited for Lord Dufferin's arrival with the greatest anxiety. It was not until the morning of Wednesday, the day on which Parliament was to reassemble, that the hurrying Governor reached the capital. Macdonald sought an interview with him as soon as possible. Was there, at this eleventh hour, any danger of a change in the arrangements? Could Dufferin have conceivably been influenced by the rising volume of protest against the prorogation? Macdonald was aware that the opposition leaders had prepared a petition against "any attempt to postpone this inquiry or to remove it from the jurisdiction of the Commons", and that Richard Cartwright, who was in charge of the petition, was claiming the adherence of ten ordinary supporters of government as well as that of the entire Liberal opposition.

The case against any further postponement of the investigation was so strong and so popular that it found some support inside the Conservative Cabinet. But Macdonald stuck firmly to his policy of delay; and, in any case, it was now too late to change Conservative strategy. Only about a third of the Conservative Members of Parliament were in Ottawa; and the opposition had mustered its full strength. Any change in the programme would be absolutely fatal to Macdonald's government; and he presented to Dufferin the unanimous request of the ministry that Parliament should at once be prorogued in accordance with the announcement which had been made in the Commons on the Governor-General's authority.[79]

In the next moment he could have given a great gasp of relief. Dufferin saw no reason why he should not follow the advice of his responsible ministers. He agreed to prorogue. He agreed, it was true, only on condition that Parliament should be reassembled in six to eight weeks; and it was not until a second meeting had been held in the early afternoon, with all the Cabinet ministers present in solemn conclave, that he consented to lengthen the interval to ten weeks, which he

might shorten by two if it seemed desirable. There was no
need for fear now. The Governor-General's course was decided
now, and he played his part magnificently. His extempore reply
to Cartwright and the other petitioners was carefully reasoned;
he carried out the prorogation with his usual dignity. There
was a great protesting uproar in the Commons, and only about
thirty-five Members, with Macdonald at their head, followed
the Speaker to the Senate.[80] It was a nerve-wracking, exasperating episode. But it was finished. Parliament was prorogued,
as he had said it would be; and next day the Royal Commission
was issued to Day, Polette, and Gowan. He had about two
months—two months in which the Commission could complete
the inquiry, in which the popular excitement could subside,
in which he could have a real chance to damage the opposition.

On September 4, the Commission opened its investigations
in the Parliament Buildings at Ottawa. From then on, until the
end of the month, the daily sessions continued. Macdonald
was very busy. He had decided that the government, in order
to protect its interests, must be represented at every examination;
and although other ministers, Campbell and Langevin in particular, gave him some assistance, he carried on most of the
cross-examining himself. He was determined, if possible, to
drive home the facts that the government had never promised
anything more than the presidency to Allan, that it had
compelled him in the end to break with his American colleagues, and that the campaign funds which its members had
accepted from him differed in no particular from the similar
contributions given and received in all British and North
American elections. He was eager, also, to expose the peculiarly
dirty means by which Huntington and his friends had acquired
their evidence. The opposition had trafficked with blackmailers
and thieves, and had dealt in stolen goods. If he could only
have the opportunity of cross-examining McMullen and Huntington! If they could only persuade or force George Norris,
Abbott's confidential clerk, to reveal how the theft of the
telegrams had been carried out.

But these hopes were denied. The opposition and its
creatures escaped his cross-examination by the simplest of all

methods. They stayed away from the inquiry. The morally righteous accusers decided that they did not quite like the idea of confronting the accused. Huntington, asserting that his first duty was to the House of Commons and refusing to recognize "any inferior or exceptional tribunal", declined the Commission's invitation to conduct the examination of the witnesses he had himself listed.[81] G. W. McMullen and Charles M. Smith, though summoned by a special messenger, remained prudently in Chicago; and Senator A. B. Foster, who, Macdonald suspected, had acted as the intermediary for the transfer of the Allan letters from McMullen to the Liberal chiefs, decided, with becoming modesty, that he would avoid the unwelcome publicity of the Commissioners' court. George Norris, as soon as he received the subpœna from the clerk of the Commission, fled with the utmost precipitancy to St. Albans, in Vermont, where he remained hidden for some days.[82] He had been well paid, expected a "government situation" as soon as the opposition got into power, and boasted that, if they did not, there were "lots of Liberals" in Montreal who would look after him handsomely. A detective trailed him all the way down to St. Albans and back again to Montreal. But he snapped his fingers contemptuously at both intimidation and persuasion. He would make no statement; he could not be got before the Commissioners; and Macdonald, on Abbott's regretful advice, decided that there was no use in trying to prosecute him.[83] In the end they had to fall back upon Alfred Cooper, a clerk in the office of J. A. Perkins, who had helped Norris do his copying. It was too late to produce Cooper before the Commissioners, even if it had been desirable to do so. But Cooper came up to Ottawa early in October and gave a long account of the affair as he knew it, which Macdonald thought might be used at the forthcoming meeting of Parliament.[84]

Parliament was to meet on October 23. And now that the Commission had finished its inquiry, Macdonald found himself looking forward to the new session with less apprehension than he would have believed possible two months ago. His doubts and terrors were, of course, by no means stilled. Far back, in some remote part of his consciousness, there remained a

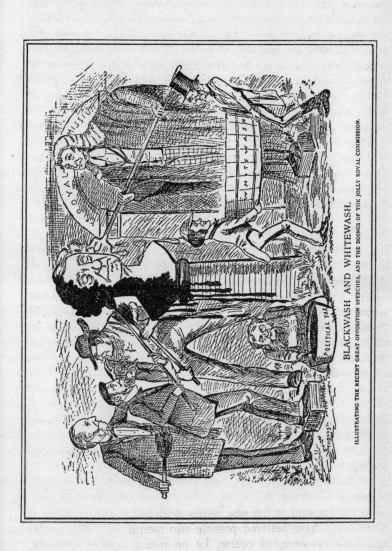

BLACKWASH AND WHITEWASH.

ILLUSTRATING THE RECENT GREAT OPPOSITION SPEECHES, AND THE DOINGS OF THE JOLLY ROYAL COMMISSION.

lingering, gnawing, unappeasable suspicion that the evidence
against him was not yet all in—that Cartier might have made
some private promise to Allan, or that he himself, in the hectic,
muddled days of the August elections of 1872, had sent still
another damning telegram, of which he now had no recollection,
to Abbott. Yet, after the prolonged inquiry by the Commissioners, this was scarcely a reasonable doubt. The scandal, down
to its last minute details, had been exposed to the public. Surely
all that could possibly be said against him had been said, and
said repeatedly. It was true that the *Globe* and the other
Reform newspapers kept denouncing "the eminently unsatisfactory and wretchedly perfunctory" character of the investigation, and threatening in plain terms that as soon as the session
opened a new and more efficient parliamentary inquiry would
be launched.[85] But neither Macdonald nor his chief, the Governor-General, was very much perturbed by these threats; the
chief results of fresh investigation, Dufferin believed, would be
the discovery of the "many dirty tricks" of the opposition.[86] The
worst was definitely over. The "glorious reaction" which
Dufferin had prophesied might even now, Macdonald considered, be setting in in his favour. The Governor-General, who
appeared to be obviously sympathetic, had asked him for a personal defence which could be used in letters to England; and on
October 9, Macdonald finished a long confidential memorandum
on his part in the whole affair. The opening of Parliament was
only a fortnight away. He was facing it almost cheerfully. "We
shall have a spicy debate and a division on the address," he
told Dufferin, "and there I think the matter will rest."[87]
Politics, of course, were completely unpredictable; but he did
not really believe that his government would be overthrown.

On Sunday, October 19, four days before the meeting of
Parliament, he was suddenly and violently jarred out of his
equanimity. On the previous Friday, Dufferin had returned
from his holiday in Quebec, had met Day and the other Commissioners, and had spent Saturday in a very careful study of
their official reports. But nothing in these outwardly formal
occurrences had prepared Macdonald for the astounding communication which he received from the Governor-General on

Sunday. The letter began reassuringly. It listed the various charges of which Macdonald had been cleared. But no kindly ending followed. ". . . It is still an indisputable and patent fact," Dufferin went on, "that you and some of your colleagues have been the channels through which extravagant sums of money, derived from a person with whom you were negotiating an arrangement on the part of the Dominion, were distributed throughout the constituencies of Ontario and Quebec, and have been applied to purposes forbidden by the statutes. . . . In acting as you have, I am well convinced that you have only followed a traditional practice and that probably your political opponents have resorted with equal freedom to the same expedients, but as Minister of Justice and the official guardian and protector of the laws, your responsibilities are exceptional and your personal connection with what has passed cannot but fatally affect your position as minister."[88] Macdonald stared at the conclusion of the long sentence. ". . . *fatally affect your position as minister.*" It was true that the disturbing words were followed by warm professions of Dufferin's personal attachment and of his belief in Macdonald's great ability and patriotism. But these assurances, though perfectly genuine no doubt, did not affect the purpose of the letter. The Governor-General was plainly conveying a warning. Did he intend, as final guardian of the constitution, to intervene? And if so, should not he, Macdonald, resign instantly?

The next morning at half past twelve, he faced his chief. It was a curious interview, at once painful and ceremoniously polite, a civilized interview, in which both participants played their parts with exquisite correctness. Dufferin hated the task he had in hand. He had come to have a great respect for his Prime Minister—a more affectionate and less critical respect than perhaps his Prime Minister had for him. The Governor-General's highly complimentary style of address sometimes seemed a little "gushing" to Macdonald; but Dufferin, with his generous, romantic nature, had been almost completely won over by this exceptional colonial, who was so attentive and considerate, whose manners were so ingratiatingly charming, and who, at the same time, seemed so markedly superior to his contemporaries in ability and patriotic spirit. "Sir John is by far the ablest public man in Canada," he told Kimberley within the first year of his governorship, and time did not alter his opinion.[89] He had looked forward with "eager expectation" to Macdonald vindicating himself from the "damnable accusations" of the "Pacific Scandal". He had been only slowly and very reluctantly convinced that there was something decidedly wrong. But once this conclusion had been reached, his high standards of political conduct prompted him to act, as much for Macdonald's sake as for his own. "I had gradually brought myself to the belief," he told Kimberley, "that under certain circumstances it might eventually become my duty to intervene and to prevent the conscience of Parliament and of the country from being forced by the mere brute strength of party spirit."[90] He could not permit his present ministers to retain office by "a vitiated parliamentary majority". This was the reason for the letter and the interview. He wanted to warn Macdonald and reserve future liberty of action for himself.

Macdonald was very agitated. He might have displayed his feelings to Dufferin in some emphatic manner. But what in fact he showed was "great dignity, courtesy, and self control". He did, indeed, reproach Dufferin mildly that this important announcement had been so long delayed; and Dufferin explained that he thought it necessary to wait until he had received his Prime Minister's confidential memorandum, had seen the Commissioners personally, and had had time to study the official evidence. Macdonald accepted the explanation graciously. His first impulse after receiving the communication, he told Dufferin, was to resign. Dufferin replied that his letter had been intended not as a dismissal but as a warning, that he wished to save his Prime Minister humiliation, and that he hoped he would fall by his own hand, not another's. Carefully, as in his letter, he reviewed the situation. It had been proved beyond all question, he admitted, that the government had not had any reprehensible dealings with the Americans, and that it had not corruptly modified the Canadian Pacific railway charter in the interest of Sir Hugh Allan. But there remained Huntington's fourth charge —the charge that Macdonald and other ministers had received very large sums of money from Allan for election purposes; and this, Dufferin pointed out, had been proven and must be admitted. Macdonald could accept the minimum of blame, and beat an honourable retreat. His recovery, if he adopted such a course, even his return to power, might be remarkably swift. He himself, the Governor-General repeated emphatically, had no desire to intervene. He would intervene only if Macdonald persisted in braving out the ordeal, and in the end escape parliamentary censure only by "the skin of his teeth".

The next day, Tuesday, October 21, Macdonald and his Cabinet considered resignation. Early on Wednesday, Alexander Campbell, meeting one of the permanent heads of departments, informed him confidentially that things were "stormy", and added that Sir John was going out again that morning to Rideau Hall to see the Governor-General.[91] Macdonald could not understand the reason for this mysterious second summons. He entered Dufferin's room in some trepidation. But it was plain, from the beginning, that the Governor had a very much more agreeable duty to perform than that which he had carried out two days before. The English mail, he informed Macdonald frankly, had arrived Tuesday night. There were private letters from Kimberley in the diplomatic bag, and in one of these the Colonial Secretary had laid down the general principle that it was the business of the Canadian Parliament to decide whether it wished to withdraw its confidence from the Governor-General's responsible advisers.[92] Dufferin generously admitted that, on the basis of this opinion, he was "more straitened by the voice of Parliament" than he had imagined himself to be. Macdonald might consider the previous letter "as in some degree cancelled, although, of course," the Governor subsequently reported to Kimberley, "I did not in any sense surrender my liberty of action . . ." for the future.[93]

Still, the immediate crisis was over. The ministry must hang on, Macdonald decided, and fight out the storm. He was even confident of the outcome. Dufferin reported that the government was "very cock-a-hoop" at the opening of Parliament on Thursday, October 23; and when, after a brief adjournment to the following Monday, the debate on the address finally began, the Conservatives were described as "jubilant" and confidently predicting a majority of sixteen to eighteen. Macdonald, the Governor-General informed Kimberley, "came up to the scratch fresh and smiling". And for a little while at least, this mood of jocular equanimity lasted. Then a change, an increasingly marked change, became apparent. The strain of the debate began to tell upon Macdonald with unnerving force. He lost a supporter, then another. The majority upon which he had counted was no longer quite so certain; and, worst of all, the Liberal tactics in the debate had become a maddeningly insoluble puzzle to him. Blake, the best speaker on the Reform side, the man who had made himself master of all the intricate complications of the "scandal", had not yet spoken. What could his silence mean? Was he waiting deliberately to speak after his great opponent? What could be the motive behind such a manœuvre? Was Blake in possession of some last damning piece of evidence, some hitherto unrevealed document of a fatally compromising character, which, once Macdonald had made his defence, he would deliver like a knock-out blow to complete the rout of the Conservatives and the ruin of the government? This had been Macdonald's secret fear for months. It came back now with paralysing force. He remembered that, even after the publication of his private telegrams to Abbott, the opposition press had continued to drop hints of "fresh revelations". Had he, during his repeated insobrieties at the time of the August elections, telegraphed another terrible, though forgotten, message to Abbott?[94] Or had Cartier, in his extremity, been forced to make one last private engagement to his insatiable tormentor, Allan?

He kept silence. The debate was wearing him down, steadily demoralizing him with its unrelieved, intolerable tension. But he would not speak. His followers, with frantic and in the end almost angry entreaties, begged him to make his long-awaited statement and bring the debate to a close while there was still a chance of victory. Dufferin believed that if he had spoken in good time and forced an early division on the address, he might have won "by double figures", if not by the majority of eighteen which had been originally predicted. But Macdonald, white and shaky, sat on in silence. His strained eyes seemed fixed, with a curious dull fascination, upon a deadly blow which might yet come and which, in some way, he must try to parry or counter. All the time his majority was steadily dwindling. It sank to eight, then to six, and finally, on Friday, the last day of October, to two. On Friday afternoon, he came again to see the Governor-General. It was obvious that he had been drinking steadily and too much; but he was entirely coherent, and what he had to say was clear and only too startling. He confided to the dismayed Dufferin his fear of the final, crushing revelation which Blake might be holding in reserve.[95] He had no knowledge of the existence of another compromising document, and no notion of what its contents might be. He realized that he was lessening his chances by every hour of delay. Nevertheless he must wait until Blake had spoken. He simply would not dare to precede him.

On Monday, after a week-end for reflection, he seemed stuck in the same obstinate and dangerous inaction. His decision to wait was apparently unaltered. His physical condition was as bad as it had been. He was pale, haggard, blunderingly weak; and the muddled ineffectiveness of his direction, which was in such strange contrast with his usual superb generalship in the House, drove his followers and the Governor-General to despair. ". . . He had a preliminary skirmish with Blake," Dufferin reported to Kimberley, "on a point connected with the presentation of my dispatches to Parliament, in the course of which he said exactly the wrong things, made two or three great blunders, compromised me, and showed to everyone, as his colleague and doctor, Tupper, admitted to me, that he was quite tipsy."[96] It was a deplorable exhibition about which everybody was gossiping freely during the recess for dinner. What was going to happen? At this catastrophic rate, the long agony of the previous week would be very quickly over. The government was drifting steadily towards the rocks, and all the while the unguarded tiller swayed drunkenly from side to side.

Then, as he sat in his place after the House had reassembled that evening, a sudden and tremendous transformation came over Macdonald. He grasped the useless, ruinous folly of further delay. He began to realize, what others had suspected for days, that Blake had held back, not because he had any sensational *coup de grâce* to deliver, but simply because he hoped to unnerve his opponent with delay, and break him down through his own indulgence. Blake had almost succeeded, Macdonald reflected grimly. But he would show Blake that a moral victory was not so easily gained as that. His defence, prepared as much as he ever prepared, or believed in preparing, a speech, was ready in his mind; and he felt returning confidence, like a great masterful wave of water, roaring through his body. The packed House lay spread out round him, the packed galleries soared above his head. They were waiting, waiting for him, and for him alone. They would not be disappointed. He would speak and speak his best. He was on his feet now, his face drawn and white, his body slight and curiously frail. The applause swelled into a roar which maintained itself for long clamorous moments, and then died slowly and utterly away. He could feel the silence of acute physical tension settle like a burden upon the great room. He could see the last laggard member tip-toeing softly to his place, the reporters settling down to their note-books, Lady Dufferin bending eagerly over the railing, and Agnes watching him, her dark features strained with painful expectancy. He wetted his lips in the nervous, involuntary manner that had become habitual with him. Now.

It was nine o'clock.

VIII

"I leave it to this House with every confidence. I am equal to either fortune. I can see past the decision of this House, either for or against me; but whether it be for or against me, I know—and it is no vain boast for me to say so, for even my enemies will admit that I am no boaster—that there does not exist in this country a man who has given more of his time, more of his heart, more of his wealth, or more of his intellect and power, such as they may be, for the good of this Dominion of Canada."[97]

It was over. He had spoken for nearly five hours. The crashing roar of applause, the brief beginning of Blake's reply, the adjournment, the hand-shakings, the fervent congratulations, the pledges of unchanging support—they were all over. It was half past two o'clock, and somehow he was out of the building and driving away over the canal to the house on Chapel Street. At the street corners there were little knots of people talking excitedly. The gas lamps in many houses would burn for a long time yet while families and friends talked over every point in the speech to which they had just listened. At Rideau Hall, the Governor-General was waiting up expectantly when his wife and her guests arrived at three o'clock in the morning; and for two hours, with many dramatic gestures, Lady Dufferin retold the long argument of Macdonald's defence.

Next day, Macdonald was literally ill with fatigue. He came to the afternoon session of the House; but in a very little while he was obliged to retire, and for several hours he lay stretched out, utterly exhausted, on a sofa in one of the committee rooms.[98] He heard hardly anything of Blake's reply; he was only dimly aware of what was going on. But, through the haze of his semi-consciousness, the realization was coming home to him that, in one supremely important way, his speech had been a tremendous success. It had been—whatever its political consequences—a personal triumph, a personal victory. At six o'clock on Monday, he had been, and he knew it, a muddled, irresolute, and uninspiring leader. "Yet three hours afterwards," as Lord Dufferin privately confided to Kimberley, "he rose—pale, haggard, looking as though a feather would knock him down—and electrified the House with this tremendous oration."[99] He had done it again. He had dipped deep into those reserves for which neither he nor anybody else had ever really found the measure. He had recovered himself. He had regained and consolidated that dominion of affection and loyalty which the Canadians were so willing to concede to him. From all over the country the congratulations were pouring in; even the supposedly impartial Rideau Hall was ardently, if privately, partisan. Lady Dufferin wrote to Lady Macdonald, confiding her enthusiasms; and the Governor-General reported that "round the breakfast table at Rideau this morning there was a continuous chorus of admiration from all my English friends".[100]

It had been a personal triumph. But he knew, even as he had made the speech, that he was facing political defeat. He had regained his command. But he could not stop the rout. The defections continued. On Tuesday, he was deserted by two more followers, one of them Donald A. Smith; and on Wednesday, November 5, he and the Cabinet decided that they could no longer hope to win a majority and that they might as well anticipate defeat. That morning he waited on Lord Dufferin to submit the resignation of himself and his colleagues, and the House had barely met at half past three in the afternoon when he rose to announce the results of his interview with the Governor-General. "I have it, therefore," he said, "in charge from His Excellency to state that he has accepted the resignation of the present administration, and I have his authority to state that he has sent for Mr. Mackenzie, the leader of the opposition, to form a government."[101] It was finished. In a few minutes the House was adjourned. In forty-eight hours more or less he would have packed up his personal belongings, said good-bye to his staff, and walked out of the East Block into private life.

His government was defeated and his projected railway had been ruined. Who had won? Not Macpherson and the Interoceanic Railway Company, for their project was involved with Allan's in a common disaster. Not the Liberal party, for it had acquired power for which it was fundamentally unprepared and which it would have to exercise in most unfavourable circumstances. Not Canada as a whole, for its consolidation by means of transcontinental railways had been indefinitely postponed. The real victor was McMullen. It was the directors of the Northern Pacific Railroad, the inevitable rival of the Canadian Pacific, who had alone scored a triumph. They had discredited a Canadian Prime Minister, overthrown a Canadian government, humiliated a great Canadian party. Above all, they had postponed—for how long?—the construction of the railway which could alone defend the Canadian north-west from the economic domination of the United States. British Columbia was still an isolated outpost on the Pacific slope; the empty prairies would have to

LADY MACDONALD

Public Archives of Canada

wait yet for their settlers; and the ridges of the Laurentians, primeval and unconquered, still stretched away, mile after mile, towards the north-west.

Chapter Six

The Forked Road

I

On November 6, the day after the resignation of the government, Macdonald met the Conservative Members of Parliament in caucus.[1] He hoped, if he did not really expect, that the meeting would end in the choice of a new leader. There were all sorts of reasons—cogent, solid, unanswerable reasons—for his own retirement at the moment. He had compounded great mistakes with little ones. He did not know, of course, that so close a friend as Alexander Campbell had been privately declaring that the ministry would not have been defeated "if Sir John A. had kept straight during the past fortnight".[2] But he could see the unspoken criticism of the "dull defensive" tactics of the government in the eyes of many of his followers; and he knew, too, that the miscalculations which he had made during the past two weeks were only a small part of the long and heavy count against him as the future leader of the Liberal-Conservative party. He had led it for nearly twenty years, through countless vicissitudes, and at last into a complete disaster. Around him had inevitably gathered the emotional accretions of two decades of constant struggle—the envy and hatred of his prolonged success, and the stigma and calumny of his final failure. He could never be free from the past, as a young man would be; and the past, with all its fighting, had left him tired. He would be fifty-nine years old in another two months, and he had earned a rest. He faced the long, silent rows of listening Conservatives earnestly. He begged them, for the sake of the country and the party, to choose a younger man.

The caucus refused. With an earnestness equal to his own, the assembled Conservatives insisted that they preferred to fight under his leadership. He could not help but be moved by this unanimous declaration. Even if it had been prompted merely by a generous impulse not to abandon him when he was down, it touched him, and touched him deeply. But, even in that moment of pride and gratitude, he made no permanent engagement. He told the Conservatives that he would continue to lead the party as long as they thought he could be of service; but he obviously thought—and continued to think— that his part was now a purely temporary one. A few days later, at a public dinner, given for himself and some of the other retiring ministers at Russell's Hotel in Ottawa, he returned, with as much frankness as he had shown in caucus, to the subject of his own retirement and the future leadership. "I cannot last much longer," he told his audience bluntly. "You will find young men of your party that you will be proud to follow with the same undeviating constancy that you have followed me. . . . I hope that out of the party to which I belong, there will rise a strong and successful administration. I have no doubt there will, but I hope I will never be a member of any administration again."[2]

He wanted a youthful leader. He wanted a long-term policy for the future. The Liberal-Conservatives had sustained a dreadful humiliation; and within a few months—for a general election was a certainty in the near future—they would indubitably experience a dreadful defeat. In all probability it would be years before the party could recover its self-confidence and regain the esteem and affection of the Canadian people. The last thing it could afford to do, Macdonald insisted—and the caucus agreed with him—was to risk its slowly reviving popularity by an irresponsible, factious course in opposition. "You will find," he told his audience at Russell's Hotel, describing the rôle which the Conservatives had decided to play, "that they will conduct matters differently from the late opposition. . . . You will never find us opposing any measure in the interest of the nation for the sake of opposition. I don't believe our party patience will be taxed, because I think their good measures, like angels' visits, will be few and far between; but if they are few and far between, they will be the more welcome, and we will support them accordingly. So far as I am concerned, that will be no vague promise. I have proved that before."[4]

He had indeed proved it before—during the Macdonald-Sicotte ministry. The pious resolution not to offer "factious opposition" was a highly appropriate pledge for a humiliated party to make. It was an acceptable form of public repentance; but, at the same time, it was probably the wisest decision which the Conservative party could have reached. The Conservatives would do very well to lie low for a while. They needed time to recover from defeat and to reorganize for victory. Time would give them a very necessary breathing-space. Time might also, and very rapidly, involve their opponents in most embarrassing difficulties. Already, in the light of the economic circumstances of the late autumn of 1873, it was possible to argue that if the resignation of the Conservative government was unavoidable, it could hardly have come at a more fortunate moment. The collapse of the "Prussian boom" in Europe during the spring had been followed in late September by an ominous financial crash in New York; and the record of the next two months had been a gloomy tale of financial and industrial failures, slackening trade, and falling prices. Nobody could realize as yet that this was the beginning of the "Great Depression" of the late nineteenth century. But everybody knew by now that Canada, as well as the rest of the western world, could probably expect a period of very hard times. The Conservatives were well out of it. They had troubles enough as it was. The party could not expect to take the offensive for months, and perhaps years, to come. All it could hope to do at the moment was to endure, to survive, and to wait in patience for the future.

Almost immediately, the tribulations began to descend. In December, in a by-election in Toronto, the Canadian public had a first chance to show the weight of its pent-up moral disapproval. The Liberals, with the help of a small group of patriotic, youthful publicists who denounced the corrupt partisanship of Canadian politics and described their own body as "Canada First", captured the riding easily for the Reform candidate, Thomas Moss; and this defeat in single combat foreshadowed with unhappy accuracy the virtual annihilation that was to come in the greater encounter of the following month. In the general election which took place in mid-winter, 1874, the Conservative strength in the House of Commons was reduced to about seventy seats.[5] "We have met the enemy," wrote C. H. Mackintosh of the Ottawa *Citizen* to Macdonald, "and we are theirs."[6] A little group of veterans had alone survived the fleeing disaster of the rout. A solitary square had maintained itself; but it had almost lost its weary and unwilling commanding officer. Macdonald, it was first announced, had won in Kingston over his previous opponent, Carruthers, though by only a trifling majority. The majority did not matter. The victory did. But, to the consternation of the Conservatives, the victory was immediately and sharply challenged. A formal petition, charging bribery and other electoral malpractices, was filed against Macdonald.[7] He might win the seat. But a long and exasperating legal wrangle would have to be fought out before he could prove his claim to it.

For some weeks after the election he was laid up with a bad cold, caught while he was canvassing in the rigours of mid-winter. At Kingston he had presented himself once again as an old man, who would stand faithfully behind the next Liberal-Conservative government but would not become a member of it. The idea of his approaching retirement had been very firmly planted in the minds of his fellow-countrymen; and people, including the Governor-General, were beginning to talk about his career in a retrospective, judicial fashion, as of something which must very soon be brought to a close. "It would be premature to forecast the future," Dufferin wrote cautiously about his late Prime Minister, "but I should be sorry to think that his public career was over. His health, however, is very precarious, otherwise he would be sure to come to the front, as he is certainly the best statesman in Canada. . . ."[8] A regretful, elegiac note sounded unmistakably in this generous estimate. But surely it was appropriate? In the first brief session of the new Parliament, Macdonald played a waiting, unobtrusive, non-committal rôle; and when summer came, he went off to Rivière du Loup for a long holiday, from which the importunate appeals of his followers failed to drag him. He told Tupper that the Conservatives in Toronto were pressing him to come up for a meeting or two, but that he frankly did not feel up to it. "My fighting days are over, I think," he wrote.[8]

A temporary commander, with a badly beaten army at his back, he was in no mood for adventurous forays. At Russell's Hotel he had cautioned his followers against an excess of party spirit; and he continued to keep them strictly and silently upon the defensive, even when, during the summer of 1874, an issue arose in which the national interest was clearly involved, and in which, so he was convinced, the new government was making a serious mistake. The public debate which followed must have seemed certain to tempt him to intervention. The new government—he might have argued—had blundered because it had presumptuously imagined that it could improve upon the concessions which he had wrung from the Americans in the Washington Treaty. The Liberals had always been inclined to explain the surrender of the inshore fisheries for a money payment simply as the natural result of Macdonald's diplomatic weakness and ineptitude. A satisfactory Reciprocity Treaty would have been perfectly possible—with the right negotiators! A Liberal could have obtained it—if only he had had a chance! And since, luckily enough, there was still a chance, for the amount of the money payment had yet to be settled by arbitration, George Brown, a robust and extremely optimistic diplomatist, was sent down to Washington to transmute this give-away sale into a profitable commercial arrangement. Fish, who was still Secretary of State, could hardly have been more uninterested, unco-operative, and unenthusiastic during these new negotiations; and the resulting draft treaty, which was made public during the summer, was really Brown's personal achievement. It provided that the Canadian and American duties on a wide variety of commodities, including manufactured goods as well as raw materials, were to be reduced gradually, by stages, over a period of years. From the point of view of the new industrial Canada, which Macdonald had recognized in the election of

1872, the treaty was highly contentious; and it had no sooner been made public than Canadian manufacturing associations and boards of trade began to criticize it emphatically and in detail.[10]

It seemed an obvious opportunity, particularly for a party which had appropriated the phrase "National Policy" and which had talked so much about incidental protection in the election of 1872. Tupper, sanguine and impetuous as always, was eager to accept speaking engagements and to denounce the treaty in public; but Macdonald hung back cautiously in a prudent reserve. He agreed with Tupper that the agreement was a bad one, which deserved thoroughly to be condemned; but he argued that the popular protest against its terms ought to be permitted to develop freely, irrespective of party, before the Conservatives made any too open attempt to turn it to their own uses. "The Boards of Trade and industrial meetings," he reminded Tupper, "have, without reference to politics, gone against it. Some of the leading Grit newspapers in Ontario are opposed to it. It is causing a decided split in the Grit ranks. The only thing that will heal that split is any attempt of the opposition leaders to make political capital out of it." The Conservatives would do well, he thought, to insist that they would not interpret rejection of the treaty as the defeat of the government. They would benefit themselves as well as the nation in the event. "The opposition would gain greatly by their patriotic course," he reminded Tupper, "and would prove the sincerity of what I said on behalf of the party, that our motto was country first, party afterward. This sown upon the waters would come back to us, and not, I think, after many days."[11]

It might have been a patriotic course. It was certainly a cautious, if not a timorous, policy. All during the autumn, the popular criticism of the draft treaty grew sharper, and an occasional Conservative, such as Thomas White of Montreal, sought to make its rejection an objective of the party.[12] But Tupper, who had been assigned the rôle of chief budget critic for the opposition, remained discreetly silent on the subject, as his chief had suggested; and Macdonald, when he discussed the proposed treaty early in the autumn with the Governor-

General, was still in a very "cautious and moderate" frame of mind. He criticized some of the treaty's definitions. He thought the "sliding scale" for the gradual reduction of duties on both sides of the border would operate unfairly on Canada. He seemed to expect that the smaller Canadian manufacturing concerns at least would almost certainly be wiped out. But, the Governor-General noted, his ex-Prime Minister was still in no mood to begin a passionate Canadian nationalistic crusade. "My impression is," Dufferin concluded shrewdly, "that Macdonald is waiting to see whether the opponents of the measure will prove sufficiently strong to make it worth his while to enter into an alliance with them. . . ."[13]

It seemed a chastened and intimidated state of mind, at once uninspired and uninspiring. "Sir John Macdonald and his party," Dufferin wrote to the new Colonial Secretary, Carnarvon, on December 8, "are entirely routed, and nobody expects them to rally during the present Parliament."[14] A year after the resignation of their ministry, the Conservatives had done almost nothing to lift themselves out of the despairing torpor of their repeated reverses; and in November, Macdonald himself met a new and sharply personal humiliation. The long dispute over the contested Kingston election case ended against him and he was unseated. In the new election, which was held the following month, in a subdued, repentant fashion, without speeches, expenditures, or any excitement, he ran again against Carruthers, and was elected.[15] But his majority—lower than it had ever been—was only seventeen! He had escaped by the skin of his teeth. And his prestige, weighed down by a year of misfortunes, had sunk lower than ever before.

He did not appear to care. For the moment he seemed sick of the ceaseless, grinding attrition of politics, and eager to be out of it. His plans for the future had been made long ago. He still kept his house in Ottawa, perhaps because property was hard to sell during the depression, and perhaps because he wanted a quiet place in which to recuperate before beginning the next phase of his existence. But there was no doubt about what the next phase was to be. He was determined to move to Toronto with his family, in the near future, and to take up the law again where he had dropped it, so many, many years ago. His law firm had already been transferred to Toronto, in the wake of its principal client, the Trust and Loan Company; and the partners—Macdonald himself, Patton, Robert M. Fleming and Hugh John Macdonald—were now established in the Trust Company's building, at 25 Toronto Street.[16] Hugh, who had joined the firm immediately on the completion of his terms at Osgoode Hall, was now twenty-three years old—a charming, friendly, warm-hearted young man, with a good deal of his paternal grandfather's easy-going amiability and something also of his grandfather's enterprise and independent spirit.[17] Hugh, Macdonald hoped and expected, would succeed him in due course as one of the senior partners. The peaceful continuity of the firm and the family could now be depended upon, and the move to Toronto was simply a natural incident in a matured plan. There was a comfortable settled air of finality about the arrangements.

II

Appearances were oddly deceptive. As the year 1875 opened, the main trend of events appeared to be carrying Macdonald irrevocably away from public affairs. But beneath the main trend there was another, subterranean movement, unacknowledged as yet and almost unnoticed, which was dragging him in exactly the opposite direction. It was not so much that the Conservatives, encouraged by the appearance of a new and favourable set of circumstances, were recovering their confidence and clamouring for more vigorous leadership. It was rather that the new Liberal government had run at once into difficulties which deepened its divisions and exposed its weakness in a fashion that almost invited attack. Everybody knew, of course, that the Liberals had not won office in the autumn of 1873 by virtue of their own strength or merit. They had been swept into power as the only available alternative to a régime which had been rejected in a great national outburst of revulsion and shame. The Reform party, in various important ways, was still an Ontario rather than a Canadian party. In Nova Scotia, its leadership since the defection of Howe had been feeble; and in Quebec its members were now being pursued with undisguised hostility by ultramontane bishops and priests determined upon the extinction of "Liberalism" in all its forms. The party was still in the process of becoming a national organization; and it had taken up the burden of office at a moment when all problems of government would be hideously complicated by the coming of the depression. The completion of Confederation was the great task facing any Canadian government; and in a time of deflation and financial stringency, it was a task which had obviously become more difficult of achievement than ever.

All these facts were interesting. But there was one aspect of the Liberal party's position which interested Macdonald more than any other. A leader himself, he was incurably absorbed in problems of leadership; and for him the problem of the Grit high command had always had an irresistible fascination. He had given years of patient and rewarding study to it. It was a complex problem, of infinite ramifications, for at all times the Reform party had been, not so much a truly national or provincial political organization, as a loose association of separatist groups, of passionately independent individualists, who combined only with difficulty and usually at the tense moments of assault. The Liberals, in fact, had never solved the problem of leadership. Brown had come nearest to it. In those wonderful years from 1854 to 1858, when he had stood at the height of his enormous physical powers and at the triumphant crest of his political confidence, Brown had been a terrific, an almost unexampled, force in Canadian politics. Yet he had failed. He had remained a sectional, not a provincial, leader. He had not succeeded in welding the disparate, intractable elements of Reformism in the Province of Canada into a single efficient fighting machine. And, in Macdonald's opinion, his failure was traceable ultimately to the defects of his own impulsive and undisciplined character. He had spent himself in vain, and he had now retired into the honourable obscurity of the Senate. Alexander Mackenzie, who had succeeded him as leader, had become the First Minister in the new Reform government.

Would Mackenzie, upon whom had devolved the larger problem
of creating a national Canadian Reform party, succeed where
Brown had failed?

At first sight it looked as if Mackenzie would bring to the
task of leadership exactly those moderating, unifying qualities
which every other Reform leader, including Brown himself, had
so conspicuously lacked. An obviously honest man, sensible,
straightforward, caustic and pugnacious in debate, yet not too
deeply committed to convictions and antipathies, Mackenzie
seemed to combine authority and conciliation in exactly the
desired quantities. The slight ageing man, with the wispy
fringe of grey beard, the long, bleak, severe Scottish countenance, and the direct, intense blue eyes, could surely be counted
upon to command respect and impose order upon his wayward
and unruly followers. He was good, stout, serviceable Scotch
tweed, which would wear well, stand up to hard usage, and
outlast more stylish materials two to one. It ought to have
been true; but, unfortunately, it was not. And the real truth,
which was quite different, became rapidly apparent to a number
of people, including that strategically placed but not entirely
impartial observer, Lord Dufferin. "The fear has been gradually
growing upon me," he wrote to Lord Carnarvon, "that my
Prime Minister is not 'strong enough for the place'. He is honest,
industrious, and sensible, but he has very little talent. He
possesses neither 'initiative' nor 'ascendancy'."[18] It was a bluntly
realistic judgment; but it was not peculiar to the Governor-
General. It was held by others. It was even held by Reformers
who, Macdonald noticed with delight, made little effort to
conceal their opinions. He began to realize that the good old
days were back again, that the Liberal party was as hopelessly
divided as ever, and that the incompatibilities, jealousies, and
antagonisms, to which he was so accustomed, might once
again destroy a Reform government.

The new régime had begun badly. The Cabinet which poor
Mackenzie had scraped together was a strangely nondescript,
unimpressive group of men. Holton was not a member of it.
Huntington, the "letter-stealer", at first declined a place; and
Dorion, the old leader of the *Rouges*, resigned his office in a

few months to become Chief Justice of the Province of
Quebec. These were serious defections. But the most strangely
dismaying case of all was the case of Edward Blake, the member
for South Bruce. Blake, by general agreement, was the ablest
of all the Reformers. High-minded, serious, widely read and
extremely intelligent, he was everywhere regarded as the
greatest asset that the new government possessed. Yet he had
resigned his post early in the spring of 1874, after only the
briefest of tenures, and just at the moment when J. D. Edgar
was sent west with instructions from the Canadian government
to negotiate a new agreement with British Columbia for the
construction of the Canadian Pacific railway. This first hasty
resignation naturally roused some doubts of Blake's fitness for
the exacting and thankless tasks of party government in Canada.
He suffered from bad health. He found the dull routine of
administration a daily exasperation to the spirit. A reserved,
sensitive, and temperamental intellectual, he was apt to feel
slights keenly, and almost equally apt to hurt others by what was
thought to be a distant and supercilious manner. His elaborate
arguments and fine-drawn distinctions sometimes bored or puzzled his associates. His adventurously radical opinions were
voiced without much apparent concern for the conventional
party line. It was suspected that neither George Brown nor
Alexander Mackenzie entirely approved of him, and that he
repaid the disapproval of these two seniors with a not very
good-natured contempt.

From the beginning, Macdonald had had high hopes of
Blake. Early in 1874, several months before Blake's resignation,
the inner circle of the Conservative party had become complacently aware of Edward's mutinous attitude to the Liberal
leaders. "No doubt Blake is not with *us*," Patteson observed
with great satisfaction to Macdonald in February, "but it does
no harm for people to begin to think that he is. It all goes
to undermine their stability."[19] It did indeed. People began
to speculate about the warmth of Blake's party loyalty. As
soon as he had resigned from the government, they passed
quickly from speculations to suspicions. And in October, 1874,
these suspicions became certainties. In October Blake delivered

at Aurora, Ontario, a notoriously disturbing speech, and at once everybody realized that a serious revolt had broken out inside the Reform party.[20]

Macdonald was apt to regard speeches such as the Aurora speech as mere tedious irrelevancies. But he saw that on this occasion the academic exercise had its point. The address would certainly arouse the deepest antagonism in Alexander Mackenzie and George Brown. It was the speech of a worthy, serious, "progressive" undergraduate, a catch-all for most of the vaguely forward-looking ideas of the time, from Senate reform to proportional representation. It reproduced many of the notions of that other very undergraduate production, the manifesto of the Canadian National Association, the new organization of the young men of Canada First. And—what was of more interest to the *Globe* and its proprietor, George Brown—it seemed in places to reflect the influence of Goldwin Smith, the radical ex-Professor of History at Oxford, the most vehement of all the Manchester anti-colonial theorists, who had recently arrived in Toronto. In England, Smith had criticized the imperial connection from the point of view of the overburdened Mother Country: in Canada he continued the attack from the opposite approach of the colony aspiring to nationhood. He and a number of the young Canada Firsters whom he gathered about him looked hopefully to Blake as the potential leader of their movement for Canadian autonomy. Blake was a nationalist, a legal and constitutional nationalist, deeply concerned about the remaining badges of Canada's subordination to the imperial Parliament and government. But for the other form of nationalism, which emphasized the territorial expansion and integration of the country, he had little more than a parochial Ontario suspicion. He was utterly opposed to any more generous proposals for the appeasement of British Columbia. To Macdonald he must have seemed a "little Canadian"; and both aspects of his little Canadianism—his suspicion of the imperial connection and his fear of transcontinental development—were emphatically revealed in the Aurora speech. The speech would certainly annoy Brown, who twenty years before had painfully eradicated the separatist and republican notions from the great Reform party he was building. It would seriously embarrass Mackenzie, who realized that the pacification of British Columbia was a national duty of first importance.

Macdonald studied Blake and Blake's ideas with curious interest. He gave the ex-Minister, from the moment of his resignation, a separate and specially important place in all his political calculations. He had Blake's influence in mind when he suggested to Tupper that the Conservative party should not make the draft reciprocity treaty the excuse for a frontal attack on the Mackenzie administration. "The Blake section," he observed to Tupper, "would then probably be induced to vote against the treaty and thus kill Brown without killing the government."[21] Blake, Blake's abilities, Blake's prestige, and the importance of Blake's following were all, in Macdonald's opinion, worthy of the most assiduous cultivation. A little carefully tended jealousy was a wonderful solvent in politics. There would be endless opportunities for its encouragement. And one of the first occurred early in the session, when Mackenzie got up unhappily to explain the resignation of his two senior ministers, Dorion and Blake.

Macdonald was in his best jocular mood. He told the House that the government which had gone to the country a year before had been, in effect, a Mackenzie-Blake government. Blake's well-known and much respected abilities had largely ensured the success of the Liberals at the polls. Yet, once the election had been safely won, and the new government solidly established, Blake had inexplicably resigned. Was there not here more than a hint of false pretence? "Everyone knew," Macdonald went on, "what the lawyers termed the principle of 'selling by sample'. The administration goes to the country and asks—'Will you buy this article? Here is an excellent article, and one of the strongest claims of this cloth to the good house-wife is that there is a strong fibre in it, coming all the way from South Bruce.' And when the people of this country, believing this to be a good kind of cloth, that would stand sun and wind or anything else, found that fibre drawn from it immediately after purchasing, it seemed, as the honourable member for South Bruce would observe, that the government had been guilty of selling under false pretences, and the people would say 'Here we have pawned off upon us the old brown stuff.'"²²

III

The clash between the "old brown stuff" and the stout material from South Bruce was a disturbing factor in an otherwise apparently settled state of affairs. It was the one hopeful change that had taken place since the autumn of 1873. It opened up delicious possibilities. But they were possibilities only. Macdonald had no intention of altering the cautious line of conduct which he had laid down for himself and his colleagues in the bleak days following the resignation of his government. He had taken it for granted that his own leadership was merely temporary, and that the Conservative party would do well not to advertise its weakness and incur further odium by following a factious course in Parliament. Here were two good reasons for a prudent, waiting policy. The possibility of a first-rate quarrel between Mackenzie's Reformers and Blake's Liberals was obviously a third. It would never do for the Conservatives to try to exploit this internal division too swiftly. Their premature intervention would, in all probability, merely unite Blake and Mackenzie against the common enemy. No, the apple of discord must be allowed to ripen quietly and without disturbance. The Conservatives must wait.

Macdonald waited through the session of 1875 in an attitude of almost amiable expectation. He spoke less frequently and more briefly than Tupper. When he did speak, it was often upon a subordinate rather than a major aspect of the matter in hand, and what he had to say frequently amounted to little more than a jocular comment upon the conduct of the ministry in general, or a facetious flick at the sensitive relations between Mackenzie and his temperamental and imperious lieutenant, Blake.²³ There were comparatively few subjects that came up during the session which roused him to really determined opposition; and of these the most important was unquestionably the bill for the Supreme Court of Canada, which Fournier, the not very distinguished French Canadian who briefly occupied the post of Minister of Justice, introduced towards the end of the session.

Macdonald was deeply interested in a Canadian Supreme Court. The establishment of a Supreme Court and the assimilation of the laws relating to property and civil rights in the common-law provinces, and the transference of that subject to the powers of the federal Parliament had always remained in his mind as achievements which were absolutely necessary for the completion of the grand scheme of Confederation. He had himself introduced bills for the establishment of a Supreme Court in the sessions of 1869 and 1870;[24] and the speech from the throne which had opened the fatal autumn sessions of 1873 promised yet a third measure for the same purpose. All these efforts had failed. The jealous concern for provincial rights, which awoke with such mysterious suddenness after Confederation, and which was felt and voiced not only by French Canadians but also by representatives of the English-speaking provinces, had held up this whole programme. There was almost no hope that the laws relating to property and civil rights would ever be assimilated; and it began to look for a while as if the establishment of a Supreme Court was also to be indefinitely postponed. But now a reversal of fortune had come. The huge Reform majority, and the sponsorship of Fournier, a French Canadian, would almost certainly ensure the passage of the bill.

It was really Macdonald's bill. It was based upon his drafts of 1869 and 1870; and he gave it his best support in the various stages of its passage through the Commons. There was, in fact, only one feature of the Supreme Court Bill to which he objected, and this feature, strangely enough, had not been present at all in Fournier's measure as originally submitted. It had been first introduced in the debate on the third reading as an amendment, a very belated amendment, which provided that the judgment of the new Supreme Court of Canada was to be final, and that no appeal could be made from it to "any court of appeal established by the Parliament of Great Britain and Ireland, by which appeals or petitions to Her

Majesty in Council may be ordered to be heard, saving any right which Her Majesty may be graciously pleased to exercise by virtue of Her Royal Prerogative".[25] As soon as this amendment had been moved by a Liberal member named Irving, Fournier got up to announce that he would be willing to adopt it; and his endorsation converted the new clause into an integral part of the government bill. At once Macdonald's opposition awoke.

Why was he so disturbed? The proviso at the end of the Irving amendment—"saving any right which Her Majesty may be graciously pleased to exercise by virtue of Her Royal Prerogative" might seem, on the face of it, to have saved the appeal to the sovereign in council unimpaired. This became, in the end, the correct interpretation. But it was not the interpretation placed at the time upon the amendment by others as well as by Macdonald. They assumed that the new clause—the Irving amendment became clause forty-seven of the Supreme Court Bill—would stop appeals to British courts in all but a few extraordinary cases; and their misapprehensions are easily explicable in the light of the great reorganization of the judicial system which was then being carried forward in the United Kingdom.[26] In his Judicature Act of 1873, Lord Selborne had established a great new court of appeal, to which he intended ultimately to transfer the jurisdiction of the Judicial Committee of the Privy Council as well as that of the other appeal courts and of the House of Lords. If, in accordance with these plans, the new statutory tribunal had become the single and final court of appeal in the United Kingdom, then clause forty-seven of the Canadian Supreme Court Act would undoubtedly have prevented appeals to it. This was what Macdonald feared; but his fears, which were well founded at the time, turned out in the end to be groundless. Lord Selborne's original design was never completed; and the Judicial Committee of the Privy Council was permitted to retain its historic form and its ancient jurisdiction.

Legally, the right of appeal to the sovereign in council was one and indivisible. There could be no real distinction, as Macdonald and other Canadians had assumed, between ordinary and special appeals; and, in the end, therefore, the concluding proviso of clause forty-seven ensured the continuance unchanged of the right of petition to the sovereign in council, and the practice of a reference to the Judicial Committee. The fact that the effort of the Mackenzie government to stop appeals had become inoperative as a result of the abandonment of part of the British scheme of judicial reform, was gradually realized in the next twelve months. But it was not realized in March, 1875. Macdonald attacked the Irving amendment in the light of the existing expectations and assumptions. He attacked it vehemently and repeatedly. He was obviously more moved than he had been in any previous debate in the session. He denounced the Irving amendment as "a surprise to the House, and forced upon it with indecent haste".[27] He told the Members bluntly that the amendment would probably ensure the disallowance of the Act by the imperial government, that the objectionable clause would no doubt be regarded in England as an evidence of a growing Canadian impatience with the imperial connection, and that the ultimate result of the adoption of the change might very well be the "severance of the Dominion from the Mother Country". "Those who disliked the colonial connection," he informed the House proudly, "spoke of it as a chain, but it was a golden chain, and he, for one, was proud to wear its fetters."[28]

Emphatic declarations such as this were rare. He could be counted upon to be himself, to speak his mind forcibly on basic issues. But laying down the law about the imperial connection was no real part of the game he had elected to play. His game, as he conceived it, was patiently to await the development of the discord between Mackenzie and Blake, and to promote it inconspicuously, if he could. The Supreme Court Bill was useless for this purpose, for, although Blake had taken little part in the debate on the measure, it was obviously the kind of constitutional advance in national status of which he was certain to approve. It was not here, but in the realm of territorial expansion and economic integration, that the best chance of open disagreement lay. Before the session was out Mackenzie would have to bring down his plan for the pacification of British Columbia; and its terms, Macdonald knew, were certain to be more generous than those which Edgar had been authorized to make in the spring of 1874. The Province had never given the Edgar offer any serious consideration at all. Walkem, the British Columbia Premier, had appealed over the head of the Canadian government to Lord Carnarvon at the Colonial Office; and Carnarvon, accepted reluctantly and not without qualification by Mackenzie as an impartial arbiter in the dispute, proceeded to lay down the terms of a new agreement between the Province and the Dominion.[29] The date for the completion of the Pacific railway was postponed until 1890; but, on the other hand, the federal government was required to prosecute its surveys, to spend at least two million dollars annually on the railway on the mainland of British Columbia, and, in addition, to construct immediately a line from Esquimalt to Nanaimo on Vancouver Island. Mackenzie, hedging slightly in a fashion which seemed oddly at variance with his reputation for simple honesty, accepted these terms, and on March 19 he introduced the Esquimalt-Nanaimo Railway Bill in the House of Commons. The issue was now joined. What would Blake do—Blake who had declared at Aurora that the Edgar terms went to the extreme limit of concession, who had announced that if the British Columbians were determined on secession, he was prepared to let them go?

Macdonald settled down with curious interest to await developments. For a while the domestic Liberal quarrel could hardly have been developed more promisingly. The Reform leaders were behaving like a group of eccentrically individualistic relatives, who, five minutes before giving a formal dinner party, suddenly discover that they have been plunged into a furious family row. Mackenzie and Blake went about their parliamentary affairs with the strained inattention of men who are inwardly torn between the wisdom of a compromise and the luxury of a knock-down fight. As late as the end of March it looked as if Mackenzie were still determined to resist. He had taken his stand upon the principle that the pacification of British Columbia was more important than the pacification of Blake. Would he be able to convince his own party, the

Parliament, and the nation that, in the national interest, he was right? Blake and two other prominent Liberals spoke and voted against the Esquimalt-Nanaimo Bill; but it passed the Commons with relative ease. Mackenzie was almost through his difficulties. And then, when perhaps he least expected it, he was met by a jarring, violent check. At the very last moment, when the session was almost over, the Bill was rejected in the Senate and there was no doubt that Liberal Senators had contributed to its defeat.

Macdonald had taken only the smallest part in the debate. He did not believe in interfering in the disputes of Reform leaders any more than in the quarrels of husbands and wives. He had voted for the Esquimalt-Nanaimo Bill, though most of his followers in the House and the Senate had voted against it. But he was very well aware of the important consequences that might flow from its rejection. On the one hand, the defeat of the Bill might arouse a tragic conflict between British Columbia and the Dominion; but, on the other, it might also bring the promising rift in the Liberal party to a quick conclusion. A real crisis in the life of the new transcontinental Canada could give the Conservatives their best chance of political recovery; but the first instinct of the Liberals, in the face of such a crisis, would almost certainly be to compose their differences. If the Esquimalt and Nanaimo Bill had passed the Senate, Mackenzie might have been emboldened to press forward and defy Blake. But such a course was now difficult, if not impossible. A new agreement with British Columbia was absolutely necessary. Mackenzie would need all the assistance he could get to push it through. He would need the help of the Blake wing. He would almost certainly have to come to terms with Blake; and, only a few weeks later, it was revealed that this was exactly what he had done. On May 19, Blake re-entered the Cabinet as Minister of Justice. The breach in the Liberal ranks was ended. And Macdonald was brought to the unwelcome conclusion that if the Reform government were to break up, it would break up not because of inward divisions, but because of outward attacks. How should Conservative strategy be revived in these circumstances? And how must he settle the problem of the leadership?

IV

That autumn, after another long and peaceful summer at Rivière du Loup, he moved up to Toronto. For the past eighteen months, he had been spending a good deal of time there, but as a guest and lodger, not as a householder; and in the city directory, he was listed discreetly, without specific residence, as "of Ottawa and Toronto". Now at last the definite move was made, and the transplanted Macdonald family established in a house, belonging to T. C. Patteson of the Toronto *Mail*, which stood on the east side of Sherbourne Street, a little north of Carlton Street.[30] It was a long, low, flat-fronted place, built of grey stock brick, with a single gable over the central entrance. The grounds were spacious and gently rolling; Sherbourne Street was only a peaceful sandy lane; and away to the north-east, towards Parliament Street, were open commons where Patteson had exercised his horses. It was comfortable and quiet enough on Sherbourne Street; but Macdonald had taken the house on only a short lease, and he had no intention of staying there permanently. He had his eye on a large property on St. George Street, close to University College, in a suburb which was distinguished, though perhaps not so fashionable as Jarvis Street. The St. George Street house would certainly be a large investment. But was not everything really settled? It was so obviously sensible for him to establish himself in Toronto. His firm had its head office there. He had scores of amusing friends and acquaintances in the city; and one of his old colleagues in the Conservative Cabinet, Charles Tupper, had also moved to Toronto and resumed his medical practice. They were both settling down into a species of comfortable semi-retirement. And why not?

Macdonald was getting on. They were all getting on. He was conscious of his sixty years, of time's increasingly peremptory reminders of its passage, of the disappearance of comfort-

ingly familiar circumstances, of the arrival of strange and
disturbing problems. "We are all getting old," he told his
brother-in-law, Professor Williamson, "and have earned rest."[31]
His sister Margaret, Williamson's wife, was seriously unwell
that autumn; and he was worried by the prospect of the
Williamsons and his sister, Louisa, continuing to live, winter
and summer, in the big old farm house, Heathfield, which
stood in relative isolation some distance from Kingston. It would
be better, he thought, if they would all get "decent lodgings in
town" during the winter.[32] He could understand the problems
of the ageing, for they were, though he did not always admit
it, close to his own. The needs of youth inevitably perplexed
him more. Mary, the child of his mature years, made no youthful demands or assertions; but she was the tragic exception to all
rules of growth and life. A wheel-chair carried her about;
standing, she had to be supported; and every significant development of human childhood came to her with difficulty, imperfectly, or not at all. He fussed over her health, worried about
her childish illnesses—about the painful appearance of her new
teeth; and on most afternoons, in the still hour before dinner,
she waited, in her heart-breaking pose of stiff composure, while
he told or read her a story.

At that moment Hugh was also giving him concern. Hugh
had been taught a certain independence very early by the odd
circumstances of his family's existence; and as a young man he
had continued to go his own way with a charming air of easy
confidence. He had, it was true, dutifully accepted a place in
the Macdonald-Patton firm, first as pupil and then as junior
partner; but so long as Macdonald remained in Ottawa and
Patton acted as the real authority in the Toronto Street office,
this professional connection did not draw the father and son
much closer. For years Hugh had had his own lodgings in the
city and had been living a busy and agreeable existence as
a sought-after bachelor and knowledgeable young man about
town. Then, in the autumn of 1875, the Macdonald family
arrived at Sherbourne Street. The fact that his son was now
a mature man of twenty-five was forcibly borne in upon Macdonald. He became aware that Hugh was a very popular young

man who had hosts of friends and knew his way about the city
with practised ease. He discovered something else—something
much more surprising and dismaying. He discovered that Hugh
was engaged to be married.

He did not like the proposed match; and, in his characteristic
brief and candid fashion, he told his son so. But it soon became
clear that Hugh had not the smallest intention of altering
his decision. He was obviously distressed and unhappy, for he
was a warm-hearted person who had no wish to cause anybody
pain; but it was also obvious that he was determined to live his
own life in his own way. He would not give in, and Macdonald
equally could not be won over. The atmosphere in the office
in the Trust and Loan Company's building became unpleasantly,
and then intolerably, strained; and Hugh, who in any case may
have already reached the conclusion that it would be better for
him to escape from the deep shadow of his father's immediate
presence, now announced that he would leave Macdonald and
Patton at the beginning of 1876 and start out on his own
account. "I hope, too," he wrote at the end of the letter in
which he told his father of his decision, "that you know that
wherever I may pitch my tent I will always be both ready and
willing to do your bidding and will always hold myself in
readiness to advance your interests in any way in my power,
for although I think you are acting in an unnecessarily harsh
manner towards me respecting my engagement, I have no doubt
that looking at the matter from your standpoint you are justified
in the course you are taking, and I certainly can never forget the
numbers of kindnesses done to, and favours conferred upon me,
in times past."[33] Hugh was doing his best not to part in anger.
But Macdonald was too wounded and annoyed to respond in
kind. His note, acknowledging Hugh's letter and accepting his
resignation, was curt and cool.[34] Yet, in other circumstances and
different moods, he would have been the first to admit that no
more frequently repeated, romantically banal situation could
exist than the one in which he found himself playing the
heavy father at the expense of two devoted and defiant lovers.
He was getting on. All this was part of an old and endless
process—of the trampling arrival of new generations, of the

resigned yet protesting withdrawal of his own seniors, of his contemporaries, and even of himself.

He had said that he was going to go. He had announced, in the most public manner, and with all possible definiteness, that he hoped and expected to retire from public life. But that was two years ago; and he still led the Conservative party. It was true that many people had not yet revoked the sentence of political banishment which they had passed upon him at the time of the Pacific Scandal. It was true that even so close a friend and colleague as Alexander Galt had openly declared, in a letter made public early in September, that he thought the selection of Macdonald as leader of the opposition had been a "grave mistake".[35] Galt, of course, had found it difficult to forget the jealousy and resentment he had felt in 1867; and, within the last few months, he had been seriously displeased once again by his old leader's bland refusal to emulate his own romantic devotion to principle. Alarmed by the increasing political activities of the ultramontane priests in Quebec, Galt had sought to enlist Macdonald's help in a passionate anticlerical crusade. But Macdonald, though sympathetic, had proved extremely wary. Obviously the Conservative party benefited— though how much it would have been difficult to say—from the influence of the ultramontanes. But obviously also the political advantage of the Conservatives was only one of several very good reasons for desiring to prevent a revival of the terrible old issue of the relations of church and state.

"Mind you," Macdonald wrote shrewdly, showing more knowledge of European affairs and Roman Catholic politics than Galt would ever take the trouble to acquire, "ultramontanism depends on the life of two old men, the Pope and Bishop Bourget (in Canada). Now there can be no doubt that there is an agreement between Catholic powers that the next Pope shall not be ultramontane. In fact it is absolutely necessary for Europe that he should be a liberal Catholic, who will cure the split in the church and bring back the old Catholics to the fold."[36] For all these reasons Macdonald had advised patience. Galt, as usual, had found the advice damping to the spirit. It no doubt confirmed his belief in Macdonald's inadequacy.

PITY THE DOMINIE; OR, JOHNNY'S RETURN.
CANADA—"HERE'S OUR JOHNNY FOR YOU AGAIN, MR. MACKENZIE! YOU'LL FIND HIM APT ENOUGH, BUT FRANKLY, SIR, HE'S FULL OF MISCHIEF!"

And, at the first opportunity, he spoke out. Macdonald was wounded by his old colleague's bluntness. Yet had he the right to be hurt, when less than two years ago he had himself been publicly declaring his unfitness for the post of leader?

The truth was that in the autumn of 1875 his position in

Canadian politics in general and the Conservative party in particular had become puzzlingly ambiguous. In November, 1873, he had pleaded with his followers to choose a younger man; but by November, 1875, reference to his own imminent retirement had temporarily ceased. He had come to Toronto, was thinking seriously of buying a large property, and seemed determined to settle down gratefully in the professional and social life of the city. It was all true; but it was also true that in the autumn of 1875 he was appearing in public more frequently and speaking at greater length than anybody would have believed possible two years before. In the previous February, he had written to Dalton McCarthy, the promising young Conservative barrister in Barrie, urging him, in his own interest as well as in that of the party, to run in North Simcoe. "The reaction has certainly set in . . . ," he argued persuasively.[37] Had the events of the last session convinced him that the waiting game he had counselled would have to be drastically and immediately revised? Had he decided that a real offensive must be mounted at once? Had he really changed his purpose? Or was his new activity the result simply of the chance that had brought on several political contests together and plagued him with invitations to speak which he could not well refuse?

Certainly, the by-elections of that autumn aroused unexpected interest. They did more. They encouraged Conservative hopes. A victory in Toronto, a defeat in Montreal—at first sight there might have seemed little to awaken great enthusiasm. But the Conservatives were tremendously exhilarated by the results. It was good merely to break even with the Grits; it was better to win a seat in Toronto, where all three constituencies had gone against them in the last election; and even in Montreal there was some encouragement, for Thomas White's defeat had a curiously heartening epilogue, like a story which at the last moment is given a sudden happy twist. Macdonald went down to Montreal for the dinner given to White, as a kind of consolatory festivity, after the election was over. These dinners to defeated candidates, with their transparent excuses

and vainglorious prophecies, were often extremely depressing
affairs; but the White dinner was not. Macdonald, in a speech
which was more obviously the speech of the evening than even
the dinner committee had probably expected, fell upon the
Reform party and the record of the Reform administration
with the fury of a young recruit and the skill of an old
campaigner.[38] No such verbal attack had been heard for years
before. Yet what did it portend? Did it mean that Macdonald
had now accepted the leadership on a new lease, with a permanent tenure? There were congratulations from many who looked
hopefully to the future. There was grudging recognition from
a few who could not forgive the inactive, waiting past. Mackenzie Bowell wrote to say that he was very pleased to learn that
Macdonald had made the Grits feel that he was not "politically
dead" yet. "And I am also glad to know that you have broken
a silence which was being misunderstood."[39]

V

Yet how could he break silence effectively? Even if he
tacitly accepted a slight extension of his "temporary" leadership,
how could he escape from the cautious, defensive, waiting
policy which he had followed for two years? He had never
been much interested in small affairs, minor mistakes, trifling
scandals. He wanted something big. And something big could
be found only in the broad lines of Reform administration, in
the general policies by which Mackenzie and his colleagues had
tried to carry forward the task of building a separate and distinctive nation on the northern half of the North American
continent. Mackenzie had certainly failed. At the end of his
second year of power his failure was abundantly obvious. His
growing unpopularity, his accumulating afflictions, his sheer
bad luck were all plain to be seen. Yet Macdonald had to see
further than this. He had to discover Mackenzie's positive
mistakes. He had to offer alternatives to Mackenzie's mistaken
policies. He had to persuade the Canadian people to accept

his different version of the national interest. How could he yet be sure where exactly he must strike?

There was one very obvious opening. The simple-minded "little Canadianism" implicit in the amendment to Fournier's Supreme Court Bill would certainly be defended and continued by Fournier's successor, Blake; and here Macdonald decided to hit with all the strength he had. "The cardinal point in our policy is connection with Great Britain," he told the audience at the White dinner in Montreal. "I am a British subject, and British born, and a British subject I hope to die."[40] The British connection was a precious cultural inheritance. But it was also an essential political defence; and beneath the few insignificant remaining forms of the old colonial relationship, there lay the reality of a diplomatic and military alliance by which alone Canada could maintain its separateness and its autonomy on the North American continent. The potential danger to that separateness and autonomy from the United States was still very great. Before the American Civil War, he reminded his listeners at Montreal, Canada had had at least some protection in the mere fact that the southern states were strongly opposed to the annexation of more free northern territory. But now the southern confederacy had been crushed; the last inhibition had been removed from American expansionism; and the whole American people believed, as in an article of faith, in the "Manifest Destiny" of its conquest of the entire continent.

Canada could escape this peril only through the British alliance. Through the British alliance alone Canada could build up its own north-west and consolidate its transcontinental dominions. Alliance! It was the word which he had been using most frequently over the last decade to describe the probable future relationship between the United Kingdom and the country which he had wanted to call the Kingdom of Canada. England, he of course assumed, would still be the "central power" and Canada, as well as Australia, New Zealand, and South Africa, would remain "auxiliary nations". But these auxiliary nations were ceasing to be dependencies; they were becoming associated and allied powers. It would be a great

mistake to imagine that their unity could be promoted by giving
them representation in the imperial Parliament, or by establishing
a new federal legislature for the entire Empire. These were
not advances towards the future, but retreats into the past. The
auxiliary British nations would be "ranged about a central
power", but they would remain "separate nations" nevertheless.
At Toronto he spoke of Queen Victoria as the "Queen of
Canada".[41] At Montreal he told his listeners that England,
Canada and the other auxiliary kingdoms would be united
under the same sovereign, owe allegiance to the same crown,
and be "bound together by an alliance offensive and defensive".[42]

The alliance would help to ensure the expansion and
consolidation of Canada on a transcontinental scale. This was
his fundamental objective; it was the end towards which the
building of the Canadian Pacific railway was the most important
means. And, in the failure of the Liberals to carry the design
of a transcontinental railway forward very vigorously, he found
the second major opening for his attack against the Mackenzie
government. The Pacific Scandal had turned out to be almost
too embarrassingly complete a success. It had destroyed the
particular railway corporation of which Sir Hugh Allan was
the head; but it also seemed, at times, to have ruined the very
project of the railway itself. The scheme lay in the splintered
pieces of a wreck; and when the Liberals tried to reassemble
it, they found themselves embarrassed by the depression, by
the quarrel with British Columbia, and by the lukewarm paro-
chialism with which some of their ministers regarded the very
idea of a transcontinental Canada. The Mackenzie government could not persuade a new group of capitalists to pick
up the scheme where Sir Hugh Allan had dropped it; and, in a
time of straitened finances, it could not push the railway
forward too energetically as a government work. The best
plan that Mackenzie could devise was to build the railway in
sections, as revenue permitted, using water and road transport
as far as possible meanwhile.

It was hardly a very heroic policy; and Macdonald did not
fail to draw the contrast between it and the policy which he
himself had been prevented from carrying out. The Conserva-

tive plan, he told his Toronto audience, would have peopled the west and kept Canadian business humming even in depression; the Liberal scheme was not really a railway at all; but simply the "pieces" of one.[43] Yet—though nobody in the Reform Cabinet appeared to be properly conscious of the fact—the transcontinental railway was still vitally necessary in the national interest. "Until that road is built to British Columbia and the Pacific," he informed his auditors at the White dinner in Montreal, "this Dominion is a mere geographical expression. . . . Until bound by the iron link, as we have bound Nova Scotia and New Brunswick by the Intercolonial Railway, we are not a Dominion in fact."[44]

Western settlement and the Pacific railway were his first two national policies. Protection to Canadian industry was again becoming the third. During the summer of 1874, when the Brown-Fish draft treaty had revived the whole question of Canadian commercial policy, he had kept silent, torn between his wish to defeat the treaty and his desire to exploit the divisions in the Reform ranks. But early in 1875, before the Canadian Parliament had even tackled the question itself, the Senate of the United States rejected the draft agreement, and it became obvious that the third effort which Canada had made since Confederation to renew the vanished Reciprocity Treaty had failed as completely as its predecessors. There was now no reason to reserve judgment; there was, on the contrary, a real opportunity for the Conservative party to declare itself, for the depression, which during 1875 began to exert its full paralysing force upon the economy, was now arousing among Canadians a passionate interest in the economic future of their country.

Macdonald felt the wind of opinion change and freshen. The public debate on commercial policy, which had begun with the publication of the Brown-Fish draft treaty, was continued in more vehement and angry accents, as Great Britain and the United States began dumping some of their surpluses on the Canadian market, and as the incidence of bankruptcies and the level of unemployment grew. Late in November the Manufac-

turers Association of Ontario held a special, largely attended
meeting to concert efforts for the increase of the tariff;[45] and
in January, the Dominion Board of Trade, a conservative body
which had hitherto been more influenced by importers than
by domestic manufacturers, decided to give its support to a policy
of protection.[46] Long before this the Conservative party had
definitely committed itself. Macdonald's pronouncements on the
subject of commercial policy were more laconic and less emphatic
than those made by Tupper and the Conservative candidates
in the by-elections in Toronto and Montreal, J. B. Robinson
and Thomas White.[47] But there was no doubt at all about his
meaning. In Toronto he attacked the first Liberal budget
("It made the fortunes of the railways by the deputations that
came down to protest against it") on the ground that its tariff
increases imposed heavy additional charges on the consumer
without affording corresponding protection to the Canadian
manufacturer.[48] At Montreal he reminded his audience that
the policy of incidental protection had first been introduced by
the Liberal-Conservative government in the Cayley-Galt tariff
of 1858-9. The party, he declared, continued to believe that
the duties necessary for revenue should be imposed so as to
provide incidental protection to the native producer. It was
also, he insisted, a matter on which the Conservatives differed
essentially from the Grits.[49]

The last point was a crucial one, which he and other Conservatives were becoming increasingly anxious to establish.
There was no doubt that the Conservative party was committed
to a policy of incidental protection. The only question was
whether the Reform party would soon be committed to incidental protection as well. In all previous debates on the subject
of commercial policy, the Reformers had certainly opposed
protective duties. But now, with the loud and increasingly
popular demand for a retaliatory tariff against the United
States ringing through the land, they showed some signs of
relieving the stiff angularity of their devotion to the principles
of free trade and the practice of revenue tariffs. The Reform
candidates in the Montreal and Toronto by-elections went

furthest in unequivocal declarations of protectionism; but Blake
was also revealing a guarded interest in the "home producer";[50]
and Mackenzie, who had declared on a visit to Scotland that
"the principles of Richard Cobden were the principles of civilization", returned to Canada to announce that his government
would consider the wisdom of revising the tariff if the needs of
the revenue seemed to require an increase.[51] The hideous
possibility that the Reform party, spurred on by the "Protectionist Liberals" in the chief Canadian cities, would shamelessly
appropriate the popular demand for protection in its own
interest now confronted Macdonald and his outraged Conservatives; and all during that autumn a frantic attempt was made to
persuade the electors that the Reform party, despite the eccentric
utterances of a few of its members, was really, on its record, a
free-trade party, and that nothing could be hoped from it in the
present economic crisis. At the White dinner, Macdonald
ridiculed the "three economic faces"—free trade at Dundee,
incidental protection at Sarnia, full protection at Montreal—
which Mackenzie had successively exhibited.[52] Mackenzie would
apply any make-up for the sake of votes. The candid record
of the Conservatives could alone be trusted.

Yet the Reform party could still falsify these confident
predictions. Would it do so? The torturing uncertainty continued
all autumn. It lasted into the winter. Tupper believed that
the Mackenzie government had come at length to realize the
peril of its situation and that it was ready to risk a *coup*
to extricate itself.[53] Macdonald heard an incredible story that
the administration was about to abandon the Pacific railway
completely in order to claim the credit for the millions of savings
which would result;[54] and in Montreal, Workman, the new
Liberal member who had defeated White, announced, with
the greatest possible confidence, that there would be a large
increase in duties in the budget which the Finance Minister,
Richard Cartwright, would bring down in February.[55] Macdonald and Tupper were convinced that the Liberals had in fact
decided to raise the tariff—though Cartwright subsequently and
categorically denied that such a decision had ever been taken.

JOHN A. MACDONALD

the fixed devices with which they began
them, and when the demand for certain

In any case, there was nothing that the Conservatives could do about it. They were already irrevocably committed; and a long article supporting incidental protection appeared in the *Mail* two days before Cartwright's budget speech.[56] Macdonald and Tupper could criticize in detail, but not in principle. The Grits had been too cleverly accommodating for them. The greatest electoral opportunity of the Conservatives had been snatched away.

But had it? As February 25, the day appointed for Cartwright's budget speech, drew closer, the pressure of interested propagandists mounted steadily in Ottawa. A deputation of the "Protectionist Association" arrived from Montreal;[57] another was expected from Toronto. But these extraordinary envoys, these visitors from the outside world, were not the only advocates who worked their hardest to influence the policy of the government. While the industrial lobbyists were being received with formal politeness in government offices, Alfred Jones and the low-tariff Liberal members from Nova Scotia were threatening, in the frank intimacy of caucus, to desert the government. By the morning of February 25, the rumour was general on Parliament Hill that there was disagreement in the Liberal ranks and that the commercial policy of the government had been changed at the instance of the Nova Scotia Reformers.[58] When they walked into the Commons chamber that day, Macdonald and Tupper probably expected nothing more than a small upward increase of duties in the interest of revenue. But, as it turned out, Cartwright had rejected even such advances as these. He took his stand immovably on the existing policy. He told the House very firmly that he regarded "every increase in taxation as a positive evil in itself". "This," he announced with finality, "is no time for experiments."[59]

"This is no time for experiments." Could the Finance Minister have uttered a more inept and provocative sentence? The present was a time of profound depression, a time of unemployment and acute distress, a time when the baffled Canadians were ready to use the fiscal devices which had been so long employed against them, and when the demand for some positive attack upon the miseries of the slump had become a chorus of millions of voices. Macdonald had found his cause. He would overwhelm Mackenzie's government with the national policy of protection. With the national policy he would revenge the humiliation of the Pacific Scandal and reverse the verdict of the election of 1874.

Chapter Seven

The Picnic Grounds of Ontario

I

He took up his new position circumspectly, with an air of cautious reconnaissance. Tupper, who was the first to reply to the budget speech, moved no amendment to Cartwright's resolutions;[1] and it was left to the back-benchers, the protectionist Liberals in particular, to sponsor the first formal protests against the government's fiscal policy. Their intervention, they declared, had been prompted by the failure of the Conservatives to meet the budget with an instant challenge. They begged Macdonald to declare himself; and one of them—Devlin of Montreal Centre—promised that if the leader of the opposition would only put himself at the head of the protectionist movement, he could "catch" the entire parliamentary delegation from Montreal.[2] It was not a very tempting trap; and Macdonald avoided it with genial contempt. "I heard the threat—the dire threat—," he answered jocularly, "that the members from Montreal would go into opposition, and yet I did not see a change in my honourable friend the Premier's countenance. He did not seem to be very much frightened. . . . I thought I could see a smile—a gentle, placid smile—pass at the time over the countenance of my honourable friend who knows his power. My honourable friend from Montreal Centre is like ancient Pistol—he can speak brave words, but like the same ancient Pistol, he can eat the leek. . . . If the government are never displaced until through the aim or accident of my honourable friend from Montreal, they will remain in office much longer than either the wishes of the opposition, or the good of the country require. . . . My honourable friend from Centre Montreal gave me a warning that unless I accept his offer at once, there would be no use in my throwing my net for him. Well, Mr. Speaker, I have caught some queer fish in my time, but I am afraid that my honourable friend—as during the previous session when he sat over in that corner—is too loose a fish for me ever to catch."[3]

The insubordination of the protectionist Liberals was valuable, for it was one more indication of the growing divisions in the Reform party. The support of these rebels might be useful. But he would have them—if he had them at all—on his own terms, not on theirs; and the terms of his proposal were certain to be vaguer and more comprehensive than any they were likely to suggest. He thought their amendments incomplete and partial, for they concentrated on manufactures and neglected agriculture. He promised something more satisfactory; but it was not until March 10—a fortnight after Cartwright's speech had been given—that he formally moved the resolution which became the official opposition amendment. It was most discreetly phrased. The word "protection" was actually used, but no special prominence was given to it. There was no demand for "protective duties", but only a modest and inoffensive request for a "readjustment of the tariff". The resolution criticized the absence in Cartwright's budget of a readjustment which would "not only tend to alleviate the stagnation of business deplored in the gracious speech from the throne, but also afford fitting encouragement and protection to the struggling manufacturers and industries, as well as to the agricultural products of the country."[4]

Macdonald's intention was obvious. He hoped to occupy middle ground, with a view of two different kinds of countryside, and the best of two possible worlds. His resolution combined the not entirely compatible interests of the manufacturer and the primary producer. It sought to reconcile the logically contradictory ideas of revenue and protection. He started with the assumption, which was common to all his contemporaries, that it was impossible to impose income taxes and other forms of direct taxation in a new country like Canada and that in consequence a tariff was the only feasible method of getting revenue. Customs duties, levied at fairly high rates, could alone finance the roads, canals, and railways which were required for the opening up of the country. Public works were essential for Canadian expansion and consolidation at all times; but they had, in times of depression, the additional advantage of providing jobs for the unemployed; and to curtail or postpone such enterprises at such a moment in the interests of "retrenchment" would, Macdonald assured the House, be "a lamentable state of affairs". Money was vitally necessary; and there was only one way in which it could be got. "We must trust to our customs, therefore," he summed up, "as the principal source of our future revenue. Now, what can be more reasonable than to so adjust the tariff for revenue purposes that it will enable us to meet our engagements, and to develop our resources, the duties falling upon the articles we ourselves are capable of producing?"[5]

The "articles we ourselves are capable of producing" were not merely manufactured goods. They were also agricultural products; and one of Macdonald's first tasks was to prove to the Canadian farmer that the policy of "incidental protection" had been designed just as much in his interest as in that of the industrial enterpriser. It was true, of course—and he admitted it freely—that Canada was on an export basis so far as wheat and flour were concerned, and that the prices of these commodities were largely set in the international market at Liverpool. But he insisted that Canadian coarse grains were in another and a quite different category. They could be protected, as they were already protected in the United States; and their protection would give to the Canadian farmer his own local market, while at the same time the protection of manufactures would ensure that market's steady enlargement through the growth of Canadian industry. At the moment, the manufactures of Canada were still in their infancy. The state of the Canadian economy, in fact, corresponded exactly with that hypothetical economic condition in which—so John Stuart Mill had fortunately argued—protecting duties were justifiable. On the one hand, Canada lay open to the dumping of American

goods; on the other, the United States was securely guarded
against Canadian imports, despite the repeated efforts of the
Dominion to negotiate a new trade treaty on mutually advant-
ageous terms. "We are informed in the speech from the throne,"
Macdonald rounded off his argument by an appeal to the stern
facts of the depression, "that there is a stagnation in trade.
We are informed also that this has arisen, not from any fault
of our own, but in consequence of the depression in trade that
has taken place in the neighbouring country. That is the statement which His Excellency the Governor-General was advised
by the honourable gentleman opposite to make to this House,
and if it be true, I say that if there is ever a time when it is
lawful, or allowable, or wise, or expedient for a government
to interfere, now is that time."[6]

The issue was joined. "Never since the settlement of the
great questions of the Clergy Reserves and Seigniorial Tenure,"
declared the editor of the Montreal *Gazette*, "have party lines
been so distinctly drawn upon a clear and easily understood
principle as they have been by these discussions and by the
recent vote."[7] Macdonald had taken up a commodiously broad
and defensible position; and the Reform government had been
edged into cramped quarters, in which there was little ground
for manœuvre. It was the biggest and most promising success
that the Conservatives scored during the session; but at the same
time it was not the only way in which their fortunes were being
improved. The unhappy divisions in the Reform party, marked
occasionally by the most gratifying outbursts of open quarrelling,
still continued. The protectionist Liberals were openly critical
of the fiscal policy of the government. Huntington, who had
attacked the ultramontanism of the Roman Catholic clergy at
a public meeting during the Argenteuil election, was bluntly
called to account by Luther Holton, the senior English-speaking
Liberal from Quebec, in the debate on the address. "Holton's
escapade," Macdonald wrote to Dalton McCarthy, "has finished
Mackenzie's government in Quebec, and I think the retention
of Huntington in the cabinet must destroy it with the Roman
Catholics all through the Dominion."[8]

Prospects were good, but not, as yet, excitingly promising.

Chance had tossed the Conservatives some unexpected favours. "Incidental protection" showed signs of becoming rewardingly popular. But it had not yet definitely proved itself; and, as for the other causes which Macdonald had tried to launch in the previous autumn, there had not, so far, been much profit in them. No new controversial measure, such as the Supreme Court Bill, had appeared to reawaken interest in the problem of the imperial connection. And the issue of the Canadian Pacific railway had become so dangerously complicated that Macdonald and Tupper, in their efforts, at one and the same time, to support the project and criticize the government, began to take refuge in the most contorted arguments. In a time of financial stress and falling revenues, British Columbia, which had captured the imagination of central Canadians a few years before, had now become a tiresome and demanding bore; and the promise to build the transcontinental railway ceased to be regarded as a statesmanlike undertaking and threatened to be damned as an utterly insane commitment. What were the Conservatives to do? They could not disown an engagement to which they had bound the country. Yet they did not want to go on supporting the increasingly costly commitments which the Mackenzie government had accepted in its reluctant and fumbling efforts to satisfy British Columbia. They were caught in a cleft stick. All that Macdonald and Tupper could do was to insist that the Conservative plan, which had been wrecked in the Pacific Scandal, of building the railway through a private commercial company would have been far more successful and far less costly than the piecemeal process of government construction into which Mackenzie had been betrayed. Macdonald believed in the railway. He believed in the pacification of British Columbia. He believed so strongly in the union and integration of the country that he may have found it difficult to criticize Mackenzie's painful but well-intentioned efforts. Perhaps significantly he had little to say on the subject. It was Tupper, more vehement and verbose than usual, who did most of the talking for the Conservatives.

Yet, despite these discouragements, Macdonald's purpose remained settled and firm. He would defeat the Reformers

and restore the Conservatives to office. And after that? Had
he really altered his decision to retire? There were signs,
during the winter and spring, that the plans he had made in
the autumn of 1873 would still be carried out. In April
occurred the death of his elder sister, Margaret, the wife of
Professor Williamson. She had been only eighteen months
older than he; and although during all the long years of his
absence from Kingston, he had been careful to keep equally
in touch with both sisters, Margaret naturally held for him a
special place. They had grown up together, and in the far-off
faded days at Hay Bay and Kingston they had shared games
and small responsibilities, from which the "baby", Louisa, had
of course been excluded. "She is my oldest and sincerest friend,"
he wrote to Williamson, "and has been so through life."⁹ And
now she was dead. Should he regard her departure as one
of those reminders, those significant taps on the shoulder,
which time seemed to make so often these days? Would it not
be better for Louisa, and Williamson, and also for himself,
to admit the approach of old age, to change their lives where
it was necessary and still possible, and to give up the tasks and
properties of their prime? In Toronto, he was settling down
into an easy professional existence, as into a well upholstered
arm-chair. The new house on St. George Street, in its pleasant
rural and academic setting, with University College nearby and
the open countryside to the north and west, was at last nearly
ready for occupation. A swarm of carpenters and painters had
invaded the building and every day Agnes went up the
muddy road to mark their progress.¹⁰ By May, he hoped, the
place would be ready for them.

Spring came, the removal was accomplished, the morning
and evening journey between St. George Street and Toronto
Street became the steady habit appropriate to the householder
and the professional man. But he could not settle down. He
did not want to settle down. The newspapers, with increasing
interest, continued to debate the merits of "incidental protection"; and, as spring waxed into summer, the first real tests of
the popularity of the new Conservative commercial policy drew
rapidly closer. By-elections were scheduled for the two con-

stituencies of North and South Ontario in the first week in
July; and the Gibbs brothers were the Conservative candidates
in the two ridings. The party had a new policy. But it needed
a new device, a new method of presentation, which would be as
fresh, as striking, as irresistibly attractive as the substance of the
new policy itself. And by good luck, and at almost the last
moment, the device was discovered. One hot day in June, a
small deputation of the Toronto Liberal-Conservative Association presented itself in Macdonald's office. They were planning,
in collaboration with the Conservatives of North Ontario, to
hold a political picnic at Uxbridge, on July 1, the ninth anniversary of Confederation. Would Macdonald consent to come
and address the crowd?

II

On Saturday, July 1, at half past eight in the morning, a
special train of the Toronto and Nipissing Railway pulled out
from the Berkeley Street Station for Uxbridge.[11] It was definitely not one of the most certain days of summer. The horizon
was doubtfully smudged with clouds; but the possible un-
pleasantness of the weather had not apparently affected the
popularity of the excursion in the slightest. There were between
three and four hundred Liberal-Conservative picnickers and
their ladies in the train; and the special carriage at the end,
with its deep rose carpet and walnut fittings and furniture,
was agreeably crowded with a little group of the more prominent guests. Macdonald and Agnes were there; so was John
Beverley Robinson, the new Conservative member for Toronto
West; and so were the various dignitaries of the Toronto Liberal-
Conservative Association. Charles Tupper and William Mc-
Dougall, who had been campaigning in Ontario South, were
not of the company. But they had planned to drive north over
the country roads, and it was expected that they would arrive
in time for the picnic.

It was eleven o'clock when the train reached Uxbridge.
During the last hour of the journey the sky had become

perceptibly more threatening, and shortly after the arrival a little light rain fell. This was certainly discouraging, it promised badly for the main events of the afternoon; but it did not spoil the roaring enthusiasm of Macdonald's reception. Two brass bands—one had come up from Markham—crashed into a march tune, and before the station platform was a wide semi-circle of waiting and applauding people. The president of the Liberal-Conservative Association of Ontario North read an address of welcome; Macdonald replied gracefully for himself and the other guests; and then they all got into carriages, and the procession, with the bands at its head, moved slowly through the streets under triumphal arches, which shoùted "welcome" and promised "victory". It was over half an hour before they reached the grove at the other side of the village, called Elgin Park, where the picnic was to be held. There, under the tall elms, long tables, crisp with newly-ironed cloths, had been laid out for those serious picnickers who, despite the weather, had come determined to lunch in a genteel fashion *al fresco* rather than in the steaming dining-rooms of the hotels. The tables were loaded with all the "substantials" and "delicacies" of a hearty meal—with plates of cold sliced chicken, ornamented tongues, hams in aspic, Milan soufflés, red mounds of strawberries, elaborate moulds of flummery and charlotte russe, tipsy cakes, pound cakes, piles of tea- and cheese- cakes, great misted jugs of iced lemonade and raspberry cordial, and clusters of bottles of wine.

It was high noon. Before the speeches—the main event of the occasion—were scheduled to begin, there was to be a luncheon interval of at least an hour. And, as the fickle sky gleamed and gloomed capriciously overhead, Macdonald lunched, and passed from table to table, and threaded his way from group to group, and gossiped, shook hands, acknowledged introductions, and welcomed uproarious salutes. These were the Canadians. They had come in an amiable holiday mood, to relax and chatter, to see each other, but, above all, to see him. They had dressed themselves in their best, for a memorable occasion, at once serious and entertaining; and they greeted him with a curious mixture of awe, as for a reigning monarch, and joyous familiarity, as for a beloved friend. It was a slice of the community, a cross-section of the nation, a sample of town and village and countryside.

They were all there—from the elegant young barrister, with his brocaded waistcoat and fashionably checked trousers, who had come out in the train from Toronto, to the thick-set, bearded farmer from Greenbank or Blackwater in his sagging "best" black coat and rusty top hat. Here was the wife of the harness-maker at Port Perry, in her snuff-coloured taffeta gown, with the bustle and the golden-brown satin trimming, made at home by the visiting dress-maker, on the "Little Wanzer" sewing-machine; and there was the banker's lady, expertly fitted in the "tied-back" dress that had been made for her in Toronto or London, in all the modishness of smoked pearl buttons, pleats and bows and laces, dagged edges and chenille fringe. Macdonald met them all. He shook hands with boys in wide-brimmed boater hats, and knickerbockers, and long black stockings, who were led up to him, blushing with embarrassment. He greeted little girls in two-piece taffeta costumes with miniature bows and fringes that were virtually replicas of mamma's. He bent graciously over babies in long elaborately embroidered gowns. He had a word for almost everybody. He knew so many names, remembered so many faces, recalled so many circumstances that usually, in the flashing second of a greeting, the entire form of his interlocutor's existence would miraculously take shape in his mind. He knew the Canadians better than anybody had ever known them before—and better than anybody would ever know them again.

By this time it was after half past one. He climbed the fresh pine steps of the temporary platform, crowded already with speakers, officials, and their ladies. Before him was a crowd of several thousand people—good-humoured, expectant people, who reclined on the grass, or sat on the insufficiently numerous chairs which the Conservative Association had provided, and waited for the instruction and the entertainment of the afternoon. There were several acres of hats—silk top hats, small, close-fitting feminine hats with feathers draped modishly between the curls and ringlets, old-fashioned brightly coloured sun-bonnets, curly bowlers, straw boaters, and here and there, like other enormously expanded hats, provident umbrellas and fringed pink parasols. As he watched the crowd and listened to the long succession of introductory speeches, Macdonald glanced occasionally and surreptitiously up at the grey uncertain sky. But Tupper, whose voice was hoarse with previous efforts, spoke very briefly; and McDougall, who was well aware that his speech could be only a curtain-raiser, was almost equally short. A few drops of rain had fallen, but that was all. The shower still held off relentlessly when Macdonald got up to speak.

He was at his best—easy, conversational, discursive. He made some jokes. He told a few stories. He accepted occasional interruptions readily, as if they had been expected cues. His plan—if he had one—seemed infinitely flexible, his manner amiable and rambling. Yet, hidden beneath the jocular good humour of the speech was a clear and aggressive purpose. Every word was designed to put the Liberals upon the defensive. The Liberals, he told his listeners, were still harping upon the extinct issue of the Pacific Scandal, with the obvious purpose of disguising the simple fact that it was their government that was on trial. The weakness and ineptitude of the Mackenzie administration had been exposed by many tests. But its incapacity had been revealed above all by the challenge of the depression; and the mere presence of a few protectionists among the Reformers should not obscure the government's refusal to accept its economic responsibilities. "The great question now before the country," Macdonald insisted, "was as to the best means to relieve it of the existing commercial depression. And there was no use looking to Mr. Mackenzie because he was a free trader . . . and there was not the slightest use in voting for a man who said he was a protectionist unless he said he would vote to put down a government which was opposed to protection."[12]

As they drove back to Toronto in the "cars" through the long summer evening, Macdonald could feel agreeably satisfied. A smart shower of rain had come down after his own speech was finished; but the spectators, instead of bolting for cover, had stayed for the end of the proceedings. The picnic had been an unqualified social success. But—what was far more important —it had also been a huge political triumph, as the by-elections of July 5 quickly demonstrated. In South Wellington, where the Conservatives had backed a man whose protectionist principles were more certain than his party loyalty, the Reformers won; but in the Ontarios, T. N. and W. H. Gibbs were triumphantly elected. That night Macdonald went down to the United Empire Club, a club which had been founded as a Conservative counterpoise to the National Club of the Canada Firsters and Blake Liberals, and which on Wednesday was gay with lights and riotous with celebrations. "Were there ever such victories as those of N. & S. Ontario?" he wrote excitedly to Tupper two days later. "Our friends write me that W. H. owes his triumph to the Uxbridge picnic. There was a gain of eighty votes in Uxbridge alone. . . . The enthusiasm here on Wednesday night was intense. The U.E. club looked magnificent, illuminated as it was from 'turret to foundation stone'. . . . The Grits by some accident selected yesterday, the day after these elections, for a great convention for organizing. They are thoroughly alarmed by our successes, and met by G. B.'s summons. Never did a more downcast set of men meet together, jeered and laughed at as they went about the streets."[18]

It was exaggeration, of course. But it was very nearly true. Everywhere there was a sudden sharp realization that fortune, who was always unpredictable and who for a long time had been bafflingly unrevealing, had at length and decisively made up her mind. Macdonald had found his theme—the relief of the depression through a change in fiscal policy. He had discovered his method—the political picnic. All over the province, the Liberal-Conservatives were suddenly alerted, like soldiers who had been roused to action or jobless men fired by the prospect of employment. For over two years they had been sunk in apathetic discouragement. Now they were aroused and hopeful. They had a cause and a way of promoting it. Of course there had been political picnics before; but they had been local, isolated, occasional affairs, completely without general significance. The Uxbridge picnic was different. It inspired imitations throughout the province. It was the first of a long procession. On July 27, there was a picnic at Colborne, in Northumberland county; and Macdonald spoke to a huge crowd of over five thousand which had come from Belleville, Port Hope, and Cobourg.[14] On August 9, he was at Guelph and Fergus; on August 23, at St. Catharines; and a week later, on August 30, at Milton, in Halton county.[15] The picnics were becoming general, regular, frequent. They had become at once a grand circuit of entertainment and a network of musters of the Conservative clans.

The sixth picnic was at Woodstock and Ingersoll.[16] Five miles east of Woodstock, on the Governor's Road, was the village of Eastwood; and here, set in its own finely wooded park, stood Vansittart House, the comfortable red-brick country house with the tremendously thick walls and double windows which T. C. Patteson had recently acquired. Macdonald and Agnes were guests of the Pattesons for the occasion; and Patteson drove over to Woodstock in the stylish imported phaeton which he had purchased from Sir Allan MacNab's estate to bring Tupper, McDougall and the Gibbses back to Vansittart House for dinner. Macdonald drank large quantities of wine and became noisily jovial during the evening. His high spirits had been constant all during the summer. So far the picnics had drawn big crowds and awakened enormous enthusiasm. And he had no doubt that next day's affair would be fully up to the established standard of success. He was not disappointed. On Wednesday, September 6, a long procession, composed of every conceivable kind of vehicle—victorias, barouches, landaus, phaetons, buggies, surreys, democrats and spring waggons—moved slowly forward, encouraged by the blaring music of four brass bands, down the road which led from Woodstock to Ingersoll, where the speeches were to be given.

The climax of the whole series of picnics came less than a week later at Belleville.[17] The Reformers, realizing at length that jeers were hardly a satisfactory retort to these social successes of the Conservatives, began a competing series of Liberal picnics; Mackenzie, Blake, and Cartwright fired fusil-

lades of denunciations and challenges from their summer plat-
forms at Macdonald; and, as the speeches followed every few
days or every week at least, the picnic grounds of Ontario
became a kind of vast provincial debating hall in which the
accusations and rejoinders followed each other with much of
the rapidity, and with all of the appositeness and sharpness, that
would have ruled in a single debate. Each side struggled
harder and harder, as the season declined and the end of
September approached, to outdo the other in the size of its
crowds, the splendour of its arrangements, and the fighting
quality of its speeches. Undoubtedly the climax of the Conservative efforts came at Belleville. There were supposed to
have been nearly fifteen thousand people there on September
12; and, although Reform editors could very easily discount this
huge total as outrageous Conservative exaggeration, the plain
fact remained that a vast crowd—larger than any that Belleville had seen since the Prince of Wales's visit over fifteen years
before—had been at the fair grounds that September afternoon. Macdonald was elated. And one of the most welcome
sources of his satisfaction was a letter of congratulation from
Hugh. Hugh had married and had moved back to his favourite
Kingston to practise law. But he had also resumed his old
affectionate correspondence with his father as if the break of
the previous autumn had never occurred.[18]

September saw the end of the picnics. Macdonald settled gratefully down for the first autumn and winter of life in
the new house on St. George Street. He could relax and take
stock. The picnics had proved the power and popularity of
his new policy of economic nationalism; and they had awakened
and reanimated Conservatives throughout the entire province.
They had done all this. But had they not done something
else—something a good deal less eagerly acceptable—as well?
Had they not enabled the Liberal-Conservatives of Ontario to
reclaim John A. Macdonald as their political leader? In
the first of his summer speeches, he had made a few guarded,
indirect allusions to his age and the need of fresh, young blood
in the leadership of the party; but as the season went on, and
competition developed and he warmed to his work, these hints

grew less frequent. The end of the summer's campaign found him in a state of hope and well-being such as he had not known for years; and when Lord Dufferin came up to Toronto in January to deliver some speeches, he told the Governor of his exuberant good health.[19] Yet could he really lead the party again? Could he take up the burden of office again, even if only for a brief while, so as to superintend the installation of the Conservatives in power once more? In January, 1877, he became sixty-two years old. He was very nearly an old man now. He did not feel old—far from it. But the fact of his age was there. And it had been driven home to him recently with frightful force by the death of the man who was almost his exact contemporary, John Hillyard Cameron.

Cameron's death was tragic in its suddenness, as his life had been tragic in its prolonged misfortune and struggle.[20] He had spent himself in a vain effort to carry the load of obligation which he had incurred twenty years before, in the depression of 1857; and now, with some of his debts still unpaid and his family in serious trouble, he was dead.[21] Significantly, ominously, he was dead. And he was not the first of Macdonald's contemporaries to go. There was nobody but Macdonald left of all that little group of Conservatives who had gathered about "Sweet William" Draper during the troubled 1840's. William Boulton, "University Bill" as the *Globe* had once called him, had died less than three years before; but Sherwood, the arrogant, intriguing Sherwood, was over twenty years in his grave. They had both been a part of Macdonald's life; but of them all, Cameron had paralleled his own career most closely. He remembered Cameron, the prosperous and hospitable host of "The Meadows" in the brave years before the crash of his fortunes. He recalled how the kindly Rose Cameron had looked after Hugh on the days when Isabella lay utterly prostrated in the rooms in Wellington Place. He could see this, and he could see far beyond this, and back into the shadowy spaces of Owen McDougall's shop on Store Street, where John Cruickshank had opened his school for "classical and general education" nearly fifty years ago. He could see the crowded room, and the desks, and the forms, and the children, and

Cameron and himself—big boys then, and promising—sitting in lordly pre-eminence.

Cameron was gone now. But once he and Cameron had competed for Draper's approval; and Draper, after having examined their credentials, had appointed them his joint heirs. Was it not time for Macdonald to begin to consider the problem of his own successor? For some time he had been regarding young Dalton McCarthy, the Barrie lawyer, with a favourable eye, with exactly the kind of benevolently appraising eye that Draper had once turned upon himself. He had been pressing McCarthy, in a flattering fashion, to enter politics. "We in the opposition are in want of a legal man of good debating power," he had written McCarthy as far back as February, 1875, "and you would have an opportunity of securing at once a status in Parliament which you may never have again."[22] Nearly two years later, in December, 1876, the Cardwell constituency became vacant, and McCarthy agreed to contest the seat. It was regarded as a relatively safe riding; but Macdonald flung all his influence behind the candidate; and Tupper— whom he regarded as "unequalled on the stump"—went up to Cardwell to give McCarthy the benefit of his energy and experience in the campaign.[23] McCarthy was elected. McCarthy, Macdonald was convinced, had patriotism and genuine ability. And in a few years, if the Conservatives were returned to power, he might be able to lay a convincing claim to office. Yet, in the politics of the moment, these were still distant possibilities. McCarthy had yet to prove himself. And if Macdonald could persuade his followers to let him resign—and could steel himself to insist on resignation—he would need a veteran as his immediate successor. There could be no real doubt who the veteran should be. Charles Tupper would be his successor, once the Mackenzie government was overthrown and the Conservatives were back in power once more. The defeat of the Reformers, Macdonald privately decided, was something which he must accomplish himself. He must reverse the verdict of the election of 1874, as the last act of his political life. Then he could retire.

III

The Conservatives came down to Ottawa for the session of 1877 with all the superabundant confidence of a football team which has won every game in the series, or a theatrical company fresh from a successful tour in the provinces. It was a lively, argumentative, acrimonious session, crowded with accusations, revelations, scandals, and all kinds of excitement. Ever since Huntington had read his notorious resolutions in the spring of 1873, the Conservatives had burned to revenge the humiliation of the Pacific Scandal. They had almost come to believe that a victory over the Reformers would be incomplete unless it were accompanied by the discovery of a scandal among the Liberals as appalling—or nearly so—as that which had caused their own ruin. They waited with breathless eagerness for a real opportunity for moral denunciation, and in the session of 1877 they thought that they had at last discovered it. They demanded a variety of parliamentary investigations into the letting of government contracts and the uses of government patronage. They made charges against a number of prominent Liberals, including the Speaker. The Reformers ought to have been intimidated and silenced by these awful revelations. But they were not. Yelling *"tu quoque"*, they rushed forward, their faces red with righteous indignation, and laid new and similar charges against the Conservatives. They were even successful in putting Macdonald into a fresh state of embarrassment by revealing the very awkward fact that he had kept some formal control, for two years after he had left office, over a fairly large balance of secret service money.[24] He was obliged to refund a sum which had been paid out from this balance, on a claim preferred by Alexander Campbell. It was all deplorable; and the Governor-General wrinkled his nose in fastidious disgust. "It has been a very unsatisfactory session," he told Carnarvon, "the two parties bespattering each other with mud in view of the dissolution two years hence."[25]

The dishonours were even. Yet somehow Conservative prestige stood higher. Conservative purpose seemed firmer, though on both sides there was unhappy perplexity about a few great questions of national policy. The problem of the Pacific railway had divided and weakened the Liberals; but Macdonald did not dare to challenge his opponents directly and unequivocally upon the subject. He had told the audience at the picnic at Ingersoll that he did not believe British Columbia would secede; he was sure, he said, "that so strong was the feeling of the people that at the next general election they would show that the desire of the eastern provinces was to keep faith with their fellow countrymen in the west."[26] Yet he had privately informed Dufferin that, in his opinion, the famous "taxation resolution" which had been passed at the time when Parliament accepted the terms of union with British Columbia, was a gloss upon the original contract which effectively limited Canada's resulting financial obligations;[27] and in the House he made no appeal whatever for the sacrifices necessary to satisfy British Columbia. On the whole, he maintained an unrevealing silence on the subject. But his taciturnity and Tupper's garrulously involved arguments were not ineffective, from a political point of view. The Conservative criticism of government railway policy, while not aggressive enough to arouse the suspicions of central Canada, was at least sufficient to win the devotion of British Columbia. "I do not think," J. H. Gray wrote to Macdonald from Victoria, "that the people here regretted when your administration fell, because rightly or wrongly they thought they had been trifled with, but if the present one were to fall, there would be shouts of triumph and bonfires, because they believe they have been *tramped* on, *slighted*, and *deceived*."[28]

These, however, were minor triumphs. The new policy of "incidental protection" was certainly the biggest Conservative success. Macdonald had laid down propositions so broad that they could be attacked only with great difficulty. He had hoped to profit from his own flexible moderation. But he had scarcely expected to gain an additional and perhaps even more important advantage from the extreme rigidity of his opponents. Yet so it was. As Conservative policy grew more broadly accommodating, Cartwright's budgets became more narrowly doctrinaire. In 1877, he announced two new excise duties on the production of Canadian malt and beer; and the only important increase which he proposed in the tariff was a small additional specific duty on the import of tea—which, of course, the Canadians could not produce.[29] It was exactly the kind of duty in which free-traders most delighted; it could not have followed free-trade principles more undeviatingly, Macdonald claimed, even if it "had been drawn by the most rabid free-trader, the most fanatical admirer of what Carlyle called the 'dismal science'".[30] It began to look as if the Reformers had chosen the inappropriate moment of the depression to acquire the fervour and dogmatism of converts to a new religion. They had declared for *laissez-faire* at a moment when Macdonald could denounce *laissez-faire* as criminal apathy. He could stigmatize the Reformers as "flies on the wheel", who believed that economic remedies were useless and who had no remedial measures to propose. He himself had put forward a possible remedy—a remedy which was fortified by a strong infusion of nationalism. He had told his audiences at the picnics that he believed in "Canada for the Canadians". He appealed at once to their growing consciousness of national unity and their frustrated desire for economic relief.

As the session ended Macdonald was in the best of spirits. In its headlong career onward, the party had been suddenly tripped up on more than one occasion during the past session; but on each occasion also it had recovered itself quickly and pressed on. The Conservatives knew that they had got the Reformers on the run. They were aware that in the popular imagination of the Canadians the Liberal party had become the hunted and they themselves the pack in full cry. The Governor-General, watching the political chances of the future with a speculative eye, shared the common belief in the decline of the Liberals. "They have certainly lost ground at a more rapid rate than is usual," he told Lord Carnarvon.[31] He read a dull, hopeless anticipation of defeat in the obvious evidences of their fatigue and nervous strain. "Blake," he informed the Colonial Secretary, "is ill, thoroughly broken down with overwork and excitement and irritability of the brain. . . . As for

Mackenzie he looks like a washed out rag and limp enough to hang upon a clothes line."[32]

Macdonald contemplated his harried and exhausted opponents with sympathetic interest, almost with pity. His own physical and mental state was excellent. Perhaps the hard campaigning of the past year ought to have tired him. But he did not feel tired. He had never felt better. And, according to the testimony of Dr. Grant and Dr. Tupper, this sense of returning well-being had its origin in a definite physical improvement. The doctors, he told Lord Dufferin, had assured him "that his constitution has quite changed of late, and that his general health would be likely to improve from henceforth for some years to come".[33] The Governor-General himself noted slight, significant differences. During the long session, with all its dinners and entertainments, Macdonald had never once drunk wine to excess. The ex-Prime Minister had been in his best form and on his best behaviour during the session of 1877. After the prorogation, when he came to pay a polite farewell call on Dufferin, there was an air of jaunty confidence and youthful high spirits in his manner.

He was beginning to feel like a proclaimed king who was waiting only for the formality of his coronation. His journey home had much of the enthusiasm of a royal progress, and at Toronto a great reception awaited him.[34] The long platform at the Berkeley Street station, the surrounding streets, and even the roofs of the standing freight cars, were crowded with an enormous welcoming mass of people. Five hundred torch-bearers marched in the procession which escorted his carriage through the heart of the city, past rows of shops and houses which were blazing with illuminations and "transparencies"; and when he came out on the balcony of the United Empire Club to address the crowd, the spring darkness was so brightly lighted with these countless fiery points of illumination that he could see the long stretch of King Street, packed and jammed with citizens. "There were ten thousand people to meet me here last Wednesday," he wrote to J. A. Macdonell. A royal welcome, which could be compared only with the welcome to royalty! "No reception like it," he continued proudly, using the now familiar comparison, "since the Prince of Wales in 1860."[35]

He was eager to get to work. "I am satisfied no time is to be lost," he confided impressively to J. A. Macdonell, "as we must have an election before another session. . . . The Grits are organizing and may make a midnight march as before. Not a moment is to be lost."[36] It was true, of course, that the Parliament elected in the winter of 1874 had still well over eighteen months of its allotted existence to run; and, although the Conservatives kept up a cheerful clamour about a dissolution, there was no certain prospect of an election before the next session. But time was running rapidly away, if it had not yet run out. The whole party must be put in a position of alert readiness for action. His second series of picnics would have to be very carefully arranged so as to cover the most ground, and do the most good, with the most economical expenditure of time. In the first week after his return from Ottawa, he sat down with Tupper to plan the summer campaign.

Tupper would be his chief aide. Tupper was his probable successor. It was time to present Tupper formally to the Ontarians, who, up until the previous summer, had never had much opportunity of appreciating his fighting qualities as a speaker. Early in June, the two friends went down to Kingston for the meeting which was to inaugurate the summer series; and Tupper, introduced as the heir-presumptive to the Conservative leadership, delivered the principal speech of the evening.[37] The town hall was packed with Macdonald's old friends and devoted followers, with people who refused to believe a syllable to his discredit, and who rejected the entire Pacific Scandal as a baseless slander. "The moral assassination policy cannot kill Sir John, Canada's ablest statesman," announced a long streamer loyally from one of the walls. It was like bringing a friend into one's parents' house, and introducing him to the family circle. As he warmed to his work, Macdonald grew more confidentially prophetic. He had long wished, he said, to retire from public life; and his friends had long resisted his retirement. "I tell you," he promised the Kingstonians, "that until my friends say that they think I have served long enough—so long as they

think I can be of any use to them—it will be but a just return
for what they have done for me not to desert them. I have long
been anxious to retire from the position I have held, and I am
sure you will say, from the acquaintance that you have formed
tonight with my friend, the honourable Charles Tupper, that
when I do retire, he is a man who will well fill my place."[38]

Less than a week later, on June 12, the picnics began. The
tour swung west and north of Toronto, though in not too wide
a range, from London, Brampton, Gorrie, Orangeville, to
Markham. But this was only the prelude to more ambitious and
far-flung engagements. Before the end of the month, Tupper
had left for Nova Scotia, and Macdonald was ready for a new
political experience—a political experience so strangely new
that it might be called a political adventure. He had made
speeches in Quebec city and in Montreal; but never in other
parts of Quebec. Quebec was Cartier's and Langevin's territory,
not his own; and even now, when, on July 4, he set out from
Montreal on the afternoon train for Sherbrooke, his tour was
planned to cover only the predominantly English-speaking
Eastern Townships.[39] The Quebec politicians—White, Masson,
Chapleau, and Langevin—accompanied and supported him on
his journey; and at St. Hyacinthe, the first stop on the way to
Sherbrooke, Chapleau spoke for him in French. There were
other stops and speeches at Actonvale and Richmond, and
darkness had fallen long before they reached Sherbrooke. But
Sherbrooke was crammed with people and blazing with lights.
"Sandy is no sic man as our Sir John," proclaimed one "trans-
parency"; and another asserted that "The weevil came in with
the Grits and prosperity with John A." There was a long
processional carriage drive through the streets that night; and
next morning Macdonald set out over the lovely countryside,
with its little lakes and sudden high hills, on a packed programme of train rides, carriage drives, picnics, dinners, and
endless speechifying. It was not until late on Saturday night,
July 7, that he arrived back in Montreal, and at Montreal the
tour climbed to its crashing crescendo of success. Five thousand
torch-bearers paraded through the streets, and at Dominion

Square, where the procession ended at eleven o'clock at night, a crowd of fifty thousand people roared applause.[40]

Then, during July and early August, while Macdonald took a holiday, he and his friends tried to estimate the effects of the first phase of the campaign. "A tidal wave seems to be setting in up here in our favour," Dalton McCarthy wrote to Tupper in Nova Scotia, "and opposition stock has gone up and is going up in a manner which appears to be extraordinary. The Montreal reception seems to have capped the climax, and Mackenzie and company have returned in a very bad temper to the capital. . . ."[41] What were Mackenzie and company going to do, Macdonald asked himself curiously? Early in May, he had half expected a general election in late summer or early autumn. But August came, there was no sign of a dissolution, and Mackenzie went off on a speaking tour of Nova Scotia. Was it a reconnaissance? What kind of reception would Mackenzie get? He need hardly have wondered. "I never was at a sadder meeting—a few funerals excepted—," wrote McLelan of the Reform demonstration at Truro.[42] Confronted with these ominous signs of unpopularity, would Mackenzie dare to dissolve? Would he not postpone the general election until after another session of Parliament, in the hope of a return of better times? It was possible—even probable. Yet Macdonald had heard another and a very contrary rumour that the Reformers intended to go to the country in January. He could not be certain. The Conservative meetings, he decided, would have to continue their triumphal course through September and into October. He wrote to Tupper, begging him to return and give him his support in the autumn picnics. "My hands," he admitted wryly, "are very full of these infernal things."[43]

His hands were very full indeed. The picnics kept him so much away from Toronto during the early autumn that Mary wrote him, by dictation, begging him plaintively to return. "The house seems so dull and lonely without you," she said, "and I miss my evening stories very much. . . . Dear Father, when are you coming back?"[44] He was back for only the briefest of intervals during most of September and the early part of October. "I wish to Heavens I had your vitality," his old friend

John Rose wrote to him, "but I could no more face what you are going through than I could earn Paradise."⁴⁵ Macdonald himself, in his detached, half-amused fashion, was impressed by his own energy. "After my Eastern Townships experience," he told J. A. Macdonell, "I begin to think highly of my powers of endurance."⁴⁶ He tried to insist that the meetings at which he spoke must not follow each other on successive days, that intervals for rest and recovery were absolutely essential. But too often these precious intervening hours were taken up with conferences, private discussions, carriage drives, and long and exhausting train rides. He travelled as far north as Lindsay, Barrie, and Owen Sound. He touched the western end of the province in Essex county and its eastern extremity in Dundas and Glengarry. Early in October, as he turned from southwestern Ontario towards Toronto and home, the good weather, which had smiled so sunnily on so many of his meetings, at last began to break. His much-abused voice grew hoarse and faint. The rain poured down at Chatham on October 10, and at St. Thomas on October 12; and two days later, at Hagersville, in Haldimand county, he could make only the briefest of speeches.⁴⁷ The tour had faltered. Yet in the end it finished strong. At Hamilton, where the last great meeting was held, the sun shone once more and with the steadfast warmth and brightness of a midsummer day. Agnes came up from Toronto to meet him, and she was presented with a necklace, and made her own speech of thanks, and the crowd was greater than any he had seen outside of Montreal.⁴⁸

IV

He carried the war aggressively into the last session of the third Parliament of Canada. It was, appropriately enough, a tense and angry period in international affairs; and the bloodless battles of Canadian politics were fought out under the lowering danger of a real conflict. Once again, twenty years after the Crimean War, Great Britain faced the real possibility of becoming involved in the quarrels of Russia and Turkey.

Late in January, 1878, Disraeli ordered the Mediterranean fleet to steam through the straits to Constantinople. In England there was immense popular support for this armed defiance of the advancing Russian armies; and for some weeks a fight on a very large scale seemed possible. Canada, which now had a coast-line on two oceans, was very much more conscious of its alarming proximity to this huge northern country, Russia, than it had been at the time of the Crimean War; and during the winter and spring occasional exciting rumours of impending attacks by Russian naval and land forces ran through the Dominion. In June, when the Congress of Berlin met to make a new settlement of the affairs of south-eastern Europe, the agitation suddenly subsided; but it had been the first serious international crisis which Canada had experienced since Confederation.

It stirred many people. It deeply affected Macdonald. He had founded the Canadian permanent force in 1871 with the establishment of the first two artillery batteries. He saw now that the existing crisis offered a favourable opportunity for strengthening and enlarging this small nucleus of a "standing army". "In a time of profound peace such a proposition would be unpopular—," he wrote to Sir Stafford Northcote, "would be objected to by the opposition of the day, and could not be carried by any ministry. And yet I am satisfied that the time has come for the formation of a regular force—closely connected with the imperial army, and worked up to the same standard of training and discipline. Without this, Canada will never add to the strength of the Empire, but must remain a source of anxiety and weakness."[49]

He was looking forward eagerly to the assumption of power. He had all sorts of things that he wanted to do with power. But power could be won only through a final, approaching struggle; and now his confidence was mixed with a tense realization that the desired trial was terribly close, that there remained only a few months in which he could make or mar his chances of victory. He was strung up to a high pitch of nervous excitement. Everybody on the Conservative side seemed in a fever from the same infection; and it was an extraordinary session, barren of any constructive legislation, yet crowded with acrimonious arguments and violent personal attacks. "There is the most devilish spirit with the opposition this session that was ever seen," wrote Alexander Mackenzie severely, as if denouncing a manifestation of original sin. "I never knew anything like it before."[50]

Even Macdonald seemed to have changed. He was strangely unlike the self-effacing, repentant, ageing man of four years ago. There were moments when he seemed to resemble much more closely the high-spirited, hard-drinking, hot-tempered young politician who had fought George Brown fifteen and twenty years before. It was true, of course, that his easy-going urbanity never entirely departed. He intervened at moments in the debates to soften asperities and to recall the House to its sense of dignity. He made occasional jokes. He told stories. He twitted Mackenzie amiably on the dizzyingly frequent changes in his Cabinet—including the second and definitive resignation of Blake; and when "Joe" Rymal, who was the homespun humorist of the House, dropped his good-humoured jibes for somewhat more acrid criticisms of the Conservative picnics of the previous summer, Macdonald merely retorted with one of those eighteenth-century anecdotes which he enjoyed so much. Rymal's departure from his usual, and acceptable, type of humour reminded him, he told the House, of Boswell's conduct on an occasion when he and Dr. Johnson had gone to the theatre and had seen a somewhat disappointing play. The audience made a great many noisy protests, and Boswell imitated the lowing of a cow with such success that the spectators encouraged his efforts by calling out *encore, encore*. Boswell lowed two or three times; and then, in the pride of his heart, he was emboldened to try to imitate other animals. But now there was no applause. The attempts were ghastly failures. "My dear Boswell," said Johnson turning impressively to his friend, "confine yourself to the cow."[51]

It was all very agreeable—at intervals. But this note of genial raillery was not dominant. Something harsher and more primitive sounded repeatedly. Macdonald tried his hardest to convict Vail, the new Nova Scotian member of the Cabinet, of disloyal utterances at the time of the secessionist movement. He disliked Vail. He disliked Donald Smith still more, for Donald Smith, his agent and confidant at the time of the Red River troubles, had gone over to the Reformers at the crisis of the Pacific Scandal in the autumn of 1873. Smith was now supporting a bill which the government had introduced to authorize the lease of the newly constructed Winnipeg-Pembina branch of the Canadian Pacific railway to a north-western American railway company, which would thus be enabled to provide through communication by rail from Manitoba to the east. The name of the American railway was not specified in the bill, but the government revealed the fact that it had been negotiating with a group of capitalists, headed by George Stephen of the Bank of Montreal, which was at that moment acquiring control of the St. Paul and Pacific Railroad; and Donald Smith was popularly and correctly believed to be a member of the Stephen syndicate. Macdonald attacked Smith for advocating a lease in which he had a personal interest. He attacked the government for rewarding Smith's political support in such a scandalous fashion.[52] It was a determined onslaught. Yet its bluntness and severity were hardly exceptional. Every contract, every item in the appropriations, was bitterly criticized or disputed. The debate on the tariff was endlessly prolonged. And when—as if Mackenzie had not had trouble enough at Ottawa—an important constitutional crisis erupted in Quebec, the Conservatives, with Macdonald at their head, leaped upon this new, heavensent issue with the evident intention of exploiting its possibilities to the full.

It was a peculiar case. Letellier de St.Just, the newly appointed Lieutenant-Governor of the Province of Quebec, had just dismissed his Conservative *Bleu* ministry, headed by de Boucherville, on the ground of its deliberate and contemptuous neglect of his office. On April 11, in a long and elaborate speech, Macdonald attacked the dismissal as a violation of the principles of responsible government.[53] Mackenzie, in his reply, took the position that the purely provincial politics of Quebec were no concern of the Parliament of Canada. He hoped to choke off the debate as soon as possible. But the Conservatives were just as anxious to prolong it. And since the government would not grant an adjournment for a third day's discussion, they continued to debate all through the night of Friday, April 12, and all through the following day until six o'clock in the evening. It was an increasingly fatigued, meaningless, and disorderly debate. Macdonald, who had directed the Conservative attack all through Friday night, had a sherry and some oysters early on Saturday morning and went to sleep on a couch in a committee room. On Monday, the *Globe* explained in scandalized tones that he had retired because he was "simply drunk, in the plain, ordinary sense of that word". Inevitably, some of the leading Conservatives got up in the House to refute these baseless slanders.[54] And inevitably the notorious debate on the Letellier affair received a fresh burst of publicity.

All this was bad enough. But there was more to come. The scandalous climax of that extraordinary session was reached on its very last day, at the moment when Black Rod was already on his way to summon the Commons to the Senate chamber for the closing ceremony of the session. On the previous evening Macdonald had reiterated his charge that the passage of the bill for the Pembina branch of the Canadian Pacific railway had been intended as a reward to Donald Smith for the "servile support" which he had given the ministry. As soon as the House met on the final afternoon, Smith rose indignantly to deny these accusations. He insisted that he had never asked or received a favour from either government, and that, at the crisis of the Pacific Scandal, he had decided to vote against the Conservative administration on grounds of conscience alone. Tupper denied his statements; Macdonald branded them as falsehoods; and in an increasingly staccato interchange which lasted through the final moments of the session, the two Conservative leaders and Smith argued furiously over the events which had preceded the fall of the Conservative government in 1873. Tupper, explosive and domineering as always, was more prominent in the mêlée than his chief. He was still shouting "coward, mean, treacherous coward!" at his opponent after the Sergeant-at-Arms had announced the messenger. But it was Macdonald who had the last word—the literally last recorded word—of the session.

"That fellow Smith," he cried hotly, after the Speaker had given orders for the admission of Black Rod, "is the biggest liar I ever met!"[55]

He might have been back in that old milling-ground—the Assembly of the Province of Canada. He might have been the still youthful Macdonald who, white with passion, had denounced George Brown on the dreadful evening of February 26, 1856! As the session ended, as the probability of an early autumn election grew more and more assured, he seemed to have recovered a young man's compelling sense of urgency, a young man's reckless determination to win at all costs. "If we fail in Ontario in the next election," he wrote to J. A. Macdonell, "then 'good-bye' to all hopes for the Conservative party. I, for one, shall give up the fight in despair."[56] This was a final effort into which he put everything of his strength and ability with hardly a moment's impatient consideration for his health. Above all, the party must be kept united; there must be no ruinous "splits" in its tightly drawn ranks. "Let us not, like the hunters in the fable," he pleaded, "quarrel about the skin before we kill the bear. It will take our united efforts to kill the bear." All that summer, while the very atmosphere seemed ominously disturbed, and periods of intense oppressive heat alternated strangely with days of frightful floods and wind-storms, he stuck to his self-appointed task. At the very beginning of the season, and again in the first fortnight of July, there were a number of huge Conservative open-air meetings and celebrations at which he spoke;[57] but this year the grand circuit of picnics was not to be so prolonged or so extended. During a great part of the summer he stayed in Toronto, dealing with his enormous correspondence, presiding over conferences, having interminable private discussions. He was the theorist of the Conservative party's strategy, the improvisor of its tactics, the arbitrator of its disputes, the prophet of its victory.

On August 17, the *Canada Gazette* announced that the third Parliament was dissolved, and that the general election would take place on September 17, exactly a month later. Immediately the tempo of the campaign quickened for the last time. Macdonald began to fit the final speaking engagements into his crowded time-table, and on August 21 he left on the night train for Kingston.[58] He was worried about his old constituency. Of his two probable opponents, one, Stewart, he had beaten before, but the other, Gunn, was an unknown and reputedly a dangerous quantity. Dalton McCarthy, who had heard a grim rumour to the effect that the Grits were boasting that Kingston would be carried against Macdonald, begged his leader to run in Cardwell, where he would hardly have to put in an appearance, and where his friends could carry on the campaign on his behalf.[59] But Macdonald considered, hesitated, and declined. He would stick to Kingston. "I shall have hard work here," he admitted, "but prospects are good."[60] On August 22, a night of thick, clinging heat, he spoke for two hours in Kingston's town hall.[61] Before the month was out, he had travelled westward as far as Toronto and eastward as far as Cornwall, was back in Kingston, and had spoken, on still another oppressively sultry night, with what the newspapers called his "vaunted vigour".[62]

What were the chances for the Conservative party? Would he really be able to revenge the defeat of 1874? Tilley, whose term as Lieutenant-Governor of New Brunswick had ended just in time, was coolly realistic about the prospects in his own province. "In viewing the position, as I see it today," he wrote to Macdonald, "we may hope to divide New Brunswick, and I say frankly that I will be satisfied with that. . . ."[63] Flour and coal duties for the benefit of Ontario millers and Nova Scotian mine-owners were not popular in the province. Tilley admitted that New Brunswick was a dangerous "weak point" for the opposition; but on the other hand he was convinced that the Maritime Provinces as a whole were sure to return a Conservative majority. Tupper agreed with him. "We have the current of public sentiment strongly in with us," he reported from Amherst, "and I will be greatly disappointed if we do not do *better* than I promised you. . . ."[64] More than sixteen out of the twenty-one Nova Scotian seats was what Tupper now predicted;

and from Langevin came a confident estimate that, in the
Quebec district, the Conservatives would increase their strength
from ten to fifteen or sixteen.[65] Optimism was almost everywhere. Yet what of Ontario? In Ontario he had fought the
hardest battles and incurred the greatest defeat of his career.
What would Ontario do now? There were some who predicted
that the Reform majority would merely be reduced, others who
argued that the two parties would about break even. Only a
few people—such as Dalton McCarthy and Macdonald himself—
really believed in their heart of hearts that the Conservatives
would win a decided majority of seats in Ontario. Yet he hesitated to speak. He had an almost superstitious dread of seeming
to anticipate events. Prophecies about the results in either the
province or the country as a whole were foreign to his nature.
And it was not until well on in the summer that Agnes, who
not unnaturally wished to know whether she would be required
to superintend a household removal to Ottawa in two months'
time, finally persuaded him to make a sober estimate.

"If we do well," he answered briefly, "we shall have a majority
of sixty; if badly, thirty."[66]

He was in his committee rooms, in Kingston, on the night
of September 17, when the first returns began to come in.[67]
Alexander Gunn had beaten him, and by a majority of one-
hundred and forty-four! For the first time in his thirty-four
years of political life, Kingston had deserted her son. He could
not help but feel regret; but, within a few hours, his regret was
whirled away like a drop in the vast, rushing spate of his
triumph. The whole province, the whole country had declared
for him in an avalanche of votes. He had sworn to defeat the
Grits, and he had brought about their complete downfall. He
had regained power. He had revenged the defeat of 1874.

Chapter Eight

The Plan in Realization

I

"I am waiting to be summoned," he wrote to Goldwin Smith on October 1, "Lord Dufferin (*entre nous*) having told me, when here, to keep my carpet bag ready."[1] It was the end of his freedom, the end of the tranquil, almost carefree, life in the St. George Street house. "I am in good health," he reassured his sister Louisa, "but have not yet *quite* regained my strength."[2] He had certainly overtaxed himself during the election, and he spent the last few weeks of his time in Toronto in recuperative idleness, varied by busy letter-writing and by long meditations on his new government and its programme. Politically, he could hardly have asked for better fortune. The results of the general election had been favourable in every province but New Brunswick. His own check at Kingston had been retrieved by election to the two constituencies of Marquette, Manitoba, and Victoria, British Columbia; and the choice was pleasantly easy, for the appeasement of British Columbia would be one of the first tasks of his government. He would sit for Victoria; and in the Commons he would have a majority very nearly as large as that which he himself had faced in the dismal dispirited session of 1874. "I resolved to reverse the verdict of 1874," he declared proudly to Cyril Graham, "and have done so to my heart's content."[3]

On October 9, in Ottawa, at half past one o'clock, he met the Governor-General for the expected interview. It was the first official meeting in close to five years. It was also very nearly their last. Dufferin's term of office was virtually over, and he had spent a good part of the spring and summer in making a series of superlatively gracious farewell appearances. He had stayed, of necessity, to see the results of the general election; and now the installation of a new and very acceptable government was to be the last act of his governor-generalship. He greeted Macdonald warmly. He told him—with perhaps a slight enhancement of the charm of his complimentary manner—that "on personal grounds the warmest wish of his heart was gratified".[4] Macdonald, in a private letter to Tupper, dryly described the Governor-General's welcome as "gushing"; but, at the same time, he was impressed by Dufferin's good opinion, and he set a high value on Dufferin's services to Canada. He had valued them so highly, in fact, that in the previous spring he had ventured to write to Sir Stafford Northcote, suggesting that the Governor-General's term of office might be lengthened by another two years.[5] Nothing had come of this suggestion. Dufferin was going back to England in a few weeks. But he had been a good friend to Macdonald and a good friend to Canada. It was important to retain his support.

In the agreeable atmosphere of this official reunion, Macdonald was his most urbane and ingratiating self. Yet, in his usual fashion, he remained cautious. He was anxious to prepare Dufferin for the Conservative programme—to reassure him about Conservative intentions. He sketched the new government's policies in a few simple and highly tentative strokes.[6] The hope, which he had confided to Sir Stafford Northcote in the previous spring, of laying "the foundation of a standing army" had now become a more definite plan; and he suggested to Dufferin the establishment of a small permanent force of three battalions. He told the Governor-General that he was "very keen" about the Canadian Pacific railway, and eager to begin it, as a commercial enterprise, in accordance with the plan which the Conservatives had always preferred; but he also admitted that the chances of a successful company flotation were extremely small in the existing depression. He hinted that he intended to ask the British government for a guaranteed loan in aid of the railway, and he was plainly aware of the unpleasant fact that the moment when the Canadian government was contemplating an increase in the tariff was hardly the most suitable moment at which to apply for an imperial guarantee. He seemed anxious to assure the British government that Canada would not sink too deeply into the "economic depravity" of protectionism. He told Dufferin that his government planned to raise the level of the tariff to approximately twenty and twenty-five per cent, to give England a preference of about one quarter to one fifth, and to submit all its fiscal proposals to the British government before introducing them into the Canadian Parliament. He ended by insisting—not, perhaps, to Dufferin's complete satisfaction—that in all his resolutions and speeches on the subject of the tariff, he had never committed himself to pure protectionist principles.

Then they turned to the subject of the new government, and Dufferin asked Macdonald for his nominations. Macdonald told the Governor-General that his proposed Cabinet was not "cut and dry", and he went away to finish his selections. Most of the veterans were recalled to office. Tupper had confirmed his claim to the Ministry of Public Works by his sledge-hammer attacks on the railway policy of the Mackenzie government. Tilley's restoration to his old post as Minister of Finance would help to quiet the Maritime apprehensions about the fiscal policy of the new government. Prince Edward Island, in the person of J. C. Pope, was given a place in the Cabinet, and New Brunswick, which had done comparatively so badly in the election, had to be content with one portfolio, instead of two as before, and with the Speakership of the Senate generously thrown in as a solatium. John O'Connor stood for the Roman Catholics of central Canada; and another Pope, John Henry, who was not related to the Prince Edward Island family, represented the English-speaking minority of the Province of Quebec. Langevin, who would never enjoy so much of Macdonald's confidence as Cartier had done, was now the chief of the French-speaking ministers; and from Ontario came a respectable but rather humdrum contingent, with Alexander Campbell as its senior member.

Macdonald himself took the post of Minister of the Interior.

It was a relatively new portfolio, created as late as 1873, and invested with the management of all the important aspects of Canada's programme of expansion in the west.[7] The great main purpose for which the new office had been established was obviously the promotion of western settlement; and, in the autumn of 1878, when Macdonald assumed control, the Department had at last reached the point at which it could make an effective beginning on its real task. The painfully difficult preliminary problems, which had appeared dramatically even before the acquisition of Rupert's Land, seemed at last to have been solved. In 1876 the claims of the half-breeds and the other squatters to land grants in the new Province of Manitoba had been largely settled; and in 1877, with the signing of the last of the seven treaties with the Indians, the aboriginal title to the Canadian north-west had been extinguished, and the prairies were freed for white settlement. The task which faced Macdonald was the task of surveying this vast western empire and throwing it open for occupation. As late as April of that year, in a debate in the House, he had admitted frankly that he knew little about the provisions of the Dominion Lands Act of 1872, which was the legal framework of the settlement organization.[8] Undoubtedly he was unacquainted with the detail of the operations of the Department of the Interior. But he did not for a moment underestimate its importance. Its tremendous importance was obvious. Along with the Departments of Finance and Public Works, it was one of the three ministries specially concerned with the great business of Canadian expansion. Tupper would sponsor the Canadian Pacific railway; Tilley would introduce the new tariff; and western settlement, which was the third of the great trio of national undertakings, would have a spokesman more politically powerful than either of the other two.

On October 19, the Cabinet, now virtually complete, was announced. The new government began to settle down into harness. Macdonald had been so long away from the exasperating routines, the repeated daily annoyances, of office that he had almost forgotten their existence. But now they punctuated his days with a quickly restored irksomeness. A whole host of devoted but unemployed Conservatives hastened to present themselves as candidates for jobs in the Canadian civil service. "Five years opposition have made our friends rather hungry," Macdonald remarked to Dalton McCarthy, "and they are worrying me about office, but the departments have been all crammed by the Grits so that it will be some time before there will be any vacancies."[9] It was usually fairly easy to end the importunities of the office-seekers by a laconic and vaguely sympathetic letter, or by a short and genial interview; but, as Macdonald quickly discovered, there were some desperately immediate problems of government policy which could not be dismissed so easily. Rose, who had retained his position, all during the Mackenzie régime, as Canadian financial agent, wrote over in some haste and with all possible urgency, to remind Macdonald that in a few months' time the Canadian government would have to meet obligations amounting to over three million pounds in London.[10] Obviously there must be new financing. Obviously also a government which had sworn to use its best efforts to alleviate the slump must make a bold and impressive beginning in commercial policy; and here Macdonald gratefully picked up an idea which the Reformers had considered but never carried out. Sir A. T. Galt, who had won a title and a considerable diplomatic reputation as a result of his services in the Fisheries Commission of 1877, would be sent over to negotiate trade treaties with the principal countries of western Europe.[11] Sir Alexander's mission would, Macdonald considered, serve a double purpose. It might widen the scope of Canada's trade. It would serve notice of Canada's intention to take a more active part in the conduct of her own foreign policy.

About the middle of November, the transatlantic migration began. Dufferin said his last farewells and departed. Galt and Tilley set out for Paris, Madrid, and London. It was almost time for Macdonald to leave for Halifax, where the new Governor-General, the Marquess of Lorne, the son of the Duke of Argyll, and his wife, the Princess Louise, were expected to arrive before the end of the month. The appointment of a nobleman whose consort was a princess—the gift of a daughter, if not of a son, of the reigning Queen—was the highest compliment which Great Britain had yet paid to the young Dominion. Dufferin, as soon as he heard of it, had instantly revived his earlier suggestion that Canada should be converted into a vice-royalty;[12] and the new Colonial Secretary, Sir Michael Hicks Beach, making light of the objection that the United States might dislike the title, passed on Dufferin's suggestion with his approval to Lord Beaconsfield.[13] But Canada could no more be made a vice-royalty in 1878 than she could be made a kingdom in 1867; and in each case the fear of outraged republicanism determined the decision. The hopes of a new title were dashed; but the coming of a real princess was a certainty at any rate. At his first interview with Dufferin, Macdonald took up the problem of appropriate etiquette, and promised to have a special railway carriage built for the new exalted tenants of Rideau Hall.

Royal carriages were for royalty. His own accommodation for the journey down to Halifax was comparatively simple. "We are not going to travel to Halifax like princes but like ordinary mortals," he wrote a little tartly to an eager inquirer who was no doubt seeking a place on what he expected to be a particularly luxurious excursion.[14] There would be a Pullman, Macdonald explained, which would probably be inconveniently crowded with officials who had to be present to swear in Lord Lorne. He was tired after weeks of strenuous effort; he badly wanted a little peace on his travels; and he boarded the Intercolonial Railway train with relief—and with some bottles of brandy in his luggage. Tupper, Brydges, Hugh Allan, and an agreeable and entertaining secretary were also on board; and in this congenial company Macdonald started drinking a little too frequently and too much. The arrival at Halifax and the obvious need of putting in a presentable appearance at the Lieutenant-Governor's house, where he was to stay until Lord Lorne's ship arrived, ought to have sobered him up. But these social obligations scarcely appeared to interest him. He kept his room, in cheerful disregard of all Lieutenant-Governor Archibald's carefully arranged hospitality. He kept on drinking, to the embarrassment of the whole household, including the tremulously curious Miss Archibald. The hours—the days—went by. The ship was expected and at last announced. The reception, with all its heightened formalities, was imminent. And at last Miss Archibald, daring to do what her father no doubt considered to be beneath his own and his guest's dignity, went in the greatest agitation and implored the secretary's help. The secretary arrived, knocked boldly at the closed door and entered. Macdonald, pale, haggard, "looking more dead than alive", lay in bed; and the counterpane was strewn with a muddle of books, documents, and newspapers. The secretary stuttered out his important message. The Governor-General's ship, he quavered, was nearly in port and Macdonald must get up and prepare for the reception.

Macdonald raised himself in bed, regarded the secretary with extreme distaste, and pointed with an imperious finger to the door.

"Vamoose," he said, "from this ranch!"

II

He seemed a strange mid-Victorian statesman. Lord Dufferin, in his tactful and sympathetic fashion, had tried to explain his Prime Minister's regrettable spells of "transient weakness" on grounds of overwork, anxiety, and sorrow. Lord Kimberley, the Colonial Secretary, was inclined to be more blunt and matter-of-fact on the subject. Yet even he had confessed that it almost took his breath away to read Dufferin's account of Macdonald's extraordinary behaviour during the last days of the crisis of the Pacific Scandal. "He should have lived," Kimberley declared in amazement, "in the good old times of two bottle men, when one of the duties of the Secretary of the Treasury is said to have been to hold his hat on occasion for the convenience of the First Lord when 'clearing himself' for his speech."[15] The good old times of the "two-bottle men" had not perhaps vanished so completely as Lord Kimberley seemed to suggest. The features, soon to become almost fabulous, of eighteenth-century political

life—the bibulous politicians, the drunken, corruptible elec-
torates, the bribery, intimidation, and open violence—lingered
on, in England as well as in Canada, far into the reign of the
Good Queen. They lingered on; but they lingered rather as
survivals which increasingly required explanation or apology.
A more decorous manner of political behaviour was gaining
in authority. Macdonald accepted the new austerities. But he
had come of age in the florid maturity of an older and more
baroque style. And in the polite, sober, provincial world of
Ottawa or Toronto there were still moments when he looked
oddly out of place.

Where did he belong? Lord Dufferin's comment—"Sir John
is a thorough man of the world"—suggested a cosmopolitan
breadth of knowledge and experience.[16] He was pleasantly
at home in very different kinds of company. He knew and
enjoyed different kinds of climate, mental as well as physical.
He read a lot, roving freely backward in time and outward in
space; and his innumerable stories—which ranged from the
perfectly proper through the marginally respectable to the
definitely scabrous—were not infrequently drawn from far lands
and past ages. He compared Mackenzie with the Mikado,
who enjoyed the prestige, and Blake to the Tycoon who had
the power.[17] During one of the debates on the National Policy,
he told the House cynically that the Canadian manufacturers
who wanted protection reminded him of the Indian squaw
who reflected sagely about whiskey that "a little too much was
just enough".[18] A harsh, native, western taste sharpened some
of his ancedotes; but more often their flavour was agreeably
mature and subtle. He was always culling absurdities from
eighteenth- and early nineteenth-century biographies, journals,
and memoirs. He enjoyed repeating a blunt, teutonic comment of old George II on one of his generals, or a bantering
exchange between Lord Melbourne and Sidney Smith, or a
clever defence by Charles James Fox of the inconveniences
and inefficiencies of the parliamentary system.[19] When he
wanted to illustrate the appropriate form of retaliation against
American commercial selfishness, he made use—rather free use
—of Canning's famous rhyming dispatch to the Hague:[20]

In matters of commerce the fault of the Dutch
Is offering too little and asking too much.
The French are with equal advantage content,
So we clap on Dutch bottoms just 20 per cent.
  (*Chorus*) Twenty per cent, twenty per cent.

(*Chorus of English Customs House Officers and French
  Douaniers*)

  (*English*) We clap on Dutch bottoms just 20 per cent.
  (*French*) Vous frapperez Falck avec 20 per cent.

Lord Kimberley had placed him, with the "two-bottle men",
in the eighteenth century. There were more than a few times
when he seemed to belong most appropriately to the reigns of
George III and George IV, to the age which had closed in
1832 with the passage of the Reform Bill. He had its grace,
its urbanity, its intelligence and reasonableness, its freedom
from sanctimoniousness and cant. "Charming in conversation,
gentlemanlike, with excellent manners, quick apprehension",
he had, according to Lord Dufferin, all the surface character-
istics of the age of good talk and good breeding.[21] He had its
generous liberality of spirit as well. Poor Mackenzie, according
to the retiring Governor-General, had the "narrowness and want
of lofty generosity inherent in a semi-educated man"; but
Macdonald had always been "good-natured, placable, and mag-
nanimous". Macdonald had never taken himself or his affairs
too seriously. In a more solemn age, he still kept something
of the jaunty eighteenth-century assumption that politics were
the affair not of ponderously instructed professionals, but of
gifted amateurs; and his successes were gained, not so much
through study and expert knowledge, as through tact, insight,
and imagination—through what Dufferin called his "great
faculty for managing other people". Here, in contrast with the
manly downrightness and simplicity which the Victorians believed they admired, his methods often seemed devious and
subtle. He could rapidly and expertly disguise his mind in the
intellectual garments of others; and it was suspected that he

adopted, almost as a matter of course, the views of his last caller, merely for the purpose of drawing out the next one. "You are sometimes, I think, oddly credulous," Alexander Campbell declared in a moment of bewildered exasperation, "or you have some arrière pensée which you do not explain —I seldom know which."[22] Yet this affectation of guileless simplicity, this shameless adoption of the mental habits of others, these clever devices of evasion and postponement were not, in the eyes of some of his contemporaries, the most puzzling features of his character. It was not merely—so they thought—a question of his occasional casual deceptions. They knew all about casual deceptions. What they could not be sure of was the fundamental seriousness of his purpose. To these mid-Victorian critics it seemed almost incredible that a man who enjoyed life so obviously, who was so frequently lacking in respectable earnestness, who seemed so ready to give up sober work and quiet repose for mere empty enjoyment, should have a really solid claim to be considered a great national statesman. He seemed to be made so incongruously for the task which he had taken up. He wore the dignity of a Prime Minister much too gaily. Surely it was a mask and he an actor.

At moments—and not only around Reform tea-tables or after family prayers in Liberal households—the dreadful charge of levity was accepted as proved. Macdonald might have been the ghost of a lean, hard-drinking eighteenth-century squire who had imprudently haunted nineteenth-century parliaments so long that he had suffered the penalty of life. Yet he did not seem bewildered or abashed by his new surroundings. If some of the mid-Victorians regarded him as the incongruous relic of an intemperate and disreputable past, he himself seemed to feel completely at home in the world in which he found himself. He got on admirably with his fellow Canadians; he evidently loved the country of his adoption. He had, in fact, a curiously sympathetic, deeply imaginative understanding of Canada and its national requirements—an understanding which seemed oddly at variance with his Regency attitude to the state and his un-Victorian want of earnestness. It was true that he looked with sceptical tolerance upon the imperfections of humanity and the limitations of government. In different circumstances he might have believed merely that the state should keep the peace and protect the frontiers; and to all projects of further governmental intervention he might have said, with Lord Melbourne, "Why can't you leave it alone?" But the circumstances which surrounded him were not those of England in the 1830's. They were the circumstances of Canada in the 1870's. And Canada was a new, huge, undeveloped, yet potentially mighty, country, where little had yet been done, and where so much might be accomplished. The only effort which was valid for his generation was an enormous positive effort on the part of the state. The only task which was relevant for his age was the continental task of nation building.

He had become a nation builder. The federal union of British North America was very largely his creation. In a national government which was as strong as he could make it, he had maintained British parliamentary institutions; and, with the help of British diplomatic and military support, he had sought to extend the territory of the new nation to its final transcontinental limits. Newfoundland alone remained aloof. He still hoped, as he had reminded Sir Stafford Northcote in the previous spring, to make his structural design complete by the addition of Newfoundland. But, apart from the second of the two island provinces, the whole of British North America had now been definitely staked out in a single claim. More, the claim had been formally acknowledged by the United States as well as by Great Britain. And the task which remained was to bind this huge, divided country together with railways, to people its empty spaces with settlers, to diversify and strengthen its simple economy with varied commercial enterprises. This was the work which he had undertaken in 1871, and dropped abruptly in 1873 because of the Pacific Scandal; and now, after five long years, he had picked it up again. It was still unfinished. If anything it had grown more difficult with the passage of time, the worsening of economic circumstances, and the mounting national feeling of frustration and failure.

As he lay in the disordered bed in Lieutenant-Governor
Archibald's house on that day in late November, 1878, the
annoying sounds which had issued from the secretary's lips
reshaped themselves into a coherent and important message.
He must get up—and at once. A new governor was about to
arrive. A new government, of which he was the head, had
taken office; and the whole programme of national integration
and development, which, five years before, he had given up in
a mood of shamed, disgusted finality, was now once more his
responsibility. For many of its details he had only an unin-
structed amateur's competence. He was not by inclination
or training a financier, and he disowned, with cheerful frankness, any particular expertise in commercial matters. Tupper's
lengthy, highly technical, immensely detailed criticisms of
the Liberal government's railway policy were quite beyond him.
He was not interested in the minutiae of the Canadian Pacific
railway; but nobody ever saw more clearly than he the central
significance of the project. "Until this great work is completed,"
he had told Sir Stafford Northcote, "our Dominion is little
more than a 'geographical expression'. We have as much
interest in British Columbia as in Australia, and no more. The
railway once finished, we become one great united country
with a large inter-provincial trade and a common interest."[23]
Once again, the realization of his goal and the consciousness of his purpose grew clear and certain. He got up and
began to dress rapidly. Lord Lorne would be arriving at any
minute. And, in a curious way, the immediacy of the Governor-
General's arrival was like a peremptory reminder of the
urgency of his great task. There was no time to lose. He had
been given one chance and had failed. And then, by luck,
and skill, and untiring effort, he had won the right to a second
try. But it had taken five years to establish his claim; and
now he was nearly sixty-four years old. The second chance
would be the last chance. It had come late. It could not be,
in the nature of things, as good, as favourable a chance as
the first. But it was the last opportunity he would ever get. It
lay waiting for him, and the new Governor-General, with whom,
in his effort to exploit this final opportunity, he would have

to be associated for the next five years, was about to make his appearance and begin their partnership. . . . He gave a few final touches to his necktie, and then, pale but erect and confident, he walked out of the room.

III

The omens seemed auspicious, as the new government and the new Governor-General settled down together in Ottawa. The immediate goals were certainly being attained. Tilley was able to dispose of his loans in London at a briefly favourable opportunity, an exceptionally favourable opportunity, Rose insisted;[24] and Galt, who was about to leave England for trade negotiations with France and Spain, seemed highly pleased with the prospects of his mission. He and Hewitt Bernard, who was to accompany him to Paris and Madrid, had found lodgings in the very London hotel in which the British North American delegates had planned Confederation in 1866. "We are all together in your old rooms at the Westminster," Galt wrote happily. "I accept this as an augury of success."[25] For a while, the augury seemed a true one. The Colonial Office was pleasantly helpful; the Foreign Office was graciously co-operative; and it was not until the eager and hopeful diplomatists reached Paris that Galt began to encounter real difficulties. Lord Lyons, the British Ambassador, who seemed to have been imperfectly instructed by the Foreign Office, met the roving Canadian Commissioner in a cool and unco-operative mood. The usual "conventional courtesies" were withheld. He "has treated me," the hypersensitive Galt raged to Macdonald, "with marked discourtesy".[26]

Macdonald smiled wryly. His old colleague's moods, he was well aware, could hardly be called lasting. And, in fact, within little more than forty-eight hours, Galt's first Parisian impressions had completely altered.[27] Lord Lyons began to be praised for his hospitality and helpfulness; and Galt discovered, to his rueful surprise, that the difficulties of making trade treaties with foreigners were not entirely attributable to the alleged dilatoriness and unconcern of the Foreign Office. The French, it appeared, had a strong bias toward protectionism. The Spaniards were worried about the position of their colonies. It was all going to be very slow and difficult, Galt began to realize; and Macdonald agreed with him. Yet Macdonald had no intention of dropping his plan for taking the initiative in the conduct of Canada's commercial relations. Galt's limited success was an argument, not for the abandonment, but for the continuation, of his mission. Perhaps the temporary appointment should be made permanent. Perhaps—over ten years after Confederation—it was now time for Canada to establish an officer, diplomatic in character and exalted in status, who would reside permanently in London, and busy himself with the promotion of Canadian interests in England and Europe.

These were matters of importance. They would have to be dealt with in the very near future. But undoubtedly the most pressing affair, the affair of the moment, was the tariff which Tilley would have to present in his budget speech. "Incidental protection" had been the main political pledge of the Conservatives, and, in all probability, the main reason for their electoral success. The promise would have to be carried out in the very first session; and late in December, when Tilley at length returned from England, the ministers settled down to the serious consideration of their plan. There were interminable sessions, beginning early in January, with the increasingly exigent representatives of the Manufacturers' Association;[28] and slowly, rate by rate, the complex schedules of the new tariff were built up. Macdonald, on the whole, took little part in these technical discussions. General policy was what interested him. Details were the concern of Tilley's department. And yet, as the details were slowly assembled and fitted together, it became gradually apparent that a certain significant change of emphasis in general policy had occurred.

What was the new tariff to be like? During the election campaign Macdonald had been usually, if not invariably, cautious and moderate in all his statements on fiscal policy. Once, at the height of the contest, he had publicly protested that he had never proposed "an increase but only a readjustment of the tariff".[29] In October, when he had accepted the task of forming a government, he had told Lord Dufferin definitely that his purpose was not protection; and on the way back from Halifax with Lord Lorne, he had insisted that the British press was quite mistaken in its assumption that the Canadian government intended anything but a tariff for revenue.[30] Literally, of course, this protest was quite justified. Revenue was bound to remain a principal object of the Canadian customs duties, for the simple reason that other forms of taxation, including income taxes, were then considered impossible of application in Canada. Money was desperately necessary. The new government had committed itself to the most costly enterprises. It had sworn to carry out the great national projects which Mackenzie and his colleagues had not been able to complete. It could not get along without a substantially larger revenue; and the only "readjustment" of the tariff which would produce the necessary funds was a "readjustment" imposing stiffer duties. The needs of the state dictated the increase; but at the same time the increase largely met the requirements of the manufacturers. The tariff became the means which would enable government and industry to co-operate in the creation of a transcontinental Canadian economy; and as the winter went on, the pressure, both inside and outside Parliament, in favour of higher duties, began to increase. The bias of government policy became clear and emphatic.

This government had, in fact, committed itself to a strongly nationalistic commercial programme.[31] It had rejected British economic theories and copied American fiscal practices in a spirit of independence and competition. The new *ad valorem* rates were fairly high; they were strengthened not infrequently with specific duties which, unlike *ad valorem* rates, would increase protection during a period of falling prices; and the twenty to twenty-five per cent British preference which Macdonald had discussed with Dufferin and Lorne was, for the moment, dropped. It was true that it had been dropped only when the preparation of the tariff was well advanced. Early in January Tilley had requested Lord Lorne to find out whether the British government would have any objection to the proposed preference.[32] But the non-committal British reply and the theoretical British dislike for differential duties of any kind were not the only reasons for the Canadian government's change of plan. The Canadian government was becoming aware of the fact that in Great Britain, as well as in France and Germany, the great depression in agriculture had awakened a new interest in the protection of farming. Both France and Germany were moving towards the imposition of tariffs which would defend their farmers against the importation of cheap American cereals. What if Lord Beaconsfield, the old defender of the Corn Laws, should follow the same course? If duties were imposed on breadstuffs in the United Kingdom, then Canada and Great Britain would be in a position to exchange preferences in their respective markets; and, as Macdonald and the Conservatives had hoped in vain for years, the countries might conclude a mutually beneficial reciprocal trade agreement. It was a tempting prospect. It was all the more tempting since the grant of an unearned preference to Great Britain might provoke retaliation from the United States; and Tilley was frankly frightened of a prohibitory American duty on the import of Canadian lumber.[33] The Canadian government drew back; and early in February, when the Governor-General made a last effort to save the preference, Macdonald and Tilley refused. They were eager to discuss an exchange of tariff concessions with Great Britain. They were prepared, even with no prospect of compensation, to give England every possible advantage through favourable rates on her manufacturing specialties. But a gratuitous British preference was politically dangerous, and for the moment would have to be given up.[34]

On February 13, Parliament opened. It was extremely cold weather, with flawless blue skies and glistening white snow—"royal weather", the newspapers called it, and fit for the Princess who now ruled the household at Rideau Hall.[35] The incoming trains were stuck for hours in snow-drifts; but, despite these interruptions, Ottawa was crowded with people, and for years there had not been so much stir and circumstance at the capital. On opening day, Macdonald drove his own "modest trap" up to the great entrance of the central building; and when, a few days later, he rose to speak in the debate on the address, he was at his best—laconic, easy, and humorous.[36] He could afford to be confident. The new tariff was to be the great measure of the first session; and for the new tariff he thought he could predict a tremendous reception. He had, on his side, a sympathetic governor, a large parliamentary majority, and, in Canada as a whole, an expectant and hopeful electorate. There was only one unknown element in a highly favourable situation. He did not know what England's attitude to the new tariff would be. He was concerned about England's attitude. England was such an immensely important factor in all his plans for the future that he could not afford for a moment to take her views for granted.

He expected, of course, that the British government would express a theoretical disapproval of a protective tariff. But, at the same time, he did not believe that there was the slightest likelihood of British opposition to the new duties. Yet he could not assume acquiescence. He had promised to submit his fiscal proposals to the Colonial Office for approval before introducing them into the Canadian Parliament. He would have to do so. But time was running extremely short. The deputations of manufacturers were still arriving at Ottawa. Tilley, his eyes red and inflamed with his work, was still bending over the complicated schedules. It was not until the very last moment that Lorne was able to dispatch the new tariff to London for imperial examination;[37] and the telegraphic reply was received in Ottawa only forty-eight hours before the time scheduled for Tilley's budget speech. What a characteristic reply it was! In a tone of resigned submission to invincible economic error, Sir Michael Hicks Beach informed Lord Lorne that Her Majesty's government regretted that the general effect of the new tariff appeared to be an increase of duties already high. "They deem however," he went on, "the fiscal policy of Canada to be a matter for decision by the Dominion legislature subject to treaty obligations."[38] It was the inevitable, the only possible, answer. There had been pained disapproval at Whitehall. There would probably be grumbling protests from Birmingham, Manchester, and Glasgow. But Tilley was at work on a detailed memorandum which would show how, through the determination of specific rates, the Canadian government had tried to give British manufacturers a concealed but real advantage over their American rivals.[39] And, once the memorandum was handed in, would not the matter be tactfully permitted to drop?

Macdonald had expected an easy course that session. So far as his own policies were concerned, it was all very plain sailing. But the small, local, utterly gratuitous disturbances of the Letellier affair aroused nearly as much anxiety as a first-class tempest in national politics. The Quebec Conservatives, despite the defeat of the motion of censure in the previous Parliament, continued to nurse the most rabid hatred of the Liberal Lieutenant-Governor of Quebec. Their fanatical determination to have his head, far from being diminished, seemed actually to be increased by the inconvenient constitutional fact that he had secured a premier, Joly, who, in accepting office, had assumed responsibility for the dismissal of de Boucherville and who had so far managed to retain a majority in the provincial legislature. Early in December, J. A. Chapleau wrote to Macdonald, enclosing a protestation against the action of the Lieutenant-Governor and demanding his political execution on the ground that all forty-seven of the Quebec Conservative members of Parliament were heartily in favour of it.[40] Before the month was out a deputation from Quebec arrived in Ottawa to press the same demand orally and with the greatest possible emphasis.[41] It was inevitable now that the matter would be brought up again in the new Parliament; and early in the session Macdonald's motion of censure of the previous year was introduced by Ouimet. On March 13, the night before Tilley's budget speech, it passed the Commons by the crushing majority of one hundred and thirty-six to fifty-one.[42]

What could be done? Macdonald was in a highly uncomfortable position. In his opinion, the Lieutenant-Governor of Quebec had acted in an arbitrary fashion. He told Lord Lorne that he thought Letellier had "behaved as badly as any man could".[43] Moreover, his dislike of this particular Lieutenant-

Governor was not mitigated by an extreme veneration for the office which he held. It was no part of Macdonald's creed to exalt the political consequence of lieutenant-governors. His inclination had always been to look on provinces virtually as subordinate municipal institutions; and nobody was readier than he to emphasize the fact that the lieutenant-governors were responsible "officers of the Dominion". Yet, at the same time, he knew very well that since Confederation the affairs of the provinces had been carried on in accordance with the "well understood principles of responsible government", and that, in a system of responsible government, responsibility for the actions of a lieutenant-governor was borne by his constitutional advisers. He was inclined, for this very good reason, to leave the quarrel between Letellier and his ex-ministers to the judgment of the Quebec legislature and the Quebec electorate. The other English-speaking members of the Cabinet would also have preferred to keep away from something which was not strictly their business. But the French-Canadian ministers, with what Lord Lorne deprecated as "Gallic violence", insistently demanded Letellier's dismissal. Macdonald resisted; but he could not resist indefinitely. He confided privately to the Governor-General that "it was impossible to make Frenchmen understand constitutional government".[44] But he did not propose to make the Letellier affair an occasion for imparting forcible instruction in parliamentary rules to his Quebec colleagues. Towards the end of the month the Cabinet finally decided to advise the dismissal of the Lieutenant-Governor; and on March 29 Macdonald presented their decision to Lord Lorne.[45]

He was not surprised—for he had talked the whole matter over with the Governor-General as early as their train ride up from Halifax—to learn that Lord Lorne was not prepared immediately to act on the Cabinet's advice.[46] The Governor-General was aghast at the vindictive partisanship of the French-Canadian ministers and members. The dismissal of Letellier seemed to him to be at once a repudiation of responsible government and an invasion of provincial autonomy; and he requested Macdonald to give his reasons in writing for advising such an extreme step. There was no doubt, of course —and Lorne knew it—that he would have to yield in the end or run the risk of a constitutional crisis far more serious than that which Letellier had provoked. But Macdonald was not in the least eager to apply the collective pressure of the Cabinet on his unwilling chief. He pondered the matter for a few days; and then on April 2, he returned and suggested that since the Letellier case presented a new problem, for which there were no precedents, in Dominion-provincial relations, it should be referred to the British government for settlement. The Governor-General closed readily with this offer.[47] He did not like the thought of arguing formally with his Prime Minister in documents which would have to be made public; but on the other hand he believed that somebody in authority should read the Canadian government a serious lecture on the constitutional unwisdom of the step it proposed to take. The reference to England seemed a highly convenient device to him; and for somewhat different reasons it appeared equally serviceable to Macdonald. What Macdonald wanted was delay. A delay of a few months, or even of a few weeks, might see the downfall of Joly, the return of the triumphant Conservatives to power in Quebec, and the consequent disappearance of all real reason for the political execution of Letellier. It was a definite possibility—a perhaps too obvious possibility— and the French Canadians were by now too determined, excited, and suspicious to accept postponements readily. They may have smelt a calculated delay in the wind; and they insisted that Langevin be sent over to London to urge the British government to reach a quick decision.[48] Macdonald yielded; Lorne yielded; and Langevin—with J. J. C. Abbott for company —set out.

In the meantime, the interminable debate on the tariff went on. All the conceivably relevant arguments had already been repeatedly rehearsed, on countless occasions, since the great discussions had begun in the winter of 1876. But the relentless talk continued. "Another day of profitless debate on the tariff . . .;" Macdonald reported to Lorne on March 28, a fortnight after Tilley had delivered his budget speech;[49] but nearly another month went by before the House disposed of the resolutions in committee and the bill introducing the new duties was read the first time. Macdonald took little part in these protracted proceedings; and it was not until the comparatively short debate on the third reading of the Bill that he intervened at any length. It was the kind of opportunity that always tempted him. Alexander Mackenzie, as if he too had become bored to tears by the subject, devoted most of his final speech on the tariff to a discussion of constitutional points and economic theories as advanced by such writers as John Stuart Mill and Goldwin Smith. Macdonald made the obvious retort that Goldwin Smith, who had made a stump speech in aid of the Conservatives on the eve of the election of 1878, was a repentant ex-free-trader, who had been converted from his previous doctrinaire Liberalism by the bitter experience of five years of Liberal rule. The memory of those five appalling years, Macdonald insisted, would keep the Canadian people safe in the "abiding city" of Conservatism for a good many lustrums to come. It might be, he went on, that in some distant future, and from some height of lofty impartiality, he would look down and see the position of the parties in the Canadian Parliament reversed. But that spectacle, he concluded, would not be in his time.

Mackenzie was on his feet in a moment. A thin, tight-lipped smile appeared and vanished on his face.

"I would merely remark," he said briefly, "the honorable gentleman does not mean he would look downwards. He would look upward."

The House laughed. But Macdonald would not permit this laugh to be the last.

"I always look up to my honorable friend," he answered urbanely, and the incident closed.[50] That night the Tariff Bill passed its third reading.

He had done what he had promised to do. The first session of the new Parliament ended triumphantly; and, as John Carling assured him privately, he stood at the very pinnacle of his prestige.[51] But the new tariff was only the beginning. The most difficult part of his programme still lay ahead; and, since

CLOSE OF THE PLAY AT OTTAWA.

GRAND TABLEAU.—THE TRIUMPH OF VIRTUE.

there was no time now to waste, he had planned a most strenuous summer. Parliament had authorized renewed negotiations for the construction of the Canadian Pacific railway; the Cabinet had decided to establish an important and permanent Canadian agency in London; and it was arranged that he, and Tilley, and Tupper—the most impressive Canadian delegation to cross the ocean since 1866—were to set out for England late in June to discuss these and other matters with the imperial authorities. Agnes, who was to visit England with her husband, and little Mary, who was to spend the summer at Rivière du Loup in the care of her two devoted servants, left Ottawa for Montreal on the morning of June 26.[52] Macdonald had expected, of course, to sail with his wife. But at the last moment his departure had been postponed because of the imminent dismissal of Letellier. The delay, however, would be for a few days only. He would follow in the next ship. And his mind was filled with pleasant anticipations of his near release from work, when the hard blow fell. Only a few hours after Agnes had said good-bye to him, he was struck down by a terrible attack of cholera—cholera accompanied by agonizing cramps and spasms which reminded him horribly of the pains which nearly ten years ago now had almost ended in his death.[53]

The medical men—Doctors Grant and Tupper—energetically took control. The frightened servants looked after him devotedly; and, through the hot, windless days of early July, he lay in bed in the empty house on Sandy Hill, trying impatiently to get well and worrying about the future. Only two years ago, he remembered, he had been boasting to Lord Dufferin about his good health, and the definite change for the better which had taken place in his constitution. He had relied upon the doctors, and the doctors had been proved wrong. He and they had built far too much upon the temporary well-being which he had enjoyed during the years in opposition. Had he not been well largely because he had been free from responsibility? And how far was this present attack the result of the incessant strain and overwork of the last eight months? The disappearance of the frightening cramps reassured him, and he recovered fairly quickly from the cholera. But his strength did not come back at once. He tried to shake off his weakness, as he tried to forget its ominous significance. Would he ever be able to finish the work he had set himself to do? Surely he ought never to have accepted office. He had come back, against his better judgment, because of an irresistible inner compulsion. He had realized that he alone could do the work that Canada needed at that moment. He had realized that the Canadian people believed that he alone could do it. He had come back; and in eight months he had been struck down with one of his worst attacks. How could he go forward confidently? Yet how could he give up the task? He had not much strength. And equally he had not much time.

IV

He sailed from Quebec on July 26—nearly a month later than he had planned to do;[54] and on Monday, August 4, he was comfortably established at Batt's Hotel, Dover Street, Piccadilly.[55] It was very late in the season. The House was about to prorogue, holidays and shooting beckoned delightfully ahead, and, as John Rose explained regretfully to Agnes, "all the world are flying". In fact, the days before the general exodus were so few that those who wished to show the Macdonalds some hospitality had actually to compete with their invitations. Rose, who expected to leave London in the following week for a pleasant series of visits to Scottish country houses, was quick to arrange a dinner party in his old friend's honour for Thursday, August 7. "It is entirely a scratch affair," he explained, "but the best that could be done at this season."[56] And, in order that he and his wife Charlotte, before their departure for Scotland, might both see something of the Macdonalds, he invited them down to his Surrey house, Loseley Park, for the following weekend. Saturday night could have been happily spent at Loseley. But Saturday night happened to be the night on which the much-engaged Colonial Secretary, Sir Michael Hicks Beach, had also planned to entertain the Canadian Prime Minister.[57] It was his one free evening, he confessed in some embarrassment. He had ventured to invite a few friends in to meet Macdonald; and Lord Beaconsfield would be there. As a matter of fact, Lord Beaconsfield was not there, for, as he explained to Hicks Beach, he had received "a peremptory summons to Osborne" from the Queen.[58] But it was obvious that the Colonial Secretary had done his best under difficulties and

that the Conservative political world would be largely represented at his dinner table. Macdonald made his excuses to
the Roses and dined that night at the Hicks Beach house in
Portman Square.

Already, late in the morning of the same day, he had had
his first long, confidential interview with Sir Michael at the
Colonial Office. He had faced this meeting with real trepidation.
As always in the past, so much depended upon the reception
which his plans might get in England; and this time, as he
knew very well, he had some daring proposals to make. From
what Lord Lorne had told him and from what he had himself
surmised, he knew that he had no excuse for being over-
confident. But still he hoped. For the first time since 1868 he
would have Conservatives, not Liberals, to deal with in Whitehall. His chief, Lord Lorne, had written ahead—to no less a
person than Disraeli—bespeaking a friendly welcome for his
Prime Minister and a sympathetic consideration for the Canadian projects. "Sir John Macdonald," he wrote tactfully, "is
perhaps the last Canadian statesman who entirely looks to
England, and who may be believed to be devoted to imperial
interests—notwithstanding the present tariff which is not in
accordance with recent British doctrine."[59] The present tariff,
Macdonald was quick to explain to the Colonial Secretary,
had been framed entirely to obtain revenue and to stop the
inundation of American imports. Even in its present form,
through "a somewhat complex classification of imports", the
tariff gave discreet but real advantages to British manufacturers; and these advantages could be openly and greatly
extended provided Great Britain were prepared to reciprocate.[60]
An imperial preferential system was, in effect, Macdonald's
first proposal. His second was a request for British financial
aid for the Canadian Pacific railway.[61] The railway, he tried
to impress upon Sir Michael, would for the first time provide a
safe route through British territory to the Pacific and the Far
East. It was essentially a great imperial undertaking, more
deserving of British support than either the construction of
the Intercolonial Railway, or the transfer of the Hudson's Bay
Company's territories had been.

Hicks Beach was interested, and not definitely negative in his responses. But at the same time he was hardly encouraging. Already, in two speeches given early in the spring, Lord Beaconsfield had publicly pronounced against the re-introduction of protection for British agriculture. France and Germany would try to defend their farmers with tariffs; but Great Britain, at this decisive crossroads in the history of her commercial policy, decided to take the other turning. There would be no new Corn Laws; there would therefore be no possibility of imperial preferences for cereals; and an Anglo-Canadian reciprocal trade agreement was really out of the question. An imperial guarantee in aid of a Pacific railway loan was a possible subject for discussion; but a favourable outcome of the discussion, the Colonial Secretary implied, could hardly be expected at the present moment. The Conservative government, he confided to Macdonald, had been terribly harassed recently by obstruction in the Commons; and the unpopularity of the new Canadian tariff in England would certainly be used to the full by the opposition against any government measure in aid of the Dominion. It would be quite impossible to push through a guarantee act before the close of the session, even if the British Cabinet agreed to sponsor one.[62] The whole subject had perhaps better be postponed until after the prorogation— possibly until after the now rapidly approaching general election. Macdonald resignedly accepted the suggestion of delay. He had expected, from what Lord Lorne had told him before he left Canada, that the Colonial Secretary would look unfavourably on his proposal.[63] To press it now would be to court a definite refusal.[64] He preferred to wait and pick the matter up again.

With this—and it was not very much—Macdonald had for the moment to be content. The next morning he travelled down to Guildford, and Rose's country house.[65] Loseley Park was one more proof—if, indeed, one more proof were needed —of how successfully the clever and engaging John Rose had fitted in to the second land of his adoption. It was an old, spacious stone house, built during the decade of the 1560's, at a time when the English Gothic tradition was being rapidly modified in accordance with Renaissance ideas, and when feudal irregularities were yielding place to more restrained lines and stricter symmetries. It had a special historic interest, for it had once belonged to Sir William More, kinsman of Sir Thomas More, Henry VIII's chancellor; and its great hall was beautifully decorated with the carved, inlaid, and painted panels which had been acquired from Henry VIII's fantastic palace of Nonsuch. A fairly large party, including the Galts and Hewitt Bernard, had already assembled at Loseley by the time the late guest arrived. Macdonald would have a good time —he always did on these occasions. But he had another and a more particular reason for welcoming the Roses' week-end invitation. In his long conversation with Sir Michael he had brought up the third project—the project of a Canadian "diplomatic" representative in London—which he had come to England to urge.[66] About this he was terribly in earnest. But at the same time he realized that he could hardly make any definite decision in the matter until he had talked it over thoroughly with John Rose. It was the simplest essential of courtesy and friendliness to inform Rose; and since Rose expected to leave on the following Tuesday for holidays in Scotland he would have to be told at once.

As Macdonald sat in the cool, shadowy library at Loseley, he was unhappily aware that the approaching conversation would be difficult and might be positively painful. Rose was one of his best friends. Rose had for years served the Canadian government well and faithfully as its confidential agent in London. As far back as the autumn of 1869, immediately after he had resigned his post as Canadian Minister of Finance, Rose had been "accredited to Her Majesty's government as a gentleman possessing the confidence of the Canadian government"; and six years later, during the Alexander Mackenzie régime, he had been appointed to the newly created post of Financial Commissioner for the Dominion of Canada.[67] Two governments had employed him and valued his unostentatious services. But if a Canadian "mission" were to be formally established in London, a Scotsman who had become a permanent resident of England could hardly be appointed as

its first head. Indeed, Rose's name had not even been considered, and the Canadian government had selected Galt as its
first choice. Galt, Macdonald knew only too well, was ambitious for himself and sensitive to the rivalry of others. He
would try to extend the boundaries of his diplomatic domain
to the furthest possible limits. But Rose, on the other hand,
had financial connections which Galt could not hope to
acquire in a hurry. Macdonald thought he saw a way of
retaining Rose's services. He was extremely anxious to do
so. And it was, therefore, with an extra measure of circumspection that he approached the subject of the Canadian "Resident Minister" to his old friend.

The next morning, when he took the train back to London,
he felt sure that Rose's acquiescence—regretful, if not exactly
reluctant—could be counted upon.[68] It had been necessary to
be delicately tentative with Rose. With the Colonial Office
he could press his point in a more forceful and outspoken
fashion. What he had to propose was certainly extraordinary.
But, then, Canada itself, in the state to which he had now
brought it, was something utterly unparalleled in British colonial
history. "Canada," as Galt was pointing out in the round,
mouth-filling phrases of his memorandum, "has ceased to occupy the position of an ordinary possession of the Crown. She
exists in the form of a powerful central government, having
already no less than seven subordinate local executive and
legislative systems, soon to be largely augmented by the development of the vast regions lying between Lake Superior and the
Rocky Mountains."[69] Canada had grown immensely in
importance. She was developing her own identity and character.
And the existence of the new tariff was only one proof of the
unquestionable fact that her interests—now essentially different
from those of the United Kingdom—required different promotion and special advocacy. She must have a new and important
representative in London—"Resident Minister" would be an
appropriate title—who could speak with authority on her behalf
to the imperial government, and who could promote her interests
in the chancelleries of Europe.

Macdonald knew what he was about. He realized that his

proposal meant the extension of colonial responsible government into the hitherto unoccupied territory of foreign affairs. He knew, as the Governor-General knew, that this was "the beginning of a difficult question, for Canada will more and more wish to make her own treaty arrangements".[70] He did not wish to break up the diplomatic unity of the Empire. The diplomatic unity of the Empire was still essential to Canada; and he believed, as the Governor-General believed, that it might be possible "to stave off for a very long time to come any wish on the part of Canada for a separate set of representatives in foreign countries". But the existing diplomatic unity could not be maintained unless Canada were satisfied; and Canada would be satisfied only if her interests and her representatives were given the prominence and the consideration which they now desired. "The sooner the Dominion is treated as an auxiliary power rather than as a dependency," Macdonald wrote in an assertive final paragraph to Galt's memorandum, "the sooner will it assume all the responsibilities of the position including the settlement of its contribution to the defence of the Empire whenever and wherever assailed. A precedent may to some extent be found in the position of Hungary with respect to the Empire of Austria." He paused a moment, considered the last sentence thoughtfully, and slowly drew his pen through it. Yet the words remained to suggest the ultimate goal of his thoughts.

Whether that ultimate goal were ever reached or not, there could be no doubt that the nation he was creating now enjoyed a new and vastly enhanced prestige in England. He accepted the civilities and honours that were given to him as, in large measure, a tribute to Canada. But there was one distinction which he could not help regarding, in some degree at least, as a vindication of himself. It was eight long years since Earl de Grey had delicately hinted in Washington that imperial Privy Councillorships might occasionally be bestowed on particularly distinguished colonial public men. It had been eventually decided to make him a member of the imperial Privy Council, as a reward for his services on the Joint High Commission of 1871. But the honour could be conferred only by swearing in the recipient at a meeting of the Council; and it was obviously impossible for Macdonald to come to England before he had fought and won the election of 1872. The award was to be a post-electoral triumph. But fate, unfortunately, disposed of matters rather differently. The sequel of the election of 1872 was not the honour of admission to the imperial Privy Council but the public disgrace of the Pacific Scandal; and as soon as the full, dreadful enormity of the Pacific Scandal began to be appreciated in England, Sir John Macdonald's still ungranted honour became the subject of shocked and per- plexed review. The whole question was, Lord Kimberley admitted to Mr. Gladstone, a "very delicate one";[71] and Mr. Gladstone agreed that it was so. Could the Queen's consent, once granted, be withdrawn? It was hardly possible. But it was even less possible for Her Majesty's government to be put in the equivocal position of seeming to reward corruption. Sir John Macdonald could hardly come over to England now and claim admission to the Privy Council. If, unhappily, he did, his imprudence would give rise to "very unpleasant discussions". He would have to be asked to wait.[72]

Well, he had waited. He had waited for six long years. And now he had come back, his disgrace obliterated in the triumph of a new election, his place in the trust and affection of the Canadian people emphatically re-confirmed, to obtain his re- ward. This time there were no doubts or reservations; there were no hints of delay. On Thursday, August 14, ten days after he had landed in England, he took an early morning train down to Osborne. And at two o'clock in the afternoon, at a meeting which was attended by the Duke of Northumber- land, the Duke of Richmond, the Lord Chancellor, and Mr. Home Secretary Cross, he was formally sworn in as a member of Her Majesty's Privy Council.[73] He had an audience of the Queen; and by evening the new Privy Councillor, who could henceforth prefix the words "Right Honourable" to his name, was back in London and dining with the Scotts, who were connections of Agnes, in Onslow Square.

He was pleased with his new honour—with the fact that it had come, in the end, from a Conservative government. He was gratified by the flattering reception he and Agnes had been given in London. And Agnes, of course, was enchanted by it. "It would amuse you to see how Agnes swells it . . .," he wrote happily to his sister Louisa.[74] They went again and again to the theatre; there were frequent dinner parties; they spent a pleasant week-end at Highclere Castle, as guests of Lord Carnarvon; and both Lord Monck and Lord Dufferin sent hearty invitations, which in the end had to be regretfully declined, to visit their houses in Ireland. It was, as he told his sister, a highly agreeable succession of "civilities"; and its climax came, appropriately enough, in the first days of September, when his time in England was drawing to its close. "Lord Beaconsfield asked me to-day to give you a message . . .," Sir Michael wrote. "He hopes you will go to dine and sleep at Hughenden on Monday next, if that day should suit you."[75] Macdonald was both surprised and delighted. When Disraeli had failed to appear at the Hicks Beach dinner, he had given up hope of meeting him. Beaconsfield was an old man. He had gone off, very soon after the session ended, to rusticate quietly at his country house, Hughenden Manor. But—and it was a new sensation in British Prime Ministers—he still felt a sense of obligation to pay some attention to the "Canadian chief". The Queen regrettably had not invited Macdonald to stay to dinner at Osborne the day he had been made a Privy Councillor; all the great houses in town were shut; the Salisburys were away at Dieppe. "This vexes me," Beaconsfield wrote in embarrassment to Lord Lorne, "as I feel your ministers ought to have been festivaled and banquetted, but what are we to do with guests who will visit London in August?"[76] There was only one thing to do, and he knew it. He invited Macdonald to come to Hughenden and Macdonald delightedly accepted.

Hughenden Manor lay in the Chiltern Hills, close to the market town of High Wycombe. Macdonald travelled down by the late afternoon train on Monday, September 1; and Lord Beaconsfield's carriage was waiting for him at the Great Western Railway station. Hughenden stood on high ground, overlooking its own park, and a small church and

churchyard. Built in the 1780's, with clean lines, sparse ornamentation, and pleasantly spaced sashed windows, it had begun
life as a typical Georgian house, unremarkable in all respects
save one. Its single peculiarity then was that it was built of red
brick with blue headers. But Disraeli was an ardent follower
of the fashionable Gothic revival; and at his orders the property
had been altered, with misplaced ingenuity, to present a spurious
Tudor appearance. Inside was a rather ornate drawing-room
with blue damask hangings and French rococo furniture, and a
small, rather ugly dining-room, where Macdonald dined alone
with Disraeli and his young secretary, Daly. After dinner they
climbed the stairs to the smoking-room, which was a kind of
auxiliary library, on the top floor of the house, and there they
talked until well after midnight.[77]

"He is gentlemanlike, agreeable, and very intelligent; a considerable man . . .," Disraeli wrote of his guest next day in
a letter to Lady Bradford.[78] It was not a bad tribute from
one veteran to another. Macdonald was certainly acquiring a
new reputation and his country a new prestige; and, as the
visit to England drew to its end, he had reason to feel not
entirely dissatisfied with its results. It was true—and he admitted it regretfully—that he had not attained the three objects
he had come to London to seek. The British government obviously considered preferential tariffs an utter impossibility;
and it had postponed consideration of both the railway guarantee
and the resident Canadian minister. Yet, on the other hand,
Tilley had had no difficulty in borrowing another three million
pounds for his immediate requirements; and from the replies
which the Canadians got to their tentative inquiries in the
city, it seemed likely that there would be capital available,
at reasonable rates, to build the Canadian Pacific railway.
London was deep in the despondency of the depression; but,
at the same time, Macdonald was conscious of a new respect
for Canada and a new interest in its future. He carried that
pleasant impression back with him, across the Atlantic, along
with the warm memory of his visit to Lord Beaconsfield; and
on September 23 he was back in his new house, Stadacona
Hall, on Sandy Hill, in Ottawa.[79]

V

Almost immediately it began—the event for which he and so many others had hoped and prayed so hard for five long and terrible years. Times began to improve. The first signs of change were admittedly timid and tentative, and he watched developments anxiously, sceptically. He had waited so long. So much depended upon a real economic recovery that he could not permit himself for a minute to indulge false hopes. And yet, as the long, warm, golden autumn of 1879 drew placidly on, he began at last to concede, even to himself, that the improvement was a miraculous certainty. Everything showed it. The harvest had been bountiful. Prices were going up. The volume of imports slowly declined, while that of exports began to rise steadily upwards. "Trade is recovering wonderfully . . .," Lorne wrote proudly to Hicks Beach.[80] The ministers gloated. And Macdonald knew that the whole future of his government had been dramatically changed. Within a year of his accession to office, his commercial programme had been vindicated by a demonstration as convincing as it was fortuitous. The National Policy was borne away towards success on the swift wheels of an accelerating prosperity. For a time, while this good fortune lasted, he would be able to do almost anything successfully. He might even succeed—it would be the supreme piece of luck—in inducing a commercial company to take over the whole gigantic project of the Canadian Pacific railway.

If only he felt better physically . . . But somehow, despite the agreeable holiday in England, he had not recovered completely from the sharp, sudden attack of the early summer. His strength had not entirely come back; he seemed to tire easily. It was nothing serious, but it kept him depressed, and, at times, suddenly and painfully eager to be free of the cares of office. All autumn he waited, almost impatiently, for the British government's decision on the Canadian proposal for a resident minister in London. He almost persuaded himself that it would be favourable. He was fairly sure that he could count on Beaconsfield's good will. In September, soon after he had left for Canada, Beaconsfield, in a speech at Aylesbury, had spoken at some length and very favourably of Canada. Macdonald was highly delighted to know that the information which he had imparted that night at Hughenden had been used so quickly and so effectively by the British Prime Minister; and he wrote Disraeli a letter of warmly sincere thanks.[81] Surely the British Conservatives had begun a new era in colonial history. Surely they would see the needs of the "auxiliary kingdom" of Canada, and realize that "allied powers" such as Canada and Great Britain really required a "semi-diplomatic" relationship. Yet they seemed to take an incredibly long time to make up their minds. October went by. It was not until nearly the end of November that the Governor-General called in Macdonald, Tupper, and Tilley—the three ministers who had gone to England the previous summer—and laid before them a long dispatch from Sir Michael Hicks Beach.[82]

As he read it, Macdonald could not help feeling a little disappointed. The dispatch was not ungracious in form or negative in substance.[83] It merely exhibited a lack of imaginative understanding of a new and developing situation. Yet it was obvious that the British ministers believed they had gone very far—and had in fact gone quite a long way—to satisfy the Canadian demands. They graciously welcomed the appointment of the new Canadian "representative"; they predicted that his services would be valuable to both Canada and England. But he could not be, they insisted politely, an officer truly diplomatic in character. ". . . His position," Sir Michael's dispatch went on to explain, "would necessarily be more analogous to that of an officer in the Home Service than to that of a minister at a foreign court." His chief business would be to communicate with the Colonial Office on Canadian affairs; and if Canadian interests were found to be involved in any negotiation with a foreign power, it would, of course, rest with the Foreign Secretary to determine in what capacity the representative could best render his assistance. For all these obvious reasons his status could hardly be regarded even as "quasi-diplomatic" in character; and the title "Canadian Commissioner" or "Dominion Commissioner" would describe his position more accurately than the somewhat grandiose designation which the Canadian government had suggested.

To Macdonald the reasoning which lay back of this cautious, well-meaning document was obvious. The British government was frightened of condoning even the semblance of a separate foreign policy in a country for which it still felt politically responsible in the eyes of the world. There remained, as Lord Salisbury indicated emphatically to Lord Lorne, the "solid and palpable fact that if they are attacked England must defend them"; and it followed, as an inevitable corollary of this indefinite liability, "that England must decide what their foreign policy shall be".[84] No body could be more anxious than the British government, Hicks Beach insisted, to know the views of Canada and to consult her interests in every imperial negotiation affecting her. "But," he went on, "the Dominion cannot negotiate independently with foreign powers, and at the same time reap the benefit which she desires in negotiations from being part of the Empire."[85] No direct formal communication could possibly be set up between a colonial government and foreign powers. The foreign powers would certainly not accept it. Neither could the British government.

Macdonald was a little disappointed, but he did not feel that he had suffered any serious defeat. He was simply encountering the inevitable misunderstandings which await the political innovator. It was a question of words as much as of facts; and in letter after letter to his superiors in England, the Governor-General tried to ensure that his ministers' wishes were not misinterpreted. "Among sensible men here," he wrote to the Marquess of Salisbury, "there is no wish to conduct negotiations separately, but only that the interests of what Sir J. Macdonald calls 'this auxiliary kingdom of the British Empire' be pushed as the interests of an integral part of the whole."[86] The last thing that Macdonald desired was a separate foreign policy for Canada. For him the diplomatic unity of the British Empire remained at once a reality and an ideal. But, at the same time, he was convinced that it was only through a recognition of the existing political plurality of the Empire that a real and effective diplomatic unity could henceforth be achieved. The duties which had been transferred from the British government to the Canadian government, the tasks which Canada, as heir to half the continent of North America, had assumed since Confederation, were of such obvious and increasing importance that, as the Canadian Council observed in its formal reply to the Hicks Beach dispatch of November, "their discussion and settlement have become subjects for mutual assent and concert, and thereby have, it is thought, assumed a quasi-diplomatic character. . . ."[87]

The general superintending authority of Great Britain would remain formally undisturbed; but in actual fact, as the Canadian Council pointed out, the imperial government would now be "more correctly defined as representing the United Kingdom than the Empire at large". The diplomatic system of the Empire must be adjusted so as to admit these incontrovertible facts. The foreign policy of the Empire must become a collective enterprise, in which Canada and each of the other great colonial governments would have the influence which its strength and importance required. Canadian interests must from now on be accepted as a major concern of British diplomacy; Canadian representatives must henceforth play an increasingly important part in the conduct of British diplomacy; and the Canadian government, through "constant and confidential communication", must be kept at all times thoroughly informed of all that concerned it in the realm of foreign affairs. "If these essentials, proper backing and equal opportunities be given," Lord Lorne wrote to Salisbury, "we may hope to keep public men here content with the present system."[88]

The Canadian reply to the views of the British government was made at length in the formal report of the Privy Council as well as in the letters and dispatches of the Governor-General. Macdonald was determined that the Canadian case should be fully stated; but he had no intention of getting into an argument over the matter with the British government. The new Canadian representative in London would prove himself by deeds, not words; and there was no point in quarrelling about the importance of his office before it was established.

Having won the main point in the argument by getting his new officer accepted by the British government, Macdonald was quite ready to make concessions. He was even prepared to concede something in respect of the new representative's title —something, but not very much. "Resident Minister" was the title which the Canadian government had first proposed. Because of its obvious implications of diplomatic status, "Resident Minister" was plainly unacceptable to the British government. But, on the other hand, "Dominion representative" or "Canadian representative"—the pale alternatives suggested by the Colonial Office—were completely unsatisfactory to the Canadians. Instead they proposed a new designation, "High Commissioner of Canada in London". The British government considered this suggestion for some time in silence; and then, on the last day of January, 1880, the Colonial Office replied that, unless Canada considered the matter of very great importance, the title "Special Commissioner" might be preferred as more appropriate.[89]

Macdonald would have nothing to do with this last tentative proposal. Galt, he informed Lord Lorne bluntly, was not going to England for any special purpose, "but to represent Canada's interests generally". "Resident Minister" was the best designation on all counts, and since it would have to be conceded some day in any case, why should it not be conceded now? "It seems to me," he wrote tartly to Lord Lorne, "that it is a matter of no importance to the imperial government what title we may give our agent. We might call him 'nuncio' or 'legate a latere gubernatoris' if we pleased. It is, of course, for the imperial government to settle the status of our agent in England, under whatever title he may present himself. Since the title of 'Resident Minister' is objected to, I think we must adhere to that of High Commissioner."[90] They did adhere to it. They suggested, indeed, that the British government might reconsider favourably the designation "Resident Minister". Failing that—their first choice—they announced that they were prepared to accept their own alternative of "High Commissioner for Canada in London". On February 7, one week before the opening of the Canadian Parliament, the Colonial Office telegraphed that "the title of High Commissioner will be recognized under the Great Seal of Canada".[91]

It had come—and much as he wished it. One more point in his programme had been dealt with. Canada was prosperous at home and recognized abroad; and, during the winter months of December and January, while he prepared for the second parliamentary session of a successful government, his thoughts kept turning repeatedly, almost longingly, towards retirement. He did not feel quite right yet. He needed and deserved rest; and since, after a year in office, his government was even more securely established than it had been in October, 1878, he could now—and never more appropriately—step out of office. Tentatively he began to sound out his friends. What did McCarthy, and Galt, and Rose think of his intentions? It was plain, unfortunately, that McCarthy, Galt, and Rose did not take him very seriously. McCarthy, who evidently considered that Macdonald was merely tired and needed a rest, invited him up to Barrie for a few days' holiday.[92] Galt, who had himself undergone a recent and reassuring medical examination, observed philosophically that perhaps, in both their cases, the machinery was getting a little worn down. "As the old saying is, however," he concluded cheerfully, "it is better to wear out than to rust out."[93] Rose, as was his nature, offered perhaps the most consolation. Yet even Rose seemed to regard Macdonald's decision with real if unexpressed incredulity. "I am not surprised," he conceded, "that you long for a rest. Though I am six years behind you, my longings are in the same direction, but worries and responsibilities seem to thicken as one gets older. But you are a *marvel*; and how you have survived and kept up your energies and vigour, in spite of the increasing and arduous cares that have pressed upon you is hardly short of a miracle. I am not half the man that you are, and will be far less so six years hence."[94]

It was complimentary, but, at the same time, slightly exasperating. Everybody seemed to count upon his inextinguishable vitality, to rely upon his indefinite continuance in office. He pushed the matter of his retirement away—but not very far. It lay in the top drawer of his mental cupboard, as he prepared in a leisurely fashion for the new session. Parliament opened on February 12. The House of Commons proceeded onward in its usual unremarkable fashion through its usual unremarkable activities. Galt, who, in his characteristically impatient fashion, had somewhat prematurely made all arrangements to sail for England on March 26, was to be given a farewell dinner in Montreal two days before his departure. Macdonald planned to attend; and the Galt dinner was the only special event to which he was looking forward when he took his place in St. Alban's church on the morning of Sunday, March 21. He never heard the end of the service. Suddenly, with the same mysterious and frightening absence of warning, he slumped forward in weakness. He had to be helped from church.[95] His carriage brought him swiftly back to Stadacona Hall.

The faithful Dr. Grant, hastily summoned, was soothingly reassuring. The attack, in itself, was not serious. The newspapers barely mentioned it. He could return to the House almost immediately and outwardly things would go on for a while much as they had gone on before. Outwardly only. The attack had shaken him terribly. He had survived it, as he had survived others before; but it was one more unmistakable indication of the steady worsening of the general state of his health. He could not go on. He must retire now—while there was still time. Only a few weeks ago, he had been called upon to pay the government's tribute on the sudden death of Luther Holton; and Holton, the senior English-speaking member from Quebec, was almost exactly the same age as himself. As he lay on the sofa, gradually recuperating, that Sunday morning in March, he came to a tremendous decision. He would act now—at once. Within forty-eight hours the ministers were all informed of his decision. Tupper would have to represent him at the Galt dinner, and the next day, March 25, a Cabinet would consider the whole matter of the leadership.

Macpherson's letter reached him before Council met. Macpherson, Minister without Portfolio, who had been ill and was only slowly recuperating, had realized that he could not attend the Cabinet meeting; and he had spent the morning of March 24 setting down in writing his reflections on the astonishing revelation that Macdonald had made to him the night before. The words of Macpherson's letter were emphatic; its tone was one of deepest concern. "The step you said you meditated taking," he wrote, "seems to me to be fraught with such grave consequences to the Conservative party and the country that I will not allow myself to believe in its possibility. The consternation it would cause in Parliament and throughout the Dominion in the Conservative ranks would equal that which reigned at St. Petersburg on the occasion of the explosion in the Winter Palace."[96] At the moment, Macpherson insisted impressively, Macdonald's retirement was quite literally unthinkable. His work could be lightened. The Conservative majority was surely big enough to give him all the help he required. But he could not retire during the session. He ought not to think of retiring for years to come.

The next day Macdonald met the Cabinet. It was a company of Macphersons. The other ministers repeated Macpherson's words; they echoed his tone of incredulity and consternation. And, as he looked at their appalled and beseeching faces, Macdonald realized that he would have to give in. His impulsive decision to retire at once—a product of weakness and apprehension—was already losing the original force of its conviction. How could he possibly retire in the middle of the session? The bill establishing the High Commissioner of Canada in London had not yet passed the House of Commons. In England a general election was to take place within a week, and the possible return of Gladstone and the Liberals to office might complicate and embarrass Galt's assumption of his new duties. Galt—the sensitive and unpredictable Galt—would require watchful coaching for weeks. His labours had not yet been successfully started. Things were never really finished and done with. There was so much of Macdonald's programme that had not been completed. And above all there was the Pacific railway.

The railway was the one absolute essential for the Canada he hoped to build. The railway would be the means of peopling the western prairies and promoting eastern industry. It would ensure both national integration and national development.

It was the track of the future—the track of destiny. It had beaten him once. It had plunged him and his party into the worst disaster of their joint career. And the triumphant completion of the railway was something which he owed alike to each member of that indivisible trinity—Canada, the Conservative party, and himself. Now the whole country was quickening with renewed prosperity and reviving confidence. Now the chance of success was greater than it ever had been. How could he give it up?

Chapter Nine

Contract for Steel

I

It was at this point that George Stephen re-entered his affairs. He had, of course, known George Stephen before. He had known George Stephen for the sufficient reason that he knew everybody of any real importance in the business world of Canada. And George Stephen was undeniably important. Since 1850, when, a young man not yet twenty-one, he had arrived in Canada from Scotland, Stephen had certainly enjoyed an impressively solid and impressively swift success. Beginning modestly as a junior partner in a Montreal importing house, he had gradually developed a substantial interest in a variety of Canadian manufactures—textiles, steel, and railway rolling-stock; and in 1876—it was the highest distinction which the business community of Canada could award—he had been made president of the Bank of Montreal. He was a tall, thin man, with a long oval head, sunk slightly forward on his chest, a pair of deep-set, brooding eyes, and a thick beard and drooping moustaches which seemed to emphasize his melancholic and watchful air of reflection. Nobody could doubt his financial sobriety and wisdom; he would not otherwise have been made president of the Bank of Montreal. But at the same time his prestige was not founded solely on a sober record of prudence, probity, and hard work. There was about him an air of distinction which was apparent not only in externals—he was a bit of a dandy and had for some time employed a valet—but also inwardly in the imaginative daring and originality of his mind. He trusted to his first illuminating impressions; he relied upon his insights. He had courage, resolution, and unflagging enterprise. He had a sense of the present and an eye for the future.[1]

The departure of John Rose had left a gap in the circle of Macdonald's mercantile friendships; but George Stephen was not destined immediately to fill it. Macdonald got to know him well, though not with any affectionate intimacy; and their acquaintanceship, an agreeable and intellectually stimulating association, continued uneventfully until it began to be affected, in various curious ways, by still another relationship, a close, family relationship, of Stephen's. Donald A. Smith, the Hudson's Bay Company officer who had gone up to Red River in 1869 as the representative of the Canadian government, and who in 1873 had abandoned Macdonald at the final crisis of the Pacific Scandal, was a first cousin of George Stephen. The family connection, as always in Scottish households, was strong; but it was not the only tie which drew Smith and Stephen together. They became good friends, and close business associates. They prospered together—and not unequally. The knowledge and experience of the one complemented those of the other. Stephen's main interests lay in the St. Lawrence valley; Smith's beyond Lake Superior. And it was Smith who performed the crucially important office of awakening Stephen's interest both in railways and in the north-west.

The chain of events was so natural as to seem inevitable. Donald Smith, who was frequently obliged to make the long journey from Montreal to Winnipeg on Hudson's Bay Company business, acquired a deepening interest in the problem of communications between eastern Canada and the Canadian north-west. Some day, perhaps, in some dim future, a great Canadian Pacific railway would provide a transcontinental all-Canadian system of transport. But that stupendous project had been postponed—how long?—by the Pacific Scandal and the depression. Must the Canadian west wait until more favourable circumstances permitted the revival of the great scheme? Or was there another and a much simpler way of providing at least provisional communication with the settlements on the

Red and Saskatchewan Rivers? Smith was firmly convinced
that there was. The materials for such a provisional system
were either already in existence or soon would be. The Mackenzie government was building a branch of the future Canadian Pacific from Winnipeg south to Pembina at the international boundary. An American railway, with the ambitious
title of the St. Paul and Pacific Railroad, was feeling its way
slowly and with difficulty northwards towards Canada. The
St. Paul and Pacific, like its great rival, the Northern Pacific,
and like the Canadian Pacific itself, had passed through a
series of involved financial calamities during the years of the
depression. Would it not be possible, Donald Smith reasoned,
to get control of it at a bargain, to persuade the Canadian
government to lease running rights over the Winnipeg-Pembina branch, and thus to complete railway communication—
though admittedly through American territory—between eastern
and western Canada?

This was the proposal which Smith persuasively presented
to Stephen; and Stephen, after a journey out to St. Paul and
a trial run over the lines of the St. Paul and Pacific, eventually
decided to join his cousin in the enterprise. He had begun his
apprenticeship in the financing and management of western
railways at a most favourable opportunity and with the most
suitable associates. Donald Smith knew the west as well as
any Canadian then living. James J. Hill, a Canadian by birth,
and his partner, N. W. Kittson, who both became members of
the new syndicate, had already had a great deal of experience
in north-west transport; and Richard B. Angus, the first general
manager of the organization, had acted for years in the same
capacity in the Bank of Montreal. It was a tight, efficient
combination of practical experience and financial power; and
in the next few years it swept forward, in an easy and assured
fashion, towards success. The St. Paul and Pacific Railroad
was acquired, renamed, with a more precise indication of its
real purpose, the St. Paul, Minneapolis, and Manitoba Railway,
and pushed rapidly northward towards the Canadian border.
In the meantime, the promoters, with Donald Smith acting the
part of an enthusiastic and highly imprudent advocate in the

Canadian House of Commons, proceeded to negotiate with the Mackenzie government for the lease of the Winnipeg-Pembina branch.[2]

It was at this moment that Macdonald had intervened. He had the best of reasons, political and personal, for attacking the Pembina lease. The Pembina lease was a vulnerable feature of the railway policy of the Mackenzie government; and ever since the catastrophe of the Pacific Scandal, he had cordially acknowledged Donald Smith as his enemy. On the last scandalous day of the session of 1878, he and Tupper had leaped, with avenging fury, upon the Pembina lease and its defiant parliamentary defender. At the moment it was beyond their power, of course, to prevent the Mackenzie government from transferring the branch to the control of the St. Paul, Minneapolis, and Manitoba Railway. But that autumn the Mackenzie government went out of power; and Macdonald and the Conservatives were presented with an opportunity of wreaking an appropriate revenge on Donald Smith and his friends. They did exactly what might have been expected of them. They got authority from Parliament to effect a change of plan. They dispensed with the assistance of the St. Paul, Minneapolis, and Manitoba Railway and made other interim arrangements for the running of the Pembina branch.

Curiously enough, this seemed to end the whole episode. Macdonald's anger was apparently appeased. Yet, at the same time, the fortunes of Stephen, Smith, and Hill did not seem to have been adversely affected. What remained, after all the quarrelling over the Pembina branch had died away, was a growing awareness among Canadians of the opening of a new and extremely exciting chapter in the history of their own north-west. Early in December, 1878, the first train pulled out from St. Boniface, across the river from Winnipeg, for St. Paul. In retrospect, it must have seemed the train which carried the whole project of western development up the shining tracks of prosperity to success. Since then settlement had advanced on both sides of the international boundary; both divisions of the new railway system had prospered; and in the spring of 1880, after Stephen's company had been in operation under

its new name for only a little less than a year, it triumphantly
published a first annual report, which disclosed a considerable
profit, not only from railway traffic, but also from sales of land.
Stephen, who only a few years before had been as ignorant of
the west as he was uninterested in railways, stood suddenly
revealed, in the eyes of interested North Americans, as a tried
and successful veteran of western transport. With the help of
a land grant from the Minnesota legislature and a prudent
reduction of the fixed charges borne by his reorganized company,
he had driven a railway across the prairie and into the heart of
the north-west. He had opened a whole empire for settlement.
Exactly the same kind of effort—enormously, portentously magnified—must be made in the Canadian north-west, if ever the
hopes of the Fathers of Confederation were to be realized. Had
not Stephen shown that he was capable of it? Inevitably
Stephen became the focus of the long-locked-up hopes and
aspirations of those who were concerned in the project of the
Canadian Pacific railway. A new future seemed to open up
before him, and he began to realize his destiny. So also did
Macdonald.

II

In the spring of 1880, Macdonald stood at a significant
middle point in his new lease of power. It was getting on for
two years since the election of 1878. It would be a good two
years more, at least, before he would have to submit his record
to the verdict of the Canadian people. He had not done too
badly. A good part of his programme was now complete. The
return of prosperity, about which even the most confirmed
cavillers could hardly express a doubt any longer, had confirmed
and generalized the complacent feeling of satisfaction throughout Canada; and abroad, in Great Britain and the United
States, the two countries which counted most in the external
affairs of Canada, conditions, though not so reassuring as at
home, were certainly not serious enough to cause any real
alarm.

It was true that the recent general election in England had brought Gladstone back for the second time to power, and that the approaching presidential contest in the United States had once again encouraged Republicans and Democrats to display their rival prowess in the heroic republican exercise of twisting the British lion's tail. The American government and the American Congress were in their usual state of pre-election belligerency. There had been a protest about the movement of a group of western Indians across the international boundary. A loud complaint had been made over the seizure of an American fishing vessel in Fortune Bay off Newfoundland; and it had been announced that the Bulwer-Clayton Treaty of 1850, by which Great Britain and the United States had formally agreed to a joint control of the future Panama Canal, could no longer be regarded as compatible with the oracular injunctions of the Monroe Doctrine. Macdonald refused to be alarmed by this intimidating series of demonstrations. "I have seen many presidential elections in the United States," he explained resignedly to Lord Lorne, "and at every one of them the rival parties tried to excel each other in patriotism, and that patriotism always consisted of attempts to bully England. Hence just now the angry discussion of the Fortune Bay affair, the proposed abrogation of the Bulwer-Clayton Treaty, the threatened cancellation of the fishery clauses in the Washington Treaty, and this discussion about Sitting Bull and his Sioux. All that England has to do is to play with these questions till the new election comes off and then all will be quiet until the spring of 1884 when these, or other subjects which will answer the same purpose, will be revived."[3]

England was more important. In this second, western phase of Macdonald's programme of national expansion, the attitudes of the British government and of British finance counted enormously: the view which the great mass of the British people took of Canada as a home for emigrants might make or mar the whole great scheme of western settlement. For the next few years or decades, the High Commissioner of Canada in London had a rôle of great significance to play. That was why the office had been established at that particular moment, and why Galt had hastened over to England. Macdonald took the intellectual abilities of his new High Commissioner very seriously; but Galt's personality never ceased to afford him entertainment. "Some touches of character will amuse you—if they don't bore you," he wrote jocularly to Lord Lorne, enclosing a great sheaf of Galt's letters from London.[4] Galt was always writing letters. He was the highly articulate romantic who is constantly pouring forth his soul on paper. From the moment he landed in England, he had experienced the most intoxicating succession of hopes, doubts, slights, encouragements, anxieties, and mental excitements generally. He worried about his house, his family, his expenses, his "status" in the "corps diplomatique", and the delicate problems of his introduction into the society of official London. He was appalled to discover that his present spouse, being his deceased wife's sister, could be presented at Court only with the special permission of the Queen. With remarkable precipitancy he came to the conclusion that the new Gladstone government was coldly antagonistic to the Canadian High Commissionership and that the Colonial Secretary and his whole department would do nothing whatever to enhance the importance of his office.[5]

Macdonald always placed a heavy discount on Galt's copiously temperamental effusions. Galt, he explained dryly to the Governor-General, was inclined to be a little "fidgety". "His letters show how impulsive he is," he went on. "Lord Kimberley is not celebrated for cordiality of manner and Galt jumped at once to the conclusion that the government were unfriendly. He is, I suppose, reassured by Mr. Gladstone's remark that he was glad Canada had taken the step of creating the office. That awkward business of Lady Galt's presentation has ended happily."[6] It had ended in the Queen's reaching the grave conclusion that since Galt's second marriage had been contracted in the United States, where marriages with a deceased wife's sister were unaccountably legal, Lady Galt's case might therefore be regarded as an exception from the general rule; and Lady Galt herself might be received at a royal Drawing-Room. Many—if not most—of Galt's problems were either solved or forgotten in the short interval which

elapsed before their victim took up his busy pen to write
again. Macdonald could afford to treat these small chronic
alarms and despondencies rather cavalierly. But there were
other disappointments, closely related to the principal objects of
the High Commissioner's office, which aroused his serious concern. "Most unsatisfactory interview with Colonial Minister
respecting emigration," Galt cabled on June 7. "He holds out
no expectation of assistance. . . ."[7] Here was an important and
disconcerting check. Galt's prime function in England was
to arouse the interest of the British people in the Canadian
north-west, and enlist the assistance of the British government
in its settlement. "The most important subject which can
engage the attention of the High Commissioner in England,"
Galt's instructions declared emphatically, "is the development
of the North-West Territory."[8]

The development of the North-West Territories had become
Macdonald's main concern. For a Prime Minister whose programme was national expansion on a continental scale, the
settlement of Canada's prairie empire stood out obviously as the
great remaining task. The preliminary work had all been done.
The aboriginal title to the land had been extinguished, and
the Indians—or most of them—had been settled on the reserves.
The claims of the *métis* to a secondary aboriginal title, and
their demand for its extinguishment by special additional grants
of land or scrip had been the subject, during the winter of 1879,
of prolonged inquiry and consideration.[9] All the western
authorities who were consulted had pronounced firmly against
the policy, which had been tried out with such very mixed
results under the Manitoba Act, of making a general grant of
negotiable scrip. In the old days when the west was free, the
métis had been able to fend for themselves very well. But they
were bewildered by the approach of North American civilization
and vulnerable to its devices; and, according to experienced
westerners, a grant of negotiable paper would merely make them
easy marks for the land speculators without bringing them any
permanent benefit. The negative testimony was impressively
unanimous. But there was no comparable agreement among
the experts as to the positive policy which the Dominion should

adopt; and the small but naggingly insoluble problem of the satisfaction of the half-breeds' claims remained.

It was one of the few—the very few—complications, Macdonald could proudly boast, which troubled Canada's management and disposal of the quarter-continent which had fallen to it with the cession of the Hudson's Bay Company's territories. Whereas a good part of American expansion towards the Pacific had been piecemeal, unplanned, and haphazard, Canada was fortunately in a position to organize and prepare in advance for almost the entire process of settlement. A system of free homestead farms, comparable to that of the United States, but with somewhat easier terms and conditions, had been adopted as the staple of the federal land policy in the west; and a great, single, uniform survey for the entire region, based accurately upon the astronomical system, was being pushed forward efficiently but at headlong speed.[10] The land was ready—or nearly ready—for occupation. It needed settlers to people it and transport to get them there. The Canadian government had spent, and was prepared to go on spending, lavish amounts on immigration propaganda. Galt himself was the visible embodiment of a great new effort to capture the imagination of Great Britain and Europe for Canada and Canada's unoccupied west. Immigrants were vitally necessary. But immigrants would be helpless without transport for themselves, their effects, and their future produce. At the moment Winnipeg was the furthest outpost of the communication system. It could not be permitted to remain so. The immigrants must be carried westward to the valleys of the Saskatchewan. And for that last advance there was only one possible vehicle—the Canadian Pacific railway.

Here again Macdonald's luck held. For seven long years, despite all the lavish inducements which his and Mackenzie's governments had held out, no capitalists worthy of consideration had come forward to claim the privilege of building the Canadian Pacific railway. He had almost reached the gloomy conclusion that, even though the depression had lifted, there would never again be any offers. And then, just when the need had become really imperative, when the delay had been stretched out until it could be stretched no longer, the offers began. They were tentative, exploratory offers—in some cases mere suggestions or whispers of offers; but all during that happy June of 1880 they kept stealing in. Galt reported that the shareholders of the old Canada Company were showing a curious interest in the Pacific railway project; it was rumoured that Brassey, the fabulously successful English railway contractor, had been making inquiries; and on June 22, when the Canadian Cabinet was actually in session considering the subject, Macdonald received a telegram from a certain Lord Dunmore, announcing that he had just arrived in New York from England and was hastening up to Ottawa with an offer to build the railway.[11] After the long neglect and discouragement of the past, this sudden respectful attention was highly gratifying. Moreover, these hints and promises of British offers were not all. There was still another proposal—which had originated in Canada. It was presented by Duncan McIntyre, who now controlled the Canada Central Railway, a railway which had been planned to run from Ottawa to Lake Nipissing, and which would thus provide a vitally important link in extending the future Canadian Pacific eastward to the head of navigation at Montreal.[12] Duncan McIntyre was the principal in the conduct of the negotiations; but, as everybody knew, back of him were the directors of the St. Paul, Minneapolis, and Manitoba Railway. Back of him, and towering above all the others, was George Stephen.

It was the most important single decision of the second half of Macdonald's career. He had chosen wrongly the first time—he had chosen Hugh Allan; and total disaster had been the result. He had won the right to a second choice. It was upon him now; and this time there must be no mistake. He must not try to hurry. Every consideration must be weighed, every aspect of the problem must be thoroughly investigated; and he himself would reserve judgment until the end. He baffled his colleagues, through long days of Cabinet discussions, by his bland impartiality. He found virtues in every offer; his references to that amiable, aristocratic figure-head, Lord Dunmore, were gravely respectful. "You spoke of Lord

Dunmore," Campbell wrote, a bewildered and accusing note in his words, "as if his name added weight, great weight, to the proposal made by him and Mr. Brown, whereas it seemed to me just the sort of thing men of business and of means would not resort to, and tricksters and stock-riggers would—I mean to put forward a nobleman. And besides that he is, if I rightly understand it, a spendthrift and most probably a dupe of some knaves or other."[13]

It was all, or most of it, true, Macdonald reflected. Lord Lorne was warning him very impressively that Dunmore was a notorious speculator with "a very good heart, no head, and no money".[14] The firm which sought to impress gullible colonials with such an emissary was obviously suspect. But was Puleston, Brown, and Company, the company which Dunmore represented, to be dismissed solely on that account? Nobody in Ottawa, Macdonald discovered, could tell him anything of importance about Puleston, Brown, and Company; and this lack of significant information was another serious element of uncertainty in a foggy and treacherous situation. The hints of further British offers persisted; and now it was rumoured that Andrew Onderdonk, the contractor for the government-built section of the Canadian Pacific in British Columbia, was about to tender still another proposal.[15] Everybody was aware of Stephen's experience, immense ability, and great financial strength; and at least a few members of the Cabinet were in favour of coming to terms with his syndicate at once. But McIntyre and Stephen demanded a cash subsidy of twenty-six and a half million dollars and a land grant of thirty-five million acres. Was it possible to accept such an offer at this stage of the negotiations? Could a decision be reached while other proposals remained unexplored?

Macdonald realized that it would be highly dangerous to decide at once. The maximum terms which could be offered, the Cabinet decided, were a cash subsidy of twenty million dollars and a land grant of thirty million acres.[16] Macdonald did not believe that he could risk a subsidy of more than twenty millions. Yet McIntyre and Stephen inflexibly refused to consider anything less than the sum which they had demanded. It was a stalemate which neither side dared immediately to break; and on July 5, McIntyre wrote to Macdonald, informing him that it was the wish of his syndicate "that the subject may be considered as being closed for the present".[17] *For the present.* The words were significant. A phase of the negotiations had certainly been terminated. But it was the first phase only. Already the Cabinet had decided that the negotiations would be suspended only to be renewed in England;[18] and a committee, consisting of Macdonald, Tupper, and John Henry Pope, had been appointed to proceed to London and to examine the various offers in greater detail there. Macdonald planned to leave within a week, on July 10. He knew that Duncan McIntyre was sailing on the same day, and on the same ship; and when he left Quebec he carried with him a reassuring message from George Stephen. "Although I am off the notion of the thing now," Stephen confided to him, "should anything occur on the other side to induce you to think that taking all things into consideration our proposal is better upon the whole for the country than any offer you get in England, I might, on hearing from you, renew it and possibly in doing so reduce the land grant to some extent."[19]

Macdonald reached London and the Westminster Palace Hotel on July 19.[20] Agnes had not accompanied him; she had stayed behind at Rivière du Loup with Mary; and the journey which he had undertaken was severely, peremptorily, practical in its nature. There were few theatres and concerts; there were still fewer public dinners, and agreeable, lazy week-ends at country houses. He had come to negotiate a contract for the Pacific railway, not to renew his previous siege of the Colonial Office; and the only event of any political importance in his visit was his appearance before the Royal Commission on the Defence of British Possessions and Commerce abroad. This Commission had been established largely as a result of the Russian scare of 1878, and one of its principal objects was to investigate the division of imperial and colonial responsibilities in defence. Macdonald's evidence was cautious, and non-committal in character. With the Russian crisis safely over, and with the prospect of an enormously costly railway contract immediately before him, he knew that, at the moment, he could not run the risk of making heavy military commitments. He had not yet felt it possible to carry out the plan he had formed in 1878 of increasing the small nucleus of the Canadian permanent force; and although he had often talked in the past of an "alliance" between the "central power" and the "auxiliary kingdom" of Canada, he did not fall in with the Commissioners' evident desire to define more exactly the reciprocal obligations of the colony and the Mother Country. In his view, there already existed a moral engagement for defence between England and Canada. The pledges which had been exchanged during the conference of 1865 and the arrangements which had been made in 1871 when the imperial troops were withdrawn from Canada, constituted, as he saw it, an informal treaty for the defence of British North America. He did not believe that these commitments could be safely extended or generalized at that particular moment. It would surely be extremely unwise, in a period of peace, to raise the question of Canada's possible contribution to a hypothetical European war in which Great Britain might be engaged. That discussion, he told the Commissioners firmly, had much better be postponed until the conflict had come or was imminent.[21]

This interview was the only important interruption in his negotiations for the railway. He stuck closely, pertinaciously, to the mission which had brought him to England. He had, as he told his sister Louisa, allowed himself six weeks', or two months', absence from Canada, in which to settle the business. Time was of the essence. He hunted up John Rose, got in touch with Sir Michael Hicks Beach, the ex-Colonial Secretary, whose opinion he had come to value highly; and on the Friday of his first week in London he had a long talk with Sir Henry Tyler, president of the Grand Trunk Railway Company.[22] It was mere prudence to give the Grand Trunk one last opportunity to consider the project; but it was plain at once, if there had been any doubt about the matter, that the Grand Trunk was not, and could not be, seriously interested. So long as the old railway held to the strategy on which it had originally been planned, the natural extension of its lines

was from Sarnia to Chicago and so westward south of the
Upper Lakes. "I have no belief myself in any line of railway
running to Fort Garry for a long time to come through British
territory," Brydges, the general manager of the Grand Trunk,
had written in 1872, at the time of the contest between Allan
and Macpherson for the first Pacific railway charter.²³ Eight
years later, as Macdonald sat in Sir Henry Tyler's office, it was
plain that a railway running north of Lake Superior was just
as inconceivable to Grand Trunk officialdom as it had been
eight years before. In effect this settled the matter. Macdonald
was prepared to compromise about many things. But he had
no intention of making the slightest compromise about the
route of the Canadian Pacific railway. The Canadian Pacific
was to be a national railway. It must run—every inch of it—
through Canadian territory.

The Grand Trunk Railway dropped out. The Onderdonk
group decided that it could not compete in the short time
available.²⁴ The other offers, of which there had been so many
rumours, failed to materialize. It was—or seemed to be—a
straight contest between Puleston, Brown and Company on the
one hand, and McIntyre and his associates on the other. And
Puleston, Brown and Company, which had seemed such a
dubious organization in Ottawa, certainly took on weight and
stature in London. Lord Dunmore, the agreeable and impecunious peer, faded discreetly into the background; and J. A.
Puleston, who appeared to be a much more substantial and
influential person, energetically took command of the negotiations for his company. On the very day of Macdonald's arrival
in London, he carried the Canadian visitor off to the Speaker's
gallery in the House of Commons and kept introducing him to
what seemed quantities of highly important friends. He was
reputed to have vast, if somewhat mysteriously undefined, backing in the City. He could apparently rely upon the support of
certain influential European bankers—Baron Erlanger, M.
Demère of the Société Générale, and the Reinachs of Paris and
Frankfort—whose names gave to his syndicate an air of truly
continental distinction. His scheme was admittedly somewhat
complicated; but it had features which were extremely attrac-

tive politically. In place of the cash subsidy which he had
at first requested, and which was considerably smaller than
that asked by McIntyre and Stephen, Puleston finally agreed
to substitute a government guarantee, for a term of years, of
the interest on the very large bond issue which he proposed to
float. It was attractive—it was undeniably attractive; and on
one of the last days of August, Macdonald tentatively drafted
a significant cable to Tilley. "Almost agreed," he wrote, "with
Société Générale of Paris, equal in standing to London and
Westminster Bank, at nineteen millions cash, thirty-two millions
land. Instead of cash may agree to equivalent guarantee of
interest for term of years not exceeding twenty. Deposit of one
million sterling as forfeit. Do Council concur? Answer quick."[25]

Yet, at the last moment, he hesitated. The cable was apparently not sent. Only a few days later, on September 2, Puleston
reported that the Société Générale had decided not to go ahead
with the venture;[26] and this refusal, as he himself recognized,
brought his scheme as a whole to an end. Had Macdonald
ever really seriously considered Puleston as the principal promoter of the national transcontinental railway? There were
those in the City who doubted it. "In plain English," one of
Puleston's supporters wrote angrily to Macdonald, "it has been
said that it was a foregone conclusion from the beginning that
a certain set of people should get the business and that Puleston
could not under any circumstances have got it, and much more
of a stronger character."[27] It may all—or most of it—have been
true. Certainly Puleston was not essential as a principal. His
backers were more important than he was; and, as the event
proved, they could be got without him.

But there was more than this. Puleston was an ordinary promoter. Stephen was a man of exceptional ability who had just
achieved a ringing success in the very kind of enterprise which
was at stake. He had, moreover, identified himself very closely
with the land of his adoption; and Macdonald wanted a truly
Canadian leader. The negotiations with Puleston may have been
at least half serious; but early in August Macdonald and his
colleagues recommenced their long discussions with McIntyre,
and on August 12 the Stephen-McIntyre syndicate offered to

build the railway for a cash subsidy of twenty-five million dollars and a land grant of twenty-five million acres.[28] As August drew towards its close, and Puleston was finally eliminated, Macdonald came rapidly nearer to an agreement with the Canadians; and on the morning of Friday, September 4, he sat down with McIntyre and the two Roses—John and his son Charles—to settle the provisional terms of the contract.[29] That afternoon the cable which he had come to England to send and for which all his colleagues in Ottawa had been waiting, was finally dispatched. "Best terms can be got," it read, "are twenty-five million cash, twenty-five million acres. . . . Four colleagues here concur. Hope you concur. Absolute secrecy. Answer quick. Telegraph Tilley. Sail next Thursday."[30]

III

It was done. And despite the long, grinding labour of the summer and the awful sense of his responsibility, he felt positively elated by his achievement. "I had a very pleasant trip to England and back," he reported laconically to his sister, "but was obliged to work very hard. I have been rewarded by success. And am in good health and spirits."[31] Everybody seemed to be in good spirits. There were no second thoughts, or regrets, among any of the principals involved. George Stephen wrote him, warmly welcoming him back, and assuring him that he thought there would be no difficulty whatever in coming to a final agreement on all points. "I want whatever arrangement is made," he wrote, "that it shall be *fair, creditable* to both the government and ourselves, and that not a *day* should be lost in the preparation of the contract and the act of incorporation."[32] The preliminary agreement had been signed before the delegation left England. Only a little more than a month later, on October 21, at Ottawa, Tupper, Stephen, and a few of the other principals affixed their signatures to the greatest contract in the history of Canadian transportation.

Stephen, who was to be the railway's first president, stood out from the start as the recognized leader of the syndicate.

Duncan McIntyre, who had been so prominent in the preliminary negotiations, was to be the first vice-president, and Richard B. Angus the first general manager. The other directors of the St. Paul, Minneapolis, and Manitoba Railway, Hill, Kittson and Donald A. Smith, were all important members of the new syndicate, though Smith's name, for obvious political reasons, was prudently omitted from the contract—an omission which unexpectedly infuriated the temperamental Smith and caused him to behave, so Stephen wrote disgustedly, "like a baby over the thing". The only London financial house which entered the syndicate was Sir John Rose's firm, Morton, Rose and Company. New York was represented by Morton, Bliss and Company, which was the senior of the two Morton firms, and by John S. Kennedy and Company, the organization which had been so deeply concerned in the financing of the St. Paul, Minneapolis, and Manitoba Railway. From Europe came a French-German group, headed by Kohn, Reinach and Company of Frankfort and Paris, and including the French Société Générale. Their stake in the affair was small; but Macdonald, believing that the presence of the European names would help to conciliate public opinion in French Canada, attached great importance to their inclusion.[33] But they proved suspiciously, mulishly difficult; and they finally agreed to sign on the somewhat ominous condition that if, after more mature consideration, they decided in the end to back out, Stephen would assume responsibility for their share.

Macdonald was committed now—and to the hilt. He had gambled everything on the choice of the right men. He had bought ability, energy, and experience at the expense of every other consideration. The personal rivalries and sectional interests which had counted for so much in the negotiations with Allan and Macpherson eight years before had not, on this new occasion, had any appreciable weight with him at all. He had insisted that every effort should be made to bring round Kohn, Reinach and their French associates; but this was almost his sole concession to the small tactics of Canadian political manœuvres. He had swallowed his own personal dislikes, and thrown his record for political consistency to the winds. In the

past, he had attacked the St. Paul, Minneapolis, and Manitoba
Railway as an alien and sinister corporation, intent upon the
ruin of a truly Canadian transcontinental railway; and he had
publicly denounced Donald Smith as "the biggest liar he ever
saw". Yet now he had made an agreement with the very directors whom he had previously exhorted the Canadian House of
Commons to repudiate. The fact that Stephen, Angus, and
McIntyre were all Montrealers, that not a single Torontonian
was included in the original membership of the syndicate, would
make it easy for the Liberals to goad a large and important
part of Ontario into opposition. It would be even easier for
Blake and his supporters to reverse the rôles of the past two
years, to adopt Macdonald's previous attitude to the directors
of the St. Paul, Minneapolis, and Manitoba Railway, and to
hold up Stephen and his friends as a gang of Americans in all
but name, who were intent upon appropriating the Canadian
Pacific Railway for their own alien purposes, in much the
same way as McMullen and his conspirators had tried to do
eight years before. In fact, of course, Stephen, Smith, and
Angus were not American railwaymen attempting to invade
Canada, but Canadian railwaymen who had successfully invaded the United States. It was an important difference; but
it was a difference which the Liberals would try to obliterate
under cartloads of abuse. There was no blinking away the plain
fact. The whole scheme was vulnerable at half a dozen different
and obvious points.

Yet these, as Macdonald knew very well, were not the most
important defects of the scheme. Its most important defect
was something far more fundamental. The project of a Pacific
railway through Canadian territory was a project only less
formidable than that of the Dominion of Canada itself. The
Dominion and the railway would both encounter the same
acute difficulties for they shared a common ultimate objective.
The prime purpose of Canada was to achieve a separate political
existence on the North American continent. The prime function of the Canadian Pacific Railway was to assist in this effort
—to help in the building of the national economy and the

national society which alone would make this ambition possible of achievement. Like Canada itself, the railway would find its most powerful rivals, its most dangerous enemies, in the continent of North America. It was, by the basic intention of its planners, in competition with all the American transcontinental railway systems in general, and with the Northern Pacific in particular. Any close or important association with American railwaymen or financiers would, as the tragic case of Sir Hugh Allan had so conclusively proved, endanger, if it did not ruin, the railway's essential character and purpose. Neither the company nor the government which sponsored it could dream of accepting too substantial an amount of capital from the United States. Neither the company nor the government could expect real friends or genuine support in any part of North America beyond the boundaries of the Dominion. The Canadian Pacific was, by design, a contender for the traffic of a continent. American railways were its natural enemies. British finance was its natural support.

Yet, at the beginning at least, British finance declined to play its necessary rôle. The Anglo-Canadian alliance, which was the basis of Canada's independence in North America, was still effective in politics. But in finance, at this stage, it exerted little force. The polite indifference to Canada which, under the Gladstone régime, ruled at Whitehall, was translated, in the City, into a cold and critical suspicion of Canadian enterprises. Morton, Rose and Company, a relatively small and inconspicuous firm, alone joined the original Canadian Pacific syndicate. No important British financial house gave the project the slightest support or encouragement at the beginning; and at least one company, the Grand Trunk Railway Company, which had its headquarters in London, maintained an unrelenting and influential opposition for years to come. The great centres of English-speaking finance, London and New York, were either indifferent or hostile to the Canadian Pacific; the press of England and of the United States varied, in its attitude, between contemptuous neglect and active malevolence. *The Times*, which had not even troubled to consider the appointment of a correspondent at Ottawa, exhibited a "sneering indifference and superciliousness" to all things Canadian, which surprised and shocked Lord Lorne.[84] The American press associations, as their record amply proved, had never missed a chance of minimizing Canada's achievements and exaggerating its troubles and difficulties.

Abroad there was little help. Help would have to come from home. And at home the nation itself was the only organization which could possibly render the required assistance. In Canada, as Macdonald had the best of reasons for knowing, the mingling of railways and politics was inevitable. The subsidy of twenty-five million dollars and the land grant of twenty-five million acres, which, in effect, made company and government the joint proprietors of the enormous patrimony of the north-west, were simply the first and most impressive pledges of a partnership which grew tighter and more inextricable with the passage of time. The government relied upon the railway for the realization of its national purposes; the railway depended upon the government for financial support and political protection. By the terms of the contract it was exempted from most forms of taxation; it was permitted to import required materials duty free; and it was given complete liberty to build what branches it desired, while at the same time it was completely protected, by one of the most controversial clauses in the contract, from all railway competition south of the international border. "For twenty years from the date hereof," the notorious clause ran, "no line of railway shall be authorized by the Dominion Parliament to be constructed south of the Canadian Pacific Railway, except such line as shall run south-west, or to the westward of south-west; nor to within fifteen miles of latitude forty-nine."[85]

To this provision, the so-called "monopoly clause", which he always regarded as the translation into railway terms of the main principle of the national policy of protection, Stephen attached, from the first, an enormous importance. "Now what do you think," he wrote bluntly to Macdonald, three days before the contract was signed, "would be the position of the C.P.R. or of the men bound to own and operate it, if it were tapped at Winnipeg or at any point west of that, by a line or lines running towards the United States boundary? What would, in such a case, be the value of the C.P.R. line from Winnipeg to Ottawa? No sane man would give a dollar for the whole line east of Winnipeg. I need not say more on this point, as it must be clear to you that *any and every line south* of the line of the C.P.R. running towards the boundary line must be owned and controlled by the C.P.R., otherwise the C.P.R. would be strangled. The fact is, that if any doubt should exist in the minds of any friends on this point I could not carry them with me, and I need not say to you, that now I am into this thing, I would not like to be forced to give it up."[36]

No, Macdonald realized, Stephen could not be forced to give it up. His company was the one potentially successful company which, in all the thirteen years since Confederation, had come forward requesting authority to build the railway. Concessions would have to be made to it, for concessions were economically vital to its success. Yet every concession, Macdonald recognized, would make his own task so much more difficult politically. The railway's privileges, powers, and exemptions were such that it could all too easily be made to appear as a gigantic and overbearing monopoly. The terms of the contract could be used to give it the dreadful aspect of a leviathan. Yet, at the moment, it was nothing but a contract. It had only a fragile paper existence. And years must pass and anything might happen, before it took concrete shape in a glittering and unbroken track of steel. Until the goal of the Pacific was reached, the partnership of government and railway, necessary but embarrassing to both, must continue. At one stroke, Macdonald had assumed a double burden. Until the success of this huge dependency was assured, he would never be free from anxiety. And he could not give up until the Canadian Pacific Railway was complete. Could he survive the ordeal? He was old and he was not too well. But in George Stephen he had acquired a helper of quite extraordinary ability. He had chosen Stephen deliberately, and he had chosen better than even he knew. Stephen was perhaps the greatest creative genius in the whole history of Canadian finance.

IV

Until the act of incorporation had been passed and the charter granted, the syndicate was really helpless; and Stephen was importunate in his demands that Parliament should be called as quickly as possible. The session opened on December 9, a good two months earlier than usual. All during the protracted and nerve-wracking negotiations of the summer and autumn, Macdonald's health had remained surprisingly good; but now at length the strain began to tell, and he fell ill again.[37] He made light of his trouble at first, assuring Louisa that it was nothing but a touch of liver, and denouncing the "confounded newspapers" which always magnified his slightest malaise.[38] But Dr. Grant counselled him not to attend the ceremonial opening of Parliament, and the Governor-General wrote a kindly note begging him to follow his doctor's advice.[39] It was Tupper, the Minister of Railways and Canals, who rose on December 14 to move the adoption of the two basic resolutions, authorizing the cash subsidy and the land grant to the Canadian Pacific Railway;[40] and although Macdonald was in his place to hear this first, formal presentation of the government's case, he did not trouble to attend when Blake and Cartwright made their prolonged and passionate attacks upon the contract. He was still not completely recovered when the House adjourned for the brief Christmas recess. Hugh and his wife and their small daughter, Daisy, came down to Ottawa for the Christmas holidays;[41] and Macdonald watched his own child, Mary, who would never properly grow up, play contentedly with the little granddaughter who was so much her junior. The brief rest helped him a little. He told his sister that he was "pretty well now". But when the House re-opened, all too quickly, on January 4, he was still, in accordance with Grant's orders, staying at home as much as possible and avoiding exposure to the cold.[42]

In the meantime the opposition to the contract had been gaining in strength and pugnacity. The company's exemption from taxation, its privilege of importing materials duty-free, its unlimited authority to construct branches, and its monopolistic control of the whole traffic of the north-west, were all vulnerable features of the agreement which perturbed even good Ontario members of the Cabinet such as Campbell and Macpherson. Blake, Cartwright, and Laurier kept hammering away at these not too easily defensible points. Yet the opposition did not by any means confine its attacks to the admittedly debatable features of the contract. Criticism was at once more positive and more basic. Once again, as in the battle over the protective tariff, the Liberals set themselves in fundamental opposition to Macdonald's whole conception of Canada's future as a nation. They had opposed the National Policy with the principle of international free trade; they now resisted the all-Canadian railway with a policy of continental transport. It would be monstrous folly, Blake and Cartwright argued, to build a railway through the unprofitable, infertile country north of Lake Superior. This criminal absurdity of nationalism ought to be abandoned at once; and instead the Canadian Pacific Railway must find its way westward through American territory south of the lake.[48]

It was this continental, anti-national position which gave the Liberal party its principal allies and its main sources of strength in the prolonged battle against the Canadian Pacific Railway. The route to which the Liberal leaders now so publicly gave their blessing was, with variations, the route which the Grand Trunk Railway had always advocated, the route which existing American railways, including the St. Paul, Minneapolis, and Manitoba, had already appropriated. At one stroke Blake and his followers found themselves reinforced by the all too powerful interests in the United States and England which were determined to spoil the chances of a national transcontinental on Canadian soil. The great American press associations began to report the speeches of Her Majesty's loyal opposition at Ottawa in the most flattering detail. The Grand Trunk Railway, which had a considerable influence in

SIR CHARLES TUPPER

From Tupper's *Recollections of*
Sixty Years in Canada

England, as well as the power of an extensive patronage in the newspapers of Quebec and Ontario, exerted itself to ensure that Liberal criticisms of the Canadian Pacific were given the widest possible publicity. "Reports appearing English press only mention doings of opposition," Charles Rose cabled in consternation from London. "Nothing mentioned other side. Suggest seeing Associated Press."[44] Macdonald must have smiled grimly. He had been through this so often before. It was only too probable that the Associated Press was feeding England with a string of biased and disparaging cables. It could be confidently assumed that the Toronto *Globe, The Times* of London, and the American Associated Press would become partners in an unofficial but none the less extremely effective alliance to injure the Canadian Pacific Railway and the government which had sponsored it. But what could be done? He had tried often before to get a fair hearing for Canada in England; and he had failed.

The climax of the Liberal opposition was reached about the middle of January with the sudden submission of a rival and —on the face of it—a much better offer to build the railway. It came from a group of Canadian capitalists, resident chiefly in Ontario, who declared they were ready to accept a smaller cash subsidy and a smaller land grant than Stephen and his associates had demanded, and who professed themselves willing to forgo all the principal exemptions and privileges which had aroused so much criticism against the original contract. Macdonald regarded this proposal as a transparently fraudulent manœuvre of party politics. Up to this point he had taken only the smallest share in the debate; but, on Monday, January 17, as soon as Tupper had formally presented the new offer to the House, he arose to defend his scheme at length and to quiet the growing doubts of his followers. "We have had," he declared, recounting the history of the Liberal opposition up to the moment of the introduction of the new offer, "tragedy, comedy, and farce from the other side. Sir, it commenced with tragedy. The contract was declared oppressive, and the amount of money to be given was enormous. We were giving away the whole lands of the north-west . . . this was the tragedy . . .

The comedy was that when every one of the speeches of these honourable gentlemen were read to them, it was proved that last year, or the year before, and in previous years, they had thought one way, and that now they spoke in another way. . . . Now, Sir, the last thing that came was the farce. We had the farce laid on the table today. The tragedy and comedy were pretty successful; but the farce, I am afraid, with an impartial audience, in theatrical phrase, will be damned."[45]

He went on to damn it. The new offer was, he claimed, a flimsy imposture, concocted in Ottawa by politicians rather than capitalists, and with politics rather than transport in mind. Some of its terms were, on the face of it, an improvement on those of the government scheme. But there was a simple explanation for these bargain figures. The irresponsible authors of the new proposal had not the slightest expectation of ever being called upon to build the railway. They could promise anything. They were perfectly free to offer the most absurd conditions. Most of the new scheme could be dismissed contemptuously as mere bluff; and the features which alone gave it its semblance of authenticity were precisely those which every patriotic Canadian ought decisively to reject. The new offer, Macdonald declared, was not for a transcontinental railway at all, but simply for a prairie section, which would be connected with the American railways and from which the trade of the Canadian north-west would be run off into the United States. "Mr. Speaker," he concluded, "the whole thing is an attempt to destroy the Pacific railway. I can trust to the intelligence of this House, and the patriotism of this country, I can trust not only to the patriotism but to the common sense of this country, to carry out an arrangement which will give us all we want, which will satisfy all the loyal, legitimate aspirations, which will give us a great, an united, a rich, an improving, a developing Canada, instead of making us tributary to American laws, to American railways, to American bondage, to American tolls, to American freights, to all the little tricks and big tricks that American railways are addicted to for the purpose of destroying our road."[46]

"Your speech," J. A. Donaldson wrote him from Toronto

on January 18, "was the whole topic of conversation through the whole city today . . . the champagne corks were flying like a humming fire of artillery."[47] He had made a great effort, for the importunities of Stephen and the restlessness of his own followers had convinced him that a great effort was necessary; and once again, from some mysterious source in his being, he had drawn the necessary strength. "I was luckily strong and well when I spoke," he told Galt, "which I did in the fashion of twenty years ago."[48] The praise of his friends and the satisfaction which he himself felt in his speech helped to carry him forward. He still hoped to pull through the session. But every day his health grew more shakily unreliable; and the business of piloting the Canadian Pacific Bill through the House kept nagging at him like an obsession. "It has kept me constantly at work," he told Galt, "to the exclusion of everything else, to strengthen the weak-hearted in both Houses." The pressure from the opposition was savage and intolerably persistent. "It was six o'clock this morning before I got home from the House," he wrote to Lord Lorne on January 26.[49] The next day the Liberals occupied the whole night with a long succession of futile amendments to Tupper's main motion, and the House did not rise until eight o'clock in the morning.[50]

The pace was a killing one, but somehow he contrived to carry on. On February 1 the Bill finally passed the Commons on a division of one hundred and twenty-eight to forty-nine; and next day the congratulatory telegrams and cables began to pour in. Even Baron Reinach sent his felicitations. But the message which perhaps pleased Macdonald most was one from Alexander Morris, who, twenty years before, had preached the creation of a greater British North America and who, in June of 1864, had helped to bring Brown and Macdonald together in the coalition which had made Confederation. "I write to congratulate you," Morris declared warmly, "on the second crowning triumph of your more recent life, second only to that of Confederation. You have now created the link to bind the provinces indissolubly together, and to give us a future and a British nationality."[51]

It was done, but the doing had nearly finished him. The

illness which in some incredible fashion he had managed to keep at bay for these vitally necessary weeks, now overcame his resistance and threw him. "The long sittings at last broke me down," he wrote to Galt, "and I had to betake myself to my bed for a fortnight and am only now beginning to crawl about."[52] It was quite impossible for him to be present on the momentous occasion when the Governor-General gave the royal assent to the Bill—the Bill which, in the eyes of a good many people, would probably bring political or financial ruin to all those who had conceived it. But the thoughtful Alexander Campbell, who had kept a close superintending eye on the final adjustments to the terms, hastened to give him an account of the last episode in the story. "It will do you good," he wrote, "to know that the Pacific Railway matter is through all the stages. We had the Governor-General down yesterday. I thought it more respectful to go out to Rideau than to write, and I found him quite ready."[53] Lord Lorne had inaugurated still another of the great national policies of the transcontinental Dominion. "At last the C.P.R. is a fixed fact," Macdonald wrote from his sick-bed almost jubilantly to Galt. "Royal assent given, royal charter under the act issued, company organized, and it now remains for Stephen and Company to show what metal they are made of."[54]

The first struggle was over. But it had been a costly one. It had damaged his health badly and it had lasted an unconscionable length of time. The impatient Stephen, who had gone to England to raise funds and encourage immigration, kept insisting, in explosive and angry letters and telegrams, that the "senseless" interruptions of the "malignant" Blake and his followers had put back the whole Canadian Pacific enterprise a full year. Macdonald was not disposed to take Stephen's romantic exaggerations too seriously; but he knew that their joint programme of western development had certainly been held up by the delay. Immigration on a large scale was essential to the success of the Canadian Pacific and to the triumph of his own plans; and, in this year of rising values and exuberant economic recovery, immigration was certainly flooding into the west as it had never come before. But Macdonald was anxious, in co-operation with the British government and the Canadian Pacific, to work out a great concerted scheme of organized settlement; and before he left England in the previous September, he had handed in a long confidential memorandum on the subject to the Colonial Secretary.

He had counted upon Galt to push the plan forward. But Galt disappointed them both. The High Commissioner had spent the autumn and winter in vain attempts to interest the British Cabinet in a government-supported immigration society; and in the end he reached the characteristically gloomy conclusion that Gladstone would never consent to put a copper of public money into such a project.[55] Stephen, though he was not so easily discouraged, was no more successful; and at length he too decided that it would be better to postpone the campaign for a while and to renew it again in the autumn. "It takes time," he wrote resignedly, "to create anything in this slow moving country."[56] Another season had gone by, and one whole phase of Macdonald's policy of western expansion had scarcely even been approached. Yet he and his colleagues seemed exhausted by their efforts. Tupper was ill. John Henry Pope was ill. Galt, who was disgusted with the English climate, the cost of English living, and his own miserable want of success with the English government, begged to be permitted to resign his post.

The worst of it all was that Macdonald could not seem to make any real recovery of his own health. Parliament prorogued on March 21, and he rallied for the closing. "We had last week a parting caucus," he wrote Tupper. "It was a most enthusiastic one, and I talked to them like a Dutch uncle about working in their counties."[57] It was his last stout effort of the season, and a few days after the closing ceremonies he suffered a sudden and serious relapse. "There was no ascertainable cause for it," he wrote Tupper a little later, "but suddenly I broke down—pulse at forty-nine, and great pain and disturbance in liver and bowels."[58] Dr. Grant was obviously very much alarmed. Apparently also he was out of his depth in the complications of the case; and, perhaps as a result, was inclined to be pessimistic and discouraging. He kept fussing nervously

over Macdonald, discovering new symptoms, and reaching new
and increasingly doleful diagnoses: he told his patient frankly
that the disease might be a cancerous affection of the stomach
and that he had better put his affairs in order.[59] Macdonald
could not believe that the time had come when he must take
these gloomy warnings literally. There were days when he
felt quite well enough to escape from his bedroom, and on
one occasion at least the ministers gathered round the dining-
room table at Stadacona Hall and a Cabinet council was held.[60]
But the improvement was not continuous and steady; and
though time drifted on and May succeeded April, he still felt
appallingly tired and weak. His sister Louisa, when she came
up from Kingston for a brief visit, was shocked to see him. "I
never saw John looking what I would call old till this time,"
she wrote to Professor Williamson. "His hair is getting quite
gray."[61]

Agnes, Hugh, and Louisa were all convinced that, as soon as
he was strong enough to travel, he must sail for England in
search of better medical advice and perfect relaxation. The
Cabinet ministers emphatically agreed. "My colleagues, en
masse, insist on my crossing the sea," he wrote to Tupper, "and
I propose crossing in the middle of May." His condition, he
realized, was far more serious than it ever had been since the
crisis of ten years before; but, despite his weakness and the
ambiguity of the future, he had no thought now of giving up
his task. The Globe, with its usual tender solicitude for his
welfare, announced that his recovery could now hardly be
expected, and that he was going away for an indefinite period,
"leaving the party without a head, and still torn by dissensions
as to the succession". He authorized C. W. Bunting, who had
succeeded to the control of the Toronto Mail, to make a public
denial of these insinuations;[62] and, in private, he was still planning for the future of the country and the party as if he expected
to continue indefinitely in office. He begged Tupper to hurry
home, for he was worried by the uncertain Conservative prospects in the approaching by-elections in the Maritime Provinces;[63] and he assured Stephen that he intended to take advantage of his visit to England to have a long talk with Bright,

Gladstone, and W. E. Forster, the Irish Secretary, about immigration.[64]

Only a little over a year ago, he had firmly determined to resign. But now, though his physical condition was much worse than it had been then, the thought of retirement did not apparently cross his mind. Strange! But it was so. The Pacific Railway, in some mysterious fashion, had settled his resolution. He would not admit that he was finished. He could not desert Stephen. He would stay until the completion of the railway was assured. "As to myself," he told Tupper, "my remaining ambition is to see that our policy is not reversed and that the National Policy and the C.P.R. are safe from 1883 to 1888."[65]

He sailed from Quebec on May 21, and eight days later was in Liverpool.

V

The first benefit of his arrival was a blessed reassurance from the consultant of his choice. Dr. Andrew Clark would not hear of Macdonald coming to see him; he came instead to Batt's Hotel to see Macdonald; and on June 1 he gave him a long and searching examination. The results were better than anybody had dared to expect. Clark told both Macdonald and Galt, who hovered anxiously in the background, that he saw no evidence of organic disease, and did not suspect any. But he also admitted that there was great functional derangement. "My complaint," Macdonald reported to Tupper after the examination was over, "is catarrh of the stomach, with a gouty state of body, not amounting to gout."[66] Clark prescribed a rigidly simple diet, but otherwise did not order any special treatment. The great thing, after the long and unbroken ordeal through which Macdonald had passed, was rest.

Yet rest, if he remained in a London hotel, the easy victim of callers, was the last thing he could expect. Galt begged him to get out of the city as soon as possible;[67] and Agnes and Hewitt Bernard began energetically to search for a

suitable place in the outskirts of London, where he could get
the desired seclusion. In the end he and Bernard rented
Denmark House, a furnished cottage in Upper Norwood, for a
couple of months. The place gave him suburban quiet and
fresh air, it was easily accessible to London, and, as he explained to Lord Lorne, he could take a walk through the
nearby Crystal Palace when it rained.[68] When they moved
out there and began their temporary housekeeping, Macdonald
was still extremely weak. He had, of all misfortunes, caught a
bad cold soon after his arrival in England, and he could not
seem to shake it off.[69] For a while Clark visited him every
day and kept "stethoscoping" him regularly. The doctor was
obviously concerned, but he still insisted that things would
soon be all right.

July came. Macdonald had been in England nearly six weeks,
and the catarrh of his chest and stomach still troubled him.
"I live according to a written regimen and dietary given me by
Dr. Clark," he told Alexander Campbell. "I avoid as much
as possible all invitations but those that are commands."[70] Yet
the commands seemed to be fairly numerous. The Duke of
Argyll gave a dinner specially for the Macdonalds. They had
lunch with Princess Louise, the Marchioness of Lorne, who was
back in England for a visit; and there were receptions at
the Gladstones' and the Salisburys'. "You will say this is a
pretty good list for an invalid . . .," he admitted to Campbell.
But the invalid seemed to benefit from these agreeable diversions
as well as from the peaceful regularity of the life at Upper
Norwood. From then on he steadily and rapidly improved; and
soon the pattern which had become characteristic of his later
visits to England, and which he and Agnes frankly enjoyed
so much, began to re-establish itself. He dined out, he went
to theatres, he met his friends and acquaintances of both political
parties, he attended a royal levee and a state ball. The weather,
for a good part of the summer, was dry, sunny, and even, at
times, decidedly hot. There were garden parties in the
sunshine, week-ends in the country, elaborate dinners with
the Drapers' Company and the Lord Mayor; and on July 21,
he went out to Wimbledon to a party in honour of the visiting

team of Canadian marksmen who had won the Kolapore cup the day before.[71]

Yet, even in the midst of the relaxation which he had earned so dearly, he did not neglect Canadian interests. His main concern was immigration. He talked it over again with Kimberley; he tried to put in a word about it with Gladstone; he went to Lansdowne House to discuss the subject informally with the Marquess of Lansdowne and a group of large Irish landowners; and he appealed to Cardinal Manning for the support of the Irish Roman Catholic hierarchy in a plan of assisted emigration from southern Ireland.[72] The utmost the Gladstone government was prepared to do in aid of overseas settlement was to appropriate a small amount of money, in the Irish Land Act, to assist Irish peasants who wished to emigrate. The amount seemed negligible to Canadians, and the aid was just as available to emigrants who intended to settle in foreign countries as it was to those who wished to go to British colonies. Lord Carnarvon suggested that Macdonald should attend the debate on the Bill in the House of Lords, in the hope that his testimony might inspire an amendment favourable to Canada. But early in August the clause slipped through, completely unaltered, much to Carnarvon's and Macdonald's disappointment, and to Galt's angry disgust.[73]

Yet, in the main, the summer in England was an extremely happy one. Almost every mail from Canada brought reassuring news. Tupper, a burly and extremely belligerent campaigner, flung himself into the by-election contests in Nova Scotia; and on June 18—victories worthy of Waterloo day, Macpherson called them—the Conservatives captured the two constituencies of Colchester and Pictou. Tupper and Tilley went on from these successes to address a series of political meetings in New Brunswick; and Tupper, who was never inclined to underrate the good effects of his own exertions, predicted confidently that "New Brunswick would be carried tomorrow if there was an election".[74] "Governmental prospects are bright here," Alexander Campbell assured Macdonald happily, "the elections go with us, prosperity continues in business and manufacturing centres, and there is every reason, so far, to anticipate a good harvest. . . ."[75] What could Macdonald desire more? There was absolutely no reason whatever, the entire Cabinet insisted, for him to make an early return home. Tilley, Macpherson, and Campbell all urged him to prolong his stay until the middle of October. "You could not do a better thing," Campbell wrote, "for yourself or the country."[76]

But he booked a passage on September 8. He knew he must go home. George Stephen was undisguisedly pleased to hear of his early return; and George Stephen's satisfaction was significant. The Canadian Pacific was just entering upon the long period of struggle and effort which must precede its completion. The whole process might take the full ten years which were specified in the contract. He might never live to see it finished. But he was determined that he would watch over the growth of his great creation until he could watch no more. He must win the next general election. He must have another five years of power. "I have no pleasure nowadays but in work," he told Alexander Campbell, "and so it will be to the end of the chapter."[77]

Chapter Ten

Good Times

I

On the voyage home, he presided over the *Sardinian*'s ship's concert—"his first appearance before the public", the programme proudly announced;[1] and when the vessel docked at Quebec on Saturday, September 17, his alert eyes and easy movements convinced the curious Canadians that he was back again on an indefinite engagement. Everybody noticed how much better he looked. His old buoyancy, the newspaper correspondents informed their readers, was back again unimpaired.[2] And, as he hurried to Ottawa and began, in his usual easy, effortless fashion, to acquaint himself with the moods of his fellow-countrymen, he realized that his own restored well-being was matched and exceeded by the exuberant high spirits of the country as a whole. Far from exhibiting any unpleasant signs of diminution, the boom was obviously at its height. Immigrants had been pouring into the west all summer. The decennial census, which had been taken during the summer of 1881, had revealed the fact that the population of the Province of Manitoba had risen in ten years from 18,995 to 65,954.[3] A veritable mania of speculation in land—something strangely new in the history of British North America—reigned at Winnipeg; and in the eastern cities, though their mood was more sedate than that of the youthful and excited west, business was obviously in a most flourishing condition. David Macpherson, who, Macdonald considered, was a sound judge in these matters, summed up the general feeling, rather regretfully, by announcing that it would

317

have been a great year for a general election. "If circumstances should be favourable next year," he suggested, "why not have it then?"[4]

Why not, indeed? Macdonald began to make preparations for a provincial Liberal-Conservative convention which was to meet in Toronto late in November, as a first important strategic move in a rapidly approaching national campaign. In the meantime he settled down to a careful examination of the state of the Canadian Pacific Railway. The first summer's operations were over. The organization which the genius of George Stephen had called into being was grappling with the basic problems of its task; and as, one by one, the fundamental decisions were made, the grand strategy of the railway became more and more clearly apparent. Already it was evident that in the far west the directors were contemplating a line a good deal south of the route which had been projected as a result of the original surveys.[5] A main line which ran towards the future Calgary rather than towards the future Edmonton would obviously provide a better basis, both for the protection of the railway's Canadian business and for the struggle with American rivals for the traffic south of the border. This change of direction required the abandonment of the Yellowhead Pass, the relatively easy northern route, and the discovery of a new way through the Rockies and the Selkirks. It was the most daring, but not the only, innovation which the company made in its first year of operation. There was a change of nearly equal significance north of Lake Superior. There the route had been provisionally planned, in accordance with the first of Sandford Fleming's surveys, to run well inland, north of Lake Nipigon. But Stephen and his directors, in the interest of economy and speed of construction, decided to move south and build close to the shore of Lake Superior. Their first idea, which was subsequently given up, was to follow the lake-shore throughout and thus to make the branch which they intended building to Sault Ste. Marie a part of the main line. This drastic change, Stephen argued persuasively, would cut costs, and shorten time.[6] It might enable the company to complete the railway to the Pacific in only five years.

The advantages of Stephen's proposed "new departure" were not lost on Macdonald. He had been the tenacious and unyielding sponsor of the line north of Lake Superior. He had insisted upon it, without qualification, as an absolute essential of the national transcontinental. The officials of the Grand Trunk Railway had rejected the mere idea of such a line in contemptuous disbelief; even George Stephen had originally viewed it with unhappy misgivings. But within a year of the signing of the contract, Stephen had completely changed his mind. As he warmed to his work, he began to realize the enormous potentialities of the all-Canadian route. "I am sure you will be glad to hear this from me," he wrote to Macdonald, "because I do not think but for your *own* tenacity on that point, would the line north of the lake *ever* have been built."[7] It would have to be built, Macdonald had always insisted. But the prospect of the cost and labour involved had been a formidable one. It was a task which might drag on interminably, which might exhaust the patience of the Canadians, ruin the railway company and destroy his own government. The thought had haunted him with disquieting persistence. But now, was he not half free of its terrors? The lake-shore route might cut the labour north of Lake Superior by as much as a half. The entire railway might be finished in 1886.

He became a convert to the "new departure".[8] It bettered his own chances, and those of the railway. But at the same time it helped, along with other developments since the signing of the charter, to strengthen the opposition to the Canadian transcontinental. It was becoming increasingly clear that there was a very real likelihood of the Canadian transcontinental becoming a real transcontinental. It was pledged to reach the Pacific Ocean, through territory which might have become the easy monopoly of the Northern Pacific; and it was compelled to seek an outlet on the Atlantic seaboard, through a long-settled region which had been dominated by the Grand Trunk. From the point of view of these two rivals, the nature, and the danger, of the competition which the Canadian Pacific would offer, were becoming clearer every day. In Ontario and Quebec, and London, the Grand Trunk began slowly marshalling its forces and organizing its propaganda. It could afford to take its time, for it was already solidly established on the ground in dispute. But the Northern Pacific could not permit itself such deliberate tactics. Unless the Northern Pacific could speedily effect an entrance into Canada, its hopes of gaining a substantial part of the Canadian traffic were lost. It must act, and act at once.

Macdonald watched the onward career of the Northern Pacific with growing uneasiness. He had good cause for alarm. The railway, which had been plagued for long years by recurring financial crises, emerged successfully from a final reorganization, acquired new capital, and proceeded to build westward towards the Pacific at headlong speed. The tentacles of its lines were creeping eagerly, possessively, towards the international boundary. If it could win the co-operation of some impecunious Canadian province, with a provincial railway to dispose of, or if it could get control of the interests of some Canadian railway speculator who had a charter or a half-built line that he wished to sell at a good profit, then, at a bound, it would be past the frontier and into Canadian territory. Macdonald knew that there were two or three small railways in Manitoba which could very easily be connected with the Northern Pacific, to the utter undoing of the Canadian transcontinental. He also knew that the Province of Quebec, which had relapsed from its earlier fiscal rectitude into a state of acute budgetary embarrassment, was anxious to be relieved of the burden of its provincial system, the Quebec, Montreal, Ottawa, and Occidental Railway. Chapleau, the Premier of the province, had announced flatly that he intended to sell to the highest bidder. What if he sold the Quebec lines to the Northern Pacific Railroad?

It was a frightening prospect. It meant, as Macdonald earnestly warned Stephen, grave danger ahead. The purchase of the Quebec provincial railway would place the Northern Pacific in a commanding position in the heart of central Canada. It would be put in possession of the only route by which the Canadian transcontinental could find its outlet on the Atlantic Ocean; and, by extending its Canadian lines across northern Ontario, it could connect them with the American part of its system at Sault Ste. Marie. All this was bad enough; but it was not the only mischief which could be expected to flow from this deplorable transfer of Canadian property to American hands. The Northern Pacific, by handsomely assuming the financial burdens of distressed Quebec, would ingratiate itself not only with the provincial legislature, but also with Quebec's Conservative Members of Parliament at Ottawa; and the French-Canadian bloc at Ottawa might quite possibly try to prevent the Dominion government from disallowing the legislation by which Manitoba would certainly attempt to empower its provincial railways to build to the international boundary. "The Northern Pacific," Macdonald wrote earnestly to Stephen, "are very anxious to get into Manitoba and the North West, and they think that by coming to the rescue of the Province at a moment when the syndicate people are supposed to be unwilling, they can secure a solid Quebec vote in the House of Commons against any veto of provincial legislation in Manitoba in the interest of the Northern Pacific connection."[9]

There was only one thing to do, Macdonald knew. All possible connections between the Manitoba railways and the Northern Pacific must be quickly and firmly stopped, and Stephen must be induced to prevent the Quebec, Montreal, Ottawa, and Occidental Railway from falling into the hands of his great American rival. Macdonald wrote to Stephen, informing him of the sinister rumours; he told Chapleau that the Dominion government would prefer to see the Canadian Pacific obtain the sale or lease of the Quebec lines.[10] In the meantime, the government was already proceeding, in a summary and effective fashion, to ward off inroads through the Province of Manitoba on the domain of the Canadian transcontinental. In November, Charles Tupper, as Minister of Railways and Canals, reported against the Manitoba and South Eastern Railway; and early in the new year its charter was disallowed. Macdonald had no doubts or hesitations. The Canadian Pacific must be protected, for a long time to come, against incursions from the south. The Dominion had the will to disallow. It had the power to disallow. And John Norquay, the Premier of Manitoba, had privately agreed some time before that he would do his best to prevent any interference by the province with the Dominion's railway policy.[11] "As to the monopoly cry," Macdonald wrote firmly to Martin Griffin, "it is all nonsense."

But it was dangerous nonsense, nonsense pregnant with trouble. It was no time to be getting into a row with the first prairie province. Yet, given his national policies and his commitments to the Canadian Pacific Railway, how could he possibly avoid doing so? Manitoba, which had enjoyed the comfort of steam transport for less than three years, had suddenly developed a voracious appetite for railways. There was no hope of its remaining contented with the main line of the Canadian Pacific and the main line of the St. Paul, Minneapolis, and Manitoba Railway. It would certainly want to promote settlement and to encourage competition in transport by laying down a positive network of provincial railways; and of these several might provide—and might be designed to provide—a connection with the Northern Pacific or other American systems. How often hereafter would Manitoba charter railways to the international border? How often would he be obliged to use the power of disallowance? He looked into the future with a shiver of apprehension. He began to realize how formidably complex the resistance to his grand national scheme was likely to be. He had expected the economic rivalry of the Northern Pacific; but he had not entirely foreseen how quickly it would be linked with the political opposition of discontented and ambitious Canadian provinces. Even in this year of plenty and prosperity, he was aware of the slow marshalling of the forces against him. Manitoba, he knew very well, was by no means the only malcontent province. British Columbia was not yet completely pacified. Quebec was nursing a growing dissatisfaction. But the most mutinous province of all was Ontario. Ontario had literally raised the red flag of revolt.

Macdonald was determined to fight the battle of the unified nation and the strongly centralized constitution. He made no attempt to avoid an encounter with Ontario. In fact, he appeared to welcome it. Oliver Mowat, the Premier of the province, his old pupil-at-law, was an antagonist with whom he had always found it a positive pleasure to do battle; and the provincial government at Toronto, a wealthy and powerful government, arrogantly conscious of its wide territories and its large population, assumed an independent and assertive rôle in the Dominion which it was surely in the national interest to combat. For three years now, ever since his return to power in the autumn of 1878, Macdonald had been getting more and more deeply embroiled with Oliver Mowat's government. There had been disputes over both territorial boundaries and jurisdictional limits. Macdonald believed that Mowat, in his exercise of the province's licensing power, had assumed an unwarranted legislative authority in the matter of temperance and public morals. He was convinced that Ontario, in its determined attempt to extend its boundaries to the north and north-west, was claiming territory for which it had no legal and historical right, and which would give it a dangerous preponderance in the Dominion. He believed that Mowat's Liquor Licence Law of 1877 was (constitutionally) subordinate to the federal statute of 1878, the Canada Temperance Act. He refused to accept the boundary award, favourable to Ontario, which had been made with such suspicious swiftness in the summer of 1878 by commissioners appointed by the Liberal government, just one month before that government went out of power. He demanded instead that the whole question should be referred for a final legal settlement to the Judicial Committee of the Privy Council.[12]

In the meantime, while these disputes were simmering away in exasperation, Oliver Mowat's government had acquired a new and colossal grievance. In the session of 1881 the provincial legislature had passed an act which regulated the public use of the rivers and streams of Ontario; and this, like every other provincial statute, had been sent to Ottawa for review by the Department of Justice. The British North America Act gave the Dominion the power to disallow any piece of provincial legislation, within one year of its receipt at Ottawa; and Macdonald had always intended that this power should be used, in the national interest.[13] For him—and it was one of his most deeply held convictions—Canada was one community, with common interests, common rights, and common ideals.

"Sir," he said later in Parliament in the debate on the disallowance of the Rivers and Streams Bill, "we are not half a dozen provinces. We are one great Dominion."[14] The Canadian Pacific Railway was a material interest which concerned the whole of Canada; property rights were rights which should be equally protected throughout the nation; and unquestionably the guardianship of these common rights and interests against provincial encroachment was a duty which the federal government could not escape.

In Macdonald's view, the Rivers and Streams Bill peremptorily called for action by the Dominion. He regarded it as an iniquitous piece of legislation.[15] It opened to public use the dams, timber slides, and other "improvements" which individual proprietors had constructed at their own expense for the floating of their saw-logs. It had been introduced while a Conservative lumberman was contesting in the courts the claim of a Liberal lumberman to make use of his "improvements" and it had been passed by a legislature with a Liberal majority, in which a relative of the Liberal lumberman concerned had a seat. To Macdonald it seemed an arbitrary and confiscatory enactment which violated existing property rights in an outrageous fashion. "The credit and fair fame of Canada," he told Meredith, the leader of the Conservative opposition in Ontario, "are under the charge, of necessity, of the general government and Parliament, and a law of confiscation by its chief province is prejudicial and might be ruinous to the credit and best interests of every man, woman, and child in the Dominion."[16] For these reasons the Rivers and Streams Act had been disallowed; and at once a thunderous roar of protest split the cloudy skies of Ontario. It was apparent that Mowat would not be intimidated into an immediate surrender. Obviously a new fight was on.

Macdonald was concerned about Ontario. Ontario was very much in his mind when he came up to Toronto towards the end of November to attend the provincial Liberal-Conservative convention. General elections were not very far away in both the province and the Dominion; and the delegates who had come in hundreds from all over Ontario must be sent back to their constituencies bursting with fighting spirit. He shook

hands with them, called them by name, talked with them,
watched them benevolently and hopefully as they listened to
speeches and applauded the passage of resolutions; and at the
end of the second day's proceedings, they crowded, nearly a
thousand of them, into the pavilion of the Horticultural Gardens
for the final dinner at which Macdonald was to speak. The

ANOTHER MILE-STONE PASSED; or, FATHER TIME AS SPRY AS EVER.

walls were hung with Union Jacks and decorated with mottoes, portraits, and coats-of-arms; and over the platform, the crown and the inscription "God Save the Queen" were picked out in flaring gas jets. The diners rose, as one man, when he entered the room; and the band crashed into "See the Conquering Hero Comes".

His theme, when he got up to speak, was the theme of the nation he was creating. He had made a reality out of a dream; and the miraculous success of his policies seemed, to his auditors, to supply an incontrovertible argument against any alternative conception of Canada and its future. He dismissed, as equally false and delusive objectives, Canadian "independence" and imperial federation. Canada must remain, what it had become, an autonomous nation inside the British imperial system; and if it kept steadfastly to its first and true course, the certainty of transcontinental nationhood lay before it. He contrasted his own national policies with the international trade and railway policies of Mackenzie and Blake. He talked about his schemes for western settlement; and he revealed, for the first time, the great change of plan by which the Canadian Pacific Railway hoped to hasten the completion of the north shore route. The whole transcontinental, he told his audience —and the whole pavilion yelled applause—would now be finished in five years instead of ten. "I now have some chance," he said proudly, "if I remain as strong, please God, as I now am, of travelling over it in person before I am just quite an angel."[17]

II

As he watched over the domestic scene, and prepared for the next session of Parliament and the general election which probably lay beyond it, he looked up, every now and then, for a quick glance at the horizon of international affairs. In one direction at least, there was hardly a cloud in the sky. He had predicted that once the presidential election in the United States was safely over, the pre-election sabre-rattling against Great Britain and Canada would suddenly and mysteriously subside. He had been nearly right. Nearly, but not quite.

Most of the American crusades and grievances appeared to be forgotten; but the prospective Panama Canal, in which an interest had been revived by the activities of de Lesseps, was a clear and somewhat startling exception. Blaine, the new American Secretary of State, laid claim, in contravention of the terms of the Bulwer-Clayton Treaty, to an exclusive protectorate over the canal. The pretension irked Macdonald. For a while he contemplated the formality of a minute of council protesting against Blaine's demand. "England was an American power," he argued to Lord Lorne, "quite irrespective of the Thirteen Colonies before the United States existed; and Canada having now a larger population than the United States when the Monroe Doctrine was announced, and the certainty (humanly speaking) of a great future, has precisely the same interests to guard as the United States. That government claims the protectorate from the necessity of keeping open under all circumstances the water communication between the Atlantic and Pacific portions of their territories *via* the canal. The same necessity exists as to Canada."[18] The same necessity existed, no doubt; but Canada, independently of Great Britain, had very little power of impressing others with the importance of its requirements. The idea of a Canadian minute of council was given up;[19] and instead Lord Lorne was requested, when he went over to England in the autumn, to put the point of view of the Dominion to Lord Granville at the Foreign Office.[20]

The Anglo-Canadian alliance remained the basis of Macdonald's foreign policy. It could hardly be called a very cordial alliance during the second of Gladstone's administrations. There was a frigid air of grim historical necessity about it which seemed to chill most attempts at hearty co-operation. Macdonald drew no inspiration from Gladstone's unbenevolent detachment. He felt he could expect little good from the Liberals; he sometimes thought despairingly that all that was possible was to prevent them from doing Canada positive harm. And yet, in his heart of hearts, he knew all the time that he must not let this negative, defeatist attitude get control of his mind for a single minute. He must keep on trying, as he had tried so often before, to arouse British interest in the country he was creating. Canada wanted immigrants. She needed capital. And she saw in Great Britain the safest and most natural source of both. Great Britain must somehow be induced to believe in the Canadian north-west and to support the Canadian Pacific Railway. The brawn of British immigrants, the funds of British investors, the co-operation of the British government —they were all necessary.

It was for these purposes, in large measure, that Macdonald had established the office of High Commissioner for Canada and had sent Galt to England. But he was beginning to suspect that Galt, for all his very real talents, was not very likely to achieve the desired results. That autumn, after a highly diverting but extremely expensive tour in western Canada, the High Commissioner had gone back to his post in London. He went; but he went reluctantly, unenthusiastically, with little of his old romantic zeal for diplomacy; and in London he began once again to experience the familiar dismal succession of discomforts, illnesses, disappointments, and frustrations. Yet, curiously enough, his woes seemed to have no effect whatever on his irrepressible imprudence. He had been back in London only a month when he informed Macdonald that he intended to re-open the subject of assisted immigration with Kimberley, and that he proposed to take part—on the side of protection, of course—in the somewhat academic controversy then going on in England between "fair trade" and "free trade".[21]

Macdonald was aghast. Gladstone, for whom the verities of free trade were only slightly less impregnable than those of Holy Scripture, might take the deepest offence at Galt's bumptious hardihood. "Gladstone, if I read him aright," Macdonald wrote to Galt, deliberately exaggerating Gladstone's malignancy in order to frighten his High Commissioner, "is governed by his hates, and is as spiteful as a monkey. In a fit of rage he might denounce Canada and its future, and show the danger continually hanging over England by Canada's proximity to the United States, and the necessity of her fighting our battles. In fact there is no knowing what he might do. . . ."[22] A "fair trade" pamphlet by the High Commissioner of Canada— an intervention in British domestic politics by a colonial who claimed to be a diplomat—was an unthinkable enormity. A premature re-opening of the immigration question was, of course, a good deal less dangerous; but, even so, it would probably do some harm.[23] Macdonald had become convinced that an assisted immigration scheme, even if it were designed mainly to relieve the congestion and misery of troubled Ireland, could not be proposed, with any hope of success, unless it were preceded by a good deal of careful diplomatic preparation. Galt had already done his best; but Galt's efforts alone were plainly not sufficient. He must be assisted by others; and Macdonald had two people in mind, as unofficial and semi-official envoys. One was Archbishop Lynch of Toronto, who, he hoped, might win the good will and support of the Roman Catholic hierarchy of Ireland. The other was George Stephen.

Early in 1882, in a mood of superb assurance, Stephen departed for England. Before he left he had begun negotiations with Chapleau for the sale or lease of the Quebec provincial railways. The fact that the Canadian Pacific had now acquired a through line as far east at least as Montreal was, of course, highly distasteful to the officials of the Grand Trunk Railway. But there were other activities of Stephen's which offended them even more. The Grand Trunk Railway looked upon the territories of southern Ontario and Quebec with a jealously proprietorial eye. There were times when its spokesmen seemed almost to imply that the terminus of the Canadian Pacific ought to have remained fixed at Callander, by the east end of Lake Nipissing, exactly at the point specified in the charter. Callander had, in fact, been chosen originally as a neutral point, midway between Toronto and Montreal. Obviously the great national transcontinental could not remain suspended in the wilds of northern Ontario; and if there was any doubt on this point, it had been effectually removed by other clauses in the charter which empowered the Canadian Pacific to acquire the Canada Central, and "to obtain, hold, and operate" other railways from Ottawa as far as the Atlantic seaboard.[24] These facts were given only the most pained and loftily distant recognition by the officials of the Grand Trunk Railway. The Canadian Pacific, they seemed to say, might be permitted, if it was good, to advance respectfully from Callander as far as Montreal. But this was the absolute limit of indulgence! Yet it was a limit which Stephen seemed already to be transgressing. He and his associates were known to have acquired a considerable interest in several eastern railway properties which would give the Canadian Pacific a competitive line from Montreal into south-western Ontario, as well as a bridge across the St. Lawrence into southern Quebec. The consternation and fury of the Grand Trunk directors mounted. Their opposition to their young rival became more vehement and undisguised.

The facts had to be recognized, Macdonald knew. The Grand Trunk, despite its pious disclaimers, had become the avowed and determined enemy of the national transcontinental. "Tyler did all he could, per fas et *nefas*," Macdonald wrote angrily to Galt, "to kill our attempts to form a syndicate in 1880. . . . I have heard Tyler in a speech at the Trinity House attack our Lake Superior route, and I know he is endeavouring to keep the syndicate out of the English market. If I *live* I shall pay Sir Henry off."[25] This threat could hardly be carried out in any simple and literal fashion, for the Grand Trunk Railway had an important function to perform in the Canadian economy and Macdonald could not afford to alienate its direc-tors, even if he had wanted to do so. But it was obvious that some kind of defence must be marshalled at once against Grand Trunk propaganda in England, for it threatened the gravest possible damage to the Canadian Pacific and the Canadian north-west. T. C. Patteson, the ex-editor of the Toronto *Mail*, had already been sent over to London to reply to the vicious attacks of what Stephen called the Grand Trunk's "paid ink-slingers". Stephen himself, who haughtily declared to Macdonald that he had gone to England to advertise his lands, not to beg for money from British investors, threw himself, with his usual furious energy, into the task of promoting the Canadian north-west as a home for British emigrants. Yet these efforts were curiously ineffectual. It was almost impossible to get any favourable publicity for Canada in the English press. "'Jumbo', the big elephant recently bought by Barnum," declared Stephen disgustedly, "is a matter of ten times more interest to London than twenty colonies. . . . The fact is that emigration is not popular, there is an instinctive feeling that they are losing national power when they decrease in numbers, even when the emigrant goes to a British colony, and the genuine insular Britisher hates all emigration efforts, and would rather have the people remain to struggle and sometimes starve than to emigrate."[26]

If any emigration could be justified, it was emigration from over-populated and agitated Ireland. A nation of peasant farmers, Ireland had suffered far more than England from the great depression in agriculture. Widespread distress had been followed by widespread violence; and in two years the organization of the Land League and the genius of Charles Stewart Parnell had raised the problem of rural Ireland into one of the most imperatively urgent questions of the day. W. E. Forster's Coercion Bill was one answer; another was the great measure of Irish land reform which Gladstone had introduced in the session of 1881. But was there not, argued the Canadian and some British imperialists, another possible solution, a solution which would apply neither coercion nor concession, but which would solve the problem of Ireland's over-population and misery by removing its victims to a land of better opportunity? Ever since Macdonald's talk with Cardinal Manning in the previous summer, he had been hoping to persuade an influential Irish-Canadian priest to go to Ireland and enlist the support of the Irish Roman Catholic hierarchy in a scheme of assisted emigration. He invited Archbishop Lynch of Toronto to found "a new Ireland"— tempered slightly by representatives of other British nationalities—in the Canadian north-west;[27] and late in February Lynch reported that he had received permission to undertake the Irish mission.[28] He was likely to be a rather expensive representative. He hinted delicately to Macdonald that on long journeys he usually travelled with a secretary and a personal servant. "His Grace is fond of attention . . . ,"[29] Macdonald remarked significantly to Galt; and Galt dutifully busied himself in arranging courtesies in official London. Then Lynch went off to Dublin, and Macdonald waited anxiously. The appalling state of Ireland was surely, he told himself, an irrefutable argument in favour of his plan. "It seems to me," he wrote to Galt, "that Gladstone and Forster must now in desperation look to emigration as a remedy."[30]

III

At this point, there occurred a contretemps which had the most unfortunate effects on the cause of emigration in particular and Anglo-Canadian relations in general. Parliament had opened, as usual, in mid-winter. It was by now an open secret that this session was to be the last before a general election took place. "I have a sort of idea," John Rose had written early in February, "that you will take advantage of the flood tide of popularity and success and dissolve after the session."[31] It was the right decision—the only possible decision, Macdonald knew. The flood-tide of popularity and success was at its golden full. "Money is rolling in on the treasury," the Governor-General wrote complacently to the Colonial Secretary. "The number of people going to the west from Ontario alone will probably be twenty thousand this year."[32] Many old Canadian homes were affected by this exodus; Macdonald's own home was affected; and Hugh's decision to move with his wife and their small daughter to Winnipeg in the spring of 1882 was, in its way, the Macdonald family's personal endorsation of the promise of the Canadian north-west.[33] Everybody, surely, was convinced of the success of the national policy of protection. Proudly and enthusiastically the Canadians had accepted the transcontinental nation which Macdonald was bringing into being with a few triumphant passes of his enchanter's wand. He was at the height of his success. The time for him to dissolve was now.

Everybody knew it. The session was tense with the excitement of expectation; the days were full of acting, advertisement, and self-glorification. Both sides—and particularly the opposition—were striking attitudes, making declarations, and laying down general principles with the greatest possible fervour and conviction. On April 14, the Commons stayed up all night to finish its discussion of the disallowance of the Rivers and Streams Act;[34] and within the next week two slightly less prolonged debates on two equally exciting subjects had taken place. Blake proposed an amendment on the motion to go into supply, affirming Canada's right to negotiate its own commercial treaties;[35] and John Costigan, an Irish Roman Catholic member, introduced a set of resolutions on the unhappy state of Ireland which respectfully but none the less definitely requested Her Majesty to restore Irish civil liberties and to grant Ireland Home Rule.[36] Blake's motion, which revived the old theme on which Galt and Huntington had expatiated over ten years before, would, Macdonald knew, give some aid and comfort to the anti-colonials in Great Britain. But he also suspected that the consequences of the Costigan resolutions might be much worse. The Costigan resolutions, advanced at this of all inappropriate moments in Ireland's history, might drive Gladstone and his Liberal government into a state of revengeful fury.

How could he head Costigan off? Costigan was the rival of the Liberal, Timothy Anglin, for the leadership of the Irish Roman Catholics of eastern Canada. The Irish Roman Catholic vote in the approaching election was trembling in the balance; and Macdonald was well aware of the fact that if Costigan did not raise the Irish issue, Anglin or some other Liberal would unquestionably do so, and in a much more provocative fashion. Besides, why should it be contemptuously assumed that Canadian reflections on the state of Ireland were a mere impertinence? Canadians believed that their happy experience under the federal system was a strong argument in favour of a measure of Irish home rule; and, as Macdonald pointed out to Lord Lorne, a country which had suffered repeatedly from Fenian raids, felt not unnaturally that it had a legitimate interest in the solution of the Irish problem.[37]

He expected trouble. And trouble came. He thought the Costigan motion ill-timed; but he could not anticipate the full horror of its tragic inappropriateness. The resolutions passed the Canadian House of Commons on April 21. On May 6, barely a fortnight later, a new Viceroy, Lord Spencer, and a

new Chief Secretary for Ireland, Lord Frederick Cavendish,
arrived in Dublin to begin an era of conciliation and co-operation. Dusk was falling on that day of procession and ceremony when Lord Frederick Cavendish and his Permanent
Under-Secretary, Thomas Henry Burke, were horribly murdered in Phoenix Park, within sight of the Viceregal Lodge,
by a gang of murderous Irish extremists who called themselves
"Invincibles". Even before the hideous tragedy in Phoenix
Park occurred, there had been critical comment in England
about the Costigan resolutions; but after May 6, the request of
an irresponsible colonial legislature for clemency to the murderous Irish ceased to be a mere impertinence and became a
positive outrage. "The people of this country," wrote Lord
Kimberley coldly to Lord Lorne, "have shown wonderful calm-
ness under immense provocation, but they are not in a temper
to be trifled with by anglers for Irish votes at elections for
colonial legislatures."[38] Mr. Gladstone and the Colonial Secretary made no attempt to hide their displeasure. The discussion of the Irish immigration scheme degenerated into argument
and angry futility.[39] Galt was furious. He was, he declared
emphatically, coming home to Canada again for the summer.
He had already resigned—for the second time!

Macdonald shrugged his shoulders. He had no time for
annoyance or regrets. Galt's temperament was a nuisance and
assisted immigration seemed an insoluble puzzle. But the
general election, on which everything depended, was now only
a couple of months away. He was already deep in preparations
for it; and on April 28, when the murders in Phoenix Park were
still over a week away, he introduced in the House of Commons
a measure which, in the eyes of his followers if not entirely
in his own, was to have a decisively favourable influence upon
the outcome of the election.[40] It was a Representation Bill,
made necessary by the results of the decennial census of the
previous year. The British North America Act provided that
each province was to have as many seats in the House of
Commons in proportion to Quebec's fixed number of sixty-five
as its population warranted; and the census now revealed that
Manitoba must be given one additional constituency and Ontario

four. How, in the absence of precise instructions in the British North America Act, was this to be done? In 1872, when the first post-Confederation changes in the representative system were made, Macdonald had explained that, although population had been regarded as the basic principle of the adjustment, other factors—"interests, classes, and localities"—had also been given consideration; and, as a result of this deference to local feeling, the boundaries of the constituencies had not been permitted to cross municipal or county lines.[41] In the redistribution of 1882, on the contrary, numerical equality triumphed over local patriotism. Local divisions were cheerfully disregarded in Ontario; and townships were freely transferred, for electoral purposes, from their own to neighbouring counties. As a result of these complicated exchanges, approximate equality of population was certainly achieved. It was Macdonald's avowed object. But he had another object which, though undeclared, was no less real. The redistribution was designed to secure a party advantage. Liberal voters were to be concentrated in as few ridings as possible, thus increasing the Conservatives' chances of success. Macdonald intended, in short, to "hive the Grits".[42]

This, the opposition declared in a paroxysm of moral indignation, was a *gerrymander*. It was, the *Globe* observed, a piece of political trickery so base and shameless as to win for Macdonald "an immortality of infamy". These scarcely novel maledictions left Macdonald unmoved. He was unabashed and unrepentant. "I will unwhig that honourable gentleman," he said, quoting with relish Pitt's taunt to Fox, "if ever he goes back on Whig principles."[43] And now the preposterously incredible had happened, and the Liberals had abandoned the ancient Reform doctrine of representation by population. ". . . We, the majority of the Ontario representatives in this House," Macdonald declared with ironic unction, "are fighting the battle of representation by population against the indignant protests of the honourable gentlemen opposite." It was a diverting position to be occupying; but Macdonald evidently did not take the battle too seriously and did not mean to let it go on too long. His introduction of the bill and his rebuttal on the first evening were brief; he did not speak on the second reading at all. And he infuriated his

opponents by opposing their lugubrious prophecies with comforting realism. Voters, he explained reassuringly to the opposition, could not be carted off with impunity like cabbages.
The political consistency of districts was a myth which had
been completely exploded by the history of the elections of the
1870's. "It shows," he concluded with smiling common sense,
"that the argument to be drawn from the supposed political
proclivities of any locality is worthless—there is nothing in it."[44]

He hoped and believed, of course, that there was something
in it. He must win the election of 1882. Five more years of
power were necessary to complete the work that he had set
himself to do. "You will not forget the fact," Stephen reminded him significantly, "that the Canadian Pacific Railway
is in reality in partnership with the government in the construction of the national railway. . . ."[45] It was true; but the
national railway was only one of the enterprises to which his
government stood committed. Macdonald's whole programme
had now been presented to the Canadian people; and what he
wanted, at this crucial point of mid-passage in the nation's
career, was the confirmation of an overwhelming vote of approval. He could carry the huge project forward to its desired
conclusion only if he had the confidence born of an emphatically favourable judgment. The judgment must confound all
his enemies. It must be rendered, not only against Blake, but
also against Blake's scarcely less dangerous ally, Oliver Mowat.
Blake was opposing the national railway and the national
policy of protection with continental transport and international free trade. Mowat was combating the ideal of a
great united Dominion with provincial rights and territorial
aggrandizement. Mowat threatened the division of powers
which he had laid down nearly twenty years before at Quebec.
The preponderance of Ontario endangered the economic and
political equilibrium of the whole Dominion.

The election was now only a month away. But he felt fit
and ready for it. Earlier in the spring there had been a disquieting return of his old symptoms. "I have had a warning against
overwork," he had written Lord Lorne early in April, "by an
attack similar to one of last spring and have been at home

since Saturday last. I hope to get out tomorrow."[46] He had taken precautions then and the precautions had more than sufficed; and on May 17, when the session and the Parliament came to an end, he felt well and fairly confident. No election was ever a certainty, of course, and he knew that in Ontario he would be fought with the fury of desperation. But on the whole, he and his intimates faced the contest with comparatively light hearts. "I have no misgivings about the result of the elections," Stephen wrote robustly. "I cannot believe that the country which is now prosperous beyond all precedent wants any change in its rulers."[47] Macdonald did not really believe it either. His own position, he knew, was very strong, and Blake's recent manœuvres were a tacit admission of the fact. The acknowledged success of the national policy of protection had compelled the leader of the opposition to modify the stiff-necked rigidity of Mackenzie's and Cartwright's free-trade principles. Blake—it was a highly gratifying sight—was hedging about the tariff!

He was eager to be away—many of the ministers had already left town—but he characteristically remained until May 25, when the Royal Society of Canada, the nation's first learned association, held its first meeting in the Senate chamber. He looked his old self—genial, gracious, oddly youthful—as he and Agnes greeted the Fellows and listened to the Governor-General's opening address.[48] That night they left for Kingston; and the next afternoon, after only a brief visit to the Williamson house and a luncheon with a few personal friends, they were off again for Napanee, where Macdonald was to make the first speech of the campaign. He had decided to give up his British Columbia seat, and to return to Ontario—not, indeed, to Kingston, but to the region of the old Midland District, of which Kingston had once been the capital. He would run for Lennox, where he had lived as a boy; and he would give his first speech in Napanee, where he had gone, nearly half a century before, to establish the branch law office for his master, George Mackenzie.

The place was packed that Friday afternoon with his admirers. The main hall in town was secured, and then rejected

as inadequate. The theatre, hurriedly substituted as a place
of meeting, was in turn abandoned for the same reason. In
the end he faced the great crowd in the open air of the market-
place. It rained—a patter of drops towards the close of his
speech. But the crowd did not budge. It listened in silence
while he dealt faithfully with both Blake and Mowat, with
national policies and Dominion-provincial relations. It was
attentive. But it was far more than attentive. It was interested,
warmly sympathetic, and, at the right moments, vociferously
responsive. And, as the bursts of laughter and applause followed
in swift and encouraging sequence, Macdonald's confidence
mounted. He had been right. This time, the game was really
in his hands. He had flushed Blake from the prickly covert
of free-trade dogma, and the hunt was up. Blake, he told his
audience, had discovered that the national policy was now
enthusiastically accepted by the entire country. Blake knew
that he must change his views. But he could not admit that
he had changed them. "He therefore tried to hedge," Macdonald told his delighted listeners. "He tried to wear two
faces under one hat—or, as the Yankee sailor said—'to steer
south by north'."[49]

That night he left for Toronto. From Toronto, the capital
of his rival, Oliver Mowat, he would direct the struggle for
that politically dominant but politically uncertain region, the
central and western part of Ontario.

IV

"We have had a hard fight in Ontario," he wrote to Lord
Lorne on June 22, two days after the election, "and had to
face the sectional and independence cries raised by the opposition. Still we are the victors."[50] They were indeed the victors.
With one hundred and thirty-nine seats to seventy-one, they
had yielded only a few inches of their commanding position.
They had won in every province but Manitoba. In Ontario,
where it was so important to combat Mowat's pugnacious provincialism, they had lost seats, but still retained a substantial

THE MARQUESS OF LANSDOWNE

THE MARQUESS OF LORNE

Public Archives of Canada

majority; and the defeat of some of the more prominent of the
Liberal leaders would certainly weaken, for a while at least,
the attacks which the opposition could mount in the new Parliament. "The victory is complete," Tilley wrote jubilantly
from New Brunswick.[51] Macdonald, who had made good his
return to Ontario, was pleased with the results, and pleased too
that he had not broken down in the struggle. But at the
moment his exhaustion was extreme. "I am completely used
up," he wrote to Lord Lorne. "Travelling night and day and
continual 'field preaching' have been too much for a man of
sixty-seven. I shall, however, soon pull myself together again."[52]

The "pulling together" process took longer than he had anticipated. In another ten days, he left for Rivière du Loup. But
late in July a series of Council meetings, at which, among
other things, Joseph Chapleau was made a minister and the
other new appointments to the Cabinet were decided upon,
called him back to Ottawa; and this brief return to the stifling
summer capital ended unhappily in another prostration. "As
I am not quite right yet," he wrote to Lord Lorne on July 28,
immediately before his departure, "I intend to stick to the rail
until I arrive at Rivière du Loup. I shall thus be able to maintain a recumbent position which is so desirable to me just
now."[53] At Rivière du Loup he recuperated slowly but surely.
He had promised himself a lazy, substantial, satisfying holiday
—a holiday long enough to conceal for a while the inexorably
rapid return of duties. And although there were often callers,
and the post-bag was always full, nothing of great importance
arose to trouble him. There was some discussion of the British
proposal to remove the imperial garrison at Halifax for service
in Egypt;[54] and, together with Lord Lorne and the Duke of
Cambridge, the imperial Commander-in-Chief, he earnestly
debated the unfortunate case of Major-General Luard, the
officer commanding the Canadian militia, an elderly military
man, who seemed imperfectly aware of the fact that he was
the servant of the Canadian government, and thus subordinate to
the new and energetic Minister of Militia, Adolphe Caron.[55]

Still, these were relatively minor affairs. They were small
vexations in a very general contentment. It seemed that

summer that nothing could go wrong with the programme of
the Conservatives. Macdonald had won the general election;
he was winning transcontinental dominion with the railway;
and over in London he had just emerged successfully from an
important round in the fight for the Canadian constitution. On
June 22, two days after the general election, a crucial decision
respecting the powers of the Dominion under the British
North America Act was handed down by the Judicial Committee of the Privy Council.[56] The suit had been brought by
an innkeeper named Russell, who had resisted the enforcement of the Canada Temperance Act on the ground that it
conflicted with the provincial right to impose licences and to
legislate in respect of property and civil rights. For years Macdonald had been arguing that the Canada Temperance Act
was well within the authority of the Dominion and that the
Ontario Licence Law was an unwarrantable exercise of provincial power. Early in the election campaign, provoked by a
direct question on the subject, he had expressed his opinion
openly and in the most unequivocal terms. He had boldly
told his audience at Yorkville that the Ontario Licence Act was
"not worth the paper it was written on". And he had gone
on to promise—and the promise was not forgotten—that "if he
carried the country, as he would do, he would tell Mr. Mowat,
that little tyrant, who had attempted to control public opinion
by getting hold of every little office from that of Division
Court bailiff to a tavern-keeper, that he would get a bill passed
at Ottawa returning to the municipalities the power taken
away from them by the Licence Act".[57]

Now he could make good his promise. He had insisted on
the constitutionality of the Canada Temperance Act. He had
boasted that his judgments on constitutional questions had
never been reversed. And now, apparently, he had been completely vindicated. In its decision in Russell *v.* the Queen,
the Judicial Committee of the Privy Council had declared that
the Canada Temperance Act was *intra vires* of the federal Parliament.[58] It was a judgment based upon an ample interpretation of the Dominion's residuary power to legislate for the
"peace, order, and good government of Canada" in all matters

not exclusively assigned to the provinces. The Judicial Committee had, in fact, decided that the federal Parliament could legislate under the residuary clause for genuine national objects even though such legislation might incidentally affect "property and civil rights in the province". No judgment could possibly have given Macdonald more satisfaction. For him the residuary power had always been the great determining fact in the distribution of powers at Confederation. And now it was freed from the dangerous encroachments of "property and civil rights". He could carry forward his programme of national legislation unimpeded. He could brush that obstructive provincialist, Mowat, out of his path.

It was a lucky summer. The Conservative party was victorious and its national policies were in the ascendant. Everything seemed made for success; and the climax of the whole long record of accomplishment was the stupendous progress of the Canadian Pacific Railway. Nothing like such speed of construction had been expected, or had, indeed, been conceived. To Canadians it seemed a miracle, and so, in a sense, it was. But it was a miracle performed by a very human agent; and in him fortune had granted the Canadian Pacific Railway its second great gift of extraordinary ability. Macdonald had found a financial genius in George Stephen; George Stephen had discovered a genius for construction in William Cornelius Van Horne. And under Van Horne, who had joined the company early in 1882, the work of exploration, survey, and construction was pushed resolutely ahead at all points. All that summer, as Macdonald rested in the hot sun at Rivière du Loup, the reassuring and triumphant reports kept coming in. On August 19, Stephen telegraphed that construction on the north shore of Lake Superior east of Port Arthur had been begun and was being prosecuted by a large force of men.[59] Five days later he transmitted an even more portentous piece of information which had come in from beyond the end of steel just a few minutes earlier. "Just heard from Major Rogers," Stephen's telegram read. "He has found a good line through the Selkirk range. No tunnel. This is good news."[60] It was better news than they had a right to expect, for they had been committed to the southerly route for a year, and only now had they found a practicable pass through the towering masses of the Selkirks. But Stephen and his associates assumed success; and in this golden high noon of the enterprise they seemed to be able to command it at will. Everybody marvelled at the swiftness of their progress. A long succession of important visitors—Galt, Tupper, Brydges, of the Grand Trunk Railway, and Sir John Rose—all went west that summer, inspected the miracle of construction, and reported their admiration to Macdonald. "The railroad is really most creditably built," Galt wrote from Qu'Appelle, "and being pushed with great energy. Brydges (who is not a partial witness) says he never saw such complete organization as the track laying."[61]

Yet the very speed and thoroughness of the construction hastened the arrival of a new and terrible problem—the problem of finances. From then on it was to haunt Macdonald and Stephen like an implacable and malevolent ghost. The partnership of government and company was, as Macdonald knew very well, limited sharply to a few by no means inexhaustible sources of revenue. The financial immaturity of Canada, the indifference or hostility of the important financial interests in London and New York all combined to reduce the support which the Canadian Pacific might hope to obtain. But the problem of its finances was also, and no less significantly, complicated by the methods which Stephen had deliberately adopted. Stephen was vulnerable before short-term difficulties precisely because he was a man of long-range views. His intention from the first had been to build a railway for the future. He had contemptuously rejected the practice, all too common in North American railway financing, of taking a quick and easy profit from the work of construction or the flotation of bonds. "The other plan, and the one I should have followed, had we been able to come to terms," he had explained to Macdonald in July, 1880, when his first offer to build the railway had been withdrawn, "would have been to limit the borrowing of money from the public to the smallest possible point . . . and to have looked for the return of our own capital and a legitimate profit entirely to the growth of the country and the development of the property—after the work of construction had been fully accomplished."⁶²

This was the plan which had been followed in actual fact. It ensured the railway's future strength, Macdonald believed; but it also meant an initial and terrible period of weakness. The sale of common stock, the gradual acquisition of the government subsidy and the government land grant as the building of the line progressed—these were the means by which the railway obtained the sinews of construction and operation. Only twenty-five millions of common stock had been sold, at less than half of its par value; and government assistance, in lands and money, had to be earned. Inevitably a heavy initial burden rested upon the principal members of the syndicate; and, as the vastness of the whole enterprise was gradually unfolded, this burden grew even heavier than Stephen had anticipated. "The road is going to cost a great deal more money than we calculated on," he warned Macdonald, late in August, when he had just returned from a visit to the north-west;⁶³ and during September and October, while the work of construction was pushed forward, expenditures continued to soar in a frightening fashion. The strain upon the young organization grew heavier; the burden of responsibility which Stephen carried was never out of his mind. He became more exacting in his requirements, more impatient of government delays and technicalities, more suspicious of Cabinet ministers who did not exhibit a constant and almost uncritical devotion to the Canadian Pacific, and more furiously angry with outrageous neutrals such as Galt, who, he suspected, was secretly hostile under a mask of judicious impartiality.

Macdonald bore with it all. He knew that Stephen was a person of great creative power, infinite resource, and enormous courage. But he knew also that he was a sensitive, impatient, self-centred, and imperious man. For the task which Macdonald had entrusted to him, Stephen's good qualities vastly outweighed his defects. Yet his defects—his quick pugnacity, his arrogant self-confidence, his angry impatience with criticism—were precisely those which were most likely to increase the dislike and suspicion of the enterprise which he represented. "As I remarked to you on a previous occasion," Hickson of the Grand Trunk Railway wrote to Macdonald, "your government has created a power which believes itself to be not only stronger than the Grand Trunk, but stronger than the government."[64] The arrogant autocracy of Stephen was, as Macdonald knew very well, a favourite theme of Liberal politicians. The whole opposition press had combined to hold up the Canadian Pacific as a frightful monster which would devour Canada's resources and enslave its people. Obviously the government would have to proceed with infinite caution; and the last thing which it could contemplate at the moment was the grant of further financial assistance to the Canadian Pacific Railway. Political support was another matter. Macdonald could—and did— maintain the political defences he had promised; and three more Manitoba railway charters were disallowed that autumn. But it was beyond his power to add, by so much as a dollar or an acre, to the company's financial strength. Stephen—and Stephen alone—must pull the railway through the first crisis of its difficulties.

He counted upon Stephen, and Stephen did not fail him. In December the president of the Canadian Pacific Railway left for New York; from there, after a few strenuous days of negotiations, he sailed for England. Early in 1883, it was revealed that a strong stock syndicate had been formed in New York, that its members had agreed to underwrite thirty millions of Canadian Pacific stock at an average price of slightly over fifty-two cents on the dollar, and that large blocks of the new issue were being disposed of in London and Amsterdam. "I must at the outset say," John Rose reported admiringly from London, "that the result is almost wholly due to the untiring efforts of our friend Stephen, whose zeal, energy, confidence in himself and the enterprise seem to inspire everybody with the like confidence."[65] Macdonald nodded happily. Stephen might be a tempestuous and difficult colleague. He might be, as John Rose admitted judiciously, an imperious man, intolerant of opposition and almost incapable of compromise. He might be all these things. He very probably was. But he was a great man as well. Macdonald knew it; and despite the persistent and malignant criticism of Blake, the *Globe*, and the "G.T.R. scribblers" the world would know it too in the end.

V

He caught a chill in December, and there were days when he felt far too ill to go to Council. He was sixty-eight years old on January 11, 1883; and although the chronic feebleness of his health was not likely to finish him off suddenly, it was something that he would have to make shift to live with to the end of his days. Ever since his terrible illness in the spring of 1881, he had realized that, if he wished to survive and complete his work, he must take systematic precautions to guard his health. He had always been a light eater; he was becoming an abstemious drinker. He kept a good cellar and when a correspondent in England recommended a bargain in claret, he was quick to order a couple of dozen of bottles. But the great drinking-bouts, the gargantuan insobrieties of his middle years were dwindling away now into memories. Time was galloping on. It seemed almost incredible that he had been married to Agnes for more years now than he had been married to the long-dead Isabella. "Little" Mary was a tall girl, nearly fourteen years old, and still heartbreakingly unstable and clumsy, despite all the special treatments that had been lavished upon her. Hugh, who came east for a brief visit during the winter of 1883, was now a man of nearly thirty-three. His first wife had died and he was soon to marry again.[66] How far away already that quarrel over his first engagement seemed! How incredibly distant were the days when he had been a boy in Kingston, left behind by a busy father in the care of his tall, raw-boned Aunt Louisa. And now Louisa herself was ill—so ill that that winter Macdonald nearly despaired of her life.

He knew that he must spare himself as much as possible; and he welcomed the coming of the expected mid-winter relaxation of tension. There was always a short period, between Christmas and the normal February opening of Parliament, when a brief and blessed lull occurred; and this year the session itself—the first session of a new Parliament from which some of his leading opponents had been extruded—promised to be a relatively mild affair. Throughout the country good times still continued. In Manitoba, John Norquay won a general election against an opposition, led by Thomas Greenway, which had vigorously attacked federal disallowance of Manitoba's railway charters. And in Ontario, where a provincial election had been set for February 27, the Conservative opposition was battling with such a lusty confidence that, in Macdonald's view, there was at least a chance of Mowat's defeat. A good many Ontario members of both parties were away from Ottawa, taking part in the provincial campaign; and for the first few weeks of the session, a curious holiday atmosphere pervaded the House of Commons.

Macdonald was in a most affable mood. He greeted Blake with indulgent geniality. Blake had complained, during the debate on the address, of the tedious brightness of the Conservatives' picture of the state of the nation, and had himself supplied corrective quantities of gloom. Blake, Macdonald told the House pleasantly, was darkness rather than light, shadow rather than sunshine, Rembrandt rather than Turner. "My honourable friend," he continued, "put me much in mind of an old Newcastle collier who had been boxing the compass for many years and in the exigencies of the last long voyage he had been in almost every foreign country. After a visit of seven years to the West Indies he came back to England, and when his ship was approaching the land, and when he felt the familiar sleet and storm and saw the familiar clouds, he put on his sou'wester and his peajacket and said: 'This is something like weather; none of your infernal blue skies for me'."[67]

For Macdonald, the good weather still lasted. He was determined to take advantage of it. For the session of 1883 he planned two important measures which would, in their different ways, assert the independence and authority of the Dominion. One was a Franchise Bill, designed to substitute a single, uniform federal franchise for the various provincial

franchises which up to this time had been used in federal
elections. The other was an Intoxicating Liquors Bill which
would transfer to commissioners appointed by the federal government the whole business of the regulation of the sale of
beer, wine, and spirits. A uniform, regulatory system, in the
interests of national peace and order, was the avowed aim of
the Bill. Its undeclared but very real enemy was Oliver
Mowat and his Ontario Licence Act; and its triumphant justification was the decision in Russell v. the Queen. In Macdonald's opinion, Russell v. the Queen had confounded his
opponents in Ontario. Mowat and his friends were now in
disorderly retreat. Would the election of February 27 bring
about their complete downfall? For a few hours, during that
late night in February, it almost seemed that it might.[68] Seat
after seat was falling to the Conservatives! Mowat was only
a half-dozen constituencies ahead! Hopes rose dizzily—only to
fall once more. The "little tyrant" was back in office again.
But he was in by a greatly reduced majority. As Macdonald had
predicted, he had been "run very close".[69] His complacent
confidence had been rudely shaken. And Macdonald pressed
his advantage and pushed his Liquors Bill forward.

Dominion-provincial relations were important. But so also
were imperial relations. And ever since the passage of the
Costigan resolutions and the collapse of the negotiations for
assisted immigration in the previous spring, relations between
Canada and England had remained in a sensitively delicate
state. Improvement was urgently necessary if the Dominion
was to get any effective British help in the settlement of the
north-west. But how could improvement be expected from
the astonishing diplomacy of Sir Alexander Galt? Galt
was a highly unconventional ambassador with an irrepressible
interest in new ideas and an incorrigible urge towards self-
expression. A year ago Macdonald had persuaded him only
with difficulty to refrain from publishing a pamphlet on "fair
trade". But this time Galt evaded soothing admonitions by the
simple expedient of accepting speaking engagements without
notifying his home government. At Greenock, Edinburgh, and

Liverpool, he discoursed at large upon such controversial subjects as protection, Home Rule for Ireland, and Imperial
Federation. The disconcerting news of his Edinburgh speech
reached Ottawa late in January, barely a week before Parliament
opened.

Macdonald was mildly alarmed. He told his High Commissioner that he awaited the arrival of his full report of the
speech "with some little anxiety". "I hope," he went on, "you
have not committed yourself too much to the project of
Imperial Federation which, in my humble opinion, can never
be worked out."[70] It was not that he disbelieved in the objects
for which Galt had urged a federal Parliament for the Empire.
He was just as firmly convinced as Galt that Canada must
acquire more power and assume more responsibility in respect
of those two exalted spheres of government activity, defence
and foreign policy. He had established the High Commissioner's office in London. The Dominion's tiny regular force
—the unostentatious, almost surreptitious "standing army" which
had hitherto been composed only of artillery batteries—was
now about to be augmented, as he had long intended, by the
addition of small infantry and cavalry units. He entirely
agreed with Galt that imperial defence and foreign policy must
become a collective system; but he was sure that this could be
achieved through the co-operation of autonomous governments,
and not through the establishment of new federal institutions.
He had no belief whatever in a Parliament for the whole
British Empire. He had already said so publicly at the Liberal-
Conservative Convention in Toronto over a year before. He
would say so again.

Galt's direction was emphatically wrong. But so also was his
pace. Galt, as usual, was in a hurry. But there was no need
for hurry. There was never—or almost never—any need for
hurry. Canada might spoil everything by hasty nationalistic
demands or premature assertions of maturity. During the idle
days of the previous summer, when, as Macdonald said, there
was little else to do, a few newspapers had discussed the exciting
possibility of his appointment as the next Governor-General of
Canada. It would be a good time now, while Galt was talking

airily about imperial reorganization in London, to spike these
rumours effectively; and early in the session, in response to
what was no doubt a prompted question, he dismissed the
whole idea of his elevation to the vice-regal throne as a preposterous invention.[71] In his view, the office of Governor-General
was the most important, but by no means the only, outward
manifestation of that deep inner necessity, the Anglo-Canadian
alliance. There were other public evidences of this vital connection; and he was equally reluctant to tamper with them.
Old General Luard had now become so thoroughly disliked
that during the winter, when the Militia Act was up for revision,
the Cabinet actually considered a daring amendment which
would have made imperial approval unnecessary for future
appointments to the command of the Canadian militia.[72] But
Lord Lorne became alarmed at this extremism, and Macdonald
drew back in apprehension. He was reluctant to cut the connection between the two divisions of a unitary defence system.
"The section in the Militia Bill relating to the Major-General
commanding," he wrote to Lord Lorne, "will remain unaltered."[73]

Galt's pronouncements on the imperial connection had certainly been gratuitous and indiscreet; but they need not be
regarded too seriously, for Imperial Federation remained a highly
theoretical subject. It was very different with the burning topic
of Home Rule for Ireland. Macdonald had good reason to
suspect that the British press and the British government
might be resentfully on the watch for unwanted Canadian
advice about Ireland. "I don't know that the allusions to the
Irish question and Home Rule were necessary," he told Galt,
"and think that on the whole they had better, as the Yankees
say, 'have been hired out'."[74] It was, on the surface, a mild,
characteristically jocular rebuke; but it marked, nevertheless, a
definite change in Macdonald's mind. He had at length become
weary of Galt's extravagances. Galt seemed incapable of learning
the first duty of a diplomatist—the duty of not meddling in the
politics of the country to which he was accredited. And he
had again suggested resignation—for the third time! Macdonald
decided to take him at his word. "Arrangements made," he

cabled, "Tupper your successor."[75] It would be very hard to let Tupper go. Everybody knew that he was not as clever as Galt; but he was loyal, and he had earnestness and force of character. "Sir C. Tupper is a man of strong temper and character," Lord Lorne warned the new Colonial Secretary, Lord Derby, "and in debate here has always been a violent and voluble speaker."[76] Macdonald would have put it differently. To him Tupper had been, quite simply, a tower of strength. He needed his support badly enough in Canada. But perhaps, in Canada's interests, it was better to have it employed in England.

The winter and the session grew old. Spring broke through the ragged drifts of snow and prorogation drew closer. He was overburdened with work, but then, at this time, he was always overburdened with work. It had not been a bad session. The Franchise Bill had run into difficulties and there would be no Factory Act. But most of his programme of domestic legislation was through; and in England the frightful consequences of Galt's indiscretions had not materialized. A mood of paternal forgiveness seemed to have extended its gentle sway over Gladstone and his colleagues. The British government appeared actually to be interested in Canada and in the settlement of its north-west. It was even possible that the British government might make a contribution in aid of emigration. A few important Cabinet ministers—including, of course, those most directly concerned with Ireland—were known to be favourable; and George Stephen, who had remained in London to promote the sale of his new issue of stock, was pressing a practical and attractive plan of assisted Irish emigration upon the attention of the Cabinet. Even so Macdonald was unprepared for the speed with which a decision was reached. On May 11 Stephen cabled giving him unofficially the gist of the British offer.[77] Gladstone's Cabinet was prepared to advance a million pounds in aid of the new company which Stephen proposed to establish as the representative of the land-holding interests of the Canadian Pacific Railway and the Hudson's Bay Company.

Macdonald hesitated. The offer was, on the face of it, exactly the kind of offer which he had been hoping for years to

persuade the imperial government to make. Yet now it was his
turn to exhibit something of the imperial government's calcu-
lating, self-interested detachment. "Parliament near prorogation," he cabled Stephen. "No legislation possible this season.
Government favourably inclined. Await details."[78] He would
await details, of course; but was he or his government likely to
be very favourably inclined to such a proposal? Obviously the
new interest displayed by the Gladstone administration in emigration had been largely prompted by the murderous violence
which reigned in Ireland; and the very considerations which
suggested the removal of Irishmen from the United Kingdom
hardened the hearts of the Canadians against their reception
in the Dominion. Why, Macdonald reasoned, should Canadians incur heavy additional obligations in order to transport the terrible Irish problem to Canada? Yet heavy additional
obligations certainly seemed to be involved in the British proposal. The million pounds was to be advanced not directly to
Stephen's new land and immigration company, but to the
Canadian government; and, in Macdonald's view, Canada
would therefore have to accept responsibility not only for the
payment of the debt to Great Britain but also for the collection
of the loans to the individual settlers. It was preposterous!
Why should Canada welcome an offer of aid made partly at
her own expense? It was Great Britain's responsibility and
wholly within Great Britain's power to give unconditional support to Irish emigration.[79]

The argument over the assisted immigration scheme continued all during the spring and early summer. But it was an
increasingly futile argument. Macdonald was not to be budged,
and his mind soon turned to other things. It was July now,
and he was anxious to get away for the long holiday at
Rivière du Loup without which he was perfectly certain he
could not carry on. He had been ill again after the prorogation.
It seemed that the end of every session was punctuated by one
of his break-downs; and his worried colleagues were once again
taking precautions to relieve him. The burden of representing
Canada abroad was being borne that summer by Tilley, Tupper,
and Macpherson; and it had been arranged that when Macpher-

son came back, he would take over Macdonald's portfolio of the Department of the Interior. Macdonald intended to keep the superintendence of Indian affairs and the control of the Mounted Police; but the whole enormous business of land granting in the north-west, which, as he assured Lord Lorne later, was "enough for any one man—and more", would henceforth become Macpherson's direct responsibility.[80]

He had slipped from under a great load of routine. But would these—or any other conceivable arrangements—really lighten the general burden of his labour and anxiety? Tupper had told him frankly that he could not hope for real relief until he stopped work. Was the time come when he should follow Tupper's advice? At the end of the session he had faced the Commons in his usual jaunty fashion. But the effort had cost him a good deal, and more than once during the early weeks of summer he wished devoutly for complete rest. "I have nearly made up my mind to get out of office," he told Plumb. "This is a good time for it and I am breaking down. I can't conceal this from myself, perhaps not from my friends."[81]

"This is a good time for it." A year ago, even six months ago, the statement might have been true. Then he could have ended his career in a real blaze of glory. The general election had been won; the success of the National Policy and the national transcontinental had been assured; the country was gratefully rich with prosperity. But those times were irrevocably gone now, and he faced a very different future. He had delayed too long; and when the summer was over and he got back to Ottawa, it was too late.

The boom began to peter out.

Chapter Eleven

Stand Fast, Craigellachie!

I

The recession had no dramatic beginning. There was no "Black Friday" to date it, no collapse of some venerable bank or commercial house to fix its commencement in popular memory. It just began. Unheralded, unannounced, unspectacular, it could hardly have made a more unobtrusive appearance. Only gradually did people become conscious of the fact that the grey, chill, all-too-familiar presence was there. A slow but persistent decline of prices set in. The stock-market at New York began to behave in an unconvinced and highly nervous fashion; and suddenly—it was a grim foreshadowing of future deficits— J. H. Pope, who was in control at the Department of Finance during Tilley's absence, reported that the government was suddenly hard up for ready cash.[1] Macdonald, who, in the last few years, had almost come to assume that annual surpluses were a Conservative prerogative, brought the matter up, in a slightly accusing fashion, on Tilley's return; and Tilley was, of course, ready with a long and somewhat involved explanation, full of references to current and capital accounts.[2] It was not entirely reassuring; and what was happening out in the north-west was far less so. The events in the north-west were ominous, for, as Macdonald knew very well, the success of his national policies and the prestige of his government depended, to a very large extent, upon the rapid and prosperous settlement of the prairies. And out on the prairies everything seemed suddenly to have gone wrong. The hectic land boom dwindled away into

a sickening stagnancy. The wheat crop of 1883 was ruined
by frost.

Lord Lorne and his consort were going home. Their tenure
at Rideau Hall had spanned the gay morning—the forenoon
and the high noon—of Macdonald's second government. They
had come to stand for good times, "royal weather", blue smiling
skies, favouring breezes, and beneficent showers. The country,
like a hardy plant, had shot up towards maturity. Its clumsy
energies had flowed vigorously into a half-dozen huge and
varied undertakings. Lord Lorne had sponsored the Royal
Society of Canada and the Royal Canadian Academy; he had
seen the start of the "National Policy" of protection and the
Canadian Pacific Railway; he had watched, with curious and
sympathetic interest, the establishment of the High Commissioner's office in London, and the first beginnings of what was
ultimately to become the new diplomatic system of the Empire.
Everything had gone well. In those first years of the administration, success had come to seem the order of nature and
failure a preposterous abnormality. Lord Lorne had brought
good luck. And now he and his royal lady were departing.
Macdonald watched them take their leave of Ottawa with real
regret, and with something, too, of an ageing man's reluctance
to accept the departure of familiar faces. "We were all unaffect-
edly sorry to part with you yesterday," he wrote the Governor-
General, "and even the apathetic Ottawa people were stirred to
the depths."[3]

The final farewells were to be said at Quebec. There the
old and the new governors would exchange their powers, and
the new régime would be set in motion by the usual elaborate
ceremony of swearing in. Lord Lorne had gone on in advance
to await the arrival of his successor; and, in a few days,
Macdonald and the entire Cabinet hastened after him. It was
past seven o'clock of a cool, clear evening in late October when
they all put out in the government steamer *Druid* from the
Queen's Wharf at Quebec to greet the new Governor-General,
the Marquess of Lansdowne.[4] Far down the river, above a point
of land, Macdonald could see the tremulous top lights of the
Allan steamer *Circassian*. To the north, the sheer cliffs of

Quebec soared abruptly into the sky. The winking lights of the town climbed upward until they seemed to mingle with the stars; the blazing lamps on Dufferin Terrace glittered like some strange and brilliant constellation; and higher still, on both sides of the river, the sky-rockets broke in the darkness like tiny meteors. The *Circassian*, its port-holes gleaming in long, beaded rows, crept gradually, deceptively, closer to the steamship wharf on the Point Lévis side; and then, suddenly, when Macdonald hardly expected it, the huge ship was upon them, its long, sleek, darkly majestic hull towering above. There was a roar of cheers from the land; and high overhead, in the lighted quarter-deck, a tiny figure could be seen acknowledging the welcome. The *Druid* puffed importantly closer; a gang-plank was flung across the chasm between the two vessels; and Macdonald, looking tall and slim and strangely boyish in the darkness, jumped lightly into the big steamer after Lord Lorne.

Macdonald had greeted more Governors-General than he cared at the moment to remember; but, though he had no reason to expect it, he was to find in this slight dark man one of the two ablest chiefs under whom he had ever served. Now he greeted him with a formal politeness which was stiffened, at least slightly, by the very real anxiety that he felt. If he had had a voice in the selection of the Crown's representative in Canada—and he had always insisted that he preferred to have nothing to do with the matter—he would certainly never have thought of including Lord Lansdowne's name in a short list of ten. Lansdowne was an Anglo-Irish peer, with extensive estates and many tenants in Ireland, and inevitably, during the growth of the violent agrarian troubles in the island, his name had become unpleasantly well known to many Irishmen on both sides of the Atlantic. Macdonald knew that there were fierce and angry Fenians in the Canadian cities and millions more of them in the United States. "There is just a possibility," he had written to Lord Lorne soon after Lansdowne's appointment had been announced, "that, as shooting landlords is not a safe game in Ireland now, the Irish American ruffians might try it on here, trusting to our unfortunate proximity to the United States, for a chance to escape."[5]

He had carried this additional worry about with him during the summer and early autumn. He had tried, with some success, to influence the attitude of the press to the new Governor; and on the night before Lord Lansdowne's arrival, he and the other ministers had met in the Hotel St. Louis to go carefully over the arrangements for his reception. It had been decided that the swearing-in ceremony was to be hedged about with a good many careful precautions, suitably disguised with pomp and circumstance. "I think it would be well," he had written Lord Lorne, "to make a considerable demonstration on the new Governor-General's assuming the government under present circumstances."[6] When Lord Lansdowne came ashore, early in the morning of October 23, he was waiting anxiously for him. He was on pins and needles of nervousness all through the formal installation at Quebec and all during the long train journey up to Ottawa. But nothing marred the ceremonious inauguration of the new Governor's reign; and at Ottawa, which they reached just as dusk was falling, the reception on the station platform could hardly have been more satisfactory.[7] The guards and the police, he noted carefully, were out in full force; but the crowd seemed orderly by inclination and even enthusiastic in its welcome. "There was not a single sign of dissent to the cheers which rang along the platform," he reported proudly to Lord Lorne.[8]

It was a good enough augury. And yet, on the whole the auguries for Lansdowne were less hopeful than they had been for Lorne. Lorne had been accepted rapturously, on trust; Lansdowne would have to make his own way by merit. And was it not only too clear already that he would have to break a path through difficulties to win his reputation? "I fear," Macdonald had written back in July, "Lord Lansdowne will have an unpleasant reign of it."[9] Had he not spoken more truly than he knew, and with more reason than at that time he could have foreseen? Was it not growing more and more obvious all the time that the coming of the new Governor had marked a real change of circumstances, a sharp and definite

shift in the winds of fortune? For weeks the signs of trouble
had been accumulating on all sides; and now the final and conclusive proof of approaching misfortune had come with a crisis
in the finances of the Canadian Pacific Railway. The railway,
Macdonald sometimes thought, was an organization secondary
only in national significance to the government itself. It was
Canada, with all its aspirations, energies, and weaknesses, in
little; and no barometer would ever record the vagaries of the
national climate with such sensitive fidelity. Everything that
happened to the railway was significant, for better or for worse.
And was it not a tragic coincidence that on October 24, the
day after Lord Lansdowne arrived in Ottawa, George Stephen
should lodge with the Minister of Railways and Canals at
Ottawa a formal petition for financial help?

Six months before there had not been the slightest sign of
such weakness. Six months before, it was true, Stephen had
very nearly concluded a general settlement of all conflicting
interests with the Grand Trunk Railway Company in London.
It was a settlement which unquestionably would have ensured
a prolonged peace, for it involved the surrender of most of the
Canadian Pacific's subordinate railway properties in southern
Ontario and Quebec to the Grand Trunk. These were large
concessions; and Stephen, at the instigation or with the approval
of his associates in North America, decided in the end that
he could not make them. The reconciliation was never carried
through; the conflict between the two railways was renewed
with greater intensity than before; and Stephen carried everything before him with a high hand. All that summer, construction was pushed forward with the furious energy which,
under Van Horne, had come to be associated with the Canadian
Pacific; all that summer the money which had been obtained
from the sale of the thirty million dollars of stock drained cease-
lessly away; and with every week that passed Stephen was
driven closer and closer to the necessity of fresh financing. He
still had resources left; but the time was very near when he
would have to augment them largely. And, as the autumn went
on, and September drifted away into October, he began to
realize that the best chance had already slipped by. The New

York market was always mercurial; but that autumn it seemed
to have grown more capriciously, more perversely unstable than
ever. Railway stocks were in general unsettled. In September,
there came a sharp break in the price of Northern Pacific, which
had a damaging effect upon the quotations of other transcon-
tinentals; and there were times also when the "bears" seemed
to have picked out the Canadian Pacific as the sole victim of
their rage. Yet Stephen would have to have more working
capital, and quickly. Fifty-five million of the Canadian Pacific's
authorized capitalization of one hundred million had already
been issued. Forty-five million dollars' worth of stock was still
available to him. Somehow he must convert a part, or all of it,
into cash.

Late in October, immediately after Lord Lansdowne, Macdonald and the other ministers had arrived in Ottawa, Stephen
reached the capital and booked a room at the Rideau Club.
In the next few years the Rideau Club, Wellington Street, and
the broad prospect of Parliament Hill were to become weari-
somely familiar to him; but now he was only at the beginning
of his prolonged ordeal of waiting upon governments and
haunting Council chambers. On October 24, he talked his
problems over at length with Macdonald.[10] He was seriously
worried, for the first time in the history of his presidency, and
he made no attempt to disguise the fact. But he was still
robustly confident of ultimate success and fertile of expedient;
and the plan which he presented for the solution of his difficulties was worked out in all his usual careful detail. Its
essence was simple. Stephen proposed to prove, by the most
convincing of all possible demonstrations, that Canadian Pacific
Railway stock was a stable five per cent security. The company
had, of course, decided at the beginning to pay a five per cent
dividend even during the period of construction; and the dividend had so far been regularly paid. But Stephen realized
that this good record could not of itself create the necessary
amount of public confidence in the future of his property. He
needed that confidence desperately at the moment. He could
not hope to get a large supply of fresh working capital without
it; and it seemed to him that the only body which could give

the public the necessary assurance was the Canadian government itself. If the Canadian government could be induced to contribute for ten years a three per cent dividend on the hundred million capital stock of the Canadian Pacific, then surely he would have given the necessary proofs of permanence and stability. The company would be left to supply only two per cent, which, on its record, it had amply demonstrated it could do; and Canadian Pacific shares would appear proudly before the world as a solid, gilt-edged five per cent investment. The government guarantee was the vital essential of the plan. Stephen wanted it badly, and he was prepared to pay for it. He never dreamed that he could expect any part of it as a gift. He proposed to buy it, with cash and securities, precisely as he might have bought an annuity for himself. As he pointed out to Macdonald, it would take twenty-five million dollars to pay a dividend of three per cent for ten years on the capital stock of the Canadian Pacific Railway. He was prepared to pay fifteen million dollars at once, and another five million on February 1, 1884, the balance to be made up of securities and other assets, including the government postal subsidy.

Macdonald looked favourably upon Stephen and his plan. The Canadian Pacific, in this sudden onset of tribulations, must be given government support. "The attempts to ruin that enterprise and *bear* the stock are most atrocious," he told Tupper indignantly.[11] He was angry with the unfriendly railway speculators in New York; he was even angrier with Sir Henry Tyler and the Grand Trunk propagandist "scribblers" in London. That the Grand Trunk should dare to attempt to undermine the Canadian Pacific and, indirectly, the government which had created and supported it, was a piece of effrontery so colossal that it could not be borne for a moment. The Grand Trunk Railway was itself a stupendous monument to government generosity and indulgence. As he reminded Tupper, it owed Canada a debt of three and a half million pounds sterling, together with a mere thirty years of unpaid interest. Much of this financial support had been supplied by Macdonald himself, in the days when he had been one of the joint heads of the government of the old united Province of Canada. He had never repudiated his action, never regretted it; government assistance had been necessary for the Grand Trunk Railway, just as it was now necessary for the Canadian Pacific, and for much the same reasons. But if the Grand Trunk's obligations had been waived with repeated generosity, they had never been cancelled or written off. Why, if the malicious attacks on the Canadian Pacific were kept up, should he not announce that he would enforce the collection of Canada's debt? "A threat of that kind judiciously used at the right time," he told Tupper, "would soon bring those people to their bearings."[12] He would carry the war into the enemy's camp! He urged Tupper and Rose to furnish him with proofs of the Grand Trunk's propagandist activities. There was certain to be a good opportunity of making use of such evidence during the next session.

In the meantime Stephen and his railway must be rescued. He was worried about Stephen. For the first time since that famous day in October, 1880, when the contract had been signed, Stephen looked depressed; and this, in a person of his "enormous pluck", was ominous. Action was obviously necessary at once; and the Cabinet decided without delay to accept Stephen's proposal, which, among other things, was easily defensible politically. Stephen's mercurial spirits rose with a bound; and it was with all his old gay confidence that he set out for New York on the afternoon of October 29 to get, as he told Macdonald, "Tilley's fifteen millions".[13] He never got them. At New York he was brutally awakened from his over-confident illusions. It was true that Canadian Pacific shares, like his own spirits, had jumped upward briefly.[14] For a day, on the announcement of the "new departure", they stood at nearly sixty-three dollars. But this, to a considerable extent, was because the government guarantee had been misinterpreted and magnified. The error was corrected; the price began to sag; the New York market became again what it had been for months, grudgingly unfavourable at best, and, at worst, malignantly hostile. Stephen, with despair in his heart, realized that in these circumstances it would be quite literally impossible to convert the huge total of forty-five million dollars of stock into working capital. He had grasped too far. He must be content with much, much less; and, within a week, he was back in Ottawa once more with a greatly reduced programme.[15] The government contribution of three per cent interest was now requested, not for the whole authorized capital stock, but for sixty-five million dollars only. It was a drastic change. It would mean, of course, that a much smaller deposit would be sufficient to buy Stephen's "annuity"; but it would also mean—an extremely important point—that he would have, in effect, only ten million dollars' worth of shares to convert into ready money. Yet, for all his searching, he could see no better course. Nor could the government. The bargain was concluded; Stephen paid over his money; and, early in November, the guarantee was announced.

For a while Macdonald hoped against hope that it would do all that Stephen had at first expected of it. "The stock ought to find a ready sale at seventy or more in the English market," he assured Tupper confidently as late as November 22.[16] But he was whistling to keep his courage up. The stock was not rising. It was falling, persistently. The government of Canada had given its guarantee, and the guarantee had availed almost nothing.[17] There was no public confidence to which the Canadian Pacific could appeal; there was only doubt, indifference, malice, and jealousy. Stephen did not dare to issue the new ten million dollars of stock, even though it bore the government's guarantee for interest at three per cent. He could do no more than pledge it in New York for a loan of five million. His plan had failed; and he and Macdonald knew it. The whole idea of purchasing public confidence and support with a government dividend had proved a complete and overwhelming failure.

Financially, the company was much worse off than it had been before Stephen had ever conceived the notion of the guarantee. It had paid out nearly nine million dollars—the first instalment of the purchase price; it had given security for the payment of the remainder; and all that it had got—or seemed likely to get—from the whole transaction was a loan of five million dollars. The prestige of Canada had unquestionably suffered. The company had been dealt a savage blow; and, from the beginning of December, its position rapidly and steadily deteriorated. Stephen was appalled by the number and the venom of his enemies. He began to realize—what Macdonald had known from the beginning—that there were powerful interests in the world which had deliberately determined to effect the ruin of his railway. "You are right," he wrote to Macdonald. "We have nothing to look for from the Yankees but jealousy and bitter hostility, and as to London our friends there will do their best to feather their own nests without caring much what happens to us here."[18] He did what he could to avert disaster. He battled against his enemies with passionate energy. While the market went to pieces, he kept rushing back and forward between Montreal and New York, trying to restore confidence and stop the spreading damage. But it was hopeless and soon he knew it. "Something must be done at *once*," he wrote urgently to Macdonald, "to put the company out of discredit or we had better give up and let the government step in and carry on the business. . . ."[19]

A fortnight before this, Macdonald had made his decision. He knew what he must do. New York, London, Paris, Amsterdam—the whole investing world—had failed the Canadian Pacific. But the Canadian Pacific was a project of the Canadian nation; and, in its extremity, it had turned back to the Canadian nation for support. The support must be granted. But to push it through the Canadian Parliament would require the help of the railway's every friend and well-wisher. On December 3, he cabled to Charles Tupper in London, begging him to return to Canada. Only a few months before, Tupper had sailed for England to become the second Canadian High Commissioner. It was a job to which he had looked forward, which he was certain to enjoy. But he was not to spend the winter of 1884 in London, making the pleasant acquaintance of his new duties. He was still a member of the Canadian Cabinet and still Minister of Railways and Canals; and his place, in this new crisis, was elsewhere.

"Pacific in trouble," Macdonald wrote on the cable form. "You should be here."[20]

II

The soft, comfortable, easy-going days of the administration, the days when he had always done right, when it had been hardly possible for him to do wrong, were gone, and probably for ever. Something harder and infinitely more exacting confronted him. How would he be able to face it? Yet he assumed, and almost as a matter of course, that he would have to face it. Another year had vanished, another parliamentary session was rapidly approaching; and he was no nearer to retirement. That autumn he moved his household again and for what he must have felt obscurely was the last time. He had been a tenant, not a proprietor, during all the long years at Ottawa; but a year ago he had purchased what had once been known as "Reynolds' house" and which he renamed "Earnscliffe", the eagle's cliff. It was a roomy, rambling, gabled house which stood close to the edge of the great cliff of the Ottawa River, about a mile or so out of town.[21] He had lived there, over ten years before, during the winter between his long convalescence in Prince Edward Island and the meetings of the Washington Conference in the spring of 1871; and a year ago, in the autumn, he had moved in again for a few months while Stadacona Hall was in the throes of a thorough redecoration.[22] He liked the house, the peace of its isolation, the view up the river towards Parliament Hill, and the sombre prospect of the dark blue Laurentian Hills to the west.

The Macdonald family occupied the last weeks of 1883, with pleasant deliberation, in settling in.[23] There was nothing wrong with him that he or the medical men could detect; but he could hardly claim to feel very robust or energetic. "I am in pretty good health," he wrote to Tupper, "but feel tired every night."[24] He was not the most obvious leader for a hard parliamentary campaign; but even so, he was in as good a case as many of his colleagues. Sometimes it seemed as if the entire Cabinet had taken to haunting doctors' offices. Pope was wretchedly ill, Tilley feared diabetes, Campbell was afflicted with frightful headaches, and Macpherson had to go off every once in a while to get the "knots" taken out of him at some German spa. Even Tupper, who was so tough and resilient that he seemed at times to be made of steel and rubber, had been seriously ill in the previous spring. But Tupper had recovered. Tupper was the most vital, the most youthfully buoyant member of what Macdonald was beginning to consider a gang of old crocks. And Tupper had responded instantly to Macdonald's appeal for help in the Canadian Pacific crisis. He had left London for Liverpool at midnight on December 5; and the next day he had sailed for Montreal on the Allan liner *Parisian*.

Christmas was only a week away when Tupper reached Ottawa. At once he and Macdonald grappled with the crisis in the Canadian Pacific's affairs. By this time Stephen was nearly frantic. Railway shares in general, and transcontinental railway shares in particular, had been terribly shaken by the sudden bankruptcy of the Northern Pacific, the Canadian Pacific's chief rival. The price of Canadian Pacific stock had gone down to fifty-four; and everywhere that Stephen turned he met the bland, confident, contemptuous assumption that the company had run through its money, that it was finished, and that in a mere matter of days it would have to stop. His creditors, the owners of the floating debt that was killing the company's credit, were after him like a pack of wolves. He had run through all expedients. "Now there is no way in God's earth," he wrote, and even on paper his words were shrill with urgency, "by which these debts can be paid off but by a loan to the company by the government. . . ."[25] Even government, by itself, could not act swiftly enough for him now. He needed an immediate advance from the Bank of Montreal; but even more, if that were possible, he needed the large-scale assistance which only the Canadian Parliament could authorize.

Macdonald knew that he must intervene. The Bank of Montreal had reached its limit. It was terrified to advance a copper more. "The danger is a bear raid on the bank stock," Stephen explained to Macdonald, "on the ground of heavy advances to the C.P.R. without cover."[26] In private, Tupper assured the Bank's representatives, Smithers and Buchanan, that the government was ready to stand behind the Canadian Pacific for the repayment of the necessary advance. But Smithers and Buchanan intimated politely that Tupper's verbal assurance was not enough. They wanted more. Nothing less than a secret memorandum, initialed by Macdonald as well as by Tupper and Tilley, would satisfy the directors, so Stephen informed Tupper in some embarrassment on December 28.[27] The next day Buchanan came up to Ottawa. In the end he seemed satisfied with a letter, signed by the Minister of Railways and Canals, supporting Stephen's application; and in the end the Bank granted the advance, though only, as Stephen found out later, by the narrowest of squeaks, and over the strong opposition of several of the directors.[28] Yet the deed was done. Stephen had his money. He could meet the loans which matured in New York on January 8. But this, as Macdonald knew only too well, was only the beginning, the first slight instalment of the Canadian Pacific's bottomless necessities. There was more—vastly more—to come; and, in the middle of January, Stephen formally presented his scheme for the satisfaction of his requirements. He asked a government loan of twenty-two and a half million dollars; and for this he was prepared to mortgage the main line of the railway and all its lands not so far appropriated.

As he gazed at these stupendous totals, Macdonald was appalled. It was not that he doubted the reality of Stephen's necessities or questioned the wisdom of his plan. He and Tupper and Tilley and Pope and Schreiber had been over the mass of evidence till the figures danced before their eyes. The plan might be modified in detail; in order to improve its political defensibility, the conditions imposed upon the railway might have to be made more rigorously exacting. But that was all. In essence, the plan would have to stand, for there was no other way out. For the Canadian Pacific, the scheme was a proved financial need. But, for the Canadian government, was it not an obvious and utter political impossibility? Macdonald did not know. There was no certainty ahead. Less than two years ago, in the general election of June, 1882, he had won a majority which was amply sufficient for all ordinary purposes. But this was not an ordinary purpose of government. In the history of Canada, it was something out of all reason and all precedent. He could no longer rely upon mere parliamentary majorities for a solid basis of support. He was up against something which might cut through all parliamentary majorities, which might transform a disciplined army of Conservatives into a panicky mob of deserters. Yet how, at this stage, could he give up? He could not abandon the railway yet. He must go forward. And he knew it.

"We are going to stand by the C.P.R.," he wrote to Lord Lorne early in January, "but anticipate great opposition in Parliament, and fear some defection of own friends. But we shall face the opposition manfully."[29] In part, of course, the opposition would be real and sincere; in part it would be purely political; but, in addition, to some extent at least, it would not be opposition at all, but simply a self-interested determination to exact a suitable reward for support. In a federal and continental state such as Canada, every national undertaking seemed fated to be weighed down with a variety of embarrassing and often inappropriate additional projects, imposed on it by demanding provinces and regions. A Canadian national enterprise was like a medieval cargo which had to pay tribute to every robber baron along the toilsome trade route to its destination. This time, with an issue so tremendous and a sum so huge at stake, it was certain that every local interest, like so many steel-eyed, rubber-necked vultures, would be implacably waiting. In the previous summer, at long last, the Dominion had finally patched up a settlement with British Columbia. But, in these days, the straitened Province of Quebec seemed to have its tongue perpetually hanging out for more; and in the Maritime Provinces, which derived no obvious benefit from the new national highway, there was already a sinister suggestion that the Canadian Pacific should undertake the construction of a new line, a "short line"—shorter than the Intercolonial—to the sea.

There would, Macdonald knew, be threats, and sulks and importunities all round. Yet these, for all their exasperating complexity, were not the worst test that he faced. The worst test was something much more serious. He would have to gamble upon the belief which Canadians—and outsiders—held in the future of the Dominion. The Pacific railway, which was the condition of successful expansion across the continent, had reached the limit of its resources and credit. It had turned, in desperation, to the state which had given it birth. But the state was Canada, a country of a few millions of people scattered across half a continent; and Canada's resources and credit had their sharply defined limits too. Was Macdonald in danger of plunging beyond these limits to disaster? Every sign on the commercial horizon suggested the approach of bad times, the return of declining revenues and niggardly markets, the deepening of a depression which would be unfavourable for even the smallest project, and might prove fatal to a giant enterprise like the Canadian Pacific. The tests, in the next few months, would be pitilessly severe; but a real faith would survive them. It all depended on faith in the end. Could the Canadians—and those who could be persuaded to support the Canadians—be kept steadfast in the conviction that the Canadian north-west was a real homeland and that a transcontinental Canada was a viable state?

Here was the real test that he would face in the next few months. In the next few months every propagandist device would be employed, with all malice and without scruple, to undermine Canada's prestige and prospects. Blake, the Grits, the Grand Trunk "scribblers", the speculators in New York, the correspondents of Reuters and the great American press associations—the whole great watching ring of his enemies—would do everything in their power to misrepresent, belittle, and defame the plan which he would have to sponsor. Every trumpery criticism, every local protest, every sign of provincial or regional discontent—anything and everything which could be used to injure his scheme through the very destruction of Canada's credit—would be picked up, magnified, exaggerated, twisted out of all recognition of the truth. Provincial governments, provincial legislatures, regional conventions and associations—all bodies in which men gathered together as political animals—were potential sources of danger. A serious sign of disaffection in any part of the country would betray him. But there was one region, above all others, in which he was vulnerable. It was the north-west. Without a successful north-west his whole great plan of national expansion and integration was meaningless. If it began to seem really probable that the north-west would not become the homeland of a prosperous and contented population, then there could be no justification for the loan he was about to propose in aid of the Canadian Pacific, and no reason for the Canadian Pacific itself. It was as simple as that. Here lay the real crux of his difficulties. For, in the north-west, everything had changed in the last four months. The north-west had ceased to be his best asset, and had become his most serious liability. What he faced in the west now was failure, discouragement, and discontent.

He was not very surprised. He had always known that the elements of real trouble existed in the north-west. The Indians, the half-breeds, and the new settlers—each group represented a different but an equally explosive problem. For the first time in nearly a century, a Canadian government had been obliged to negotiate with large, organized tribes of Indians, and to attempt their settlement on reserves. The elaborate process by which this had been carried out was, of course, an old one; it had been worked out by Sir William Johnson in the eighteenth century and had been passed on, a valuable administrative inheritance, to the Canadian government in 1860, when the imperial authorities gave up the administration of Indian affairs.[30] There was nothing new about Indian reserves; but in the Canadian north-west the size of the areas involved, the numbers of Indians affected, and the solemnity and comprehensiveness of the treaty engagements accepted all helped to transform an old and rather simple undertaking into a new and awful responsibility. The costs were certainly high. During this and the previous fiscal year, the Dominion government had been spending at the rate of slightly over a million dollars a year on Indians. But it was barely six years since the last of the treaties had been signed with the Blackfoot in the autumn of 1877; and nobody as yet could feel any certainty that the new system was a success. The reserves remained an experiment—difficult, unpredictable, and highly dangerous.

Here the fears which Macdonald felt were the fears inspired by novelty. In the case of the half-breeds and the new settlers, they were the apprehensions of well remembered experience. The *métis* thought of themselves as a "nation". In the settlement process they were a nation of squatters. Macdonald knew, as any lawyer knew, that squatters were notoriously suspicious, impatient, and stubborn people, and that the settlement of their ill-defined claims was probably the most exasperating and difficult problem that could confront a land-granting department. He knew too—for the Red River Rebellion had demonstrated it with ugly conclusiveness—that the French half-breed squatters of the north-west were a sensitive, proud, impulsive lot, with a tradition of co-operation, semi-military in character, which made them extremely formidable in opposition. He knew all this; and he knew too that the dangers in the north-west must certainly have been magnified by the arrival of the great masses of settlers, who had been coming in ever since 1879.

"Settlement" was a process which he understood by experience. He had grown up in Upper Canada in the immense, unhappy disturbance of its "settlement" period. He, and his relatives and friends, had lived through privation, failure, pestilence, agitation, and actual rebellion. The troubled course of colonization could not have altered very radically in half a century; and the change, where it had occurred, was, he was inclined to believe, decidedly for the worse. Settlement had become a business, extremely commercial in character. The speculators, the land-grabbers, the predatory transients who exploited town-sites, accumulated homesteads, battened on honest and unwary settlers, were more numerous than they had ever been before. Politically they were dangerous, he was convinced, for they were skilful at organization, and ready to exploit popular discontent for their own purposes. "The truth is," he had written Lord Lorne over a year before, at the time of the disallowance of the three Manitoba railway statutes, "there is yet no real public opinion in Manitoba. The men who now lead the agitation are a ring of land sharks and homestead jumpers. In a year or two the solid mass of settlers will outvote and override the gang of speculators who now pose as 'the people of the north-west'."[31]

And now—far too early—the first great test of the north-west had come. The land boom had collapsed with demoralizing suddenness; the killing frost of September 7 had virtually ruined the crop of 1883. "Times could not be much worse than they are," Aikins, the Lieutenant-Governor of Manitoba, reported from Winnipeg on the last day of November.[32] The grumbling and dissatisfaction were very real, Aikins insisted; but he had no doubt also that they were being vigorously promoted by the new Liberal opposition, which, with Thomas Greenway as its leader, had arisen as a result of the controversy over federal disallowance. Macdonald braced himself for trouble. He had not long to wait. On December 19 and 20 a convention of westerners assembled at Winnipeg, and proceeded to organize themselves in the Manitoba and North-West Farmers' Union.[33] The "Declaration of Rights" which they adopted after a long discussion of their troubles was a comprehensive enumeration of grievances. They attacked high freight rates, the tariff on agricultural implements, the administration of the public lands, the Canadian Pacific monopoly of transport, and the Ogilvie monopoly of grain elevators. The principal author of all their misfortunes was, of course, the government of Canada.

Macdonald was worried. The agitation could hardly have come at a more unfortunate time. It coincided exactly with the crisis in the finances of the Canadian Pacific; and in both cases, unknown but obviously influential persons hastened to give the bad news as much damaging publicity as possible. Over a week before the convention held its meetings in Winnipeg, J. G. Colmer, who presided over the High Commissioner's office during Tupper's absence, telegraphed in great excitement that a dispatch had appeared that morning in all the London newspapers announcing a movement for redress of grievances among the farmers of the north-west. The agitation, the English readers were assured, was assuming "gigantic proportions"; and one inflammatory speaker was alleged to have threatened that, if grievances were not redressed, the agitators would

"look to Washington". "Such reports," Colmer concluded
gravely, "very harmful here."[34] They were deliberately, mali-
ciously harmful, Macdonald knew. The propaganda against
Canada was now being disseminated almost without interruption. It had become a conspiracy. John Rose reported, towards
the end of December, that hardly a day passed without some
dispatch injurious to the Canadian Pacific or Canadian interests
in general appearing in the London newspapers. "I believe myself," he wrote, "and am assured by others, that this is part of the
'bear' movement in New York, aided by confederates here,
against Canadian Pacific and all its collateral interests."[35]

Macdonald hesitated. He knew that in order to save the
Canadian Pacific he must act as quickly as possible. Yet he
shuddered at the possible consequences of action. He had
never before performed such a crucial operation, in such unfavourable circumstances, and before the vigilant eyes of so
many enemies. Adverse reports of government intentions were
being carefully prepared in advance; hostile rumours of government policy were flying about from lip to lip. Stephen
and John Rose begged him in desperation to maintain secrecy.
He had to work out the complicated provisions of the relief bill
with a wary eye for inevitable criticisms; and when Parliament
met on January 17, he had to persuade his dubious and frightened followers that further aid on a vast scale could alone save
the Canadian Pacific Railway. It all took time. It would take far
more time—how much time he could not tell—before the measure could be pushed through Parliament. And, in the meantime, it might be too late. Stephen was at the end of his tether.
When, at length, he began to realize how long it would take to
grind out the relief bill, he became nearly frantic. He told
Tupper bitterly that he would never have attempted to carry
on if he had suspected for a moment that help might not
reach him before March 1. "I am going down in the morning,"
he wrote Macdonald from the Rideau Club as he prepared once
more to return to Montreal, "and you may be sure I will do all
I can to keep things moving and in life till relief arrives, but
you must not blame me if I fail. . . . I am getting so wearied

ANOTHER CASE OF "OPEN YOUR MOUTH AND SHUT YOUR EYES."

and worn out with this business that almost any change would
be a relief to me."[36]

Macdonald was worn out himself. Stephen seemed to be
failing him; the whole over-ambitious enterprise of Canadian
nationalism was breaking apart in his hands. But his scheme was
ready, and he was determined to go through with it. On the

afternoon of Friday, February 1, after routine business had been finished, Charles Tupper rose in his place and introduced the eleven long resolutions for the relief of the Canadian Pacific Railway.[37]

III

The debate which followed was one of the longest and most acrimonious in the long and acrimonious history of the Canadian transcontinental railway. The opposition was determined to resist to the utmost. It was true, as Blake admitted with cynical frankness in the House, that he expected the relief bill to pass; but he and his friends and associates, in and out of Parliament, saw in the distress of the railway and the embarrassment of the government an opportunity which they could exploit with telling effect in the nation as a whole. The whole enormous indictment against the Canadian Pacific could now be presented to the Canadian people; every individual, agency, and interest which was opposed to the railway could now unite in a supreme and final effort to effect its undoing. Brydges, who had been general manager of the Grand Trunk Railway, hastened to Ottawa to "post" Sir Richard Cartwright on the iniquities of his company's terrible rival. Joseph Hickson, who had succeeded to Brydges' position, published the letters he had written to Macdonald in protest against the unjust and baneful relief bill.[38] In the Commons, Blake, Cartwright, and a long succession of Liberal speakers were attacking Tupper's resolutions with all the moral indignation of righteous men invited to condone a political abomination. To Blake the history of the Canadian Pacific was an unrelieved and unending chronicle of misdeeds. He denounced its dubious financial devices, its monopolistic methods of construction, its reckless changes of route, its lavish expenditures on railway properties outside its legitimate contract, its arrogant invasion of the territories of other railways in the east, and its own jealously guarded monopoly in the north-west.

But attacks from the outside were not the only danger which

Macdonald had to meet. He also had to cope with threatened defections from within. On February 14, while the vote on Tupper's resolutions was still some distance away, a large deputation of provincial ministers from Quebec appeared before Council to present the claims of their province for further federal assistance.[39] Four days later, John Costigan, who had sponsored the resolutions on Ireland two sessions previously, and who had, for some time, been a member of the Cabinet, sent in his resignation to Macdonald.[40] This action had nothing directly to do with the Canadian Pacific Railway; but it was timed to coincide with the crisis in the railway's finances and with the climax of Macdonald's difficulties. It was serious enough, for Macdonald had no wish to risk the alienation of the capricious Irish Roman Catholic vote. But the threatened revolt of the forty-odd Conservative members from the Province of Quebec was more serious still. The Quebec members vigorously supported the financial claims made by the government of their province, and a few obstreperous secondary leaders seemed prepared to make the satisfaction of these demands a condition of their vote in favour of the Canadian Pacific relief bill. Moreover, the news of the incipient insurrection got about, and was promptly given the widest publicity. "Further most injurious messages through Reuter," John Rose cabled from London, "stating resignation two ministers account Pacific and that forty-two French members vote against."[41]

Macdonald was not to be frightened or intimidated. He drove the Canadian Pacific loan forward with all the force which he could command. There was not a moment to lose. For the company, time was now literally of the essence. It survived from day to day, and lived from hand to mouth. "Meantime," Stephen wrote on February 16, "I do not see how we are to squeeze through and keep everything moving till relief reaches us. Our individual means of helping the company are exhausted and if we do not get help now, we must stop and the effect of that would be simply fatal to the company."[42] It would, indeed, be grotesquely tragic if the company, on the eve of its salvation, should be forced to incur the stigma of some temporary stoppage or default; and Macdonald and Stephen bent themselves to avert this disaster. Yet it was perilously close. The air was poisoned with rumours. The Cabinet, it was reported, was torn by dissension; Tilley was about to be impeached; the government would certainly fall. The campaign of misrepresentation and abuse was, John Rose insisted, terrifying the British investors all too successfully. It was even intimidating the banks. Tupper wrote to the Bank of Montreal, as he had written six weeks before, giving government backing to Stephen's request for a loan which would tide the company over the last few days until the bill was through Parliament. The bank refused the request. "McIntyre goes down to New York tonight," Stephen wrote after giving Macdonald this piece of news, "to raise by way of loan for a few days $300,000 which we think will keep us out of the sheriff's hands till Tuesday or Wednesday. I hope he will manage this, though he may not be able. In that case I do not know what we shall do. . . ."[43]

Macdonald scarcely intervened in the long debate; but he pushed the relief measure onward without pause and against all interruptions. He persuaded Costigan to withdraw his resignation. He smothered the incipient rebellion among the French-Canadian members. He wired Rose requesting him, in the name of the Canadian government, to remonstrate against the injurious dispatches which were appearing in the British press. "Message false," he cabled. "No ministers resigned. Pacific resolutions passed committee yesterday, yeas one hundred and thirty-six, nays sixty-three. Concurrence probable today."[44] It was only a day later, on February 22, that the House gave its concurrence to the resolutions; and the bill based upon them passed the Commons less than a week later, on February 28.[45] It was a Thursday, late at night; and Stephen believed that with the loan which McIntyre might obtain he could hold out until the following Wednesday. In the meantime the bill would have to pass the Senate. "I trust the Bill will get into the Senate tomorrow night," Stephen wrote urgently, "and I write this to ask you if you will kindly take such measures with your friends in the Senate as will induce them to give the Bill the utmost despatch consistent with decency, so that we may be sure of getting the money on *Wednesday*. I trust Tilley will be ready. . . ."[46] Wednesday, March 5, came; and in the afternoon the Commons trooped up to the Senate chamber to hear the Deputy-Governor, Sir William Ritchie, give the royal assent to the Pacific Railway loan.[47] It had been done, and done just in time.

At once, the tension eased. The floating debt in Montreal and New York, which had embarrassed Stephen so much, was paid off. "The Yankees are all happy now," Stephen wrote to Macdonald from New York, "having got their money from the C.P.R. . . ."[48] The repayment of the American creditors and the Bank of Montreal—the support of the Canadian Pacific credit in the international money markets—was the first object of the government loan; and it had certainly been achieved. But there was a second and still more important object, which was to ensure the successful completion of the railway, without further governmental assistance, by the spring of 1886 at latest. And as yet, as Macdonald knew very well, nobody could confidently predict that this goal would be attained. He could count upon nothing, really, but George Stephen's courage and ingenuity. The future of the railway was cloudy with doubt. But even this dark prospect was not the worst of his uncertainties. He could not yet be sure that he had not risked too much in granting the loan. At one stroke he had very nearly doubled the subsidy which had been given to Canada's first transcontinental railway. Would it be possible to convince Canada in particular and the world in general that these huge expenditures, on the part of a few millions of people, were justifiable? Would the Canadians be willing and able to prove to Western Europe and the Americas that his conception of a prosperous transcontinental Canada was a valid one? There was no sign of the depression lifting; there was every prospect of increased difficulty ahead. Could the Canadians, in time of trouble, support the burdens of nationhood? Or would this half-formed, half-empty country break apart under the strains which he had imposed upon it?

He could not begin as yet to frame an answer to the question. Political circumstances were already unfavourable.

By the time the session ended, on April 19, they had grown
more unfavourable still. Organized regionalism or provincialism
offered the most serious threat to the national unity upon
which he had to rely for success; and organized provincialism
seemed rampantly on the increase throughout the Dominion.
"I had to circumvent a rather ignoble plot to cause a stampede
of my French friends," he informed Lord Lansdowne in a letter
recounting some of the secret history of the session, "by offering
them, for their semi-insolvent province, large pecuniary aid.
The plot failed, but this combination of the French to force
the hand of the government of the day is a standing menace
to Confederation."[49] It was not the only standing menace to
Confederation at that moment, he knew very well. The
country seemed full of provincial animosities and discontents.
British Columbia had been pacified, New Brunswick and Prince
Edward Island were quiescent; but it was nearly two years now
since Nova Scotia had passed into the control of the enemy,
and the government of Manitoba, though outwardly loyal, was
in a restless and demanding mood. The quarrel with Ontario,
and its "little tyrant", Mowat, still continued. He was so deeply
committed to this struggle, and so much was now involved on
both sides, that the outcome was certain to be of major significance in the political and constitutional history of the
Dominion. He had hoped for a complete victory; but the time
had gone by when he could indulge these hopes any longer. He
could not win now. He might lose completely. The best he
could do was draw even.

Over a year ago he had faced Parliament with the superb
confidence born of the Dominion's constitutional triumph in the
case of Russell v. the Queen. Then Mowat had been on the
defensive, and Ontario's Liquor Licence Act had seemed to be
in jeopardy. But now the whole position of affairs was exactly
reversed. During 1883, the Judicial Committee of the Privy
Council had, in its judgment in the case of Hodge v. the
Queen, affirmed the complete validity of the Ontario Liquor
Licence Act. It was now Blake's turn to gloat over Macdonald
and cast doubts upon the constitutionality of the Dominion
Licence Act of 1883. It was now Mowat's opportunity to take

the offensive in support of his legislation against the pretensions
of the federal act. Promptly and pugnaciously he had taken
advantage of this new turn of fortune. In the course of the
winter of 1884 the legislature of Ontario enacted still another
provincial licence law which, among other things, imposed heavy
supplementary duties upon all those who took out licences
under the Dominion statute. Obviously, as Macdonald pointed
out to Campbell, these differential duties were imposed, not for
revenue, but as a penalty for any person who dared to obtain
a federal authority. "Now the idea that any subject is to be
punished in a heavy fine for obeying the law of the land," he
went on angrily, "is monstrous and cannot be put up with for
a moment."[50] In due course, the new Ontario licence law was
disallowed; but meanwhile Langevin yielded so far as to
announce that the question of the constitutionality of the federal statute would be submitted to the courts "with all convenient
speed".[51] A contest which revolved round taverns and tavern-
keepers, and which had been undertaken at least partly for the
sake of the patronage involved, was obviously nearing its end;
and the Dominion's early advantage was being steadily whittled
away. It had been a comically disreputable controversy; but
Macdonald had always regarded it seriously. He saw—and
saw correctly—its underlying significance. In the end it was
to go a long way towards deciding the interpretation of the
British North America Act.

The Licence Act of 1884 was the last Ontario statute which
was disallowed by Macdonald's government. He still believed
firmly that the Rivers and Streams Bill was an iniquitous
measure; and that winter the Rivers and Streams Bill had been
enacted for the fourth time by an invincibly determined Oliver
Mowat. Macdonald had disallowed it thrice. But on this
fourth occasion he held his hand. The whole ground of further
action was being cut away beneath his feet. The dispute between
the two contentious lumbermen, which had prompted Mowat's
legislation in the first place, had all this time been travelling
through the courts. It reached the Judicial Committee of the
Privy Council, that tribunal of curiously arbitrary and contradictory judgments, early in March, 1884; and on March 7,

Dalton McCarthy, who acted as counsel for the Conservative lumberman, wrote Macdonald a long, gloomy account of the proceedings, stressing the enormous difficulty of conveying any real understanding of Canada and its economy to the minds of the members of the Committee. "In this case," he explained, "they are, I think, much influenced by an erroneous notion that they have taken up that Canada is mainly a lumbering country, and lumbering the chief employment of its inhabitants, and that the consequent use of its streams as public highways is of the first consequence to us all."[52] Whatever their notions may have been, there was no uncertainty about their verdict. They decided in favour of the Liberal lumberman. He could float his saw-logs over his Conservative competitors' "improvements" freely and without benefit of the legislation which Ontario had tried vainly to pass on his behalf. Disallowance could not alter this decision. Disallowance could affect nothing. And it was given up.

Macdonald emerged from these encounters badly mauled. The Dominion had been beaten—almost humiliated. At a moment when it desperately needed national support, it had unquestionably lost moral authority. It had failed to vindicate the cause of unity at a time when half the provinces in the union seemed bent on pursuing a disruptive course of bluster and bullying. Quebec had got its money, Ontario had won its cases; and now Manitoba seemed quite prepared to carry its agitation to the point of endangering the Canadian Pacific and threatening the cause of western settlement. In February a delegation of the Manitoba and North-West Farmers' Union had come down to Ottawa to discuss western grievances with Macdonald; and early in March, a second convention of the union, with several hundred delegates in attendance, was held in Winnipeg to receive the mainly negative report which the delegation had brought back.[53] This time the proceedings were distinctly more alarming. A resolution was passed bluntly warning prospective settlers to stay away from the north-west until its wrongs were righted. There were threats of rebellion and secession. In the pages of the newspapers, it all looked extremely formidable.

Macdonald was not yet very seriously worried. "The speculators," he wrote to Lord Lorne, "who were ruined by the collapse after the boom of three years ago, and are of desperate fortunes, with some democrats, have attempted to get up a row, blustered, talked secession, and all that sort of thing; but the reaction has set in and Norquay who, with many faults and weaknesses, is loyal to the Dominion, has been sustained by an overwhelming vote, twenty to six, on certain factious amendments to the address in answer to the speech at the opening of the Manitoba session. We are doing all that we can to help them within reasonable limits, and at the opening of spring, when the people are on their farms, the agitation will be forgotten."[54] At the time it seemed a not-over-confident prediction. The Farmers' Union had discredited itself by its excesses and its flagrantly partisan tone. Tupper made a definite concession to western feeling when he announced in the House that as soon as the Canadian Pacific line north of Lake Superior had been constructed, the government would cease to prohibit by disallowance the building of railways with American connections in Manitoba.[55] Finally, interrupting the session of the Manitoba legislature for the purpose, Norquay came down to Ottawa to discuss provincial grievances in general. Late in April, after the prorogation of Parliament, Macdonald sat down with the western delegates to negotiate "better terms".

And then an unaccountable and dismaying event occurred. Norquay returned to Manitoba in May. He may have felt dissatisfied with the concessions he had secured from the federal government; he probably feared that his opponent, Greenway, would make bountiful political capital out of their alleged inadequacy. In any case, he defied Ottawa, and disavowed his own agreement; and the legislature, with the hearty concurrence of both parties and the applause of the whole province, rejected the "better terms" in their entirety. It was a hard, unexpected blow, coming at a time when the Dominion was vulnerable, and from a source which would be seriously regarded. Macdonald was dismayed and indignant. He was angry with Norquay for succumbing so tamely to the mere threat of pressure from the "demagogue", Greenway. He was frightened of the damaging publicity which would infallibly be given to this utter miscarriage of his efforts to pacify the discontented north-west. But at the moment anger triumphed over apprehension. He would show Norquay that the Dominion was not be scorned! The youngest and most insignificant of the provinces would not bully his government into submission! "As matters now stand," he wrote furiously to Aikins, "our offers for the sake of peace have been rejected, and therefore do not exist, and may never be repeated. At all events, everything is thrown over for a year."[56]

Could the Canadians, in time of trouble, support the burden of nationhood? Could the outside world be induced to believe that a transcontinental Canadian state was possible? He did not dare to attempt an answer now. Everything had gone against him in the past eight months. There was widespread discontent in Canada, hostility in the United States, and in England indifference and disbelief. He was still convinced that the surest source of support for Canada lay in the United Kingdom. But he realized that the long record of recent Canadian misfortunes seemed to deny the validity of his goal of nationhood; and he knew that virtually everything that had been said or written about Canada in England in recent years had helped to build up a solid wall of doubt and scepticism through which it seemed almost impossible to hack a way. John Rose discovered that Reuters' organization, which distributed Canadian news to many British newspapers, got its despatches exclusively from the hostile Associated Press, and had accepted this arrangement for no better reason than that the material was supplied free, or nearly so.[57] George Stephen, who, after the fiasco of the previous autumn in the United States, was anxious to secure more financial support in Great Britain, reported gloomily from London that Canada had not yet been lifted from its state of discredit, and that things Canadian were still regarded with profound distrust.[58]

But this was not all, as Macdonald soon discovered. Tilley was to meet the same distrust, in the most frighteningly serious form which it could assume. Early in June, at the moment when the legislature of Manitoba was pugnaciously

rejecting its agreement with the Dominion, the Minister of
Finance sailed for England, with the object of floating a new
loan of five million pounds sterling, and of arranging for the
conversion of an old and slightly larger loan at a reduced rate
of interest. He arrived in London to find an efficiently organized
propaganda campaign against Canada in vigorous operation.
"A desperate effort is being made here, and successful too," he
informed Macdonald indignantly, "to force down both government and Canadian Pacific Railway stocks, and the knowing
ones say they will be forced still lower. All kinds of unfriendly
statements are sent here from the United States and Winnipeg
touching the C.P.R. and I fully expect that when the prospectus
of our loan appears tomorrow we will have a heavy Grand
Trunk Railway blast against it."[59] The blast was quite as heavy
as Tilley expected it would be. A defamatory article in one of
the financial papers described the loan as "another crutch for
the C.P.R."; and a sandwich-man, advertising this diatribe,
paraded for several hours in front of Barings', where the bonds
were being offered to the public.[60] "Tilley has got his money,"
Rose explained ruefully to Macdonald, "but it required a strong
whip, and we met with great opposition from certain quarters,
and great lukewarmness in certain others where he and the
government had the right to expect better things."[61] Macdonald
had certainly expected a better rate than Tilley had been able
to obtain. The whole operation, he reflected gloomily, was
nothing to boast about; and it was decided to postpone the
floating of the conversion loan to a more propitious time.

Before the end of June, Macdonald left Ottawa for his new
summer house, "Les Rochers", at Rivière du Loup. "I was
obliged to hurry away from Ottawa," he told Chapleau, "as
I felt myself on the eve of breaking down. . . ."[62] He had no
end of worries; and once again his physical distresses had become
acute. "I am suffering much from stomachic disturbance,"
he wrote Tupper, "and can't throw it off, and must put up
with it as best I may, but it makes life not worth living. I would
leave the government tomorrow, if it were not that I really
think George Stephen would throw up the sponge if I did. He
was so worried and sleepless that his wife became alarmed and

sent him off to the seaside."[63] Obviously Stephen was far
from through his difficulties. The credit of Canada had been
strained. And out in the north-west, there was an ominous
fermentation, still unpacified.

He had troubles enough. But now there came an aggrava-
tion of his western difficulties which certainly he had never
expected. It was ten years and more since Louis Riel had left
Canada. Riel would never be forgotten, of course. He had
been the creative mind and the evil genius of the Red River
rebellion; he would remain an ineffaceable picture in the
collective memory of the Canadians. But Riel, the man, had
vanished; and the last thing that Macdonald ever anticipated
was his return. He had foreseen many things. But he had
never foreseen such an incredible misfortune as that. Yet now
it occurred. Early in July, Louis Riel returned to the Canadian
north-west.

IV

All during July and August, while he tried to rest and recover
his strength, Macdonald studied the reports from the north-west
with curious interest. The weather was atrocious. It teemed
with rain at Rivière du Loup during most of July; it rained
without ceasing when he and Lady Macdonald spent a long
week-end with the Stephens at Causapscal. And, while the
trees dripped and the skies gloomed overhead with sullen persistence, his own health did not noticeably improve. Campbell
wrote him affectionately expressing regret at his continued illness. "If we only had a week of sunshine, we should all be
better," he declared. "Why do you not relax the bow? There
is no use in keeping it always bent. I would shut off everything
for a month. Can you not manage this?"[64] Of course he could
not manage it. His summer holidays were no longer real holidays. Fifteen years ago Rivière du Loup had been a quiet and
retired village; now it had become a popular and populous summer colony. And there, as Tupper shrewdly surmised, he was
"exposed" to too much work. Visitors and mails kept continually

arriving. Besides, he wanted them to arrive. He would have been deeply disturbed if there had been any serious interruption in the regularity of their arrivals. His interest never ceased. He had half a dozen major problems and any number of minor difficulties to keep him constantly occupied. He could never really forget these things. He had come to live for them. And one of the most serious of his major problems during the summer of 1884 was the increasingly serious situation in the north-west.

"The news from the north-west," he admitted to Lord Lansdowne, "is a little disquieting."[65] Riel, at the request of a deputation of English and French half-breeds, had arrived in the vicinity of Prince Albert, in the District of Lorne, where the *métis* agitation had its focus; and, as Macdonald confessed, his arrival had created "rather a panic".[66] But Edgar Dewdney, the Lieutenant-Governor of the North-West Territories, wrote that he did not anticipate any real trouble; and Macdonald himself was not unduly alarmed. Yet he remained watchfully on the alert. He insisted that Riel must be kept under close observation. Riel had proved himself a successful organizer of discontent, and organizers of discontent were to be feared in the north-west, for there, as Macdonald reminded the Lieutenant-Governor of Manitoba, there were "certain uneasy elements". Inevitably, the Indians had found it terribly difficult to accommodate themselves to the revolutionary change which had taken place in their mode of existence. The *métis*, who before had been hunters of the buffalo, and carriers for the Hudson's Bay Company, had seen these old means of livelihood vanish and had betaken themselves reluctantly, and with dangerous sullenness, to the uncongenial business of farming. Even the latest arrivals, the new white settlers, had experienced a demoralizing change when they had passed, suddenly and almost without warning, from the good crops and high prices of the boom to the frosts, and failures, and deflated land-values of the depression. Every important group in the north-west had been forced to adjust itself to a new and highly unpleasant set of conditions; and the experience had been a painful one. In Macdonald's mind, this was the fundamental explanation of the unrest on the prairies. The north-west was full of disap-

pointed and dissatisfied men. They were troubled. They were
perhaps ready to make trouble for others.

Yet Macdonald did not really expect any serious disturbance.
Of the three "uneasy elements" in the north-west, he put the
Indians at the bottom of his list. "The last—the Indian element—," he wrote to Lieutenant-Governor Aikins, "is not to
be dreaded unless there is a white or half-breed rising."[67]
The Indians would do no more than follow the leadership of
others; and Macdonald was inclined to believe that, if they
waited for the white settlers to start a revolt, they would wait
in vain. The white settlers, it was true, had blustered and talked
secession; and late in June Norquay had sent Macdonald a
copy of an intercepted letter from one Mack Howes to George
Purvis, the President of the Farmers' Union, advocating nothing
less than armed revolt. Macdonald took steps to secure the
arms which Howes had proposed seizing; and he heartily
approved of Norquay's decision to set detectives to watch the
two agitators closely.[68] Yet he had been through these meaningless paper conspiracies often enough before. "I don't attach
much importance to these plots," he wrote to Aikins, "but my
experience of the Fenian business has taught me that one
should never disbelieve the evidence of plots or intended raids,
merely because they are foolish and certain to fail." He would
keep a sharp watch out, but he did not really expect to see
Howes and Purvis charging about, armed to the teeth, at the
head of great masses of insurgent white settlers. Early frosts,
high duties on reapers, and a railway to Hudson Bay, were the
stuff of general elections, rather than revolts. There was very
little afflicting the new settlers of the north-west which a
bumper crop would not cure.

The half-breeds were another matter. The problem of the
French-speaking half-breeds in particular stood, as he knew very
well, in a category of its own. Riel was a dangerously enigmatic
character; his fellow *métis* were impressionable and unpredictable people. "One cannot foresee what he may do," he warned
Aikins, "or what they, under his advice, may do."[69] They had
revolted once in the past; they might revolt again in the future.
But Macdonald did not really fear that the Red River rising

would be repeated on the banks of the Saskatchewan. He did
not believe that the materials of a real revolt existed. The
half-breeds had been treated with great consideration. They had
been given many concessions, including the vitally important
concession respecting land tenure. The holdings of the original
métis settlers on the two branches of the Saskatchewan had
been surveyed in long, narrow river lots, in exactly the fashion
they desired. It was true that subsequent to the original survey,
other half-breeds had squatted on lands, beyond the original
métis settlements, which had been divided on the rectangular
system of sections and townships. During 1883 and 1884
these squatters had been petitioning for a complete re-survey in
accordance with their wishes. The federal government had no
intention of denying these people their river lots; but the land
officers believed that the existing rectangular sections could be
readily divided, without the trouble and expense of a new
survey, into long narrow strips, each with a river frontage.[70]
They were now trying to explain their plan to the impatient
and suspicious half-breeds.

There remained only one problem; but it was a problem of
supreme importance. It arose out of the conviction of the
métis that they shared with the Indians in the original title
to the land of North America, and could prefer an equally
valid claim for compensation. The Manitoba Act, they argued,
had tacitly acknowledged this claim. The 1,400,000 acres of
the half-breed grant, set aside by the Manitoba Act, had, after
years of delay, uncertainty, and vexation, been finally divided;
and two hundred and forty acres of land had been granted to
each half-breed child, and negotiable scrip for one hundred
and sixty acres to each half-breed head of a family. The
troubled history of the disposition of the half-breed grant had
been a most unfortunate experience which nobody, with any
experience in the north-west, had any desire to see repeated.
Moreover, the federal government saw no need for repetition.
There was a superabundance of land for the métis of the north-
west on whatever terms they wished to claim it. If, as
Macdonald informed Lord Lansdowne, they decided to plead
their Indian blood, they could obtain their share of the reserve

and of the annual benefits provided by the government. If, on the other hand, they preferred to maintain the status of independent white farmers, they could acquire a homestead, and the pre-emption to another quarter-section of land on the same generous conditions as anybody else. But did the *métis* want farms? Or did they want free transferable lands and negotiable scrip, which they could sell easily for a little ready money? And was this the kind of compensation which the Dominion should think of granting to them?

Macdonald and the officials of the Department of the Interior had taken their responsibilities very seriously. They knew they were dealing with a restless and improvident people. They believed that any concessions which brought no permanent benefit to the *métis* were really valueless; and for this reason they had long ago rejected the idea of negotiable scrip. The experts were opposed to it. The whole history of the half-breed land grant in Manitoba was a warning against another such issue of paper; and those who were now demanding it in the north-west were, on the whole, an extremely doubtful lot. The émigré *métis* from Manitoba, who had squandered their previous grants and who could have no claim whatever in any future distribution, were suspiciously prominent in the agitation which was going on on the banks of the Saskatchewan; and they were aided and abetted, Macdonald was convinced, by the land sharks who had everything to gain and nothing to lose from a new distribution of negotiable scrip. "The scrip is sold for a song to the sharks and spent in whiskey," Macdonald explained to Lord Lansdowne, "and this we desire above all things to avoid."[71] It was a miscarriage of good intentions which any responsible government would try to avoid. What real benefit would these unstable and thriftless people derive from such a perfunctory solatium?

The demand, in the form in which it had been made, could not wisely be granted. Yet this did not mean that Macdonald considered the matter closed. The half-breed claims could be settled in another and a more beneficial fashion. The whole issue was a proper subject for compromise. And to Macdonald, the final proof that a satisfactory compromise was possible lay

in the wise moderation of Riel's conduct since he had received
the appeal to go to the north-west. The man was certainly a
born leader. He had no sooner reached the settlements on the
Saskatchewan than he began, with great energy and address,
to knit together the various discontented elements—half-breeds,
Indians, and white settlers—in one close union of protest. But
he had preached only lawful courses. He gave every evidence
of intending a peaceful settlement. And Macdonald was reassured. "There is, I think," he wrote to Lord Lansdowne,
"nothing to be feared from Riel. In his answer to the invitation
sent to him, which was a temperate and unobjectionable paper,
he spoke of some claims he had against the government. I
presume these refer to his land claims which he forfeited on
conviction and banishment. I think we shall deal liberally with
him and make him a good subject again."[72] In such a programme, the first and most obvious need was, as Lord Lansdowne suggested, to "obtain touch" of Riel. French-speaking
priests in the disaffected areas and French-speaking officials in
the north-west administration were instructed to approach Riel
and his discontented *métis* quietly and to sound them out.
"I think the true policy," Macdonald wrote to Lansdowne
after he had dismissed the idea of an issue of scrip, "is rather
to encourage them to specify their grievances in memorials and
to send them with or without delegations to Ottawa."

At the end of the summer, this was still the position of
affairs. He lingered as long as he possibly could at Rivière du
Loup; and when, after the middle of September, he at length
returned to Ottawa, he carried with him the unhappy knowledge
that his long holiday had not brought the hoped-for improvement in his health. The irritation of the "coats of the stomach",
as Tupper professionally described it, kept him in a state of
grumbling physical discomfort. All too frequently he felt
wretched. He needed rest, he needed help; and all the time
difficulties were multiplying, and the opposition was exploiting
them outrageously for its political advantage. In August, Oliver
Mowat, his old rival, had won what was perhaps his greatest
triumph from the Judicial Committee of the Privy Council.[73]
Against a battery of lawyers, led by Dalton McCarthy, who

acted for Manitoba and the Dominion, he had made good
Ontario's claim to the vastly extended boundary on the north-
west which had been awarded by the arbitrators in the summer
of 1878; and early in September he returned to Toronto in
triumph, like some fabulous eastern war-lord, laden with booty
and rich in territorial conquests. Yet even this—bad as it was—
was not all. During the summer Macdonald had come to read
the secret which was half-revealed in Stephen's disquieting
hints. He knew now that the enormous aid granted in the
last session would not be enough to secure the completion
of the Canadian Pacific Railway.

"Meanwhile," he had confided to Tupper in August, "things
are not going right. At every by-election, Dominion or local,
we are fought with the whole strength of the Grits. My
colleagues, excepting Pope, Langevin, and Caron, are not
worth a cent in counteracting this tremendous effort, and with
my failing strength and advancing years, I cannot do everything.
Next month I shall have a clear understanding with my colleagues, and they *must* work or others will."[74] Brave words!
But how could he back them up with action? Bowell, Carling,
Macpherson, and Campbell, all freely offered their resignations
in order to assist him in the work of Cabinet reconstruction.
"Take my word for it, Sir John," wrote Tupper, characteristically
stating the obvious as if it had been a discovery of his own,
"you want some fresh blood in the cabinet—young, active,
vigorous men, who, with you to advise and direct them, will
give a vigorous impulse to the party."[75] Macdonald wearily
agreed with him. He longed for young, active, vigorous men.
But where were they to be got? For years Dalton McCarthy
had seemed by all odds the most promising prospect in a small
field; and Alexander Campbell had come to assume that Macdonald's "mantle" would eventually fall upon the not unwilling
shoulders of the Barrie lawyer. But McCarthy, who had been
approached in the previous spring with an informal offer of
the portfolio of Justice, had replied, much as John Hillyard
Cameron had replied decades before, that he could not give up
his lucrative private practice while his large debts remained
unpaid. Macdonald tried him again hopefully in September;

and again he was turned down. "I am still of the same opinion," McCarthy wrote, "as to the impossibility of my giving up my business, and joining the ministry; and therefore you must re-arrange without me."[76]

There was a cold conclusiveness about this final reply which was profoundly discouraging. Macdonald realized that he had no hope whatever, for years to come, of obtaining McCarthy's assistance. He was sick and tired of the whole difficult business of Cabinet reconstruction; and, besides he still felt physically unwell. Agnes kept insisting that he must take his condition more seriously and seek more expert advice; and towards the end of September he consulted a new medical man, a Dr. Howard of Montreal. Howard prescribed a fresh treatment, seemed reasonably optimistic about his case, and then, with impressive seriousness, urged him to take a complete holiday, in the only way in which it was ever possible for him to take it, by going overseas. Macdonald pondered. Could he go? The news from the north-west had suddenly become disturbing. The growing uncertainty of the finances of the Canadian Pacific was an unutterable secret which he shared only with George Stephen. He would have to cope with these things, and cope with them soon, for there was apparently nobody else who could do so. But if the vigorous young men had failed him, if he must carry on much as he had done before, then obviously what remained of his health must be guarded jealously. Rivière du Loup had not helped him much. Perhaps London would.

He suddenly decided to follow Howard's advice. "I am obliged to go off to England," he wrote to a supporter. "My health, I am told, imperatively requires it. But I shan't give that as a reason, for it would discourage our friends."[77] There were, of course, other reasons, equally valid and much more publishable, for a visit to England. Tilley's large-scale conversion operation had still to be carried out; and Stephen, who was preparing to cross the Atlantic once again himself, argued persuasively that Macdonald could do far more good for himself, the country, and the Canadian Pacific Railway by a six or eight weeks' visit to England than he possibly could by staying unhappily at home. Macdonald yielded with a sigh of relief.

On October 8, he left Ottawa; and two days later, in the pleasant company of Stephen, he sailed for England.

V

He enjoyed a holiday in England more than any other holiday that could possibly have been offered to him. It gave him what no vacation in Canada could ensure—complete release from most of the responsibilities of office. But this great, though negative, gift of peace was not the only benefit to which he looked forward expectantly when he sailed for Liverpool. The life which opened up before him as soon as he set foot on the station platform in London was as agreeable as any he had ever experienced. He enjoyed theatres, concerts, and dinner parties. He liked good company and good talk. And every time he came to England, there were more people—old friends, new acquaintances, and unknown admirers—who were eager to welcome him back or to greet him for the first time. In the past, of course, it had been the Conservatives who had given him the most cordial formal receptions; the Liberals, except in the way of official business, had paid as little attention to him as they conveniently could. But in 1884 a strange change seemed to have come over Mr. Gladstone and his Cabinet. They had, apparently for the first time, become aware of Macdonald's existence. They began to take in the fact that here was a man who had given a lifetime of public service to a country which might, in the end, become a great North American power. Despite all their confident prophecies and candid preferences, and despite the uniformly unfavourable publicity of the Liberal press, the Dominion of Canada still seemed determined and able to enjoy an independent existence in the New World. It was odd—almost incredible! But there it was! The British Liberals came to the conclusion that the fact of Canada must be admitted, and the presence of her Prime Minister suitably acknowledged. This curious change of attitude was in part the result of the mere passage of time—time which had at least made Sir John Macdonald a familiar figure, if not exactly a

colonial institution. But it may have been, to an even larger
extent, the consequence of a still more fundamental change, a
change in the attitude of the British people to their Empire. The
foundation of the Imperial Federation League in 1884 was
an evidence of this change; and it had to be admitted that there
were highly respectable Liberals, such as Mr. Forster, who took
a prominent part in the affairs of the Imperial Federation
League. The Empire was ceasing to be something to be
ashamed of, to apologize over. It was almost—if not quite—
becoming a subject of pride.

Macdonald had arrived suddenly, unannounced and unexpected; and it took Mr. Gladstone, whose reflections on the
subject may have been assisted by others, a little time to decide
what he would do. On November 15, which was nearly a month
after Macdonald had arrived at his old quarters in Batt's Hotel
in Dover Street, he wrote to the Canadian, offering him, in
recognition of his "long and distinguished services", the Grand
Cross of the Bath.[78] A week later, on Sunday, November 23,
the most memorable week that Macdonald ever spent in England
began. He stayed on Sunday with the Prince of Wales at
Sandringham. On Monday he was entertained at dinner in
London by the Beaconsfield Club; and on Tuesday, by royal
command, he went out to Windsor to receive his new honour
and to dine and sleep at the castle. He was the guest of honour
at a dinner given by the Empire Club, the day after his return
to London from Windsor. The Marquess of Lorne—"What a
good and true 'Canadian' he is!" Stephen had exclaimed—presided on that occasion; and over eighty peers and commoners
were present at what was undoubtedly the most elaborate and
the most enthusiastic tribute which had yet been paid to a
Canadian statesman. The chairman spoke handsomely in Macdonald's praise. So did Lord Salisbury for the Conservatives,
and Lord Kimberley for the Liberals. Afterwards Lord Lorne
told Tupper that "no one, except a foreign potentate, had ever
had such a reception".[79]

Macdonald was pleased and touched. Physically he was feeling enormously better. He had gone, of course, as soon as he
had arrived, to consult his old physician, Dr. Andrew Clark;

but it was London, even more than medical advice and treatment, which brought back his sense of well-being. He recovered his normal buoyant spirits far more quickly than he had in the summer of 1881—so quickly, indeed, that Stephen was conscious of just a shade of apprehension. He inquired solicitously, after one large dinner which they had attended together, whether Macdonald felt any the worse for the previous evening's turtle soup. But Macdonald, for a man who had been suffering all summer from a grievously "deranged stomach", accommodated himself to the rich dishes of a succession of lavish ceremonial dinners with extraordinary rapidity. He felt very nearly at the top of his form. He was conquering the Liberals in 1884 as he had conquered the Conservatives in 1879. It was true, as had been amply evident at the Empire Club dinner, that in Great Britain he was still, to some degree at least, the special protégé of the Conservative party. But his new honour had been recommended by a Liberal government. Mr. Gladstone had unbent so far as to be positively amiable at the time of his investiture at Windsor; and Lord Kimberley had paid him compliments in public at the Empire Club. The amazing fact was that for the first time Liberals and Conservatives had combined to do him honour on an impressive scale. It was—or it could reasonably be interpreted to be—a recognition of the validity of his national policies, an acceptance of the idea of the transcontinental Canada which he was trying to create.

No recognition could have come more pat. No honour could have been bestowed at a more appropriate moment. It was ironical, of course, that these tributes to his political wisdom, these acknowledgments of his country's brilliant prospects should have been made just at the moment when the materials of the national structure seemed to be breaking apart in his hands. In retrospect, after the possible disaster of the future, his ovation might appear a terrible mockery. But in the meantime it was still possible that his dream might be converted into reality; and so long as he could struggle to achieve it, every expression of approval was of value to him. He needed confidence as he had rarely needed it before. Ever since the autumn began, Canada's position had seemed to be steadily worsening.

On the way over on the boat George Stephen had revealed to him in detail the desperate urgency of the Canadian Pacific's necessities. But this was not the only troubling knowledge which he carried with him across the Atlantic. Just before he left Ottawa he had received a most disquieting piece of information from the north-west.

It had come in a bulging private letter from Edgar Dewdney, the Lieutenant-Governor of the North-West Territories.[80] The plan, which Macdonald and Lord Lansdowne had advocated, had been carried out. "Touch" had been obtained with Riel. Early in September, two unofficial French-speaking emissaries, Bishop Grandin and Amédée Forget, the Clerk of the North-West Council, had sought out the *métis* leader and had persuaded him to make a statement of his demands. Dewdney had enclosed the reports of this curious interview in his letter. Macdonald studied the documents with increasing dismay. There seemed no end to Riel's incredible demands. He asked for special land grants, not only for the half-breeds then living, but also for each future generation, at intervals of eighteen years. He demanded that two million acres of land should be set aside as an endowment for the building and maintenance of half-breed schools, hospitals, and orphanages. "This is what we request for the present," ran the postscript to Bishop Grandin's memorandum of the interview, "until Canada becomes able to pay us each year the interest of the sum which our country is worth and until public opinion consents to recognize our rights to their full extent."[81] The "sum which our country is worth" was calculated in a simple and generous fashion. The value of the North-West Territories was estimated at forty cents an acre for the entire area; and the resulting capital sum was to be divided between Indians and half-breeds, at the rate of twenty-five cents an acre to the half-breeds, and fifteen to the Indians![82]

All this was disturbing enough. But there was something which disturbed Macdonald even more. The gravest revelations in the documents concerned Riel himself, his purposes and ambitions. In the presence of his fellow half-breeds, he had blustered, had insisted excitedly that his mission was purely altruistic and that he was not to be bought. Yet in private his manner significantly altered. He was much quieter. His own personal grievances were carefully enumerated. Hints were dropped about jobs for himself and his principal confederates. There was a vague suggestion of "a sum of money". What did it all mean? All during the summer Macdonald had felt certain that he could rely upon Riel's good will and his desire for a peaceful settlement. But now, in the face of these preposterous demands and this equivocal behaviour, all his confidence in the future vanished. Did this strange half-breed desire peace? Or did he intend mischief? Was he the leader of a constitutional agitation? Or was he a selfish, anarchic, black-mailing adventurer?

The problem of Riel and the north-west would confront him as soon as he got home. But so also would the problem of the Canadian Pacific Railway. All during the summer he had tried to dismiss this problem from his mind. He had sought to convince himself that somehow or other George Stephen would find a solution. He had tried to ignore George Stephen's hints and covert appeals. He could ignore them no longer. By the time he reached London, he knew the railway's real position in all its gloomy detail. Once again, after a short period of barely eight months, the company was in desperate financial straits. The government loan had saved it; but the government loan had also imposed crippling conditions which had embarrassed it ever since. Macdonald had considered it essential to prove to the hesitant and doubtful Canadians that he was not throwing quantities of good money after bad. He had guarded his invest-ment with stiff securities. Virtually all the assets of the company were pledged in a first mortgage to the government of Canada.

The thirty-five millions of unissued common stock remained, of course. But in the circumstances of the moment they were almost useless. The government lien was too intimidating to investors. The shares were quoted at forty-five, before Mac-donald left for London, and nothing that Stephen could do seemed to arrest their slow, persistent decline. New York had failed the railway. London was still coldly unresponsive to its appeals. Morton, Rose and Company was the only British

firm which had so far backed the company; and Stephen was
convinced that Morton, Rose and Company were giving only
a timorous and ineffectual support. He and Macdonald tried,
through the kind offices of a young member of the Baring clan
who was a junior partner in a friendly New York firm, to
secure the financial backing of the great house of Baring.[83]
But these first approaches were failures. Macdonald did not
know where to turn. Stephen assured him that the government
subsidy and loan, paid out as the progress of the work merited,
would suffice to keep construction going. But beyond this were
the fixed charges of interest and dividends. And Macdonald
knew now that the company could not go on meeting these
payments without fresh funds. Where were fresh funds to be
got?

He had talked the whole portentous problem over at great
length with Stephen during the journey across the Atlantic;
and once he reached London, he began another set of equally
lengthy discussions on the same subject with Tupper. Tupper
emphatically agreed with him that a final effort to save the
railway must be made. Neither of them had the slightest
doubt on that score. It was a question rather of what was the
most politically acceptable form that aid could take. It was
also a question—an even more fundamental question—of
whether or not aid in any conceivable form could be pushed
through the Dominion Parliament at its next session. Macdonald was profoundly doubtful. He shrank from the exhausting
and exasperating labour involved. After only a year's respite,
he must begin his work all over again, and this time under
much more unfavourable circumstances. The government was
not so well off as it had been in the autumn of 1883. Temporary
arrangements, it was true, had been made for the loan that
matured in January, 1885; but current revenues, Tilley reported
from Canada, had been declining ever since the fiscal year
began in July.[84] The slump had finally hit the treasury. They
could confidently expect financial difficulties from now on. But
grave as these financial difficulties might be, they were not
likely to be so baffling as the political problems which Macdonald
was certain to encounter. How was he to convince his followers
—his own Cabinet—that government aid to the Canadian Pacific

was necessary once again? The burly Tupper had always been a stout supporter of the railway, and Tupper could, and did, despatch a long letter to Tilley, warmly advocating the plan of relief which he and Macdonald had tentatively sketched out.[85] But this time Tupper must remain in England; and Macdonald, burdened by the momentous decision which they had taken together, must go home to face his colleagues alone. What the issue would be he literally had not the faintest idea. But he had given his word to Stephen. And perhaps at some dreadful moment in the shame and defeat of the Pacific Scandal he had made a vow with himself.

VI

Stephen sat in the pleasant library of his house in St. James's Place. He felt triumphantly elated. Even in that autumn of disasters, there was still hope; and today was a day of hope confirmed. He and his cousin, Donald Smith, by pledging their own personal credit once more, had just secured a loan of fifty thousand pounds for the railway. And now, with Macdonald committed in principle to a further instalment of government aid, Stephen could almost bring himself to believe that a way would be found through the blind jungle of difficulties which faced him. Once again the partnership of company and government, the partnership of Donald Smith, John A. Macdonald, and himself, had triumphed. They were all Scotsmen, all Highlanders, all, ultimately, sons of the same river valley. Macdonald's ancestors, on his mother's side, had come from Strathspey; and Stephen and Smith had been born in little towns close to the river in the land dominated by the Clan Grant. Stephen's fierce hatreds, his black discouragements, his radiant exaltations, were all legitimate parts of the rich inheritance he had received from Speyside; and unlike Macdonald, who had no personal memory of the country of his forbears, he was steeped in recollections of the land by which he had been shaped. He remembered the river itself, winding onward, peat-black between the high banks, and brown, like old ale, over the shallows. He remembered the great rock which had given the Clan Grant its rallying-place and its battle slogan. The rock of defiance. Craigellachie.

Stand fast, Craigellachie!

He would beat them! He and Macdonald and Donald Smith would beat them yet! Blake, the hated *Globe,* the Grand Trunk Railway scribblers, the "bear" speculators in New York—the whole malignant host of the Canadian Pacific's enemies—he would beat them all. He took a telegraph form, addressed it to Donald Smith in Montreal, and wrote a message of three words only:

"Stand fast, Craigellachie!"[86]

Chapter Twelve

Triumph and Disaster

I

The dusk of the brief January day had fallen long before the train reached Montreal. A curious balmy softness, like a false, delicious breath of spring, was in the air. The long queue of carriages moved off easily through the streets which were strangely unencumbered with snow; and the crowd waited comfortably as if it had been a night in April. There were masses of people everywhere. Macdonald could sense the enormous presence of the crowd all along the packed roads to the drill hall. The roar of welcoming applause was unbroken. There were two miles of flaming torches. High up, against the blue-black, velvety sky, the rockets burst in little showers of rose pink and daffodil yellow; and, at the Place d'Armes, a fountain, fed with hundreds of Roman candles, soared upwards and fell in cascades of golden stars. The drill shed was jammed with people. He knew he could not possibly make them hear. He told them he could have wished for a trumpet to carry his voice to all. Only a few heard his apologies and his thanks. But the rest did not seem to care. They had come, French and English, not so much to listen to him speak, as to honour him, and swell his triumph. They waited patiently and sympathetically, applauding loudly whenever there seemed a suitable opening.[1]

The day before, Sunday, January 11, he had reached the age of seventy. Two months ago, while he was still in England, he had passed the fortieth anniversary of his entrance into public life. The great celebration at Montreal was intended

399

to commemorate these two tremendous events; but it was not
the first triumph that had been spread before him since his
return from England. Less than a month before, on December
17 and 18, a great convention of more than four thousand
Conservatives from all over Ontario had assembled at Toronto.[2]
Toronto and Montreal—the two principal cities of Ontario and
Quebec, the two political divisions which nearly twenty years
ago had been Canada West and Canada East. Macdonald
had lasted all through these political permutations and com-
binations. His career had spanned the history of the two sections of the old Province, and the history of the two provinces
of the new Dominion. And for most of the men who crowded
into the drill shed at Montreal and the Opera House at Toronto,
there was no clear political memory in which his big nose,
and bushy hair and tall, slight figure were not prominent.
That autumn, for the first time, apparently, the English had
really discovered the Canadian Prime Minister. But for the
Canadians themselves there was no need of discovery or re-
discovery. For forty years they had laughed at him, criticized
him, forgiven him, believed in him, and followed him.

They could scarcely remember a past without him. They
could hardly conceive of a future in which he would cease
to be. The feebleness of his health was, of course, well-known
and deeply lamented. But how could the Canadians look too
seriously upon something which he himself made light of and
cracked jokes about? "If John A.'s stomach gives in," he told
them at Toronto, repeating a famous medical diagnosis of the
political situation, "then the opposition will go in; but if John
A.'s stomach holds out, then the opposition will stay out." They
had not the slightest doubt that the opposition would stay out.
John A. was politically indestructible. He was the monarch
who had become so necessary that he would surely live for
ever. And when, at Toronto, he told them that he had reached,
or even passed, the culmination of his career, the great national
Conservative disbelief found utterance in a single protesting
cry which was heard, when it so easily might not have been
heard, throughout the whole of the great auditorium.

"You'll never die, John A.!"

He had, in fact, become an old man. But, like a young man, he lived for the present and the immediate future. He rarely spoke of death; he had no interest in dwelling in the past. And it was, sometimes, with a sudden, grinding pain of recollection that he remembered what he had been through. Once, in the early days at Earnscliffe, when Agnes was still unpacking and arranging their household goods, she came upon a small mysterious box of children's toys. There was a broken rattle, a little cart, a few wooden animals. They were not Mary's—Agnes was certain of that. They seemed oddly old-fashioned to have been left behind by Daisy or some other small visitor to Earnscliffe. Whose could they be? She took them to Macdonald who was lying resting upon his bed. He looked at the box perfunctorily, incuriously, and then with a sudden pang of interest. Raising himself on his elbow, he took the small cart in his hand.

"Ah!" he said, "those were little John A.'s."[3]

And suddenly thirty years had rushed away, and he was back in the "Italian villa" Bellevue, and the soft summer breeze from Lake Ontario was blowing in from the open window, and his first-born was playing boisterously on the bed by Isabella's side . . . He did not notice Agnes's departure. The room was empty. And he was staring at the floor.

There were moments when for him, as for anyone else, what he had been through seemed too terrible to be borne. But mainly he carried the burden of his existence easily, even jauntily. There were more frequent reminders now of its dreariness; he was increasingly conscious of the almost frightening depth of experience upon which he could draw. Once, as he was on his way to his office past the rows of portraits of ex-Speakers in old Canadian Parliaments, he told his new secretary, the suave and impeccably correct Joseph Pope, that whenever he came that way he felt as if he were walking through a churchyard. Time and again there kept coming back to him the story of the old monk in the ancient monastery in Europe who had the care of the portraits of the departed members of his order, and who said one day to some visitors, pointing to the pictures of the dead, "I feel sometimes as if, after all, they were the realities, and we are the shadows."[4] Macdonald knew that there was solid reality in what he had done in the past. But it was imperfect reality—imperfect because incomplete. Deep within him there lay the inarticulate assumption that the history of Canada during its most important half-century was a plot which he, as its author, must hasten to complete. He had always known what he wanted to do. The design had been there from the beginning. All he needed now was a few years in which to finish it.

II

And yet, as he admitted to himself, the difficulties in the way of its completion were larger and more numerous than ever. The dignities which had been offered to him, the celebrations which had been given in his honour had, he knew very well, encouraged him more than he could say. But was it not a false, a fatally delusive encouragement? Had not the whole history of Canada for the past twelve months been a steady, unbroken, disheartening record of deterioration? The depression, far from lifting, had in fact steadily deepened. Manitoba had broken with the Dominion; Ontario had defied it with triumphant impunity; Nova Scotia was ominously rumbling with dissatisfaction. Some kind of trouble was brewing—was perhaps being deliberately brewed—in the north-west; and the railway which was to link all the wrangling and disconnected sections of the trans-continental Dominion together had for the second time run through all its resources, and was back once more, an embarrassed and embarrassing mendicant, upon the national doorstep. The state of the nation could hardly be worse. There could hardly be more problems than there were in domestic affairs. But, of course, domestic politics were not the only politics. There were also foreign relations.

Relations with the United States were almost never in a happy state of health. Good neighbourhood on the North

SIR GEORGE STEPHEN

American continent was troubled by a succession of chills, fevers, and other maladies; and one of the worst of these afflictions was the everlasting problem of the fisheries, which periodically returned, like a severe case of rheumatism contracted unhappily in early childhood, to trouble the body politic with its agonies. Over twelve years ago, when he had persuaded the Canadian Parliament to accept the Washington Treaty, Macdonald had perhaps hoped that the problem of the fisheries had been successfully banished, at least for his own political lifetime. But the ancient affliction had appeared once more. It had come back in fact at the earliest possible moment at which the American government could insure its return.

In 1883, at the first legal opportunity, it had announced the abrogation of the Washington Treaty in the briskly conclusive fashion in which it had ended the Reciprocity Treaty twenty years before. The reasons for this determined haste were not, in Macdonald's opinion, hard to seek. The Washington Treaty had provided that the excess value of the Canadian over the American inshore fisheries was to be settled by arbitration; and in 1877, the arbitration at Halifax had ended in the award of five and a half million dollars to the British North American provinces. For the United States this was a preposterous sum, the payment of which was neither forgotten nor forgiven. "The truth is," Macdonald explained to Lord Lansdowne, "that the United States government have so often overreached England in diplomacy that they are dissatisfied with any treaty in which they have not gained a decided advantage."[5] Obviously the republic had not gained a "decided advantage" in these sections of the Washington Treaty. It had not got the fisheries for nothing —or next to nothing; and therefore, on July 1, at the earliest possible moment, the fisheries clauses of the treaty were to come to an end.

What to do? Macdonald had begun the consideration of this problem in the summer of 1884, when the American presidential campaign was just getting nicely under way; and he took it up again, at Lord Lansdowne's request, in December, after Grover Cleveland had been elected for his first term as President. A fair amount of time had already elapsed since the American announcement had been made; the Governor-General and Sir Lionel Sackville-West, the British Minister at Washington, were anxious to have a declaration of Canadian intentions; and Macdonald called the Cabinet together on the day before Christmas to consider the matter. Neither he nor any of the other ministers saw any reason why Canada should hurry forward anxiously with a new policy. The United States had announced the abrogation of the fishery clauses for its own purposes and without troubling itself to suggest any alternative settlement of the question. There was no need for the Dominion, like an agitated suitor desperately seeking a favourable answer, to prostrate itself in humility in Washington. Canada would always be ready to discuss a reciprocal trade treaty with the United States; it would even be willing to prolong the privileges of the Washington Treaty, for the benefit of the citizens of the republic, until January 1, 1886, in order to give another six months for negotiation. And if the negotiation failed—well, it would always be possible to fall back on the Convention of 1818, and the defence of the inshore fisheries against American depredation. Besides, there were particular as well as general reasons for waiting to discuss the matter with Cleveland rather than with Arthur. "Mr. Arthur," Macdonald confided to Lord Lansdowne, "is now engaged in the amiable work of embarrassing his successor. . . . We have a much better chance of better treatment from the new than from the moribund government."[6]

Here there was still a fairly ample margin for most contingencies. But, in the matter of the Canadian Pacific Railway, Macdonald had become a desperate prisoner of circumstances, hemmed in savagely on all sides. "I feel," Stephen confessed unashamedly, "like a man walking on the edge of a precipice, with less 'nerve' than is comfortable or even 'safe' in such a case. . . ."[7] And Stephen's feeling of inadequacy and apprehension was, at bottom, very much like his own. Two months ago, when he had been in England, talking the whole problem over with Stephen and the positive and optimistic Tupper, he had still hoped that a way out could be found. The difficulties were formidable, and he had never dreamed of underestimating them; but he had still believed that they might be overcome. He could indulge this belief no longer. It had become a stupid delusion. The financial ruin of the railway was at hand. It must have government aid. It could survive only with government aid. Yet its relief by government seemed a political impossibility.

As the January days went by and the opening of Parliament drew closer, Stephen's appeals grew more and more shrilly importunate. He kept insisting, with ever increasing vehemence of emphasis, that "the object of the present application to the government is to save the *life* of the company".[8] Late in December, the workmen at Port Arthur struck because of the delay in the delivery of their pay, and before the end of the year the stock was down to forty-three and a half at New York. There was no telling, Stephen assured Macdonald with gloomy savagery, how far it might drop. Once again the small creditors were clamouring for their money; and over in London, so John Rose telegraphed in dismay, a well organized propaganda was once more employed in battering down the credit of the company.[9] Stephen had virtually become a permanent resident of Ottawa. He drafted memoranda, arranged and rearranged figures, haunted committee rooms, and besought ministers. It was the unlimited government lien, he was convinced, which had been fatal to the success of the company; and, in his view, the only effective remedy was a measure which would pay off the government loan and convert the thirty-five millions of unissued stock into ready money. He proposed, in place of the unmarketable stock, to issue thirty millions of four-per-cent bonds; and for these, as the essential condition of their success, he begged a government guarantee of principal and interest. It was one plan for the salvation of the doomed railway. But it was only one. There were other and slightly different schemes proposed by McIntyre and Tupper. And all during January the government considered them, deliberately, critically, unenthusiastically. Stephen was nearly beside himself. "What alarms me," he wrote indignantly to Macdonald, "is the apprehension that the patient will die while the doctors are deliberating on the remedy to be applied."[10]

Yet Macdonald was convinced that haste would be far more dangerous than delay. He had expected that any proposal of further aid to the Canadian Pacific would be met by opposition; but even he had not foreseen how determined and implacable that opposition was likely to be. Before his return to Canada, a rumour of impending government assistance had begun to run in a sinister fashion through the country and, by the beginning of the New Year, a wail of alarm and protest, in which the Conservative newspapers somewhat shamefacedly joined, was ringing through the Dominion. Thomas White, the editor of the Montreal *Gazette*, wrote to say that he did not believe a measure of relief could be carried; and Macdonald's colleagues in the ministry, with their ears cocked sensitively to the protests of the back benchers and the complaints of the electorate, were convinced that such legislation could not be attempted with success. Campbell, McLelan and Bowell were all opposed to a new loan; Tilley was highly dubious. "I have heard all Stephen has to say," he wrote to Macdonald, "and I confess I cannot see how we can go to Parliament next session and ask our supporters to vote for it."[11]

At the moment, Macdonald could not see either. With a doubtful press and an unwilling Cabinet at his back, he realized that he could not risk too much too soon. "I myself fear," he wrote to Tupper on January 24, 1885, five days before the opening of Parliament, "that the *Week* is right when it says that however docile our majority, we dare not ask for another loan. The thing is hung up until next week. How it will end I don't know."[12] It was obvious by that time, at any rate, that it was not going to end in any immediate parliamentary action in favour of the Canadian Pacific. Stephen, who, with Donald Smith, had just borrowed, at the eleventh hour, the six hundred and fifty thousand dollars necessary to pay the January dividend, was begging Macdonald despairingly to assert himself. "The question is too big for some of our friends," he wrote, "and nothing but your own authority and influence will carry anything that will accomplish the object."[13] It was useless. Macdonald declined, for the moment, to impose a favourable decision. Yet, at the same time, he did not finally reject the possibility of relief. His language on the subject was curiously indecisive and non-committal. He informed Stephen, by telegraph, that there was "little chance" of any aid that year;[14] and when Blake, in the debate on the address, congratulated him ironically on the absence of all mention of the Canadian Pacific in the speech from the throne, Macdonald took the first opportunity of referring to the omission, and in phrases which were perhaps deliberately ambiguous. "There is no necessity for mentioning it," he told the Commons, "inasmuch as there is no legislation that we are going to lay before the House—that we propose to lay before the House just now."[15]

For the moment he kept his cards close to his chest. He was determined to delay. He could not be any too sure of his own strength, and he could not form an accurate estimate of the forces arrayed against him. In the game he was playing, the stakes were far too big for him to risk a false move. He would make no move at all so far as the fisheries and the railway were concerned. But there were other things in his varied and long-range programme besides fisheries and railways; and it was not the first time that he had refused an engagement at one point in order to press forward at another. He knew now where he wanted to advance. He would shake himself free, at one important point, from the hampering clutches of the provinces. For years he had disliked the fact that federal elections were held in accordance with franchises determined by the different provincial legislatures. "It is impossible, of course," he had written to Brown Chamberlin over fifteen years before, "that the elective franchise should be at the mercy of a foreign body."[16]

Fifteen years had gone by, and his conviction had simply been strengthened. The struggle between the Dominion and those "foreign bodies", the provinces, had simply grown in intensity. Mowat's victory in the boundary dispute had been followed, only a short while before the session opened, by a decision in the Supreme Court of Canada against the validity of the federal Licence Law of 1883. Mowat had successfully defied the Dominion; and Mowat's triumphant audacity seemed likely to become the fashionable model for every discontented province in the country. It was intolerable! Twice before, in two successive speeches from the throne, the government had promised a measure "for the assimilation of the electoral franchises in the several provinces". Now, for the third time, the promise was made, and this time he meant to keep it. He would prevent those insolent provincialists from meddling any longer with the laws by which the Dominion Parliament was elected!

III

The "waiting game", which he believed he so infinitely preferred, was a game played with big risks for high stakes. The stakes were nothing less than a unified, transcontinental Canada; the risks were a fatal inward division of the country, abandonment by Great Britain, and annexation by the United States. He had not thrown in his hand. With a small, but not seriously diminished, pile of chips, he was still in the game. His principal companions were players of enormously greater resources. The very fact that he continued in the game at all was a colossal gamble. He played each hand with infinite caution. His hesitations and postponements had by now become notorious. The practical man who had built a nation in a quarter century was getting to be known as a procrastinator. The realist who had always lived intensely in the immediate present had come to be called affectionately "Old Tomorrow". It was a grotesque but not unkindly misconception of which he was well aware, which did not entirely displease him; and it was never better illustrated than in the odd little episode, which prefaced, with such ironic incongruity, the most strenuous and most dangerous year in his entire political career.

It happened on the afternoon of Thursday, February 5, a week after the session opened. Blake was asking for information. Blake, like the good leader of the opposition he was, was always asking for information, on the most improbable subjects and on every possible occasion. This time his inquiries took a sharply personal turn. He wanted to know how much of the interval between the sessions of 1883 and 1884 had been spent in Canada by the ex-Minister of Railways and Canals, Sir

Charles Tupper. When, he further inquired, had Sir Charles resigned his portfolio, and when would his successor be appointed?[17] Macdonald promised that the information about the length of Tupper's residence in Canada—he had, of course, been mainly in England, beginning his new duties as High Commissioner—would be supplied "tomorrow". J. H. Pope, Macdonald went on, had been acting Minister of Railways and Canals since Tupper's resignation in June, 1884. "It is intended," Macdonald finished his reply, "to fill the office of Minister of Railways ere long." At this point, an unidentifiable voice, which the official reporter did not even notice, called out "tomorrow"![18] The House smiled. And Blake went relentlessly on with his questioning. When, he asked, had the office of Librarian of Parliament become vacant and when would a successor to Dr. Todd be appointed? "A librarian has not yet been appointed," Macdonald replied amiably, "one will be appointed ere long—I was going to say 'tomorrow' only I knew the honourable gentleman would laugh."[19]

Tomorrow was February 6; and on February 6 the news of the tragedy of Khartoum and the death of General Gordon was made public in Canada.[20] It was only the first of the military crises of 1885. But it came out of a sky which most people still thought was clear, and it shocked the conscience and stirred the indignation of the whole Empire. For a while, a great war seemed closer than it had ever done since that time, almost exactly seven years before, when the "Jingoes" had clamoured for resistance to Russia, and Disraeli had ordered the Mediterranean fleet to steam through the Dardanelles to Constantinople. What was to be done this time? Should Great Britain withdraw from the Sudan, as, indeed, Gordon had been instructed to do, or was there now any real alternative to an advance for the reconquest of Khartoum? And if a great and popular effort at retribution was to be made, what part would the Empire as a whole and Canada in particular play in it? Canada, of course, had already made a small distinctive contribution to the expedition which, in the previous October, had started up the Nile under General Wolseley for the relief of the beleaguered General Gordon. A party of Canadian "voyageurs"—lumbermen and

Indians experienced in the treacherous furies of Canadian water-
ways—put their knowledge at the service of the columns which
toiled up the uncharted Nile.[21] But the voyageurs, despite their
usefulness and, indeed, their bravery, had been non-combatants.
Was it not time for combatants, in numbers, to take over?

Macdonald remained unsympathetically aloof from the mood
of belligerent patriotism which seemed for a while to be sweeping the Dominion. He held back for reasons both general and
particular, theoretical and practical. As he told Tupper, the
question of the mutual assistance to be given by the Mother
Country and the Colonies was a question which could not be
answered satisfactorily until a settlement of the much more
general problem of the organization of the Empire had been
carried out. Like most members of his generation, he had ideas
about the organization of the Empire; but his views were not
the fashionable views of 1885. He had no faith in an imperial
federal parliament; what he hoped for was a league or alliance
of Great Britain and the "auxiliary kingdoms" of Canada and
Australia. As he saw it, a pact between England and Canada
for the defence of British North America already existed. Its
bases were the pledges which the two countries had exchanged
in 1865, and the arrangements which they had agreed to in 1871
when the imperial troops were withdrawn from central Canada.
Was it possible, now that the Dominion had so nearly come
of age, to extend this agreement so as to cover other areas and
other contingencies? Macdonald had always hoped that Canada
would be a source of strength, not weakness, to Great Britain.
At the back of his mind there had long lain the conception
of a great, formal association of the self-governing kingdoms of the
Empire.[22] But he knew that in this, as in so many other things,
haste would be perilous. It had taken him years to establish
the bare nucleus of a Canadian permanent force. It would,
in all probability, take far longer to secure an acknowledgment
of Canada's external obligations. He did not want to prejudice
the issue by premature action. He wanted to launch his appeal
when he could be certain of a favourable response.

In the meantime, in the absence of a formal agreement, each
case would have to be considered on its merits and in the light

of the circumstances of the time. A general war, which threatened any substantial portions of the Empire, was a war in which
all its self-governing communities would obviously take part.
But local defence against minor disturbances was a different
matter; and Great Britain had in effect insisted upon this
difference when she withdrew the garrisons from central Canada
in 1871. If—which was now unhappily possible—serious trouble
should break out in the Canadian north-west, Macdonald had
no intention of requesting imperial military help as he had
done so anxiously in 1869-70. The maintenance of peace in
the north-west of North America was now Canada's business;
and similarly the suppression of a small uprising in the interior
of Egypt was an affair in which Great Britain and possibly
Australasia might interest themselves. "England is not at war,"
he reminded Tupper, "but merely helping the Khedive to put
down an insurrection, and now that Gordon is gone the motive
of aiding in the rescue of our own countryman is gone with
him. . . ."[23] This was not, nor was likely to become, a general
conflict. Why should the Empire pay for the incoherence of
Gladstone's foreign policy? Why should England herself indulge
in further heroics in the Sudan at a time when there was
already a prospect of serious trouble with Russia over the
delimitation of the Russian-Indian boundary?

In the end it was an affray in the north-west frontier of India
that decided the Gladstone government to cut its commitments
in the Sudan. It was fear for the peace of another north-west
frontier which, in all probability, caused Macdonald to blow
so coldly upon the zeal of Tupper and the Canadian Militia
colonels for Egyptian adventures. For over six months now,
ever since Riel's return in the previous summer, Macdonald had
been worried about the north-west. Since Christmas of 1884
his anxiety had been rapidly increasing. On December 30,
a petition had arrived from the District of Lorne, accompanied
by a covering letter from a certain W. H. Jackson, who described
himself as the secretary of the "general committee".[24] There was
no apparent connection between this petition and Riel. Jackson
was known in Ottawa as the leader of the small group of white
settlers who were taking part in the agitation and in his letter

he referred to "the Canadian and English wing of the move-ment", as if it was for this wing that he spoke. The petition was in English. It briefly recapitulated the difficulties of the Indians and made the familiar demand of the *métis* for lands and scrip. It then went on to list a number of small specific criticisms relating mainly to the operation of the Dominion Lands Act; it presented a dubious historical argument, based on the Manitoba negotiations of 1870, in support of the claims of the north-west for greater political autonomy; and it ended by requesting provincial status, responsible government, and control of its own natural resources for the Saskatchewan re-gion. Finally the petitioners asked permission to send delegates to Ottawa to lay their requests before the Dominion government in a bill of rights.

The petition was acknowledged on January 5, discussed in the Cabinet on January 9, and referred at once to the Minister of the Interior for action.[26] The period of memorials and dis-cussions, which, as Macdonald had told Lord Lansdowne during the previous summer, gave the best promise of ending the trouble, had evidently arrived. Nothing as yet had come directly from Riel. No formal statement of the objects of his mission or the claims of his followers had yet been submitted under the authority of his own name. This was disturbing, but Macdonald had not yet given up hope. If events followed the course which they had in the Red River Rebellion, the agitators on the banks of the Saskatchewan would now probably call a large meeting or convention, draw up a bill of "rights", and appoint delegates to go to Ottawa. In the meantime, the Dominion government had decided, on its part, to make an enormous concession. Early in January the ministers came to the conclusion that they must proceed immediately to an enumeration of the north-west *métis*, with a view to granting the long-requested land and scrip. Macdonald had not changed his views about the wisdom of this dubious solatium. He regarded such grants as objectionable in principle and vicious in their probable consequences. But he decided that against his better judgment he must give in. "I do not hesitate to say that I did it with the greatest reluctance," he told the House of

Commons later. "I do not easily yield if there is a better course open; but at the last moment I yielded and I said: 'Well, for God's sake, let them have the scrip; they will either drink it or waste it or sell it; but let us have peace.' "[26]

It was at this point, when the government expected negotiations and was prepared to make real concessions, that a most disquieting piece of news arrived from the north-west. Ever since, on the eve of his departure for England, Macdonald had received the account of the interview which Forget and Bishop Grandin had had with Riel, he had been very uneasy about the *métis* leader's real intentions; and now these doubts and suspicions were horribly confirmed by still another disturbing communication from Dewdney which arrived in Ottawa late in January. Once again, "touch" had been obtained with Riel. A few days before Christmas, Father André, the local priest, and D. H. MacDowall, the member for Lorne in the North-West Council, had paid a visit to the half-breed leader in St. Laurent; and the amazing revelations of the four-hour interview which followed were now spread before Macdonald's astonished eyes. Previously, in the presence of Forget and Grandin, Riel had held forth eloquently about his altruistic purposes and merely hinted about his private claims. But now, before MacDowall and André, he was cynically, almost brutally, selfish. Quite early in the interview, he announced that he had come back to Canada to press his own personal claims as well as to advocate the interests of the half-breeds; and he left his listeners clearly to infer that he hoped, by renewing and increasing his strong influence with the *métis*, to bring effective pressure to bear on the government in his own behalf. "He then proceeded to state," MacDowall continued with his incredible narrative, "that if the government would consider his personal claims against them and pay him a certain amount in settlement of these claims, he would arrange to make his illiterate and unreasoning followers well satisfied with almost any settlement of their claims for land grants that the government might be willing to make, and also that he would leave the north-west never to return."[27]

It might have seemed enough. But there was more to come. Riel had then proceeded calmly to appraise his own political value, basing his estimates on the various efforts which, he claimed, had been made to bribe him to leave the country after the Red River Rebellion. As much as thirty-five thousand dollars had, he asserted, been offered him on one occasion by an emissary from Sir John Macdonald! "His claims," MacDowall went on, "amount to the modest sum of one hundred thousand dollars, but he will take thirty-five thousand dollars as originally offered, and I believe myself three thousand to five thousand would cart the whole Riel family across the border. Riel made it distinctly understood that 'self' was his main object, and he was willing to make the claims of his followers totally subservient to his own interests." Cynically candid about his real purposes, he was equally plain-spoken about the kind of assurances he would accept. Verbal or written promises would have no effect upon him whatever; hard cash would alone induce him to play his part. "He said, 'My name is Riel and I want material', which I suppose," MacDowall added a little sourly, "was a pun."

To Macdonald it was a shattering revelation. It made the whole agitation seem a malevolent sham. It utterly destroyed his faith in Riel's good will. "I believe," he solemnly told the House later, "he came in for the purpose of attempting to extract money from the public purse. . . ."[28] How was one to deal with such a man? How was one to cope with an agitation which seemed to be so completely the embodiment of his enigmatic personality? Could the Canadian government stoop to the dangerous devices which this self-confessed political blackmailer was openly inviting it to adopt? It could not. "Of course, that could not be entertained for a moment,"[29] Macdonald declared when he told the House of Commons of Riel's offer to accept a bribe. Riel might be ready to sell himself; but Macdonald and his colleagues could not afford to buy him. They must continue to act as if they were treating not with a self-interested American adventurer, but with a legitimate Canadian movement. They must do everything possible in reason—and even out of reason—to show their readiness to remedy popular grievances. On January 28, the Cabinet accepted the formal recommendation of the Minister of the Interior that a commission of three be appointed to make an enumeration of the *métis* of the north-west for the purpose of arriving at an equitable settlement of their claims.[30] "Government has decided to investigate claims of half-breeds," Macpherson telegraphed to Dewdney on February 4, "and with that view has directed enumeration of those who did not participate in grant under Manitoba Act."[31]

He had yielded in the west. He still hoped to dissipate the murky crisis that was developing so obscurely in the west. But in the east the collapse of the Canadian Pacific Railway was drawing closer with every day that passed. Together these disasters might mean the ruin of very nearly everything he had tried to do for the Canadian prairie country. He knew it. But characteristically he could not bring himself to accept these catastrophic conclusions. Deep in the final privacy of his being, he refused to believe that a single half-breed megalomaniac could destroy the west as a homeland for British Americans or that the track which was to bind Canada together would be permitted to fail for a few million dollars. Stephen, he was aware, still counted secretly upon his own veiled, half-whispered promises; and Stephen was prepared, up to the last moment and with his utmost effort, to do everything he could to earn the assistance which he had begged from the government. He and Donald Smith had borrowed the six hundred and fifty thousand dollars to pay the January dividend; they had endorsed a five-months note for one million dollars "to provide the company with current funds to keep it going for the next few weeks". Macdonald, implicitly if not explicitly, had required proofs that Stephen and his partner were prepared to make huge sacrifices for their own creation. And proofs had been supplied. "I venture to say," Stephen wrote reproachfully, "that there is not a business man in all Canada, knowing the facts, but would say we were a couple of fools for our pains."[32]

But was the government aid which these efforts had justified, a political possibility? Macdonald was still filled with painful uncertainty. McLelan threatened resignation; most of the other Cabinet ministers were either hesitant or opposed. John Henry

Pope and Frank Smith were strong in support of relief for the
railway; and Tupper wrote from London, protesting, with more
even than his usual emphasis, that the Canadian Pacific must
not be permitted to go down, and that he himself was prepared
to go back at once to Ottawa, either to take McLelan's place,
or to give the government all the aid he could as a private
member.[33] Macdonald shook his head. He missed Tupper
terribly; but he realized that if the High Commissioner came
back he would have to get a seat in Parliament and that the
session would probably be over before the necessary by-election
could be held. No, he would have to get along without Tupper.
He would have to see the thing through himself. But he was
weary with the toil of it; and there were times also when he
was disillusioned with an enterprise which seemed such an
insatiable drain upon the country and which dragged with it
such a host of predatory parasites. "The Quebec M.P.s," he
wrote to Tupper, "have the line to Quebec up again. The Maritimes are clamorous for the Short Line, and we have black-
mailing all round. How it will end, God knows! But I wish I
were well out of it."[34]

It was on March 17 that Macdonald wrote his letter to
Tupper. During the next few days it began to seem increasingly
probable that the Cabinet could not be persuaded to grant
more aid to the Canadian Pacific. But even this was not all.
At the same time, the threat of a real storm began to roar up
over the horizon of the north-west. For some days, the news
from the Saskatchewan had been bad. Now, with terrifying
rapidity, it went from bad to worse. What was happening?
Father André had kept requesting that the "indemnity" be
paid to Riel; he and Crozier of the North-West Mounted Police
had urged that a settlement in accordance with the "confidential
communications" should be made at once.[35] Had the unbeliev-
able really occurred? Had Riel determined to pull down the
heavens because his own private demands for money were
ignored? Was this the real explanation of the curious ineffectu-
ality of the government's promise to proceed with an equitable
settlement of the *métis* claims for land and scrip? Macdonald

did not know, and the time for answering such questions had
gone by.

He must act. On the night of March 23, Major-General
Frederick Middleton, the General Officer Commanding the
Canadian Militia, was sent west to Winnipeg; and next day the
newspapers carried confused reports that Riel's *métis* were threatening Fort Carlton and its small garrison of North-West
Mounted Police under Crozier. It had come to a fight in the
west. And, at the same time, in Ottawa, the endless negotiations between the government and the Canadian Pacific Railway
slowed down ominously to a stop. Stephen faced the stark
fact that there would almost certainly be no government relief.
"I need not repeat how sorry I am," he wrote from Abbott's
office in the Parliament Buildings, "that this should be the result
of all our efforts to give Canada a railway to the Pacific Ocean.
But I am supported by the conviction that I have done all that
could be done to obtain it."[36]

It was Thursday, March 26; and all day long alarming
rumours of a clash between Riel's men and the police at Fort
Carlton swept through the cities and towns and far into the
Canadian countryside. At Ottawa there was no official news
of an engagement, and Macdonald cabled reassuringly to
London, England. But next day the telegram from Colonel
Irvine, which was to end all these comforting delusions, arrived
at the East Block; and that night Macdonald rose in his place
in the House to announce the tiny battle at Duck Lake between
the *métis* and Crozier's command.[37] The two disasters—the
revolt on the prairie and the collapse of the railway—had come
together in time. And together they might destroy him and his
Canada. Yet the blow which they would deliver was not a
single one. They were separate problems. They would have
to be dealt with separately. They could even be played off
against each other. And in that possibility did not there still
lie a real hope? He could use the railway to defend the west.
He could use the west to justify the railway.

IV

"This insurrection is a bad business," he wrote with characteristic brevity to Lieutenant-Governor Dewdney, "but we must
face it as best we may."[38] For him the great danger lay not so
much in the revolt of a few hundred *métis* as in the possibility
of a general Indian rising. He had never believed that the
Indians would start trouble; but he could not rid himself of the
fear that, if once the initiative were given by others, the whole
native population of the west might follow it in a bloody and
destructive mob. "The first thing to be done," he wrote to
General Middleton, modestly apologizing for bothering him with
his "crude" strategical ideas, "is to localize the insurrection."[39]
The government was already proceeding, by every means in its
power, to win over the waverers and to confirm the loyalty of the
well affected. Through Father Lacombe, Macdonald early
secured a promise of support from the Blackfoot tribe, which
occupied the territory of southern Alberta. General orders were
given to distribute additional provisions to the Indians; and the
investigation of the *métis* claims was now set in motion by the
appointment of the necessary commissioners.

These were pacific, conciliatory measures. But the outbreak
on the prairies was an armed uprising; and military force was
necessary to prevent its development and to crush it at its
source. For the first time in their collective history, the Canadians confidently faced a struggle on their own soil with nothing
but their own resources. Macdonald had no thought of requesting the assistance of regular imperial troops; he had no need
to wait, in angry futility, until the coming of spring and the
opening of navigation would permit a force to fight its toilsome
way through endless miles of lake and river, forest and prairie,
to an uncertain encounter with a successful rebellion. He
could act at once. The railway was there; citizen soldiers everywhere were clamouring for enlistment; and within only a few
days of the time when the incredulous Canadians had learnt
of the repulse at Duck Lake, the first national Canadian army
was assembling for its journey to the north-west.

As early as March 25, the Winnipeg militia, with Hugh Macdonald among their number, had begun to move westward; and on Monday, March 30, in all the main cities of the east, the troops marched down under grey and rainy skies to the railway stations, while the bands played "Auld Lang Syne" and "The Girl I Left Behind Me".[40] "Wish you to travel night and day," Adolphe Caron, the Minister of Militia telegraphed on March 31 to the first detachments speeding westward. "I want to show what the Canadian militia can do." It was an appeal which came home as clearly, and with quite as much force, to William Cornelius Van Horne as it did to any militia commander travelling towards Winnipeg in a flat-car north of Lake Superior. Van Horne knew, and he made every one of his subordinates realize, that not only the credit but perhaps also the very existence of the Canadian Pacific Railway depended upon the speed and efficiency with which it could complete this great effort in military transport. On the night of April 4, the first companies from the east reached Winnipeg; and less than a week later, Middleton, in command of the first of the three striking columns, set out from Qu'Appelle northward for Riel's stronghold at Batoche.

Macdonald had done his work. It was up to the soldiers now. And while Caron coped energetically with the thousand details of military organization and the columns struggled over rolling prairie through the bitter cold of early spring, he took up once more the old task of maintaining Canadian confidence at home and defending Canadian prestige abroad. At home, the nation had responded magnificently. The secret fears, which had nagged at him for years, that the country was about to split apart in jagged pieces of sectional discontent and antagonism, had, in the end, been proved false. More emphatically perhaps than ever before the Canadians had revealed a sense of their identity and a belief in their future. He had not asked too much of the Dominion; he had not overtaxed the immature but growing sense of nationalism which he had nursed so patiently for so many years. The first consequence of the rebellion, in fact, was a vigorous assertion of the national will. It was much. It was perhaps even more than he had dared to expect. But it was not all. The North-West Rebellion not only gave him his supreme vindication; it also supplied his enemies and critics, both at home and abroad, with their greatest opportunity.

Abroad, the opportunity was exploited to the full. Wherever the dispatches of the American press associations went, and they seemed to go almost everywhere, Canada's western difficulties were enormously exaggerated, and her prospects painted in the most blackly discouraging colours. The news which came out of Winnipeg and was printed in most of the Canadian newspapers was, on the whole, honest and reasonably accurate. But this was not the news which the rest of the English-speaking world got, or, indeed, appeared to want. The American newspaper correspondents in St. Paul, who were familiarly known, so one Canadian editor assured his readers, as "liars on space", apparently supplied most of the information about the North-West Rebellion which appeared in the press of both England and the United States.[41] One London newspaper actually went to the extreme length of sending out a correspondent to the Canadian north-west; but The Times did not apparently even consider such a preposterously unnecessary expenditure. It relied instead upon dispatches which were dated, oddly enough, from Philadelphia;[42] and, as late as May 5, it was confirming its previous reports of a general Indian rising and complacently assuring its readers that Canada had a long and bloody native war on its hands. Lansdowne was astonished, as other governors-general had been astonished before him, at these evidences of indifference and misrepresentation; and Macdonald and Tupper, who knew that there was not the slightest use in attempting to correct the malevolent distortions of the American press, recommenced their old efforts to get a fair hearing for Canada in England.[43]

At home, Macdonald knew, the opposition would be even fiercer and more determined than ever. He expected the longest, hardest, most contentious session since the famous session of 1882. It was nearly three years now since the last general election; and before the despondent, twice-defeated Grits there glimmered the pale hope of a new appeal to the people. They were certain to use every ounce of strength and ingenuity to turn this session to their advantage. They would exhaust themselves in efforts. And what magnificent, unparalleled opportunities lay before them! The Washington Treaty was running out, the Canadian Pacific Railway was obviously *in extremis* and the government was about to introduce a novel and highly debatable Franchise Bill. The riches of their enemies' misfortunes were spread before the Liberals! And now, as a final gift of the bounty of good fortune, came the calamity of a rebellion. It could hardly have been worse, Macdonald realized. He knew how vulnerable he was, even at the centre of power. "The government is too old," he told Tupper. He had felt this for over a year now. He grew more and more gloomily conscious of it as the session advanced. The ministers were too old for the crisis which was upon them. They were tired and ill and timid and disillusioned.

For a while at least, he must fight a defensive battle. Controversial decisions must be postponed; the country must follow moderate courses; and in a month—in six weeks—the whole frightening aspect of affairs might be utterly changed by a stroke of good fortune in the north-west. His first, his instinctive choice was for a policy of delay; and to a large extent a policy of delay was forced upon him by the opposition. The session had opened in a deliberate, argumentative fashion. Then the news of the rebellion in the north-west seemed to transform the Grits into a pack of curs, snapping at everything and everybody, worrying each legislative bone that was thrown to them for weeks; and on April 16, when Macdonald moved the second reading of his Franchise Bill, the pack rushed in baying as if for a kill. It was only after prolonged debates, over several basic amendments, that the Bill at last got into committee; and in committee it remained for week after week while the two sides wrangled endlessly over virtually every one of its terms.

Here the prolonged obstruction ended in annoying him and stiffening his determination; but in other respects he was obviously ready to accept suggested postponements and to deal in generously conciliatory gestures. It was no time, he knew very

well, to start quarrelling with the United States. The fishery
articles of the Washington Treaty would, at the instance of the
American government, come to an end on July 1; and, so far
as the law was concerned, American privileges in the inshore
fisheries of British North America would be governed once more
by the terms of the Convention of 1818. In fact, in the circumstances of the moment, it would be highly injudicious for
Canada to make a sudden attempt to keep American fishermen
outside the three-mile limit. England was still seriously concerned over the disagreement with Russia. The Dominion had
more than enough on its hands in the north-west; and, in
Macdonald's opinion, the new administration at Washington,
with Cleveland as President and Bayard as Secretary of State,
gave far more promise of a liberal spirit in commercial policy
than any of its recent predecessors.[44] He had his eye fixed, just
as in 1871, upon a generous reciprocal trade agreement with the
republic; and for this reason he was not inclined to reject Bayard's candidly self-interested request that the American fishing
privileges under the Washington Treaty should be continued for
another six months pending the possible negotiation of a new
agreement. In return for this large concession, Bayard suggested
that the American President, in his message to Congress, might
suggest the appointment of a joint high commission for the
peaceful settlement of the relations between the two countries.
Beyond this no compensation whatever was offered. American
fishermen might fish in Canadian waters until December 31;
but on July 1, the American tariff on Canadian fish would
come promptly into operation. "He appeals to us as good neighbours," Macdonald wrote dryly of Bayard to the Governor-
General, "to do what he does not offer as a good neighbour to
do to us."[45]

Here postponement and conciliation were obviously devices
of mere prudence; but, in respect of the Canadian Pacific Railway, the policy of delay had paradoxically become a gamble of
the most perilous extravagance. Within a week, the prestige
of the railway had risen enormously; but at the same time it was
rushing towards financial disaster with the speed of one of its
own trains. In the north-west it had performed a national serv-

ice with superb efficiency. The Canadian Militia had been rushed with such swiftness to their bases at Qu'Appelle, Swift Current, and Calgary that the outcome of the struggle was decided before the rebellion itself had had a real chance of getting going. In a few weeks, Macdonald was convinced, the country would begin to appreciate this; but at the moment, when the troops had not yet made contact with the rebels and when the real nature of the struggle was hardly understood, he did not believe that he could presume upon a real change in the popular attitude to the railway. Three months, two months, ago he had feared that the opposition, in the Cabinet and the party, to further aid for the Canadian Pacific was too strong for him to overcome. Now, in the face of the prodigies which the railway had performed in the national interest, that opposition was visibly declining. But had it weakened far enough to permit him to act? He did not know. He was besieged by uncertainties. And his first instinct was always to delay.

Yet, in a matter of days, delay might be fatal. The company must be saved soon or there would be nothing left to save. It was a race between the railway's creditors and the marching feet of General Middleton's militia. It was a trial of strength between the endless, acrimonious procrastinations of Canadian politics and the dauntless and devoted spirit of George Stephen. Everything he possessed had been flung into the insatiable maw of the railway's necessities. He had told Donald Smith—and Van Horne remembered it long afterwards as the finest speech he had ever heard—that if the end came they must not be found with a dollar in their pockets.[46] He had come to Ottawa because there was now no hope of assistance elsewhere; and, as he told Tupper, he had been living there almost continuously since early in December. A dozen times he had been convinced that the end had come; a dozen times he had decided that it was useless to continue the struggle further; and yet he could never quite bring himself to give in. He had sat in J. H. Pope's house, waiting for its owner, with his chin in his hand, staring into space, and muttering, "We are ruined". He had walked furiously out of the Russell Hotel, vowing that he would shake the dust of Ottawa off his feet for ever. But he had not left. He had stayed on. He had never really ceased his efforts for a moment.

Yet there were limits to human endurance; and by the middle of April he had reached the smouldering, angry conclusion that he had passed them. "It is impossible for me to continue this struggle for existence any longer," he wrote to Macdonald on April 15. "The delay in dealing with the C.P.R. matter, whatever may be the necessity for it, has finished me, and rendered me utterly unfit for further work, and if it is continued, must eventuate in the destruction of the company."[47] The destruction of the company! Was it avoidable now? "Have no means paying wages," Van Horne telegraphed to Stephen, "pay car can't be sent out, and unless we get immediate relief we must stop. Please inform Premier and Finance Minister. Do not be surprised, or blame me, if an immediate and most serious catastrophe happens."[48]

On April 24, Macdonald wrote privately to C. F. Smithers of the Bank of Montreal.[49] A plan for the financial relief of the Canadian Pacific would, he explained, be brought before Parliament in the near future. But such a measure could not be passed in a hurry, and meanwhile the necessities of the railway were becoming more pressing every day. Would the Bank consent, on the strength of his private guarantee, to grant a temporary advance to the company? The Bank declined.[50] It would probably have taken a different view, Charles Drinkwater, the Canadian Pacific's secretary, wrote to Macdonald, if the legislation had actually been submitted to the House. It was the bluntest of hints; and Macdonald realized that delay had been spun out so long that a break was inevitable if he did not act at once. Yet could it be said that circumstances were yet favourable to action? On April 25 the news of the successful arrival of Colonel Otter's column at Battleford cheered the whole of Canada's anxiously waiting people. But on the same day came the disturbing reports of the stiff, indecisive engagement between Riel and General Middleton's forces at Fish Creek; and on April 30 the heavy black headlines in the newspapers shouted that Great Britain and Russia were on the eve of war. It was on the same day that Macdonald presented his plan for the relief of the railway to the Conservative caucus;[51] and on May 1 he gave notice of the resolutions which he proposed shortly to submit to Parliament.[52]

It was, with minor modifications, the plan which he had discussed with Tupper and Stephen during the previous autumn. In place of the thirty-five millions of dormant common stock, which were to be cancelled by the proposed legislation, the Canadian Pacific Railway Company was empowered to issue an equivalent amount of first mortgage bonds. The essence of the plan was that the existing governmental lien upon the whole of the company's property was to be extinguished by the new bonds. They were to be delivered to government, and retained by government, as a security both for the loan of the previous year and for a new advance of five million dollars which was to be made immediately to the company. Tupper thought the plan excellent. He expected little opposition in Parliament or the country, "especially with the fact before them that but for the rapid construction of the C.P.R. the country might have been torn to pieces, and enormous waste of blood and treasure involved."[53] He was right, Macdonald knew. The rebellion was coming rapidly to an end, as he had hoped and believed it would. It was true that on May 2 Otter had suffered a hard check at Cut Knife Hill and had retired on Battleford; but, on the afternoon of May 13, Caron read in the House a triumphant telegram from Middleton announcing the capture of Batoche and the collapse of the *métis* resistance.[54] The issue of Canadian expansion had been settled, and settled for all time. The west had been won by Canadian soldiers and a Canadian railway.

But would the Canadian people be willing to pay the price of their own national survival? The party was now committed. But the measure of relief had still to be pushed through the recalcitrant and ungovernable House of Commons; and the whole management of the government's programme fell upon Macdonald. Macpherson and Chapleau were away for shorter or longer periods; Pope was ill and shaky; Campbell was repeatedly prostrated by his dreadful headaches; and Tilley departed, two months before the session ended, for the operation in England which was quickly to bring his political career to a close. For day after day of furious battle, Macdonald, the solitary fighting member of the Cabinet, faced the House virtually alone. He had every reason to break down. His record for the past few years must have led everybody, including himself, to expect a collapse. But, fed with some mysterious inner source of strength, he stood his ground. "I am holding out pretty well," he told his sister early in May, "in the hard fight we have here."[55]

He did not believe he had ever known such a savage conflict. On one occasion, shortly after the Franchise Bill got into committee, the House sat continuously for two and a half days. It was only the most preposterous of the excesses of this most incredible debate. All during May and into June every clause, sentence, phrase, and almost every word of the Franchise Bill was fought with the full strength of the opposition. Macdonald became convinced that the Liberals were exploiting the Bill, as a threat to provincial rights, with the deliberate purpose of panicking his French-Canadian followers into desertion. He grew more and more determined to fight the battle of the union and of the independent House of Commons which, in his opinion, was the union's necessary expression. The Franchise Bill became an obsession with him. "I shall not be baulked . . .," he wrote to Lord Lansdowne at the beginning of June.[56] Another week, full of petty verbal battles, went by; but by that time the end of the committee stage appeared dimly, promisingly, ahead. The government turned with relief to the suspended bills and half-forgotten measures of its programme; and finally on June 16, John Henry Pope arose to move the resolutions in aid of the Canadian Pacific Railway Company.

V

"On the twentieth," Macdonald wrote to Charles Tupper on July 27, "we closed the most harassing and disagreeable session I have witnessed in forty years. The Grits were desperate and acted like desperate men."[57] The long protesting retreat of the opposition had been fought fanatically and at every inch of the way. Blake's oratory, stripped, like a luxury liner, of all ornamentation for wartime service, had been crammed with vast formidable masses of government documents and statistical details. He had opposed the grant of further aid to the Canadian Pacific, and attacked the policy of the government in the north-west, in two enormous orations, each of which lasted well over six hours, wore everybody out with its tedious prolixity, and even plunged some of his own ardent followers into profound and noisy slumbers. Yet these heroic exploits, like the prolonged obstruction which had preceded them, had availed nothing in the end. In the end the government had staggered through. It had not, in many ways, been a very creditable session, for, as Macdonald reminded Campbell later on, the Treasury Bench had been obviously enfeebled, the whole burden had fallen on the Prime Minister, some of the work had not been well done, and the Conservatives had audibly complained.[58] Still, the government had survived. "The session is over," he wrote proudly to Tupper, "and the opposition didn't score a single point."

"I consider the passage of the Franchise Bill," he declared, "the greatest triumph of my life."[59] It was the triumph of an old man's enormous expertise in the fine points of parliamentary in-fighting. Macdonald would savour, and perhaps overestimate, this peculiarly personal success; but the victories which had been won for the railway, and in the north-west, were obviously of far greater national importance. Stephen, like one of his own prospectors in the Rockies, had at length found a good pass through what had seemed the insuperable mountain range of his difficulties; and the great house of Baring, which up to that time had regarded the Canadian Pacific with majestic indiffer-ence, now at last consented magnificently to act as agents for the issue of the new four per cent bonds. The support of the great English financial house had come late. How much easier so many things would have been if it had come earlier! But it had come at last. And with it came the apparent acceptance of Canada in England as a possible transcontinental state. The Canadians had made good their claim to the north-west with treasure, and toil, and blood. And, as Macdonald saw clearly, their own sense of their collective destiny had grown clearer and firmer during the long ordeal through which they had passed. "Canada as you will see," he wrote to Tupper, "is delirious with enthusiasm on the return of our volunteers. This has done more to weld the provinces into one nation than anything else could have done."[60]

He was—or so it seemed—nearly done with the north-west. And all that remained was to deal, in a spirit of reasonable, unsentimental clemency, with the inevitable consequences of a rebellion. The commission established by the government would have to complete its investigation of the claims of the *métis*; and the courts would have to settle the fate of the half-breed and Indian principals in the revolt. Macdonald had never believed that more than a relatively small part of the demand for scrip was legitimate; he had never believed that scrip would provide more than a brief satisfaction for those who could make good their claim to it. And, as the work of the North-West Commissioners proceeded, the accuracy of these realistic assumptions was conclusively established. Seven hundred and seventy-nine half-breeds had thought so highly of the *métis* title to the land, and their own right to participate in it, that they had signed petitions demanding its recognition. It was now revealed that of these seven hundred and seventy-nine, as many as five hundred and eighty-six could not qualify for scrip, either because they had already been granted it under the Manitoba distribution or because they were half-breeds from the United States, or squatters who were not half-breeds at all.[61] To only one hundred and ninety-three of the signatories had the North-West Commissioners granted scrip; and of these how many would derive any permanent benefit from the government's bounty? "In spite of the good intentions of government," Amyot, the French-Canadian member for Bellechasse, telegraphed from the west to Langevin, "work by Commission will be a farce, because crowds of speculators follow the Commissioners, intoxicate half-breeds, buy for a nominal sum their scrips."[62] It was for this, Macdonald reflected angrily, that the whole country had been thrown into a turmoil, that men had died, and that millions of money had been expended. It was for this that a handful of *métis* and Indians would have to pay with imprisonment or life. The last harsh episode in the affair was now at hand; and on July 20 the trial of Louis Riel, watched over by the whole nation with absorbed interest, began at Regina before Magistrate Richardson.

In the meantime, while he waited for the conclusion of the final scene in this unhappy drama, Macdonald tried to cope with the problems of the future. The reorganization of the Cabinet, postponed again and again during the past year, could not be held off any longer; there were several places—perhaps even his own place—which must be filled at once. "Now is the time for me to retire," he wrote to Tupper. "I have finished my work. Everything that I proposed to do from Confederation down to the present time has been completed."[63] It was all true; and his wish for retirement was all the stronger because it grew out of a satisfied sense of achievement and not out of the weakness and exhaustion of ill health. Yet how could he abandon the ministry now? Macpherson had already retired. Tilley was about to accept the lieutenant-governorship of his native province of New Brunswick; and for weeks past Campbell had been repeatedly requesting, in his lugubrious, put-upon manner, to be made Lieutenant-Governor of Ontario. If Macdonald left the Cabinet now, when so many others were leaving or threatening to leave, he might complete the disintegration and the ruin of the government. He would have to stay—for a while at least. He tried to persuade Campbell to defer his ambitions and postpone his resignation. And, on the advice chiefly of his Maritime friends, he got in touch with John S. D. Thompson, a Nova Scotian politician who was now on the bench, but who, before the defeat of the Conservatives in 1882, had been the main strength of the provincial government at Halifax.[64] For years—for as long, it seemed, as he could remember—he had been seeking a young, active, vigorous and able recruit for the reformation of a Cabinet of debilitated veterans. Was Thompson, of whom everyone spoke so highly, the man he sought?

On July 30, he escaped, at long last, from the stifling heat of Ottawa, and hurried down to Rivière du Loup. By now the summer was half over; and what remained of it seemed never free from the preoccupations of public affairs. The reorganization of the Cabinet, the delicate negotiations with Judge Thompson, the preliminary arrangements for a conference with the United States on the fisheries, all combined to crowd the last few golden weeks of August with their anxieties; and when, early in September, he got back to Ottawa, full of an annoyed feeling that he had earned and had been cheated out of a holiday, it was only to discover that a new and most painful difficulty was awaiting him. Campbell, who had been persuaded with considerable difficulty to remain in the Cabinet, naturally assumed that he would retain his present portfolio as Minister of Justice; but the Ministry of Justice was the one department which Judge Thompson had insisted quietly but firmly he must have if he were to enter the Cabinet. Macdonald was determined to secure Thompson's services.[65] But Campbell was a surprised and unwilling sacrifice;[66] and it was only after the most painful recriminations and reproaches that Macdonald persuaded him to accept the office of Postmaster-General. The whole episode left him feeling emotionally worn out; and he began to long once more for the only real holiday which he had ever seemed to enjoy, a holiday in England. "I have had no rest this summer at all," he wrote to Tupper, "and am half inclined to take a run across the sea. But this Riel business must be settled first, and the arrangements for the negotiations at Washington."[67]

The import of "this Riel business" had certainly increased with great rapidity during the past few weeks. On August 1, the trial of the *métis* leader at Regina had come to an end. The defence, which had been conducted by a group of the most distinguished counsel in the country, had been mainly based on the contention that the accused was of unsound mind. But Riel himself expressly and vehemently rejected the plea of insanity; the medical evidence was contradictory; and, as B. B. Osler pointed out at the time of the trial, there was a curious inconsistency between the prisoner's alleged "megalomania" and the hard, persistent shrewdness with which he had bargained for the betrayal of his "mission". "He seems," the Chief Justice of Manitoba said later, in affirming the verdict, "to have had in

· GRIP · SATURDAY, 29TH AUGUST, 1885.

A RIEL UGLY POSITION.

view, while professing to champion the interests of the *métis*,
the securing of pecuniary advantage for himself."[68] In the end,
the half-breed leader had been convicted of treason; and in the
time-honoured and terrible phraseology reserved for such occa-

sions he was sentenced to death by hanging. It was this sentence, with its awful definiteness and finality, which hastened the expression of a clear and sharply divided public opinion. In Quebec a protesting demand for clemency began to be heard; in English-speaking Canada, and particularly in the Province of Ontario, it was assumed, as something about which there was no room for argument, that there would be no interference from government and that the law would be permitted to take its course.

Macdonald himself was very much of the same mind as his fellow-citizens of Ontario. Riel had been sentenced to hang on September 18; and he saw no reason why the state should make any effort to alter the infliction of this penalty. There was, on his reading of the evidence, no need for a new trial. He had confidently expected that the Appeal Court of Manitoba would confirm the decision reached at Regina; and he did not believe that the government, of its own motion, should do anything to invite further proceedings. "I don't think," he wrote to Lord Lansdowne towards the end of August from Rivière du Loup, "that we should by a respite anticipate—and as it were court—the interference of the Judicial Committee."[69] There was no appeal, as a matter of course, to the Judicial Committee of the Privy Council in criminal cases; and if the government took any special steps to "facilitate" such an appeal, English-speaking Canada, in Macdonald's opinion, would certainly take violent exception. He knew, of course, that a section of opinion in Quebec would warmly approve such a move. But he was convinced that Riel, in abandoning the faith of his fathers, had forfeited his strongest claim upon the sympathies of his French-speaking fellow-subjects. The emotional feeling in his favour did not go very deep and it could not last very long.

VI

As soon as he got back to the capital on September 10, these reasonable conclusions were shattered. At Ottawa a sense of impending crisis was in the air. Petitions for the commutation of Riel's sentence were already beginning to arrive; and—what was much worse—it was known that Langevin, with the probable support of Chapleau and Caron, would in all likelihood press for a commission of inquiry into Riel's mental state. Campbell, who was continuing as Minister of Justice pending Thompson's election in Nova Scotia, was strongly opposed to such an investigation. Riel's defence, he argued, had been based on the plea of insanity; and judge and jury, after hearing a mass of evidence on the subject, had rejected it. "How can medical men now look into Riel's mental state as it existed in February and March last?" he inquired. "We can give them no authority to hear evidence on oath which would be trying him over again and the inquiry would almost inevitably end in disagreement amongst the doctors; and leave, as regards the fate of the prisoner, 'confusion worse confounded'. . . . I do not think that such an inquiry should take place, unless the alleged insanity has intervened since the trial. . . ."[70]

With all this Macdonald agreed. But, at the back of their minds, both he and Campbell had the uneasy suspicion that for the sake of their French-speaking colleagues, the commission of inquiry would have to be granted in the end. Campbell argued that if they must yield, they had better yield at once. But Macdonald was determined, as long as possible, to avoid interference by government in the normal processes of justice. There was still a final court of appeal left, though less than a fortnight before he had counselled against inviting an application to it. On September 11, the Department of Justice telegraphed Magistrate Richardson to reprieve the prisoner; and immediately Riel's lawyers appealed to the Judicial Committee of the Privy Council in London.

In the meantime, the Governor-General left by train for the north-west. This was the journey, long planned and long and eagerly awaited, which was to be signalized by the driving in of the last spike of the completed Canadian Pacific Railway. "With that railway finished and my Franchise Bill become law," Macdonald had written, early in September, to his old friend Lord Carnarvon, "I feel that I have done my work and can sing my *nunc dimittis*."[71] There was now, he realized bitterly,

not the slightest chance of his immediate retirement from the
government. His work was not finished. He was caught in
the toils of the Riel affair; and the Riel affair, which had arisen
with such mysterious suddenness and violence, was big with
menace for the future. It threatened possible ruin for much of
his work. It threatened, incidentally, to spoil the ceremonial
completion of the railway, for which he had struggled so long
and so hard. Far out, in the mountains, construction was being
held up by bad weather. The gap in the line was closing, but
it was not closing fast enough; and early in October it became
clear that the last spike could not be driven in before the end
of the month and that if the Governor-General wished to be
present for the final decision concerning Riel, he must change
his plans and start east at once. Lansdowne began to hurry
home; and on October 22, three days before his arrival in
Ottawa, a cablegram from the Colonial Office informed Macdonald that the Judicial Committee of the Privy Council had
heard counsel on behalf of Riel and had advised the Queen
to dismiss his petition.[72]

Responsibility had been flung back upon Ottawa. And once
more Macdonald faced the question of a special commission of
inquiry into Riel's mental state. Caron was critical of the
proposal; but Langevin believed that a final investigation was
necessary to quiet public opinion in Quebec; and Macdonald
and Campbell, who had already privately decided that they
would accept Langevin's plan, if he urged it strongly, reluctantly
consented.[73] A governmental interference in the administration
of justice was something which Macdonald disliked on grounds
both general and particular. Against his better judgment he
agreed to it; but he was determined that the inquiry should be
strictly limited in time, and that it should be directed towards
the one question which, in the light of the legal precedents,
constituted the real point of issue.

The great leading case in the whole problem of crime and
insanity was the McNaghten case of 1843. In answer to a
series of questions put on that occasion by the House of Lords,
fourteen British judges had replied, in part, that a man must
be presumed to be sane until he was proved not to be so, and

EARNSCLIFFE

"that to establish a defence on the ground of insanity it must be clearly proved that, at the time of committing the act, the accused was labouring under such a defect of reason, from disease of the mind, as not to know the nature and quality of the act he was doing; or, if he did know it, that he did not know he was doing what was wrong". The question of insanity, the judges continued, must not be put in any general or abstract fashion, but with reference to the accused's knowledge of right and wrong "in respect of the very act with which he is charged". Finally, in the fifth and last of what became known as the Mc-Naghten Rules, the judges affirmed that a medical man, even if he had been present throughout the trial and had heard all the evidence, could not in strictness be asked his opinion of the state of the prisoner's mind at the time of the commission of the crime unless the facts in the case were admitted or not disputed and the problem had thus become substantially scientific in character.[74]

On the last day of October, Macdonald rapidly completed the arrangements for the inquiry. Three medical men—Dr. A. Jukes, surgeon at the Regina prison, Dr. F. X. Valade of Ottawa, and Dr. M. Lavell, the Warden of the Kingston Penitentiary—were appointed to examine Riel. They were not invited to express an opinion on the question of the prisoner's accountability at the time of the rebellion; they were simply asked to report upon his present mental state. Lavell and Valade left Ottawa at once for the west; and to them both Macdonald gave precise and unambiguous instructions. "Remember," he pointed out to Lavell, "that the jury have decided that he was sane when his treasons were committed, and at the time of his trial. The judge approved of the verdict and the Court of Queen's Bench at Manitoba on appeal confirmed it. You cannot therefore go beyond that verdict and your inquiry will be limited to the simple question whether he at the time of your report is sufficiently a reasonable and accountable being to know right from wrong."[75] If, he continued, in explanation of the purpose of the inquiry, a criminal after conviction was found to be suffering from "raging dementia", the law was accustomed humanely to postpone the execution of his sentence; and since representations had been made that Riel's mind had lately given way, the government had decided to make an investigation into his present mental state. "I need scarcely point out to you," he reminded the two medical men, emphasizing once again the main point of the McNaghten Rules, "that the inquiry is not as to whether Riel is subject to illusions or delusions but whether he is so bereft of reason as not to know right from wrong and as not to be an accountable being."⁷⁶

The doctors departed. There was nothing to do but wait. He was waiting now for two very different but oddly associated things—for the last act in the building of the railway, and for the final verdict in the case of Riel. It was strange how all during the troubled year of 1885 the drama of the railway and the drama of the North-West Rebellion had been so often intertwined, and now, in the last moments of the dénouement of each, they were twisting together once more. "Doctors arrived this morning," Lieutenant-Governor Dewdney telegraphed from Regina on November 7;⁷⁷ and on the same day, far out in Eagle Pass, at the spot which Stephen had determined must be called Craigellachie, a group of intent men were watching the bearded Donald Smith drive home the last spike in the Canadian Pacific Railway. "Thanks to your far-seeing policy and unwavering support," Van Horne telegraphed from Craigellachie, "the Canadian Pacific Railway is completed. The last rail was laid this (Saturday) morning at 9:22."⁷⁸

Van Horne's telegram reached Macdonald in Ottawa on Monday, November 9. If it had come a year ago, or at any time before the outbreak of rebellion in the north-west, the news from Eagle Pass would have made the day memorable with unqualified satisfaction. But now there was little spirit, and no time, for congratulations or rejoicings. Riel had been reprieved until November 16. It was only a week away now; and the final decision on the fate of the *métis* leader was at hand. Campbell had completed his report for the Cabinet. It was, Macdonald informed Lansdowne, "a bold recommendation that Riel's sentence be carried out".⁷⁹ A telegram from Dewdney, which reached Ottawa that same Monday morning, informed Macdonald that Jukes, the doctor at the Regina gaol, had found the prisoner "perfectly accountable for his actions"; and within the next twenty-four hours the opinions of both Lavell and Valade arrived by telegraph. Lavell's examination had convinced him that Riel was a responsible being;[80] Valade drew a distinction between "political and religious subjects", on which he did not believe the prisoner to be accountable, and "other points", about which Riel seemed quite capable of distinguishing right from wrong.[81] By Tuesday, November 10, the evidence was all in; and Macdonald had made up his mind. Six weeks before he had told the Governor-General that a prerogative interference in the administration of justice was justifiable only in a case of "supreme necessity". No case of "supreme necessity" had been made out for Riel. No conclusive case of any kind had been made out. Macdonald would stick to the courts and their decisions. He would take his stand on their verdict and their sentence. And he was not to be budged.

One day later, on Wednesday, November 11, the Cabinet decided that Riel must hang. No very prolonged period of anxious debate had been necessary to reach this decision. The issue was never really in doubt. And the important question was not whether Riel's sentence would be altered or its execution postponed, but whether Macdonald would be able to carry all his French-Canadian ministers and the bulk of his French-Canadian supporters with him. Caron remained firm; Langevin was not prepared to desert his chief; and Chapleau, having spent the night after the Cabinet's final decision in composing a long memorandum in support of his dissent, decided on Thursday morning that he could not incur the responsibility of handing it in and thus helping to promote a racial war.[82] By the time Langevin left Ottawa later in the same day, Macdonald was certain that a united Cabinet would confront the mounting clamour of protest from Quebec. The French-Canadian leaders would remain faithful. But what of their followers? Langevin was met on the station platform at Montreal by five mutinous French-speaking members of Parliament. And next day nineteen Quebec members telegraphed Macdonald that they would not accept responsibility for Riel's execution.[83]

On Thursday, November 12, a special messenger, bearing the

Governor-General's warrant for the execution, left Ottawa for Regina. It was irrevocable now; and the strain and fatigue of the last few days of decision dulled Macdonald's eyes and deepened the lines on his face. His colleagues pressed him to cross the ocean for a brief rest; and he told Lord Lansdowne that he hoped to slip away so quietly that he would be aboard the ship before anyone noticed his departure. He was worn out with what he had been through; he dreaded the trouble that he knew was certain to come. But there was no panic in his heart, and no apprehension in his words. "Keep calm resolute attitude—all will come right," he wired Langevin at Quebec.[84] ". . . We are in for lively times in Quebec," he warned Lansdowne in his dry, laconic fashion, "but I feel pretty confident that the excitement will die out."[85] He could not really believe that the devotion of Quebec could be won by a man who had abjured his religion, renounced his citizenship, and shown himself perfectly prepared to abandon his followers for money. He could not really believe that the death of a single *métis* could seriously damage the work of unity through diversity which he and Cartier had carried out twenty years ago. Yet with what frightening swiftness this dreadful commotion had arisen in Quebec! Would it long survive Riel's death? Would his execution be a nine-days' horror, to be soon superseded by other excitements? Or would it remain as an indefinitely remembered injury to a people? Macdonald would soon know— or soon begin to know. "Messenger arrived seven this evening," Dewdney telegraphed on November 15.[86] Tomorrow was Monday, November 16. Tomorrow Riel was to die.

On the morning of November 16 the autumnal sun rose late but brilliant over plains which all about Regina were white with hoar frost.[87] The glare filled the land to the horizon; it formed a glittering frame for the little group of figures, dressed in sombre garments, who stood together, in still attitudes of portentous gravity, at the top of the tall structure inside the Regina gaol. And in the centre of the group Father McWilliams and Riel were saying the Lord's Prayer.

Our Father, who art in heaven, Hallowed be thy Name, Thy kingdom come, Thy will be done, in earth as it is in

*heaven. Give us this day our daily bread; And forgive us our
trespasses, As we forgive them that trespass against us; And
lead us not into temptation, But deliver us from evil . . .*

And then the sprung trap gave and Riel dropped to his
extinction.

Chapter Thirteen

The Revolt of the Provinces

I

WHEN the Allan liner *Polynesian* docked at Liverpool on December 1, Macdonald was greeted by two warmly cordial invitations. Both George Stephen and John Rose wanted the visitor to spend his time in London at their houses. Anne Stephen promised, her husband wrote, to "do" Macdonald quite as well as Batt's.[1] "I am all alone," John Rose assured his old friend. "You can have the whole house to yourself, breakfast and dine when you please. . . . I know it is rather far, but it may keep too many people from boring you, and there is a brougham which shall be at your sole disposal, and get you anywhere in ten minutes."[2] Even the brougham could not tempt Macdonald away from Batt's Hotel in Dover Street. Rose was one of his oldest and closest friends; and, as the postscript in Rose's letter of invitation reminded him, it was over forty-two years since they had first "foregathered". But Batt's had virtually become his London house; and part—and possibly a not unimportant part—of London's charm lay in the delicious irresponsibility which Batt's engendered. The small obligations of a private house might prove faintly irksome. He excused himself gratefully to the Stephens, and declined Rose's affectionate hospitality. He would see all three of them—and many more. But he would stop at Batt's.

London was full of excitement. The general election—they were still long-drawn-out affairs in England, lasting several weeks —had just got nicely under way; and the movement and dramatic suspense which Parnell had mysteriously succeeded in imparting to British politics, were at their height. By December 19, when the last returns were in, the English people learnt, to its consternation, that the Liberals had a majority over the Conservatives of eighty-six seats, and that Parnell's Irish Nationalists totalled exactly the same number. For the moment, the political ascendancy of the Irish leader seemed complete. Yet his "overruling position", which Macdonald bewailed in a letter to Lord Lansdowne, threatened the Conservatives much more seriously than it did the Liberals. Parnell could keep either one of the great English parties out of office; but he could not put, and keep, either one of them in. The only party to which he could give effective power was the Liberal party; and the approaching downfall of Lord Salisbury and the Conservatives seemed the one real certainty in a highly tense and ambiguous situation.

Macdonald was gravely disappointed. He had lived through the five years of the second Gladstone government without developing any overwhelming feeling of respect or gratitude; and when, in June, 1885, while the North-West Rebellion was coming to an end, Lord Salisbury had formed his first Cabinet, Macdonald had regarded the triumph of the Conservatives proudly as virtually a second Canadian victory. Now, after only six months, it was clear that the victory would likely be very short-lived. The Conservatives, almost certainly, were going out of power; and they were going out of power at a time when Canada urgently needed their support in her external relations. There was every prospect of serious negotiations, if not of actual disputes, with the United States over the inshore fisheries; there was a faint hope, which Macdonald and Stephen held in common, of an imperial mail subsidy for the Canadian Pacific steamer service between British Columbia and the Far East. In Macdonald's eyes, as well as in Stephen's, the Canadian Pacific was potentially a vast transoceanic and transcontinental system stretching all the way from Liverpool to Hong Kong. He believed that the British Conservatives would be far readier than their opponents to appreciate the importance of a great northern imperial route for traffic and defence; and he had no doubt at all, after the experience of the past, that the best hope of a vigorous defence of the fisheries lay not in Gladstone but in

Salisbury. As soon as the Colonial Secretary, Sir F. A. Stanley, got back to London after the election, he began to discuss with him the proposed joint commission with the United States.[3] He spent the New Year's week-end with W. H. Smith, the Secretary for War, at Greenlands, Henley-on-Thames; and on Monday, January 4, he went to see Lord Salisbury himself at the Foreign Office.[4]

In the meantime, in the intervals of theatres, dinner-parties and interviews, he kept reflecting on the absorbing news which was arriving from home. There was no longer the faintest doubt about the matter—Riel's execution had aroused a thunderous agitation in the Province of Quebec. On November 22, immediately after Macdonald's departure for England, an enormous mass meeting of protest had been held in the Champ de Mars, in Montreal; and a total of thirty-seven speakers competed with each other in ferocious denunciations of the "hangman's government" at Ottawa. Honoré Mercier, the provincial Liberal leader, informed the multitude that Riel was a Christian martyr sacrificed to Orange fanaticism; and Wilfrid Laurier, who for some years had been attempting to transform the anticlerical and revolutionary *Rouges* into respectable English Liberals, made the heroic but somewhat un-Gladstonian announcement that if he had lived on the banks of the Saskatchewan he would have taken up a rifle himself. The direct and immediate outcome of the meeting in the Champ de Mars was the creation of *Le Parti National*. Liberals and Conservatives co-operated in its establishment; and thus it appeared that the always dreaded, but never yet embodied, monstrosity of Canadian political life, the purely "racial", purely French-Canadian party, had at last come into existence.

Obviously, there were two important questions to be asked about *Le Parti National*, "the party of race and revenge", as the *Mail* of Toronto christened it. Would it remain a real union of Liberals and Conservatives? Would it exert any real influence in Canadian politics? As he scanned the reports in the newspapers, and read the reassuring letters from his colleagues, Macdonald began to suspect that the answer to the first question was a fairly definite no. It was surely significant that Mercier had accepted the leadership of *Les Nationalistes,* after two French-Canadian Conservatives had modestly declined it. The character of the agitation, Pope wrote to say, was becoming "more and more decidedly Rouge every day".[5] Caron was sure that the bolting Conservatives were beginning to realize that a trap had been laid for them by the opposition;[6] and Langevin believed that not more than twenty Quebec members would vote once against the party and that fewer than ten would keep up any further opposition.[7] No, it was obvious that *Le Parti National* was not going to swallow up Quebec Conservatism. *Le Parti National* was, in fact, becoming fairly rapidly a mere belligerent *ultra* wing of the Liberal party.

But were all its dangers disappearing in the process? Might not this resurgent nationalism revive the Liberal party in Quebec and fortify it for future provincial or federal victories? For this question, which was plainly the more important of the two, Macdonald had no ready answer; and it was obvious that his colleagues in Canada were equally uncertain, despite their confident predictions that the Riel agitation was a nine days' wonder which would be completely forgotten by the time Macdonald was back in Ottawa. The ministers in general, and particularly the French-Canadian ministers, wanted time. They wanted far more than nine days for the subsidence of the vast upheaval which Riel's execution had created. They suggested tentatively that "a short delay" in the opening of Parliament might strengthen their hands. Macdonald agreed with them. He told Lord Lansdowne, who was anxious to transfer the angry public debate over Riel to the legitimate theatre of Parliament, that the wishes of Langevin and the other French-Canadian ministers should be followed if possible. They had had a hard time of it, he added sympathetically. "They deserve well for the manly stand they have taken."[8]

He himself was having anything but a hard time of it in London. As usual, he had shrugged away his anxieties with enviable ease. As usual, his incredible resilience, his marvellous powers of recuperation had come effectively to his rescue; and, after a few days of complete relaxation, he emerged, as he had so often done before, looking as fresh and vigorous as if he had never seen really hard service before. He was enjoying himself immensely. He dined out night after night; he went repeatedly to the theatre; he spent two week-ends in the country; and on New Year's Eve, he was one of a large party that watched the pantomime *Aladdin* at Drury Lane. He caught a slight cold waiting on a station platform in Kent because he would insist on hurrying back to London from Lord Brabourne's country house despite the infrequent train service on Boxing Day. But this was the only misadventure which befell an elderly gentleman who had been rushing about with unsuitably youthful gusto and in apparently complete forgetfulness of the fact that he would be seventy-one on January 11 of the new year.

"What are you going to do on Christmas Day?" "little" Mary wrote to him from Canada. "I will miss you very much. I suppose you will be out in time for your birthday. . . ."[9] But by January 11 he was only two days away from Liverpool on the Cunard liner *Oregon*; and it was not until the afternoon of Tuesday, January 19, that he finally reached Ottawa. There was a welcoming reception at the City Hall; the band played "When Johnny Comes Marching Home"; and then Pat Buckley, Macdonald's favourite Irish cab-driver, drove them out along Sussex Street in his splendid four-in-hand to Earnscliffe.[10] Macdonald looked well—remarkably well. He looked, the friendly newspapers announced enthusiastically, "as ruddy as a red apple". And for once, Agnes realized gratefully, the newspapers had not exaggerated the miraculous transformation which a few short weeks had brought. "He was so tired and worried when he went away," she wrote to Louisa in Kingston, "that it quite enspirits me to see him so cheery."[11]

II

Only six months ago he had decided that the time had come for him to resign. He had told Tupper and Lord Carnarvon that he had finished his work. He had meant it; and the Canada which he had brought into being was the solid justification of his claim. The great design, sketched out gradually in the long frustrating years before 1867, had now been realized in actuality. With the exception of Newfoundland, the destined territorial limits of Canada had been reached. ". . . The Dominion cannot be considered complete without Newfoundland," he reminded Lord Lansdowne. "It has the key to our front door. . . ."[12] Some day, he was convinced, Canada must put this key in its pocket. But here his dreams of territorial expansion ended; and although he was perfectly prepared to give polite consideration to plans for the union of one or more of the British West Indies with Canada, he looked upon such proposals with inward doubt and misgiving.[18] In his view, the original provinces and territories of British North America were Canada's lawful inheritance. And in this wide, transcontinental domain he had established the institutions of a strongly centralized federal government. For nearly two decades while the law and custom of the constitution were being slowly clarified, he had watched over and defended the interests of the Dominion. He had worked out the three great economic policies—the settlement of the west, the development of eastern industry, the building of an all-Canadian transcontinental railway—by which a truly national economy, diversified and integrated, would be slowly realized. He had done his best. And his work at last was done.

Yet—and he knew it very well—he could not possibly give up at that moment. He had finished the design called Canada. But only the gaunt skeleton of the structure had been raised; and he was now called upon, almost literally, to save the half-finished fabric from abandonment or destruction. The plans, the surveys, the transport routes, the political institutions—the whole machinery of nationalism—had all been completed. But the nation itself, the populous and prosperous nation, had not yet come into existence. The meagreness of the accomplishment seemed to be a mocking refutation of the validity of the original design. In the past two years every circumstance had turned unfavourable. The depression still continued; immigration had faltered; most of the north-west was empty yet; and the country was racked with rebellion and cultural conflict. He had lost the initiative. He had been slowly and relentlessly forced back upon the defensive; and from all sides there appeared enemies

who seemed determined to exploit the country's adversities and
to launch the most fundamental attacks upon everything he had
achieved in the past two decades.

There was danger from abroad, for the American Senate
rejected the President's recommendation of a joint commission
to settle the problem of the fisheries; and early in February, the
inevitable occurred in England, the Salisbury government was
defeated, and Gladstone formed his third Cabinet. Once again,
Canada would have to defend the inshore fisheries with the
uncertain co-operation of the English Liberals; and the Anglo-
Canadian alliance, under the pressure to which it would certainly be subjected, might weaken or even break. The foreigners to
the south, who had only grudgingly admitted Canada's separate
existence and who were quite prepared to use diplomatic force
to advance their annexationist ambitions, were always dangerous.
In the circumstances of the moment, they were perhaps more
dangerous than they had been for the past fifteen years. But,
even so, were they as immediately and obviously dangerous as
the enemies at home?

Macdonald did not think so—yet. Ever since he had assumed
power in 1878, the enemies at home had been gradually accumulating. Everything he had done since 1878—the tariff, the
transcontinental railway, the settlement of the west, the assertion
of the Dominion's superintending control over the provinces
—everything had provoked protests and strengthened regional
discontents. Ontario had successfully defied the federal power
of disallowance; Manitoba seemed determined to destroy the
protection which had been granted to the Canadian Pacific
Railway; and Nova Scotia was becoming more angrily impatient
with her commercial and financial position in Confederation. It
would never do, of course, to exaggerate the importance of these
affairs. They were the ordinary sour bread and rancid butter
of Canadian politics; and the one really frightening abnormality
of the past year, the North-West Rebellion, had been crushed
before it had had a chance to develop into a serious danger.
It had been crushed. But, in dying, had it left another and
possibly even greater danger behind it? The "nationalist" agitation in Quebec might provoke an equally parochial "nationalist"

response in Ontario; and these two explosions of primitive feeling might destroy the cultural concord which had been one of the principal benefits of Confederation. The North-West Rebellion had begun by uniting the country in a burst of patriotism. Was it to end by dividing the nation in an outbreak of "racial" hatred? And how could a young and undeveloped country, already weakened by internal dissensions, survive a renewal, on a grand scale, of this old cultural conflict?

One thing at a time. The first issue was the issue of Riel's fate. Parliament met on February 25, and on March 1, C. J. Coursol moved for the report of the medical commission on Riel's mental state. No "medical commission" had, in fact, been appointed, as Macdonald's reply clearly revealed;[14] and there had been no formal collective "report". The government had simply requested three medical men to examine the prisoner and to give their opinion of his existing mental condition; and the replies, which were sent in separately, arrived in a very informal and piecemeal fashion, with letters following telegrams. In a twentieth-century treason case, such private and highly confidential communications would almost certainly be withheld from publication; but Macdonald's government, which dispensed information with a swiftness and a completeness rarely known in modern democracies, decided to give the substance of each expert's opinion to Parliament.[15]

It was not an unfair exercise in condensation. The omitted portion of Dr. Jukes's letter to Lieutenant-Governor Dewdney bore much more heavily against Riel than in his favour.[16] Lavell, in his telegram, had pointed out the pertinent fact that Father André was still admitting the prisoner to the sacraments, and, in his subsequent letter to Macdonald, he had described Riel as "a vain ambitious man, crafty and cunning, with powers in a marked degree to incite weak men to desperate deeds".[17] "He seeks his own aggrandisement," he concluded, "and, in my opinion, if he can attain his own ends, will care little for his followers." All these sentences, which would, of course, have given the greatest satisfaction to believers in Riel's guilt, were completely omitted from the printed version of Lavell's opinion. So also was Valade's opening statement that he did not believe

Riel to be an accountable being. But the distinction which the French-Canadian doctor had drawn between the prisoner's views on "political and religious subjects" and "other points", though blurred, had not been erased; and it was evident that he considered Riel responsible within the latter category only. The government, in short, had tried to give briefly, and in unprovocative language, the gist of each expert's opinion.

A debate was inevitable on the fate of Riel. It would, Macdonald knew, be a hazardous episode. It might bring serious trouble. But equally, with a little careful manipulation, the threat of misfortune might be turned into the gift of good luck. A debate which would satisfy the French-speaking Conservatives and embarrass the English-speaking Liberals was certainly conceivable. It would need careful planning. But planning was a congenial exercise, and early in the session Macdonald was ready with his plan. Landry, a Quebec Conservative member, gave notice of a motion deploring the fact that the government had permitted the sentence passed on Louis Riel to be carried out. There was, as Macdonald saw quickly, a good deal to be said for this particular resolution. It would give the "bolting *Bleus*" a chance to voice their dissatisfaction, and to cast what Langevin regarded as their one necessary vote against the government. It would do more than this. It would force the unhappy Liberals of Ontario to expose their serious disagreements over Riel.

On March 9, forty-eight hours before the day appointed for the debate on the Landry motion, Macdonald became ill. "I am afraid," he informed the Governor-General on March 9, "that I shall be obliged to lay up to get rid of my cold which threatens congestion."[18] The cold, which developed into bronchitis and then began to be accompanied by sciatic pains, kept him, an increasingly unhappy prisoner, in bed. But from his sick-room he could still direct the dispositions of the Landry debate; and there was a final ingenious and effective device which he now decided to use. At his request, Caron asked Langevin to move the previous question immediately after Landry had made his motion. "I shall be ready to take the floor immediately after Landry," Langevin promised.[19] And next day, as soon as Landry had sat down, he got up, defended the government's decision in a brief and somewhat formal reply, and ended by moving the previous question. At once the limits of the debate were firmly and narrowly set. The long string of fiendishly ingenious amendments by which the opposition would have continued to torture the subject and the government was abruptly cut short. The debate was focused not upon government policy in the northwest, which most Liberals could have agreed in condemning, but upon Riel's mental state and the commutation of his sentence, about which English-speaking and French-speaking Liberals were hopelessly divided.

Macdonald kept his bed. Instead of getting better, he grew steadily worse. Night after night he lay sleepless, racked with coughing or sciatic pains. The doctors prescribed sedatives and hypodermic injections; and after a brief respite of drugged sleep, he lay for long hours somnolent, his head "buzzing with opiates".[20] Yet, despite his pain and confusion, he never completely relaxed his hold on affairs. He could not help feeling worried when the Governor-General sent him a long letter questioning the wisdom of the bill which the government proposed to introduce for the better protection of the fisheries; and he was deeply suspicious of a sudden American proposal to establish a joint commission for an examination of the Canadian-Alaskan boundary. Why should such an offer be made with such zealous eagerness by a nation which seemed so strangely reluctant to accept a joint commission on trade and fisheries? Despite his pain and torpor, he was instantly alert and on the defensive; and, in a few letters to Lord Lansdowne, he quickly worked out all the main arguments on which Canada relied nearly two decades later in the final settlement of the Alaskan boundary dispute.[21]

Yet the main focus of his troubled and wavering interest was not here, but on the fate of the Landry motion. The debate—there was no doubt about it—was going well. Laurier made an eloquent speech for the opposition; and on March 17, Blake delivered a characteristically enormous oration, seven hours in length, and exactly twice as long as the speech with which a few weeks later Gladstone introduced his first Home Rule Bill. But, despite these big efforts, the opposition attack was not well sustained. The principal English-speaking Liberal leaders remained conspicuously and significantly silent; and Thompson, upon whom, as Minister of Justice, fell the main burden of the government defence, rose magnificently to his first great debating opportunity. Even Campbell was impressed; and only a few months before Campbell had observed coldly that Thompson had "the air of a man educated for the priesthood, with a nervous look and subdued manner".[22] The debate on the Landry motion changed Campbell's opinion. There was praise on all sides for Thompson's speech; and Campbell had even heard an unhappy Grit admit that the new Minister of Justice had "really smashed Blake".[23] It was true, Macdonald reflected, and true in a special sense. Thompson had "smashed" Blake in the way that Blake could be most decisively smashed—by the deeply felt but unspoken arguments of Blake's own followers. And a few days later, when the vote on the Landry motion was finally taken, it was revealed that the disaffection in the Liberal camp was even more serious than that in the Conservative. The Landry motion was defeated by one hundred and forty-six votes to fifty-two.[24] Seventeen French-speaking Conservatives voted against the government; but twenty-three English-speaking Liberals deserted the opposition.

It was, as he would have said himself, "altogether satisfactory". And, as he lay in bed and tried to cope with the gnawing pain in his leg, he could not help feeling that there were other and more general reasons for satisfaction. The session, despite his absence, was moving smoothly forward. The new and younger ministers—John Thompson, George Foster at Marine and Fisheries, and Tom White in the Department of the Interior—were all performing with tolerable efficiency; and McLelan, who had succeeded Tilley as Minister of Finance, was able to bait his budget with what everybody would certainly regard as a delectable tid-bit. The twenty million dollars' worth of bonds which the government held as security for its loan to the Canadian Pacific had now been converted into cash as a result of Barings' successful flotation of the bond issue of the previous year; and with this money, together with lands to the value of over nine million dollars, the government would be able, McLelan announced proudly, "to settle all accounts with the Canadian Pacific Railway Company".[25] The loans which every Reform politician and every Grit newspaper had denounced as a sheer gift to the railway and a total loss to the country, had been repaid within less than a year after the last spike had been driven in at Craigellachie. And Canada, fortified with twenty millions of hard cash, would be able to pay off its floating debt and escape fresh financing.

It "took well" with the public, McLelan informed Macdonald complacently. It took so well that the Liberals treated the proposal in a discreet and respectful fashion. The Liberals, in fact, were in general behaving in an unheroic and disunited way; and in comparison with the repeated and prolonged excitements of 1885, the new session was plainly a fairly tame and easy affair. "The best thing you can do for us all," Campbell wrote wisely, "is to get strong again, and in the meantime to allow us to conduct public affairs on our own judgment."[26] It was plain good sense; and despite his lust for information and his instinct for management, Macdonald let himself relax in a slow and not too easy recuperation. At the end of March he had to undergo the painful process of blistering; and a fortnight later he was admitting that a slight imprudence, such as resting incautiously on his lame leg, seemed "to awaken the sleeping demon" of his pain.[27] Yet slowly he improved. On April 20, he ventured, he told the Governor-General, to "try the atmosphere" of the House;[28] and two days later he rose in his place to propose the government bill for the representation of the North-West Territories in the Dominion Parliament.

III

The spring days lengthened, the unremarkable session drew slowly towards its close. Obviously the opposition in the House was divided and inhibited; but obviously also, as Macdonald realized very clearly, the parliamentary opposition was only a very partial expression of the dissatisfaction in the country as a whole. Resistance to the Conservative programme had not really slackened, still less had it disappeared. It had simply taken the different and possibly still more dangerous form of cultural antagonism and provincial discontent. Provincial protests were like *leit-motifs* which kept on being repeated, with incredibly persistent reiteration, by strings and brass and wood-winds, through endless varieties of orchestration, but always with the same hostile and minatory note.

The possible variations of the main themes of provincial discontent seemed literally endless. The ugly sounds kept coming back, and back, and back. Manitoba, despite the supposedly "final" settlement of its claims which had been patched up the previous year, was clamouring excitedly against the Canadian Pacific's "monopoly clause". Ontario and Quebec were quarrelling with a pugnacity which seemed to imply that "race" and religion were newly discovered subjects of dispute; and early in May, the *Mail* of Toronto which had been established fourteen years before to represent Conservatism with completeness and fidelity, began to print a series of articles on the Roman Catholic Church which sounded altogether too much like George Brown's diatribes of a quarter century ago. On May 7, the provincial legislature of Quebec began a long debate on the execution of Riel. The Quebec Liberals, with "nationalist" support and with the energetic Mercier as leader, were obviously waxing lusty and confident on the Riel issue. And everybody began to be gloomily apprehensive that the days of the Conservative government in Quebec were numbered.

Even this was not all. In the east, an angry chorus of protest grew steadily more determined and more shrill. It was over fifteen years ago that Macdonald, with Howe's help, had "pacified" Nova Scotia. But certainly no province was showing more restiveness and impatience in the spring of 1886 than Nova Scotia. Her troubles were mainly economic and financial in origin; the main objects of her dislike were the federal tariff and the insufficient federal subsidies. Certain long-run changes in the Maritime economy, such as the contraction of wooden-ship building and the relative decline of the old West Indies markets, had been unhappily accompanied and emphasized by the short-term distresses of the depression. The awful sense of permanent stagnation which resulted had bred in many people a conviction that some fundamental mistake had been made; and the old belief, which had never really died out, that Nova Scotia had been tricked into Confederation against her will and her best interests, began rapidly to gain converts once again. A new movement for Howe's old objective, the repeal of the union, was once more in being.

Macdonald had been watching the development of this agitation for some time with curious interest. The Liberal leader, W. S. Fielding, who had succeeded to the premiership of Nova Scotia two years before, had obviously been trying to make profitable political use of the movement, without identifying himself too closely with it. But his early efforts to use the bogey of secession to frighten the Dominion government into a grant of "better terms" had been unsuccessful; and in the spring of 1886 he decided upon a bolder and more aggressive thrust. On May 7, he himself moved a set of government resolutions for the repeal of the union so far as Nova Scotia was concerned. In a few days the resolutions were passed with large majorities; the provincial government announced an appeal to the people on the issue of secession; and despite Macdonald's advice to Lieutenant-Governor Richey to delay the dissolution as long as possible, the general election was fixed for June 13.[29]

"Are Nova Scotia secession resolutions serious?" Rose inquired anxiously from London. "Have they been influenced by Home Rule views here?"[30] Macdonald was always eager to counteract anti-Canadian propaganda in England, and he knew that he could return a short answer to the second of Rose's questions. "No connection between Irish Home Rule and resolutions," he cabled back. "Province applying for better terms—looks like blackmail."[31] Of course it looked like blackmail. But it was highly dangerous blackmail—how dangerous he had no means of telling as yet. He knew only that since the establishment of Confederation, and the pacification of Nova Scotia, in 1869, this was the first open attempt at the repeal of the union. He knew also that, although there might be no connection between Irish Home Rule and Nova Scotia secession, the fact remained that Fielding's agitation was reaching its climax at a time when the Liberals were in power in England and when the "Grand Old Man" of British politics

was passionately espousing the cause of local liberties within
the Empire.

The disaffection of Manitoba and Nova Scotia, the open
quarrelling of Ontario and Quebec, all spelled trouble for the
future. But this long concatenation of domestic misfortunes
was not the only source of worry. There was an equal, or
nearly equal, danger in the unsolved problem of the fisheries
and in the unsettled relations with the United States. During
the winter, Canada had decided that since all its proposals for
a settlement had been uniformly rejected by the United States,
it would proceed henceforth by the very different method of
enforcing its treaty rights. By the Convention of 1818, American
fishing vessels were permitted to enter the inshore waters of
British North America for wood, water, shelter, and repairs,
"and for no other purpose whatever". Why not stand on the
plain meaning of these words, particularly since every invasion
of the three-mile limit, for whatever purpose, made clandestine
fishing ridiculously easy? The bill for tightening up the enforcement of the fishery regulations, about which Lord Lansdowne
had expressed such grave doubts, was pushed forward without
alteration; and in the meantime, out on the Atlantic coast, Canadian coast-guards and customs officers began to apply the existing
legislation with a new vigour. Early in May, the American
fishing schooner, *David J. Adams*, was seized in Digby harbour
for buying ice and bait; and in the next few weeks, a few other
seizures for similar infractions of the Convention of 1818
followed.

At once a great, angry roar of protest shook the United States.
What did these bumptious colonials think they were doing?
Bayard, with a ready reliance on the American assumption that
Canada was a primitive colonial dependency, refused to concede
that the Dominion had any authority whatever to give either
legislative or executive effect to treaties entered into by the
imperial government. Great Britain was immediately and
urgently requested to prevent the offending measure from going
into operation. Lord Rosebery put Canada's case forcefully to the
American Minister in London; but Granville who, after an
interval of fifteen years, had briefly returned to the Colonial

Office, was plainly very anxious that the seizures of American fishing vessels should cease and that the new Canadian Fisheries Bill should not become law. Macdonald was stubbornly recalcitrant under this Colonial Office pressure. Bayard's contemptuous dismissal of Canada's legislative powers had put his back up. "The present denunciation of those powers by Mr. Bayard," he told Lord Lansdowne, "is really audacious."[32] He insisted that in the circumstances Canada had no option but to protect her own property, and that the new Fisheries Bill was an entirely legitimate attempt to increase the efficiency of the protection. "After all," he reasoned with the Governor-General, "this legislation does not attempt to extend our rights but simply to improve our procedure by giving the means of enforcing those rights."[33]

The session was nearly over. Macdonald may have begun to feel that he would get the Bill through in safety. But at the last moment he had to yield. Only a few hours before the prorogation a cable arrived from Lord Granville instructing the Governor-General to reserve the Fisheries Bill.[34] "In the face of the rather impudent protest from Mr. Bayard, it will put us in a rather humiliating position," Macdonald wrote from his place in the Commons, in a final effort to avert the blow, while the last debate of the session was raging round him. "He protests against our power to legislate and we will appear tamely to acquiesce."[35] Only a few minutes later, against his own better judgment, the Governor-General did in fact publicly "acquiesce"; and although he begged Granville to explain that the Bill had been reserved solely because it was thought that it might embarrass the somewhat hypothetical "negotiations" then in progress, both he and Macdonald realized that the prestige of Canada had been dealt a heavy blow.[36] The Dominion had suffered a serious diplomatic reverse. It had been compelled to endure a grave affront to its constitutional pride.

It was bad. But it was not by any means the only misfortune of the early summer of 1886. The swift current of cultural dispute and provincial protest seemed quickening to a mill-race. The *Mail*, despite Macdonald's private protests to its editor, continued to foment religious and cultural warfare. In Quebec, Mercier's "nationalist" crusade was making such rapid progress that a Liberal victory in the approaching provincial election was now a distinct possibility; and in Nova Scotia the cause of Canadian unity was about to meet the most complete and unequivocal repudiation that it had yet encountered. Immediately after the prorogation of Parliament, McLelan and Thompson hastened down to Nova Scotia to throw the weight of their influence into the provincial electoral campaign. They utterly failed to avert the victory of the Liberals. Fielding won, won handsomely, and won on the simple and catastrophic proposal to repeal the union. "You will have seen long ere this reaches you," Macdonald wrote to Tupper on June 21, "that Fielding has defeated the Conservatives on the secession cry —horse, foot, and artillery. Never was there such a rout. McLelan has come back from this inglorious campaign and gives no intelligent account of the disaster."[37]

It was in the gloomy light of these misfortunes that Macdonald sat down, after the prorogation had brought its welcome lull, to a serious consideration of the political future. The existing Parliament was now four years old. In another twelve-month there would have to be a general election; and Lord Lansdowne was already inquiring whether he was likely to ask for a dissolution before 1886 was out. On the whole, Macdonald was inclined to favour postponement. The clean sweep which Fielding had made in Nova Scotia on the repeal issue had surprised most people, including probably Fielding himself. It was too early yet to be at all confident of how serious the secession movement might prove to be; and the fact that Gladstone, after the defeat of his first Home Rule Bill, was about to go to the country added a further and grave element of uncertainty. "A good deal will depend on the results of the elections in England," he wrote to the Governor-General. "If Gladstone succeeds, Heaven knows what he may do, if a petition is presented to the Queen asking for relief and separation."[38] Gladstone, in his infatuation with Home Rule, might give serious consideration to the Nova Scotian demands. And if so, nobody could tell what might happen to Confederation. In the meantime, however, it would be madness for the Dominion government to anticipate such a catastrophe, to challenge Nova Scotia in a general election before Fielding's purpose was made quite clear. It would be better to wait—for a while at least. And there were too many other good reasons —Riel, the racial and religious conflict, the depression and the unrest of labour—for delay. "We have rocks ahead," he wrote to Tupper, "and great skill must be exercised in steering the ship."

The work of the next six months must be a great organized effort of patient preparation. He would have to begin by giving ground. It would be highly dangerous, in the uncertain state of affairs in both Canada and England, to put too great a strain upon the Anglo-Canadian alliance; and Canada, having made its position abundantly clear in test cases such as that of the schooner *David J. Adams*, could afford to relax a little the rigour of its enforcement of the Convention of 1818. Fishing by American vessels inside the three-mile limit would, of course, not be permitted for a minute; but for the present season at least there would be no more seizures on the ground of the purchase of supplies or provisions.[39] "I have thoroughly frightened Foster," he told the Governor-General, "as to his proceedings as possibly leading to war, and he is I believe energetic in his instructions that there should not be any exhibitions of too much zeal."[40]

"This wretched fishery imbroglio", as Stephen called it, kept Macdonald preoccupied and perturbed for most of June. He could do nothing until the excitement caused by the seizures had subsided a little. He did not dare to leave Ottawa. Yet he was already planning a programme of pre-election activities which would occupy many weeks and take him very far afield. He realized that what he faced was not an election, like that of 1882, which could be carried in a rush of confident enthusiasm. The campaign which was looming up before him now would almost certainly be much more like the long and carefully organized struggle which had preceded the triumph of 1878. He invited Tupper to come back to Canada for a serious stocktaking of the wretched state of affairs in Nova Scotia. He began to feel that it might be wise to undertake a series of political meetings, something like the famous picnics of 1876 and 1877, in Ontario during the coming autumn. For the summer, his plans were made. He would go west. The Canadian Pacific was about to inaugurate its regular passenger service between Montreal and Port Moody, and what more fitting than that he, of all the ministers, should travel by the first train? The journey would give him a badly needed holiday, a knowledge of the great new country he was creating, a chance to show himself to its new inhabitants and to quiet the rising storm of their protests in Manitoba.

It was not until June 23 that Lord Lansdowne finally authorized the "western expedition". There was no hope now that Macdonald would be in time for the first "ocean to ocean" train that pulled out from the Dalhousie station in Montreal at eight o'clock on the evening of June 28. He was still working determinedly on the late afternoon of Saturday, July 10, which was the day finally set for his departure. "Awful hard work to get away," he wrote briefly to Thompson. "I have written three letters to Lord Lansdowne today."[41] It was late at night when the little party—Macdonald, Agnes, Agnes's companion, the invaluable secretary, Joseph Pope, Fred White of the Mounted Police, and the two servants—assembled in the Ottawa station. The departure had been kept a close secret until the last. There were few people in the station; and they settled themselves happily in the *Jamaica*, the special carriage, with the wonderful fine-meshed window screens to keep out the dust and mosquitoes, which Van Horne had thoughtfully provided for their comfort.[42] Then at last they were off. The lights of Ottawa dropped behind them. They were out in the open countryside, in the rich darkness of a summer night, racing north-west towards the rock and forest of the Canadian Shield. The train gathered speed. The long, lugubrious whistle of the engine died slowly and mournfully away in their wake.

IV

Macdonald watched the rapid approach of Winnipeg through the wide, curtained windows of the *Jamaica*. It was nearly nine o'clock on Tuesday morning, July 13. For two days the train had been threading its way through the dense forests

of the Shield, or hugging the long, looping curves of the north
shore of Lake Superior. They had done little travelling at
night, for Van Horne was anxious to ensure Sir John's rest
and to enable him to see the whole line by daylight. They had
seen it all; and now, within the last few hours, they had watched
it change suddenly and with mysterious completeness. The
trees thinned out, the great scarred rocks dwindled and disappeared, the land flattened out in dead levels that stretched
towards an incredibly remote horizon. The train slowed down
gradually to a stop, and Macdonald got to his feet. The painful
awkwardness of his leg, the unhappy, lingering after-effect of
his winter's illness, still nagged at him a little. But, after only
two days of holiday, he was already feeling better; and in his
morning coat, grey trousers, grey top hat and favourite gay necktie, he looked very nearly his usual smart and jaunty self.[43]
He moved quickly towards the end of the carriage. The first
of the prairie public appearances had begun. There on the
platform outside were the faithful Conservatives of Winnipeg,
headed by Lieutenant-Governor Aikins and "Honest John"
Norquay.

For three days they were Lieutenant-Governor Aikins's guests.
They went on one long excursion, over a branch line of the
Canadian Pacific, to the south-western part of the province, and,
for a good part of the journey, Agnes rode adventurously in the
engine. At Winnipeg there were receptions, with long queues
of smiling Conservatives who wanted to shake hands, and a
public meeting at the "Royal Roller Rink", which was the
largest hall in town. Macdonald told his audience that when
the contract for the Canadian Pacific was being negotiated in
1880 he had scarcely dared to hope that he would live long
enough to travel in the flesh along the entire railway to its
terminus. His friends had regretfully expected that he might
have to view the completed work from the serene heights of
heaven above. His enemies had naturally supposed that he
would be compelled to gaze upward at it from the pit beneath.
"I have now disappointed both friends and foes," he continued
gaily, "and am taking a horizontal view."[44] His horizontal view,
he explained, did not end at Port Moody or Victoria, but
continued westward, in imagination at least, across the rim

of the Pacific Ocean to the Far East. When he was last in England he had interested Lord Salisbury in a line of steamers running between British Columbia and China; and now that the elections in England were going so well for the Conservatives and the prospect of Lord Salisbury's return to power was so certain, there was a real hope that a Pacific steamship service would be soon established.

On Friday, July 16, at the very early hour which became characteristic of their morning departures, they left Winnipeg. A long, comfortable, lazy week-end was spent with the Dewdneys at Government House in Regina;[45] and it was not until Tuesday that they set out westward again. Over the gently rolling interminable prairie the train picked up speed, and they raced into Medicine Hat, in mid-afternoon, at a rate of forty miles an hour. But the darkness of the long summer day had already fallen when the train finally pulled up at Gleichen, the little station, east of Calgary, in the heart of the Blackfoot country. Chief Crowfoot, who in the dark days at the beginning of the North-West Rebellion had pledged the loyalty of his tribe to Macdonald, was waiting, a little on his dignity, for he had been led to expect the visitors nearly three hours before; and it was not until very early the following morning that the Indians, who had come to the rendezvous in full force, began to assemble for the pow-wow. The lesser chiefs—Old Sun, Eagle Rib, Medicine Shield, Running Eagle, Little Plume —sat about portentously in full war-paint and feathers. Crowfoot alone was in his oldest clothes—in memory, he informed Macdonald, of the dead Poundmaker. His face, with its well shaped features and fine lines, was shrewd and proud and intelligent. He told the listening Indians that Macdonald was the "biggest man" they had had among them for a long time. He begged Macdonald to banish the fears of the Indians for their children's nourishment and welfare. Then the Indians did a dance, and presents were distributed; and Macdonald gave Crowfoot a dark broadcloth suit with silk facings—a proper suit of mourning.[46]

Beyond Calgary the land lifted into foothills, and the foothills broke apart and thrust themselves furiously upwards in mountains. The train was stopped. Agnes and Macdonald seated themselves securely on the buffer bar—the "cowcatcher" —in front of the engine; and the wheels began to move again. The wind tore past their faces. The Kicking Horse River wound about, with sinuous agility, below them. The valley contracted menacingly into what seemed an impassable gorge and then broadened out into lush and placid meadowlands. The enormous, uninterrupted prospect began to make the view from the windows of the *Jamaica* seem narrow and unsatisfying. Agnes, with her inexhaustible vitality, preferred the hot sun and the rushing wind; and Macdonald, though he was a less frequent and less indefatigable passenger on the "cowcatcher" than his wife, kept his precarious perch for longer than he might have believed possible four months before. They travelled through Rogers Pass and past Craigellachie on the buffer bar; from it they watched the great coiling valleys of the Thompson and Fraser Rivers. On the distant sides of the canyons, the great cascades hung trembling like threads of silver. The colours of the rock-face—green, and rose, and amethyst, and deep purple—melted and mingled. Even the coming of sunset did not end the excitements of the ride; and after dinner, on the last evening of the journey out, they took their accustomed places on the buffer bar. It was black dark by now. The train was racing down the Fraser canyon towards Lytton. Above, the gloom was lit by a few stars; hundreds of feet below was the river; and the locomotive, feeling its way experimentally with the great beam of its headlight, laboriously skirted the edges of the chasm, roared through tunnels, and rattled over creaking bridges.[47]

Early on Saturday morning, July 24, they reached Port Moody; and late that night the steamer *Princess Louise* brought them to their journey's end at Victoria. "Sir John looks as gay as a lark," the correspondent of the Port Moody *Gazette* informed its readers.[48] The first, most exhilarating part of the trip was over; but its welcome relaxations were just beginning, and for over a fortnight they rested contentedly at Driard House, Victoria's most pleasant hotel.[49] Then, in a leisurely fashion, the return began. There were visits to the principal British Columbian towns. There were several stops and speeches, as they worked their way slowly back across the prairies, for the benefit of the newly enfranchised citizens of the North-West Territories. And then, at Winnipeg, came the first sharp foretaste of the hard political campaigning that lay ahead. A provincial Conservative convention had been convoked, in the hope of restoring the declining strength of Norquay's government and the waning popularity of Conservative policies at Ottawa. Macdonald defended the "monopoly clause" of the Canadian Pacific charter. It would, he hoped, be given up "speedily". But in the meantime, the national railway must be defended—and if necessary by federal disallowance—from the premature encroachments of its American rivals.[50]

On Monday, August 30, at about half past four in the morning, the Canadian Pacific engine brought the sleeping inmates of the *Jamaica* to rest at Ottawa; and the long journey, which had occupied over fifty days and covered over six thousand miles, came at last to an end.[51]

V

Back in his office in the East Block, Macdonald gazed speculatively at the hazy political horizon. "Now, I suppose," Rose wrote admiringly from England, congratulating him on his safe return, "you are like the old war horse, keen for the assault again; and may you have the fullest measure of success."[52] Macdonald was by no means sure of success. Time had crept up upon him once again; and time and the bag of troubles he carried on his back could not be shaken off now. He would have to remain in office until he had reached some kind of agreement with the United States over the fisheries; he would have to attempt to cope with the ominously spreading protest movement of the provinces. Fielding's victory in Nova Scotia had been an unqualified repudiation of the very idea of British North American unity; and Macdonald's whole conception of the national interest faced a long series of similar electoral ordeals. It had been announced that the dreaded provincial election in Quebec would take place on October 14. Beyond that there was a possible election in Manitoba and a very probable election in Ontario. And beyond all these was the definite necessity of a federal general election within the next nine months.

During September he made a few short forays of investigation into the debatable territory of southern Ontario. Ontario and Quebec were the great powers of the Dominion; and he knew that he was losing Irish Roman Catholic votes in Ontario just as he was losing French Roman Catholic votes in Quebec. At a political meeting at London, on September 16, he pointedly informed his audience that the Conservative press was completely free from party control and that he had no responsibility whatever for the editorial policies of the *Mail* of Toronto.[53] It was, he reflected gloomily, an almost wholly useless exculpation. The vast rumbling religious and racial agitation was not to be settled by such easy disclaimers. And the question was not whether he would lose support—which he was certain to do—but whether he would lose more than he gained. If Mercier and his Liberal-Nationalists triumphed on October 14, the Conservative cause in the Dominion would be seriously endangered. But if the Conservative government at Quebec were sustained, then surely Blake had no great chance of success in the approaching federal election. "A great many Protestant Liberals, especially the Presbyterian Scotchmen," Macdonald explained to the Governor-General, "are incensed at his course on the two questions of Riel and Home Rule and will only pardon him if his game succeeds in carrying Quebec. If not they will say that he sold himself without getting the money."[54] Without getting the money! If that were the result, Macdonald would be through in safety. If Quebec remained firm in its allegiance, his system of government could be maintained intact. There were times when it seemed that everything depended on the retention of Quebec.

In the meantime, while he waited apprehensively for the fateful October 14, there were other breaches in the authority and prestige of the Dominion which he must try to repair. He wanted the Fisheries Bill of last session removed from its state of suspended animation and given the force of law; he wanted a pledge of the assistance of the Atlantic Squadron of the Royal Navy in the defence of the fisheries for the season of 1887.

Lord Lansdowne, who had gone to England in the late summer, had been pressing the British government to yield on both these points;[55] and the fortunate return of Lord Salisbury and the Conservatives to power had strengthened Macdonald's hope of British support in a policy of protection. He set himself to win it. Protection, he was convinced, would now have to be continued for years. The Americans would be in no mood for diplomatic concessions for some time to come. Having just finished one presidential contest, they were virtually embroiled in a new one.

"For the next three years," he argued to Lord Lansdowne, "neither party will take any step to affect its popularity, and a supposed leaning towards England or her colonies, or the settlement of any treaty not obviously disadvantageous to England, would be unpopular. Bayard, contrary to my expectations, is endeavouring to out-jingo Blaine, both in Canada and Mexico, but neither he nor Cleveland will go in for war or interruption of diplomatic intercourse. Were Blaine in power he would do everything disagreeable short of war, and perhaps, if England had trouble elsewhere, go further. If I am right in this, the true policy would seem to be to pursue a steady course of protection to our waters, and condemnation of vessels committing undoubted breaches of the Treaty of 1818, for the next three years, before the presidential election. By that time the American fishermen will have learnt that every breach involves seizure and forfeiture and that their only course is to keep out of our waters and get their supplies elsewhere. If any weakness is shown on the part of the British government or of ours, our waters will be continually invaded and we shall have to submit to a series of diplomatic bullyings which if Blaine, or any Republican like him, is elected President, may culminate in a cessation of friendly intercourse. Nothing *can* be gained by submission. Much *may* be gained by a calm but firm assertion of our rights and their enforcement."[56]

At length, on October 14, the Province of Quebec voted. The results were certainly mixed and none too clear; but it was obvious that the Conservatives had lost and that the Liberals and Nationalists had substantially gained. There was still some hope, of course; and Langevin was inclined to believe that the Conservative government would somehow contrive to pick up a majority by the time the session began.[57] Macdonald's assessment of the future was much more blunt and gloomy. "The triumph of the *Rouges* over the corpse of Riel changes the aspect of affairs, *quoad* the Dominion government completely," he wrote to Tupper. "It will encourage the Grits and opposition generally; will dispirit our friends, and will, I fear, carry the country against us at the general election."[58] The worst—or very nearly the worst—had happened. The general election could not be delayed longer than six months; and everywhere the prospects were steadily worsening. Nova Scotia had gone. Quebec was almost certainly going. Norquay's power was obviously tottering in Manitoba; and in Ontario, Mowat stood a very good chance of improving his position at the next general election.

"What prospect your coming over?" Stephen cabled him from London.[59] "No prospect," Macdonald replied flatly. On Saturday, October 30, the Cabinet spent a long afternoon discussing the prospective dissolution, and, with only three dissentients, it was decided that the general election must take place before another session.[60] On Wednesday, November 3, Macdonald left for Toronto, to begin the rallying of the Conservative forces.[61] And less than a fortnight later, when the Conservative speaking tour in southern Ontario had just begun to get nicely under way, Mowat suddenly announced that the Ontario legislature would be dissolved and a general election held at the end of December. The tests, both federal and provincial, were coming—and coming very soon—in Ontario; and, now that Quebec was wavering uncertainly in its allegiance, the retention of Ontario began to seem the condition of Conservative survival. With White, Thompson, and Meredith, the opposition leader in Ontario, for company, Macdonald plunged into the real ordeal of a series of autumn speaking engagements. He stood the fatigues and discomforts—the long hours, the milling crowds, the suffocating rooms—with the cheerfulness of a born, and a seasoned, campaigner. "Sir John surprises me—," Thompson wrote to his wife in wonderment, "he goes through all these hardships quite gaily. . . ."[62] Even a bad cold, which unfortunately became bronchial, did not seriously interrupt the tour; and it was not until December 20 that he finally turned his face towards home.[63]

Back in the East Block, with the new year rapidly approaching, Macdonald anxiously considered the state of the nation once more. Internationally, the Dominion had gained. Late in November the imperial government agreed to give the royal assent to the Canadian Fisheries Bill; and at the same time it was decided that if an agreement with the United States had not been reached by the beginning of the next fishing season, the Royal Navy would send a cruiser to assist in the protection of the fisheries.[64] These were resounding diplomatic successes for a persevering but hard-pressed government. In the approaching general election they could be of real value. But, unfortunately, they stood virtually alone. In domestic affairs the unbroken tale of calamity had continued with the Manitoba general election on December 9 and the Ontario general election on December 28. In Manitoba, Norquay was "saved" but only, as Lieutenant-Governor Aikins admitted, after an "agony" of uncertainty; and in Ontario Mowat more than doubled his previous majority. The battered Norquay's survival could be explained, Aikins considered, by Macdonald's efforts on his behalf at the Manitoba Conservative convention of the previous August. But all during November and December, Macdonald had been expending himself, without stint, and apparently without any effect, in William Meredith's support. It was extremely discouraging. It was nearly as bad as it could be. Of the four provincial general elections of 1886, the Conservatives had lost two, drawn one, and emerged, dubious and bloody victors, from the fourth.

Yet Macdonald decided to go ahead. Postponement of the federal general election would now be regarded simply as a public admission of the gravity of his position. He might as well take the initiative with all the confidence he could muster. On Saturday, January 15, he sent the order-in-council authorizing the dissolution to Lord Lansdowne; and on Monday morning the newspapers announced that the election would be held on February 22.[65] The last fortnight of January was spent in final, frantic efforts to collect the Conservative team and put the players in good heart. Tupper, who had with

THE DOCTOR ARRIVES!

difficulty been persuaded that his presence was absolutely essential for the recovery of Nova Scotia, did not leave England until January 12; and Chapleau, choosing this most appropriate

moment for a violent assertion of his personality, threatened
resignation if a long list of his demands were not met.[66] The
team had its unwilling and refractory members. But ten days
later they were all present and ready to take the field. "You
may like to know," Macdonald informed the Governor-General
on January 24, "that Chapleau is back into the fold."[67] And
next day Tupper, looking as hearty and pugnacious as ever,
arrived in Ottawa ready and willing for service.

On the last day of January, Macdonald left for Toronto by
the midnight train.[68] The day had brought the news of a
final and crushing misfortune. In Quebec, Mercier had finally
emerged triumphant from the political muddle produced by
the October election; and on January 30 a new provincial
government of Liberals and Nationalists had taken office at
Quebec. The governments of the two central provinces—of
the "great powers" of the Dominion—were now in the hands
of Macdonald's enemies. Every circumstance seemed to be
in Blake's favour. Every event of the past twelve months seemed
to promise his success. And yet, as the short campaign proceeded on its agitated way, Macdonald began to realize that
Blake was unaccountably failing to take advantage of his
enormous opportunities. The country was full of economic
depression, of cultural conflict, of a sense of national frustration
and discouragement. But Blake was not exploiting these possibilities. He was not making capital gains for the Liberals out
of the growing volume of national discontents.

His attitude to the depression and to the vexed question of
commercial policy, Macdonald noted, was characteristically
uninspiring. People were now in the mood for desperate
remedies—just as they had been in the years from 1873 to
1878. Macdonald had met that irrepressible human demand for
action with his proposal of the national policy of protection.
But Blake, in similar circumstances and with a similar opportunity, had nothing comparable to offer. In the Maritime
Provinces and in certain parts of Ontario, a significant number
of people, unconnected with politics, were already beginning
to advocate the abandonment of protection and the substitution
of a radically different policy, commercial union with the
United States. Obviously no more frontal attack upon Canadian

economic nationalism could have been devised. But, if Blake was aware of the political possibilities of the proposal, he chose to ignore them. At Malvern, in one of his first campaign speeches, he informed the audience that in his opinion the size of the Canadian debt made any reduction in Canadian taxation impossible and that therefore the tariff would continue to give "a large and ample advantage to the home manufacturer over his competitor abroad".[69]

It was a safe, sober, sensible announcement. But it could hardly arouse people with the hope of drastic remedial action; and it enabled Macdonald to hold up his opponent to ridicule as a reluctant, half-hearted, last-minute convert to a religion which he had previously reviled and still secretly abhorred. Macdonald dealt largely in this kind of burlesque during the campaign. He usually spoke last, after the other members of the Conservative team had finished their speeches, and in a more informal and jocular fashion. Early in the campaign the *Globe* had informed its readers very impressively that the Prime Minister was in his dotage, that Tom White had become his virtual keeper, and that Tupper was hurrying home to take his place. Macdonald made the most of this inspired diagnosis. The *Globe*, he reminded his listeners genially, had reported his suicide in 1873 and, on various occasions since, had announced his approaching demise through cancer of the stomach or paralysis of the brain. He had mysteriously survived all these gloomy predictions. And, he concluded, "as he was enjoying a few lucid moments just then before an attack of frenzy came on," he would proceed to discuss a few of the questions of the day.[70]

He did not usually discuss them at any length. But he stuck to the campaign, despite its winter rigours, until the very end. At Brockville, on Friday, February 11, the Conservative procession, reception, and speeches all took place to the accompaniment of a howling blizzard. The roads and railways were so thickly blocked with snow that he did not reach Ottawa until Saturday afternoon, and then he was so worn out that he could do nothing but tumble into bed.[71] Some day he would injure himself beyond recovery by these tremendous exertions. Some day, perhaps; but not yet. Once again, after only a few hours' respite, his marvellous vitality reasserted itself. That very Saturday night he addressed a crowded meeting in Ottawa. On Monday he took to the road again. And it was not until Saturday, February 19—three days before the election—that he reached Kingston, where he was once more a candidate, and finally came to rest.

VI

"After all the lies and abuse, your reward has come," the faithful Campbell wrote triumphantly on February 23. "I am fairly delighted, more I think than I felt in previous struggles. I hope Blake has a bad head-ache . . . and yourself again member for Kingston. Hurrah! Hurrah! Confound their politics, frustrate their knavish tricks!"[72] Part of their knavish tricks, Macdonald assured the Governor-General, was an unabashed reliance upon the vast organized patronage of the Grand Trunk Railway Company, and an even more deplorable acceptance, in Montreal alone, of nearly a hundred thousand dollars from the Chicago meat-packers, who had formerly controlled the Canadian market and who had evidently not taken Blake's promise about the tariff too literally.[73] Yet despite the foreigners and their gold, the "national" Canadian party had won. The old man's audacity had succeeded. "We fought with great odds against us," he wrote to G. T. Blackstock, "and would have been beaten if the elections had not been brought on when they were. With another session we were gone. I know many of our friends thought I was too bold, but boldness carried the day."[74]

It had indeed. The Conservatives, Macdonald predicted to the Governor-General, would have a majority of between thirty-five and forty when all the returns were in. This, of course, was too optimistic; but it was not a gross overestimate, and the early divisions in the first session of the new Parliament gave Macdonald majorities of thirty or slightly over. In Nova Scotia, Ontario, and Manitoba—the three "oppressed" provinces which were popularly supposed to be ripe for rebellion and secession—

the Conservatives had won; and in Quebec, despite all the efforts of Mercier and his Nationalists, they had done a little better than break even with their opponents. National unity had evidently not died on the Regina scaffold; the country was not going to split apart immediately in cultural and sectional fragments. Canadian politics—with minor changes, it was true— were apparently proceeding in their accustomed way. Things were surely as they always had been. And was not the re-election of John A. Macdonald for Kingston a significant proof of the fact?

And yet, despite this immediate and surprised sense of relief, there was something curiously unsatisfactory about the election of 1887. What, after all, had it decided? Had it done anything more than leave unsettled the question of Liberal leadership and the problem of the future programme of the Liberal party? Blake, who had now endured two defeats since he had succeeded Mackenzie, was obviously sunk deep in the gloom of disappointment and frustration; and towards the end of March he sent out a circular letter to his followers, proposing resignation from the leadership. Macdonald viewed this development with very mixed feelings. It was, of course, agreeable to have this public admission of Blake's chagrin; but, on the other hand, the prospect of Blake's retirement was definitely a disquieting one. "I hope he won't resign," he told Blackstock. "We could not have a weaker opponent than he." He had grown accustomed to Blake and Blake's little idiosyncracies. He felt that he could go on beating Blake, every four or five years, until the end of the chapter. But a new Liberal leader was an unknown and highly unacceptable quantity. A new leader might quickly succeed in representing the vital opposition of the country far more completely and effectively than Blake had done.

In the meantime, while the Liberals were hesitating unhappily about their leader and their programme, the national dissatisfaction continued to assume different but no less dangerous forms. On March 16, in the speech from the throne which opened the new session of the Quebec legislature, Mercier announced that he intended soon to call a conference of the provinces and the Dominion to consider "their financial and other relations".

A few weeks later, on April 4, he wrote to Macdonald, drawing
his attention to the announcement, and requesting "a confidential interview" on the subject.[75] This communication put
Macdonald instantly on the alert. He did not like it. It seemed
to him that in view of the fact that Mercier had formally made
public his proposal, the time for "confidential interviews" had
gone by; and, as for the proposed conference itself he viewed
it from the first with the deepest suspicion. There was no
provision in the constitution for such meetings and no necessity
for them. Why should he negotiate with the provinces collec-
tively rather than individually? Upon what grounds and for
what reasons was this strange and unprecedented proposal
being made?

He had only too much reason to question Mercier's good faith.
He could not know, of course, that early in March Mercier
had written to Mowat of Ontario, arguing strongly that "there
should be an understanding between the provincial governments
with a view to the organization of a system of common defence".[76] But he instinctively suspected that the conference
would be nothing more or less than a league of malcontent
provinces in organized opposition to the national policies and
national leadership of the Dominion. Mercier, who owed his
office to his abuse of the "hangmen" at Ottawa, was the self-
confessed ringleader of this obvious conspiracy. Mowat, who
had been fighting the exercise of Dominion disallowance for
years, would probably be an eager partner in the alliance.
Fielding, who had prudently hesitated in his campaign for
secession as a result of the Conservative success in Nova Scotia
in the federal general election, would no doubt gladly accept
Mercier's conference as a convenient way out of his perplexities;
and even Norquay, the unhappy Conservative Premier of
Manitoba, who seemed to cling so desperately to office, might
be driven, by the sheer weight of the anti-disallowance agitation
in his province, into identifying himself with Mercier's league
of discontent.

There was danger in the organization of this league. There
was danger also in its basic assumption—hinted at in the Quebec
speech from the throne—that Confederation was a compact

which it was open to the contracting provinces to review and revise at their discretion. Macdonald replied with distant politeness to Mercier's first letter.⁷⁷ And when Mercier renewed his request, with effusive protestations of good will, Macdonald consented to an official, but not a confidential, interview.⁷⁸ This the Premier of Quebec declined; but it was plain that he intended, with or without Macdonald's co-operation, to go ahead with his project of an interprovincial conference.

No, the general election had not settled everything. It had certainly not settled everything in Macdonald's favour. He was aware of certain painful uncertainties in the political situation. He suspected that there might be lurking menaces ahead. But he had no intention of letting these possibilities intimidate him. It was spring now; and on April 13, the new Parliament met for its first session. He felt supported and comforted by its solid, manageable presence. Once again the people of Canada had sustained his government; and once again he had a comfortable majority at his back. He saw no reason at all why he should modify his conception of the rôle of the Dominion in national affairs, or alter the policies which he had devised for the nation's enlargement and integration. The Canadian voters had emphatically endorsed these policies. Why should he change them? The insurgent provinces might try to undermine the national economy, wreck the transcontinental railway, and dethrone the Dominion from its pre-eminence. But he would resist all this. They were *his* national policies. They were popular. And he would stand by them.

He could not stand by them, however, without a fight. Norquay, after a final unsuccessful visit to Ottawa, returned to Winnipeg and obviously abandoned all effort to support Dominion railway policy in the west. On April 19, he served blunt notice that Manitoba would submit no longer to federal interference with its railway legislation, and announced that a new railway, the Red River Valley Railway, from Winnipeg to the international boundary, would be built immediately by the province as a government work. The issue was now clearly and sharply joined. Inevitably it came up in Parliament, for one of the western members introduced a resolution for the deletion of the monopoly clause from the Canadian Pacific Railway charter; and inevitably Macdonald had to make a new declaration of government policy. The whole ugly business worried him. He began to discuss various possible concessions, including new Manitoba branch lines and lower freight rates, with Stephen. But he knew that at the moment he could not yield on the main point.

He defended the Canadian Pacific Railway as a great national undertaking, the axis of a transcontinental, east-west Canadian trading system, in which every province and every citizen had an interest, and which the Dominion was bound to protect and defend. "Every province," he told the Commons, "is interested in keeping that trade for ourselves, and no one knows better than the honourable gentleman opposite that the Pacific Railway charter would not have been granted, that the land would not have been given, that the money would not have been voted, and the loans would not have been made, if it had been understood by the representatives of the older provinces that the money was to be expended on an enterprise which might be bled at one hundred different points, so that by the time the traffic arrived at Montreal, it would be a miserable fragment of the magnificent stream of commerce that we had a right to expect to pass through Canada from one end to the other. . . . No; we are convinced our policy was right. We have confidence in it."[79]

He had a similar confidence in the national policy of protection. The national policy of protection, he reminded the Commons, had won an equal endorsation at the general election. There were, to be sure, increasingly disturbing signs, as spring went on, of a growing interest in complete free trade, or commercial union, with the United States. Even the Toronto *Mail* was showing a perverse interest in this new heresy. But the *Mail's* deviations from rectitude were now so numerous that they had ceased to be shocking. The paper had become a confirmed and incorrigible renegade; and Macdonald was already discussing arrangements for the establishment of a new and orthodox journal in Toronto.[80] He was not greatly impressed by the fashionable and no doubt ephemeral interest in commercial union with the United States; and the only changes which he contemplated in the protective system were changes which would round it out, strengthen it, and increase its popularity. Nova Scotia, under the tempter Fielding, had wandered away into error. Nova Scotia had been led back again into virtuous ways by Tupper at the last election. It was now the Dominion's opportunity to reward the province that had been lost, and then found, by a suitably generous treatment of her interests; and, on May 12, as the main innovation of his budget speech, Tupper proposed a scheme of substantially increased iron and steel duties.[81]

Macdonald's design was what it always had been. The country, with the Canadian Pacific Railway as its principal axis, was conceived commercially as an east-west trading system, protected mainly against competition from the south, and open at the Atlantic and Pacific coasts for the movement of men and goods and capital. The United States had always been the chief rival of this national organization; and England had been, and remained, its only great ally. Macdonald had always been deeply interested in the present and future form of the Anglo-Canadian alliance; but the imperial connection had only lately become fashionable in England; and it was not until 1887, the year of Queen Victoria's Golden Jubilee, that the British government decided to accord a new and formal recognition to the self-governing and dependent Empire. In 1887, the recently formed Imperial Federation League achieved its greatest triumph; and the Salisbury government invited representatives of the "auxiliary kingdoms" and Crown colonies of the Empire to assemble in London for a Colonial Conference. If it had been any time but the spring, Macdonald or Tupper would almost certainly have attended. But the Conference opened early in April, when the Canadian Parliament was just about to meet for the session; and it was utterly impossible for either the Prime Minister or the Minister of Finance to leave Ottawa. Alexander Campbell and Sandford Fleming, who had been the original government surveyor for the Canadian Pacific Railway, went instead.

Macdonald was well aware of the fact that Fleming had had no political experience whatever and that Campbell had resigned from the ministry and was about to become Lieutenant-Governor of Ontario. He knew that they were very unlikely to act with any great initiative or energy at the Colonial Conference. He was not dissatisfied. He did not particularly want them to play a constructive part. With a country economically depressed, provinces apt for quarrelling or secession, a north-west rebellious and still half-empty, and an enormously costly railway barely completed, he was not in the mood for daring or expensive innovations. This, he considered, was definitely not a propitious moment for the working out of ambitious plans for imperial defence or imperial preferential trade; and in any case, as he had told the Royal Commission on the Defence of British Possessions and Commerce Abroad in 1880, he preferred separate arrangements between England and the individual colonies rather than a common system which bound them all. Campbell and Fleming were instructed, not to offer any new Canadian assistance to a general scheme of imperial defence, but to emphasize the contribution which Canada had already made in the assumption of new military burdens at home and in the unaided construction of the Canadian Pacific Railway. At the moment Canada still needed more help that she could possibly give. She needed it for the promotion of communications and trade on the Pacific. Above all she needed it for the defence of the North Atlantic fisheries.

As May slipped away, and Parliament adjourned for a brief spring recess, it was this final feature of Macdonald's national plan—protection against the United States—which occupied him most. A new fishing season was beginning; and, until an agreement with the United States was reached, every fishing season was full of potential trouble. But Macdonald faced the season of 1887 with much greater equanimity than he had that of 1886. His position was definitely stronger than it had been in the previous summer. During the winter months there had been some talk about a proposal of Bayard's which Lord Lansdowne found "one-sided and disingenuous" and which, he claimed, decided against Canada "all the debatable points and some which are not debatable at all".[82] Quite early in the discussions Macdonald briefly pronounced that most of Bayard's scheme was "altogether inadmissible", and there was never any real chance of its adoption.[83] No further concessions to the Americans had been made. The Fisheries Act of 1886 was law; British naval protection had been promised. In 1887 the defence of the fisheries would be stronger and more united than it had been since the Washington Treaty had been abrogated by the United States.

But defence, however concerted and successful, was not Macdonald's object. He did not want a permanent state of diplomatic friction any more than he wanted a permanent state of economic vassalage. He had always hoped for a sensible, satisfactory settlement of the fisheries dispute. He had always believed that a sensible, satisfactory settlement would be hastened if Canada only showed that she meant business about defending her property; and in the spring of 1887 the truth of this simple proposition seemed to be demonstrated. After two years, during which Bayard had "tried on" a variety of methods of settling the dispute, out of hand, in favour of the United States, the American Secretary of State finally made his first large conciliatory gesture. Through Erastus Wiman, a Canadian resident in the United States, who was soon to become notorious as an advocate of commercial union, he intimated that he would be glad to receive Macdonald or Tupper for the purpose of discussing Canadian-American relations. Macdonald accepted this indirect invitation readily enough. It was arranged that Tupper, under the guise of a holiday visit to the United States, should pay an informal call on Bayard in Washington.[84] A week after Tupper's return to Ottawa, a letter from the American Secretary of State seemed to clinch the prospect of a favourable settlement. "I am confident," Bayard wrote, "we both seek to attain a just and permanent settlement; and there is but one way to procure it—and that is by a straightforward treatment on a liberal and statesmanlike plan of the entire commercial relations of the two countries."[85]

VII

Macdonald had taken his stand. It was essentially the old ground—he saw no real reason to change it. And the question was not whether he would shift his position, but whether he could be dislodged from it. The opposition that session in Parliament was negligible; the Reformers were preoccupied with the distracting business of changing their leader. Early in June Blake finally resigned, and the Liberal and Conservative press joined in paying polite tributes to his services. The disgusted Stephen was infuriated by these respectful estimates of Blake's contribution to the national welfare. "He has done more harm to Canada ten times over than any man living," he raged, "and his record shows it."[86] Did it? Macdonald shook his head. Blake may have been politically malignant. But the record proved that he had been a singularly unsuccessful politician. Would his successor, the bookish, agreeable, and elegant Wilfrid Laurier, be any better? And would Laurier's elevation to the leadership mean any radical change in the essentially subtle and cautious policy which Blake had pursued?

On June 23, amid the festivities of Jubilee Week, Parliament was prorogued. For Macdonald there was no hope yet of an escape to the St. Lawrence. July, he knew, would have to be "sweltered out" in Ottawa. A somewhat ominous hush—the hush appropriate to anxious discussion and planning—descended upon the Liberal party. But, in the meantime, the air was loud with other ringing protests. Resistance to the Dominion and its national policies was continuing to develop outside Parliament and in virtual independence of the existing party system. In Ontario, Farmers' Institutes and Commercial Union Clubs were discussing economic partnership with the United States in a mood of growing enthusiasm; and out in Manitoba, Norquay, the renegade Conservative, was apparently preparing to carry out his provincial railway policy by main force. On July 2, in conscious defiance of the Dominion, he turned the first sod for the Red River Valley Railway. Macdonald was very angry. He determined to put a stop to these insolent proceedings at once. "Your bankrupt population at Winnipeg must be taught a lesson," he told Aikins severely, "even if some of them are brought down to trial at Toronto for sedition."[87] Peremptorily he ordered the Lieutenant-Governor to send down the offending statutes at "the first convenient opportunity"; and on July 16 the Red River Valley Railway Act was disallowed.[88]

He had, he told Aikins, no fear at all of the consequences of this uncompromising policy. But in his heart he thought differently. There was, of course, no doubt at all about the criminal lunacy of Manitoba's conduct. "When you reflect," he expostulated to John Rose, "on a legislature of thirty-five members, with a population of one hundred and ten thousand, coolly devoting a million of dollars to build a railway from Winnipeg to the frontier, between two lines owned by the C.P.R., running in the same direction, one on the east and the other on the west side of the Red River, when there is not business enough for one of the two existing lines, you can understand the recklessness of that body."[89] It was almost incredible! Nobody seemed to have the faintest sense of responsibility! Norquay was acting at least partly in self-interest; the motives of the Liberal politicians and railway speculators who were egging him on were obviously suspect; and the whole insane enterprise would very probably end in the bankruptcy of the province. Manitoba might fall. But, if she did, she would drag others down with her. Already the Canadian north-west, Canadian railways, and Canadian credit were plunging down again into ruinous disrepute. Lansdowne was gravely worried for the future. Stephen, sick at heart with the renewed and sharp decline of Canadian Pacific stock, had come to the conclusion that the monopoly clause was not worth the appalling price he had to pay for it.

When, late in July, Macdonald left for a holiday in New Brunswick, the Manitoba agitation was at its height. When he returned to Ottawa early in September, its shrill excited intensity had not diminished in the slightest. He could see no pleasant prospect anywhere. Stephen was bemoaning the fact that the drop in Canadian Pacific stock had cost the shareholders nearly twenty million dollars. The opposition newspapers—now including the *Mail*—were doing their best to whip up an interest in Mercier's approaching interprovincial conference; and there could be no doubt that the popularity of commercial union with the United States had been steadily rising all summer. The only really satisfactory intelligence that reached Macdonald during August was the news from England that Tupper's unofficial

visit to the United States had resulted in an agreement to
appoint a new Joint High Commission for the settlement of the
outstanding Canadian-American disputes. Even the gratification
produced by this announcement was qualified immediately and
sharply by the darkest misgivings. Another conference at Washington! Was Canada once again to be laid as a burnt offering
on the altar of Anglo-American friendship?

He was instantly on the defensive. He kept putting a long
series of searching questions to the Governor-General and himself.[90] Who was to represent Canada at Washington? If he
did not go himself, could the "impulsive" Tupper be trusted
to act alone? Was it not probable that Joseph Chamberlain,
who had been announced as the principal British Commissioner,
would act in accordance with Liberal anti-colonial theories and
would be ambitiously eager to get back to England as quickly
as possible with a treaty in his pocket? Would the terms of
reference include commercial relations as well as Atlantic and
Pacific fisheries? And would the Commission be empowered
to settle the controversy over Bering Sea, where the United
States had been busily seizing Canadian sealing vessels as if
the open ocean were a private American lake?

Obviously the powers of the Commission were the vital
feature of the arrangement. Macdonald wanted them to be as
wide and as explicit as possible; and when, towards the end
of September, he first saw the terms of reference, he was disappointed and annoyed both by their limitations and their
vagueness. "'Dolus latet in generalibus'," he wrote to the
Governor-General, "and the whole thing seems to be a snare
laid by the United States government to entrap England into
a commission to consider the expediency of relaxing the terms
of the Convention of 1818. This has long been their aim and,
as it is the Magna Carta of the Maritime Provinces, must be
resisted. You may think me too suspicious, but I have a lively
recollection of the manner in which the United States Commissioners in 1871 at Washington, after getting the article settled
respecting the *Alabama* claims, coolly refused to consider
Canada's claim for Fenian invasions and outrages, on the ground
that they were not authorized by their government."[91]

As October drew on, it became clear that the uncertainties of the last six months were ending. The time for expectation and apprehension was over: the time for action had come. On October 13, the Cabinet decided that Tupper would be Canada's representative at the Washington Conference and that Thompson would act as his legal assistant. "So that matter may be considered as settled," Macdonald wrote to Lord Lansdowne.[92] Once again, for the second time since Confederation, he had to face a crucially important diplomatic encounter with the United States; and at the same embarrassing moment, almost as if their movements had been deliberately timed, his domestic opponents emerged from cover to renew their attacks. On October 12, in a speech to his constituents at Ingersoll, Sir Richard Cartwright, who, since Blake's retirement from the leadership, had become the principal Liberal leader in Ontario, committed himself unequivocally to the support of commercial union with the United States;[93] and on October 20, Honoré Mercier welcomed the delegates to the interprovincial conference at Quebec.

Chapter Fourteen

The Renewal of Cultural Conflict

I

During the autumn of 1887 the newspaper attack against Macdonald's national design reached a harsh crescendo of intensity. Never before had there been such a heavy bombardment of his whole position; never before had the bombardment been sustained by so many thundering pieces of journalistic artillery. In French-speaking Canada and the Maritime Provinces, the principal newspapers had largely gone over to the opposition. In English-speaking Quebec, the Montreal *Gazette* maintained a stout defence virtually alone; and in Toronto, the capital of the "banner" province of the Dominion, the two most popular and most frequently quoted newspapers, the *Globe* and the *Mail*, had now united in opposition to everything for which Macdonald stood. In desperation, the Conservatives had decided that a new ministerial paper, the *Empire*, must be founded in Toronto; but the response to an appeal for financial support was at first so unsatisfactory that for a while Macdonald considered the still more desperate expedient of a new attempt to propitiate the *Mail*. Dalton McCarthy would have nothing to do with this proposal. "No," he wrote firmly to Macdonald, "we must start the *Empire* or prepare for defeat at the next general election —if not before that."[1]

In the meantime, the chorus of denunciation grew more shrill and sustained. The attack was now directed, not merely against this or that national policy, but against the whole conception of a separate Canadian nationality in the North American continent. Every disappointment, every misfortune, every evidence of cultural division and religious antagonism was carefully enumerated in one long, comprehensive indictment of Confederation. "Our enormous debt," the *Mail* began its portentous list, "the determination of the people of the north-west to break loose from trade and transportation restrictions in defiance of the federal authority; the exodus of population from the north-west and the far larger stream pouring out of the older provinces; the threats of secession heard in the three Maritime Provinces; the decline in our exports which are less today by five dollars per head of population than they were in 1873, although since then we have spent no less than one hundred and twenty millions of borrowed money in developing our resources; the gathering of the local premiers at Quebec to devise ways and means of allaying provincial discontent and averting provincial bankruptcy—these, to go no further, are phenomena, which, if they presented themselves in any other country, young or old, we should regard as the forerunners of dissolution."[2]

Approaching dissolution had become the main theme of the opposition press; but not of the opposition press alone. The prophecies were uniformly gloomy, the desperate significance of the existing state of affairs was emphasized by all. "It is not improbable," wrote the editor of the Montreal *Gazette*, "that the people will, sooner than many now imagine, be called on to determine whether the work accomplished in 1867 is to be undone, whether the Confederation is to be preserved or allowed to lapse into its original fragments, preparatory to absorption into the United States. The signs of the times point to the imminence of so momentous an issue."[3] The signs of the times seemed to make clear that the hour of decision was close at hand. Gloom and doubt and consciousness of failure were widespread. The air was full of a sense of impending crisis. Was it not better, argued many, to cut the national losses and to admit that the whole attempt to found a transcontinental Canadian economy had been a gigantic mistake?

It was in this despairing atmosphere that the interprovincial conference met. The circumstances of the moment gave a sinister significance to its declared purpose of amending the

British North America Act. Macdonald did not underestimate the potential danger of the conference, for he had good reason not to underrate the power of the provincial governments. In the last two decades, he had seen them become something very different from the glorified county councils which he had expected after the union. Provincial governments had grown greatly in constitutional authority, in political influence and prestige. Provincial loyalties seemed to have remained steadfast, while truly national sentiments had apparently declined in strength. Finally—and this was, perhaps, the most important point of all—some of the provinces had acquired a territorial extent and a physical power which utterly invalidated the picture which he had drawn tentatively at Confederation of the future map of British North America. He had, in all probability, looked forward to the emergence of a number of provinces, not too large and not dissimilar in size and consequence. But in the past ten years this dream of relative territorial equality had been completely shattered by the triumphant expansion of Ontario and Quebec. The final settlement of the north-western boundary of Ontario had not yet been effected by the imperial Parliament. But the enlargement was inevitable now; and, as Macdonald pointed out to Campbell, it was obvious that if Ontario were to extend as far north as Hudson Bay, so must Quebec.

"Now if you will look at the map," he continued earnestly, "and see the enormous extent of country proposed to be added to the two provinces, you will see what vast preponderance it gives them over the other provinces in the Dominion. History will repeat itself and posterity will find out that the evils that exist in other federations from the preponderance of one or more members will again happen. It is our duty as founders of a nation to look far into the future. I know it will be said that the additional territory desired by Ontario and Quebec is inhospitable in climate and ill adapted for settlement, but we used to hear the same thing of the Red River country and the north-west. I have little doubt that a great portion of the vast region asked for by the two provinces will be capable of receiving and will receive a large population."[4] The two central provinces

would become empire provinces—powerful metropolitan governments with enormous hinterlands. And Quebec, with a population of millions owing allegiance to its special customs, might
prove a barrier fatal to national unity. "I look to the future in
this matter . . .," Macdonald repeated, "farther ahead perhaps
than I should. But are we not founding a nation? Now just
consider for yourself—what a country of millions lying between
English Canada and the Atlantic will be. I have no objections
to the French as French or as Catholics, but the block caused
by the introduction of French law and the Civil Code would
be very great."⁵

He had looked into the future farther perhaps than anybody.
He had tried, with every ounce of his strength and every device
at his command, to sustain the national interest. Repeatedly he
had had to give way. The long series of engagements which
he had fought with provincial governments in the 1880's had
resulted in as many losses and draws as wins. He had had to
yield to Ontario. He was beginning to suspect that he might
have to yield to Manitoba as well. The whole difficult and
ungrateful effort to preserve the east-west transport system
from the damage which Manitoba seemed determined to inflict
upon it was breaking against Manitoba's unreasoning, almost
maniacal resistance. It was not, of course, that Norquay had
succeeded in his insane design of building a third railway from
Winnipeg to the international border. He had utterly failed
to obtain capital; and the scheme had collapsed in angry frustration for at least a season. "Norquay," Macdonald wrote wearily
to Lieutenant-Governor Aikins, "seems to have run himself
quite aground in his selfish eagerness to retain his place."⁶
But Norquay could not retain his place, Macdonald knew. He
was sinking, and sinking fast. The trouble was that he would
not sink alone.

In all probability, the Manitoba government and the Manitoba Conservative party would be dragged down with him.
He had discredited the north-west, frightened away the immigrants and capital that were necessary for its development, and
brought the Canadian Pacific Railway staggering to its knees.
"Your railway development," Macdonald declared emphatically

—◆GRIP◆—

PROVINCIAL RIGHT IS FEDERAL WRONG.

Sir John—How dare you fellows meet to conspire against me?

Mowat—Pardon me, we met simply to take measures to preserve the rights of the provinces.

Sir John—Just so! That's what I say. It's the same thing, you little tyrant!

to a correspondent in Winnipeg, "has been paralysed and the C.P.R. prevented from getting the means to build the branches which it was their interest and their desire to build in order to bring the necessary traffic to their main line. . . . Now so great is the distrust in England as to your future that not a pound, not a cent, can be got on pledge of land grants to railways."[7] A year ago the company's common stock had been selling at the proud sum of seventy-five dollars a share; at the end of September it was quoted at a new low of forty-nine and a half. "Yesterday's advices from England about the position of the C.P.R. securities are most discouraging," Stephen wrote to Macdonald on October 4. "Barings are annoyed beyond endurance by anxious inquiries, and between one thing and another I am nearly off my head."[8] The monopoly clause, Stephen was now nearly convinced, must be given up. But he was determined not to surrender it cheaply. And Macdonald began to realize that once again, after an interval of only three years, he might have to ask the Canadian Parliament and the Canadian people to make another large concession to the Canadian Pacific Railway.

Unquestionably there were places where he would have to yield. He had given in to individual provinces before now; he would very possibly have to give in to individual provinces again. But an organized conspiracy of provincial governments was a different, and a much more scandalous, affair; and to such a conspiracy he refused to surrender. He would simply decline to recognize the interprovincial conference; he would not, by the slightest sign, admit its existence. And such a defence, though it might seem weak and ineffectual at the moment, could in the end prove completely devastating. Up to this moment, the provincial premiers had had everything their own way. They had met, to the accompaniment of a fanfare of opposition trumpets, on October 20. They had strutted about the centre of the stage in a bright spotlight of publicity, laying down general principles, formulating resolutions, and talking, with interminable volubility, about their virtues and their woes. They had abolished the federal power of disallowance, reformed the Senate in the interest of the provinces, and voted themselves a large increase in the subsidies payable by the Dominion. They had done all this with a bustling, self-important, consequential air which temporarily obscured some inconvenient but highly important facts about their conference. The Dominion, of course, had not been represented: British Columbia and Prince Edward Island had neither of them put in an appearance. The interprovincial conference was not a meeting of all the governments—nor even of all the provincial governments—of Canada. Constitutionally, it was nothing.

Herein lay the masterly effectiveness of Macdonald's uncooperative silence. In the absence of support from the Dominion, what were the five malcontent provinces to do with their precious resolutions? Upon what grounds, failing the adhesion of British Columbia and Prince Edward Island, could they demand a change in the established procedure for the amendment of the British North America Act? Except on one occasion in 1875, when the Mackenzie government had acted independently of Parliament, requests for the amendment of the British North America Act had been presented to the imperial Parliament in a joint address of the Senate and the House of Commons of Canada; and, obviously, so long as Macdonald and the Conservatives retained control of the two houses, no joint request for the incredible amendments proposed by the interprovincial conference would ever be sent. It was as simple as that. Macdonald waited imperturbably within the impregnable wall of his defences. It would need a revolution to destroy them. And would the Quebec Conference—this Grit caucus, this conspiracy of the discontented five—ever have the stomach to begin a real revolution? Macdonald smiled sardonically. He did not believe it.

II

In the meantime, while he waited for the provincial premiers to make the next move, he busied himself with still another section of the defence of his national system. Relations with the United States had obviously entered a most critical phase. The Joint High Commission was about to meet in Washington; and all autumn commercial union or unrestricted reciprocity with the republic had been apparently winning a great army of supporters. Unrestricted reciprocity, which was distinguishable from commercial union only by much pretentious hair-splitting, and which, like commercial union, threatened Canadian fiscal autonomy and political independence, was in fundamental opposition to Macdonald's whole conception of a separate Canadian nationality in North America. Its dangerous political implications must certainly be exposed. But at the same time it must be admitted that there lay back of it a legitimate and important aspiration, which was the natural desire of Canadians for reasonably good trade relations with the United States. Could he satisfy that aspiration? In the light of Bayard's promising letter to Tupper, was there not a real chance that it might be satisfied in the approaching negotiations at Washington?

Macdonald looked forward to the meeting of the Washington Conference with a curious mixture of eagerness and apprehension. He had worked for this conference for nearly three years. But now that it was about to assemble, he was full once more of suspicion and disquietude. He could not help but be deeply, incurably sceptical about all Anglo-American negotiations in which Canada was involved. He hardly dared to permit himself to hope for good results. And yet, on the face of it, the omens seemed undeniably favourable. The Cleveland administration appeared genuinely eager for a broad trade agreement between the two countries. Tupper, who had spent a week-end with Chamberlain talking over the Canadian case, reported that he was much pleased with the British Commissioner, and that he thought Canada had been "fortunate in his selection".[9] Thompson, who was immensely learned on the subject of the fisheries, had been placed in charge of the legal aspect of the negotiations, as principal expert adviser. Macdonald at first told the Governor-General bluntly that he hoped "no legal man will come out from England"; and when Lord Lansdowne mildly protested, Macdonald replied that Canada could have no objection to an English counsel accompanying Chamberlain, provided he kept to a properly subordinate rôle. "I want to guard against the legal conduct of matters being taken out of Thompson's hands," he wrote frankly to the Governor-General.[10] Thompson must be in control. And how strange and wonderful was the contrast between Thompson's acknowledged pre-eminence and the dubious and embarrassed status of the representatives of the Department of Marine and Fisheries whom Macdonald had had the effrontery to bring with him to Washington in 1871!

He was certainly less apprehensive than he had been in 1871. He said good-bye to Tupper almost confidently on November 15. But doubts—unpleasant, irrepressible doubts—still lingered. He had seen too many demonstrations of what he called roundly "the faithlessness of the American government". "There is no fair dealing to be expected from them," he declared emphatically to the Governor-General.[11] And within a few days—within a time so short that the event may have anticipated even his gloomiest predictions—the truth of this generalization seemed to be borne out once again. Tupper's first letters from Washington were disconcerting in the extreme. It was not, Macdonald noted gratefully, that there was any sign whatever of a break in the solidarity of the British delegation. Tupper reported that "our party is working most harmoniously and pleasantly" and that "nothing could be more satisfactory than the manner in which Mr. Chamberlain sustained our position".[12] No, thank God, the trouble was not here! The trouble was with the Americans who were conforming, in an absurdly literal way, to their reputed standard of behaviour. They had given every indication of desiring a generous trade agreement. Their Secretary of State, Bayard, had informed Tupper that, in his opinion, a satisfactory settlement of Canadian-American difficulties could be reached only through a straightforward and liberal treatment of "the entire commercial relations of the two countries". Yet now, and at the very first official meeting of the Joint High Commission, the American plenipotentiaries flatly announced that the terms of reference did not include commercial or tariff questions and that the work of the conference must be limited to the question of the proper interpretation of the Convention of 1818.

Macdonald was exasperated, extremely disappointed, but not really surprised. "All our prognostications as to the course of the United States government are more than verified," he wrote disgustedly to Lord Lansdowne, "and Mr. Bayard does

not come out of it in a very creditable manner."[13] He had, of
course, some sympathy for the Secretary of State's position.
"I have little doubt," he remarked in a letter to Tupper, "that
both he and the President were sincere at first in their desire
to extend trade relations with Canada, but they feel Congress is not with them, and they wish now to avoid a second
snub from the Senate."[14] The Americans, he thought, were
endeavouring to extricate themselves from these political difficulties by humiliating disavowals of their past professions; and
at the same time they were evidently quite prepared to use the
hostility of the Senate in order to extract concessions from
Canada at no expense to the United States. "The manner in
which Bayard attempts to set aside his letter to you," he wrote
to Tupper indignantly, "is most disingenuous. His letter should
be read, not only according to its plain meaning, but also by the
light thrown on it by the previous negotiations for a commission."
The whole purpose of the conference, for which England and
Canada had now been pressing for nearly three years, was a
broad consideration of the commercial relations of the two countries. But at the last moment, and with fatal results, England had
characteristically put her trust in the general declarations of a
gentleman's agreement. "It is a pity," Macdonald lamented to
Lord Lansdowne, "that Her Majesty's government wouldn't
listen to our request to have the question of commercial intercourse specially mentioned as a subject of reference in the
agreement for a conference. At present it would appear that we
have fallen into a trap set for us by the United States and are
now forced to enter into a discussion confined to the subject of
the meaning of the Convention of 1818."[15]

This, it appeared, was exactly what the American plenipotentiaries had in view. They professed themselves to be uninterested
in the privilege of fishing inside the Canadian three-mile limit.
The Canadian inshore fisheries, they explained, had ceased to
be of any great value to American fishermen, and what they
wanted, as a support for their deep-sea fishery, were the privileges which the Canadians claimed were denied by the Convention of 1818—the privileges of buying bait, ice, and other
supplies, and of transhipping fish in Canadian Atlantic ports.

Would it be possible for Canada to grant these privileges, provided the American fishing vessels took out licences for the
purpose, and provided the licences were paid for, either by fees
imposed on the vessels themselves, or by the free admission
of Canadian fish into the American market? Tupper believed
that this would be a wise arrangement to make. He drafted an
alternative proposal—a bad second-best to his original offer—
along these lines; and on December 7 he telegraphed to Macdonald for permission to submit it to the conference.

Macdonald felt extremely uncertain. For a fortnight now,
with increasing annoyance and disgust, he had been coping
with the spate of letters and telegrams from Washington. "I
am chained by the leg here just now," he wrote to his sister
Louisa, who had been pleading with him to pay a visit to
Kingston, "and cannot leave town for a moment, as the negotiations with Washington are going on and I am receiving cypher
messages hourly which require immediate answer."[16] Tupper's
request required an answer—an answer given soon, if not immediately. What was he to say to it? He hardly knew. The blunt
disconcerting diplomatic manœuvres at Washington had left
him with a profound feeling of discouragement. There was no
hope now of tariff concessions in the American market. He
would have no means of quieting the general economic unrest
which, for the moment, seemed to have been captured so completely for the commercial union movement. Tupper's proposal
aroused no enthusiasm whatever. The Governor-General was
critical of it; the ministers differed widely in their opinion of
it.[17] On December 8, after a prolonged discussion, the Cabinet
divided against it, five to four.[18]

But could he risk a complete break-up of the Conference
thus early in the proceedings? What did the British plenipotentiaries think of the proposed offer? Above all, did the Canadian
Cabinet ministers now in Washington, Tupper, Thompson,
and Foster, concur in its presentation? "Do you three agree to
proposal?"[19] he telegraphed to Tupper late on December 8.
Tupper's reply was definite and reassuring. "All three plenipotentiaries and Minister of Justice and Foster concur in the
proposal," he answered briefly. The addition of these three

names converted the narrow majority against the offer into a slightly larger majority in its favour; and on December 10, after another long discussion, the Cabinet reluctantly decided in favour of the plan.[20] The Governor-General agreed that his government could not take the responsibility of letting the negotiations fail at this stage;[21] and on December 10 Macdonald finally telegraphed to Tupper authorizing the submission of the proposal. He was at once dissatisfied and apprehensive. "The greatest care should be taken in the draft of your offer," he warned Tupper. "As you know they will make the most ungenerous use of any omission or careless expression."[22] He feared the textual chicanery of the Americans. He was worried about the reception which the Canadians would certainly give to such a niggardly settlement of the fisheries dispute. It was therefore with a real sense of relief that on the night of December 10 he received an unexpected telegram from Tupper, informing him that the Conference had adjourned for the Christmas holidays, that Chamberlain would stay a further few days in Washington for private discussions with Bayard, and would then come up to Ottawa.[23]

III

In the brief holiday interval, Macdonald had time for an anxious casting-up of the national accounts. Canada incorporated was by no means bankrupt yet; there were even a few encouraging items to be put down on the credit side of the ledger. But these were balanced by equally serious losses; and, on the whole, his position was no better than it had been in the early autumn. There was now not the faintest hope of a popular trade agreement with the United States. There was, on the other hand, every expectation of renewed trouble with the disgruntled provinces. He had no means of knowing what moves those adroit players Mowat and Mercier had in contemplation; but it was certain now, at any rate, that the game was up in the west and that the long effort to maintain a Conservative interest in Manitoba had ended in failure. Norquay, having staggered on blindly and ineffectually for so many years, finally resigned office a few days before Christmas; and although his successor, Harrison, was a Conservative, it was plain that the new government was an extremely feeble one, and that Greenway and the Liberals were certain to gain power in short order. The western attack upon Macdonald's national policy would now be directed by a new and vigorous leader, a leader uninhibited by past pledges and old political sympathies; and every effort would be made to press it home to success.

But even this was not all. The Liberal leaders were obviously continuing their absorbed, their positively fascinated contemplation of the political possibilities of commercial union or unrestricted reciprocity. Macdonald's best defence against it had now gone. He had little hope of quieting the agitation with a good trade treaty with the United States.

But, on the other hand, if the legitimate commercial aspirations back of the movement could not be satisfied, its dangerous political implications were certainly being exposed, and realized, much more fully than before. The *Empire*, the new Conservative Toronto newspaper which finally made its appearance towards the end of December, began a sustained attack on North American continentalism; and on December 30, in a speech before the Toronto Board of Trade, Joseph Chamberlain frankly assured his audience that a North American customs union would instantly compromise Canada's fiscal freedom and might pave the way for the loss of its political independence.[24] Chamberlain, Macdonald predicted gaily to Tupper, could be elected in the most Tory constituency in Canada! The whole country, he felt certain, had connected commercial union inextricably with annexation and was prepared to repudiate both. "All the federal elections," he informed Tupper complacently—too complacently, "have gone against commercial union. . . . Leading men of the opposition like Alexander Mackenzie, James Young, and John Macdonald of Toronto, and Edgar, Blake's *fidus Achates*, have denounced commercial union. The rural press of Ontario on both sides oppose it. Commercial union is a dead duck, and I think Lord Lansdowne sees now that my policy, as announced to him last spring, of allowing the cry

of commercial union to blaze, crackle, and go out with a
stink, without giving it undue importance, was a wise one."[25]

On the whole, his reflections, though mixed, were not more
depressing than they had been. The holiday season was a
pleasantly restful one. Chamberlain came up to Ottawa and
there were official dinners and some long discussions of the
fisheries question; but for a good part of the time he remained
agreeably settled at Earnscliffe. For the first time in years,
nearly all the members of his family were collected about him.
Agnes, who had been west again on a visit, had brought his
grand-daughter, Daisy, back with her;[26] and Hugh, who had
been ill and out of sorts in the early autumn, returned to spend
Christmas at Earnscliffe. It was pleasant to have the quiet,
sombre house full of people and gay with children's talk; but
though he loved to have the children and grandchildren about
him, their presence did not make him forget his own generation.
One day late in December, he and Agnes and Hugh went up
to Kingston in the *Jamaica* to see Louisa. For years Louisa
had been an invalid, whose hospitable instincts were excited to
frenzy by the mere suggestion of a visit of her relatives. "*Now
mind*," Macdonald warned her with mock severity, "if you
make any attempt to provide beds for us we will turn round
and return at once to Ottawa."[27] They spent the day with her,
and in the evening they all went over to visit Aunt Maria
Macpherson. Macdonald thought his sister looked very frail;
but her courage and good spirits were as indomitable as ever.[28]

In the meantime, the second Canadian plan for the settlement of the fisheries dispute was being gradually worked out in
detail. It was a comprehensive proposal which, among other
things, included arrangements for a final decision of the vexed
question of what bays were included in Canadian territorial
waters. Its principal feature was a provision that American
fishing vessels, on obtaining licences, could enter Canadian
ports to buy supplies and tranship fish, and that these licences
would either be issued at a substantial tonnage fee, or would be
free so long as the United States repealed the duty on Canadian
fish. The scheme left Macdonald coldly unenthusiastic. He
considered fees for licences a troublesome, inadequate, and

unpopular return for the Canadian concessions. "I would suggest," he argued to Tupper, "that if the Americans agree to a licence system at all it should be provided that licences should be issued free so soon as by treaty or tariffs we have free fish, and not before, and that the licence system should cease whenever any duties are re-imposed. . . . The Americans would pride themselves on their cleverness in getting a surrender of our claims on the bait question in such a manner that we could not terminate it, and then please the fishermen by re-imposing the duty on fish."[29] A free market for Canadian fish—the last vestige of his original idea of a trade treaty—was the only thing that really interested him. And he was reconciled to licence fees only because Chamberlain repeatedly assured him that they were a necessary part of a final settlement to which he had secured Cleveland's and Bayard's informal approval in advance.

The opening of Parliament had been set for February 23. "The fate of the conference," Macdonald wrote confidently to Lord Lansdowne, "will be determined long before this. The points for discussion are so few that they will be disposed of in a fortnight and the results, if they amount to a treaty, will at once be laid before the Senate."[30] It was, for Macdonald, a curiously naïve assumption. The State Department of the United States still had enlightening experiences in store for him, as well as for Tupper, Chamberlain, and Thompson. On January 9, the day on which the conference reconvened, the Anglo-Canadian delegates presented the proposal for which, they imagined, American approval had been secured in advance. But instead of a ready and gratified acceptance, there were unexpected requests for adjournments. The adjournments became prolonged delays; and the delays were followed by critical and inconclusive answers. The angry climax of the British delegation's bewilderment came when Bayard objected that the Canadian proposal was defective in that it did not give American fishing vessels the privilege of fishing in Canadian territorial waters. At this abrupt resurrection of a claim which the American plenipotentiaries had repeatedly and emphatically declared they had no intention of making, the burly Tupper exploded.

Chamberlain, he reported to Macdonald, was "wildly indignant".[31] The leader of the British delegation had come to the
angry conclusion that the American plenipotentiaries were
"a lot of dishonest tricksters". "I am afraid," Thompson wrote
sardonically to his wife, "nothing will come of our mission but
the board bills. These Yankee politicians are the lowest race
of thieves in existence."[32]

Macdonald accepted this second revelation much more
equably than the furious diplomatists in Washington. He
had been disillusioned by the whole wretched business. The
treaty—if a treaty were ever signed—would be of almost no
value to Canada and would bring no prestige to the Canadian
government. He did not much care whether an agreement was
reached or not; but since Canada had been manœuvred into
such restricted and unfavourable ground, he was determined to
dispute every remaining inch of the way. "I think the Americans
are merely bargaining like costermongers,"[33] he wrote to Lord
Lansdowne on February 1. He resolved to be equally tenacious.
The conference, after its first salutary explosion of temper,
settled down into an extremely suspicious, close-fisted examination of the Canadian draft treaty, and of its much abbreviated
version, the *modus vivendi*, which dealt merely with the commercial privileges of American fishing vessels in Canadian ports.

Virtually nothing else was discussed. Macdonald was not
anxious to hasten the settlement of the Alaskan boundary.[34]
Neither were the Americans. And when Tupper and Chamberlain brought up the question of the American seizures of
Canadian sealing vessels in Bering Sea, the American plenipotentiaries, in exact imitation of their predecessors when confronted by the Fenian claims, replied very firmly that the
Bering Sea matter was not within their terms of reference.
There was nothing to do but talk of the North Atlantic fisheries
—of fish, fishing vessels, fishing licences, fishing supplies, and
tariffs on fish. For another ten days the mean, trivial argument
continued, and then it drew sluggishly to a close. ". . . You
will see that we are to have a treaty," Macdonald wrote unenthusiastically to the Governor-General.[35] On February 15, the
much-debated document was signed. On February 20, it was

transmitted, with a letter of recommendation, by President Cleveland to the American Senate.

Three days later, the second session of the sixth Parliament of Canada opened at Ottawa.

IV

"I hope that you three will be able to return soon to prepare for Parliament," Macdonald wrote to Tupper on February 6. "We are quite at a standstill about legislation. I don't know what to put into the speech from the throne."[86] Two days before the opening he was still apparently undecided, for on February 21 he wrote to Lord Lansdowne, promising to settle the topics of "the speech" that afternoon and to send the draft over the next day.[87] His embarrassments and uncertainties were real, and curiously revealing. He had half a dozen subsidiary projects, most of them postponed and far from completion, by which he hoped to extend and develop the main lines of his programme. But the main lines of his programme had been laid down long before this. His most creative period as a legislator was over. All he could do—if he could do that—was to save an achievement threatened by adverse economic circumstances and fanatical human attacks. All he could do was to hang on, in the hope of better times, in the hope that his efforts would be finally justified by success. He had lost the initiative. And the initiative had been ruthlessly grasped by much more extreme and violent men. These new men were beginning to appear in federal politics. They were already very prominent in provincial affairs.

The five provincial conspirators who had met at Quebec had spent a part of the winter in glorifying the new "Quebec Resolutions" to their respective legislatures. Mowat was perhaps the most formidable member of the gang, Mercier the most sinister, and Greenway, who had replaced the luckless Norquay, would in all probability prove to be the most obstreperous. "He is so thoroughly unprincipled," Macdonald wrote of Greenway to one of his supporters in Manitoba, "that he would be sure to play a game similar to that of Norquay and be quite regardless

⋆GRIP⋆

SIR JOHN'S DELICATE SITUATION.

Greenway.—Drop your Disallowance Policy in Manitoba or——!!!

Stephen (C.P.R.)—Don't drop your Disallowance Policy in Manitoba or——!!!

of the evil consequences of the agitation on the Province so
long as he is able to retain office."[88] It was quite certain that
Greenway would quickly signalize his elevation to power by
a violent effort to end the Canadian Pacific monopoly. What
was the Dominion government to do? Macdonald was embarrassed by Tupper's unguarded promise, made several years ago
in the House, that the monopoly would be surrendered as soon
as the road was finished. He was still more embarrassed by his
knowledge of the evil effects which the Manitoba agitation was
having upon the Canadian Pacific, the Canadian west, and the
Canadian government. But there was only one way in which
the monopoly could be ended. He would have to make a
financial agreement with the Canadian Pacific Railway Company—an agreement which, in the end, would probably not
cost the country a copper but which, at the moment, might be
very unpopular politically. Could he risk it? He decided that
he would have to take the chance. And in the week before the
opening of Parliament he sat down with J. H. Pope and George
Stephen to work out an arrangement.

It was at this point that Thomas Greenway, accompanied by
his Attorney-General, Joseph Martin, descended upon Ottawa
to effect the economic liberation of his province. Greenway's
arrival, which occurred early in March, could hardly have
been more unfortunately timed. Macdonald and the Canadian
Pacific officials had not yet by any means reached an agreement.
Stephen demanded a Dominion guarantee of the principal and
interest, at four per cent, of a bond issue of twenty-two and a
half million dollars, based on the unsold lands of the company.
Macdonald was convinced that the country could not support
an issue of more than fifteen millions. The lands, he thought,
must be valued at one dollar rather than a dollar and fifty cents
an acre; and he and Pope and Tupper were determined that
the guarantee should cover interest only, not principal, and that
the rate would not be higher than three and a half per cent.
Laboriously, through a series of lengthy conferences, they were
working their way towards a settlement along these lines.[89] They
were making progress; but unfortunately the rate of progress
was not rapid enough to please the impatiently waiting Thomas
Greenway.

A theatrical diplomatist, with a relish for stormy exits, Green-way suddenly and ostentatiously left Ottawa for Toronto. "I regret your hasty departure," Macdonald patiently telegraphed to him at the Queen's Hotel. "Matters making as rapid progress as possible. I hope you will return and stay for a few days. Please answer."[40] Greenway magnanimously answered. And after the receipt, by telegraph, of a further instalment of Macdonald's regrets and assurances, he still more magnanimously returned to Ottawa.[41] But he let it be known that he was in no mood to tolerate shilly-shallying; and when, on March 30, it was learnt that his departure could not be postponed much longer, Macdonald wrote a semi-official letter, informing him that there was "a good prospect of legislation by the federal Parliament during this session which will almost if not entirely remove the reasons for the exercise of disallowance" against Manitoba railway charters.[42] This was a guarded assurance; but even so, it anticipated the solution of Macdonald's difficulties. On the very day it was sent, Stephen telegraphed from Montreal that he must ask for more time for consideration. In the end, however, his resistance was overcome; and on April 26, Langevin rose to introduce the measure which granted the government guarantee in exchange for the surrender of clause fifteen of the Canadian Pacific Railway charter.

In the meantime, while a provincial Premier was breaking through the defences of the all-Canadian transport system, two different sets of extremists, utterly opposed in character, were beginning an attack on the national policy of protection. The agitation for commercial union had not blazed, crackled, and gone out with a stink. On the contrary, the Reform caucus, at the opening of the Parliamentary session, decided to adopt unrestricted reciprocity as the official trade policy of the party; and on March 14, Sir Richard Cartwright, the "Blue Ruin Knight" as the Conservatives loved to call him, moved in the House for "the largest possible freedom of commercial inter-course" between Canada and the United States in all the manufactures and natural products of both countries.[43] The management of the Liberal party had passed out of the control of sober nationalists like Blake and Mackenzie and into the hands of adventurous opportunists such as Cartwright and the inex-

perienced Laurier. Moreover—and this, to Macdonald, was not
the least important consequence of the new Liberal programme
—one form of politico-economic extremism inevitably provoked
another. Commercial union and unrestricted reciprocity, with
their obvious threat to Canadian autonomy, naturally forced
people back upon the support of England and the Anglo-
Canadian alliance. North American continentalism found its
logical opposite in British imperialism; and Richard Cartwright,
the renegade Tory who had been so strangely transformed into
a continental unionist, was now confronted by Dalton McCarthy,
the Macdonald Conservative whose zeal for imperial federation
seemed to be outrunning his party loyalty. Ever since the
autumn, when the strength and political significance of the
commercial union movement had begun to become apparent, the
Imperial Federation League had been developing a new zeal
and popularity in Canada. McCarthy was the president of the
League; he became its parliamentary spokesman; and on April
30, he delivered in the House a considerable speech in favour
of imperial preferential trade.[44]

Macdonald took no important part in the long debate on
Cartwright's motion or in the short discussion which followed
McCarthy's speech. He was trying to delegate more of the work
of the House to his subordinates; and, in any case, his opinions
were well known. He had no objection whatever to a broad
commercial agreement with the United States or to an extension
of preferential trade within the Empire. He had tried hard
enough in the past, and would try again in the future, to secure
them both. But he disliked both continental union and imperial
federation, and for much the same reasons. He was convinced
that each carried a threat for Canadian nationality; and in both
the Cartwright and McCarthy resolutions there were, it seemed
to him, serious political implications which he and his followers
could not accept. Most of the Conservatives listened in discreet
silence to the lame debate on McCarthy's motion. Cartwright's
resolution was obviously much the more serious of the two
attacks on the national policy of protection; and it was countered
by an official Conservative amendment which welcomed freer
trade relations with the United States provided they did not

conflict with the policy "which was adopted in 1879 and which has since received in so marked a manner the sanction and approval of the people."[45] Macdonald had not the slightest intention of making any fundamental alteration in the national policy. The Canadian people had supported it in three general elections, and in both good times and bad. And now, after four stagnant years of depression, it almost looked as if good times were coming back again with a rush.

The fact was that he was beginning to feel that at least a phase of his long ordeal was over. Another parliamentary session was coming to an end. For two and a half years—ever since Riel's execution in the autumn of 1885—he had been standing with his back to the wall, warding off a ring of assailants; and now at last it began to seem that the fury of the assault was slackening. The combined onslaught of the provincial premiers had not as yet resulted in anything serious. The new Liberal leaders, like the old, had so far failed in their attacks. Best of all, there had been a sudden revival of business activity; and prices, depressed and lethargic for so long, were beginning to climb upward in a lively fashion. "The honourable gentleman," said Macdonald, referring to Wilfrid Laurier, during the debate on the speech from the throne, "has remarked the marvellous tenacity with which we proclaim the prosperity of this country. We proclaim it with considerable tenacity because we believe we are justified in doing so."[46] For the past few years the justification of this belief had been an article of Conservative faith and the substance of Conservative hopes. But had not circumstances changed at last? And was not prosperity again becoming a demonstrable fact?

Time was getting on. The great companions of the last five strenuous years of nation-building were leaving him, for their work was done. Stephen announced that he would resign the presidency of the Canadian Pacific Railway some time during the summer; and Lord Lansdowne had arranged long before to leave as soon as the current session was over. On May 22, he prorogued Parliament. He and Lady Lansdowne paid a last unexpected visit to Earnscliffe to say good-bye to Agnes and Mary;[47] and on May 23, Macdonald faced "the ablest chief"

under whom he had ever served, for the last time. "I am a bad
hand at leave-taking," Lansdowne had written only a few hours
before in a brief note of farewell, "and my difficulty does not
diminish when I feel deeply what I have to say. I do not, therefore, like to trust to this afternoon for an opportunity of saying
good-bye to you and of telling you how sorry I am to part with
you and how much I have appreciated your kindness and confidence. . . . Nor am I using an idle phrase when I say that
it has been an advantage to me not only in respect of the government of Canada to be in constant communication with one
whose experience of the public affairs of the Empire has been
as wide as yours. . . . I will not ask you not to forget us, because
I am quite sure you will remember us and not unkindly. I wish
you good-bye and as much happiness as is compatible with a
servitude from which your country will, I suspect, not allow
you to emancipate yourself."[48]

They had gone. They—and so many others—had gone or
were going. They were going with regrets or, as in Stephen's
case, with bitter resentment at Canadian ingratitude. They were
going in weariness, in illness, or in death. Thomas White, the
new Minister of the Interior, who had proved himself such an
excellent debater and administrator, died suddenly when the
session had still a month to run. John Henry Pope was ill with
what he as well as others suspected was a mortal illness. McLelan
was anxious to resign. Tupper wanted to get back to the well-
liked duties of the High Commissionership in London; and
Thompson was hopefully hinting that Macdonald might soon
find a way to fill his place and thus enable him to take advantage of an expected vacancy in the Supreme Court of Canada.
They were failing, or giving up, or backing out, or wanting to
be away. He had the disheartening and not unfamiliar sensation
that the human resources that he had painfully scraped together
were running away out of his hands.

Why should this always be so? Why was there not a small,
well-knit group of able ministers, with one recognized principal,
to whom he could surrender his leadership? His work was done.
He had created the Canadian nation. For three desperate years
he had been defending it against inward disintegration and

outward attack. Only a little over a year ago, a general election had been triumphantly won. There was still ample time for a new leader to take over, before the government would have to go to the country once more. And if he was ever to retire, if he was ever to get relief before death claimed him, this, in all probability, was his last real chance.

He talked the matter over with Stephen and with Tupper. But he could see no clear way stretching ahead. Who was to succeed him as leader? Ten years ago he had told a cheering audience at Kingston that Tupper was his appropriate and worthy successor. But that was back in 1877, and in the meantime many things had happened. Tupper had begun a new career as a Canadian diplomat; Tilley had definitely retired from public affairs; and Langevin, the only other minister whose political career stretched back into the pre-Confederation days, had become, after Macdonald, the senior member of the Cabinet. Langevin's influence and prestige, of course, had never equalled Cartier's; but during the perilous days of the Riel crisis he had definitely grown in stature. His loyalty had preserved the solidarity of the Cabinet and prevented the open declaration of a racial war; and in gratitude Macdonald may have agreed that these services gave Langevin a good claim to the succession of leadership. But was this agreement—if it existed—still valid? And, above all, was this the moment to bring it into effect? The jealousies and antagonisms which divided the French-Canadian leaders were notorious. "The mutual distrust among them is apparently irreconcilable,"[49] Macdonald reminded Tupper ruefully. And Stephen, after a long conversation with a French-Canadian politician, reported that the Quebec members would probably prefer Tupper to any leader of their own.[50] Was this a possible solution? Before the end of the session Macdonald talked the matter over once again with the Nova Scotian leader.[51] But Tupper apparently did not believe that the understanding with Langevin should be broken, and probably preferred to go back to his London job. It was settled. Tupper resigned his office as Minister of Finance, was reappointed High Commissioner, and immediately after the session was over, left for England.

The best and most reliable of Macdonald's captains had gone. He was virtually the solitary active survivor of his generation of British North American politicians. How could he give up now? He would have to hang on, for a while at least. He would have to finish the toilsome and ungrateful job of reconstructing the Cabinet once again, and he would have to see the new Governor-General, Lord Stanley of Preston, suitably welcomed and installed. "I am afraid," he wrote to Lord Lansdowne, "that Lady Lansdowne and you have rather spoiled both my wife and myself, and that it will be some time before we become reconciled to the newcomers."[52] There were so many newcomers these days! There were so many strange faces! He was an old man with a strangely youthful elasticity of spirit. And he had stretched it to the utmost.

V

The summer was a dull and unexciting one, spent quietly at Dalhousie in New Brunswick and in a tour of Cape Breton Island. Stephen resigned the presidency of the Canadian Pacific Railway early in August and for a while Macdonald hoped vainly, longingly, that he might pay a long-desired visit to England in the ex-president's company. But this was not to be. There were far too many dangerously unpleasant situations in Canada that summer to permit his slipping away. And if the Canadian troubles had not been enough, and more than enough, by themselves, there were also the extravagances of an approaching American presidential election. American presidential elections often saw the emergence, for the benefit of millions of Anglophobe Irish Americans, of at least one or two highly acrimonious contentions between the United States and Great Britain or British North America. Macdonald took the appearance of these contentions for granted. He was convinced that they were frequently drummed up, if not virtually invented, for election purposes. But in 1888 there was no need for Democrats or Republicans to exercise their creative powers. Issues already existed. They were the still undecided fate of the Chamberlain-

Bayard Treaty and the increasingly contentious dispute over the fur-seal fisheries of Bering Sea.

The Senate had not yet accepted the Chamberlain-Bayard Treaty; and the fur-seal dispute was apparently no nearer solution than it had been in the summer of 1886, when the first Canadian sealing vessels had been arrested on the high seas. During the spring the American Department of State proposed the establishment of a close season, which would last from April to November, and during which no pelagic or open-sea fishing for seals could be carried on. This was a humane proposal ostensibly advanced with an anxious desire to protect the seals from destruction; but to Lord Lansdowne and his ministers it seemed probable that the principal beneficiaries of the plan would, oddly enough, be the American fur-seal fishermen rather than the seals themselves. The prohibition of pelagic fishing alone would totally prevent fishing on the high seas by Canadian vessels while at the same time it would generously permit the wholesale slaughter of the animals on the Pribilof Islands by the American Alaska Fur Company. The magnanimity of this offer did not greatly impress Macdonald. He somewhat grudgingly agreed that Canada was ready "to join with other governments in providing means to prevent extermination of the fur seal in the North Pacific";[53] and the negotiations dragged on inconclusively into the summer. "*Quoad* Bering's Sea*," he wrote to Lord Stanley from Inch Arran House, the hotel at which he stayed in Dalhousie, "I think I can read between the lines that Mr. Bayard desires to play with the subject and postpone the settlement until after the presidential election in November. . . . Bayard or rather Cleveland dare not give the least evidence of concession now, as it would at once be used as a cry against him at the polls."[54]

He had warned the Governor-General that English-speaking countries could expect little more than calculated snubs from the United States during election time. He had learnt the truth of this by frequently repeated and bitter experience; but even he was somewhat surprised to see the completeness with which American foreign policy had apparently become the sport of American domestic politics. Cleveland and his Republican

opponents were equally determined to pose as the vindicators
of American rights; they were equally prepared to make use of
the fisheries issue for an exhibition of republican valour. On
August 21, the Senate rejected the Chamberlain-Bayard Treaty;
and two days later—with the plain intention of outdoing one
piece of heroics by another still more sensational—President
Cleveland sent Congress a message requesting the power to
proclaim a state of complete commercial non-intercourse with
Canada.

It was true that the advantages of the Treaty were not completely lost, for the *modus vivendi* accompanying it was put into
force; and it was almost certain that the Senate, whose anti-
British thunder had been so neatly stolen, would not give its
support to Cleveland's sweeping measure of economic retaliation.
But it was not altogether surprising that the Canadians were
somewhat alarmed by a declaration so unequivocally truculent
that it might have served as a suitable preliminary to war. Macdonald characteristically tried to make light of the matter.
"Cleveland, I fancy," he wrote realistically to Lord Lansdowne,
"had ascertained that the Irish vote would carry New York
against him, and so in desperation took an extra twist at the tail
of the British lion."[55] Yet the violence of this "extra twist"
settled Macdonald's plans for the late summer. "I had almost
made up my mind to take a run to England," he told Stephen
regretfully, "when the President's message came out. It was
impossible to foresee what would be the action of the President
or the Senate, and I thought it necessary to be on the spot, so
that Canada might be ready to take any step that might be
forced on us by such action."[56]

The American presidential election was the most important,
but by no means the only, reason for his remaining on sentry
duty at Ottawa. The titanic engagements of American national
affairs had their minor equivalents in the alarms and excursions
of Canadian provincial politics. It was a noisy and quarrelsome
summer—a still more noisy and quarrelsome autumn. Collect-
ively the provinces seemed quiescent. They were making no
obvious moves to implement the reforming resolutions of the
interprovincial conference. But individually the more obstrep-

erous among their number were creating as large a commotion
as ever. The legislature of Quebec had been recently passing
some very controversial statutes; and the national stage continued
to resound to the turbulent activities of Thomas Greenway. As
soon as the monopoly clause had been repealed, he proceeded,
as Stephen had always feared he would, to make an agreement
with the Northern Pacific Railroad for the completion and operation of the Red River Valley Railway. And when the Canadian
Pacific officials attempted, by means of an injunction, to prevent
the construction of a branch of this new system, Greenway's
Attorney-General, Joseph Martin, called out volunteer police
to protect the work. For a brief while, there was a threat of a
mimic civil war.

Macdonald kept trying, with extreme difficulty, to maintain
his precarious position between these two embittered opponents,
and to force each one of them to keep the peace. "The more
I think over the course of Manitoba, and especially of the Win-
nipegers, the more astonished I am," he wrote to John Schultz,
the new Lieutenant-Governor of the Province. "They seem
resolved upon driving the C.P.R. into a hostile position, as they
treat the company as though it were an enemy of their Province,
and so blind are they to the consequences of their acts that they
are urging the C.P.R. to extend their lines and build additional
branches at the same time that they are passing charters and
entering into negotiations with a foreign corporation to build
rival lines."[57] Obviously the conduct of Manitoba was inexcus-
able; and if Greenway undertook to defend his extravagances
with a questionable use of legislative power, Macdonald was
quite prepared to resort to disallowance once again.[58] He would
stand no nonsense from Greenway; but equally he was not
entirely convinced by the lugubrious air of injured virtue adopted
by Stephen. He reminded the ex-president that the Canadian
Pacific had, on its part, been busily acquiring railway properties
in the United States, and that Greenway could not be greatly
blamed "for desiring to get as much railway accommodation
for his Province as he can". Stephen's pessimism and Stephen's
bitter disappointment at the black ingratitude of the Canadian
people both betokened, he thought, a far too sensitive state of

mind. "Meanwhile," he wrote with cheerful cynicism, "don't be disgusted at the ingratitude of the Manitobans. I have been long enough in public life to know how little of that commodity there exists in this world."[59]

There was another and a still harder test for his political realism that autumn. The American presidential election was rapidly approaching; and there were so many unsettled accounts between Canada and the United States that he waited for it with perceptibly more anxiety than he had four years before. "I hope Cleveland will succeed," he wrote to Lord Lansdowne, "as if Harrison is President Blaine will be, as Secretary of State, the actual government. This means continual discomfort for Canada not only for four years, but Blaine will work steadily for the presidentship for the following term, and will therefore throw himself into the arms of the Irish Americans."[60] The abandon with which both sides flung themselves into the arms of the Irish Americans and the confidence with which they both relied upon the vote-getting power of unfriendliness to England and Canada surprised and dismayed the Governor-General;[61] and even Macdonald, who thought he knew a great deal about American politics, was somewhat disconcerted by the astounding climax of the campaign. It was a relatively unknown Republican voter who succeeded in applying the methods of the *agent provocateur* to the business of bedevilling Anglo-American relations. Pretending to be a naturalized Englishman named Murchison, he wrote to the British Minister at Washington, asking his advice on how he should vote; and Sir Lionel Sackville-West—he became Lord Sackville of Knole about this time—unguardedly replied that he thought the Democratic party was still desirous of maintaining friendly relations with Great Britain and still ready to settle all questions with Canada. On October 24, the Republican managers published this letter; and two days later, annoyed with the British Minister's interference in American politics and well aware of the fact that to be credited with friendly feelings towards England and Canada was the political equivalent of a criminal charge, Cleveland kicked Lord Sackville back to England with what a supporter enthusiastically described as "your biggest boot of best leather".[62]

Macdonald had reminded Stephen that "there is no saying what the Yankees may do in stress of politics".[63] He was sorry for Lord Sackville, though he thought the net in which he had been caught was a flimsy one;[64] and he was not surprised to see Cleveland defeated and Blaine installed as Secretary of State. ". . . We must take things as they come," he had characteristically written to Lord Lansdowne, early in the campaign, when he still hoped that Cleveland would be elected; and he now tried to draw some comfort for himself and Tupper from the fact that Harrison had the two houses of Congress with him and that, if he wished for conciliation, he would not have to face the organized obstruction which had so troubled his predecessor. The ultimate fate of the Fisheries Treaty still rested in suspense. The settlement of the Bering Sea dispute had not even been begun. Altogether there were half a dozen problems in trade, transport, and communications which Macdonald still had to keep regretfully in the category of unfinished business. He was still interested in a Pacific cable and a subsidized steamship service from Vancouver to Australasia and the Far East; he was prepared to give considerable assistance to a fast line of Atlantic steamers to Montreal and Halifax. He had any number of things that he wanted to talk over with the members of the British government. Most unfortunately his visit to England, projected for that autumn, had had to be postponed. But, as he told Tupper, he had some faint hopes that the session of 1889 might be a short one. And if happily it turned out to be, he would hurry over to England in the spring.

Meanwhile, at home, there was some ground for encouragement. There were some good reasons for believing that the organized opposition which he faced was not nearly so formidable as it had been twelve months ago. The provincial premiers, having made one last vain effort to inveigle Macdonald into a discussion of the resolutions of the interprovincial conference, tacitly abandoned their attempt to reform the constitution.[65] The formal attack against the primacy of the Dominion had failed. The angry excitement over railways in Manitoba seemed to be gradually subsiding. And, best of all, the popularity of unrestricted reciprocity was apparently receding before the onrush of returning prosperity. There could surely be no doubt about it now. Times were definitely improving. "The crop in Manitoba and the north-west is very good on the whole," Macdonald wrote to George Stephen late in October, "and, as prices are good, the whole country is happy except at Prince Albert and along the North Saskatchewan where the crop can't be brought out." There were troubled spots, of course; but, on the whole, the Dominion was regaining zest and confidence. The time soon came, early in January, when he could actually inform Stephen that there was "quite a revival of a spirit of enterprise in Canada".[66]

Another year had gone by. "Today I am seventy-four years old," he wrote to Professor Williamson on January 11, "a fact which brings serious reflections. I am in fairly good health for my age, but can't expect that to last very long, as my work increases faster than my years. I must soon call a halt."[67] He must soon call a halt or death would take him before he ever had a chance to enjoy a holiday. Death had taken his sister Louisa that autumn. For long years she had been a chronic invalid; and he had fussed over her and scolded her affectionately for her imprudence, just as, in the old days at Hay Bay and the Stone Mills, he and Margaret had protectively looked after baby "Lou". Only last April the doctor had given him a fairly satisfactory report on her condition. "He speaks, however," he chided her gently, "in the strongest terms of your refusal to keep quiet. Complete rest, he says, is your best medicine, and you won't take it. . . . Now, my dear Louisa, you really must take better care of yourself, or you and I will quarrel."[68] She had resembled him physically. She had had more than a little of his gay vitality of spirit; and she had lingered on, frail, cheerful, indomitable, through years of weakness and suffering. Now she was gone; and Maria Macpherson, the dead Isabella's sister, was the last link with the past.

Everything was changing—even the physical circumstances of his daily life. Late in 1888 they moved back, from the rented quarters in which they had been living during the autumn, to an enlarged, improved, and redecorated Earnscliffe. "Reynolds' house," though comfortable enough, had been anything but spacious when he bought it six years before; but now, with a handsome new dining-room, and a small additional office built specially for himself, it had become a much more suitable residence for a Prime Minister who had many visitors, a lot of correspondence to keep up, and a great deal of entertaining to do. "It is the pride of Agnes's heart," he wrote to Professor Williamson;[69] and he himself was pleasantly satisfied with his recreated property. After three-quarters of a century he had finally secured a house which was fit for the job to which he had given his life. He had lived here for the last five years. He would probably die here. He might—who could tell?—retire to enjoy its quiet for a few years in peace.

The improvement of Earnscliffe was, in its way, the Macdonald family's farewell to the drab, defeated days of the immediate past. Macdonald could not live in the past. He had to live in the present and future; and his own and his country's perspectives were brighter and more spacious than they had been. Prosperity was coming back, and prosperity was a wonderful solvent of obstinate difficulties, a wonderful pacifier of unruly spirits. Would it not drop a golden curtain of oblivion over such extremist politicians as Honoré Mercier and Thomas Greenway? Macdonald began to indulge the hope that it would. "Mercier is killing himself in the east," he informed Stephen fairly confidently, "as Greenway is doing in the west. I hope, ere long, to get rid of both those scamps."[70]

No hope could have been more delusive.

VI

Honoré Mercier was the perfect example of the new generation of Canadian politicians, the men of provincialism and vehemence who had been flung up by the vast upheaval of the Riel agitation. In 1887, he had sought to organize a constitutional attack upon the unity of the Dominion; and now, by pushing through a settlement of the dispute over the estates of the Jesuits, he had suddenly raised an issue which seriously threatened the cultural concord of the country. The Jesuits'

Estates controversy was, in fact, exactly the kind of politico-religious dispute which had set French-speaking and English-speaking Canadians against each other in the 1850's, and against the resurgence of which the Fathers of Confederation had tried to guard in the provisions of the British North America Act. Yet here once more, its malevolent aspect apparently unaltered, was the old problem of the relation of church and state. In the past few years, all kinds of inward weaknesses and outward attacks, constitutional, political, and economic, had threatened Macdonald's national structure. And now at last had come a renewal of the old and most terrible calamity, the cultural conflict.

It was a complex matter, bristling with highly debatable points. The original Society of Jesus, which had been suppressed by papal brief in 1773 throughout the entire Roman Catholic world, had been granted large estates in New France before the British conquest of 1763. In 1800, after the last surviving Jesuit had died, the estates were confiscated to the Crown; and in 1831 they were transferred, as an endowment in support of education, to the control and management of the legislature of Lower Canada. It was not until the 1860's, when the Jesuits had re-established themselves in Canada East, that their demands for compensation for their lost estates began to be seriously pressed; and then the claims of the Society were vigorously challenged by the counter-claims of the Roman Catholic bishops, who argued that the property of religious houses suppressed by papal brief reverted to the hierarchy of the dioceses in which they were situated. Mercier determined to end the resulting controversy by a final settlement which would be backed by the authority of the Pope; and the resulting Jesuits' Estates Bill, which was passed by the Quebec legislature during the summer of 1888, settled the conflicting claims for compensation in accordance with the Pope's decision. The Act provided four hundred thousand dollars to be divided among the various rival claimants. It also put sixty thousand dollars at the disposal of the Protestant Committee of Public Instruction for Quebec.

The opposition to this measure developed slowly, but it

developed surely none the less. During the autumn and winter of 1888-9, it gradually gathered force and conviction. Why, asked Protestant newspaper editors and clerical leaders, should either the bishops or the Jesuits be given any compensation whatever? A papal brief could not confer any property rights in a British country; a new Society of Jesus could not revive the claims of a defunct corporation simply because it had appropriated its name. The whole question of the public endowment of religious bodies had been finally settled, once and for all, by the secularization of the Clergy Reserves. It was unfair and unwise to depart from this decision for the benefit of one religious communion only; and it was particularly objectionable to waive the rule in respect of property which had been transferred in trust to the province for the support of education. Finally—and this was, perhaps, the gravest part of the indictment—the authority of the papacy had been invoked to effect the settlement, and the correspondence between the Pope and Mercier had actually been printed *in extenso* in the preamble to the Bill. For all these good and more than sufficient reasons, the opponents of the Jesuits' Estates Bill began to urge the Dominion government to intervene to prevent the operation of this most iniquitous law. And in January 1889, the first important petitions requesting disallowance arrived in Ottawa.

"Am I safe in assuring the Duke of Norfolk," Tupper had inquired by telegraph a week before Christmas, "that the Jesuits' Act will not be disallowed?"[71] Macdonald replied that the matter would be settled by the middle of January. For some reason which he could not, or did not want to, explain, a few ministers evidently desired a short delay for consideration.[72] But by the middle of January, with petitions already arriving in Ottawa and a dangerous agitation under way, there was no more time for temporizing or delay, and the government hastened to announce that it had no intention of disallowing the Jesuits' Estates Act. With this decision Macdonald was in complete agreement. He did not at all approve of some of the expressions used in the preamble of the Act; he suspected that they had very possibly been placed there with the express purpose of provoking him into an unwary and unjustifiable exercise of the power of disallowance. But he was not to be caught. Disallowance was unnecessary and would be unwise. There was, as he told one Protestant clergyman, no need for the Dominion to take action in the national interest against a statute which did not in any way affect any other of the provinces.[78] The Dominion would take no action. And surely, once this decision had been firmly announced, the excitement would rapidly die away.

But it did not. Instead it grew more general and more passionate. The issue of the Jesuits' Estates Act and its disallowance would now very probably become a parliamentary matter; and—what was much more painful to bear—there was a very real probability that it would be raised, not by some Calvinistic Reformer, but by that lost leader of the Conservatives, Dalton McCarthy. McCarthy, like Mercier and Greenway, was a typical politician of the new age. Less than five years ago he had brusquely declined Macdonald's offer of the Ministry of Justice. He had evidently found a much greater interest and a more important meaning in the turbulent politics which had come into being with the depression and the North-West Rebellion than he ever would have done in the routines of administration and compromise. He had opposed Cartwright's North-American continentalism with imperial federation. Now he and his friends would confront Mercier's French-Canadian Catholic separatism with the ideal of a unified English-speaking Canada under the British Crown. "I have been asked to let you know," he informed Macdonald by letter on March 1, "that at three o'clock—or when the orders for the day are called— O'Brien proposes to say that he will take an early opportunity of moving respecting the disallowance of the Jesuits' Estates Bill."[74]

Parliament had opened on January 31. Macdonald had not looked forward to it. "I am in good health, but rather dread another session," he admitted to George Stephen; and now, when the spring and prorogation were still far away, the real trouble which justified his vague apprehensions had come. On March 15 he called a party caucus. The vast majority of the Conservative members joined him in appealing to W. E. O'Brien to drop his motion requesting the Dominion government to disallow the Jesuits' Estates Bill. But these entreaties were useless. Despite the fact that their resolution virtually expressed a want of confidence in the Conservative government, O'Brien, McCarthy and their small group of associates persisted in their decision.[75] They offered, indeed, to resign from the party; but this, of course, was the last thing that Macdonald wanted. He hoped to maintain the strength and unity of Conservatism and to prevent Canadian party politics from becoming the fanatical politics of "race" and religion. "I should be sorry," he wrote to Colonel O'Brien on March 20, "if any member should think himself bound to sever from the Conservative party because he voted for your motion."[76]

In the great debate which began on Tuesday, March 26, Macdonald took only a relatively unimportant part. The main defence of the government's position was made by Sir John Thompson; the moderate who had succeeded to the post of Minister of Justice, answered the extremist who had declined it. It was not until late on Thursday night, at the close of the third day of debate, that Macdonald rose to speak. For a few minutes he amused himself and the House by congratulating the Liberals upon the unanimity with which they were about to support the government's policy of non-interference in provincial affairs. But most of his speech was given over to an account of the politico-religious quarrels of his young manhood and to a reasoned appeal against the renewal of the desperate antagonisms of race and religion. "What would be the consequences of a disallowance?" he asked the House rhetorically. "Agitation, a quarrel—a racial and religious war would be aroused. The best interests of the country would be prejudiced, our credit would be ruined abroad, and our social relations destroyed at home."[77] That was why he hoped that the revolt of McCarthy and his independent followers would not spread. That was why, when, one hour later, the final vote was taken, he could not help feeling an enormous sense of relief. Only thirteen members— eight Conservatives, including O'Brien himself, and five Liberals —had voted in favour of the motion; and one hundred and eighty-eight had voted against it.[78] The whole difficult business was over—and well over. The "noble thirteen"—or the "devil's

dozen"—had declared themselves. The statement of their con-
scientious convictions was to be respected. There would be no
expulsions and no recriminations. And now, having talked the
whole matter over sensibly and decided it sensibly, the nation
would be at peace.

But peace did not come. On March 25, the day before the
debate began in the House of Commons at Ottawa, a great
mass meeting in Toronto resolved that it was the duty of
Canadian citizens to use all legitimate means to prevent the
Jesuits' Estates Bill from being carried into effect. Another
still larger meeting was planned for April 22; and the Toronto
Citizens' Committee announced that on this occasion Dalton
McCarthy would speak. It was a plain intimation that McCarthy
proposed to carry the issue of the Jesuits' Estates from the
Canadian Parliament to the Canadian people. And early in
April—as if to make the meaning of his independent course
still more explicit—he resigned from the presidency of the
Liberal-Conservative Union of Ontario. Macdonald, in a final
appeal to an old and admired friend and follower, begged him
to withdraw his resignation and to give up a senseless, primitive
agitation which threatened to divide the party and the country.[79]
But McCarthy was adamant. The fundamental question in
Canadian politics, he told Macdonald in reply, was not whether
Canada was to be annexed to the United States or not, "but
whether this country is to be English or French".[80] It was a
vague, inflammatory issue on which scores of thousands of
excited people seemed determined to take a stand. Early in
June, eight hundred representatives from Ontario met in
Toronto to form the Equal Rights Association; and on June 24,
St. Jean Baptiste's day, Mercier and a score of French-Canadian
speakers thundered a defiant rejoinder.

Macdonald's summer was settled. The Jesuits' Estates Bill
had been received in Ottawa on August 8, 1888; and for a year
from that date the Governor-General in Council could disallow
it. As the fatal, final day approached, the agitation grew shriller
and shriller. ". . . One of those insane crazes," he wrote to
Lord Lansdowne, "has taken possession of the ultra Protestants
which can only be compared with the Popish Plot or the papal
aggression agitation which ended so ingloriously in the Ecclesi-

astical Titles Act of Lord John Russell. The drum ecclesiastic is beating in all parts of Ontario. Dislike of the French has much to do with the excitement, which I think will soon die out, but I shouldn't like a general election just now."[81] For a few weeks anything might happen. He would have to stay and keep up his protective watch over the country. Thompson pressed him to go to England, adding reassuringly that the ministers would "promise not to fight *much* until you could return".[82] But Macdonald realized that the English mission would have to be postponed once more. Would he ever see London and the sedate, familiar front of Batt's Hotel again? There would never be another welcoming letter from John Rose awaiting him at Liverpool. Rose was dead. And Rose's departure had darkened his own life and driven home the terrible uncertainty of his hold upon it. One day, nearly a year ago now, in a moment of depression, he had written to Lord Lansdowne that he feared they had met for the last time. What if it should turn out to be true?

He had disappointments and worries enough. But on June 7, when he appeared before Convocation of the University of Toronto to receive an honorary degree from its President, Sir Daniel Wilson, he seemed as unconcerned and sprightly as ever.[83] His physical alertness still matched his astounding buoyancy of spirits. When Sir Daniel had finished his presentation, Macdonald jumped up, with almost "youthful alacrity" to receive his degree; and when the ceremonies were over, he smiled, and laughed, and shook hands with scores of people, while the students cheered him loudly. "I wonder," he inquired gaily of W. R. Meredith, as they were leaving the hall together, "if this war between Queen's and Toronto will supersede the Jesuit agitation, eh?" If only it were true! But the Jesuit agitation was something very different from a debate over matriculation examinations. August 8 was approaching, and with it the last demonstrations which the Equal Rights Association was certain to make. He would await these final ructions imperturbably; and before the end of June he was back at "Les Rochers", at Rivière du Loup. "The weather is delightful," he wrote to Thompson who was still sweltering away at his desk in the capital, "and it is all the more enjoyable when we know that there is only a sheet of brown paper between you Ottawaites and Hell."[84]

He had one strong card yet to play in the acrimonious game of the Jesuits' Estates Bill. As early as May 31, he had written to Tupper, urging him to obtain from the imperial Attorney-General and Solicitor-General an official opinion "affirming the validity and constitutionality" of the much disputed act.[85] But time went by and the answer did not come; and when finally it did arrive its wording was disappointingly defective. In the meantime the Equal Rights Association requested an interview with Lord Stanley in order to present its views in favour of disallowance; and Hugh Graham of the Montreal Star offered five thousand dollars in aid of a test of the constitutionality of the act before the Supreme Court of Canada. Macdonald was not entirely satisfied with the phrasing of the answer which the Governor-General proposed to give to the deputation of Equal Righters;[86] but on August 2 the interview came off quietly enough, the petitioners behaving, Lord Stanley considered, "with great moderation".[87]

"The Governor-General's answer has taken very well," Macdonald wrote to Thompson with satisfaction.[88] He was equally pleased with the Minister of Justice's "admirable paper" on Hugh Graham's petition. Finally, towards the end of August, a revised and much more acceptable version of the British law officers' opinion of the constitutionality of the Jesuits' Estates Bill arrived in Ottawa.[89] It was published on September 3, the day after Macdonald finally left Rivière du Loup for the capital. He was almost beginning to believe that the affair was at an end. The time for disallowance had gone past. The Jesuits' Estates Act was now the law of the land. Surely the ineffectual agitation against it was over, and surely the dangerous cultural conflict which it had provoked would now die away?

He was wrong. In the meantime, Dalton McCarthy had left for the west to raise the issue of the French language and Separate Schools in Manitoba and the North-West Territories.

Chapter Fifteen

The Last Election

I

He was nearly seventy-five years old. He faced the world like an old lion, less strong than he had been and conscious of his waning strength, but still powerful and proud of his continued mastery. He was tall and slight; his carriage was erect; he held himself like a young man; and his hair, waving in a fine, thin, silvery cloud, was a not too unsubstantial ghost of the curly chevelure of his young manhood. His eyes were tired and disillusioned; but his mouth was firm with strength and humour; and there was no bitterness, no mere shrewdness, no cunning in small deceptions in his face. His face was wise, and deeply experienced, and full of battle. He offered no apologies, he suffered from no vain regrets. He stood erect and determined, with an air of debonair defiance, of jaunty courage.

He had outlasted a whole political generation. The comrades and antagonists of his young manhood—MacNab and Hincks, Cameron and Foley—were dead or forgotten. George Brown, the greatest rival of his entire career, had been ten years in his grave. Tilley and Campbell and McLelan had all retired into the honourable obscurity of lieutenant-governorships; and it was half a century now since that day in the autumn of 1839 when the young Alexander Campbell had first walked into his small office in Kingston. He had seen seven governors-general come and go. He heard from some of them still, though at longer and longer intervals; and once a letter from old Lord Monck, who was so stiffened with rheumatism now that he could scarcely get about, brought back a sudden recollection of the plans and struggles of a quarter-century ago.[1] He remembered that first of July of 1867, when they had all worked away in the humid Privy Council chamber, "setting the coach in motion" in Monck's own phrase, while outside the hot sun shimmered on the terraces of Parliament Hill.

He had outlasted them all. Yet he had not exhausted his resources. He had not yet come to the end of those reserves from which there seemed always to be something else that he could draw. Campbell had spoken of his "many-sidedness". "Often," McLelan wrote admiringly, "when Council was perplexed and you had made things smooth and plain, I have thought of the expression an old farmer made about my late father when he saw him accomplish something that had puzzled all the neighbours. 'There are wheels in that man that have never been moved yet.' And so I have thought of my leader that there is a reserve force—'wheels that have not yet been moved'."[2] He had dreamed and planned and created; and his great design for Canada had been laid down, in all its essentials, long before this. But he had not exhausted his creative impulse or his creative capacity. He was still interested in general ideas rather than in administrative detail. He had a young man's zest for new constructive policies and a young man's impatience with mere competent routines. "I told Bowell just before leaving," he wrote to Thompson during the summer of 1889, "that while all my colleagues diligently attend to their several departments I cannot get them to consider, or rather to express any opinion on the general policy of the government unless I initiated it. I instanced the question of our proposed conference with the Australasian Colonies when I four times invited the attention of Council to consider it, but got nothing more than a general acquiescence in whatever I proposed. . . . Now this acquiescence is flattering enough, but it does not help me. . . ."[3]

His greatest failure, perhaps, was his failure to obtain a copious and satisfactory source of help. The Cabinet, which a few years ago had been too old, had certainly become more youthful in character as a result of the recent appointments. But had it in the process acquired a new sense of direction and purpose? Could he place any more reliance upon its unity and wisdom? He shook his head sadly. The best of the veterans were continuing to drop out of the ranks; and John Henry Pope, one of the last of them, had died after a long illness in April. Langevin, the oldest in point of service after Macdonald, was experienced, loyal, uncomplaining; but he remained an unimpressive, unimaginative man, immersed in the humdrum routines and questionable patronage of the Department of Public Works. Chapleau had fire and eloquence; but he was always restlessly attempting to extend and strengthen his political empire. "Chapleau, as ambitious and unscrupulous as ever," Macdonald wrote to Lansdowne in the spring of 1889, "is arousing his countrymen to claim for him poor Pope's succession as Minister of Railways, which I sternly refuse him, as the office would give him unlimited opportunities to job which he would eagerly avail himself of, and he will be discontented and intriguing."[4] In the end—it was a desperate remedy, for he had not administered a department for years—Macdonald had to take over the Department of Railways and Canals himself. "I was very unwilling to do this," he told Tupper later, "but could not avoid it without a *crise ministérielle*."[5] Chapleau would probably have been quite ready to precipitate a *crise ministérielle*. He was a difficult colleague—certainly more difficult than Caron. But even Caron was always getting into scrapes through sheer imprudence and obstinacy, and then, at the last moment, "recovering himself by his remarkable power of carrying a popular audience".

The others—most of them—were not much better, if they were no worse. The Irishmen, Frank Smith and John Costigan, were temperamental and very unreliable. There were encouraging times when Costigan "affected sobriety" and maintained his affectation; and there were deplorable periods when he forgot his pledges, and Macdonald threatened to call for his resignation.[6] Dewdney, who had been Lieutenant-Governor of the North-West Territories during the troubles of 1885, was one of the newer members of the Cabinet; but his appointment as Minister of the Interior had aroused a great deal of opposition among the French Canadians. Charles Hibbert Tupper, the High Commissioner's son, was another of the younger, newer ministers, whom Macdonald admired, though in a not uncritical fashion. "Charley has got the bumptiousness of his father," he wrote frankly to Thompson, "and should be kept in his place from the start."[7] All of them—even the young-est and most promising—had their crotchets, frailties, or defects. The Cabinet was a burden as well as a support; to maintain its tranquillity, he had been obliged, at the age of seventy-five, to take over the administration of a large department himself. And of the dozen and more ministers, only one man, John Thompson, had become a really strong stay and support. He admired Thompson's state papers. He relied upon him as government spokesman in the great debates in the Commons. He valued his advice.

Yet had he the right to assume that Thompson was his logical successor? Thompson was a Roman Catholic—a convert to Roman Catholicism. Did he dare—remembering the party and the nation—to step down in Thompson's favour? Did he want to relinquish the leadership yet? Politics was his profes-sion. He had brought to it great natural gifts; he had developed them through a lifetime of experience; and there was no honourable occupation of retirement or semi-retirement which he would willingly accept in exchange for the task to which he had given his life. Tupper, who had seen more than enough of the "crass ignorance of everything Canadian" which pre-vailed at Washington, was eager to have him take the position from which Lord Sackville had been so unceremoniously dis-missed in the autumn of 1888. "If I were Her Majesty's government," he wrote, "I would offer you a peerage and the position of minister at Washington. . . ."[8] But this suggestion, even if it had been taken up seriously, would not have interested Macdonald. He wanted neither the honour nor the job.

It was not, of course, that he had the slightest objection in principle to the grant of appropriate honours to Canadians. He had, on the contrary, always believed that "the monarchical idea should be fostered in the colonies, accompanied by some gradation of classes", and he had always hoped that the subjects of the Kingdom of Canada would be encouraged "to look for-ward to the Empress-Queen as the *fons honoris*".[9] But he knew

—and Agnes knew—that he could not hope to support the dignity of a title. "You may be sure," Agnes had written to Louisa on one occasion, "that he will *never* take a peerage. It would make us both ridiculous, and though we have been both very wicked often, I humbly think we have never been ridiculous! Nothing would distress me more than to see him—that most unfortunate of men—a *very poor lord.* . . . I know his mind well on the subject and am *positively certain* that he would never make so great a mistake as to be a peer."[10] He would not willingly accept the honour which Tupper—and no doubt many others—would have been willing enough to suggest in high places; and he did not particularly like the idea of the job to which Tupper hoped to promote him as a reward for his services.

The position of British minister at Washington was, he knew very well, the only suitable position of sufficient dignity which could be offered to him if he retired from active political life. But he was not like Howe, whose life had been embittered by his unhappy, unavailing search for an appropriate imperial appointment; and he was not by any means convinced that this particular appointment at Washington was one to which any Canadian ought to aspire as yet. "I greatly doubt the expediency of having a Canadian permanent minister at Washington," he had written to Tupper. "The present system of uniting the British minister ordinarily appointed with a Canadian whenever a question affecting Canada arises works more satisfactorily than the proposed change. I won't trouble you with all the arguments, but if you sit down and think it out, I am sure you will agree with me."[11] The case against Tupper's proposal seemed to him so obvious that it scarcely merited a lengthy statement. Besides, if Tupper still remained obstinately unconvinced, there was a final, and, in Macdonald's view, unanswerable argument. How could he go? "*Quoad* the Washington embassy," he wrote to Tupper a little later, "suffice it to say for the present that neither you nor I could be spared for the mission if offered and I don't know any other Canadian fit except perhaps Thompson."[12]

He could not go. He could not leave Canada. He instinctively assumed that his one rightful place was at Ottawa. It was not, of course, that he cherished a mere naïve belief in his own indispensability. Delusions about anything or anybody, including himself, were expensive pieces of mental furniture with which his mind was not encumbered. But deep within him lay the inarticulate conviction that so long as he was physically capable of doing so he must watch over the country which he had created. A long lifetime was scarcely long enough to complete the work which he had had in mind. For five years he had been kept almost continuously upon the defensive. But there were some signs now that the disrupting turmoil in the country was subsiding, and some reason to believe that the fury of the attacks against his position had declined. During the summer of 1889, he had turned again to some major items of unfinished business. The rejection, by the American Senate, of the Fisheries Treaty, had left Canadian-American relations in a highly unsatisfactory state. The Canadian east-west commercial system, transcontinental and transoceanic in extent, with terminals in Europe on the one hand and the Far East on the other, was a great undertaking which he had not yet strengthened and extended as much as he had hoped to do.

He was not an imperial federationist; and he knew that imperial federation, partly because of the unpopularity of its principal Canadian advocates, had become deeply suspect in French Canada. Ambitious schemes for an imperial defence system or an imperial customs union were out of the question; but he was just as convinced as he ever had been that the alliance with England and the association with the other developing nations of the Empire-Commonwealth were the surest guarantees both of Canada's political autonomy and its fiscal and commercial independence. "It looks like sheer insanity," he wrote, concerning the Liberal proposal of unrestricted reciprocity with the United States, "to propose practically to limit our foreign trade to the United States when there is such an immense opening for the development of our commerce with all the rest of the world. Our true policy is to cultivate closer commercial relations with England and the British colonies. Australia is already in communication with Canada for that purpose, and, if I mistake not the signs of the times, England will ere long think more of her children and less of strangers than she has hitherto been doing."[13]

He always hoped, of course, that as soon as Canada and the other colonies had demonstrated their ability to furnish the United Kingdom with the necessary supplies, Great Britain could be persuaded to establish a preferential tariff on foodstuffs. "I fear, however," he wrote to one British correspondent, "that the fetish of free trade has as yet too many worshippers in England to hope for such a result. However, the time will come, and we must wait."[14] In the meantime, while he waited, he was determined to explore the prospect of improved communications and increased trade with Australasia and the Far East. The British Postmaster-General had finally signed the contract with the Canadian Pacific for the carriage of the China mails; and during the summer Macdonald was considering the composition of a Canadian mission, headed by J. J. C. Abbott, which would visit Australasia and the Far East and discuss such matters as a Pacific cable, the Pacific steamship service, and the possibilities of improved trade relations with the different Australian governments.[15] Before the summer was over, he had realized that the Australian political time-table differed markedly from the Canadian, that the Australian legislatures would all be in session during the autumn, and that the Abbott "expedition" to the Antipodes would have to be postponed until the early spring of 1890 by which time, it was hoped, the Canadian Parliament would be prorogued.

But there was something more immediate and more important than Australia. There was the United States. And there was the urgent preliminary necessity of establishing a common policy with the United Kingdom on all the important points at issue, before the negotiations with the United States were pushed too dangerously far. ". . . I ask you for your opinion," Macdonald had written to Thompson fairly early in the summer, "as to what course to pursue *quoad* the Yankees. From Pauncefote's note to the Governor-General, it is clear that Lord Salisbury won't move, but shall wait for a move from the United States. And *they* won't move. Now shall we? And if yes, in what mode or direction? The *modus vivendi* will expire next February and our troubles will recommence. We must not like so many foolish virgins sit with our lamps untrimmed. 'I pause for a reply'."[16]

He did not have to pause very long. In a little over a week a lengthy, considered reply had arrived from the Minister of Justice. Thompson was in favour of an immediate "forward move" towards the United States. In his view, there were at least three important questions—Bering Sea, the North Atlantic fisheries, and trade relations—whose settlement was of vital importance to Canada. Macdonald agreed; but he knew that nothing serious could be done until the autumn, and he was convinced that no preliminary moves should be made until every item on Thompson's agenda had been thoroughly discussed with the officials in London. For years now he had been hoping vainly to cross the ocean to England. "I never saw anyone improve by a voyage as he does," Agnes had once told Louisa. And the sea voyage, and the London that lay at the other end of it, was a physical and spiritual satisfaction which he had been promising himself for a long time now, and which, because of one danger after another, he had been obliged repeatedly to postpone. Why should he postpone it any longer? Why should he not go that autumn, with another minister, with Thompson preferably, and have a thorough discussion of all issues outstanding between Canada and the United States?

It was a pleasant decision. But almost immediately it was qualified by unpleasant second thoughts. Was it really safe to go? "The chief difficulty would be—for instance, if you or I went—," he wrote to Thompson, "that Council might make some mistake on the Jesuit question and commit us on other matters. There would be great pressure on Council both from Quebec and the Maritimes during our absence."[17] The Cabinet, he could not help thinking, was, at the moment, a rather unhappy mixture of unreliable veterans and inexperienced apprentices. Could he depend upon it at a time when treacherous difficulties obviously still lay ahead? The Jesuits' Estates agitation, it was true, was gradually subsiding; but, as he told Lord Lansdowne, it was not subsiding "without leaving unfortunate consequences behind". "It has revived the hostile feelings," he explained, "that time had nearly extinguished between English and French, and which may lead to disastrous results."[18] Only a little while ago he had been congratulating himself that the agitation was really confined to Ontario and Quebec. But Canada as a whole had become an inflammable country through which a high wind of excitement and disputation was fiercely blowing. And before the summer was out, Manitoba, that most excitable of all provinces, had been fired by a fresh controversy.

Dalton McCarthy had gone west that summer. Early in August, he delivered two speeches, one at Portage la Prairie and one at Calgary; and at both places he expounded his now familiar message that a narrow, parochial, French-speaking "nationalism" should not be permitted, through special schools and special language privileges, to prevent the development of a true Canadian nationality. McCarthy had, of course, already expressed these views on a number of occasions and at considerable length; and the importance of the speeches at Portage la Prairie and Calgary lay not so much in the novelty of their ideas as in their immediate relevancy to the local situation in Manitoba and the North-West Territories. In respect of both time and place, McCarthy's utterances could scarcely have come more pat. His mere presence in the west seemed to precipitate the expression of convictions which westerners had reached long before, about which they had no longer any doubts, and which they were determined to put into immediate execution. Joseph Martin, the energetic Premier Greenway's Attorney-General, who had moved a vote of thanks after the Portage la Prairie speech, took advantage of the occasion to endorse McCarthy's views most emphatically. Within a matter of days, the government of Manitoba announced that, at the next session of the legislature, it would deal with separate schools and the legal status of the French language. Within another two months, the Assembly of the North-West Territories petitioned the federal government to move for the repeal of clause one hundred and ten, which defined the privileges of the French language in the North-West Territories Act.

II

It was a frustrating, disappointing autumn. Nothing seemed to be going right. Once again the long-delayed visit to England had to be given up. The mission to Australia was postponed. The great comprehensive scheme for the extension and improvement of the Canadian commercial system seemed everywhere to be running into obstacles and disappointments. The "Short Line"—the project of a swifter railway service from Montreal through the United States to the Maritime Provinces—had been one long tale of difficulties and disputes; and in October, Anderson and Company of Scotland, a firm which had virtually agreed to establish the fast steamship service between Canada, Great Britain and Europe, surrendered its option on the contract.[19] Relations with the Canadian Pacific Railway, which, on the whole, had remained so steadfastly good during all the desperate difficulties of 1884 and 1885, now seemed to be fraying rapidly under a number of rasping disagreements. There were disputes over the Short Line, over the selection of the company's lands, and finally—this was the most dismally acrimonious contention of all—over the condition of the government-constructed section of the railway in British Columbia. A long, complaining letter from Stephen, which reviewed these matters and bewailed the "unfairness and unfriendliness" with which the company had been treated, left Macdonald really "irate". "The charge of unjust treatment of the C.P.R. at my hands, and from *you*," he wrote indignantly, "seemed to me inexplicable —but an angry discussion won't help matters. . . . I wish you would read Charles Reade's novel of *Put Yourself in His Place*. I am sure if you were one of the ministry you would act as we are doing, but you, I fear, look only on matters from one point of view."[20]

There were too many of these disagreements. There were too many disappointments at a time when one might have expected fulfilment of hopes. The country was reasonably prosperous. The worst of the internal dissensions seemed to be dying away. But on all sides Macdonald's efforts to improve the external relations of the country appeared to have been brought to a standstill. The plan of reopening negotiations

SIR JOHN THOMPSON

with the United States on a wide range of topics had been postponed because the essential preliminary discussions with the
authorities in London had not taken place, and because, until
a new British minister, in place of the ignominiously dismissed
Lord Sackville, had been appointed to Washington, the conduct
of any serious negotiations between the two countries was
virtually impossible. In the meantime, during the season of
1889, the United States had again been vigorously asserting
its claim to a superintending control over the fur-seal fisheries
of Bering Sea. "To please the Alaska Company and the Irish,"
Macdonald explained with temperate realism to Lord Lansdowne, "a revenue cutter is seizing British Columbian sealers
and to mollify Lord Salisbury it allows them to escape."[21]
No change in the existing unsatisfactory state of affairs occurred
until late in the autumn when the new British Minister,
Sir Julian Pauncefote, finally arrived in Washington. And
then Blaine, the American Secretary of State, at once proposed
a renewal of the fur-seal negotiations.

Macdonald, ill with one of his bad bronchial colds, was
confined to Earnscliffe when the dispatch, announcing the
American proposal, arrived in Ottawa. He had always feared
Blaine's elevation to the seats of the mighty. "Were Blaine
in power," he had prophesied to Lord Lansdowne over two years
ago, "he would do everything disagreeable short of war, and
perhaps if England had trouble elsewhere, go further." And
now this man, whom he had always regarded as the personifica-
tion of American jingoism and whom he suspected of a deep-
seated hostility to Canada, was firmly installed in power. Blaine
was a fact, a "fixed fact", as Macdonald would have said himself, temporarily fixed at any rate; and it had always been his
assumption that facts must be faced, with watchful cheerfulness
or resignation, and the very best made of them. He told Lord
Stanley that Canada would accept the American proposal,
but on conditions. He stipulated that the Americans must
abandon their claim to jurisdiction in Bering Sea, that Canada
must be directly represented on the proposed joint commission,
and that its conclusions, if any, must be subject to Canadian
approval.[22]

The reply, which came quickly, was highly unsatisfactory.[23]

The United States insisted that it had never asserted the *mare clausum* doctrine and would consequently make no disclaimer. A most exasperating evasion! If the government of the United States had not asserted jurisdiction over Bering Sea, why was it instructing its officers to seize Canadian vessels in mid-ocean? In the reply which he drafted for Lord Stanley, Macdonald dealt faithfully with this important aspect of the question; but there were two other points in the American rejoinder which disturbed him only less. The first was Blaine's decided preference for an informal "diplomatic conference" rather than a commission; and the second was his blunt refusal to accept an official Canadian representative in the negotiations. Macdonald was suspicious of "diplomatic conferences", the uncertain conclusions of which could so easily be disputed or repudiated by the United States; but he looked even more darkly upon Blaine's obvious effort to depress Canada's diplomatic position. Plainly, of course, it was to the interest of the United States, in this as in all other negotiations involving British North America, to deal solely with Great Britain, the country which had little direct interest in them. But was this simple and immediate end Blaine's sole purpose? On numerous occasions and over a long period of years, the Secretary of State had shown himself consistently hostile to British North America. Might not his latest refusal be a part of the more vague and general design of embarrassing, impeding and perhaps even frustrating Canada's national development?

Even so, as Macdonald knew very well, the hope of a conference could not be given up. The only alternative was open resistance to the police authority which the Americans had been exercising in the disputed area; and the talk, which had already been going on, of sending a British man-of-war to Bering Sea to give support to the Canadian sealing vessels, filled Macdonald with deep disquietude. "I don't care to say it here lest it might be misunderstood in British Columbia," he had written to Tupper towards the end of October, "but I confess that I look with dread on the advent of a British man-of-war in the Bering Sea. A collision would not be avoided by an American officer—perhaps courted. In such a case it might not produce actual war, but Blaine would or could make it the excuse for a cessation of diplomatic or commercial intercourse."[24] Blaine's calculated snubs would have to be endured for fear of something infinitely more serious. The tactful British suggestion that a Canadian could, of course, serve as technical adviser to the Minister at Washington would have to be accepted with the best grace possible. "Canada fails to understand the United States objection to a Canadian being direct representative of Her Majesty's Government," Lord Stanley telegraphed the Colonial Office on December 13, "but to avoid delay will defer to the course decided on by Her Majesty's Government without further protest."[25]

The conference, which Charles Hibbert Tupper, the son of the old "Cumberland war-horse", would attend as Canadian adviser, would not likely be held until late in the winter. In the meantime, Parliament must be called. Macdonald had planned a fairly early opening, in the hope that Abbott would be free to depart on his Australian mission about the end of March, and in the hope also that he himself might be able to slip away before the summer was too far advanced on his long-deferred visit to England. Parliament met, according to plan, on January 16. A good deal more time would be available; but already, long before the opening, Macdonald became aware that his hope of breaking the back of the session's work in the first two months could almost certainly not be realized. It would not be an easy, uncontroversial, smoothly running session at all— far from it! The cultural conflict, like a fire in a high wind, had leaped from Ontario across the uninhabited expanses of the Precambrian Shield into Manitoba. Its fury remained virtually unabated; its character had only slightly changed. So long as the Jesuits' Estates Bill dominated the scene, the tumult had centred mainly around the power and privileges of the Roman Catholic Church; but now, with the transference of the excitement to Manitoba and the North-West Territories, the attack had come to be focused upon language and education. It was certain that as soon after the opening of Parliament as possible, Dalton McCarthy would move for the abolition of the guarantees for the French language in the North-West

Territories Act, and that a prolonged and highly dangerous debate would inevitably follow.

There was, as Macdonald knew very well, not the slightest doubt about the origins and meaning of this new disturbance in the north-west. It was the nemesis of the arrogant dictatorship of Riel. Exactly twenty years before, Riel and his spiritual advisers had sought, in the interest of the *métis* in particular and French Canadians in general, to determine in advance the structure and institutions of the first western Canadian province. They had demanded and secured a particular educational system before the citizens of Red River had even considered the subject; they had imposed provincial status upon a community which had expressly rejected it after considerable debate. This determination of the constitution of Manitoba in advance of the unmistakable assertion of its real character had not been an easy matter even in 1870. It had been accomplished only through the deliberate falsification, by Riel and his advisers, of the known wishes of the inhabitants of Red River. Even in 1870, the Red River settlement had not been simply a little French Canada in the west; and, in the twenty years since the passing of the Manitoba Act, the real character of the province had asserted itself even more emphatically. "There is no especial reason," Macdonald had pointed out realistically to Chapleau, "why a French Canadian should be preferred for office in the west. The people of Quebec will not migrate in that direction. They, wisely, I think, desire to settle the lands yet unoccupied in their Province and to add to their influence in eastern Ontario. The consequence is that Manitoba and the North-West Territories are becoming what British Columbia now is, wholly English—with English laws, English, or rather British, immigration, and, I may add, English prejudices."[26]

By 1890 the clash between law and reality had become acute. And the existing agitation was the inevitable result of the efforts of the people of the north-west to free themselves from the fetters which had been so prematurely imposed upon them. For Macdonald and the Conservative party, the agitation carried a double threat. Constitutionally, Manitoba and the North-West Territories stood in two quite different positions; and it was obvious that the danger from the North-West Territories was the more direct and immediate of the two. Within the limits imposed by the British North America Act and interpreted by the courts, Manitoba had control of its own schools and language guarantees: but in the North-West Territories, which, of course, had not yet been granted responsible government, these matters were still necessarily the concern of the federal Parliament. The Dominion was certainly more deeply involved in the affairs of the Territories than in the affairs of Manitoba; but even in respect of Manitoba and Manitoba's projected radical legislation, a position of complete detachment was going to be very difficult for the federal government to maintain. The Dominion, in addition to its general power of disallowance, possessed certain specified reserve powers in the field of education; and in the now almost inevitable controversy over Manitoba's new school legislation, these powers would be unquestionably invoked. This, however, lay still in the future. The trouble over the French language in the North-West Territories was very much in the present. On January 22, six days after the session opened, Dalton McCarthy moved to delete clause one hundred and ten from the North-West Territories Act.[27]

McCarthy justified his proposal on the simple ground that it was "expedient in the interest of unity that there should be community of language". Macdonald did not believe that community of language was the necessary condition of national unity. But he also did not believe that duality of language could be preserved in the North-West Territories by constitutional guarantees to which the mass of the inhabitants were unquestionably opposed. It was a cruel dilemma—a dilemma more cruel than that in which he and his party had been forced by the agitation over the Jesuits' Estates Bill. The Roman Catholic religion was no monopoly of the people of Quebec; but on the North American continent, the French language was their unique possession. As time passed and the second reading of McCarthy's Bill drew closer, the angry determination of the French-speaking members to defend the status of their language mounted. But so also did the resolution with which the English-

speaking members prepared to ensure that the people of the
north-west should have the right to determine the character
of their own institutions. There was only one way out of this
impossible situation; and on February 11, the day before
McCarthy's Bill was to come up for second reading, the Conservative party took it. In full caucus, but with many French-
Canadian supporters deeply dissatisfied, the party decided that
the matter must be regarded as an open question.

On February 12, as soon as the debate began, Nicholas
Flood Davin, member for West Assiniboia, arose to move in
amendment that "the Legislative Assembly of the North-West
Territories be authorized to deal with the subject of this Bill by
ordinance or enactment, after the next general election for the
said Territories".[28] Here, in the eyes of the English-speaking
Conservatives, was an admirable compromise, which removed
the stigma which Dalton McCarthy had placed upon the French
language and safely transferred the whole contentious subject to
the remote control of the North-West Legislative Assembly. The
Quebec members ought to be satisfied with such a sensible solution. But plainly they were very far from being satisfied; and all
hope that they could be induced to vote for the Davin amendment was quickly ended when Beausoleil, Liberal member for
Berthier, moved, as an amendment to the amendment, that the
language guarantees in the North-West Territories had been
granted to promote good understanding and racial harmony and
that nothing had since occurred to excuse or justify their abolition.[29] Immediately it became apparent that the Beausoleil
amendment would become a battle slogan round which the
French-Canadian resistance, irrespective of party, would inevitably rally. The next day, February 13, a second long and futile
Conservative caucus failed to compose the differences between
the English-speaking and French-speaking divisions of the party.
The Quebec members were adamant. And in the days of debate
that followed, speaker after French-Canadian speaker, of both
parties, arose to identify himself with the principle of Beausoleil's
amendment.

Not until the afternoon of February 17 did Macdonald
enter the debate. It was Laurier's taunt that the McCarthy Bill

was a typical example of harsh and oppressive Toryism which brought him to his feet. He had no difficulty in proving that it was a Conservative majority under Lord Metcalfe which had first requested the imperial Parliament to amend the clause in the Union Act of 1840 which provided that the English language alone was to be used in all the written proceedings of the provincial legislature. He had no hesitation in affirming —what he had affirmed forty years before against the determined opposition of George Brown—that the cultural duality of Canada must be accepted as the prime condition of its continued existence. "There is no paramount race in this country;" he declared firmly, "there is no conquered race in this country; we are all British subjects, and those who are not English are none the less British subjects on that account."[30] These were principles which he was ready enough to assert again and without qualification. But they were not, he realized, the only principles at stake. The susceptibilities of French-Canadians were not the only susceptibilities to be considered, and the north-west was as much involved in the agitation as Quebec. ". . . We must take great care, Mr. Speaker," he reminded the House, "that while we are calming the agitation and soothing the agitated feelings of the people of Quebec, we are not arousing the feelings of the freemen of the north-west by passing a resolution which postpones for an indefinite time, it may be for a long period, a question in which we can see, from the resolution they have adopted, that they are greatly interested."[31]

He was seeking earnestly for an acceptable compromise. But obviously also he was failing to find it. He opposed McCarthy's Bill. He rejected Beausoleil's amendment. He gave general approval to Davin's plan of permitting the citizens of the north-west to decide the matter themselves. He seemed to stand on the doctrine of self-determination. And then, towards the end of his speech, he began to qualify it with the expedient of delay. During the previous day's debate, Edward Blake had suggested that the decision concerning the French language should be postponed a while longer until the character of the north-western community was still more plainly determined. Was it not possible, Macdonald asked the House, to couple this suggestion with Davin's original proposal in a reasonable compromise?

He was desperately in earnest. But he was tired, and less effective than usual. If he had hoped to win French-Canadian approval for his vague proposal, he realized at once that he had completely failed. His followers from Quebec were bitterly disappointed at his stand; and all next day, while several unsuccessful caucuses were held, the French Canadians maintained their obstinate resistance. When, a day later, the vote on Beausoleil's motion was finally taken, every French-speaking member, with the exception of Chapleau and one or two absentees, voted in its favour; and one hundred and seventeen English-speaking members voted in a body against it.[32] What had so long been dreaded in Canadian politics had come at last to happen. Party did not seem to matter. Race stood opposed to race.

Yet, in the end, after his first fumble, Macdonald found an acceptable formula of compromise. Thompson presented it that night, for he himself was worn out by the long argument; but two days later when the House, in a much better humour, resumed the debate after the brief Ash Wednesday recess, he rose at once and accepted government responsibility for Thompson's amendment. In its opening clauses, the new resolution restated and reaffirmed the covenants in respect of the French language which were embodied in the British North America Act. It then went on to declare that it was proper, expedient and not inconsistent with those covenants that the Assembly of the North-West Territories should be empowered by Parliament to regulate, after the next general election, the conduct of its own proceedings, written and oral. The use of the French language in the courts of the North-West Territories would continue to be permitted. The territorial ordinances would be printed in both French and English as before. But henceforth the North-West Assembly would have the authority to determine the language of its own records and debates. It was a compromise; but in the light of actual conditions in the Territories, a not unreal compromise. And in a formal speech, which was the principal feature of the last two days of debate, Macdonald presented it with all the persuasive earnestness of which he was capable. "Let us forget this cry," he declared in the last sentences of his peroration, "and we shall have our reward in seeing this unfortunate fire, which has been kindled from so small a spark, extinguished for ever, and we shall go on, as we have been going on since 1867, as one people, with one object, looking to one future, and expecting to lay the foundation of one great country."[33]

Early in the morning of February 22, Lord Stanley wrote to Macdonald, congratulating him on the "brilliant division" —a division which had been so largely secured by his own great effort.[34] On the previous night, at a little after ten o'clock, the vote on Thompson's amendment had been finally taken. Fifty members—a handful of irreconcilable French-Canadian *Rouges*, a few McCarthyites, a small number of Liberals who preferred Davin's motion—voted against it; but one hundred and forty-nine people, French and English, voted in its favour.[35]

III

Four days later, Charles Hibbert Tupper, the new Minister of Marine and Fisheries, arrived in Washington for the fur-seal negotiations.

Macdonald was by no means reassured by Tupper's first reports. Blaine seemed to be pursuing a steady and determined policy of reducing Canadian participation to a cipher, conducting the negotiations on a level of calculated informality, and assuming the necessity of a close season before any effort had been made to prove it. It was plain that he did not in the least welcome a Canadian representative. He told Tupper frankly, at their first meeting, that he had not expected to see him. "I understood," he declared coldly, "that the British Government and the United States administration would agree upon a close season in the interests of this great and important industry and then submit the agreement to Canada for approval."[36] Tupper valiantly took the liberty of reminding him that unless the United States assumed Bering Sea to be a *mare clausum* of its own, it would obviously have to discuss the necessity and wisdom of a close season with all the nations interested in the fur-seal fishery. "I have never claimed the sea was a *mare clausum*," Blaine retorted. "But recollect," he added quickly, "I have never abandoned that claim which my predecessor set up."[37] In the end he agreed to submit in writing the American justification for the close season; and Tupper busied himself in preparing the Canadian reply. But it was quite evident that the Secretary of State was irritated by this deliberate and carefully recorded diplomacy. He wanted to proceed immediately to the establishment of the close season. And, in Tupper's somewhat jaundiced view, the new British Minister, Sir Julian Pauncefote, was apparently only too ready to hurry obediently after him.

Macdonald had been ill at the beginning of the year. The session had tired him out already. "I am so unwell," he wrote wearily to Bowell on March 4, "that I am completely floored, and must go to bed or I shall be ill. So you must get on as best you can."[38] He had no assurance at all that Tupper was "getting on" well at Washington. An unaccountable delay in the arrival of the letters expected from the Canadian representative aroused in him the disturbing suspicion that American agents were tampering with the mails;[39] and young Stanley, the Governor-General's son, was sent down to Washington with new and important communications. But this effort to strengthen Tupper's hand by applying a little polite pressure to the British Minister had no effect. Blaine virtually refused to give any more time to a discussion of the merits of the close season, and brusquely demanded that the Anglo-Canadian representatives present their "final proposition". On March 18. Tupper left Washington for Ottawa, bringing with him a draft convention which Pauncefote had drawn up.

The work of the session was at its demanding climax, and Macdonald was none too well. But once March 28 was past and Foster's budget speech had been safely delivered, the Cabinet settled down to the discussion and detailed amendment of Pauncefote's draft. The plan which gradually took shape was a simple one. In its main essentials, it bore a fairly close resemblance—a perhaps ominous resemblance—to the North Atlantic Fisheries Treaty, which had failed in the American Senate nearly two years before. The principal provision of the Anglo-Canadian draft was the establishment of a mixed commission of experts—with final reference to an arbitrator—which was to study the conditions of fur-seal life and, within two years, to submit a plan for the control and regulation of the fur-seal fishery. In the meantime, while the commissioners were carrying on their investigations, the capture of seals on both land and sea was to be suspended.[40]

Macdonald and the Cabinet were determined to put the unargued American case for a close season to the rigorous test of a careful and comprehensive examination. The Canadian amendments were uncompromising in the strict impartiality of their proposals; and when, early in April, Tupper returned to Washington with the revised draft, Sir Julian Pauncefote was distinctly disturbed.[41] It alarmed him to discover that the Canadians had included the American-owned Pribilof Islands in the area which the Commissioners were to investigate and to which the *modus vivendi* was to apply. He objected; and his objections perplexed and annoyed both Tupper and Macdonald. If the real purpose of all concerned was the preservation of the fur seals from extinction, then what valid distinction could be drawn between indiscriminate slaughter on the islands and indiscriminate slaughter on the high seas? Why did not Pauncefote see the force of this reasoning? Why was he yielding so readily to the persuasions of Blaine? "It may be out of place for me to say it," Tupper confided to Macdonald, "but I cannot refrain from urging that in future negotiations with the United States, no British Minister at Washington should act for us. It is apparent that there is always present on his part a desire to make his future residence in Washington as pleasant as possible, and he is to some extent therefore unable to take and keep a firm and independent position."[42]

Macdonald sighed. Clearly Sir Julian Pauncefote was not Joseph Chamberlain; and clearly the Canadian government would have to take vigorous steps itself to make its position perfectly clear in Washington. On April 11, after Tupper's report of the British Minister's objections had been received, Macdonald drafted a firm telegram to his colleague in Washington. "Council wish you to impress strongly on Sir Julian," it read, "their desire to adhere as closely as possible to the lines of our proposal."[43] A fortnight later, when Pauncefote still jibbed at the inclusion of the islands in the area to be governed by the terms of the *modus vivendi*, Macdonald telegraphed that if the British Minister insisted on the original and unamended article, the draft convention could be presented to the United States only under protest from Canada.[44] At this, Sir Julian gave in; the Foreign Office finally approved the plan; and on April 29, Pauncefote presented it to Blaine. A profound silence, lasting several weeks, followed. And then, on May 22, by the highly informal means of a press release in the American newspapers, Macdonald and Pauncefote learnt that the United States Cabinet had rejected their proposal. The news that an American revenue cutter had been ordered to seize vessels carrying on sealing in the waters of Bering Sea was included in the same dispatch.[45]

By this time Parliament had been prorogued for about a week. Though it had begun nearly a month earlier than usual, the session had ended at the accustomed time. It had been a long, exacting, dispiriting session—disagreeable to the tired and ill Macdonald and, as time went on, increasingly discreditable to the Conservative party. A month after the opening, J. C. Rykert, the Conservative member for Lincoln, had been charged with using his position and influence in Parliament for his own private gain;[46] and although these charges were not in fact substantiated by the committee of investigation, the evidence uncovered was so damaging to Rykert's character and conduct that in the end he resigned his seat. Early in May when *l'affaire* Rykert was drawing to its sorry close, a yet more unsavoury scandal, involving persons still more exalted in the Conservative party, was for the first time disclosed. Thomas McGreevy, member for Quebec West, was accused of having accepted, over a period of years, considerable sums of money in return for advancing the interests of the Quebec contracting firm, Larkin, Connolly and Company, at the Department of Public Works.[47]

What made these deplorable charges all the more dangerous was that Thomas McGreevy was Sir Hector Langevin's brother-in-law and that Sir Hector Langevin's department had always been the Department of Public Works. "If you had said," Bowell wrote to Macdonald, "'Langevin cannot have too much *patronage—he likes it*', you would have hit the nail upon the head squarely."[48] As Macdonald knew only too well, the possibilities of jobbery inside Langevin's department were almost literally endless. Had he become really involved in something seriously discreditable?

The scandals were grave and becoming more serious; but they were not the only serious domestic problems to which he could look forward in the early summer of 1890. The government had emerged successfully—with a dignified air of wise statesmanship—from the great debate on the status of the French language in the North-West Territories. In the meantime, however, in Manitoba, one of the two opposing divisions in the cultural conflict had made another sudden and aggressive advance. During the session of 1890, the provincial legislature had abolished the legal guarantees for the French language and had established a new uniform system of non-sectarian schools to the support of which all citizens, irrespective of their religious beliefs, would be required to contribute. A disgruntled minority was opposed to both these changes. But, in respect of the language guarantees, it was obviously hopeless, after the amendment of the North-West Territories Act, to invite intervention from the federal government. The Manitoba Schools Act was a different matter. And the familiar petitions, requesting disallowance, began once more to descend upon Ottawa.

Macdonald was fresh from the long tribulations of the Jesuits' Estates Bill. He had no doubt as to the course he should take. "I am strongly of opinion," he wrote in March to a French-speaking supporter in Manitoba, "that the only mode by which the separate school question can be satisfactorily settled in your province is by an appeal to the courts. If the Bill were disallowed, the game of Greenway and Martin would be played successfully. They would probably summon the legislature again, and carry the Bill over again, and then dissolve and go to the country. The excitement would be tremendous and the question would remain unsettled, whereas a decision by the courts would finally dispose of it and the agitation consequent upon it."[49] This, of course, was the best that could be hoped for. But it would be a long time before the period in which disallowance could be exercised would be over. And it would be a still longer time before the test cases could end their protracted perambulations through the courts. Meanwhile, the opportunities for agitation would remain. The chances of embarrassment for the federal government were very real.

The danger was there. But—thank Heaven!—it was still distant. And the most pressing and immediate problems which confronted him lay in the sphere not of domestic but of external affairs. Late in June, Thompson departed for England to discuss copyrights and merchant-shipping regulations with the British officials, and also to bring up a matter which had long interested Macdonald, the appointment of a Canadian to the Judicial Committee of the Privy Council. The repeated postponement of the visit to England—which Macdonald still felt too tired to undertake—had resulted in a small accumulation of topics which would have to be discussed at the Colonial Office. They were all of some consequence; but obviously by far the most important was the unsolved question of the Bering Sea fur-seal fisheries. Since Blaine's rejection of the draft convention, and the public announcement of the American intention to police Bering Sea, relations with the United States had been nearly as bad as they could have been. Lord Salisbury and the American Secretary of State settled down to a long diplomatic argument over the freedom of the seas. A small squadron of the Royal Navy ominously took up its station at Esquimalt, British Columbia. The danger of war, the chance of a collision—such as Macdonald had always feared—which would lead to war or to a cessation of diplomatic or commercial intercourse, was greater than it had yet been.

Even this was not all. In the last little while, a most significant development had been taking place in Washington. It was becoming increasingly apparent that the United States was on the eve of a very considerable change in the history of its commercial policy. A new and comprehensive tariff measure, the McKinley Bill, was now well on its deliberate way through Congress; and the McKinley Bill provided, not only for a general and substantial increase in the American tariff, but also for the imposition of a few heavy specific duties on some of the most important cereals and other farm products which Canada exported to the United States. The McKinley Bill would be, in effect, a complete, unqualified rejection of the whole idea of a reasonable Canadian-American trade agreement. It would grievously hurt several Canadian export trades. It might ruin the barley industry of southern Ontario.

It was a bad, a politically dangerous, time. A general election was inevitably approaching. And despite Macdonald's still enormous vitality, he sometimes felt distressed by the decline of his own powers as well as by the persistence of his problems. He could never give up now. There was no way out for him. He would die in office. Tacitly he accepted his destiny; but he could not help being occasionally weighed down by the sense of his own age and weariness, and by the recurring gloomy reflection that his government's usefulness had been exhausted. "I am a good deal discouraged as to our future," he wrote to Tupper early in June. "Not that the country has gone or is going against us, but because our ministry is *too old* and *too long* in office. I am on the way to seventy-six. Langevin has aged very much and is inert and useless except in office, but he doesn't move in Quebec politics. He, Caron and Chapleau are allowing Mercier to carry the Province away from them by their want of harmony. Costigan and Colby have their frailties, as you know. Bowell is pretty hale, and yet shows age in some degree, and I fear for Thompson's health. But enough of this."[50]

Enough of all this, for a while. Before June was out he was away for what he told Tupper would be a six-weeks' holiday at Rivière du Loup.

IV

During the long vacation at Les Rochers, which was less interrupted and more genuinely refreshing than any he had had in recent years, he laid tentative plans for the future. The general election would almost certainly have to be held in 1891. Further delay would be dangerous, for the provincial omens, to which he paid a good deal of attention, were foreboding trouble once again. Mercier had been triumphantly returned in the recent provincial general election in Quebec. In Ontario, where the Equal Righters, under Dalton McCarthy's inspiration, had campaigned virtually as a separate group, Meredith's Conservatives had suffered accordingly and Mowat was returned to power once more with a substantial majority. These renewed provincial Liberal successes disturbed Macdonald. It was time, at any rate, he thought, to begin making a few unostentatious preparations for the future. And early in August he paid a visit to Prince Edward Island, where he had not been since 1870, when he had spent a long carefree summer in restful convalescence at Charlottetown.[51]

Yet, as summer declined into autumn, the threat of these provincial defeats seemed to recede into the background. The real danger was something quite different. The real danger was the relentless approach of the McKinley tariff. Already Laurier, Cartwright, and Charlton were predicting economic disaster for Canada as the inevitable result of the new law. They had dragged out unrestricted reciprocity from the comparative obscurity in which it had lain for the past year with all the enthusiasm of a fresh conviction. Unrestricted reciprocity, they explained in numerous speeches, was the only panacea for the calamity that was approaching Canada; and the Liberal party was, of course, the only party which could possibly negotiate unrestricted reciprocity with the United States. Late in September, when Macdonald travelled down to the Maritime Provinces for a brief speaking-tour, talk of the McKinley Bill and its consequences had become so general and so excited that he devoted all the last part of his speech at Halifax to the question of commercial policy. The fundamental purpose of the United States, he told his audience, was to starve Canada into annexation. Reciprocity on self-respecting terms was not to be obtained from the republic. If the Canadians wished to trade freely with the United States, they must—so the Americans said in effect—either accept annexation or—what would be a virtual equivalent—separate from the United Kingdom and set up as an "independent" republic.[52]

As he rode back from Saint John, over the Short Line through a golden autumnal day, the merchants and shippers in scores of Canadian ports were frantically loading the last bulging cargoes for the United States. On Monday, October 6, the McKinley Act went into operation; and it was not until a month later, when the American congressional elections were held, that the heavy gloom which had settled down over Canada was pierced by a faint ray of hope. The Democrats had gained control of the new House of Representatives. "The rising of the people of the United States against the McKinley Bill is most wonderful," Macdonald wrote to George Stephen. "What the immediate consequences may be, can't yet be foreseen. By the rotten constitution of the United States, the present Congress, although discredited, nay repudiated, by the people, has full power until 4 March next. It will assemble on 4 December and the question is whether the Republican majority can bully it through, or whether, frightened at the hostile attitude of the electors, they may track back a bit. If the Senate is firm even after March next, the McKinley Bill cannot be repealed until 1897, but I am told that the western senators, although Republicans, will back down in the face of the angry multitude. We shall see."[53]

They would. But he did not really expect to see a repeal of the law. The persistent hostility which had been displayed, over a period of years, by both the Cleveland and Harrison administrations, had convinced him that the frustration of the Canadian national experiment had become the avowed object of both the American political parties. "Sir Charles Tupper will tell you," he informed Stephen, "that every American statesman (and he saw them all in 88) covets Canada. The greed for its acquisition is still on the increase, and God knows where it will all end. If Gladstone succeeds, he will sacrifice Canada without scruple. We must face the fight at our next election, and it is only the conviction that the battle will be better fought under my guidance than under another's that makes me undertake the task, handicapped as I am, with the infirmities of old age. . . . If left to ourselves, I have no doubt of a decision in our favour, but I have serious apprehensions, which are shared by all our friends here, that a large amount of Yankee money will be expended to corrupt our people."[54] He believed that American funds would be freely used to help the Canadian opposition. He believed that the Canadian opposition was offering advice to the Americans in the conduct of their policy of calculated denial and refusal. And he knew too that the struggle for the support of the Canadian voter would, in all likelihood, have to be carried on in the dejection and wretchedness of renewed depression. On November 7, three days after the American elections, the stock exchanges of London and Paris were reported very depressed, and the next week brought a major collapse in the security markets of all important financial capitals of the western world.[55]

In these gloomy circumstances the news that Newfoundland was successfully negotiating a trade and fisheries treaty with the United States came with a profound shock of consternation and dismay. On November 15, in response to anxious inquiries, the Colonial Secretary, Lord Knutsford, telegraphed the terms of the proposed convention, added that Blaine was apparently ready to consider a separate treaty, on a wide basis, with Canada, and suggested that one or two Canadian representatives should proceed unofficially to Washington for a conference. Two days later, after a long Cabinet meeting, Macdonald waited on the Governor-General with a draft minute of council which had been hurriedly drawn up on the subject.[56] Obviously he was deeply concerned. The effect, he declared, of these separate negotiations with Newfoundland would simply be to divide and weaken British North America by setting one colony against the other. In all probability, this was Blaine's real object. Blaine, he reminded the Governor-General, had never withdrawn or qualified his frequently expressed belief that Canada must be given no commercial privileges in American markets while she remained a British possession. Public men and newspapers in the United States made no effort to conceal their hope that the present consistently hostile attitude of the American administration to Canada would weaken and break down the Canadian desire for a separate political existence.

This, Macdonald declared earnestly, was the fundamental aim against which British North America must be always on its guard. If Great Britain permitted the signing of the separate Newfoundland treaty, the unhappy Canadian feeling of isolation and misfortune would be increased; and real and substantial assistance would be given to the United States in its commercial war with the Dominion. Separate negotiations, with different advantages and unequal concessions, would arouse jealousies and antagonisms, and weaken British North American resistance. The only effective means of ensuring Canada's survival as a separate nation—and here Macdonald expressed his deepest conviction—was the maintenance of a united front by Great Britain and the whole of British North America against the United States. As for the somewhat casual invitation to "unofficial" talks in Washington, bitter experience had made him deeply suspicious of this kind of negotiation with the United States. If the Canadian representatives presented themselves unofficially, Pauncefote, who, Macdonald believed, was under Blaine's influence, would alone have any diplomatic status. "Unofficial" discussions would simply give the Canadian case away. They could, and probably would, be repudiated by Blaine at his slightest convenience.

These strong protestations had an immediate effect. It was, moreover, not simply a negative effect. And very soon it began to seem that this provoking and frightening affair might have exceptionally favourable consequences. During late November and early December, Macdonald was ill with a tenacious cold; but the news which was brought to his study in Earnscliffe appeared uniformly and—in view of all the past—almost incredibly hopeful. The Newfoundland convention was delayed until Canada could begin negotiations with the United States on its own account.[57] The United Kingdom agreed that the Canadian representatives at the proposed conference must be plenipotentiaries and not mere delegates. Pauncefote, in answer to an eager Canadian offer to start negotiations at once, reported that Blaine would not accept a formal commission until a "basis of arrangement" had first been reached, but that he had expressed "a strong desire" to conclude "a wide Reciprocity Treaty".[58] Macdonald was warily unconvinced by these characteristic evasions; but, in the critical circumstances of the moment, he knew he would have to accept Blaine's ambiguous invitation at its most favourable face value, and get the very best for Canada out of it that he could.[59] "We have held in Parliament and elsewhere," he wrote to Thompson, "that our attempts to negotiate had been so often rejected by the United States that we could not in self-respect go on our knees again, but that we were ready, whenever the United States made any sign of a desire to negotiate, to go into the matter earnestly. This suggestion of Blaine's gives us the opportunity and will prevent the opposition from stating that we have abandoned our ground and taken up theirs."[60]

On December 13, the Canadian government dispatched to London and Washington a brief statement of its comprehensive proposals for the trade discussions.[61] Three weeks later, on January 2, Lord Knutsford reported on the reception which these proposals had received at Washington. Secretary Blaine, he telegraphed, did not believe that it would be possible to obtain a formal trade commission until the prospects of its success had been assured by previous private discussions; but he was willing to enter into such private discussions with Pauncefote and one or more Canadian delegates at any time after March 4.[62] "You will observe," Macdonald explained later to Thompson, "that we had no intimation that the private and informal meeting was to be kept secret until January, when we applied for leave to publish our minute-in-council proposing a formal conference. We knew that the conference proposed by Blaine was to be unofficial and in that sense private, but had no idea that the fact of the meeting was to be kept private."[63]

The fact of the proposed meeting was, of course, not kept private. Macdonald himself made no official announcement. He did not apply to the British government for permission to publish until January 21, by which time he had nearly made up his mind to request an immediate dissolution.[64] But, in the meantime, while official statements were withheld, newspaper speculation was busy. The air was full of rumours and insinuations, for both sides felt that a general election was imminent, and each was manœuvring desperately for position. On January 14, the Toronto *Mail* announced, "on authority which leaves little reason to doubt that the rumour is true", that Great Britain had been urging Canada to compose its differences with the United States in a broad trade agreement, "and that Sir John Macdonald and his colleagues are seriously disturbed in consequence".[65] This provoked a counter-declaration from the Toronto *Empire*. The *Mail's* statement, it declared roundly, was not true. On the contrary, it was the government of the United States which had recently approached the Canadian government with a view to the improvement of trade relations.[66]

Macdonald's hand was being forced. It was of the utmost importance that he should make an official statement—and at once. He wanted permission, not merely to publish the substance of the Canadian proposal of December 13, but also to indicate that it had been inspired by the favourable attitude of the United States.[67] His necessities were the opportunities of the Liberal opposition. They were also, for somewhat different reasons, the opportunities of James G. Blaine. In these circumstances, the connection between the American State Department and the Canadian opposition, the existence of which even the Governor-General had come to suspect, was suddenly and dramatically revealed. On January 28, Edward Farrer, one of the editors of the Toronto *Globe*, had an "important though informal" interview in Washington with Secretary Blaine and Chairman Hitt of the House Committee on Foreign Affairs.[68] Blaine had found it impossible to receive official Canadian representatives until March 4; but he was evidently quite prepared to discuss trade relations with the editor of the leading Canadian opposition newspaper as early as January 28. Negotiations with official Canadian delegates must be kept strictly private; but the news of Farrer's interview was instantly given to the press and received wide publicity. The immediate consequences of the meeting—a consequence which was no doubt arranged at the meeting itself—was given wider publicity still. In a letter written on the same date, a Congressman inquired of the Secretary of State whether negotiations for a "partial" reciprocity with Canada were going on. "I authorize you to contradict the rumours you refer to," Blaine replied. "There are no negotiations whatever on foot for a reciprocity treaty with Canada. . . . We know nothing of Sir Charles Tupper's coming to Washington."[69]

All along, Macdonald had distrusted "informal" discussions. He had suspected that Blaine would repudiate them at his own convenience. Blaine had done exactly that. He had betrayed Macdonald deliberately and completely. "No, I have not seen the letter," Stanley replied, on the day of publication, in answer to Macdonald's inquiry, "but it would be quite like Blaine. . . . The more I think of the situation the more I should be disposed to advise that we should go right ahead—Blaine or no Blaine."[70] Macdonald agreed. The government was in an appalling position. It had been led up the garden path, double-crossed with cool efficiency, and then effectively prevented from uttering a word of explanation or protest. Insupportable—possibly disastrous! But there it was. Further delays or manoeuvres were pointless. The decision to dissolve, which had been nearly reached on January 21 and postponed in the frustrating days that followed, could now be confirmed. There was every reason to take the field openly, at once, and with every ounce of resolution and confidence that he could muster. On Monday, February 2, the order for the general election was signed. When he drove home that evening with his secretary, Joseph Pope, he seemed full of energy; and far into the night he was busy outlining his election address.

The address was a reasoned defence of his design for Canada, and of its two greatest foundations, the national transcontinental railway and the national policy of protection. It was a reasoned attack upon unrestricted reciprocity which, in his view, offered the most fundamental threat to the fiscal autonomy and political independence of Canada. "The question which you will shortly be called upon to determine," he told the voters, "resolves itself into this: shall we endanger our possession of the great heritage bequeathed to us by our fathers, and submit ourselves to direct taxation for the privilege of having our tariff fixed at Washington, with a prospect of ultimately becoming a portion of the American union? . . . As for myself, my course is clear. A British subject I was born—a British subject I will die. With my utmost effort, with my latest breath, will I oppose the 'veiled treason' which attempts by sordid means and mercenary proffers to lure our people from their allegiance. During my long public service of nearly half a century, I have been true to my country and its best interests, and I appeal with equal confidence to the men who have trusted me in the past, and to the young hope of the country with whom rests its destinies for the future, to give me their united and strenuous aid in this, my last effort, for the unity of the Empire and the preservation of our commercial and political freedom."[71]

On January 21, he had sent a final appeal to Tupper in England. "Immediate dissolution almost certain," he cabled. "Your presence during election contest in Maritime Provinces essential to encourage our friends. Please come. Answer."[72] Tupper had answered yes. And on February 6, the day before the election address was finished, he was back in Ottawa once more. They would fight it out together for the last time. On Saturday, February 7, Tupper departed to fulfil an engagement at Kingston which his chief was unable to keep. And eight days later, on Sunday night, February 15, Macdonald left Ottawa for Toronto.

V

He was determined to finish what Blaine and Farrer had begun. If this was the kind of warfare that was desired, then —by good luck and good management—he could carry it effectively into the enemy's camp. He was ready to change his method; but his programme remained essentially the same. The *Times* correspondent, Colmer telegraphed from England, was now asserting that the Conservative government had virtually abandoned the plan of closer trade relations with the United States on which it had first gone to the country and had returned to the old policy of protection and imperial loyalty.

This, of course, was nonsense. The Conservative government had never officially "gone to the country" on a policy of closer trade relations with the United States. It had never had the chance. Blaine had tied the hands and stopped the mouths of the Canadians while he proceeded with complete impunity to double-cross them. Yet despite the bitter humiliation of this betrayal, Macdonald was prepared to resume the postponed negotiations as if nothing had happened. "*Times* Toronto correspondent in error," he telegraphed back to England. "Government and Conservative party have not abandoned issue on which they went to the country. They still desire to negotiate for closer trade relations with the United States, but they insist on control of their own tariffs and will not discriminate against the Mother Country."[73] These, of course, were the conditions on which Macdonald had always insisted; and the speech which he gave at Halifax on October 1, 1890—the only important speech of the previous autumn—had anticipated all the main themes of the election address of February 7, 1891.

He had not changed his programme. He did not intend directly to attack Blaine. But, by good fortune, Farrer, the intermediary between the American Secretary of State and the Canadian opposition, had been delivered into his hands. On Tuesday, February 17, at a great Conservative rally in the Academy of Music in Toronto, at which he and Tupper were the principal speakers, he attacked Farrer—and through him the Liberal party—by impugning the journalist's loyalty and calling in question the motives which lay behind his advocacy of unrestricted reciprocity. Farrer, at the request of an American friend, had written a pamphlet, in which, as he himself later explained, he had tried to view Canadian-American trade relations as an American would; and from this point of view, he had suggested several methods of economic retaliation by which the United States could bring the citizens of the Dominion to a realization of the stupidity of their trade and fisheries policy.[74] Only a few copies of this pamphlet had been printed under strict conditions of secrecy. The Conservatives, through a friendly printer, had managed to secure only a part of the proofs. But the gist of Farrer's argument, and the retaliatory methods he had suggested—tonnage duties on Canadian vessels, suspension of the bonding privileges in the United States, cutting the connections of the Canadian Pacific Railway at Sault Ste. Marie—were all clearly revealed in these few precious proof sheets.

At Halifax Macdonald had hinted that the Canadian opposition was giving aid and comfort to the Americans in the conduct of their commercial warfare against the Dominion. Now these insinuations became a definite charge. The rejection of Canadian advances, the hostility to legitimate Canadian interests at Washington, were in large measure traceable, he told his audience, to the advice which traitors like Farrer had offered to the Americans. In effect Farrer and his like had presented themselves as Canadian guides to the realization of annexation. If, they had said to the Americans, you wish to obtain the Dominion, you must concede nothing to Canada, you must put the screws on Canada, you must coerce the Canadians and bully them in every possible fashion. "In fact," Macdonald went on, summarizing the general argument of Farrer's pamphlet, "the document points out every possible way in which Canada and its trade can be injured, and its people impoverished, with the view of eventually bringing about annexation. . . . I say that there is a deliberate conspiracy, in which some of the members of the opposition are more or less compromised; I say that there is a deliberate conspiracy, by force, by fraud, or by both, to force Canada into the American union."[75]

Macdonald could play the game that Farrer and Blaine had started as well as they, or better. He had turned the tables upon his opponents. But he had done more than win by means of a sharply clever trick. He had found and stated, in a simple and arresting form, the main theme of the election. Farrer, an editor of the most important Canadian opposition newspaper, had been ready, at a time of depression and great national distress, to advise the foreigner against his country's own interests. Were not the Liberals, in advocating the closest economic relationship with the United States, really playing the foreigner's game just as effectively and by only slightly less obvious means? And was not unrestricted reciprocity nothing more nor less than a vote of want of confidence in the whole idea of a distinct and separate nation in northern North America? During the last few years, under accumulated reversals and misfortunes, the Dominion had been driven in until its back was to the wall. But the impulse to resist and to survive was strong; and that impulse had become incarnate in an old man of seventy-six, who had told the Canadians, in a final manifesto, that he purposed still to continue the work of "building up on this continent, under the flag of England, a great and powerful nation", and who would never give in until he died.

For an old man of seventy-six he was going at a killing pace. Before he left Ottawa, he had told his secretary Joseph Pope that he intended to remain in Toronto and to supervise the general operations of the campaign from there.[76] But he could not keep to his plan. He began to yield to the frantic appeals that kept pouring in from every part of the province; and quickly and inevitably he was drawn into a circuit of the battlefront, with stops at every point where the fighting was hottest. On Wednesday, February 18, the day after his arraignment of Farrer, he left Toronto for Hamilton. On Thursday, he was in Strathroy; on Friday, the guest of John Carling, in London. And on Saturday, travelling eastward again, he spoke in succession at Stratford, St. Mary's, Guelph, Acton, and Brampton.

He had done the same, or nearly the same, scores of times before; and even as recently as 1886, Thompson had marvelled at the high good spirits with which he had carried on in just such a tour as this. But Saturday, February 21, was probably as hard a day's speaking as any he had ever attempted. At Brampton people noted how hoarse he had become; and when they reached Toronto late that night, it seemed to Pope that his master looked more tired than he had usually done in the past after such exertions. Macdonald rested on Sunday, but a day's rest was not enough; and he was weary still when he started for Kingston on Sunday night. After days of mild weather in western Ontario, it had turned sharply cold again; and the thermometer stood at less than ten degrees above zero when his private car came to rest at Kingston in the early hours of

Monday morning. He was chilled through by the time he reached the British American Hotel. Most of the day he spent resting in his roomy suite in the hotel; and a reporter who came to see him in the early afternoon found him in good spirits, but still wan from the fatigues of his western tour.[77]

On Tuesday, February 24, the weather changed dramatically again. The clouds that had been piling up steadily for the past twelve hours broke in the late afternoon, the rain poured down, and by night the wind had risen to a gale.[78] He spoke that evening to a huge crowd in the Kingston Opera House; and the next day, with slush and puddles underfoot and a lowering rainy sky above, he started out for Napanee. It was nearly sixty years ago that he had gone off, a lad of seventeen, to set up George Mackenzie's branch legal establishment in the tiny frontier village of Napanee. It had been the first important move of his career; and now he was bound on what was virtually its last journey. The town, that raw, unpleasant February day, was packed with people. In an open carriage he was driven slowly down the main street, through a shouting, gesticulating crowd, to the town hall. The place was full to suffocation; even the platform was crowded. In a vague, chaotic dream he was aware of a chorus of young girls singing the national anthem, of somebody speaking, of somebody else introducing him, of himself rising slowly, desperately to his feet.[79] It was as though he stood at bay. His face was flushed, his white straggling hair was disordered; and he was conscious of nothing but the heat, and the crowds, and his own appalling weariness. Then it was over; and somehow he was stumbling towards the door, past the faces, the voices, the outstretched hands, the oppressive, indistinguishable clamour all around, and out into the street, and the open carriage, and the chill and clammy air.

When at last they reached the private railway carriage, Pope left him, with a sheaf of newly arrived telegrams in his hand, at the door of his bedroom. Only a few minutes later, when the secretary entered the room again, he found the old man lying across the bed.[80] His face was grey, grey with fatigue, grey with another kind of fatigue which was the final exhaustion of a life.

VI

The tour was stopped. The remaining speaking engagements were cancelled. In his moment of extreme weakness, his old enemy, the severe bronchial cold, had clutched at him once again. His voice was almost gone, his pulse weak and irregular; and when he breathed there was often pain over his left lung.[81] For days, while the campaign roared towards its furious conclusion, he lay and rested at Kingston; and it was not until March 4, the day before the poll, that he felt able to travel back to the capital. As soon as he reached Ottawa, he went to bed. That evening, the first election returns were brought to him as he lay there. But the short, hard cough still shook him, he tired with dismaying swiftness; and it was barely ten o'clock and the results from not more than half the constituencies were in, when he turned suddenly on his side and went to sleep.

The next day the congratulatory telegrams and letters began to pour in. The Marquess of Salisbury, Lord Lorne, George Stephen and a host of other admirers all sent their felicitations. Even the Queen, so Lord Stanley informed him, "expressed her great gratification at the result of the elections". His own feelings were much more mixed. His government had been returned to power; his own majority in Kingston was the largest in his political career. But the party had lost a few seats in both Ontario and Quebec; and although it had picked up others in the Maritime Provinces, the total majority was definitely a little smaller than it had been. Still, they were the victors; and in that year of hard distress and savage discouragement, it was perhaps wonderful that the government had even survived. "The effect of the McKinley tariff is so disastrous," he wrote to George Stephen, "that if our election had been postponed until another harvest, we should have been swept out of existence. As it was, I was surprised and grieved to find the hold unrestricted reciprocity had got of our farmers. . . . I have of course pointed out that unrestricted reciprocity meant annexation, and the movements of Cartwright, Farrer and Wiman enabled us to raise the loyalty cry, which had considerable effect.

AN UP-HILL JOB.

LAURIER—"YOUR HORSE HAS WASTED AWAY TO A SHADOW. HE'LL NEVER BE ABLE TO PULL YOU THROUGH WITH THAT LOAD!"

SIR JOHN—"DON'T WORRY YOURSELF, MY DEAR SIR; A GOOD DEAL DEPENDS ON THE DRIVING, YOU KNOW."

Still, the farmers' defection, and the large sums sent, *beyond a doubt*, from the United States, have left us with a diminished majority and an uncertain future."[82]

His own future—a few of those closest to him began to realize—was still more uncertain. "I am slowly—very slowly—gathering myself together again," he wrote to Professor Williamson on March 10. "I have not been out of the house since I arrived here, but this is a fine day, and I shall drive to Council."[83] He had ventured downstairs for the first time the previous day and had begun work on the great unopened mass of his correspondence. His physician, Dr. R. W. Powell, cautioned him, reminding him, with the utmost earnestness, of his imperative need for rest. He listened with his usual genial courtesy; but it was plain that he intended to follow the advice only within limits. "I must attend to my work," he said seriously to Dr. Powell, "if I am at all able."[84] But he was not really able yet. Long before the business of Council was finished on March 10, he was overcome once again by his dreadful sense of weariness. He had to leave before the adjournment, to his own distress and to the deep concern of his colleagues.

The weeks went by. He spent them mainly in bed or indoors. At the end of March he told Stephen that he was "only now" recovering from his prostration. And meanwhile the time which was even partially free for convalescence was dwindling rapidly away. Early in April Sir Charles Tupper left to reopen the trade negotiations at Washington, received the rebuff of a fresh postponement from Blaine, returned once more and departed finally for England. By that time, Macdonald was deep in preparations for Parliament; and on April 29, almost before he knew it, the new session opened. He was going about more freely now; and it was with something of his old jaunty, defiant energy that he replied, on the first day of the debate on the speech from the throne, to Laurier's taunt about the Pyrrhic victory he had gained at the polls. "I tell my friends and I tell my foes: *J'y suis, j'y reste*," he answered with spirit. "We are going to stay here and it will take more than the power of the honourable gentleman, with all the phalanx behind him, to disturb us or to shove us from our pedestal."[85] Brave words!

But, as the days went by, everybody could see how feeble he was, and when he got back to Earnscliffe in the evening, or, more often, in the afternoon, Agnes knew that he was utterly done out.

During those long, dreary weeks of convalescence, he had often felt weariness and depression; but on May 12, not a fortnight after Parliament opened, he suddenly experienced fear. With two of his colleagues he went that morning to wait upon the Governor-General. The old problem, at once tiresome and dangerous, of the Bering Sea fisheries was up once more. A telegram of inquiry from the Colonial Office required an answer. He started to explain his views; and then, without warning, it became difficult for him to find or articulate his words. He was terribly conscious of his mysterious disability; but the Governor-General was conscious of it too; and making an excuse to take the telegram away with him to Rideau Hall, he promised that he would bring it back himself that afternoon to the Prime Minister's office in the Parliament Buildings. It was nearing the appointed hour when Macdonald hurriedly entered the apartments, crossed to his private room, called his secretary, and, explaining that Lord Stanley would be arriving almost immediately by appointment, asked him to go and request Sir John Thompson to attend without delay. Pope came hurrying back to say that the Minister of Justice would be there in a few minutes.

"He, must come at once," Macdonald said thickly and with difficulty, "because he must speak to the Governor for me, as I cannot talk. There is something the matter with my speech."[86]

A few minutes later when Lord Stanley arrived, he found his Prime Minister and his Minister of Justice waiting for him together in curious stiff attitudes of expectancy in the inner room. Macdonald looked ill. He also seemed extremely embarrassed. In a low and not very distinct voice, he asked Thompson to speak for him; and in a very few moments the wording of the telegraphic reply was determined and the telegram itself dispatched. The sense of strain and difficulty in the room seemed to deepen. There was nothing for Lord Stanley to do but go. And then, as he turned to leave, he saw what he had not observed before, that one side of Macdonald's face was slightly drawn and twisted.[87]

The door closed upon the Governor-General. Thompson departed almost immediately after. For a few moments Macdonald was left alone, and then, as if he could bear the solitude no longer, he crossed into the outer office to speak to Pope.

"I am afraid of paralysis," he said, and there was a harsh note of apprehension in his voice. "Both my parents died of it, and I seem to feel it creeping over me."[88]

Pope called a cab. Together they walked down Parliament Hill to meet it. By that time Macdonald seemed better; and at half past six, when the doctor called at Earnscliffe, he found his patient still further improved and his speech nearly restored. Together and very gravely they talked over the ominous event of the afternoon.[89] Macdonald admitted that for some time past he had felt a slight want of power in his left arm and an occasional tingling in his left hand and fingers. Powell explained his condition, pointed out the almost inevitable consequence of continued effort, and earnestly advised complete rest. It was Macdonald's last chance; but he declined to take it. Complete rest, or an absence from Ottawa while Parliament was sitting, was, he informed Powell, utterly out of the question. He stuck to his post. He came to Council; he attended Parliament. And for a while fortune seemed to favour his magnificent audacity. He grew rapidly better. And from Monday to Friday of the penultimate week in May he was almost his old gay self again.

Friday, May 22, 1891, was a day like any other day in the Commons House of the Parliament of Canada. There was nothing to distinguish it from all the other hundreds of days he had spent there since the far-off session of 1865. Late spring had come wafted in on a breeze that was as soft and warm as that of midsummer; and Parliament Hill was heavy with the scent of lilac. "Sir John is very well and bright again," Thompson wrote that day to his wife.[90] It almost seemed that Macdonald's old parliamentary form had come back once more. He did not speak at any length; but he intervened again and again in the debate with his accustomed urbane and jocular

JOHN A. MACDONALD

comments. He was still in his place when the adjournment came at eleven o'clock; and he lingered for a while on the terrace outside, chatting with his Minister of Customs, Mackenzie Bowell. It was like a summer night. The laden lilac bushes rimmed the crest of Parliament Hill, and beyond that the land fell steeply away to the river below and rose on the other side to the low dark hills of the Precambrian Shield. And somewhere out there, hidden in the rock and forest, bright under the moonlight, was the railway, his railway, the track of Canada, the track of destiny, thrusting its way forward, mile after mile, towards the north-west.

"It is late, Bowell," he said. "Good-night."

Epilogue

The Sixth of June, 1891

I

IT WAS six o'clock when he reached Earnscliffe on the evening of Saturday, May 23. Parliament, of course, stood adjourned for the week-end; but he had taken advantage of the free day to call a meeting of the Cabinet, and the whole afternoon had been filled with its prolonged deliberations. Slowly he alighted from the cab; and Agnes, who had come anxiously out to the gate to meet him, saw at once, with the familiar pang, how dreadfully weary he looked. She took his brief-case—the inevitable accompaniment of his journeys home—in her hand; and when they walked up the path together arm-in-arm, it was she who was giving support to him.[1]

It was Saturday night; and by a long established rule which had become a tradition of his premiership, Saturday night during the session was the invariable occasion of a large dinner-party at Earnscliffe. The guests were all invited; in another hour or so they would be arriving. It was impossible, he told the worried Agnes, to cancel the affair at this late hour. He would preside, as he had done so many times in the past, at his own dinner table; and with the old resilience his spirits seemed to rise instinctively to meet the occasion. He was in his best form that night. It was as though he had inwardly determined that the guests at that last dinner-party would carry away with them an unspoilt memory of the geniality of their host. When Pope left him at about ten o'clock, it seemed to the secretary that the old Sir John—the Sir John not only of a few months, but even of a few years ago—had been miraculously restored.[2]

The last guest departed. He was flushed and suddenly tired. The room was warm—warm with the quickly produced heat of a spring night when the air outside is chill enough to discourage too much ventilation. Another window was flung open; and for a few moments he sat beside it, relaxed in an easy chair, while the cool air flowed refreshingly over him. It seemed nothing at the time; but next day they remembered the tiny incident, for next day he was suddenly worse again. He had contracted a cold—a slight cold only, surely; but with it those frightening symptoms, which had troubled him so much at Kingston three months ago, seemed to reappear.[3] His voice was very weak. He felt an oppressive sense of constriction across his chest; and when he coughed there came a sharp spurt of pain.

Early in the afternoon, the now seriously worried Agnes summoned the doctor. Powell gave his patient immediate relief; and for two days he succeeded in keeping him in bed, with gradually encouraging results. On the third day, Wednesday, May 27, Macdonald could bear the inaction no longer. The thought of the vast, accumulating, and accusing pile of correspondence downstairs was too much for him. He insisted that morning on going down to his study, and there, with Pope, he worked steadily through the greater part of the day. When Powell came for his evening visit, he told the doctor that he felt fairly comfortable. He was tired and weak. But then that was to be expected. He had put in a fairly full day. And it was without much apprehension, and with even a small feeling of satisfaction at a good day's work well done, that he went to bed that night. He was awakened suddenly at about half past two in the morning. He had called aloud without realizing that he had done so. The terrified Agnes was bending over him; and in a few minutes he became aware that there was little sensation in his left leg, and that the power and feeling in his left arm seemed completely gone.[4]

He lay on the bed, stretched out in stillness, and waited. Thank God, he could talk. When the doctor, hastily summoned, arrived at a little past three o'clock, he could discuss his symptoms with him with his usual laconic clarity. The left side of his face was slightly stiffened and twisted; but there was no impairment in his speech, and before the dawn of that brief night of late spring, he had already partially recovered from the effects of his seizure. By half past nine o'clock he could, with some effort, draw his left leg slowly up towards his body; and although the numbness in his left arm was more stubbornly resistant, it also seemed to be slowly passing away as the morning wore on. When Pope arrived, after the doctor had left and the breakfast hour was over, Macdonald greeted him with his usual composure. There was no fear in his eyes, and no disquietude in his voice. He discussed at some length, and with an interest which was not in the least perfunctory, two resolutions which he intended shortly to bring before Parliament. It was as if he fully expected to be back in his place in the House of Commons by the following Monday at the latest! And in one brief episode only was there a hint of his realistic awareness of his condition. He asked Pope to bring him one of his estate documents, and Pope inquired whether he wished to sign it then or later.

"Now," he replied briefly, "while there is time."[5]

Powell had requested a consultation. In some mysterious fashion a rumour of the increased seriousness of the Prime Minister's illness was already running through Ottawa;[6] and when, in mid-afternoon, Doctors George Ross and James Stewart arrived from Montreal, the grave news was amply confirmed. By four o'clock the consulting physicians were at Macdonald's bedside. His speech was unimpaired; his intellect was unclouded. He could move his left leg fairly freely now; and although the numbness in his left arm still persisted, he could lift it to his head and extend it from his body with relative ease. He was, the doctors considered, making the most remarkable recovery. But obviously a slight lesion had occurred; and, with the utmost earnestness, they explained the real state of affairs to the patient and assured him that the only way of averting a second and probably fatal seizure was complete rest in bed and entire freedom from public business for at least some weeks to come. With grave courtesy, Macdonald thanked them for their kindness and their candour. Lady Macdonald was informed.

A bulletin was drafted for publication; and at six o'clock Dr. Powell went up to the Privy Council room, met the Cabinet solemnly assembled, and informed its members of everything that had taken place.[7]

II

Macdonald spent the evening placidly reading in bed. It was, whether he was well or ill, the normal conclusion of every day; and that night he enjoyed his usual amount—about six hours—of sleep. When morning came on Friday, May 29, he was evidently feeling better still. He had a cup of tea. He moved his left arm with considerably more freedom, Dr. Powell observed, than he had even on the previous evening; and when Pope came at about ten o'clock, he reverted, with an instinctive and incorrigible impulse, to the habit of a lifetime, and demanded to see the morning's letters.[8] Pope brought up a few of them—carefully choosing those of minor importance: and a few minutes later he came hurrying in again with a piece of information of obviously much greater interest. Sir John Thompson, the Minister of Justice, had called at Earnscliffe and was waiting below. Macdonald instantly determined to seize the opportunity which this visit afforded. It was nearly a week since he had seen any one of his colleagues. He was hungry to re-establish contact, to re-impose his accustomed control; and Thompson was his favourite minister, to whom he imparted his most intimate confidences. He gave orders that the Minister of Justice was to be shown up at once.

Thompson entered the room in some trepidation. He was a worried and anxious man. His own responsibility, which was great enough before, had been magnified to an uncertain but an enormous extent within the past few days. The rumours, the bulletins, the news of the doctors' consultation had all done their disintegrating work. In forty-eight hours the character of the House had utterly changed. The government side was weighed down with anxiety; the opposition was alive with eager expectation. "The Grits," Thompson wrote to his wife that day, "are like a lot of pirates prepared to make a rush. We will have a caucus on Tuesday and rally our men." How could it be done? Without a known and accepted leader, how could the rank and file be effectively rallied? He glanced again at the man who lay on the bed before him. Macdonald's mouth was firm, his eyes were alert. He might have been recuperating from a slight illness. He was obviously better. He might even get well again. But, in his heart of hearts, Thompson did not believe it. "The probability is," he told his wife a little later, "that he will not be in the House again this session, if ever."[9]

If ever. The wordless phrase hovered in the air between them. It was the inarticulate first premise of their speculations. Who was to succeed? There was no instantly obvious first choice. There were far too few real possibilities. For months, for years, Macdonald's thoughts had trudged wearily round and round this small, closed circle of selection. He knew everything that had been said, and that could be said, for and against every conceivable candidate. A case could be made out for Langevin, for Tupper, and for Thompson. But he was aware of the disability of Thompson's religion, of the disrepute into which Langevin had fallen as a result of the recent scandals, of Tupper's unpopularity with certain important Cabinet ministers, including Thompson, and of Tupper's own preference for his work as High Commissioner in London. The idea of a stop-gap appointment, of a temporary, provisional prime minister, who would hold the government and the party together until the issue of the leadership had been settled, was an obvious idea that had occurred to him before. Late in the spring, at one of the last Cabinet meetings that he had attended, he had suggested such a plan to Thompson. "Thompson," he said slowly, "when I am gone, you will have to rally around Abbott; he is your only man."[10] Abbott had held office for only a few years, but he was a veteran member of Parliament, and an old and loyal Conservative; and the fact that he sat in the Senate, rather than the House of Commons, would have the additional advantage of giving Thompson, in the Commons, a large measure of effective control. Abbott's honour would be titular, as well as provisional. But, even so, was he worthy of it? Macdonald was not sure. His doubts and uncertainties returned. He did not feel particularly drawn to Abbott. And, even in this last extremity, he still hesitated to perform the final solemn act of naming a successor.

"Thompson," he said faintly but firmly, "some time ago I said you would have to rally round Abbott, that he was your only man. I have changed my mind now, he is too selfish."[11]

He would have spoken more. But Thompson was anxious to end the visit. The old man must not be tired. And had he not talked enough—and more than enough—already? As gently but as swiftly as he could, the Minister of Justice brought the conversation to a close and withdrew. Macdonald was left alone; but not for long. At about midday, a second visitor— Dr. Sullivan, the physician who had attended him during his break-down in Kingston in mid-winter—paid a brief call to the sick-room. Then the patient had a little milk and a few spoon-fuls of beef-tea. He was resting and reading one of the reviews, when Powell arrived at a little after half past three. For a while the doctor and his patient talked softly together. The room was very still. The whole house was hushed in silence; and outside the lawns and terraces of Earnscliffe drowsed in the hot sun of late May. Powell was putting the usual routine questions to his patient, and Macdonald was making his usual replies. And then, as if he wished merely to dispose himself a little more comfortably during this gentle interrogation, the old man leaned his head back upon the pillow. He yawned once or twice. And, in a second, he seemed to become un-conscious.

The doctor started forward. Could it be? In an instant he knew that there was no possible doubt. The man lying on the bed before him had received a second and devastating stroke. The entire right side of his body was paralysed. He was bereft of speech.[12]

It was four o'clock on the afternoon of Friday, May 29.

III

Agnes, Hugh John, and Pope were summoned at once. Hurriedly, in low tones, the doctor explained to them what had probably occurred. The stricken man was conscious of their frightened presence. He tried desperately to speak to his son; and his utter failure brought home to them all the completeness of the tragedy that had befallen him. Time was of the essence now. Death might come in a few hours—even in a few minutes. The doctor moved swiftly to give his patient quick relief, to get immediate assistance, and to send the necessary warnings. He dispatched messengers requesting two Ottawa physicians— Sir James Grant and Dr. H. P. Wright—to come at once to Earnscliffe for a consultation. He wrote to both the Governor-General and Sir Hector Langevin informing them of the sudden dreadful change in his patient's condition.

Earnscliffe waited in the strained silence of painful expectancy. It was half past six, and the rooms were rich with the golden light of early evening when Sir James Grant and Dr. Wright arrived. They and Dr. Powell were a long time together in the silent room upstairs; but if Agnes clutched at the vain hope that the length of the consultation might mean an uncertainty of diagnosis or a division of expert opinion, she was soon undeceived. The doctors were in entire agreement. The symptoms were very marked; and as Dr. Powell explained, it was obvious that "a hæmorrhage had taken place into the left hemisphere, chiefly confined to the motor area".[13] When the stroke came, the patient had been resting quietly in bed, there had apparently been no disturbance in the heart's action, and, in Powell's opinion, the damage was somewhat less serious than might have been expected. Even so, Macdonald was in a highly critical condition; and the doctors clearly feared for the worst. At eight o'clock they issued a bulletin for publication; and a little later, in a second letter to Langevin, Sir James Grant gave, without extenuation, the gloomy conclusion they had reached. "I have just seen Sir John in consultation," he wrote. "Entire loss of speech. Hæmorrhage on the brain. Condition hopeless."[14]

It was past nine o'clock when this message arrived on Parliament Hill. The House of Commons was in evening session. For most of the day the members had been discussing a Liberal resolution deploring Sir Charles Tupper's recent participation in

the Canadian general election as a breach of his duties as High
Commissioner for Canada in London. It was the same subject
that had been up a week before, on the last day that Macdonald
had attended Parliament; but the opposition had a great deal
more to say about it, and C. H. Mackintosh, the Conservative
member for Ottawa City, was endeavouring to reply to Cartwright's attack when Sir James Grant's note was brought in.
For a moment Langevin stared at the message. He passed it
swiftly to the other ministers; he crossed the floor and whispered
the news to Laurier. The House became rapidly aware that
something gravely unusual had occurred; and a minute later,
when the Minister of Public Works got up to move the adjournment, all doubts were ended. Langevin's voice was
strangely shaken. "I have the painful duty," he said, speaking
with some difficulty, "to announce to the House that the news
from Earnscliffe just received is that the First Minister has had
a relapse, and that he is in a most critical condition. We have
reports from the medical men in attendance on the right honourable gentleman, and they do not seem to believe that he
can live many hours longer."[15]

A minute later the House adjourned. It was nearly ten
o'clock. The members crowded about the Minister of Public
Works. He repeated the news; he showed Sir James Grant's
message. When there was no more to learn, Conservatives and
Liberals stood about in little groups discussing the calamity in
hushed voices; and Langevin sat in his place, the tears running
down his cheeks. He was an uninspiring man, with no great
ability except in the routines of administration and with much
too ingrained a disposition to nepotism and jobbery. But for
over thirty years, through every conceivable situation and all
possible danger, he had been loyal to Macdonald. Commonplace, mercenary, ageing, he was the embodiment of loyalty;
and in that moment it might have seemed that loyalty would
redeem him.

"For thirty-three years I have been his follower," he kept
saying over and over again. "For thirty-three years I have been
his follower."[16]

He and Thompson and Chapleau drove out that night to

Earnscliffe. Earlier in the evening, while the House was still in session, the Governor-General had called. He had informed the Queen by cable. By ten o'clock the news was speeding over the telegraph wires to every city, town, and village in Canada; and next morning, on the front pages of scores of newspapers, it was revealed to millions of shocked Canadians. In some headlines, Macdonald was referred to by his name; in others by his official title; and in still others—as if there could not be the faintest doubt as to who was meant—by pronoun only. *He is dying.* The Canadians knew the worst now. They expected him to die. They—like the physicians who had issued the first bulletin—could not see how he could long survive such an appalling shock. The Monday morning newspapers, they felt sure, would bring the news of his death. But Monday came, and the final, fatal intelligence did not appear. He still lived. The hours went by and he still lived. And gradually, as the hours mounted into another day, the Canadians began to realize that far away, in the hushed chamber at Earnscliffe, a last struggle was being waged against death itself.

IV

It was the first of June. The Ottawa valley was bathed in heat and light. For two weeks there had been scarcely any rain.[17] The sun rose blood-red at dawn and sank at night into a blood-red sky. Behind its drawn curtains, the great dim bed-chamber at Earnscliffe was drowsy with summer heat; and there he lay, wasted, silent, somnolent, but still alive. His splendid vitality, which he had used and abused so often and which had never failed him yet, was fighting a final, involuntary battle for his existence. His heart's action was weak and irregular: his breathing rapid and laboured. It was painfully evident that his vital forces were close to the last point of exhaustion. Yet he lived on. Whether he willed it or no, his body continued its desperate fight for life. He could swallow the milk and beef tea and champagne which they gave him so carefully. He knew when he desired the slight relief of being moved from one side to the other of the bed.

What he felt was not mere consciousness of physical wants. Deep in its ultimate citadel, behind the thick walls of paralysis and silence, his mind was still working, imperfectly but coolly, reasonably, as it had always done. He could not speak. His whole right side was immobilized. But his left arm, which had first tingled with the threat of paralysis, was still unimpaired; and by the pressure of his left hand he could still communicate with the watchers by his bedside. It was his last contact with the world; and he used it surely, without the slightest hesitation and without a single mistake.[18] If a question were put by one of the doctors or nurses in such a way that the answering pressure might mean either yes or no, then his hand remained slack. It was only when the meaning of the slight movement had become plain and unmistakable that he gave it, if he so desired. His wishes, which came faintly but surely, and, as it were, out of endless distances, were commands which the watchers were anxious to carry out to the letter. There must be no mistake. What he wanted, must be done, and done exactly. And sometimes, to complete assurance, they put their questions in different ways, both positively and negatively. The response was always the same. He was never confused himself; he never confused them. He talked, in this strange way, with Agnes, Hugh John, Pope, Fred White, and the others who served him; and repeatedly, while his wife sat beside the bed, he answered her unuttered and unutterable question with a gentle pressure of his hand.

The room was hushed. The house was hushed. The grounds lay silent in the sunshine. The tugs which laboured up the river dragging the lumber barges behind them had ceased to blow their whistles; the bells had been taken off the horse-drawn street-cars which passed slowly up and down Sussex Street.[19] The world had drawn back, respectfully, reverently; but it had drawn back only a little way. A long procession of people came daily to make inquiries of the guardian at the gate. A short distance away, a bell tent had been pitched for the Canadian Pacific Railway telegraph operator: and every few hours the newspaper correspondents came down in a body to read the latest bulletin and to put their innumerable questions to the doctors. The whole country waited for news; and in the meantime, while it waited, it was consumed by curious and anxious speculation.

In Ottawa, Thompson wrote sardonically to his wife, the buzz of excitement was intense. What was going to happen? Who, if death came, would succeed the old chief? There was a movement in favour of Tupper, which Tupper himself quickly discouraged in an emphatic cable to his son. Langevin's declining chances were discussed. Thompson's name grew increasingly prominent; and Thompson himself, so he told his wife, was "trying to bring about an arrangement by which Abbott will be the new Premier".[20] It was all speculative, indefinite, uncertain. Nothing could be done until the struggle in the still room at Earnscliffe had ended; nothing would be done, Lord Stanley let it be known, until the inevitable and elaborate state funeral was over. Thompson, though he had determined to decline the succession himself, was annoyed at the prospect of this further and, to him, unconstitutional delay. The Governor-General, he reasoned, had no right to be without a government an hour longer than he could help.[21] Yet at what hour, in the eyes of the Canadians, would the government of the maker of their country really be over? He was ruling Canada from his death-bed. He would rule Canada until he had been buried in its earth.

For five days the eyes of the whole country were fixed upon Earnscliffe. And then, on the sixth day, Thursday, June 4, the unrevealing and monotonous gloom of the bulletins was suddenly interrupted by a ray of hope. In Ottawa, the weather, after the brief rain of the previous day, was slightly cooler; the horizon, which had been smudged with the smoke of bush fires, was clear once more.[22] And inside the dim room in the house by the cliff side, a remarkable, an unmistakable change seemed to be taking place. "Sir John Macdonald passed a fairly comfortable night . . . ," the medical men reported in their mid-morning bulletin. "His cerebral symptoms are slightly improved at the time of our consultation, owing doubtless to the fact that having lived six days since his seizure, partial absorption has had time to take place."[23] Was it possible? Was the hæmorrhage slowly disappearing? Had they the right to hope? Rapidly, as the news sped across the nation, the current of speculation changed and quickened. Inside Earnscliffe the little group of anxious people maintained their watch with breathless intentness. Still he seemed to improve. By mid-afternoon it was obvious that he was recognizing faces much more easily and naturally than he had yet done since his seizure; and one by one those closest to him came and lingered for a few moments at his bedside. Was it a last farewell? Or was it, perhaps, a first faint greeting?

For a few hours more the scales hung even; and then they tilted slowly against him. He was weaker again that night. He was weaker still at noon on Friday when Dr. George Ross, hastily summoned for the second time from Montreal, arrived to take part in the usual midday examination. "At a consultation today," the doctors declared in their two o'clock bulletin, "we find Sir John Macdonald altogether in a somewhat alarming state. His strength, which has gradually failed him during this past week, shows a marked decline since yesterday. . . . In our opinion his powers of life are steadily waning."[24] Hour after hour, as the long afternoon melted into evening, the slow decline continued. The little flame of his consciousness, which had flared up for the last time during the previous afternoon, died slowly down; and finally, after the true darkness had fallen, it flickered out.

There was another short, still summer night, with, far away, the faint roar of the Chaudière Falls. There was another red dawn, and another long, brilliant summer day, while the river, all splashed with sunshine as it had been on that first Dominion Day, flowed serenely past and away to the north-east. Then, when once more the sun had gone down behind the long blue line of the Laurentians, the last change came. Up to then his breathing had been shallow and rapid. Now it grew slower, slower still, and, as the watchers clustered around him, died away in the last, faint, lingering prolongations. He was going now. He was borne on and outward, past care and planning, past England and Canada, past life and into death.

V

Outside, in the grounds surrounding Earnscliffe, it was very still. At a little before ten o'clock, most of the newspaper men had given up their vigil. The watch had been left to two correspondents, who had strolled slowly over to the Canadian Pacific telegraph tent, and who were now strolling slowly back again. They had just reached the gate when quick foot-steps were heard hastening softly towards them down the path. The lantern hanging above shed a dim light; and by it they could see Joe Pope's strained, worn face. It was exactly twenty-four minutes past ten on the night of Saturday, June 6.

"Gentlemen," Pope said brokenly, "Sir John Macdonald is dead. He died at a quarter past ten."[25]

He added, in reply to the one question which the corres-pondents thought of asking, that the end had come quietly and peacefully. Then he fixed Dr. Powell's last bulletin to the gate of Earnscliffe. In a few minutes the news was flashing east and west across the telegraph wires. In a few minutes more, the bells began to toll in Ottawa; and before midnight, they were tolling in most of the cities of the Dominion.

He lay, the next day, in the room in which he had died. It was not until nine o'clock on Sunday that his body was moved downstairs to the spacious, lofty room which he had added to Earnscliffe and which was hung now with heavy draperies of white and purple.[26] In his uniform of an imperial Privy Coun-cillor and with the insignia of his orders at his side, he lay there all through Monday. The Governor-General, the ministers, a small group of his friends and associates entered one by one to stand briefly by his side. But these few people were only a small fraction of the thousands who wished to have a last glimpse of him, and who were even now hurrying towards Ottawa by train and carriage and farm waggon. A state funeral, the Cabinet had decided on Sunday night, was obviously necessary; Agnes had agreed; and as soon as Parliament opened on Monday afternoon, Langevin, the senior surviving minister, formally announced the old Prime Minister's death and formally moved that he should be "publicly interred and that this House will concur in giving to the ceremony a fitting degree of solemnity and importance". Laurier followed in support; and it was curious, and yet not inappropriate, that both the eulogies pronounced that afternoon should have been given by French-speaking Canadians. Laurier, of course, was by far the more gracefully eloquent of the two; but there was a simple, dogged sincerity in Langevin's broken, commonplace sentences and in his abrupt close. "Mr. Speaker," he said, "I would have wished to continue to speak of our dear departed friend, and spoken to you about the goodness of his heart, the witness of which I have been so often, but I feel that I must stop; my heart is full of tears. I cannot proceed further."[27]

Next day, Tuesday, June 9, the body lay in state in the Senate chamber of the Parliament of Canada. The Canadians, of all ages and every occupation, were looking their last upon him. They came all that day and far into the night; and early next morning the packed queue slowed down again to a mere crawl. It was nearly twelve o'clock and the chamber was about to be closed to the public, when Sir Casimir Gzowski, the representative of the Queen, walked solemnly forward and laid a wreath of roses upon the dead man's breast. "From Her Majesty Queen Victoria," ran the inscription, "in memory of Her faithful and devoted servant."[28] It was the ultimate tribute. The great room slowly emptied. The last preparations were made. At a quarter past one exactly the bell in the clock tower began to toll; and slowly, with majestic deliberation, the funeral procession moved forward.

The night, like so many of the nights of that early summer, had been oppressively sultry. During the forenoon it grew steadily hotter and hotter. And now the long procession moved slowly down Rideau Street under a blue and burning sky. Between the rows of shops and houses, draped in their folds of black and purple, people were massed in thousands. Around St. Alban's Church, the crowd was thickest; and as the short service drew towards its close, the tropical atmosphere seemed to grow ominously heavier. It was more oppressive still when the funeral procession laboriously reformed and started back again towards the station. A curious yellow haze hung in the air. To the west, a great black cloud soared menacingly over Parliament Hill. There came a sudden fierce gust of wind—a violent scattering of huge raindrops. And then, in an overwhelming deluge, the storm broke upon the city.

At the railway station, the Canadian Pacific engine was draped in black and purple. Every engine and every station along the long transcontinental line of his railway was hung with mourning; and as the train swept westward towards Kingston that late afternoon, under skies cleared by the storm and golden with sunset, there were crowds on every station platform, and groups by the roadsides, and lone figures standing waiting in the fields. It was late at night by the time the train reached Kingston, but the station was packed with people. People began to assemble before the City Hall where the body lay in state, at five o'clock on the morning of June 11. People kept pouring into the town in increasing numbers as the sun climbed higher in the sky; and then, on foot and in every kind of vehicle, they followed him in thousands on his last journey over the dusty roads to the Cataraqui cemetery.[29]

"I desire that I shall be buried in the Kingston cemetery near the grave of my mother, as I promised her that I should be there buried."[30] He lay close to his parents, his first wife, his sisters, and his long-dead infant. The terraced slope rose to a slight eminence; and from there, away to the south-east, a few of Kingston's tallest towers and roofs were visible. Somewhere in that huddle of grey limestone buildings was the little shop on Quarry Street where he had begun to practise law. There, overlooking the Lake, stood the Italian villa, "Bellevue", where his firstborn had died. It was nearly seventy-one years since Hugh and Helen Macdonald and their small family of children had first set foot on the dock at Kingston. Beyond the dock lay the harbour and the islands which marked the end of the lowest of the Great Lakes; and beyond the islands the St. Lawrence River began its long journey to the sea.

A NOTE ON AUTHORITIES

The second volume of this biography, like the first, is based on materials contemporary with the events described in the text. The principal sources are collections of documents which are to be found in various archives and libraries, public and private, in Canada and Great Britain. A number of these collections have been found useful in the composition of both volumes of this biography; and for a description of such materials, the reader is referred to the note on authorities which was published in *John A. Macdonald, the Young Politician*. Here it will be sufficient to comment briefly on the nature of the evidence peculiar to *John A. Macdonald, the Old Chieftain*, and to indicate the collections which have not been listed already.

In general, the sources, both manuscript and printed, are richer and more numerous for *The Old Chieftain* than for *The Young Politician*. The evidence for the last twenty-four years of Macdonald's career is, in fact, extremely large in quantity and high in quality. Most of this material has been used very little in the past; and a substantial portion of it is here used for the first time. The Macdonald Papers, which continue to be the most important single source for the biography, are much more voluminous for the post-Confederation, than for the pre-Confederation, period. They are supplemented by valuable collections of the papers of Macdonald's principal colleagues, of which the Tupper Papers and the Thompson Papers at the Public Archives of Canada, and the Alexander Campbell Papers at the Public Records and Archives of Ontario, have been the most useful. The domestic side of Macdonald's life is illuminated by a diary of Lady Macdonald, in the possession of Mrs. D. F. Pepler, which covers the early post-Confederation years; and the political gossip of Ottawa, as it came to the attention of an informed and responsible civil servant, is revealed in the diary of Edmund A. Meredith.

The papers of the governors-general and the colonial secretaries of the period have provided some of the richest sources of material for *The Old Chieftain*. Macdonald was accustomed to write regularly and frequently to his political chiefs in much the same way as Disraeli and Gladstone reported to Queen Victoria; and the governors-general, in their turn, retailed the inner history of Canadian affairs to their political superiors, the colonial secretaries. The Argyll Papers—the correspondence of the Marquess of Lorne while Governor-General of Canada— and the Lansdowne Papers both contain a substantial number of Macdonald's letters. The Earl Granville, the Earl of Kimberley, the Earl of Carnarvon, and Sir Michael Hicks Beach, later the first Earl St. Aldwyn, occupied in turn the office of colonial secretary during a large part of the period covered by this volume; and their papers have proved extremely valuable. *The Dufferin-Carnarvon Correspondence, 1874-1878*, edited by C. W. de Kiewiet and F. H. Underhill (Toronto, the Champlain Society, 1955) has been recently published; but, in *The Old Chieftain* all references are to the original manuscripts in the Public Record Office, London. Finally, the correspondence of Sir Stafford Northcote, the first Earl of Iddesleigh, who was one of the British High Commissioners at the Washington Conference of 1871 and, for some time, the Governor of the Hudson's Bay Company, has provided some interesting information concerning the fisheries negotiations and the Red River Rebellion.

NOTES

Chapter One: *The Pacification of Nova Scotia*

(Pages 1 to 32)

[1] *Globe* (Toronto), 8 November, 1867.

[2] Diary of Lady Macdonald, 7 July, 1867.

[3] *Ibid.*

[4] Public Archives of Canada, Macdonald Papers, vol. 514, Macdonald to Bischoff, 17 October, 1867.

[5] *Leader* (Toronto), 9 November, 1867; *Globe*, 9 November, 1867.

[6] Macdonald Papers, vol. 514, Macdonald to Hill, 11 November, 1867.

[7] *Leader*, 11 November, 1867.

[8] Macdonald Papers, vol. 514, Macdonald to Archbishop Connolly, 31 December, 1867.

[9] Lady Macdonald's Diary, 11 January, 1868.

[10] *Ibid.*, 7 July, 1867.

[11] *Ibid.*, 1 December, 1867.

[12] *Ibid.*, 19 January, 24, 26 March, 1868.

[13] *Ibid.*, 17 November, 1867.

[14] Norman Ward, "The Formative Years of The House of Commons, 1867-91", *Canadian Journal of Economics and Political Science*, vol. 18 (Nov. 1952), pp. 431-451.

[15] Macdonald Papers, vol. 514, Macdonald to Cook, 3 February, 1868.

[16] Lady Macdonald's Diary, 11 January, 1868.

[17] *Debates and Proceedings of the House of Assembly of the Province of Nova Scotia*, 1868 (Halifax), pp. 34-35.

[18] Lady Macdonald's Diary, 7, 27 February, 1868.

[19] Macdonald Papers, additional, vol. 2, Macdonald to Louisa Macdonald, 6 March, 1868; Lady Macdonald's Diary, 25 February, 1868.

[20] Macdonald Papers, vol. 194, Campbell to Macdonald, 28 February, 1868.

[21] *Ibid.*, vol. 514, Macdonald to McCully, 29 February, 1868.

[22] *Globe*, 20 March, 1868.

[23] *Ibid.*, 7 April, 1868; Isabel Skelton, *The Life of Thomas D'Arcy McGee* (Gardenvale, Canada, 1925), pp. 537-538.

[24] Lady Macdonald's Diary, 12 April, 1868.

[25] Josephine Phelan, *The Ardent Exile* (Toronto, 1951), pp. 296-297.

[26] *Globe*, 8 April, 1868.

[27] Journal of Edmund A. Meredith, vol. 6, 7 April, 1868.

[28] E. M. Saunders, *The Life and Letters of the Rt. Hon. Sir Charles Tupper, Bart., K.C.M.G.* (London, 1916), vol. 1, pp. 167-169, Macdonald to Tupper, 30 April, 1868.

[29] Macdonald Papers, vol. 514, Macdonald to Archibald, 4 July, 1868.

[30] *Ibid.*, vol. 115, Tilley to Macdonald, 17 July, 1868; *ibid.*, Archibald to Macdonald, 17 July, 1868.

[31] Sir Joseph Pope, *Correspondence of Sir John Macdonald* (Toronto, n.d.), pp. 67-70, Monck to Macdonald, 29 July, 1868.

[32] Macdonald Papers, vol. 514, Macdonald to J. S. Macdonald, 30 May, 1868; *ibid.*, Macdonald to Tupper, 4 July, 1868.

[33] Public Archives of Canada, Chamberlin Papers, vol. 2, Macdonald to Chamberlin, 26 October, 1868.

[34] *Globe*, 4 August, 1868.

[35] Joseph Pope, *Memoirs of the Right Honourable Sir John Alexander Macdonald, G.C.B., First Prime Minister of the Dominion of Canada* (London, 1894), vol. 2, p. 29, Howe to Macdonald, 1 August, 1868.

[36] *Ibid.*, vol. 2, pp. 29-34, Macdonald to Monck, 4 September, 1868.

[37] Macdonald Papers, vol. 115, Minutes of the Convention, August, 1868.

[38] Pope, *Memoirs*, vol. 2, pp. 29-34, Macdonald to Monck, 4 September, 1868.

[39] Macdonald Papers, vol. 115, Macdonald to Howe, 7 August, 1868.

[40] *Globe*, 8, 10 August, 1868.

[41] Pope, *Memoirs*, vol. 2, pp. 29-34, Macdonald to Monck, 4 September, 1868.

[42] Lady Macdonald's Diary, 27 August, 1868.

[43] *Ibid.*, 19 September, 1868.

[44] *Ibid.*, 21 September, 1868.

[45] Macdonald Papers, vol. 514, Macdonald to Rose, 23 September, 1868.

[46] Pope, *Memoirs*, vol. 2, appendix 18, pp. 302-303, Howe to Macdonald, 15 September, 1868.

[47] Macdonald Papers, vol. 514, Macdonald to Howe, 6 October, 1868.

[48] *Ibid.*, vol. 115, Howe to Macdonald, 13 October, 1868.

[49] Saunders, *Tupper*, vol. 1, p. 187, Macdonald to Tupper, 20 November, 1868.

[50] Macdonald Papers, vol. 515, Macdonald to Archibald, 27 October, 1868.

[51] Pope, *Memoirs*, vol. 2, appendix 18, pp. 303-304, Macdonald to Howe, 26 September, 1868.

[52] *Ibid.*, vol. 2, appendix 18, pp. 305-306, Macdonald to Howe, 4 November, 1868.

[53] *Globe*, 28 November, 1868.

[54] Macdonald Papers, vol. 202, Cartier to Macdonald, 24 December, 1868.

[55] Public Archives of Canada, Tupper Papers, Macdonald to Tupper, 2 January, 1869.

[56] Macdonald Papers, vol. 515, Macdonald to Howe, 23 December, 1868.

[57] *Ibid.*, Macdonald to Davis, 15 January, 1869.

[58] Lady Macdonald's Diary, 13 January, 1869.

[59] Tupper Papers, Macdonald to Tupper, 2 January, 1869.

[60] Macdonald Papers, vol. 515, Macdonald to White, 1 February, 1869.

[61] Lady Macdonald's Diary, 30 January, 1869.

[62] Macdonald Papers, vol. 515, Macdonald to Langevin, 25 January, 1869.

[63] Lady Macdonald's Diary, 7 February, 1 April, 1869.

CHAPTER TWO: *The West in Jeopardy*

(Pages 33 to 69)

1 *Globe*, 24, 27 February, 1869; Journal of E. A. Meredith, vol. 6, 27 February, 1869; Macdonald Papers, vol. 515, Macdonald to Howe, 8 March, 1869.

2 Lady Macdonald's Diary, 11 April, 1869.

3 Macdonald Papers, vol. 539, Allan to Macdonald, 20 April, 1869.

4 *Ibid.*, Allan to Macdonald, 24 April, 1869.

5 *Ibid.*, vol. 515, Macdonald to Doyle, 16 June, 1869.

6 *Ibid.*, Macdonald to Young, 25 May, 1869.

7 Charles Clarke, *Sixty Years in Upper Canada, with Autobiographical Recollections* (Toronto, 1908), pp. 56-59; G. W. Ross, *Getting into Parliament and After* (Toronto, 1913), pp. 23-28.

8 R. S. Longley, *Sir Francis Hincks, A Study of Canadian Politics, Railways and Finance in the Nineteenth Century* (Toronto, 1943), pp. 348-349.

9 *Globe*, 31 July, 5 August, 1869.

10 Macdonald Papers, vol. 516, Macdonald to Allan, 29 September, 1869.

11 *Ibid.*, vol. 520, Macdonald to O'Brien, 26 March, 1872.

12 Lady Macdonald's Diary, 27 February, 1868.

13 Journal of E. A. Meredith, vol. 7, 13 September, 1869.

14 *Globe*, 29 September, 1869.

15 Pope, *Correspondence*, p. 99, Rose to Macdonald, 27 September, 1869.

16 Journal of E. A. Meredith, vol. 7, 8 October, 1869.

17 Lady Macdonald's Diary, 7 November, 1869.

18 Macdonald Papers, vol. 516, Macdonald to Gray, 27 October, 1869.

19 *Ibid.*, Macdonald to Brown, 14 October, 1869.

20 *Ibid.*, Macdonald to McDougall, 8 December, 1869.

21 D. F. Warner, "Drang nach Norden—the United States and the Riel Rebellion", *Mississippi Valley Historical Review*, vol. 34 (March, 1953), pp. 693-712.

22 Northcote Papers, bundle 4, Northcote to Lampson, 20 April, 1870.

23 Macdonald Papers, vol. 516, Macdonald to Stephen, 9 December, 1869.

24 *Ibid.*, Macdonald to Cartier, 27 November, 1869.

25 *Ibid.*, Macdonald to McDougall, 27 November, 1869.

26 *Ibid.*, Macdonald to McDougall, 20 November, 1869.

27 *Ibid.*, Macdonald to Cartier, 27 November, 1869.

28 Lady Macdonald's Diary, 1 December, 1869.

29 G13, vol. 3, Granville to Young, 30 November, 1869.

30 Macdonald Papers, vol. 516, Macdonald to Rose, 5 December, 1869.

31 British Museum, Additional MSS. 44166 (Gladstone Papers), Granville to Gladstone, 29 November, 1869.

32 Macdonald Papers, vol. 516, Macdonald to McDougall, 12 December, 1869.

33 *Ibid.*, Macdonald to Archibald, 10 December, 1869.

34 *Ibid.*, Macdonald to McDougall, 27 November, 1869.

35 *Ibid.*, Macdonald to Cartier, 27 November, 1869.

36 Pope, *Memoirs*, vol. 2, pp. 59-61, Macdonald to Rose, 31 December, 1869.

37 *Ibid.*

38 Pope, *Correspondence*, p. 119, Macdonald to Rose, 3 January, 1870.

39 Northcote Papers, bundle 4, Lampson to Northcote, 31 January, 1870.

40 Macdonald Papers, vol. 516, Macdonald to Rose, 26 January, 1870.

41 Pope, *Correspondence*, p. 124, Macdonald to Brydges, 28 January, 1870.

42 Macdonald Papers, vol. 516, Macdonald to Carroll, 29 September, 1869.

43 *Ibid.*, vol. 258, Rose to Macdonald, 7 February, 1870.

44 C. P. Stacey, *Canada and the British Army, 1846-1871* (London, 1936), p. 216.

45 Northcote Papers, bundle 4, Lampson to Northcote, 31 January, 1870.

46 Macdonald Papers, vol. 516, Macdonald to Rose, 26 January, 1870.

47 Lady Macdonald's Diary, 1 April, 1870.

48 Pope, *Correspondence*, p. 120, Macdonald to Rose, 21 January, 1870.

49 *Parliamentary Debates*, 1870, pp. 449-468, 558-575.

50 Pope, *Correspondence*, p. 132, Macdonald to Rose, 25 March, 1870.

51 Macdonald Papers, vol. 517, Macdonald to Rose, 11 March, 1870.

52 *Ibid.*

53 Public Record Office, P.R.O. 30/29 (Granville Papers), Gladstone to Granville, 6 March, 1870; Royal Archives, D27, Gladstone to the Queen, 5 March, 1870.

54 British Museum, Additional MSS. 44167 (Gladstone Papers), Granville to Gladstone, 6 March, 1870.

55 G13, vol. 3, Granville to Young, 5 March, 1870.

56 Pope, *Correspondence*, p. 134, Macdonald to Carnarvon, 14 April, 1870.

57 G13, vol. 3, Young to Granville, 9 April, 1870.

58 Pope, *Correspondence*, p. 133, Macdonald to Carnarvon, 14 April, 1870.

59 *Globe*, 15 April, 1870.

60 *Ibid.*, 12 April, 1870.

61 G. F. G. Stanley, *The Birth of Western Canada, a History of the Riel Rebellions* (London, 1936), p. 95.

62 Journal of E. A. Meredith, 19 April, 1870; Royal Archives, P 24, Curle to Ponsonby, 22 April, 1870.

63 Northcote Papers, bundle 4, Northcote to Granville, 26 April, 1870.

64 *Globe*, 25 April, 1870.

65 Northcote Papers, bundle 4, Northcote to Lampson, 26 April, 1870.

66 Stanley, *Birth of Western Canada*, pp. 118-119.

67 *Ibid.*, p. 114.

68 Macdonald Papers, vol. 517, Macdonald to Young, 27 April, 1870.

69 Northcote Papers, bundle 1, Northcote to Disraeli, 28 April, 1870.

70 *Globe*, 4 May, 1870.

71 Journal of E. A. Meredith, vol. 7, 30 April, 1870.

72 Andrew Lang, *Life, Letters, and Diaries of Sir Stafford Northcote, First Earl of Iddesleigh* (Edinburgh and London, 1890), vol. 1, p. 331.

73 Macdonald Papers, vol. 517, Macdonald to Young, 4 May, 1870.

CHAPTER THREE: *Fish and Diplomacy*

(Pages 70 to 102)

1 Pope, *Memoirs*, vol. 2, p. 76; Northcote Papers, bundle 3, McNeill to Northcote, 7 May, 1870.

2 *Globe*, 30 May, 1870; Journal of E. A. Meredith, 30 May, 1870.

[3] Pope, *Correspondence*, p. 136, Blake to Bernard, 2 June, 1870.

[4] *Globe*, 18 June, 1870.

[5] *Islander* (Charlottetown), 8 July, 1870.

[6] *Ibid.*, 18 September, 1870.

[7] *Times* (Ottawa), 23 September, 1870.

[8] Macdonald Papers, vol. 517, Macdonald to Greer, 23 September, 1870.

[9] *Ibid.*, Macdonald to Mrs. Williamson, 23 September, 1870.

[10] *Ibid.*, Macdonald to Musgrave, 29 September, 1870.

[11] A. L. Burt, *The United States, Great Britain, and British North America, From the Revolution to the Establishment of Peace after the War of 1812* (New Haven and Toronto, 1940), pp. 418-419.

[12] R. S. Longley, "Peter Mitchell, Guardian of the North Atlantic Fisheries, 1867-1871", *Canadian Historical Review*, vol. 22 (December, 1941), pp. 389-402.

[13] Pope, *Correspondence*, p. 122, Macdonald to Rose, 21 January, 1870.

[14] Macdonald Papers, vol. 517, Macdonald to Macpherson, 4 November, 1870.

[15] *Ibid.*, Macdonald to O'Connor, 19 November, 1870.

[16] *Ibid.*, Macdonald to Archibald, 1 November, 1870.

[17] *Ibid.*, Macdonald to Campbell, 1 November, 1870.

[18] Kimberley Papers, Journal of Events during the Gladstone Ministry, 13 June, 1871.

[19] P.R.O. 30/29 (Granville Papers), vol. 80, Thornton to Granville, 20 September, 1870, 4 October, 1870.

[20] G. Smith, *The Treaty of Washington, 1871, A Study in Imperial History* (Ithaca, 1941), p. 25.

[21] Lady Macdonald's Diary, 3 January, 1871.

[22] *Ibid.*, 4 January, 1871.

[23] G13, vol. 4, Kimberley to Lisgar, 1 February, 1871.

[24] *Ibid.*, Lisgar to Kimberley, 2 February, 1871.

[25] Macdonald Papers, vol. 167, Macdonald to Lisgar, 4 February, 1871.

[26] Public Record Office, FO.5, 1298, Rose to Granville, 9 February, 1871; G13, vol. 4, Lisgar to Kimberley, 18 February, 1871.

[27] G13, vol. 4, Kimberley to Lisgar, 4 February, 1871.

[28] Macdonald Papers, vol. 518, Macdonald to Macpherson, 6 February, 1871.

[29] *Ibid.*, Macdonald to Rose, 22 February, 1871.

[30] *Ibid.*, vol. 167, Macdonald to Tupper, 5 March, 1871.

[31] P.R.O. 30/29, vol. 80, Thornton to Granville, 14 February, 1871.

[32] *Ibid.*, vol. 63, de Grey to Granville, 28 February, 1871.

[33] *Ibid.*, de Grey to Granville, 7 March, 1871.

[34] *Ibid.*, vol. 80, Thornton to Granville, 22 November, 1871; Northcote Papers, bundle 4, Northcote to Lisgar, 5 April, 1871.

[35] Macdonald Papers, vol. 167, Macdonald to Tupper, 5 March, 1871.

[36] P.R.O. 30/29, vol. 63, de Grey to Granville, 3 March, 1871.

[37] *Ibid.*, de Grey to Granville, 7 March, 1871.

[38] Macdonald Papers, vol. 168, Macdonald to Tupper, 8 March, 1871.

[39] *Ibid.*, Macdonald to Tupper, 9 March, 1871.

[40] *Ibid.*, Macdonald to Tupper, 11 March, 1871; *ibid.*, Hincks to Macdonald, 12 March, 1871.

[41] G13, vol. 4, Kimberley to Lisgar, 11 March, 1871.

42 Macdonald Papers, vol. 167, Macdonald to Tupper, 17 March, 1871.

43 P.R.O. 30/29, vol. 63, de Grey to Granville, 17 March, 1871.

44 Macdonald Papers, vol. 167, Macdonald to Tupper, 17 March, 1871.

45 Ibid., vol. 518, Macdonald to Tupper, 21 March, 1871.

46 P.R.O. 30/29, vol. 63, de Grey to Granville, 10 March, 1871.

47 Macdonald Papers, vol. 518, Macdonald to Lisgar, 11 March, 1871.

48 Ibid., Macdonald to Gray, 31 March, 1871.

49 Ibid., vol. 168, Macdonald to Tupper, 22 March, 1871.

50 Ibid., vol. 518, Macdonald to Tupper, 29 March, 1871.

51 P.R.O. 30/29, vol. 63, de Grey to Granville, 27 March, 1871.

52 Ibid., vol. 59, Gladstone to Granville, 12 April, 1871.

53 Ibid., vol. 63, Gladstone to Granville, 4 April, 1871.

54 Ibid., vol. 59, Granville to Gladstone, 4 April, 1871.

55 Kimberley Papers, Lisgar to Kimberley, 6 April, 1871; P.R.O. 30/29, vol. 63, de Grey to Granville, 18 April, 1871.

56 Ibid., de Grey to Granville, 31 March, 1871.

57 Ibid., de Grey to Granville, 24 March, 1871.

58 Ibid., de Grey to Granville, 11 April, 1871.

59 Northcote Papers, bundle 4, Northcote to Gladstone, 18 April, 1871.

60 Macdonald Papers, vol. 518, Macdonald to Tupper, 16 April, 1871.

61 P.R.O. 30/29, vol. 59, Gladstone to Granville, 20 February, 1871.

62 Ibid., vol. 63, de Grey to Granville, 25 March, 1871.

63 Ibid., de Grey to Granville, 15 April, 1871.

64 Ibid., vol. 59, Gladstone to Granville, 17 April, 1871.

65 Ibid., vol. 63, de Grey to Granville, 21 April, 1871.

66 Macdonald Papers, vol. 518, Macdonald to Tupper, 27 April, 1871.

67 Ibid., vol. 518, Macdonald to Morris, 21 April, 1871.

68 Ibid., Macdonald to Hincks, 29 April, 1871.

69 Pope, Memoirs, vol. 2, p. 137, Macdonald to Cartier, 6 May, 1871.

70 P.R.O. 30/29, vol. 63, Lisgar to Northcote, 6 May, 1871.

71 Ibid., de Grey to Granville, 12 May, 1871.

72 Ibid.

73 Ibid., de Grey to Granville, 5 May, 1871.

74 Lang, Northcote, vol. 2, pp. 17-18.

75 Allan Nevins, Hamilton Fish, the Inner History of the Grant Administration (New York, 1936), p. 490.

CHAPTER FOUR: *Design for the Future*

(Pages 103 to 128)

1 Pope, Correspondence, p. 145, Macdonald to Morris, 21 April, 1871.

2 Macdonald Papers, vol. 518, Macdonald to de Grey, 15 June, 1871.

3 Ibid., Macdonald to Gowan, 24 June, 1871.

4 Ibid., Macdonald to de Grey, 6 June, 1871.

5 Ibid., Macdonald to Gowan, 24 June, 1871.

6 Ibid., vol. 252, Morris to Macdonald, 1 April, 1871; Parliamentary Debates, Dominion of Canada, 1871 (Ottawa, 1871), pp. 660-765, 1027-1030.

7 Globe, 14 March, 18 July, 1873; Macdonald Papers, vol. 123, Names of the Parties present at the Meeting of 14 July, 1871.

[8] Macdonald Papers, vol. 519, Macdonald to Jackson, 17 July, 1871.

[9] *Ibid.*, vol. 77, Lisgar to Macdonald, 7 July, 1871.

[10] Kimberley Papers, Lisgar Letters, Lisgar to Kimberley, 11 May, 1871.

[11] *Ibid.*, Minute by Kimberley.

[12] *Ibid.*, Minute by Gladstone.

[13] Kimberley Papers, Lisgar Letters, Kimberley to Lisgar, 25 May, 1871.

[14] Royal Archives, R51, Gladstone to the Queen, 8 June, 1871; *ibid.*, D27, Gladstone to the Queen, 5 July, 1871.

[15] British Museum, Additional MSS. 44, 224 (Gladstone Papers), vol. 139, Kimberley to Gladstone, 7 June, 1871.

[16] Macdonald Papers, vol. 519, Macdonald to Lisgar, 21 July, 1871.

[17] Kimberley Papers, Lisgar Letters, Kimberley to Lisgar, 14 August, 1871.

[18] G3, vol. 3, Kimberley to Lisgar, 23 September, 1871.

[19] Macdonald Papers, vol. 519, Macdonald to O'Connor, 27 November, 1871.

[20] Public Records and Archives of Ontario, Campbell Papers, Macdonald to Campbell, 19 December, 1871.

[21] Macdonald Papers, vol. 519, Macdonald to Gowan, 12 October, 1871.

[22] *Ibid.*, Macdonald to Carling, 23 December, 1871.

[23] *Ibid.*, Macdonald to Bellingham, 10 October, 1871.

[24] *Ibid.*, Macdonald to Pope, 3 November, 1871.

[25] *Ibid.*, Macdonald to Lisgar, 29 November, 1871.

[26] Kimberley Papers, Lisgar Letters, Kimberley to Lisgar, 20 December, 1871.

[27] British Museum, Additional MSS. 44224, Kimberley to Gladstone, 15 December, 1871.

[28] Royal Archives, A42, Gladstone to the Queen, 18 December, 1871.

[29] G3, vol. 8, Kimberley to Lisgar, 21 December, 1871.

[30] Kimberley Papers, Lisgar Letters, Lisgar to Kimberley, 11 January, 1872.

[31] Macdonald Papers, vol. 520, Macdonald to Lisgar, 22 January, 1872.

[32] *Ibid.*, vol. 519, Macdonald to Carling, 24 November, 1871.

[33] *Ibid.*, Macdonald to Hamilton, 28 December, 1871.

[34] *Ibid.*, vol. 520, Macdonald to O'Connor, 22 February, 1872.

[35] *Ibid.*, Macdonald to Pope, 6 February, 1872.

[36] British Museum, Additional MSS., 44,224, Kimberley to Gladstone, 16 February, 1872.

[37] Macdonald Papers, vol. 167, Rose to Macdonald, 8 February, 1872.

[38] Public Archives of Canada, G13, vol. 5, Kimberley to Lisgar, 10 February, 1872.

[39] Kimberley Papers, Lisgar Letters, Kimberley to Lisgar, 22 February, 1872.

[40] *Ibid.*, Lisgar to Kimberley, 29 February, 1872.

[41] G13, vol. 5, Lisgar to Kimberley, 28 February, 1872.

[42] Macdonald Papers, vol. 520, Macdonald to Patteson, 24 February, 1872.

[43] *Ibid.*, vol. 519, Macdonald to Brown, 2 December, 1871.

[44] *Ibid.*, vol. 520, Macdonald to Stephen, 20 February, 1872.

[45] *Ibid.*, Macdonald to Patteson, 24 February, 1872.

[46] *Ibid.*, vol. 539, Macpherson to Macdonald, 21 February, 1872; *ibid.*, vol. 543, Trust Deed, 27 March, 1872.

[47] *Ibid.*, vol. 123, Macdonald to Macpherson, 11 March, 1872.

[48] *Ibid.*, vol. 520, Macdonald to Rose, 17 April, 1872.

[49] *Report of the Royal Commissioners, Appointed by Commission, Addressed to them under the Great Seal of Canada, bearing date the Fourteenth Day of August, 1873* (Ottawa, 1873), p. 195, Allan to Smith, 28 February, 1872.

[50] D. G. Creighton, "George Brown, Sir John Macdonald, and the 'Workingman'", *Canadian Historical Review*, vol. 24 (December, 1943), pp. 362-376.

[51] G13, vol. 5, Kimberley to Lisgar, 16 March, 1872.

[52] J. A. Chisholm (ed.), *The Speeches and Public Letters of Joseph Howe* (Halifax, 1909), vol. 2, pp. 639-640.

[53] Macdonald Papers, vol. 520, Macdonald to Rose, 17 April, 1872.

[54] Pope, *Correspondence*, p. 161, Macdonald to Cameron, 3 January, 1872.

[55] Kimberley Papers, Journal of Events during the Gladstone Ministry, 2 March, 1872.

[56] *Ibid.*

[57] Journal of E. A. Meredith, vol. 7, 3 May, 1872.

[58] *Parliamentary Debates, Dominion of Canada* (Ottawa, 1872), pp. 344-345.

Chapter Five: *Blackmail*

(Pages 129 to 179)

[1] Macdonald Papers, vol. 520, Macdonald to Rose, 18 June, 1872.

[2] *Ibid.*, vol. 228, Lynch to Macdonald, 9 May, 1872.

[3] Pope, *Correspondence*, p. 165, Macdonald to Rose, 5 March, 1872.

[4] *Report of the Commissioners*, p. 43.

[5] Macdonald Papers, vol. 194, Campbell to Macdonald, 7 July, 1872.

[6] *Ibid.*, vol. 520, Macdonald to Rose, 18 June, 1872.

[7] *Report of the Commissioners*, Macdonald's evidence, pp. 102-103.

[8] *Ibid.*, Macpherson's evidence, pp. 28-29.

[9] Macdonald Papers, vol. 344, Hewitt to Macdonald, 19 June, 1872.

[10] *Mail* (Toronto), 12 July, 1872.

[11] *Ibid.*

[12] Campbell Papers, Macdonald to Campbell, 12 July, 1872.

[13] Macdonald Papers, vol. 123, Allan to Macdonald, 12 July, 1872.

[14] *Ibid.*, vol. 520, Macdonald to McInnes, 17 June, 1872.

[15] *Mail*, 15 July, 1872.

[16] *Ibid.*, 16 July, 1872.

[17] Macdonald Papers, vol. 194, Campbell to Macdonald, 20 July, 1872.

[18] *Ibid.*, vol. 123, Macpherson to Macdonald, 19 July, 1872.

[19] *Ibid.*, Allan to Macdonald, 17 July, 1872; *ibid.*, Allan to Cartier, 18 July, 1872.

[20] *Ibid.*, Cartier to Macdonald, 19 July, 1872.

[21] *Ibid.*, Cartier to Macdonald, 22 July, 1872.

[22] *Daily News* (Kingston), 26 July, 1872.

[23] *Report of the Commissioners*, Macdonald's evidence, pp. 103, 199; Macdonald Papers, vol. 123, Macpherson to Macdonald, 27 July, 1872.

[24] *Report of the Commissioners*, Allan's evidence, pp. 135-136; Macdonald Papers, vol. 123, 30 July, 1872.

[25] *Report of the Commissioners*, p. 200.

[26] T. S. Webster, John A. Macdonald and Kingston (M.A. Thesis, Queen's University, 1944), p. 121.

[27] Macdonald Papers, vol. 521, Macdonald to G. Macdonald, 6 August, 1872.

[28] *Report of the Commissioners*, Macdonald's evidence, p. 118.

[29] *Ibid.*, Allan's evidence, p. 137.

[30] Pope, *Correspondence*, p. 177, Macdonald to Lisgar, 2 September, 1872.

[31] Macdonald Papers, vol. 521, Macdonald to Macpherson, 19, 26 September, 1872.

[32] *Ibid.*, vol. 123, Macpherson to Macdonald, 17 September, 1872.

[33] *Ibid.*, Allan to Macdonald, 4 October, 1872.

[34] *Ibid.*, Allan to Macdonald, 7 October, 1872.

[35] Kimberley Papers, PC/A/25a, Dufferin to Kimberley, 15 October, 1872; *Report of the Commissioners*, pp. 84-85, Campbell's evidence.

[36] Macdonald Papers, vol. 123, Macpherson to Macdonald, 16 November, 1872.

[37] Kimberley Papers, PC/A/25a, Dufferin to Kimberley, 27 November, 1872.

[38] Campbell Papers, Hincks to Campbell, 8 November, 1872.

[39] Macdonald Papers, vol. 522, Macdonald to Langevin, 28 November, 1872.

[40] Macdonald Papers, vol. 202, Macdonald to Cartier, 23 December, 1872.

[41] *Report of the Commissioners*, appendix, p. 89, McMullen's statement.

[42] *Report of the Commissioners*, pp. 170-171, Abbott's evidence.

[43] *Ibid.*, appendix, p. 89, McMullen's statement.

[44] Macdonald Papers, vol. 125, Smith to Macdonald, 20 February, 1873.

[45] *Ibid.*, vol. 224, Hincks to Macdonald, 25 February, 1873.

[46] *Ibid.*, vol. 522, Macdonald to Rose, 13 February, 1873.

[47] *Ibid.*, vol. 126, Affidavit of A. T. Cooper, 2 October, 1873.

[48] Pope, *Memoirs*, vol. 2, appendix 26, p. 329.

[49] Kimberley Papers, PC/A/25a, Dufferin to Kimberley, 4 April, 1873.

[50] Macdonald Papers, vol. 202, Macdonald to Cartier, 10 April, 1873.

[51] *Mail*, 9 April, 1873.

[52] *Ibid.*, 19, 22 April, 1873.

[53] *Ibid.*, 7 May, 1873.

[54] Public Archives of Manitoba, Morris Papers, "C", Campbell to Morris, 29 November, 1873.

[55] *Mail*, 7 May, 1873.

[56] G13, vol. 5, Kimberley to Dufferin, 12 May, 1873.

[57] Macdonald Papers, vol. 258, Rose to Macdonald, 1 May, 1873.

[58] *Ibid.*, vol. 125, Allan to Macdonald, 9 April, 1873.

[59] Pope, *Memoirs*, vol. 2, pp. 157-158, Cartier to Macdonald, 17 May, 1873; *ibid.*, pp. 158-159, Josephine Cartier to Macdonald, 22 May, 1873.

[60] Journal of E. A. Meredith, vol. 8, 20 May, 1873.

[61] Kimberley Papers, PC/A/25a, Dufferin to Kimberley, 29 May, 1873.

[62] *Ibid.*, Dufferin to Kimberley, 21 June, 1873.

[63] *Ibid.*, Dufferin to Kimberley, 13 June, 1873.

[64] Macdonald Papers, vol. 523, Macdonald to Cameron, 2 July, 1873.

[65] *Gazette* (Montreal), 3 July, 1873.

[66] *Ibid.*, 4 July, 1873.

[67] Macdonald Papers, vol. 125, Blake to Macdonald, 3 July, 1873.

[68] *Ibid.*, vol. 523, Macdonald to Dufferin, 4 July, 1873.

[69] *Ibid.*

[70] *Ibid.*, vol. 523, Macdonald to Amour, 8 July, 1873.

[71] *Globe*, 18 July, 1873.

[72] Macdonald Papers, vol. 79, Macdonald to Dufferin, 7 August, 1873.

[73] *Ibid.*, Macdonald to Dufferin, 31 July, 1873; *ibid.*, vol. 125, Campbell to Macdonald, 18 July, 1873.

[74] *Ibid.*, vol. 125, Abbott to Macdonald, 21 July, 1873.

[75] Kimberley Papers, PC/A/25b, Dufferin to Kimberley, 14 August, 1873.

[76] Macdonald Papers, vol. 79, Dufferin to Macdonald, 31 July, 1873.

[77] Kimberley Papers, PC/A/25b, Dufferin to Kimberley, 6 November, 1873.

[78] *Ibid.*, Dufferin to Kimberley, 9 August, 1873.

[79] *Correspondence Relative to the Canadian Pacific Railway Company* (London, 1874), pp. 7-29, Dufferin to Kimberley, 15 August, 1873.

[80] *Mail*, 14 August, 1873.

[81] *Report of the Commissioners*, p. 221, Huntington to Day, 26 August, 1873.

[82] Macdonald Papers, vol. 126, Ramsay to Macdonald, 22 September, 1873.

[83] *Ibid.*, Abbott to Macdonald, 10 October, 1873.

[84] *Ibid.*, Affidavit of Cooper, 2 October, 1873.

[85] *Globe*, 5 September, 1873.

[86] Kimberley Papers, PC/A/25b, Dufferin to Kimberley, 26 September, 1873.

[87] Macdonald Papers, vol. 523, Macdonald to Dufferin, 22 September, 1873.

[88] Kimberley Papers, PC/A/25b, Dufferin to Macdonald, 19 October, 1873 (enclosed in Dufferin to Kimberley, 26 October, 1873).

[89] *Ibid.*, PC/A/25a, Dufferin to Kimberley, 23 April, 1873.

[90] *Ibid.*, PC/A/25b, Dufferin to Kimberley, 26 October, 1873.

[91] Journal of E. A. Meredith, vol. 8, 22 October, 1873.

[92] Kimberley Papers, PC/A/25b, Kimberley to Dufferin, 6 October, 1873.

[93] *Ibid.*, Dufferin to Kimberley, 26 October, 1873.

[94] Morris Papers, "C", Campbell to Morris, 29 November, 1873.

[95] Kimberley Papers, PC/A/25b, Dufferin to Kimberley, 6 November, 1873.

[96] *Ibid.*

[97] *Mail*, 5 November, 1873, quoted in Pope, *Memoirs*, vol. 2, p. 194.

[98] *Mail*, 4 November, 1873.

[99] Kimberley Papers, PC/A/25b, Dufferin to Kimberley, 6 November, 1873.

[100] Macdonald Papers, vol. 79, Lady Dufferin to Lady Macdonald, 4 November, 1873; *ibid.*, Dufferin to Macdonald, 4 November, 1873.

[101] *Mail*, 6 November, 1873.

CHAPTER SIX: *The Forked Road*

(Pages 180 to 212)

[1] *Mail*, 7 November, 1873.

[2] Journal of E. A. Meredith, vol. 8, 7 November, 1873.

[3] *Mail*, 17 November, 1873.

[4] *Ibid.*

[5] E. P. Deane, "How Canada has Voted: 1867 to 1945", *Canadian Historical Review*, vol. 30 (September, 1949), pp. 227-248.

[6] Macdonald Papers, vol. 346, Mackintosh to Macdonald, 30 January, 1874.

[7] *Ibid.*, vol. 303, Petition against Macdonald's Election, 7 November, 1874.

[8] Public Record Office P.R.O. 30/6 (Carnarvon Papers), vol. 26, Dufferin to Carnarvon, 18 March, 1874.

[9] Saunders, *Tupper*, vol. 1, p. 234, Macdonald to Tupper, 24 August, 1874.

[10] *Gazette*, 13 August, 16 September, 1874.

[11] Saunders, *Tupper*, vol. 1, p. 234.

[12] *Gazette*, 19 September, 1874.

[13] P.R.O. 30/6, vol. 27, Dufferin to Carnarvon, 2 October, 1874.

[14] *Ibid.*, Dufferin to Carnarvon, 8 December, 1874.

[15] Webster, John A. Macdonald and Kingston, p. 127.

[16] *Toronto Directory for 1876, Containing an Alphabetical Directory of the Citizens and a Street Directory . . .* (Toronto, 1876), p. 281.

[17] Macdonald Papers, additional, vol. 2, H. Macdonald to Macdonald, 25 March, 1874. In this letter Hugh suggested that his father should leave the bulk of his estate to his wife and daughter, "simply giving me a trifle to show that I have not been cut off for bad behaviour".

[18] P.R.O. 30/6, vol. 26, Dufferin to Carnarvon, 16 April, 1874.

[19] Pope, *Correspondence*, p. 236, Patteson to Macdonald, 17 February, 1874.

[20] W. S. Wallace (ed.), "Edward Blake's Aurora Speech", *Canadian Historical Review*, vol. 2 (September, 1921), pp. 249-271.

[21] Saunders, *Tupper*, vol 1, p. 234.

[22] *Debates of the House of Commons of the Dominion of Canada* (Ottawa, 1875), vol. 1, p. 32.

[23] *Ibid.*, p. 649.

[24] Macdonald Papers, vol. 159. This volume contains the correspondence respecting Macdonald's Supreme Court Bills.

[25] *House of Commons Debates*, 1875, p. 976.

[26] F. H. Underhill, "Edward Blake, the Supreme Court Act, and the Appeal to the Privy Council, 1875-6", *Canadian Historical Review*, vol. 19 (September, 1938), pp. 245-263.

[27] *House of Commons Debates*, 1875, p. 980.

[28] *Ibid.*, p. 981.

[29] M. A. Ormsby, "Prime Minister Mackenzie, the Liberal Party, and the Bargain with British Columbia", *Canadian Historical Review*, vol. 26 (June, 1945), pp. 148-173.

[30] *Toronto Directory for 1876*, p. 281.

[31] Queen's University Library, Williamson Papers, Macdonald to Williamson, 27 April, 1876.

[32] Macdonald Papers, additional, vol. 2, Macdonald to Louisa Macdonald, 14 July, 1875.

[33] *Ibid.*, H. Macdonald to Macdonald, 30 November, 1875.

[34] *Ibid.*, Macdonald to H. Macdonald, 2 December, 1875.

[35] O. D. Skelton, *The Life and Times of Alexander Tilloch Galt* (Toronto, 1920), p. 468.

[36] *Ibid.*, p. 483.

[37] Macdonald Papers, additional, vol. 2, Macdonald to McCarthy, 15 February, 1875.

[38] *Gazette*, 26 November, 1875.

[39] Macdonald Papers, vol. 189, Bowell to Macdonald, 9 December, 1875.

[40] *Gazette*, 26 November, 1875.

[41] *Mail*, 8 November, 1875.

[42] *Gazette*, 26 November, 1875.

[43] *Mail*, 8 November, 1875.

[44] *Ibid.*, 29 November, 1875.

[45] *Proceedings of Special Meeting of the Manufacturers' Association of Ontario, held at St. Lawrence Hall, Toronto, 25th and 26th November, 1875* (Toronto, 1876).

[46] *Gazette*, 21, 22 January, 1876.

[47] For statements by White and Tupper, see *Gazette*, 27 September, 1875; *Mail*, 4 November, 1875.

[48] *Gazette*, 10 November, 1875.

[49] *Mail*, 29 November, 1875.

[50] *Globe*, 6 November, 1875.

[51] *Ibid.*, 28 July, 1875; *Gazette*, 14 October, 1875.

[52] *Mail*, 29 November, 1875.

[53] Macdonald Papers, vol. 282, Tupper to Macdonald, 29 January, 1876.

[54] Tupper Papers, Macdonald to Tupper, 27 January, 1876.

[55] *Gazette*, 29 January, 1876.

[56] *Mail*, 23 February, 1876.

[57] *Gazette*, 26 February, 1876.

[58] *Ibid.*

[59] *House of Commons Debates*, 1876, p. 261.

CHAPTER SEVEN: *The Picnic Grounds of Ontario*

(Pages 213 to 242)

[1] *House of Commons Debates*, 1876, pp. 262-283.

[2] *Ibid.*, p. 321.

[3] *Ibid.*, p. 340.

[4] *Journals of the House of Commons*, 1876, p. 490.

[5] *Debates*, 1876, p. 491.

[6] *Ibid.*, p. 493.

[7] *Gazette*, 18 March, 1876.

[8] Macdonald Papers, additional, vol. 2, Macdonald to McCarthy, 17 February, 1876.

[9] Williamson Papers, Macdonald to Professor Williamson, 11 March, 1876.

[10] Macdonald Papers, additional, vol. 2, Macdonald to Louisa Macdonald, 25 April, 1876.

[11] *Mail*, 3 July, 1876.

[12] *Ibid.*

[13] Tupper Papers, Macdonald to Tupper, 7 July, 1876.

[14] *Mail*, 28 July, 1876.

[15] *Ibid.*, 10, 24, 31 August, 1876.

[16] *Ibid.*, 7 September, 1876.

[17] *Ibid.*, 13 September, 1876.

[18] Macdonald Papers, additional, vol. 2, H. Macdonald to Macdonald, 22 September, 1876.

[19] P.R.O. 30/6, vol. 30, Dufferin to Carnarvon, 19 January, 1877.

[20] S. Thompson, *Reminiscences of a Canadian Pioneer for the Last Fifty Years* (Toronto, 1884), pp. 339-340.

[21] Macdonald Papers, vol. 347, Cameron to Macdonald, 4 February, 1877.

[22] *Ibid.*, additional, vol. 2, Macdonald to McCarthy, 15 February, 1875.

[23] *Ibid.*, Macdonald to McCarthy, 17 November, 18 December, 1876.

[24] *House of Commons Debates*, 1877, pp. 44-49.

[25] P.R.O. 30/6, vol. 31, Dufferin to Carnarvon, 27 April, 1877.

[26] *Mail*, 7 September, 1876.

[27] P.R.O. 30/6, vol. 29, Dufferin to Carnarvon, 9 February, 1876.

[28] Macdonald Papers, vol. 346, Gray to Macdonald, 14 August, 1876.

[29] *House of Commons Debates*, 1877, pp. 123-147.

[30] *Ibid.*, p. 402.

[31] P.R.O. 30/6, vol. 31, Dufferin to Carnarvon, 5 April, 1877.

[32] *Ibid.*, Dufferin to Carnarvon, 27 April, 3 May, 1877.

[33] *Ibid.*, Dufferin to Carnarvon, 3 May, 1877.

[34] *Mail*, 3 May, 1877.

[35] Macdonald Papers, additional, vol. 1, Macdonald to Macdonell, 7 May, 1877.

[36] *Ibid.*

[37] *Mail*, 7 June, 1877.

[38] *Ibid.*, 11 June, 1877.

[39] *Ibid.*, 5 July, 1877.

[40] *Ibid.*, 9 July, 1877.

[41] Tupper Papers, McCarthy to Tupper, 13 July, 1877.

[42] Macdonald Papers, vol. 232, McLelan to Macdonald, 20 August, 1877.

[43] Tupper Papers, Macdonald to Tupper, 22 August, 1877.

[44] Macdonald Papers, additional, vol. 2, Mary Macdonald to Macdonald, 12 October, 1877.

[45] *Ibid.*, vol. 259, Rose to Macdonald, 24 November, 1877.

[46] *Ibid.*, additional, vol. 1, Macdonald to Macdonell, 21 August, 1877.

[47] *Mail*, 11, 13, 17 October, 1877.

[48] *Ibid.*, 18 October, 1877; Macdonald Papers, additional, vol. 2, Macdonald to Louisa Macdonald, 22 October, 1877.

[49] Pope, *Correspondence*, pp. 329-342, Macdonald to Northcote, 1 May, 1878.

[50] Public Archives of Canada, Alexander Mackenzie Papers, Letterbook 6, Mackenzie to Cameron, 8 April, 1878.

[51] *House of Commons Debates*, 1878, vol. 2, p. 1796. Macdonald told this story accurately on the whole, but with one important mistake. Boswell's companion at the theatre on this occasion was not Dr. Johnson, but Dr. Hugh Blair. Johnson first heard the story when Boswell related it during the closing days of the tour to the Hebrides. See G. B. Hill and L. F. Powell (eds.), *Boswell's Life of Johnson* (Oxford, 1940), vol. 5, p. 396.

[52] *House of Commons Debates*, 1878, vol. 2, pp. 2556-2557.

[53] *House of Commons Debates*, 1878, vol. 2, pp. 1878-1902.

[54] *Ibid.*, pp. 2057-2067.

[55] *Ibid.*, p. 2564.

[56] Macdonald Papers, additional, vol. 1, Macdonald to Macdonell, 13 March, 1878.

[57] *Mail*, 25 May, 5, 8, 10 July, 1878.

[58] Macdonald Papers, additional, vol. 2, Macdonald to McCarthy, 21 August, 1878.

[59] *Ibid.*, vol. 228, McCarthy to Macdonald, 25 August, 1878.

[60] *Ibid.*, additional, vol. 2, Macdonald to McCarthy, 23 August, 1878.

[61] *News* (Kingston), 23 August, 1878; *Mail*, 23 August, 1878.

[62] *Mail*, 28, 30, 31 August, 1878.

[63] Macdonald Papers, vol. 276, Tilley to Macdonald, 26 July, 1878.

[64] *Ibid.*, vol. 282, Tupper to Macdonald, 6 August, 1878.

[65] *Ibid.*, vol. 226, Langevin to Macdonald, 22 August, 1878.

[66] Pope, *Memoirs*, vol. 2, p. 202.

[67] *News*, 18 September, 1878.

CHAPTER EIGHT: *The Plan in Realization*

(Pages 243 to 283)

[1] Pope, *Correspondence*, p. 245, Macdonald to Smith, 1 October, 1878.

[2] Macdonald Papers, additional, vol. 2, Macdonald to Louisa Macdonald, 2 October, 1878.

[3] *Ibid.*, vol. 524, Macdonald to Graham, 6 November, 1878.

[4] Saunders, *Tupper*, vol. 1, pp. 262-263, Macdonald to Tupper, 9 October, 1878.

[5] Pope, *Correspondence*, pp. 239-242, Macdonald to Northcote, 1 May, 1878.

[6] St. Aldwyn Papers, PCC92, Dufferin to Hicks Beach, 12 October, 1878.

[7] H. D. Kemp, The Department of the Interior in the West, 1873-1883 (M.A. Thesis, University of Manitoba, 1950).

[8] *House of Commons Debates*, 1878, vol. 2, p. 1651.

[9] Macdonald Papers, vol. 524, Macdonald to McCarthy, 24 October, 1878.

[10] *Ibid.*, vol. 259, Rose to Macdonald, 30 October, 1878.

[11] Skelton, *Galt*, pp. 515-520.

[12] St. Aldwyn Papers, PCC92, Dufferin to Hicks Beach, 8 August, 1878.

[13] *Ibid.*, PCC13, Hicks Beach to Beaconsfield, 26 August, 1878.

[14] Macdonald Papers, vol. 524, Macdonald to Coursal, 14 November, 1878.

[15] Kimberley Papers, PC/A/25b, Kimberley to Dufferin, 20 November, 1873.

[16] Argyll Papers, Letterbook 4, Dufferin to Lorne, 22 August, 1878.

[17] *House of Commons Debates*, 1875, p. 649.

[18] *Ibid.*, 1879, vol. 2, p. 1821.

[19] *Ibid.*, 1878, vol. 2, 2556.

[20] *Ibid.*, 1876, p. 573.

[21] Argyll Papers, Letterbook 4, Dufferin to Lorne, 22 August, 1878.

[22] Macdonald Papers, vol. 195, Campbell to Macdonald, 15 July, 1880.

[23] Pope, *Correspondence*, pp. 240-241, Macdonald to Northcote, 1 May, 1878.

[24] Macdonald Papers, vol. 259, Rose to Macdonald, 19 December, 1878.

[25] *Ibid.*, vol. 216, Galt to Macdonald, 30 November, 1878.

[26] *Ibid.*, Galt to Macdonald, 18 December, 1878.

[27] *Ibid.*, Galt to Macdonald, 20 December, 1878.

[28] *Ibid.*, vol. 524, Macdonald to Frazer, 26 December, 1878.

[29] *Globe*, 26 July, 1878.

[30] Argyll Papers, Letterbook 1, Lorne to Hicks Beach, 3 December, 1878.

[31] W. A. Mackintosh, *The Economic Background of Dominion-Provincial Relations*, Appendix 3 of the *Report of the Royal Commission on Dominion-Provincial Relations* (Ottawa, 1939), pp. 19-20; O. J. McDiarmid, *Commercial Policy in the Canadian Economy* (Cambridge, 1946), pp. 161-163.

[32] Argyll Papers, Letterbook 1, Lorne to Hicks Beach, 1 January, 1879.

[33] *Ibid.*, Lorne to Hicks Beach, 5 February, 1879.

[34] *Ibid.*, Lorne to Hicks Beach, 8 February, 1879.

[35] *Gazette*, 15 February, 1879.

[36] *Ibid.*, 17 February, 1879.

[37] Argyll Papers, Letterbook 1, Lorne to Hicks Beach, 10 March, 1879.

[38] G13, vol. 10, Hicks Beach to Lorne, 12 March, 1879.

[39] Canada, *Sessional Papers*, 1879, No. 155, Memorandum by Tilley, 19 March, 1879.

[40] Pope, *Correspondence*, pp. 251-252, Chapleau to Macdonald, 2 December, 1878.

[41] St. Aldwyn Papers, PCC61, Lorne to Hicks Beach, 26 December, 1878.

[42] *House of Commons Debates*, 1878, vol. 1, pp. 407-408.

[43] Argyll Papers, Letterbook 1, Lorne to Hicks Beach, 3 December, 1878.

[44] St. Aldwyn Papers, PCC61, Lorne to Hicks Beach, 26 December, 1878.

[45] Argyll Papers, Letterbook 4, Lorne to Hicks Beach, 9 April, 1879.

[46] St. Aldwyn Papers, PCC61, Lorne to Hicks Beach, 27 March, 1879.

[47] *Ibid.*, Lorne to Hicks Beach, 3 April, 1879.

[48] *Ibid.*, Lorne to Hicks Beach, 6 April, 1879.

[49] Macdonald Papers, vol. 80, Macdonald to Lorne, 28 March, 1879.

[50] *House of Commons Debates*, 1879, vol. 2, p. 1823.

[51] Macdonald Papers, vol. 199, Carling to Macdonald, 19 May, 1879.

[52] *Ibid.*, additional, vol. 2, Macdonald to Louisa Macdonald, 26 June, 1879.

[53] *Ibid.*, Macdonald to Louisa Macdonald, 6 July, 1879.

[54] *Gazette*, 28 July, 1879.

[55] Macdonald Papers, vol. 162, Macdonald's Memorandum book, 4 August, 1879.

[56] *Ibid.*, Rose to Macdonald, 6 August, 1879.

[57] *Ibid.*, Hicks Beach to Macdonald, n.d.

[58] St. Aldwyn Papers, PCC75, Beaconsfield to Hicks Beach, 8 August, 1879.

[59] Royal Archives, P 25, Lorne to Beaconsfield, 1 June, 1879.

[60] Macdonald Papers, vol. 162, Confidential Memorandum on the Tariff, 25 August, 1879.

[61] *Ibid.*, vol. 216, Considerations connected with the claim for an imperial guarantee, 25 August, 1879.

[62] *Ibid.*, vol. 162, Macdonald to Walkem, 23 August, 1879.

[63] *Ibid.*, vol. 80, Lorne to Macdonald, 28 June, 1879.

[64] Argyll Papers, Letterbook 4, Hicks Beach to Lorne, 16 August, 1879.

[65] Macdonald Papers, vol. 162, Macdonald's Memorandum book, 10 August, 1879; *ibid.*, additional, vol. 2, Macdonald to Louisa Macdonald, 20 August, 1879.

[66] *Ibid.*, vol. 216, Confidential Memorandum on Canada's Representative in London, 25 August, 1879.

[67] M. H. Long, "Sir John Rose and the Informal Beginnings of the Canadian High Commissionership", *Canadian Historical Review*, vol. 12 (March, 1931), pp. 23-43.

[68] Macdonald Papers, vol. 259, Rose to Macdonald, 2 November, 1879.

[69] *Ibid.*, vol. 216, Confidential Memorandum on Canada's Representative in London, 25 August, 1879.

[70] St. Aldwyn Papers, PCC61, Lorne to Hicks Beach, 25 July, 1879.

[71] British Museum, Additional MSS. 44225 (Gladstone Papers), Kimberley to Gladstone, 2 December, 1873.

[72] Kimberley Papers, PC/A/25b, Kimberley to Dufferin, 8 December, 1873.

[73] Macdonald Papers, vol. 162, Memorandum book, 14 August, 1879.

[74] *Ibid.*, additional, vol. 2, Macdonald to Louisa Macdonald, 20 August, 1879.

[75] *Ibid.*, vol. 162, Hicks Beach to Macdonald, 28 August, 1879.

[76] Argyll Papers, Letterbook 4, Beaconsfield to Lorne, 13 August, 1879.

[77] Macdonald Papers, vol. 162; Pope, *Memoirs*, vol. 2, pp. 205-206.

[78] W. F. Monypenny and G. E. Buckle, *The Life of Benjamin Disraeli, Earl of Beaconsfield* (London, 1920), vol. 6, p. 477.

[79] Journal of E. A. Meredith, vol. 10, 23 September, 1879.

[80] Argyll Papers, Letterbook 1, Lorne to Hicks Beach, 22 October, 1879.

[81] Pope, *Memoirs*, vol. 2, pp. 207-209, Macdonald to Beaconsfield, 7 October, 1879.

[82] St. Aldwyn Papers, PCC61, Lorne to Hicks Beach, 25 November, 1879.

[83] Macdonald Papers, vol. 216, Hicks Beach to Lorne, 1 November, 1879.

[84] Argyll Papers, Letterbook 4, Salisbury to Lorne, 5 November, 1879.

[85] *Ibid.*, Hicks Beach to Lorne, 7 November, 1879.

[86] *Ibid.*, Letterbook 1, Lorne to Salisbury, 29 September, 1879.

[87] Macdonald Papers, vol. 216, Order-in-Council, 22 December, 1879.

[88] Argyll Papers, Letterbook 1, Lorne to Salisbury, 28 November, 1879.

[89] G13, vol. 10, Colonial Secretary to Governor-General, 31 January, 1880.

⁹⁰ Macdonald Papers, additional, vol. 1, Macdonald to Lorne, 5 February, 1880.

⁹¹ G13, vol. 10, Colonial Secretary to Governor-General, 7 February, 1880.

⁹² Macdonald Papers, vol. 228, McCarthy to Macdonald, 28 December, 1879.

⁹³ Ibid., vol. 217, Galt to Macdonald, 9 January, 1880.

⁹⁴ Ibid., vol. 259, Rose to Macdonald, 22 January, 1880.

⁹⁵ Mail, 22 March, 1880.

⁹⁶ Macdonald Papers, vol. 247, Macpherson to Macdonald, 24 March, 1880.

CHAPTER NINE: *Contract for Steel*

(Pages 284 to 316)

¹ Heather M. Donald, Life of Lord Mount Stephen (Ph.D. Thesis, University of London, 1952).

² Ibid.

³ Argyll Papers, Letterbook 4, Macdonald to Lorne, 15 May, 1880.

⁴ Ibid., Macdonald Letters, Macdonald to Lorne, 17 May, 1880.

⁵ Macdonald Papers, vol. 217, Galt to Macdonald, 4 May, 1880.

⁶ Ibid., additional, vol. 1, Macdonald to Lorne, 25 May, 1880.

⁷ Ibid., vol. 217, Galt to Macdonald, 7 June, 1880.

⁸ Ibid., Draft Instructions to Galt, n.d.

⁹ Sessional Papers, 1885, No. 116, pp. 81-96.

¹⁰ Chester Martin, "Dominion Lands" Policy, vol. 2 in Canadian Frontiers of Settlement, ed. by W. A. Mackintosh and W. L. G. Joerg (Toronto, 1938).

¹¹ Macdonald Papers, additional, vol. 1, Macdonald to Lorne, 18, 23 June. 1880.

¹² Ibid., vol. 127, McIntyre to Macdonald, 21 June, 1880.

¹³ Ibid., vol. 195, Campbell to Macdonald, 15 July, 1880.

¹⁴ Ibid., vol. 81, Lorne to Macdonald, 24 June, 1880.

¹⁵ Ibid., additional, vol. 1, Macdonald to Lorne, 5 July, 1880.

¹⁶ Campbell Papers, Campbell to Mills, 2 August, 1880.

¹⁷ Macdonald Papers, vol. 127, McIntyre to Macdonald, 5 July, 1880.

¹⁸ Ibid., vol. 524, Macdonald to Dunmore, 3 July, 1880.

¹⁹ Ibid., vol. 267, Stephen to Macdonald, 9 July, 1880.

²⁰ Ibid., vol. 163, Memorandum book, 19 July, 1880.

²¹ Alice R. Stewart, "Sir John A. Macdonald and the Imperial Defence Commission of 1879", Canadian Historical Review, vol. 35 (June, 1954), pp. 119-139.

²² Macdonald Papers, vol. 163, Memorandum book, 23 July, 1880.

²³ G. P. de T. Glazebrook, A History of Transportation in Canada (Toronto and New Haven, 1938), p. 240.

²⁴ Campbell Papers, Onderdonk to Campbell, 3 August, 1880.

²⁵ Macdonald Papers, vol. 127, Macdonald to Tilley (draft), n.d.

²⁶ Ibid., Puleston to Macdonald, 2 September, 1880.

²⁷ Ibid., vol. 163, Cameron to Macdonald, 8 September, 1880.

²⁸ Ibid., vol. 127, McIntyre to Macdonald, 12 August, 1880.

²⁹ Ibid., vol. 163, Memorandum book, 4 September, 1880.

[30] *Ibid.*, vol. 127, Macdonald to Langevin, 4 September, 1880.

[31] *Ibid.*, additional, vol. 2, Macdonald to Louisa Macdonald, 3 October, 1880.

[32] *Ibid.*, vol. 267, Stephen to Macdonald, 27 September, 1880.

[33] Macdonald Papers, vol. 127, Macdonald to Rose, 5 November, 1880.

[34] Argyll Papers, Letterbook 2, Lorne to Walker, 26 September, 1880.

[35] Glazebrook, *A History of Transportation*, p. 302.

[36] Macdonald Papers, vol. 267, Stephen to Macdonald, 18 October, 1880.

[37] Argyll Papers, Letterbook 4, Macdonald to Lorne, 16 November, 1880.

[38] Macdonald Papers, additional, vol. 2, Macdonald to Louisa Macdonald, 2 December, 1880.

[39] *Ibid.*, vol. 81, Lorne to Macdonald, 6 December, 1880.

[40] *House of Commons Debates*, 1880-1881, vol. 1, pp. 50-74.

[41] Macdonald Papers, additional, vol. 2, Macdonald to Louisa Macdonald, 23 December, 1880.

[42] Argyll Papers, Macdonald Letters, Macdonald to Lorne, 6 January, 1881.

[43] *House of Commons Debates*, 1880-1881, vol. 1, pp. 102-106, 144.

[44] Macdonald Papers, vol. 127, C. Rose to Macdonald, 8 January, 1881.

[45] *House of Commons Debates*, 1880-1881, vol. 1, p. 488.

[46] *Ibid.*, p. 494.

[47] Macdonald Papers, vol. 128, Donaldson to Macdonald, 18 January, 1881.

[48] *Ibid.*, vol. 524, Macdonald to Galt, 24 January, 1881.

[49] Argyll Papers, Letterbook 4, Macdonald to Lorne, 26 January, 1881.

[50] *House of Commons Debates*, 1880-1881, vol. 1, p. 765.

[51] Macdonald Papers, vol. 128, Morris to Macdonald, 28 January, 1881.

[52] *Ibid.*, vol. 524, Macdonald to Galt, 27 February, 1881.

[53] *Ibid.*, vol. 195, Campbell to Macdonald, n.d.

[54] *Ibid.*, vol. 524, Macdonald to Galt, 27 February, 1881.

[55] *Ibid.*, vol. 218, Galt to Macdonald, 4 January, 1881.

[56] *Ibid.*, vol. 267, Stephen to Macdonald, 7 April, 1881.

[57] Saunders, *Tupper*, vol. 1, p. 302, Macdonald to Tupper, 21 March, 1881.

[58] *Ibid.*, vol. 1, pp. 302-303, Macdonald to Tupper, 11 April, 1881.

[59] *Ibid.*, vol. 1, p. 303, Macdonald to Tupper, 21 April, 1881.

[60] Macdonald Papers, vol. 524, Macdonald to —, 18 April, 1881.

[61] Williamson Papers, Louisa Macdonald to Williamson, 3 May, 1881.

[62] *Mail*, 24 May, 1881.

[63] Saunders, *Tupper*, vol. 1, p. 304, Macdonald to Tupper, 16 May, 1881.

[64] Macdonald Papers, vol. 524, Macdonald to Stephen, 6 May, 1881.

[65] Saunders, *Tupper*, vol. 1, p. 303, Macdonald to Tupper, 21 April, 1881.

[66] Tupper Papers, Macdonald to Tupper, 2 June, 1881.

[67] Argyll Papers, Letterbook 4, Galt to Lorne, 2 June, 1881.

[68] Macdonald Papers, additional, vol. 1, Macdonald to Lorne, 20 June, 1881.

[69] Tupper Papers, Macdonald to Tupper, 21 June, 1881.

[70] Campbell Papers, Macdonald to Campbell, 12 July, 1880.

[71] *Mail*, 22 July, 1881.

[72] Macdonald Papers, additional, vol. 1, Macdonald to Lorne, 20 June, 1881.

[73] Macdonald Papers, vol. 164, Carnarvon to Macdonald, 6 August, 1881.

[74] *Ibid.*, vol. 282, Tupper to Macdonald, n.d.

[75] *Ibid.*, vol. 195, Campbell to Macdonald, n.d.

[76] *Ibid.*, Campbell to Macdonald, 22 August, 1881.

[77] Campbell Papers, Macdonald to Campbell, 12 July, 1880.

Chapter Ten: *Good Times*

(Pages 317 to 352)

[1] Macdonald Papers, vol. 164, Programme of Ship's Concert on the *Sardinian*, 15 September, 1881.

[2] *Mail*, 19 September, 1881.

[3] A. S. Morton, *History of Prairie Settlement*, vol. 2, *Canadian Frontiers of Settlement*, ed. W. A. Mackintosh and W. L. G. Joerg (Toronto, 1938), p. 59.

[4] Macdonald Papers, vol. 248, Macpherson to Macdonald, 4 September, 1881.

[5] *Ibid.*, Macpherson to Macdonald, 9 August, 1881; *ibid.*, vol. 256, J. H. Pope to Macdonald, 19 August, 1881.

[6] *Ibid.*, vol. 267, Stephen to Macdonald, 29 October, 4, 5 November, 1881.

[7] *Ibid.*, Stephen to Macdonald, 27 August, 1881.

[8] *Ibid.*, Stephen to Macdonald, 17 November, 1881.

[9] Pope, *Correspondence*, pp. 280-281, Macdonald to Stephen, 19 October, 1881.

[10] Macdonald Papers, vol. 524, Macdonald to Stephen, 6 January, 1882.

[11] *Ibid.*, Macdonald to Griffin, 31 October, 1881.

[12] J. C. Morrison, Oliver Mowat and the Development of Provincial Rights in Ontario: a Study in Dominion-Provincial Relations, 1867-1896 (M.A. Thesis, University of Toronto, 1947), Chapter 3.

[13] W. E. Hodgins, *Correspondence, Reports of the Minister of Justice, and Orders in Council upon the Subject of Dominion and Provincial Legislation 1867-1895* (Ottawa, 1896), p. 61, Report of the Minister of Justice, 9 June, 1868.

[14] *House of Commons Debates*, 1882, p. 924.

[15] Hodgins, *Dominion and Provincial Legislation, 1867-1895*, p. 177, Report of Minister of Justice, 21 May, 1881.

[16] Macdonald Papers, vol. 524, Macdonald to Meredith, 14 January, 1882.

[17] *Mail*, 24 November, 1881.

[18] Macdonald Papers, additional, vol. 1, Macdonald to Lorne, 2 November, 1881.

[19] *Ibid.*, Macdonald to Lorne, 14 December, 1881.

[20] Argyll Papers, Letterbook 2, Lorne to Granville, 17 December, 1881.

[21] Macdonald Papers, vol. 218, Galt to Macdonald, 9, 13 December, 1881.

[22] *Ibid.*, vol. 524, Macdonald to Galt, 7 January, 1882.

[23] *Ibid.*, Macdonald to Galt, 27 December, 1881.

[24] Glazebrook, *History of Transportation in Canada*, p. 294.

[25] Macdonald Papers, vol. 524, Macdonald to Galt, 24 December, 1881.

[26] *Ibid.*, vol. 267, Stephen to Macdonald, 26 February, 1882.

27 *Ibid.*, vol. 524, Macdonald to Lynch, 9 December, 1881.

28 *Ibid.*, vol. 228, Lynch to Macdonald, 20 February, 1882.

29 *Ibid.*, vol. 524, Macdonald to Galt, 15 March, 1882.

30 *Ibid.*, Macdonald to Galt, 28 February, 1882.

31 *Ibid.*, vol. 259, Rose to Macdonald, 6 February, 1882.

32 Argyll Papers, Letterbook 3, Lorne to Kimberley, 23 March, 1882.

33 Macdonald Papers, vol. 524, Macdonald to Marsh, 28 January, 1882.

34 *House of Commons Debates,* 1882, pp. 876-926.

35 *Ibid.*, pp. 1068-1075.

36 *Ibid.*, pp. 1033-1034.

37 Pope, *Correspondence,* pp. 287-289, Macdonald to Lorne, 2 May, 1882.

38 Kimberley Papers, Lorne Letters, Kimberley to Lorne, 11 May, 1882.

39 Macdonald Papers, vol. 219, Galt to Macdonald, 27 April, 1882.

40 *House of Commons Debates,* 1882, pp. 1202-1204.

41 Norman Ward, *The Canadian House of Commons: Representation* (Toronto, 1950), p. 30.

42 R. M. Dawson, "The Gerrymander of 1882", *The Canadian Journal of Economics and Political Science,* vol. 1 (May, 1935), pp. 197-221.

43 *House of Commons Debates,* 1882, p. 1208.

44 *Ibid.*, p. 1209.

45 Macdonald Papers, vol. 267, Stephen to Macdonald, 8 May, 1882.

46 *Ibid.*, additional, vol. 1, Macdonald to Lorne, 3 April, 1882.

47 *Ibid.*, vol. 267, Stephen to Macdonald, 9 June, 1882.

48 *Mail,* 26 May, 1882.

49 *Ibid.*, 29 May, 1882.

50 Argyll Papers, Macdonald Letters, Macdonald to Lorne, 22 June, 1882.

51 Macdonald Papers, vol. 277, Tilley to Macdonald, 25 June, 1882.

52 Argyll Papers, Macdonald Letters, Macdonald to Lorne, 22 June, 1882.

53 Macdonald Papers, additional, vol. 1, Macdonald to Lorne, 28 July, 1882.

54 *Ibid.*, Macdonald to Lorne, 4 August, 1882; *ibid.*, vol. 82, Lorne to Macdonald, 5 August, 1882; *ibid.*, additional, vol. 1, Macdonald to Lorne, 8 August, 1882.

55 Argyll Papers, Letterbook 4, Cambridge to Lorne, 3 July, 1882; Macdonald Papers, vol. 82, Lorne to Macdonald, 18 July, 1882; *ibid.*, additional, vol. 1, Macdonald to Lorne, 21 July, 1882.

56 *Mail,* 8 July, 1882.

57 *Ibid.*, 2 June, 1882.

58 *Report Pursuant to Resolution of the Senate to the Honourable the Speaker by the Parliamentary Counsel relating to the Enactment of the British North America Act, 1867* . . . (Ottawa, 1939), annex 3, pp. 14-18.

59 Macdonald Papers, vol. 267, Stephen to Macdonald, 19 August, 1882.

60 *Ibid.*, Stephen to Macdonald, 24 August, 1882.

61 *Ibid.*, vol. 219, Galt to Macdonald, 16 August, 1882.

62 *Ibid.*, vol. 267, Stephen to Macdonald, 9 July, 1880.

63 *Ibid.*, Stephen to Macdonald, 27 August, 1882.

64 *Ibid.*, vol. 223, Hickson to Macdonald, 9 October, 1882.

65 *Ibid.*, vol. 259, Rose to Macdonald, 1 February, 1883.

66 Williamson Papers, Macdonald to Williamson, 19 February, 1883.

67 *House of Commons Debates,* 1883, p. 23.

[68] *Mail*, 28 February, 1883.

[69] Pope, *Correspondence*, p. 299, Macdonald to Galt, 21 February, 1883.

[70] Skelton, *Galt*, pp. 539-540, Macdonald to Galt, 2 February, 1883.

[71] *House of Commons Debates*, 1883, p. 65.

[72] Argyll Papers, Letterbook 3, Lorne to Cambridge, 10 March, 1883.

[73] *Ibid.*, Letterbook 4, Macdonald to Lorne, 10 March, 1883.

[74] Pope, *Correspondence*, p. 298, Macdonald to Lorne, 21 February, 1883.

[75] Macdonald Papers, vol. 219, Macdonald to Galt, n.d.

[76] Argyll Papers, Letterbook 3, Lorne to Derby, 22 April, 1883.

[77] Macdonald Papers, vol. 267, Stephen to Macdonald, 11 May, 1883.

[78] *Ibid.*, Macdonald to Stephen, 12 May, 1883.

[79] *Ibid.*, additional, vol. 1, Macdonald to Lorne, 26 June, 1883.

[80] Argyll Papers, Macdonald Letters, Macdonald to Lorne, 16 October, 1883.

[81] Macdonald Papers, vol. 525, Macdonald to Plumb, 24 June, 1883.

Chapter Eleven: *Stand Fast, Craigellachie!*

(Pages 353 to 398)

[1] Macdonald Papers, vol. 256, Pope to Macdonald, 23 July, 1883.

[2] *Ibid.*, vol. 277, Tilley to Macdonald, 27 September, 1883.

[3] Argyll Papers, Macdonald Letters, Macdonald to Lorne, 16 October, 1883.

[4] *Mail*, 23 October, 1883.

[5] Macdonald Papers, additional, vol. 1, Macdonald to Lorne, 9 June, 1883.

[6] Argyll Papers, Macdonald Letters, Macdonald to Lorne, 26 July, 1883.

[7] *Mail*, 24 October, 1883.

[8] Argyll Papers, Macdonald Letters, Macdonald to Lorne, 26 October, 1883.

[9] *Ibid.*, Macdonald to Lorne, 19 July, 1883.

[10] Macdonald Papers, vol. 267, Stephen to Macdonald, 25 October, 1883.

[11] Tupper Papers, Macdonald to Tupper, 22 November, 1883.

[12] *Ibid.*

[13] Macdonald Papers, vol. 267, Stephen to Macdonald, 29 October, 1883.

[14] *Mail*, 30 October, 1883.

[15] *Mail*, 7 November, 1883.

[16] Tupper Papers, Macdonald to Tupper, 22 November, 1883.

[17] *House of Commons Debates*, 1884, pp. 99-100.

[18] Macdonald Papers, vol. 267, Stephen to Macdonald, 3 December, 1883.

[19] *Ibid.*, Stephen to Macdonald, 15 December, 1883.

[20] Pope, *Correspondence*, p. 308, Macdonald to Tupper, 1 December, 1883.

[21] Macdonald Papers, vol. 525, Macdonald to Christie, 20 November, 1882.

[22] *Ibid.*, Macdonald to Bate, 25 April, 1884.

[23] Williamson Papers, Macdonald to Williamson, 21 November, 1883.

[24] Tupper Papers, Macdonald to Tupper, 22 November, 1883.

[25] Macdonald Papers, vol. 267, Stephen to Macdonald, 15 December, 1883.

[26] *Ibid.*, Stephen to Macdonald, 23 December, 1883.

[27] Tupper Papers, Stephen to Tupper, 28 December, 1883.

28 *Ibid.*, Stephen to Tupper, 5 January, 1884.

29 Macdonald Papers, additional, vol. 1, Macdonald to Lorne, 7 January, 1884.

30 G. F. G. Stanley, *The Birth of Western Canada, a History of the Riel Rebellions* (London, 1936), p. 207.

31 Macdonald Papers, additional, vol. 1, Macdonald to Lorne, 2 December, 1882.

32 *Ibid.*, vol. 186, Aikins to Macdonald, 30 November, 1883.

33 J. A. Jackson, The Disallowance of Manitoba Railway Legislation in the 1880's (M.A. Thesis, University of Manitoba, 1945), pp. 48-49.

34 Macdonald Papers, vol. 282, Colmer to Macdonald, 10 December, 1883.

35 *Ibid.*, vol. 259, Rose to Macdonald, 29 December, 1883.

36 *Ibid.*, vol. 269, Stephen to Macdonald, 22 January, 1884.

37 *House of Commons Debates*, 1884, pp. 84-85.

38 Grand Trunk Railway: *Correspondence between the Company and the Dominion Government respecting Advances to the Canadian Pacific Railway Company* (February, 1884).

39 R. Rumilly, *Histoire de la Province de Québec*, vol. 4, *Les 'Castors'* (Montreal, n.d.), pp. 132-133.

40 Macdonald Papers, vol. 206, Costigan to Macdonald, 18 February, 1884.

41 *Ibid.*, vol. 259, Rose to Macdonald, 21 February, 1884.

42 *Ibid.*, vol. 269, Stephen to Macdonald, 16 February, 1884.

43 *Ibid.*, Stephen to Macdonald, 27 February, 1884.

44 *Ibid.*, vol. 259, Macdonald to Rose, 21 February, 1884.

45 *House of Commons Debates*, 1884, p. 569.

46 Macdonald Papers, vol. 269, Stephen to Macdonald, 27 February, 1884.

47 *House of Commons Debates*, 1884, p. 664.

48 Macdonald Papers, vol. 269, Stephen to Macdonald, 21 March, 1884.

49 *Ibid.*, additional, vol. 1, Macdonald to Lorne, 26 March, 1884.

50 *Ibid.*, vol. 525, Macdonald to Campbell, 26 April, 1884.

51 *House of Commons Debates*, 1884, p. 937.

52 Macdonald Papers, vol. 228, McCarthy to Macdonald, 7 March, 1884.

53 Jackson, Disallowance of Manitoba Railway Legislation, pp. 49-53.

54 Macdonald Papers, additional, vol. 1, Macdonald to Lorne, 26 March, 1884.

55 *House of Commons Debates*, 1884, p. 109.

56 Macdonald Papers, vol. 525, Macdonald to Aikins, 6 June, 1884.

57 *Ibid.*, vol. 259, Rose to Macdonald, 23, 27 February, 1884.

58 *Ibid.*, vol. 269, Stephen to Macdonald, 26 April, 1884.

59 *Ibid.*, vol. 277, Tilley to Macdonald, 12 June, 1884.

60 *Ibid.*, Tilley to Macdonald, 19 June, 1884.

61 *Ibid.*, vol. 259, Rose to Macdonald, 18 June, 1884.

62 *Ibid.*, vol. 525, Macdonald to Chapleau, 3 July, 1884.

63 Tupper Papers, Macdonald to Tupper, 28 June, 1884.

64 Macdonald Papers, vol. 197, Campbell to Macdonald, 23 July, 1884.

65 Lansdowne Papers, Macdonald Letters, Macdonald to Lansdowne, 17 July, 1884.

66 *Ibid.*, Macdonald to Lansdowne, 10 July, 1884.

67 Pope, *Correspondence*, pp. 314-315, Macdonald to Aikins, 28 July, 1884.

68 Macdonald Papers, vol. 525, Macdonald to Norquay, 1 July, 1884.

[69] Pope, *Correspondence*, p. 313, Macdonald to Aikins, 7 July, 1884.

[70] Macdonald Papers, vol. 105, Deville to Burgess, 14 February, 1884.

[71] Pope, *Correspondence*, pp. 317-319, Macdonald to Lansdowne, 12 August, 1884.

[72] Lansdowne Papers, Macdonald Letters, Macdonald to Lansdowne, 5 August, 1884.

[73] C. R. W. Biggar, *Sir Oliver Mowat* (Toronto, 1905), vol. 1, chap. 15.

[74] Tupper Papers, Macdonald to Tupper, 13 August, 1884.

[75] Macdonald Papers, vol. 282, Tupper to Macdonald, 11 September, 1884.

[76] *Ibid.*, vol. 228, McCarthy to Macdonald, 28 September, 1884.

[77] *Ibid.*, vol. 526, Macdonald to Robertson, 4 October, 1884.

[78] Pope, *Memoirs*, vol. 2, p. 209.

[79] Macdonald Papers, vol. 282, Tupper to Macdonald, 11 December, 1884.

[80] *Ibid.*, vol. 107, Dewdney to Macdonald, 19 September, 1884.

[81] *Ibid.*, Memorandum of Conversation between Bishop Grandin and Riel, 7 September, 1884.

[82] *Ibid.*, Forget to Dewdney, 18 September, 1884.

[83] *Ibid.*, vol. 526, Macdonald to Baring Brothers, 6 September, 1884.

[84] *Ibid.*, vol. 277, Tilley to Macdonald, 3 December, 1884.

[85] *Ibid.*, vol. 129, Tupper to Tilley, 28 November, 1884.

[86] J. M. Gibbon, *Steel of Empire* (Toronto, 1935), p. 278.

CHAPTER TWELVE: *Triumph and Disaster*

(Pages 399 to 439)

[1] *Mail*, 13 January, 1885; Pope, *Correspondence*, pp. 331-332, Macdonald to Tupper, 24 January, 1885.

[2] *Mail*, 18, 19 December, 1884; Pope, *Correspondence*, p. 328, Macdonald to Tupper, 24 December, 1884.

[3] Pope, *Memoirs*, vol. 1, p. 62.

[4] *Ibid.*, vol. 2, p. 292.

[5] Lansdowne Papers, Macdonald Letters, Macdonald to Lansdowne, 7 June, 1884.

[6] *Ibid.*, Macdonald to Lansdowne, 25 December, 1884.

[7] Macdonald Papers, vol. 269, Stephen to Macdonald, 29 December, 1884.

[8] *Ibid.*, Stephen to Macdonald, 14 January, 1885.

[9] *Ibid.*, vol. 259, Rose to Macdonald, 10 January, 1885.

[10] *Ibid.*, vol. 269, Stephen to Macdonald, 14 January, 1885.

[11] *Ibid.*, vol. 277, Tilley to Macdonald, 6 January, 1885.

[12] Pope, *Correspondence*, pp. 331-332, Macdonald to Tupper, 24 January, 1885.

[13] Macdonald Papers, vol. 269, Stephen to Macdonald, 17 January, 1885.

[14] *Ibid.*, vol. 269, Macdonald to Stephen, 20 January, 1885.

[15] *House of Commons Debates*, 1885, vol. 1, p. 22.

[16] Pope, *Correspondence*, pp. 74-75, Macdonald to Chamberlin, 26 October, 1868.

[17] *House of Commons Debates*, 1885, vol. 1, p. 41.

[18] *Mail*, 6 February, 1885.

[19] *Debates*, 1885, vol. 1, p. 41.

[20] *Mail*, 6 February, 1885.

[21] G. F. G. Stanley, *Canada's Soldiers, 1604-1954* (Toronto, 1954), pp. 270-271.

[22] *House of Commons Debates*, 1886, vol. 1, p. 20.

[23] Pope, *Correspondence*, pp. 337-338, Macdonald to Tupper, 12 March, 1885.

[24] Public Archives of Canada, Department of the Interior, Dominion Lands Branch, File No. 83808, 1885.

[25] *Ibid.*

[26] *House of Commons Debates*, 1885, vol. 4, p. 3118.

[27] Macdonald Papers, vol. 107, MacDowall to Dewdney, 24 December, 1884.

[28] *House of Commons Debates*, 1885, vol. 1, p. 745.

[29] *Ibid.*

[30] *Sessional Papers*, 1885, No. 116, Order-in-Council, 28 January, 1885.

[31] Macdonald Papers, vol. 105, Macpherson to Dewdney, 4 February, 1885.

[32] *Ibid.*, vol. 269, Stephen to Macdonald, 9 February, 1885.

[33] Pope, *Correspondence*, p. 337, Tupper to Macdonald, 24 February, 1885.

[34] Tupper Papers, Macdonald to Tupper, 17 March, 1885.

[35] Macdonald Papers, vol. 107, André to Dewdney, 21 January, 1885 (enclosed in Dewdney to Macdonald, 3 February, 1885); *ibid.*, Crozier to Dewdney, 3 February, 1885.

[36] Pope, *Correspondence*, pp. 338-339, Stephen to Macdonald, 26 March, 1885.

[37] *House of Commons Debates*, 1885, vol. 2, p. 790.

[38] Pope, *Correspondence*, pp. 341-342, Macdonald to Dewdney, 29 March, 1885.

[39] *Ibid.*, pp. 340-341, Macdonald to Middleton, 29 March, 1885.

[40] *Mail*, 31 March, 1885.

[41] *Ibid.*, 25 March, 1885.

[42] Macdonald Papers, vol. 259, Rose to Macdonald, 9 May, 1885.

[43] *Ibid.*, vol. 283, Tupper to Editor of *The Times*, 20 May, 1885.

[44] Lansdowne Papers, Macdonald Letters, Macdonald to Lansdowne, 9 March, 1885.

[45] *Ibid.*, Macdonald to Lansdowne, 15 May, 1885.

[46] Gibbon, *Steel of Empire*, p. 287.

[47] Pope, *Correspondence*, p. 345, Stephen to Macdonald, 15 April, 1885.

[48] *Ibid.*, Stephen to Pope, 16 April, 1885.

[49] Macdonald Papers, vol. 129, Macdonald to Smithers, 24 April, 1885.

[50] *Ibid.*, Drinkwater to Macdonald, 27 April, 1885.

[51] *Mail*, 1 May, 1885.

[52] *Ibid.*, 2 May, 1885.

[53] Macdonald Papers, vol. 283, Tupper to Macdonald, 7 May, 1885.

[54] *House of Commons Debates*, 1885, vol. 3, pp. 1822-1823.

[55] Macdonald Papers, additional, vol. 2, Macdonald to Louisa Macdonald, 9 May, 1885.

[56] Lansdowne Papers, Macdonald Letters, Macdonald to Lansdowne, 3 June, 1885.

[57] Macdonald to Tupper, 27 July, 1885, Letter in possession of Oscar Orr, Esq., Vancouver, British Columbia.

[58] Pope, *Correspondence*, pp. 358-360, Macdonald to Campbell, 12 September, 1885.

[59] Macdonald to Tupper, 27 July, 1885.

[60] *Ibid.*

[61] *Sessional Papers*, 1886, No. 45.

[62] Macdonald Papers, vol. 106, Amyot to Langevin, 16 May, 1885.

[63] Macdonald to Tupper, 27 July, 1885.

[64] Pope, *Correspondence*, pp. 351-352, Macdonald to Thompson, 21 July, 1885.

[65] *Ibid.*, pp. 358-360, Macdonald to Campbell, 12 September, 1885; Macdonald Papers, vol. 526, Macdonald to Campbell, 14 September, 1885.

[66] Pope, *Correspondence*, p. 360, Campbell to Macdonald, 13 September, 1885; Macdonald Papers, vol. 197, Campbell to Macdonald, 14 September, 1885.

[67] Saunders, *Tupper*, vol. 2, p. 61, Macdonald to Tupper, 4 September, 1885.

[68] *Sessional Papers*, 1886, No. 43.

[69] Pope, *Correspondence*, pp. 354-356, Macdonald to Lansdowne, 28 August, 1885.

[70] Macdonald Papers, vol. 197, Campbell to Macdonald, 11 September, 1885.

[71] *Ibid.*, vol. 526, Macdonald to Carnarvon, 8 September, 1885.

[72] *Ibid.*, vol. 106, Colonial Secretary to Deputy Governor, 22 October, 1885.

[73] *Ibid.*, Campbell to Macdonald, 23 October, 1885; *ibid.*, Campbell to Macdonald, 27 (?) October, 1885.

[74] H. Barnes, "A Century of the McNaghten Rules", *Cambridge Law Journal*, vol. 88, pp. 300-321.

[75] Williamson Papers, Macdonald to Lavell, 31 October, 1885.

[76] Macdonald Papers, vol. 106, Macdonald to Lavell and Valade, 31 October, 1885.

[77] *Ibid.*, Dewdney to Macdonald, 7 November, 1885.

[78] *Ibid.*, vol. 129, Van Horne to Macdonald, 7 November, 1885.

[79] Lansdowne Papers, Macdonald Letters, Macdonald to Lansdowne, 9 November, 1885.

[80] *Ibid.*, vol. 106, Opinion of M. Lavell, 8 November, 1885.

[81] *Ibid.*, Opinion of F. X. Valade, 8 November, 1885.

[82] Pope, *Correspondence*, p. 364, Chapleau to Macdonald, 12 November, 1885.

[83] Macdonald Papers, vol. 108, Lesage *et al.* to Macdonald, 13 November, 1885; *ibid.*, Coursal *et al.* to Macdonald, 13 November, 1885.

[84] Pope, *Correspondence*, p. 365, Macdonald to Langevin, 13 November, 1885.

[85] Lansdowne Papers, Macdonald Letters, Macdonald to Lansdowne, 13 November, 1885.

[86] Macdonald Papers, vol. 107, Dewdney to Macdonald, 15 November, 1885.

[87] *Leader* (Regina), 17 November, 1885; *Mail*, 17 November, 1885.

CHAPTER THIRTEEN: *The Revolt of the Provinces*

(Pages 440 to 481)

[1] Macdonald Papers, vol. 166, Stephen to Macdonald, 29 November, 1885.

[2] *Ibid.*, Rose to Macdonald, 27 November, 1885.

[3] *Ibid.*, vol. 85, Macdonald to Lansdowne, 12 December, 1885.

[4] *Ibid.*, vol. 166, Engagement book, 2-4 January, 1886.

[5] *Ibid.*, vol. 256, Pope to Macdonald, 10 December, 1885.

[6] *Ibid.*, vol. 200, Caron to Macdonald, 26 November, 1885.

[7] *Ibid.*, vol. 227, Langevin to Macdonald, 19 December, 1885.

[8] *Ibid.*, vol. 85, Macdonald to Lansdowne, 21 December, 1885.

[9] *Ibid.*, additional, vol. 2, Mary Macdonald to Macdonald, 22 December, 1885.

[10] *Mail*, 20 January, 1886.

[11] Macdonald Papers, additional, vol. 2, Agnes Macdonald to Louisa Macdonald, 19 January, 1886.

[12] *Ibid.*, vol. 526, Macdonald to Lansdowne, 7 June, 1885.

[13] Lansdowne Papers, Macdonald Letters, Macdonald to Lansdowne, 26 May, 1884; Pope, *Correspondence*, p. 326, Macdonald to Hincks, 18 September, 1884.

[14] *House of Commons Debates*, 1886, vol. 1, p. 31.

[15] *Sessional Papers*, 1886, vol. 12, No. 43.

[16] Macdonald Papers, vol. 106, Jukes to Dewdney, 6 November, 1885.

[17] *Ibid.*, Lavell to Macdonald, 8, 9 November, 1885.

[18] Lansdowne Papers, Macdonald Letters, Macdonald to Lansdowne, 9 March, 1886.

[19] Macdonald Papers, vol. 227, Langevin to Macdonald, 10 March, 1886.

[20] Lansdowne Papers, Macdonald Letters, Macdonald to Lansdowne, 13, 17 March, 1886.

[21] *Ibid.*, Macdonald to Lansdowne, 13, 15 March, 1886.

[22] Pope, *Correspondence*, p. 360, Campbell to Macdonald, 14 September, 1885.

[23] Macdonald Papers, vol. 198, Campbell to Macdonald, 22 March, 1886.

[24] *House of Commons Debates*, 1886, vol. 1, p. 368.

[25] *Ibid.*, p. 411.

[26] Macdonald Papers, vol. 198, Campbell to Macdonald, 26 March, 1886.

[27] Lansdowne Papers, Macdonald Letters, Macdonald to Lansdowne, 14 April, 1886.

[28] *Ibid.*, Macdonald to Lansdowne, 20 April, 1886.

[29] *Chronicle* (Halifax), 10, 26 May, 1886.

[30] Macdonald Papers, vol. 259, Rose to Macdonald, 10 May, 1886.

[31] *Ibid.*, Macdonald to Rose, 12 May, 1886.

[32] *Ibid.*, vol. 86, Macdonald to Lansdowne, 4 June, 1886.

[33] Lansdowne Papers, Macdonald Letters, Macdonald to Lansdowne, 21 May, 1886.

[34] Macdonald Papers, vol. 86, Granville to Lansdowne, 2 June, 1886.

[35] Lansdowne Papers, Macdonald Letters, Macdonald to Lansdowne, 2 June, 1886.

[36] Lansdowne Papers, Letterbook 3, Lansdowne to Granville, 2 June, 1886.

[37] Pope, *Correspondence*, p. 382, Macdonald to Tupper, 21 June, 1886.

[38] Lansdowne Papers, Macdonald Letters, Macdonald to Lansdowne, 1 July, 1886.

[39] *Ibid.*, Macdonald to Lansdowne, 7 June, 1886.

[40] *Ibid.*, Macdonald to Lansdowne, 10 June, 1886.

[41] Public Archives of Canada, Thompson Papers, Macdonald to Thompson, 10 July, 1886.

[42] Macdonald Papers, vol. 288, Van Horne to Agnes Macdonald, 7 July, 1886.

[43] *Manitoban* (Winnipeg), 13 July, 1886.

[44] *Ibid.*, 15 July, 1886.

[45] *Leader* (Regina), 20 July, 1886.

[46] *Mail*, 21, 22 July, 1886.

[47] *Ibid.*, 23, 26 July, 1886.

[48] *Gazette* (Port Moody), 31 July, 1886.

[49] *Star* (Victoria), 25, 29 July, 1886.

[50] *Manitoban*, 26 August, 1886.

[51] *Mail*, 31 August, 1886.

[52] Macdonald Papers, vol. 259, Rose to Macdonald, 15 September, 1886.

[53] *Mail*, 17 September, 1886.

[54] Lansdowne Papers, Macdonald Letters, Macdonald to Lansdowne, 2 October, 1886.

[55] Macdonald Papers, vol. 85, Lansdowne to Macdonald, 20 August, 1886.

[56] Lansdowne Papers, Macdonald Letters, Macdonald to Lansdowne, 4 September, 1886.

[57] Macdonald Papers, vol. 227, Langevin to Macdonald, 15 October, 1886.

[58] Pope, *Correspondence*, p. 386, Macdonald to Tupper, 15 October, 1886.

[59] Macdonald Papers, vol. 270, Stephen to Macdonald, 4 November, 1886.

[60] Thompson Papers, Family Letters, Thompson to his wife, 31 October, 1886.

[61] *Mail*, 4 November, 1886.

[62] Thompson Papers, Family Letters, Thompson to his wife, 12 November, 1886.

[63] Pope, *Correspondence*, p. 390, Macdonald to Tupper, 20 December, 1886.

[64] Macdonald Papers, vol. 86, Colonial Secretary to Lansdowne, 26 November, 1886.

[65] Lansdowne Papers, Macdonald Letters, Macdonald to Lansdowne, 15 January, 1887; *Mail*, 17 January, 1887.

[66] Macdonald Papers, vol. 205, Chapleau to Macdonald, 20 January, 1887.

[67] Lansdowne Papers, Macdonald Letters, Macdonald to Lansdowne, 24 January, 1887.

[68] *Mail*, 1 February, 1887.

[69] *Globe*, 24 January, 1887.

[70] *Mail*, 12 February, 1887.

[71] Macdonald Papers, vol. 205, Macdonald to Chapleau, 13 February, 1887.

[72] *Ibid.*, vol. 198, Campbell to Macdonald, 23 February, 1887.

73 Lansdowne Papers, Macdonald Letters, Macdonald to Lansdowne, 24 February, 1887.

74 Macdonald Papers, vol. 527, Macdonald to Blackstock, 28 March, 1887.

75 Pope, *Correspondence*, p. 399, Mercier to Macdonald, 4 April, 1887.

76 Province of Ontario, *Sessional Papers*, 1887, No. 51, Mercier to Mowat, 8 March, 1887.

77 Pope, *Correspondence*, pp. 399-400, Macdonald to Mercier, 6 April, 1887.

78 *Ibid.*, p. 401, Macdonald to Mercier, 28 April, 1887.

79 *House of Commons Debates*, 1887, vol. 1, pp. 578-579.

80 Macdonald Papers, vol. 228, McCarthy to Macdonald, 3 April, 1887.

81 *House of Commons Debates*, 1887, vol. 1, pp. 384-407.

82 Macdonald Papers, vol. 86, Lansdowne to Macdonald, 25 December, 1886.

83 *Ibid.*, vol. 527, Macdonald to Lansdowne, 28 December, 1886.

84 Lansdowne Papers, Macdonald Letters, Macdonald to Lansdowne, 16 May, 1887.

85 Charles Tupper, *Recollections of Sixty Years in Canada* (London and Toronto, 1914), pp. 177-182.

86 Macdonald Papers, vol. 270, Stephen to Macdonald, 4 June, 1887.

87 *Ibid.*, vol. 527, Macdonald to Aikins, 25 June, 1887.

88 *Dominion and Provincial Legislation*, pp. 855-856.

89 Pope, *Correspondence*, pp. 403-404, Macdonald to Rose, 25 June, 1887.

90 Macdonald Papers, vol. 527, Macdonald to Lansdowne, 1 September, 1887; Lansdowne Papers, Macdonald Letters, Macdonald to Lansdowne, 14 September, 3 October, 1887.

91 Lansdowne Papers, Macdonald Letters, Macdonald to Lansdowne, 24 September, 1887.

92 *Ibid.*, Macdonald to Lansdowne, 13 October, 1887.

93 *Globe*, 14 October, 1887.

CHAPTER FOURTEEN: *The Renewal of Cultural Conflict*

(Pages 482 to 520)

1 Macdonald Papers, vol. 228, McCarthy to Macdonald, 3 September, 1887.

2 *Mail*, 27 October, 1887.

3 *Gazette*, 20 October, 1887.

4 Campbell Papers, Macdonald to Campbell, 3 December, 1887.

5 *Ibid.*, Macdonald to Campbell, 15 December, 1887.

6 Macdonald Papers, vol. 527, Macdonald to Aikins, 15 October, 1887.

7 *Ibid.*, Macdonald to Brown, 17 October, 1887.

8 *Ibid.*, vol. 270, Stephen to Macdonald, 4 October, 1887.

9 Pope, *Correspondence*, p. 406, Tupper to Macdonald, 15 September, 1887.

10 Lansdowne Papers, Macdonald Letters, Macdonald to Lansdowne, 18 October, 1887.

11 Macdonald Papers, vol. 527, Macdonald to Lansdowne, 3 October, 1887.

[12] *Ibid.*, vol. 176, Tupper to Macdonald, 24, 25 November, 1887.

[13] *Ibid.*, vol. 527, Macdonald to Lansdowne, 30 November, 1887.

[14] Pope, *Correspondence*, p. 406, Macdonald to Tupper, 7 December, 1887.

[15] Macdonald Papers, vol. 527, Macdonald to Lansdowne, 30 November, 1887.

[16] *Ibid.*, additional, vol. 2, Macdonald to Louisa Macdonald, 10 December, 1887.

[17] *Ibid.*, vol. 527, Macdonald to Tupper, 8 December, 1887.

[18] *Ibid.*, Macdonald to Tupper, 9 December, 1887.

[19] *Ibid.*, vol. 176, Tupper to Macdonald, 9 December, 1887.

[20] Lansdowne Papers, Macdonald Letters, Macdonald to Lansdowne, 10 December, 1887.

[21] Macdonald Papers, vol. 87, Lansdowne to Macdonald, 10 December, 1887.

[22] *Ibid.*, vol. 527, Macdonald to Tupper, 8 December, 1887.

[23] Lansdowne Papers, Macdonald Letters, Macdonald to Lansdowne, 11 December, 1887.

[24] J. L. Garvin, *The Life of Joseph Chamberlain* (London, 1933), vol. 2, pp. 333-334; W. R. Graham, "Sir Richard Cartwright, Wilfrid Laurier, and Liberal Trade Policy", *Canadian Historical Review*, vol. 33 (March, 1952), pp. 1-18.

[25] Macdonald Papers, vol. 527, Macdonald to Tupper, 15 January, 1888.

[26] *Ibid.*, additional, vol. 2, Macdonald to Louisa Macdonald, 10 September, 1887.

[27] *Ibid.*, Macdonald to Louisa Macdonald, 23 December, 1887.

[28] *Ibid.*, Macdonald to Minnie Macdonell, 12 January, 1888.

[29] *Ibid.*, vol. 527, Macdonald to Tupper, 5 January, 1888.

[30] Lansdowne Papers, Macdonald Letters, Macdonald to Lansdowne, 31 December, 1887.

[31] Macdonald Papers, vol. 176, Tupper to Macdonald, 19 January, 1888.

[32] Thompson Papers, Family Letters, Thompson to his wife, 16 January, 1888.

[33] Lansdowne Papers, Macdonald Letters, Macdonald to Lansdowne, 1 February, 1888.

[34] Pope, *Correspondence*, pp. 408-409, Macdonald to Tupper, 6 February, 1888.

[35] Lansdowne Papers, Macdonald Letters, Macdonald to Lansdowne, 11 February, 1888.

[36] Pope, *Correspondence*, p. 409, Macdonald to Tupper, 6 February, 1888.

[37] Lansdowne Papers, Macdonald Letters, Macdonald to Lansdowne, 21 February, 1888.

[38] Macdonald Papers, vol. 527, Macdonald to Daly, 31 January, 1888.

[39] *Ibid.*, vol. 271, Stephen to Macdonald, 25 February, 16, 20 March, 1888.

[40] *Ibid.*, vol. 119, Macdonald to Greenway, 20 March, 1888.

[41] *Ibid.*, Macdonald to Greenway, 21 March, 1888; *ibid.*, Greenway to Macdonald, 23 March, 1888.

[42] *Ibid.*, vol. 527, Macdonald to Greenway, 30 March, 1888.

[43] *House of Commons Debates*, 1888, vol. 1, p. 144.

[44] *Ibid.*, vol. 2, pp. 1069, 1078.

[45] *Ibid.*, vol. 1, p. 646.

[46] *Ibid.*, p. 14.

[47] Macdonald Papers, additional, vol. 2, Macdonald to Louisa Macdonald, 29 May, 1888.

[48] *Ibid.*, vol. 88, Lansdowne to Macdonald, 23 May, 1888.

[49] *Ibid.*, vol. 528, Macdonald to Tupper, 14 July, 1888.

[50] *Ibid.*, vol. 271, Stephen to Macdonald, 12 January, 1888.

[51] Saunders, *Tupper*, vol. 2, pp. 117-118.

[52] Lansdowne Papers, Macdonald Letters, Macdonald to Lansdowne, 13 July, 1888.

[53] *Ibid.*, Macdonald to Lansdowne, 24 April, 1888.

[54] Macdonald Papers, vol. 528, Macdonald to Stanley, 17 July, 1888.

[55] Lansdowne Papers, Macdonald Letters, Macdonald to Lansdowne, 6 September, 1888.

[56] Pope, *Correspondence*, pp. 429-431, Macdonald to Stephen, 22 October, 1888.

[57] Macdonald Papers, vol. 528, Macdonald to Schultz, 2 August, 1888.

[58] *Ibid.*, Macdonald to Schultz, 17 November, 1888.

[59] *Ibid.*, Macdonald to Stephen, 4 August, 1888.

[60] Lansdowne Papers, Macdonald Letters, Macdonald to Lansdowne, 6 September, 1888.

[61] Macdonald Papers, vol. 89, Stanley to Macdonald, October, 1888.

[62] Allan Nevins, *Grover Cleveland, A Study in Courage* (New York, 1933), pp. 428-431.

[63] Pope, *Correspondence*, p. 430, Macdonald to Stephen, 22 October, 1888.

[64] Macdonald Papers, vol. 528, Macdonald to Tupper, 16 November, 1888.

[65] Pope, *Correspondence*, p. 431, Mowat to Macdonald, 17 November, 1888.

[66] *Ibid.*, p. 436, Macdonald to Stephen, 12 January, 1889.

[67] Macdonald to Williamson, 11 January, 1889. Letter in the possession of W. F. Nickle, Esq., of Kingston, Ontario.

[68] Macdonald Papers, additional, vol. 2, Macdonald to Louisa Macdonald, 27 April, 1888.

[69] Macdonald to Williamson, 11 January, 1889.

[70] Pope, *Correspondence*, p. 430, Macdonald to Stephen, 22 October, 1888.

[71] Macdonald Papers, vol. 284, Tupper to Macdonald, 19 December, 1888.

[72] *Ibid.*, vol. 528, Macdonald to Tupper, 22 December, 1888.

[73] *Ibid.*, Macdonald to Hamilton, 26 January, 1889.

[74] *Ibid.*, vol. 228, McCarthy to Macdonald, 1 March, 1889.

[75] *Ibid.*, vol. 471, O'Brien to Macdonald, 18 March, 1889.

[76] *Ibid.*, vol. 528, Macdonald to O'Brien, 20 March, 1889.

[77] *House of Commons Debates*, 1889, vol, 2, p. 908.

[78] *Ibid.*, p. 910.

[79] Pope, *Correspondence*, pp. 442-443.

[80] *Ibid.*, pp. 443-444, McCarthy to Macdonald, 17 April, 1889.

[81] Lansdowne Papers, Macdonald Letters, Macdonald to Lansdowne, 14 May, 1889.

[82] Macdonald Papers, vol. 275, Thompson to Macdonald, 18 May, 1889.

[83] *Globe*, 8 June, 1889.

[84] Thompson Papers, vol. 89, Macdonald to Thompson, 4 July, 1889.

[85] Pope, *Correspondence*, pp. 445-446, Macdonald to Tupper, 31 May, 1889.

[86] Thompson Papers, vol. 91, Macdonald to Thompson, 2 August, 1889.
[87] Macdonald Papers, vol. 94, Stanley to Macdonald, 2 August, 1889.
[88] Thompson Papers, vol. 91, Macdonald to Thompson, 14 August, 1889.
[89] *Ibid.*, Macdonald to Thompson, 30 August, 1889.

Chapter Fifteen: *The Last Election*

(Pages 521 to 563)

[1] Macdonald Papers, vol. 275, Monck to Macdonald, 24 September, 1890.
[2] *Ibid.*, vol. 232, McLelan to Macdonald, 29 June, 1889.
[3] Thompson Papers, vol. 89, Macdonald to Thompson, 4 July, 1889.
[4] Lansdowne Papers, Macdonald Letters, Macdonald to Lansdowne, 14 May, 1889.
[5] Pope, *Correspondence*, p. 461, Macdonald to Tupper, 7 December, 1889.
[6] Macdonald Papers, vol. 528, Macdonald to Costigan, 2 May, 1889.
[7] Thompson Papers, vol. 72, Macdonald to Thompson, 13 June, 1888.
[8] Pope, *Correspondence*, pp. 431-432, Tupper to Macdonald, 1 December, 1888.
[9] *Ibid.*, pp. 449-451, Macdonald to Knutsford, 18 July, 1889.
[10] Macdonald Papers, additional, vol. 3, Agnes Macdonald to Louisa Macdonald, n.d.
[11] *Ibid.*, vol. 528, Macdonald to Tupper, 16 November, 1888.
[12] *Ibid.*, Macdonald to Tupper, 22 December, 1888.
[13] Queen's University Library, McLaughlin Collection, Macdonald to Hallam, 6 May, 1889.
[14] Pope, *Correspondence*, p. 449, Macdonald to Edgecome, 4 July, 1889.
[15] Thompson Papers, vol. 90, Macdonald to Thompson, 27 July, 1889.
[16] *Ibid.*, vol. 89, Macdonald to Thompson, 4 July, 1889.
[17] *Ibid.*, vol. 90, Macdonald to Thompson, 25 July, 1889.
[18] Lansdowne Papers, Macdonald Letters, Macdonald to Lansdowne, 28 September, 1889.
[19] Macdonald Papers, vol. 288, Andersons to Macdonald, 12 October, 1889.
[20] Pope, *Correspondence*, pp. 455-456, Macdonald to Stephen, 13 September, 1889.
[21] Lansdowne Papers, Macdonald Letters, Macdonald to Lansdowne, 28 September, 1889.
[22] Macdonald Papers, vol. 32, Stanley to Macdonald, n.d. (with enclosure).
[23] *Ibid.*, Colonial Secretary to Governor-General, n.d.
[24] *Ibid.*, vol. 529, Macdonald to Tupper, 22 October, 1889.
[25] *Ibid.*, vol. 32, Stanley to Knutsford, 13 December, 1889.
[26] Pope, *Correspondence*, p. 414, Macdonald to Chapleau, 6 June, 1888.
[27] *House of Commons Debates*, 1890, p. 38.
[28] *Ibid.*, p. 532.
[29] *Ibid.*, p. 557.
[30] *Ibid.*, p. 745.
[31] *Ibid.*, p. 750.
[32] *Ibid.*, pp. 875-876.
[33] *Ibid.*, p. 895.
[34] Macdonald Papers, vol. 90, Stanley to Macdonald, 22 February, 1890.

[85] *House of Commons Debates*, 1890, p. 1018.

[36] Macdonald Papers, vol. 30, C. H. Tupper to Macdonald, 27 February, 1890.

[87] *Ibid.*

[88] Thompson Papers, vol. 103, Macdonald to Bowell, 4 March, 1890.

[39] Macdonald Papers, vol. 529, Macdonald to C. H. Tupper, 11 March, 1890.

[40] *Ibid.*, vol. 31, Draft Convention for the North Pacific Seal Fishery.

[41] *Ibid.*, C. H. Tupper to Macdonald, 10 April, 1890.

[42] *Ibid.*, C. H. Tupper to Macdonald, 11 April, 1890.

[43] *Ibid.*, Macdonald to C. H. Tupper, 11 April, 1890.

[44] *Ibid.*, C. H. Tupper to Macdonald, 27 April, 1890.

[45] C. C. Tansill, *Canadian-American Relations, 1875-1911* (New Haven and Toronto, 1943), p. 311.

[46] *House of Commons Debates*, 1890, pp. 449-450, 638-650, 1713-1734.

[47] *Ibid.*, pp. 4500-4503, 4564.

[48] Macdonald Papers, vol. 189, Bowell to Macdonald, 23 July, 1890.

[49] Pope, *Correspondence*, p. 466, Macdonald to Chevrier, 25 March, 1890.

[50] Saunders, *Tupper*, vol. 2, p. 140, Macdonald to Tupper, 5 June, 1890.

[51] *Empire* (Toronto), 9 August, 1890.

[52] *Ibid.*, 2 October, 1890.

[53] Pope, *Correspondence*, pp. 477-479, Macdonald to Stephen, 10 November, 1890.

[54] *Ibid.*

[55] *Empire*, 11, 12 November, 1890.

[56] G 12, vol. 85, Stanley to Knutsford, 19 November, 1890.

[57] *Sessional Papers*, 1891, No. 38, Knutsford to Stanley, 25 November, 1890.

[58] *Ibid.*, Pauncefote to Stanley, 7 December, 1890.

[59] Macdonald Papers, vol. 530, Macdonald to Stanley, 8 December, 1890.

[60] Thompson Papers, vol. 118, Macdonald to Thompson, 9 December, 1890.

[61] G 12, vol. 85, Stanley to Knutsford, 13 December, 1890.

[62] *Sessional Papers*, 1891, No. 38, Knutsford to Stanley, 2 January, 1891.

[63] Thompson Papers, vol. 127, Macdonald to Thompson, 27 April, 1891.

[64] G 12, vol. 85, Stanley to Knutsford, 21 January, 1891.

[65] *Mail*, 14 January, 1891.

[66] *Empire*, 16 January, 1891.

[67] G 12, vol. 85, Stanley to Knutsford, 24 January, 1891.

[68] *Free Press* (Ottawa), 29 January, 1891.

[69] *Globe*, 30 January, 1891.

[70] Macdonald Papers, vol. 90, Stanley to Macdonald, 30 January, 1891.

[71] Pope, *Memoirs*, vol. 2, appendix 28, p. 336.

[72] Macdonald Papers, vol. 285, Macdonald to Tupper, 21 January, 1891.

[73] *Ibid.*, Macdonald to Colmer, 13 February, 1891.

[74] *Globe*, 18 February, 1891.

[75] *Empire*, 18 February, 1891.

[76] Pope, *Memoirs*, vol. 2, p. 257.

[77] *News* (Kingston), 23 February, 1891.

[78] *Ibid.*, 25 February, 1891.

[79] *Ibid.*, 26 February, 1891.

[80] Pope, *Memoirs*, vol. 2, pp. 257-258.

[81] Public Archives of Canada, The Last Ten Days of the Life of the Right Honourable Sir John Alexander Macdonald, G.C.B., Prime Minister of Canada, by his attending physician, Robert Wynyard Powell, M.D.

[82] Pope, *Correspondence*, p. 485, Macdonald to Stephen, 31 March, 1891.

[83] Williamson Papers, Macdonald to Williamson, 10 March, 1891.

[84] Powell, The Last Ten Days.

[85] *House of Commons Debates*, 1891, vol. 1, p. 35.

[86] Pope, *Memoirs*, vol. 2, pp. 258-259.

[87] G 12, vol. 85, Stanley to Knutsford, 4 June, 1891.

[88] Pope, *Memoirs*, vol. 2, p. 259.

[89] Powell, The Last Ten Days.

[90] Thompson Papers, Family Letters, 22 May, 1891.

EPILOGUE: *The Sixth of June, 1891*

(Pages 564 to 578)

[1] Powell, The Last Ten Days, p. 5.

[2] Pope, *Memoirs*, vol. 2, p. 259.

[3] Powell, The Last Ten Days, pp. 5-6.

[4] *Ibid.*, p. 6.

[5] Pope, *Memoirs*, vol. 2, p. 260.

[6] *Free Press* (Ottawa), 28 May, 1891.

[7] Powell, The Last Ten Days, pp. 7-8.

[8] Pope, *Memoirs*, vol. 2, pp. 260-261.

[9] Thompson Papers, Family Letters, Thompson to his wife, 29 May, 1891.

[10] Sir John Willison, *Reminiscences, Political and Personal* (Toronto, 1919), p. 193.

[11] *Ibid.*

[12] Powell, The Last Ten Days, p. 9.

[13] *Ibid.*, p. 10.

[14] *Free Press*, 30 May, 1891.

[15] *House of Commons Debates*, 1891, p. 600.

[16] *Empire*, 30 May, 1891.

[17] *Mail*, 2 June, 1891.

[18] Powell, The Last Ten Days, pp. 11-12.

[19] *Mail*, 2 June, 1891.

[20] Thompson Papers, Family Letters, Thompson to his wife, 31 May, 1891.

[21] *Ibid.*, Thompson to his wife, 1 June, 1891.

[22] *Empire*, 5 June, 1891.

[23] Powell, The Last Ten Days, p. 14.

[24] *Ibid.*, p. 15.

[25] *Gazette* (Montreal), 8 June, 1891.

[26] *Mail*, 9 June, 1891.

[27] *House of Commons Debates*, 1891, p. 884.

[28] *Empire*, 11 June, 1891.

[29] *Mail*, 12 June, 1891.

[30] Pope, *Memoirs*, vol. 2, p. 264.

INDEX

Abbott, J. J. C., 170, 174, 417; Canada Pacific Railway Co., 122, 133-4, 135, 141, 149, 150; offices rifled, 152, 156; Allan affidavit, 161; files published, 163, 167-8; Letellier, 262; Australia, 527, 533; Conservative leadership, 568-9, 574

Act for the Temporary Government of Rupert's Land, 35, 43

Aikins, J. C., 370, 459, 466

Alabama claims, 45, 74, 78, 125, 129, 480; Washington Treaty, 99; Geneva, 116-118

Alaskan boundary, 449, 497

Allan, Sir Hugh, 174, 207, 248, 293, 297, 300, 302; Macdonald's debts, 34, 38-9, 41, 57; Canada Pacific Railway Co., 112-13, 120; American intrigue, 121-2; Cartier, 123, 131, 132; Macpherson, 133-4; Conservative election funds, 140, 141, 142; presidency promise, 143; American associates, 144, 145, 146; McMullen, 148, 149, 150, 151; London capital attempts, 152, 157; select committee, 153, 154, 155, 156; affidavit, 160, 161, 162; Abbott's files, 163; Royal Commission, 167, 168, 170 172, 173

American Alaska Fur Co., 507, 531

American Civil War, 64, 74, 119, 206

American Commission in Washington, 1871, 84, 86-7, 90, 96; *see also* Fisheries question *and* Joint High Commission

American relations with Canada, *Alabama*, 116-7, 129; Bering Sea, 507, 531-3, 539-42, 544; C.P.R., 302, 306, 308, 362, 367, 371, 382; commercial union, 468, 474, 478-9, 494, 501-2; danger, 74-5, 206, 408, 483; Fenians, 61, 96, 355-6; fisheries (1870), 75-8, 80, 89, 402-4, 422, (1885), 430, 441-2, 446, 454-5, 457, 462, 464, 466, 476-7, (1887), 495-7, (1889), 526-7; Joint High Commission (1887), 480-1, 488-93, 495-7; Liberals, 548, 551, 553-5, 560;

Panama Canal, 327; presidential elections, 289, 506, 510-11; press, 303, 306-7, 367, 381, 420; Red River, *see* Red River, American involvement; trade, 119, 209, 215-16, 250, 258, 475, 508; McKinley Bill, 545-7; Blaine, 549-55; vice-royalty, 248

Amyot, G., 428

André, Father Alexis, 413, 416, **447**

Anglin, Timothy, 333

Angus, Richard B., 286, 300, 301

Annand, William, 11, 27

Anti-Confederates (Nova Scotia), 4-5, 11, 14, 16-18, 26-7, 30

Archibald, Sir Adams George, 18, **26**, 50, 76, 248-9, 254

Arthur, Chester A., 404

Assiniboia, *see* Red River

Associated Press, 307, 381; *see also* American relations, press

Australasian colonies, 521-2, **527**, 530, 533

Baldwin, Robert, 37

Bank of Montreal, 238, 284, 286, 364-5, 375-6, 424

Bank of Upper Canada, 39

Baring, financial house of, 396, **427**, 450, 487

Batoche, 419, 425

Battleford, 424-5

Bayard, Thomas F., 422; fisheries, 454-5, 464, 476-7; Joint High Commission (1887), 489-91, 493, 496-7, 506-7; Bering Sea, 507; *see also* Chamberlain-Bayard Treaty

Beaconsfield, Benjamin Disraeli, First Earl of, 28, 67, 124, 248, 266-7, 268, 409; Russian crisis, 236; Corn Laws, 258; Macdonald, 273; speech on Canada, 276

Beaty, James, 124, 135

Beausoleil, C., 536-8

Bering Sea, 480, 497, 507, 511, **528**, 531-2, 539, 540, 542, 544, 561

Bernard, Col. Hewitt, 11, 15, 19, 41, 48, 269, 313-14; Deputy Minister of Justice, 8; Washington Conference, 82; C.P.R., 146; trade mission, 255

614